NATCHITOCHES
1729-1803

"In agreement with the very reverend father curate, Fray Stanislás, I . . . consulted with the citizens, calling on each one according to his ability, regarding the building of another church, this being one of the first duties of Christians. To this they have agreed, and some with such zeal and efficacy, notwithstanding the poverty of the place, that already the alms reach the sum of seven hundred dollars. With this capital and the abundance of stone here, both for making lime and for the walls, it appears that we shall have sufficient for a very decent building, to which I am devoting my greatest care, in order that it be undertaken and finished as soon as is possible. Therefore, I beg your Lordship to please consent that I may have the honor to place the first stone of the foundations of this holy church in your illustrious name, a favor for which all of us here will be sincerely and duly thankful."

Commandant Athanase de Mézières to Governor Luis de Unzaga y Amazaga, February 1, 1770

(Papeles Procedentes de Cuba, Legajo 110, Number 189)

NATCHITOCHES

Abstracts of the Catholic Church Registers
of the
French and Spanish Post
of
St. Jean Baptiste des Natchitoches
in
Louisiana

1729-1803

Elizabeth Shown Mills

HERITAGE BOOKS
2007

HERITAGE BOOKS
AN IMPRINT OF HERITAGE BOOKS, INC.

Books, CDs, and more—Worldwide

For our listing of thousands of titles see our website at
www.HeritageBooks.com

Published 2007 by
HERITAGE BOOKS, INC.
Publishing Division
65 East Main Street
Westminster, Maryland 21157-5026

Copyright © 1977 Elizabeth Shown Mills

Other books by the author:

Natchitoches Church Marriages, 1818-1850: Translated Abstracts from the Registers of St. Francios des Natchitoches Louisiana

Natchitoches: Translated Abstracts of Register Number Five of the Catholic Church Parish of St. Francois des Natchitoches in Louisiana: 1800-1826

Tales of Old Natchitoches

All rights reserved. No part of this book may be reproduced or transmitted in any form or by any means, electronic or mechanical, including photocopying, recording or by any information storage and retrieval system without written permission from the author, except for the inclusion of brief quotations in a review.

International Standard Book Number: 978-0-931069-10-6

D. O. M. Lapis isce, in fundamentis
sacro-sanctae Ajustae Ecclesiae,
Jussû et vice Yllustrissimi domini,
Ludovici de Vnzâga, in hâc provincia
pro Catolica Majestate imperitantis,
rite, solemniterque depositus ob
aeternam ad nepotes rei memoriam.
anno salutis mdcclxxi.

[To God best and greatest. In the year of
salvation 1771, this stone was laid in the
foundations of the holy and venerable
church in due order and solemnity by command
and in the name of Don Luis de Unzaga,
ruling in this province in behalf of his
Catholic Majesty, for the eternal memory
of the event with posterity.]

(From the cornerstone of
the Church of St. François, Natchitoches, 1771.)

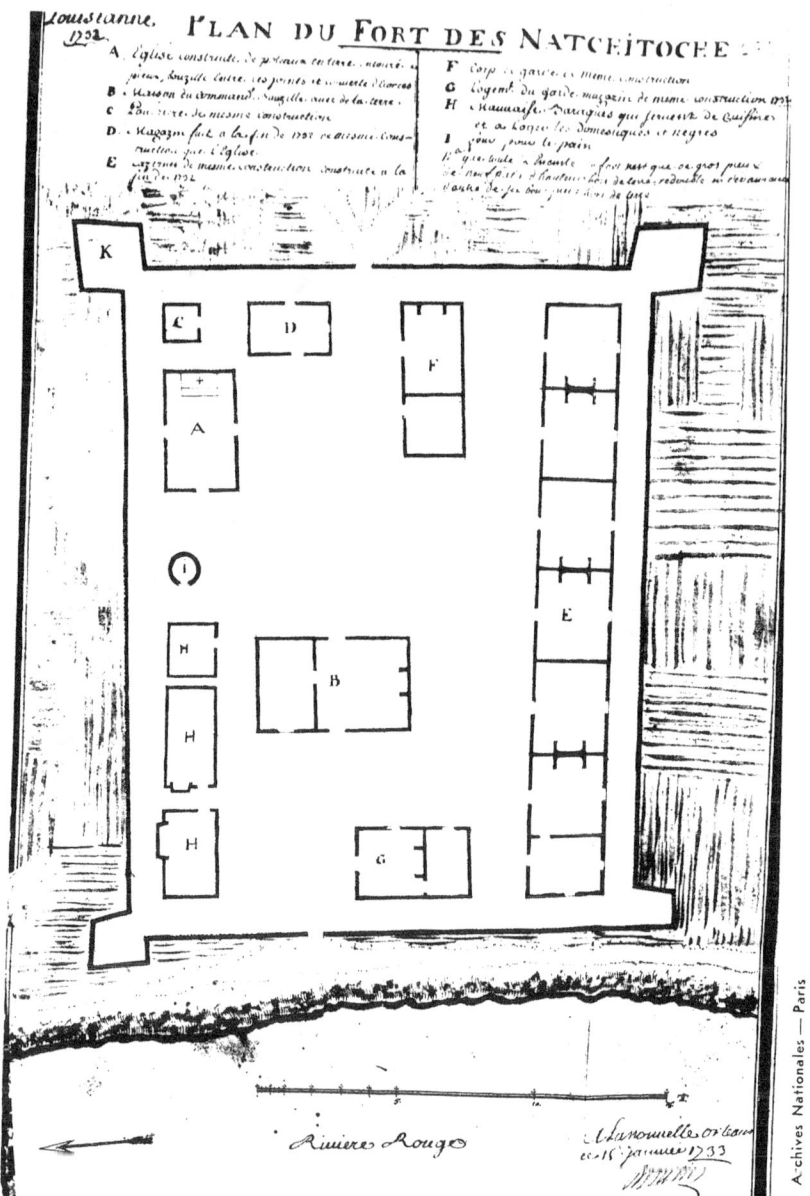

Plan of the Fort at Natchitoches A. The church constructed of posts in the ground, enclosed with stakes, mud filled (*bouzille*) between the joints, and roofed with bark. B. House of the commandant, the frame filled in with earth. C. Powder magazine of the same construction. D. Warehouse built at the end of 1732 of the same construction as the church. E. Barracks of the same construction, constructed at the end of 1732. F. Guardhouse of the same construction. G. Lodging for the warehouse keeper of the same construction, 1732. H. Wretched huts which serve as kitchen and to lodge the servants and Negroes. I. Oven for bread.

Note that the entire enclosure of the fort is only of heavy stakes, nine feet high above ground, and doubled on the inside with others six good feet above the ground.

New Orleans, 15 January 1733, Broutin

TO

GARY, CLAY, DONNA, AND DANNY

= Año de 1779 =

En el año de mil setecientos setenta y nueve dia diez y nueve de Enero Yo el infra escrito, despues de la publicacion de las tres Amonestaciones en tres dias festivos consecutivos, y despues de haber pedido, y exhibido el actual, y mutuo Consentimiento delos Contrayentes, junté en Matrimonio, y di la Bendicion nupcial a Juan Santiago David natural de Dambiersk, obispado de Leon en Francia, hijo legitimo de Juan Bautista David, y de Maria Neurin; y a Maria Ana Dartigaux natural de Bayona en Francia hija legitima de Pedro Dartigaux y de Maria Monica Duchit: Cuio Matrimonio fue Celebrado en presencia delos testigos siguientes: Dn Antonio Charbonet, Esteban Pavie, francisco la Caze, y Pedro Badin, los quales firmaron conmigo en el mismo dia, mes, y año que arriba, en fe de lo qual firmé.

fr Luis de Quintanilla Cura

A representative entry from the Natchitoches church registers. Marriage of Juan Santiago David and Maria Ana Dartigaux, January 19, 1779. Luis de Quintanilla, a Spanish priest, renders the names of the parties, who are French, in translation.

TABLE OF CONTENTS

	Page
Codes	x
Introduction	xi
Acknowledgements	xvii

THE REGISTERS:

Register 1	3
Register 2	63
Register 3	170
Register 4	200
Register 4-B	326

APPENDICES:

A. Glossary of Foreign Terms	417
B. Conversion Table for Personal Names; French - Spanish - Latin - English	420
C. Abbreviations Used within the Registers	424

INDEX — 425

Cover: Based on the May 9, 1738, inventory of the church property at Natchitoches by de St. Denis, Commandant, and sub-delegate de la Chaise, before the notary Duplessis, this drawing is by Charles Norman of Natchitoches. The structure is described as follows: "Twenty feet long and twenty four wide, built on nine foot logs with double beams filled in between with mud work. The said Church has six windows with shutters and iron work, a big double door with iron work, a small door with a lock. The said building is covered with shingles on planks without fancy work. Everything being new." Also mentioned is "a thirteen and a half pound bell, set up outside the church." The priest at the time was the Rev. Father Jean Francois de Civray, Capuchin.

CODES

The following codes have been used, for brevity, within the abstracts:

(f) indicates that a duplicate entry exists which contains one or more factual discrepancies. A detailed discussion of this problem is provided in the Introduction.

(s) indicates that an individual signed the record or that the priest noted the individual signed one copy of the record.

(x) indicates that an individual made his mark upon an entry or that the priest stated the individual could not sign.

INTRODUCTION

In 1729 the French post *St. Jean Baptiste des Natchitoches* was fifteen years old -- an adolescent settlement, daring, sassy, and eager for adventure. It was also poor, in resources and in faith. Its fatherland had failed to provide financial support. Its mother church was engrossed with more pressing concerns elsewhere. As it struggled for survival on a frontier claimed by both France and Spain, the post at Natchitoches worked out its own code of behavior and developed a distinctive lifestyle that would set it apart from the rest of Louisiana for many decades to come.

In those fifteen formative years between 1714 and 1729, this fledgling settlement had little experience with religion. The parental authorities of church and state in France had provided no religious instruction or activities for their children in this distant outpost. *Padres* from the rival Spanish post of Los Adaes, some fifteen miles to the west, had taken under their wing the spiritual orphans at Natchitoches, but their occasional visits left no lasting mark.

Between May 1729 and January 1730 a visiting priest recorded at Natchitoches the earliest extant records of the religious life of that post: three marriages, one death, and eleven baptisms. The little book that he began was preserved by the faithful, but subsequent priests who passed through the region did not deign to record in it the sacraments they administered. Not until 1734, the twentieth anniversary of the post, did a Jesuit priest arrive in this frontier settlement to tend full-time the needs of the neglected flock. By 1738, the Catholic parish *St. François d'Assisi des Natchitoches* was an established institution, with a new church of stark, crude, simplicity.

Throughout the next seventy years, as Louisiana bounced from French to Spanish to French to American control, the fortunes of the parish varied. The religious fervor of the parishioners likewise quickened and waned in cycles that corresponded closely to the political activity that enmeshed it. A strong preference was shown at the post throughout the eighteenth century for pastors of French birth, and at least one Spanish *padre* suffered such keen disrespect that he abandoned his post and returned to New Orleans. Yet, in spite of the difficulties periodically created by international politics, irreverent parishioners, and zealous priests who seesawed between the concerns of church and state, the Catholic faith remained a dominant force in the social development of the post.

Natchitoches, traditionally, has been considered a settlement of French and Spanish origins, but its colonial population was much more varied. Attracted by the free-wheeling, *laissez-faire* spirit this frontier displayed, new settlers came to Natchitoches from the farms and cities of almost every European nation -- from Great Britain to Hungary to Italy -- and from the New World colonies of Canada and the Atlantic coast. Others were brought to Natchitoches, under the bonds of slavery, from the Indian nations of the Southwestern plains and from the myriad tribes of Africa's fabled Gold Coast. Within the confines of this small outpost on the Louisiana-Texas frontier, soldiers and slaves, hunters and craftsmen, peasants and noblemen shared each other's lives and lived each other's joys and sorrows.

The Catholic registers of the parish of St. François are more than a mere list of births, marriages, and deaths. On their tattered and ink-blotched pages are chronicled the kaleidoscopic lives of the men and women who built this "oldest permanent settlement in the Louisiana Purchase." Whole families are followed through the decades as they extended themselves into the fringes of North Louisiana, yet remained within the jurisdiction of this vast parish. From the offspring settlements of Rapides, Bayou Pierre, and *St. Louis des Caddodoches* (near modern Shreveport) and from points as distant as Ouachita and Attakapas, the straying families returned to Natchitoches in quest of the sacraments.

As in most Catholic registers, the Natchitoches entries follow a basic form, but within the confines of that form an infinite variety of information is to be found. Points of origin and parental information abound. More punctilious priests recorded occupations, nicknames, and more distant relationships. Principals and witnesses frequently penned their signatures or made their marks, leaving behind a silent but certain testimony on the state of literacy at the little post. Occasional Protestants renounced the religions of their births and made a Catholic "Profession of Faith." Peons cited their ancestral origins as proudly as the rare *noblesse*. Alligators and assassins, treacherous currents and bolts of lightning appear as villains in the burial registers. Slaves and free nonwhites received the sacraments with regularity, illustrating the marked degree to which Catholic America treated nonwhites as spiritual equals.

The entries that are reproduced in this volume represent all known extant records from 1729 to 1803. They are *edited* translations, rather than complete translations, of the original French, Spanish, and Latin entries, but considerable care has been taken to include all information that might be of use to historians and genealogists. For the sake of brevity and preciseness, a few French or Spanish terms have been retained -- for example, those denoting exact racial composition and, of course, the standard *dit* and *alias*. For those readers not familiar with the terms used, a glossary is provided in the Appendix.

For the most part, the baptismal and marriage records seem to be complete for this colonial period, although a few chronological gaps do exist -- most notably the baptisms from 1770 to 1775, inclusive. Burial entries are far from complete. As the reader will soon discover, the chronological arrangement of the entries leaves much to be desired. Partly this results from the varied systems used by the priests who made these entries, and partly from the fact that the original books have been rebound in the past without proper reassimilation of loose pages. Individual pages and entries are not systematically numbered in the original; therefore the editor has chosen not to reproduce them. The numbering system used in these abstracts are numbers assigned by the editor. The order of the original entries and the separation of the volumes have been retained.

A FEW WORDS OF WARNING MUST BE MADE. The main problem that plagues researchers who work in this type of records is the inconsistency of those records, particularly with regard to names. Illiteracy and cultural differences produce a multitude of variations in spelling. The fact that these registers have been recorded in three languages greatly intensifies the problems incurred in using them. Any individual name may appear in these registers in French, Spanish, or Latin form, regardless of the person's national origins. For example, a Carolina native named John might appear as Jean, Juan, or Joannis, depending upon the preferred languages of the priests who made the entries. Occasionally, even surnames are translated; for example: the Prudhomme family appears under the Latin form of the name, Per Domo; the Frenchwoman, Jeanne de la Rivière, occasionally appears as Juanna del Rio; the Spanishwoman, Juanna de los Reyes, appears as Jeanne Le Roy upon occasion, which could easily result in her confusion with the French colonist, Jeanne Le Roy, if the researcher is not cautious.

In translating and abstracting these entries, the editor has tried to preserve original spellings as much as possible, although variations occasionally occur in such number within a single entry that it is not possible to include them all. Where spellings are so variant that they might not be recognized, the editor has inserted, in brackets, the more common spelling for that family name. Similarly, since each individual's name appears under a variety of spellings, the editor has also standardized the index listings under the most common spellings, with variations cross-referenced. In the cases of individuals who were able to sign their names, the manner in which they signed is indicated at least once, along with the spelling given by the priest. It will be noted that occasionally individuals were inconsistent, also, in the manner in which they wrote their own names.

To help the reader overcome the difficulty presented by the recording of given names in different languages -- i.e., Charles, Carlos, and Carolum -- the editor has provided a "Conversion Table" in the Appendix. In deciding which version is the preferred for any given individual, the editor suggests that the reader consider the individual's national origins. If a settler were French, he or she seldom, if ever, called himself by the Spanish version of his name. Occasional problems occur with families of mixed origins -- i.e., a French mother and a Spanish father. In such cases, it is suggested that the family historian should adopt for such an individual the manner in which he signed his own name, if he were literate, or the spelling of the society in which the individual lived.

Still additional problems are caused by the old French custom of *dits*. In brief, these may be defined as "nicknames," with one prime difference between them and their modern counterparts: a *dit* (or *alias* in Spanish) was more commonly substituted for an individual's FAMILY name rather than for a given name. Often *dits* were adopted by children and grandchildren and used in preference to the family name to such an extent that the family name was eventually abandoned. In some cases, it is difficult to distinguish exactly which name was the *dit* and which was the original family surname, as in the Pereau-Vildec family. Natchitoches registers leave considerable doubt as to which of these names was the original. When the origins of the first settler are traced back into Canada, the problem still exists. In such cases, only by tracing to the earliest known ancestor can the researcher make an accurate, or hopefully-accurate determination. (In the case of the Pereau-Vildec family, the former name is the earliest on record.) Within this present work, individuals and families appear under *dits* as well as family names. In those entries which contain only the *dit*, the editor inserts the family name in brackets. Indexing adhers to family name, with *dits* cross-referenced.

A final problem that will be incurred in using this work is *CONTRADICTORY* information. Particularly is this a problem in determining a person's literacy. On one occasion he may have signed a record, yet on a second occasion the priest may have recorded that this individual did not know how to sign. It is the editor's opinion that carelessness or haste on the part of the recorder was the main cause. Many priests did not bother to obtain signatures at all. Despite the inconsistencies, the editor has noted signatures or marks as they appear, since these frequently do help in distinguishing one individual from a second by the same name. Again, discrepancies appear in racial origins. For example, an individual might be described as a Caddo Indian in one record, a *mestizo* or *metif* in the next, and eventually as a "free *mulatresse*." Since the editor has done extensive research on almost all of these early Natchitoches families, white, black, and Indian, an editorial opinion is sometimes offered where such contradictions exist.

The most serious problems with discrepancies are found among the entries recorded by Fr. Jean Delvaux in Registers 3, 4, and 4-B for the years 1786 to 1795. French by birth, Fr. Delvaux apparently did not know Spanish, the "official" language, when he arrived at Natchitoches. Ignoring the registers already in use (those now numbered 2 and 4), Fr. Delvaux began a new register (now numbered 3) and recorded his entries entirely in French. By 1793 he appears to have learned the Spanish language and, at that time, rewrote his French entries in Spanish using Book 4 for baptisms and 4-B for marriages and deaths. He then abandoned Book 3 and the French language. In comparing the entries in Book 3 with their copies in Books 4 and 4-B, a sizable number of discrepancies are apparent. Where the editor has found such discrepancies, they have been noted and it is suggested to the reader that in such cases the entries in Book 3, the original version, are probably the more accurate ones.

The editor has sought to provide for researchers a usable, accessible, and accurate rendition of these invaluable but sometimes barely legible records. However, she is still human and subject to human imperfection. In cases where contradictions exist, or should any entry raise questions in the minds of any researcher, the editor encourages the researcher to examine the original himself -- or at second best to request a photocopy that he may examine. The editor also encourages the reader to supplement the entries in these registers with research in all available source materials for the area. Her own comparisons of church, civil, and miscellaneous records have convinced her that ANY original document well might contain error. Officials of yesteryear were human also. Only by gathering, scrutinizing, and comparing a variety of records on any individual, can a researcher "rest easy" with the "facts" he has collected.

   Photocopies or certified copies of any entry in this volume may be obtained at a nominal fee by writing: Secretary, Church of the Immaculate Conception, Natchitoches, Louisiana 91457. Please provide a stamped, self-addressed return envelope with your request.

                                                E. S. M.

ACKNOWLEDGEMENTS

In submitting this work to the public, I must acknowledge the assistance of those individuals who made this study possible. The cooperation of the pastors of the Church of the Immaculate Conception at Natchitoches, formerly St. François, has been indispensable. To Msgr. Henry F. Beckers, and the Reverend Fathers John Cunningham and Russel Lemoine, former pastors of Immaculate Conception, and the Reverend Fathers Frank S. Foret and Philip F. Michiels, now of that parish, as well as Mrs. John G. Williams, the parish Secretary, I must express gratitude. All have offered unlimited cooperation and assistance, in spite of the many inconveniences I have imposed upon them over the years this work has been in progress. Their sincere concern for the preservation of these irreplaceable records, and their interest in making their vast store of information available to the public is appreciated by all who value America's heritage.

Appreciation must also be expressed to the Clerk of Court for the Parish of Natchitoches, Irby L. Knotts, and to the capable staff who assist him in his work. They, too, have been extremely cooperative in making their records available. Were it not for the extensive supplemental work I have been able to do in the civil records of the parish, I could not consider myself qualified to undertake the responsibility of translating and editing ecclesiastical records of this type where an accurate rendition of personal and family names is mandatory.

I must also say thanks to my husband and colleague, Gary B. Mills, who has worked with me in these records to such an extent that it is often difficult for us to distinguish between his work and mine. His "professional" advice and perceptive historical perspectives have proven invaluable. To Clay, Donna, and Danny, who have doubled as cook, maid, and moral supporter during the final months of the preparation of this manuscript, I also owe a debt of appreciation and love -- which I hope I have repaid in part by preserving for them an extensive part of their own heritage.

E. S. M.

NATCHITOCHES
1729-1803

*Abstracts of the Catholic Church Registers
of the French and Spanish Post
of St. Jean Baptiste des Natchitoches in Louisiana*

REGISTER 1

1. EMMANUEL RONDIN
   March 2, 1734, baptism of Emmanuel, born February 28, the daughter of Julien Rondin and Elizabeth Dubos. Godparents: Guillaume Chever, Chevalier de St. Agnette, officer of the infantry, and Dame Emmanuel Sanchez de St. Denis.

2. JEANNE DE ARAMBOULE
   April 2, 1734, baptism of Jeanne, born February 26, 1734, daughter of Emmanuel de Aramboule and of _____ /sic/, Spaniard from the post of Adays. Godparents: Francois Goudeau, surgeon, and Dame Marie Rose /page torn/.

3. JEANNE CHEVER *dit* DUFRENE
   April 15, 1734, baptism of Jeanne, daughter of /Guillaume Chever -- page torn/ and Therese Barbier. Godparents: /page torn/.

4. ANGELIQUE
   April 27, 1734, baptism of Angelique, *negresse* of the widow d'Herbanne. Godparents: Jean Baptiste d'Herbanne (s) and /Angelique Dumont/ Verger (x).

5. MARIE LOUISE
   May 16, 1734, baptism of Marie Louise, adult, female Indian belonging to Lebrun, habitant. Godparents: Colet (s), habitant, and Marie Anne Bocquet (x).

6. FRANCOISE
   May 23, 1734, baptism of Francoise, adult, female Indian belonging to Pierre /Rachal dit/ St. Denys, corporal and soldier. Godparents: Le Roy *dit* Framboise (s), soldier, and "his wife" (s).

   NOTE: The signature of Mme. Le Roy actually does not appear in the register, although Fr. Vitry stated that she signed. There are a number of such entries in this section of the register.

7. MARIE LOÜISE DE LA CHAISE
   May 24, 1734, baptism of Marie Loüise, born May 21, 1734, daughter of Messire Jacques de la Chaise (s) and of Dame Marie Rose de St. Denys. Godparents: Messire Louis Juchereau

de /̲S̲t. Denis -- page tor̲n̲/ and Dame Emmanuel Sanchez de Navarre.

8. FRANCOIS LEMOINE
   JEANNE VICTORIA GARCIE
   July 17, 1736, after publication of bans, marriage of Francois LeMoine, soldier, *dit* La Vidette, age 40, son of Francois LeMoine and Marguerite Gentin of the town of Amboise, diocese of Tours . . . and . . . Jeanne Victoria Garcie, previously of the Spanish post of Adays, living two years in this parish, aged 13, daughter of Pierre Garcie, soldier, and of Marie Joseph Condee. Witnesses: Pierre Marets de la Tour (s/ Mariet Delatour), officer of Mr. Tourangeau; Claud Bertrand *dit* Dauphine (s/ Claude Bertrant); and Pierre Alorges (s/ Alorge), both sergeants.

9. JEAN BAPTISTE BREVEL
   ANNE
   July 27, 1736, after publication of three bans and with the permission of Commandant St. Denys, marriage of Jean Baptiste Brevel, aged 39 /̲i̲llegibl̲e̲/ . . . and . . . Anne, of the Caddoes /̲r̲emainder illegibl̲e̲/.

10. CESAR
    MARIE ANE
    January 8, 1736, marriage of Cesar, *nègre*, and Marie Ane, *négresse*, both slaves of Mr. de St. Denys, commandant, "in presence of Mr. de la Chaise and other witnesses."

11. FRANCOIS
    MARIE FRANCOISE
    January 8, 1736, marriage of Francois, *nègre*, and Marie Francoise, *négresse*, both slaves of Mr. de St. Denys, commandant, "in presence of Mr. de la Chaise and other witnesses."

12. PIERRE
    MARIE
    February 2, 1736, marriage of Pierre, *nègre*, and Marie, *négresse*, both slaves of Mr. de St. Denys, commandant, in presence of Mde. de St. Denis "and other witnesses."

13. JEAN BAPT. D'HERBANNE
    VICTOIRE MARGUERITE GONZALES
    April 8, 1736, "after publication of bans," marriage of Jean Bapt. d'Herbanne of this parish, aged 25, son of deceased Francois d'Herbanne and of Jeanne de la Grande Terre, habitants of this parish . . . and . . . Victoire Marguerite Gonzales of the Spanish post of Adaÿs, 15 years, daughter of Messire Joseph Gonzales, general of the post, and Dame Marie Gertrude de la Cerda. Witnesses: Pierre Marets

de la Tour and Jacques de la Chaise.

14. FRANCOIS
   June 9, 1734, baptism of Francois, *négrillon* of Pierre Marion, habitant. Godparents: Francois Goudeau (s), surgeon, and Jeanne Chaniau (x), wife of Pierre Marion.

15. MARIE ANNE
   June 18, 1734, baptism of Marie Anne, *négritte* of Widow la Renaudiere, habitant. Godparents: Charles La Renaudiere (x), and Marie Anne Rousseau (x).

16. MARIE DES NEGES DE ST. DENYS
   August 16, 1734, baptism of Marie des Neges, born August __, daughter of Messire Louis de St. Denys, Commandant of the post, and Dame Emmanuele Sanches de Navarre. Godparents: Francois Goudeau, surgeon, and Marie Petrone de St. Denys. Father present.

17. LOUIS JOSEPH
   September 19, 1734, baptism of Louis Joseph, *négrillon* of Mr. de St. Denys /remainder illegible/.

18. CATHERINE
   October 17, 1734, baptism of Catherine, *négritte* of Mr. d'Herbanne. Godparents: Jean Baptiste d'Herbanne and Jeanne /surname illegible -- no signature/.

19. JEAN BAPTISTE
   October 17, 1734, baptism of Jean Baptiste, *négrillon* of Mr. de la Chaise, *endoyé*. Godparents: Jean Baptiste d'Herbanne (s), and Jeanne Robert (x).

20. ANTONIA EMMANUELLE
   January 18, 1735, baptism of Antonia Emmanuelle, Indian, daughter of La Ramée and of Cecile. Godparents: Messire Loüis de St. Denys (s) and Dame Emmanuelle Sanchez de Navarre.(x).

21. JOSEPH DUPRE
   February 6, 1735, baptism of Joseph, born February 4, 1735, son of Jacques Dupre and Anne Marie Philippe. Godparents: Joseph du /illegible -- signature also illegible/ and Jeanne Riotau (x). Father present and signed also.

22. PIERRE TRICHE
   March 1, 1735, baptism of Pierre, born February 26, 1735, son of Henry Triche and of Marie /no last name given/. Godparents: Pierre de /Illegible/ and Nicola de Grenade.

23. NICOLE DES DOULEURS /SURNAME ILLEGIBLE/
April 12, 1735, baptism of Nicole des Douleurs, born and *endoyée* April 1, 1735, daughter of Therese /surname illegible/. Godparents: Louis jucherot de St Denys and Dame Emmanuelle Sanches de Navarre, his wife.

24. GABRIEL LAGÉ
April 13, 1735, baptism of Gabriel, born April 8, 1735, son of Jean Lagé and Francoise Buart. Godparents: Gabriel Buart and Marie Francoise Bourdon. Father present and signed.

25. ANNE PREVOST
April 12, 1735, baptism of Anne, born and *endoyée* April 10, 1735, daughter of _____ Prevost (x) and Yves Dubos. Godparents: Jean Bossier and Anne Chaniau, his wife.

26. JEAN BAPTISTE *dit* FLONDOR
    MARIE
June 19, 1735, baptism of Jean Baptiste *dit* Flondor and Marie, his wife, with consent of their master who was present. /Master unnamed/ Godparents: Jean Baptiste d'Herbanne (x) and Jeanne _____ (x).

27. MARGUERITTE
August 6, 1735, baptism of Margueritte, age 4, Indian female of Messire Louis de St. Denys, commandant; *endoyée* at three months of age. Godparents: Pierre de la Tour, officer (x), and Dame Emmanuele Sanches de Navarre (x).

28. ANNE VERGER
August 17, 1735, baptism of Anne who was born and *endoyée* that same day, daughter of Joseph Verger and Angelique Charles. Godparents: Henry Triche (x) and Anne Chaniau (x).

29. MARIE VERGER
August 17, 1735, baptism of Marie who was born and *endoyée* that same day, daughter of Joseph Verger and Angelique /no last name/. Godparents: Francois Goudeau (x) and Marie Triche (x).

30. JEANNE LE ROY
October 16, 1735, baptism of Jeanne, /birthdate illegible/, legitimate daughter of Etienne Le Roy and Francoise Gilot. Godparents: Robert, soldier, and Jeanne _____ /Illegible/.

31. ANNE MARIE
October 22, 1735, baptism of Anne Marie, born October 19, 1735, legitimate daughter of Julien, *nègre*, and Feliciane, Indian. Godparents: Louis de St. Denys, commandant, and Emmanuel Sanches de Navarre (x).

32. JACQUES RACHAL
    December 6, 1735, baptism of Jacques, born December 4, 1735, legitimate son of Pierre Rachal and Marie Anne Benoit. Godparents: Jacques Chevalier, soldier, and Anne Chaniau, habitant (x).

33. FRANCOIS
    December 26, 1735, baptism of Francois, *nègre* adult belonging to Mr. de St. Denys, commandant. Godparents: Francois Goudeau, surgeon, and Marie Petronille de St. Denys (x).

34. CESAR
    December 26, 1735, baptism of Cesar, *nègre* adult belonging to Mr. de St. Denys, commandant. Godparents: Gilles Francois and Jeanne de Dieu (x).

35. HYVES
    January 2, 1736, baptism of Hyves, son of Jean Baptiste and Marie, negro slaves of d'Herbanne. Godparents: Hyves du _____, *cadet*, and _____ d'Herbanne (x).

36. CLAUDE
    THERESE
    January 8, 1736, baptisms and marriage of Claude and Therese, negro slaves of Mr. de la Chaise. Godparents of Claude: Claude Bertrand and Marie, his wife. Godparents of Therese: Mr. le Brun and M^de /Lagé *dit*/ Piedferme.

37. THERESE LE VASSEUR
    January 25, 1736, baptism of Therese, *endoyée* January 24 and born January 16, legitimate daughter of Jacques Le Vasseur *dit* Jolibois and Marie Francoise Bourdon. Godparents: Guilhaume Chever *dit* Dufresne (x) and Therese Barbier (x).

38. ANNE MARIE DE LA CHAISE
    January 28, 1736, baptism of Anne Marie, born and *endoyée* January 27, 1736, legitimate daughter of Jacques de la Chaise and Marie Rose Jucherot de St. Denys. Godparents: Pierre de la Tour, officer, and Marie Petronille Jucherot de St. Denys (x).

39. JEAN PIERRE
    February 2, 1736, baptism of Jean Pierre, *nègre*, /master illegible/. Godparents: /Illegible/ and Marie Petronile de St. Denys (x).

40. JEAN BAPTISTE BREVEL
    May 20, 1736, baptism of Jean Baptiste, son of Jean Baptiste Brevel, soldier, and of Anne /no last name/. Godparents: Pierre Alorges, Sergeant, and Marie "*dite* Dauphine from the name of her husband" (x). Father present.

41. ANNE
   June 16, 1736, baptism of Anne, adult, female Indian of
   Jean Baptiste Brevel (s), present. Godparents: Claude
   Bertrand *dit* Dauphine (s), sergeant, and Angelique Charles
   /Dumont/ (x).

42. JACQUES FRANCOIS
   August 26, 1736, baptism of Jacques Francois, *negrillon* of
   deceased Mr. du Sablé. Godparents: Francois Chaniau (x)
   and Jeanne Chaniau (x).

43. MARIE FRANCOISE
   September 21, 1736, baptism of Marie Francoise, Indian of
   Mr. Cusson. Godparents: Francois Godeau, surgeon, and
   Marie Bocquet.

44. JEANOT *dit* AN_____
   November 1, 1736, baptism of Jeanot *dit* An____ /illegible/,
   belonging to Francoise Bouchon. Godparents: /illegible/.

45. GREGOIRE
   November 5, 1736, baptism of Gregoire, *négrillon* of Mr. de
   St. Denys. Godparents: Gregoire, *nègre*, and Marie,
   négresse, of Sr. d'Herbanne.

46. PIERRE
   November 8, 1736, baptism of Pierre, aged 6, *endoyé* at
   birth, son of Julien, *nègre*, and of an Indian woman. Godparents: Pierre de la tour (s), officer, and Marie Dauphine.

47. MARIE CHEVER
   November 10, 1736, baptism of Marie, born November 9, 1736,
   legitimate daughter of Guillaume Chever *dit* Dufresne (s)
   and Therese Barbier. Godparents: Jean Prudhomme (x) and
   Marie Bocquet (x).

48. MARIE GERTRUDE
   November 18, 1736, baptism of Marie Gertrude, legitimate
   daughter of Francois, *nègre*, and Marie Francoise, *négresse*
   Godparents: Louis de St. Denys (x) and Marie Gertrude de
   St. Denys (x).

49. ROBERT DUPRE
   December 6, 1736, *endoyé* on day of birth, legitimate son of
   Jacques Dupre *dit* La Suisse and Anne Marie Philipelau. God-
   parents: Robert Avare and Huves Dubos (x).

50. ELISABETH DUPRE
   December 6, 1736, baptism of Elisabeth, legitimate daugh-
   ter of Jacques Dupre and Marie Philiplau. Godparents:
   /Illegible/ and Elizabeth /Illegible/.

51. MARGUERITE VICTOIRE PRUDHOMME
December 19, 1736, baptism of Marguerite Victoire, legitimate daughter of Jean Prudhomme and Catherine Meslier. Godparents: Guilhaume Chever and Marguerite Victoire Gonzales (x).

52. FRANCOIS
January 6, 1737, baptism of Francois, *négrillon* of Mde. la Renaudiere. Godparents: Francois Chaniau (x) and Marie Francoise La Renaudiere (x).

53. JOSEPH ANTOINE
January 7, 1737, baptism of Joseph Antoine, *négrillon* of Mr. de St. Denys. Godparents: Louis Antoine de St. Denys (x) and Marie Petronille de St. Denys (x).

54. ANTOINE LAGÉ
February 1, 1737, baptism of Antoine, legitimate son of Jean Lagé and Francoise Buart. Godparents: Antoine Dupin (x) and Angelique Verger (x).

55. GUILHAUME CESAR
February 24, 1737, baptism of Guilhaume Cesar, *nègre* of Francois Barbier *dit* Marechal. Godparents: Guilhaume Chever *dit* Dufresne and Therese Barbier (x).

56. MARIE
March 2, 1737, baptism of Marie, adult Indian belonging to Mr. de St. Denys, commandant, *endoyée* in 1734. Godparents: Pierre Marais de la Tour (s), officer, and Rose de la Chaise (x).

57. FRANCOIS
March 10, 1737, baptism of Francois, adult *nègre* belonging to Francois Manne. Godparents: Francois Manne (x) and Jeanne D'Herbanne, his wife (x).

58. MARIE HENRIETTE
March 13, 1737, baptism of Marie Henriette, Indian belonging to Mr. Duplessis, born and *endoyée* March 10. Godparents: Henry Triche (x) and Louise Duplessis (x), mistress of the slave.

59. PIERRE *dit* GUERIN
March 30, 1737, baptism of Pierre *dit* Guerin, adult *nègre* belonging to Mr. St. Denis. Godparents: Pierre de la Tour (s/ de la Chaise), lieutenant of the marines, and Marie Bled (x) /Ville Blette/.

60. CATHERINE
March 30, 1737, baptism of Catherine, adult *négresse* of

Mr. de St. Denis. Godparents: Jacques de la Chaise (x) and Manuel Sanches de Navarre (x).

61. ANTOINE
March 31, 1737, baptism of Antoine, adult *nègre* belonging to Jacques de la Chaise. Godparents: Louis de St. Denys and /Illegible/.

62. NICOLAS
March 31, 1737, baptism of Nicolas, adult *nègre* belonging to Jacques de la Chaise. Godparents: Nicolas Prevot and Catherine Mesliers (x).

63. JEANNE
March 31, 1737, baptism of Jeanne, adult *négresse* of Jacques de la Chaise, having been *endoyée* when ill. Godparents: Francois Goudeau, surgeon, and Marie Louise de la Chaise (x).

64. JEAN *dit* Janot
April 7, 1737, baptism of Jean *dit* Janot, adult *nègre* of Mr. de St. Denis. Godparents: Gilles Francois *dit* Jolis Garcon (x) and Therese Charpentier (x).

65. PIERRE
April 13, 1737, baptism of Pierre, adult *nègre* belonging to Mr. Bocquet. Godparents: Pierre de la Tour (s), officer of the marines, and Marie Bocquet (x), the slave's mistress.

66. GABRIEL
April 20, 1737, a small Indian belonging to Mr. Le Brun, habitant, *endoyé* in 1736 when ill. Godparents: Gabriel Buart, soldier (x) and Marie Anne Rousseau (x).

67. CLAUDE
April 22, 1737, baptism of Claude, adult *nègre* belonging to Mr. Le Brun. Godparents: Claude /Illegible/ and Marie Francoise /Illegible/.

68. MARIE LOUISE
April 28, 1737, baptism of Marie Louise, adult *négresse* of Jean Baptiste Le Brun, habitant. Godparents: Giles Francois, *dit* Jolis Garcon (x) and Francoise Gilot (x).

69. JEANNE
May 3, 1737, baptism of Jeanne, *négrillone* belonging to Mr. d'Herbanne. Godparents: Jean Baptiste D'Herbanne and Jeanne D'Herbanne Manne (x).

70. PIERRE *dit* JASMIN
May 5, 1737, baptism of Pierre *dit* Jasmin, adult *nègre*

belonging to Mr. D'Herbanne. Godparents: Pierre Alorges, sergeant of the garrison, and Jeanne Chaniau (x).

71. MARIE ANNE
May 5, 1737, baptism of Marie Anne, adult *négresse* belonging to Mr. D'Herbanne. Godparents: Jacques Magdonogh, officer, and Marie Dauphine (x).

72. EMMANUEL TRICHE
May 6, 1737, baptism of Emmanuel, legitimate son of Henry Triche and Marie Charles. Godparents: Louis Jucherot de St. Denys, Jr. (x) and Emmanuel Sanches de Navarre (x).

73. LOUIS ANTOINE DE LA CHAISE
May 11, 1737, baptism of Louis Antoine, born March 8, 1737, legitimate son of Jacques de la Chaise and Rose Marie Jucherot de St. Denys. Godparents: Louis Antoine Jucherot de St. Denys (x) and Emmanuel Sanches de Navarre (x).

74. MARIE BARBE
May 26, 1737, baptism of Marie Barbe, adult Indian belonging to Louis de St. Denys, Commandant. Godparents: Jacques de la Chaise (s) and Marie Petronille de St. Denys (x).

75. JACQUES
LOUISE
June 2, 1737, baptisms of Jacques and Louise, adult negroes belonging to Francois Barbier *dit* Marechal. Godparents of Jacques: Jacques Le Vasseur *dit* Jolibois and Marie Francoise *dit* Bourdon; godparents of Louise: Pierre Marel de la Tour and Marie Dauphine.

76. JEANNE VERGER
July 10, 1737, baptism of Jeanne, born July 8, 1737, legitimate daughter of Joseph Verger and Angelique Charles. Godparents: Pierre Fosse *dit* Tourageau and Jeanne D'Herbanne Manne. Father present.

77. MARIE LOUISE
July 15, 1737, baptism of Marie Louise, *négresse* belonging to Pierre Marionau, habitant, born July 14, 1737. Godparents: Louis Marionau (x) and Marie Anne Lacroix Chaniau (x).

78. MARIE LOUISE RACHAL
July 28, 1737, baptism of Marie Louise, born July 27, 1737, legitimate daughter of Pierre Rachal *dit* St. Denys, corporal of the garrison, and Marie Anne Benoit. Godparents: Pierre Alorge (s), sergeant, and Marie Dauphine (x).

79. JEANNE RONDIN
September 8, 1737, baptism of Jeanne, born September 7,

1737, legitimate daughter of Julien Rondin and Jeanne Riotaur. Godparents: Antoine Dupin (x) and Martine Bonet (x).

80. CLAUDE CESAR
    LOUISE
    September 8, 1737, baptisms of Claude Cesar and Louise, adult negroes of S^r D'herbanne. Godparents of Claude Cesar: Claude Bertrand (x) dit Dauphine and Marie Dauphinée (x); godparents of Louise: Francois Chaniau (x) and Marrie Anne Marchand (x).

81. MARIE LOUISE
    September 26, 1737, baptism of Marie Louise, négritte, belonging to Pierre Marionau, habitant. Godparents: Louis Marionau (x) and Marie Anne Marchand (x).

82. NICOLAS dit DOCLA
    JUDITH
    September 29, 1737, baptisms of Nicolas dit Docla and Judith, adult negroes belonging to S^r D'Herbanne. Godparents of Nicolas: Pierre Rachal and Marie Anne Benoit (x); godparents of Judith: Pierre Besson (x) and Anne Chaniau (x).

83. MARIE LOUISE MANNE
    September 29, 1737, baptism of Marie Louise, legitimate daughter of Francois Manne and Jeanne D'Herbanne. Godparents: Jean Baptiste D'Herbanne (x) and Marguerite Victoire Gonzales (x).

84. JACQUES dit FRAPE D'ABORD
    November 24, 1737, baptism of Jacques dit Frape d'Abord, adult nègre of Jacques de la Chaise. Godparents: Jacques Magdonoch, officer, and Jeanne Chaniau (x).

85. MARIE FRANCOISE
    November 24, 1737, baptism of Marie Francoise, adult négresse of Jacques de la Chaise. Godparents: Pierre Marionau (x), habitant, and Francoise Buart (x), habitant.

86. NICOLAS PREVÔT
    December 10, 1737, baptism of Nicolas, born December 3, 1737, legitimate son of Nicolas Prevôt dit Colet and Yves Dubos. Godparents: Pierre Prevôt (s) and Nicole Prevôt (x).

87. PIERRE dit L'EVEILLES
    December 14, 1737, baptism of Pierre dit L'Eveilles "of the Tonika," nègre adult belonging to J. Bapt. D'Herbanne. Godparents: Pierre Fosse dit Tourangeau (x) habitant, and Marie Francoise Bled (x), /Ville Blette/.

88. GUILHAUME dit MALBOUROUG
    December 14, 1737, baptism of Guilhaume dit Malbouroug,

nègre adult belonging to J. Bapt. D'Herbanne. Godparents: Guilhaume Chever *dit* Dufresne (s) and Marie Charles (x) habitant.

89. PIERRE
December 22, 1737, baptism of Pierre, adult *nègre* belonging to Jean Bapt. D'Herbane. Godparents: Gaspar D'Herbane (x) and Jeanne D'Herbane (x).

90. LOUISE SUSANNE
December 22, 1737, baptism of Louise Susanne, *négresse* adult belonging to J. Bapt. D'Herbanne. Godparents: Pierre Fosse *dit* Tourangeau (x) and Louise D'Herbane (x).

91. ALEXANDRE
December 22, 1737, baptism of Alexandre, *nègre* adult of Francois Manne. Godparents: Jean Bapt. Besson (s) and Marie Dauphine (x).

92. THOMAS *dit* SANS CARTIER
December 22, 1737, baptism of Thomas *dit* Sans Cartier, adult *nègre* belonging to J. Bapt. D'Herbanne. Godparents: Julien Rondin (x) and Jeanne Riotaur (x).

93. REMY *dit* JOLI COEUR
December 26, 1737, baptism of Remy *dit* Joli Coeur, adult *nègre* belonging to Mde. de la Renaudiere. Godparents: Remy Poisot (s) and Angelique Charles (x).

94. ANGELIQUE
December 26, 1737, baptism of Angelique, adult *négresse* of Mde. de la Renaudiere. Godparents: /Illegible/ and Martine Bonnet (x).

95. ETIENNE
December 27, 1737, baptism of Etienne, born December 26, *négrillon*, son of Francois and Genevieve, negroes. Godparents: Jean Pierre *dit* Caton, *nègre* and Marie Anne, *négresse*, belonging to Mr. de St. Denys.

96. JEAN *dit* LE JEUNESSE
January 5, 1738, baptism of Jean *dit* Le Jeunesse, *nègre* adult belonging to Sieur Jean des Jeans. Godparents: Jean Lagé *dit* La Rose (x) and Francoise Buart (x).

97. ETIENNE *dit* Canon
January 12, 1738, baptism of Etienne *dit* Canon, adult *nègre* belonging to J. B. D'Herbanne. Godparents: Etienne Le Roy *dit* Framboise (x), soldier, and Francoise Gilot (x).

98. LOUISE MARGUERITE
January 15, 1738, baptism of Louise Marguerite, *négrillone*,

legitimate daughter of Joseph and Susanne, adult negroes of Sr. Jean Bapt. D'herbanne. Godparents: Pierre D'Herbanne (x) and Louise D'Herbane (x).

99. FRANCOISE
January 28, 1738, baptism of Francoise, *négrillone*, legitimate daughter of Francois and Genevieve, negroes belonging to Mr. Manne. Godparents: Toisse, *nègre*, and Francoise, *négresse*, slaves of Mr. D'Herbanne.

100. MARIE GERTRUDE
February 23, 1738, baptism of Marie Gertrude, *négrillone* born February 1, 1738, legitimate daughter of Jean Baptiste and Marie, negroes of J. B. D'Herbanne. Godparents: Jean Bapte. D'Herbanne and Marie Gertrude Cerdas (x).

101. PIERRE
March 23, 1738, baptism of Pierre, adult *nègre* of Mr. de St. Denys. Godparents: Pierre Alorges, sergeant, and Marie Charles, habitant.

102. ETIENNE *dit* PIERROT DU ST. TOTIN
March 23, 1738, baptism of Etienne *dit* Pierrot du St. Totin, adult *nègre* belonging to Mr. de St. Denys. Godparents: Etienne Le Roy *dit* Framboise, soldier (x) and Francoise Gilot.

103. MARIE
March 30, 1738, baptism of Marie, adult Indian belonging to Pierre Rachal *dit* St. Denis, corporal. Godparents: Pierre Alorges, sergeant, and Marie Dauphiné (x).

104. MARIE *dite* LA RITTE
April 13, 1738, baptism of Marie *dite* La Ritte, adult Indian belonging to Mr. de St. Denys. Godparents: Francois de Strada (s/ Franco. de esmada) and Therese Charpentier (x).

105. MARIE LOUISE LE ROY
April 20, 1738, baptism of Marie Louise, legitimate daughter of Etienne Le Roy, soldier in the company of Mr. Macarty, and Louise Francoise Gilot; baptism performed at Natchitoches by Reverend Father Marmoulet of the order of St. Francis, a missionary from Los Adayes. Godparents: Jean Baptiste Davion (x) and Marie Dumont (x).

"I, a Capuchin priest and apostolic missionary, certify that the above act of Baptism was performed, but that it was not entered into the Register by the Reverend Father Marmoulet because he does not know the French language. In faith of which I sign, at Natchitoches, July 1, 1738." s/ Fr. Jean Francois C., *curé*.

106. PIERRE
    May 27, 1738, baptism of Pierre, *négrillon* of Monsieur de
    St. Denis, chevalier and commandant. Godparents: Pierre
    Cusson (x) and Marie Francoise Brie (s/ Bled) /Ville Blette/.

107. REMY POISOT
    June 17, 1738, baptism of Remy, legitimate son of Remy
    Poisot *dit* Bourgignon, soldier in the company of Mr. Ma-
    carty, of Dijon in Burgundy, parish of Our Lady, and Anne
    Marie Philippe, German. Godparents: Henry Riche (x)
    /Triche/ and Angelique Dumont (x).

108. ROSE MARIE BOISSELIER
    August 15, 1738, baptism of Rose Marie, posthumous and le-
    gitimate daughter of Jean Boisselier, pilot /Illegible/ for
    the King at the Balize, and Catherine Le Brüe of the parish
    of St. Frond, town and diocese of Perigaux. Godparents:
    Jean Jacques Macarty (s), captain of a company detached
    from the marines, and Emmanuelle Sanches de Navarre (s).

109. LOUIS RONDIN
    October 4, 1738, baptism of Louis, born "the thirteenth,"
    a son of the legitimate marriage of Julien Rondin, native
    of the parish of St. Bernard de Dôle in Bretagne, and of
    Jeanne Rioteau, a Creole. Godparents: Louis Jobar (x),
    habitant, and Jeanne Piquery (s/ La Robert - J. Piquery).

110. CHARLES FRANCOIS LE VASSEUR
    November 5, 1738, baptism of Charles Francois, born Novem-
    ber 3, 1738, legitimate son of Jacques Le Vasseur, native
    of Paris, parish of St. Nicolas des champs, and Marie Fran-
    coise, his wife, a native of Cleville. Godparents: Fran-
    cois Manne and Jeanne Victoire Garcie (x).

111. FRANCOIS
    December 18, 1738, baptism of Francois, *négrillon* belong-
    ing to Mr. de St. Denis. Godparents: Francois Moville (x)
    and Therese Locavia (x).

112. MARIE ANTOINE
    December 18, 1738, baptism of Marie Antoine, *négritte* of
    Mr. de St. Denys, previously *endoyée*. Godparents: Pierre
    Besser (x) and Marie des Neiges de St. Denys (x).

113. MARIE ANNE
    January 4, 1739, baptism of Marie Anne, *négritte* of Jean
    D'Herbanne *dit* Des Pres. Godparents: Jean Baptiste Bes-
    con (s) and Marie Anne Rousseau (s).

114. MARIE GAUTHIER
    May 9, 1739, baptism of Marie, legitimate daughter of Jean

Gauthier and Marie Louise. Godparents: Rene du Bos (s) and Marie Francoise Renaudiere (x).

115. MARIE FRANCOISE CHEVER
May 9, 1739, baptism of Marie Francoise, legitimate daughter of Guillaume Chever (s), native of the parish of Paletne in the town and bishopric of Vannes, in Bretagne, and of Therese Barbier, native of Tulin (Tutin?) in Dauphine. Godparents: Gaspar Barbier (s) and Marie Francoise Bourdon.

116. JEAN BAPTISTE TRICHE
May 26, 1739, baptism of Jean Baptiste, legitimate son of Henry Triche, a German inhabitant of this post, and Marie du /illegible/* born May 25, 1739. Godparents: Jean Baptiste Derbanne (s) and Angelique /illegible/* (x).

*Dumont

117. FRANCOIS
May 28, 1739, baptism of Francois, adult *nègre* belonging to Robert Avard. Godparents: Jean Baptiste Derbanne (s) and Louise Francoise Gilot.

118. FRANCOIS
MARIE
May 28, 1739, marriage of Francois and Marie, negro slaves of Robert Avard. Witnesses: Jean Baptiste Derbanne (s) and Louise Francoise Gilot.

119. MARIE LOUISE BREVEL
June 19, 1739, baptism of Marie Louise, born October 20, 1738 "at the Caddoes," legitimate daughter of Jean Baptiste Brevel (s), soldier in the company of Mr. MaCarty, and Anne, Indian. Godparents: Francois Goudeau, surgeon major, and Jeanne Joseph Piquery (s/ La Robert - J. Piquery).

120. LOUIS DE ST. DENYS
July 24, 1734. Death and burial of Louis de St. Denys. Soldier at the post. Witnesses: Hymco Clilnet and Jacques Chevalier.

121. JACQUES DUBOIS
August 10, 1734, burial in parish cemetery of Jacques Dubois, blacksmith and resident of the post, age fifty years. Witnesses: Thomas Meschi? and Jacques Chevalier.

122. ELIZABETH DUBOS
September 11, 1734, death and burial in parish cemetery of Elizabeth Dubos.

123. PIERRE GUERIN
May 10, 1735, death and burial in parish cemetery of Pierre

Guerin, aged 60 years, native of Mareine near La Rochelle. Witness: Bocquet.

124. CHARLES _____ *dit* LE MAJOR
June 22, 1735, death and burial in parish cemetery of Charles _____ [*sic*] *dit* Le Major, aged sixty years, a native of Domfront in Normandie. Witnesses: Maret de la Tour and Macdonogh.

125. JEANNE
August 3, 1735, burial in the parish cemetery of Jeanne, an Indian of six or seven years who died "the night of the same day."

126. JACQUES GUAIDON *dit* NANTOIS
August 26, 1735, death and burial in parish cemetery of Jacques Guaidon *dit* Nantois, a native of Nantoine. Witness: Macdonogh.

127. OLIVIER CLINON *dit* L'OLIVE
October 10, 1735, death and burial in parish cemetery of Olivier Clinon *dit* L'Olive, aged twenty-five years, soldier.

128. JEANNE D'HERBANNE
October 25, 1735, death and burial in parish cemetery of Jeanne D'Herbanne, widow of Francois D'Herbanne. Witness: Macdonogh.

129. MAGDELEINE GAY (DUBOS)
October 28, 1735, death and burial in parish cemetery of Magdeleine Gay, wife of René Dubos.

130. NICOLE VILLE VIEILLE (NAVARRE)
November 3, 1735, burial of Nicole Ville Vieille, wife of Robert Navarre, *anspesade* of the garrison of this post, who died November 1, 1735. Witness: Bocquet.

131. JACQUES DUPRE *dit* LA SUISSE
June 26, 1736, burial in the parish cemetery of Jacques Dupre *dit* La Suisse, native of Paris, who accidentally drowned on June 25 and was found the 26th. Witness: Brevel.

132. JOSEPH DANDONAU *dit* DU SABLE
August 20, 1736, burial in the parish cemetery of Joseph Dandonau *dit* Du Sable, habitant, who died on August 19. Witness: Marel de la Tour.

133. FRANCOIS LE MOINE *dit* LA VIDETTE BOUDIN
January 4, 1737, burial in parish cemetery of Francois Le Moine *dit* La Vidette Boudin, a soldier who died that same day.

134. MARIE JUCHEROT DE ST. DENYS (DE LA CHAISE)
April 29, 1737, burial in the church of Marie Jucherot de
St. Denys, twenty-one and a half years old, wife of Jacques
de la Chaise, who died on April 28. Witnesses: Marel de
la Tour and Magdonogh.

135. XAVIER CORTINAS
August 26, 1737, death and burial of Xavier Cortinas, aged
25 years, a Spanish soldier from the post of Los Adayes.
Witness: Magdonogh.

136. ANONYMOUS
September 28, 1737, burial of a female Indian of Mr. de la
Tour, in the parish cemetery.

137. PIERRE
September 28, 1737, burial of Pierre, aged four, *négrillon*
belonging to Mr. de la Chaise.

138. MARIE CHEVER
October 5, 1737, burial of Marie Chever; remainder of entry
illegible.

139. JEANNE RONDIN
September 20, 1737, death and burial of Jeanne, eight day
old daughter of Julien Rondin and Jeanne Riotaur.

140. PIERRE BENOIT *dit* DUBOIS
December 11, 1737, death and burial of Pierre Benoit *dit*
Dubois, a soldier of the garrison at this post. Witnesses:
de la Chaise and Macdonogh.

141. PROSPERE BENOUS
July 1, 1738, death and burial of Prospere Benous, a soldier of the company of Mr. Macarty. Witnesses: de la Tour
and Macarty.

142. ANONYMOUS
July 2, 1738, death and burial of a small Indian girl of
Robert Avard.

143. CATHERINE LA BRÜE (BOISSILIER, GOUDEAU?)
August 11, 1738, death of Catherine La Brüe, widow of deceased Jean Boissilier, supply pilot for the king at the
Balise, and wife of Sieur Godeau?, surgeon major at this
post, native of the parish of St. Fran___ /St. Frond?7,
town and bishopric of Perigeau, daughter of Ferdinand la
Brüe and of Marie /remainder illegible7.

144. JACOBUNE DE LA CHAISE
MARIA ROSA DE ST. DENIS
July 6, 1733, marriage of Jacobune de la Chaise and Maria

18

Rosa de St. Denis, daughter of Louis Antoine de St. Denis
and Emmanuelle Sanchez Navarro, witnessed by Brother Jean
Gregorio de la Campa of the Los Adaes mission. Entry recorded in Latin, March 17, 1744, at the Los Adaes mission
by Father Francisco Ballejo, Spanish priest of the Order
of Our Holy Father Saint Francis, an apostolic missionary
at the mission of Saint Michael de los Adayes, province of
Los Texas.

145. FRANCOIS CHANIAU
MARIE ANNE MARCHAND
September 9, 1734, marriage, after publication of three
bans, of Francois Chaniau, habitant of this parish, 26
years old, son of _____ Chaniau, habitant, and Marie Rondau . . . and . . . Marie Anne Marchand, aged 13, habitant
of this parish, daughter of Jean Marchand, soldier, and
Jeanne Pouillet. Witnesses: Jean Bossier, Jean Baptiste
Bocquet (s), habitants, Francois Goudeau (s), surgeon, and
Claude Bertrand *dit* Dauphine (s), sergeant.

146. FRANCOIS DOMINIQUE LAYBE
JEANNE RODRIGUE
_____ __, 1735 /month and day left blank/, marriage of
Francois Dominique Laybe and Jeanne Rodrigue, Spaniards
living in this parish. Witnesses: Marel de la Tour and
Macdonogh.

147. JULIEN RONDIN
JEANNE RIOTAUR
June 21, 1735, after publication of three bans, marriage of
Julien Rondin, habitant of this parish, 39 years old, son
of Julien Rondin and Marie Joupin of St. Leonard in Bretagne . . . and . . . Jeanne Riotaur, 15 years old, habitant of this parish, daughter of Pierre Riotaur and Martinne Bonnet. Witnesses: Pierre Marels de la Tour (s), J. B.
Bocquet (s), Jacques Macdonogh (s), and Joseph Verger (s).

148. FRANCOIS MANNE
JEANNE D'HERBANNE
January 9, 1736, marriage of Francois Manne, aged 24 years,
son of Francois Manne and Isabeau Richard of Bern in
Switzerland . . . and . . . Jeanne D'Herbanne, aged 16
years, native of this parish, daughter of deceased Francois D'Herbanne and Jeanne de la Grande Terre. Witnesses:
Pierre Marels de la Tour, Jean Baptiste Bocquet, Rene Dubois, and Jacques Macdonogh.

149. FRANCOIS
GENEVIEVE
March 10, 1737, marriage of Francois and Genevieve, negro
slaves of Francois Manne, habitant. Witnesses: Francois
Manne and "his wife."

150. FRANCOIS
     GENEVIEVE
     March 24, 1737, marriage of Francois and Genevieve, negroes
     of Jacques de la Chaise. Witness: de la Chaise.

151. PIERRE *dit* GUERIN
     CATHERINE
     March 30, 1737, marriage of Pierre *dit* Guerin and Catherine, negroes of Louis de St. Denys. Witnesses: de la
     Chaise and St. Denis.

152. NICHOLAS
     JEANNE
     March 31, 1737, marriage of Nicholas and Jeanne, negroes
     of Jacques de la Chaise. Witness: de la Chaise.

153. REMY POISOT *dit* BOURGUIGNON
     MARIE PHILIPPE
     April 30, 1737, after three bans, marriage of Remy Poissot
     dit Bourguignon, soldier, aged 28 years, son of Mammes
     Poisot, royal notary at Stratsbourg and Marie _____ /sic/
     his wife . . . and . . . Marie Philippe, widow of deceased
     Jacques Dupre, aged 30. Witnesses: René Dubos (s) and
     Francois Manne (s), habitants of this post.

154. PIERRE *dit* JASMINE
     MARIE ANNE
     May 4, 1737, marriage of Pierre *dit* Jasmine and Marie Anne,
     negroes of Mr. Derbanne. Witnesses: Jacques Macdonogh (s)
     and Pierre Alorge (s).

155. JEAN
     ISABELLE
     May 13, 1737, marriage of Jean and Isabelle, negroes of
     Louis de St. Denys. Witness: Louis de St. Denys.

156. JACQUES *dit* LA RAMEE
     MARIE BARBE
     May 27, 1737, marriage of Jacques *dit* La Ramee and Marie
     Barbe, Indian slaves of Louis de St. Denys. Witness:
     Louis de St. Denys.

157. JACQUES
     LOUISE
     June 2, 1737, marriage of Jacques and Louise, negro slaves
     of Francois Barbier *dit* Marechal. Witnesses: "their godfathers and godmothers;" s/ Maret de la Tour.

158. FRANCOIS DE TORRES
     XAVIERE DOMINIQUE FLORES
     July 27, 1737, after publication of three bans in this parish

159. and in the parish of Adayes, marriage of Francois de Torres, soldier of the Post of Adayes, 25 years old, son of Marc de Torres and Luice Garcia of the kingdom of Leon . . . and . . . Xaviere Dominique Florés, widow of Joseph De Al Barado 17 years old, actually living in this parish, daughter of Christophe Florés and Nicole de Boustamente of St. Louis du Potosi, who has for godfather Pedro Sierra (x), corporal of the garrison of Adaÿes, and for godmother Nicole Cordoba (x)

160. CLAUDE CESAR
LOUISE
September 8, 1737, marriage of Claude Cesar and Louise, negroes of Mr. D'herbanne. Witness: Macdonogh.

161. NICOLAS
JUDITH
September 29, 1737, marriage of Nicolas and Judith, negroes of Mr. D'herbanne. Witness: Mr. D'Herbanne.

162. JACQUES dit FRAPE D'ABORD
MARIE FRANCOISE
November 24, 1737, marriage of Jacques dit Frape d'Abord and Marie Francoise, negroes belonging to Jacques de la Chaise. Witnesses: their godfathers and godmothers.

163. PIERRE
LOUISE SUSANNE
December 22, 1737, marriage of Pierre and Louise Susanne, negroes belonging to Jean Bapt. D'Herbanne. Witnesses: their godfathers and godmothers.

164. REMY
ANGELIQUE
December 26, 1737, marriage of Remy and Angelique, negroes of Dame la Renaudiere. Witnesses: their godparents.

165. LOUIS LA MALATHI
JEANNE VICTORINE GARCIE
April 14, 1738, after three bans, marriage of Louis La Malathi, son of Jacques de la Malathi of St. Poirier Parish, diocese of Montauban /no mother given/ . . . and . . . Jeanne Victorine Garcie, daughter of Pierre Garcie and Marie Joseph Condée. Witnesses: Guillhaume Chever (s) and Jean Baptiste Besson (s).

166. PIERRE
ANNE
June 30, 1738, marriage of Pierre and Anne, negroes of Monsieur de St. Denis, Chevalier. Witnesses. Louis de St. Denis and de la Chaise.

167. ANTOINE RODRIGUE *dit* PAGNAU
MARIE MARCELLE
September 22, 1738, after publication of bans at Natchitoches and at the mission of St. Michel des Adayes, marriage of Antoine Rodrigue, a Spanish *mulâtre* . . . and . . . Marie Marcelle, Indian slave of Signora Dona Lucretia. Witnesses: de la Chaise (s), de la Tour (s), D'erbanne (s), and Pedro Reinevint?

168. JEAN BAPTISTE DERBANNE
VICTOIRE MARGUERITE GONZALES
March 5, 1739, rehabilitation of the marriage of Jean Baptiste Derbanne (s), son of deceased Francois D'erbanne and Jeanne de la Grande Terre . . . and . . . and Victoire Marguerite Gonzales of the Post of Adayes, daughter of Joseph Gonzales and Gertrude Maria de la /Cerda/. Witnesses: Robert Avard and Jean Baptiste Besson. Marriage was originally celebrated April 8, 1736 by Fr. Vitry "against the laws of the Church and of the State" and vows were renewed June 4, 1738 before Fr. Vitry on orders of the Vicar General, Father Mathias, dated April 12, 1738.

169. GABRIEL BUARD
MARIE ROUSSEAU
April 28, 1739, marriage of Gabriel Buard, soldier in the company of Mr. Macarty, legitimate son of George Buard, a native of Morge in Switzerland, and Claudine Bachalard . . . and . . . Marie Rousseau, a Creole of the parish on the German Coast, daughter of Louis Rousseau, of the parish of le Zay? in Poitou, diocese of Poitiers, and of Marie Chaigneau of the parish of Ste. Scoule in Aunis?, diocese of La Rochelle and Leuray. Witnesses: De Corbier (s), Jean Lagé (s), Alorge (s), Besson (s). Also signed: Mari Roussau.

170. FRANCOIS BARBIER
_____ 11, 1739, /month left blank/, burial in the parish cemetery of Francois Barbier, native of the parish of Tulin in Dauphiné. Witnesses: Duplessis (s), Jean Haieszes (s), Guillaume Chevel (s).

171. MARIE ANNE
February 11, 1739, burial in the parish cemetery of Marie Anne, *négritte* belonging to Jean Derbanne *dit* Des Pres.

172. PIERRE PRUDHOMME
January 22, 1739, death and burial in the parish cemetery of Pierre Prudhomme, habitant of this post. Burial performed by Sieur Pierre Duplessis "and other inhabitants" and witnessed by Besson and Verger. Entry recorded by Fr. Jean Francois de Civary, *curé*, on March 4, 1739.

173. ANTOINE DUPIN
March 14, 1739, death and burial of Antoine Dupin, habitant of this parish, aged about 35 years, native of the city and diocese of Poitiers. Witnesses: Besson, Verger.

174. GEORGE AVENAL
MARIE FRANCOISE LA RENAUDIERE
March 19, 1739, after three bans, marriage of George Avenal (x), soldier in the company of Mr. Macarty who gives his permission, son of George Avenal and Catherine Fasecoche of the kingdom of "Hongrie" . . . and . . . Marie Francoise la Renaudiere (x), widow of deceased Pierre Benoist, soldier, legitimate daughter of deceased Philippe la Renaudiere and Perrine Piver. Witnesses: de Corbier (s), René du Bos, and Alorge (s).

175. ELIZABETH VERGER
August 15, 1739, baptism of Elizabeth, born July 16, 1739, legitimate daughter of Joseph Verger of the Rue de St. Jacques in Paris, parish of St. Nicolas, and of Angelique Demont. Godparents: Julien Rondin (x) and Marie Paschal, wife of Mr. Goudeau (s), surgeon major of this place.

176. LOUIS LAGE
December 8, 1739, baptism of Louis, born December 5, 1739, legitimate son of Jean Lage (s), of Genêsee, habitant of this post, and Francoise Buard of Morges in Bergne, Switzerland. Godparents: Louis La Malathe *dit* Joubar, absent and represented by Jacques le Vasseur (x), and Marie Anne Rousseau (s).

177. LOUIS LA MALATHI
December 21, 1739, baptism of Louis, born December 20, legitimate son of Louis de la Malathi, native of St. Poirier, diocese of Montauban, habitant of this post, and of Jeanne Victoire Garcia, a Spaniard. Godparents: Henry Trichle (x) and Therese Clare /Clairmont/ (x).

178. JACQUES
/Illegible/ 20, 1739, baptism of Jacques, *négrillon* of Mr. St. Denis. Godparents: Jacques de la Chaise (s), *garde magasin du roy*, and Marie Paschal (s), wife of Mr. Goudeau, surgeon.

179. FRANCOIS PRUDHOMME
June /blank/, 1739, baptism of Francois, legitimate son of deceased Jean Philippe Prudhomme and /Catherine Meillier/. Godparents: Francois Goudeau (s), surgeon, and Marie Paschal (s), his wife.

180. JEANNE RACHAL
August 13, 1739, baptism of Jeanne, legitimate daughter of

Pierre Rachal *dit* St. Denis of the parish of St. Denis de Leron /d'Oléron/ in St. Onge, and of Marie Anne Benoist of the parish of St. Laurens of /illegible/. Godparents: Pierre Cusson (x), habitant, and Jeanne Piquery (s), wife of Robert /Avard/.

181. GEORGE AVENAL
MARIE FRANCOISE LA RENAUDIERE
/Duplicate of Entry 174./

182. LOUIS
March 13, 1740, baptism of Louis, *nègre* belonging to Mr. de la Chaise. Godparents: Louis Joubart and Marie Francoise Le Vasseur.

183. PIERRE ANTOINE DE ST. DENIS
June 29, 1740, baptism of Pierre Antoine, born June 20, legitimate son of Louis Jucherot de St. Denis (s), commandant and chevalier, and Emmanuelle Sanches de Navarre. Godparents: Pierre Maret de la Tour (s), lieutenant commanding one comapny of the marines, and Dame Parence Garcia, sister of the infant's mother.

184. MARIE ANNE POISOT
July 6, 1740, baptism of Marie Anne, legitimate daughter of Remi Poisot (s) and Marie Philippe, born July 3. Godparents: Jean Maderne (x) and Marie Buart? (x).

185. JEANNE
July 17, 1740, baptism of Jeanne, *négresse* belonging to Sieur Marion. Godparents: Athanase Fortunat de Mezieres (s) and Jeanne Marion.

186. HENRY GILLES MORINE
September 4, 1740, baptism of Henry Gilles, legitimate son of Jean Antoine Morine and Claire Prox. Godparents: Henry Trichle (x) and Marie Dumont (x), his wife.

187. MARIE THERESE
September 11, 1740, baptism of Marie Therese, an Indian of the Cannecy nation, aged 7 or 8 years, property of Mr. de St. Denis (s). Godparents: Jean Flore (x) of the parish of the Adaies and Marie Therese Fleur (x).

188. JEAN BAPTISTE
November 13, 1740, baptism of Jean Baptiste, *nègre* of Mr. de St. Denis. Godparents: Jean Baptiste Besson and Louise Marguerite Guedon.

189. MARIE
December 13, 1740, baptism of Marie, a *négresse* of Mr.

Derbanne. Godparents: Guillaume Chever and Marguerite /illegible7.

190. MARIE FRANCOISE
January 25, 1741, baptism of Marie Francoise, Canneis Indian slave of Robert Avare. Godparents: Louis Marion and Louise Comptois.

191. MARGUERITE LE ROI
February 1, 1741, baptism of Marguerite, legitimate daughter of Etienne Le Roi *dit* Framboise, soldier, native of Paris, parish of St. Gervais, and Louise Francoise Gilot of Conflame near Charanton. Godparents: Guillaume Boisseau (s) and Dame Marguerite La Chaise (s).

192. MARIE JEANNE LE VASSEUR
March 24, 1741, baptism of Marie Jeanne, legitimate daughter of Jacques Le Vasseur, native of Paris, parish of St. Nicholas des Champs, and Marie Francoise Bourdon of Amiens, parish of St. Joachim. Godparents: Pierre Maret de la Tour (s), lieutenant, and Jeanne Marionneau (x).

193. CHARLES AUGUSTE DE LA CHAISE
April 6, 1741, baptism of Charles Auguste, born April 4, 1741, legitimate son of Jacques de la Chaise (s), *subdélégué* at Natchitoches, and of Marguerite Darensbourg. Godparents: Frederick Darensbourg (s) and Emmanuelle Sanches de St. Denis (x).

194. MARGUERITE GOUDEAU
May 5, 1741, baptism of Marguerite, legitimate daughter of Francois Goudeau (s) of La Rochelle, parish of Saint Bartholomew, and Marie Paschal, Creole of this country, habitants at Natchitoches. Godparents: Frederick Darensbourg (s), lieutenant, and Marguerite de la Chaise (s).

195. JOSEPH FRANCOIS
May 9, 1741, baptism of Joseph Francois, *négrillon* of Mr. de St. Denis. Godparents: Louis Antoine de St. Denis and Jeanne Marion.

196. AGNES GAUTIER
June 10, 1741, birth and baptism of Agnes, daughter (according to the ordinances of the king) of Jean Gautier, absent from his wife some eighteen months, and of Marie Andre. Godparents: Pierre Bossier *dit* Le Brun (s) and Agnes Bergereaux (s).

197. MARIA CECILE
GENEVIEVE
July 14, 1741, baptism of Maria Cecile and Genevieve,

négrittes belonging to Sr. Derbanne. Godparents of Maria Cecile: Louis Marionau and Marie Le Vasseur. Godparents of Genevieve: Louis Jubar and Jeanne Joubard.

198. ANNE
April 3, 1741, baptism of Anne, Indian slave of Jean Bossier of this parish. Godparents: Pierre Bossier and Anne Bossier.

199. MARIE JEANNE RONDIN
August 3, 1741, baptism of Marie Jeanne, legitimate daughter of Jules Rondin and Jeanne Riotaur. Godparents: Joseph Verger (s) and Jeanne Prevotiere.

200. PERINE AVENEL
August 3, 1741, baptism of Perine, legitimate daughter of Georges Avenel, soldier, and Marie Francois la Regnatiere. Godparents: Charles La Regnaudiere (x) and _____ La Regnaudiere (x).

201. MARGUERITE
September 4, 1741, baptism of Marguerite, Indian, belonging to Jean Boisselier. Godparents: Pierre Boisselier and Anne **Bart?**

202. LUCREIE
November 1, 1741, baptism of Lucreie, *négritte* belonging to Mr. de St. Denis. Godparents: Michel Corbier and Emmanuelle Sanches de St. Denis.

203. MARIE FRANCOISE MALATHI
November 29, 1741, baptism of Marie Francoise, legitimate daughter of Louis Jobard *dit* Malathi, native of St. Porier near Montauban, and Jeanne Victoire, Spanish. Godparents: Guillaume Chever (s) and Marie Francoise Le Vasseur (x).

204. CATHERINE ALORGES
December 1, 1741, baptism of Catherine, legitimate daughter of Pierre Alorges (s), native of Andelis, province of Normandie, and Catherine Meillier. Godparents: Pierre Laurens, officer, and Jeanne l'Abbe (s).

205. JEAN HAZES (HAZESZES)
MARIE FRANCOISE DE VILLERS BLET
/blank/, 1740, after publication of one ban and dispensation from other two, marriage of Jean Hazes* son of Jean Hazes, native of Bougival, diocese of Paris, and Catherine Edmond, native of the same place . . . and . . . Marie Francoise de Villers Blet (s), widow of Pierre Le Sage who died "at the Caddoes", a native of Paris, parish of St. Paul, legitimate daughter of Jean Baptiste de Villers

Blet, native of Chartres, and Marie Therese Martancour, native of Paris, parish of St. Paul. Witnesses: Francois Goudeau (s), Maret de la Tour (s), Claude Bertrand (s) and Guillaume Chever (s).

*Jean Hazes signed this marriage entry as "Hazeszes."

206. GUILLAUME BERGEREAU *dit* ST. ONGE
AGNES REGNAUDIERE
/Not given/ 17, 1740, marriage after publication of two bans and dispensation with third, of Guillaume Bergereau *dit* St. Onge, native of Jeannai in St. Onge, Parish of St. Sulpice, son of Nicolas Bergereau, native of Jeannai, and Jeanne Vigere of Saintaur, parish of St. Brie of the same province. . . and . . . Agnes Regnaudiere, native of Illinois, post of Kascatia /Kaskaskia/, daughter of Philippe Regnaudiere, native of Perigord, and Perine Pivert, native of Vitrei in Bretagne. Witnesses: Etienne Chaniot, Jean Lage (x), Remi Poisot, Pierre Bernardin. /Illegible signatures/.

207. ETIENNE BARBIER
LOUISE MARGUERITE DERBANNE
September 19, 1740, after three bans, marriage of Etienne Barbier (x), son of deceased Francois Barbier, native of Tulin in Dauphine, and Francoise Prudhomme, habitants of this parish . . . and . . . Louise Marguerite Derbanne (x), native of this parish, a daughter of deceased Francois Derbanne and Jeanne de la Grande Terre. Witnesses: J. B. Derbanne (s), Pierre Alorges, Guillaume Chever (s).

208. JEAN BAPTISTE BESSON
MARIE LOUISE GUEDON
February 8, 1741, after two bans and dispensation from the third, marriage of Jean Baptiste Besson (x), native of Paris, son of Jean Baptiste Besson and Marie Lefebvre . . . and . . . Marie Louise Guedon (x), of this parish, daughter of Jacques Guedon and Marie Therese Nantois. Witnesses: Pierre Alorges (s), sergeant, Guillaume Boisseaux (s), *voluntaire*, Pierre Duplessis, and Jacques Levasseur.

209. PIERRE ALORGES
MARIE CATHERINE MEILLER
February 13, 1741, after three bans, marriage of Pierre Alorges (s) and Andelis, province of Normandie, bishopric of Rouen, son of Charles Alorges and Marie Deguisancourt . . . and . . . Marie Catherine Meiller (x), native of Paris, parish of Saint Sulpice, widow of Jean Prudhomme, daughter of Joseph Picard and Catherine Meillier /sic/. Witnesses: Guillaume Chever (s), Claude Bertrand (s), Guillaume Boisseaux (s) Jacques Levasseur.

210. ROMAINE ANTOINE *dit* SOURIS?
CATHERINE
May 7, 1741, marriage of Romaine Antoine *dit* <u>Souris?</u> and Catherine, negroes belonging to de la Chaise. Witnesses: de la Chaise (s) and de la Tour (s).

211. MARIE
March 12, 1740, burial of Marie, adult Indian belonging to Mr. de St. Denis, in parish cemetery.

212. LOUISON
September 1, 1740, death and burial, in parish cemetery, of Louison, adult Indian belonging to Sieur Rondien.

213. ANONYMOUS
October 1, 1740, burial of a male, adult, Cancis Indian of Mr. de St. Denis, in the parish cemetery.

214. SANS QUARTIER
November 13, 1740, burial of Sans Quartier, Indian, aged 7 years, property of de la Chaise, in the parish cemetery.

215. MARIE THERESE NANTOIS (GUEDON)
November 20, 1740, burial in the parish cemetery of Marie Therese Nantois, a Chitimachas, wife of Jacques Guedon *dit* Nantois.

216. MARIE? ECHINE
February 26, 1741, burial in parish cemetery of <u>Marie?</u> Echine, an Indian girl aged twelve years, belonging to de la Chaise.

217. NICOLAS
April 12, 1741, burial in the parish cemetery of Nicolas, adult *nègre* of Mr. Rondin.

218. MARIE LOUISE
/no date/ 1741, burial in the parish cemetery of Marie Louise, Indian, about 8 months old, belonging to Mr. St. Denis.

219. JOSEPH VERGER
December 26, 1741, baptism of Joseph, born December 10, 1741, son of Joseph Verger (s), native of Paris, Rue St. Jacques, parish of St. Benoit, and Angelique Demont. Godparents: Thomas Leger (s) and Marie Francoise Levasseur.

220. JACQUES
January 7, 1742, baptism of Jacques, *négrillon* belonging to Mons. de la Chaise. Godparents: Jacques de la Chaise and Marguerite D'Arensbourg, his wife.

21. LOUIS ANTOINE
    April 19, 1742, baptism of Louis Antoine, *négrillon* of Mr. de la Chaise. Godparents: Pierre Maret de la Tour and Pelagie D'Arensbourg, his wife.

22. JEAN FRANCOIS
    May 6, 1742, baptism of Jean Francois, *négrillon* of Mr. de St. Denys. Godparents: Jean Baptiste Besson and Louise Marguerite Guedon.

23. ANNE ROSE
    May 11, 1742, baptism of Anne Rose, *négritte* belonging to Robert Avard, habitant. Godparents: Julien Davion (s) and Jeanne Piquery (s/ La Robert).

224. JEAN BAPTISTE ETIENNE BARBIER
    May 27, 1742, baptism of Jean Baptiste Etienne, son of Etienne Barbier and Louise Marguerite Derbanne. Godparents: Jean Baptiste Derbanne and Therese Chever.

225. MARIE THERESE
    August 24, 1742, baptism of Marie Therese, *négritte* belonging to Mr. de St. Denys. Godparents: de la Chaise and Marie de St. Denis.

226. PIERRE HENRI RICHER
    October 2, 1742, baptism of Pierre Henri, born September 29, 1742, son of Henri Richer and Marie Clermont, habitants. Godparents: Pierre Fosse and Marie Angelique Dumont.

227. MARIE FRANCOISE POISOT
    October 2, 1742, baptism of Marie Francoise, 4 days old, daughter of Remi Poisot (s) and Marie Philippe, habitants. Godparents: Guilhaume Bergereau *dit* St. Onge and Marie Francoise le Vasseur, habitants.

228. REINE JEANNE MADERNE
    February 7, 1743, baptism of Reine Jeanne, born February 6, 1743, daughter of Jean Maderne (x) and Marie Thili, habitants. Godparents: Pierre Fosse (x) and Jeanne Malathi (s), habitants.

229. MARIE MARGUERITE DE LA CHAISE
    February 11, 1743, baptism of Marie Marguerite, born February 10, 1743, daughter of Jacques de la Chaise (s), *subdélégué*, and Marguerite d'Arensbourg. Godparents: Louis Jucherot de St. Denis, commandant, and Damoiselle Marguerite de St. Denis.

230. GASPARD
    February 21, 1743, baptism of Gaspard, *négrillon* of Jean

Baptiste Derbanne, habitant. Godparents: Gaspard Barbier and Therese Chever.

231. JEANNE
February 27, 1743, baptism of Jeanne, *négritte* belonging to Jean Baptiste Derbanne, habitant. Godparents: Jean Prud'homme and Therese Chever.

232. FRANCOIS RONDIN
September 27, 1743, baptism of Francois, legitimate son of Julien Rondin and /Jeanne/ Riotaur. Godparents: /Illegible/ and Marie /Illegible/.

233. MARIE LOUISE
/No date/, 1743, baptism of Marie Louise, *négritte* belonging to Mr. de la Chaise (s), *subdélégué*. Godparents: Christophe Athanase de Mezieres (s), *cadet* of the garrison of this post, and Marie Louise de St. Denis (s).

234. LOUIS
/No date/, 1743, baptism of Louis, *négrillon* belonging to Mr. D'herbanne, habitant. Godparents: Louis Renauld (s/ Louis Renaux), habitant, and Jeanne Chagneau (x), wife of Sieur Marion.

235. ANONYMOUS
/No date/, baptism of the child of an Indian called Jeanne, belonging to Sieur Brevel, habitant. Godparents: Pierre Prudhomme, soldier of the garrison, and Marie Louise, wife of Sieur Dauffinois /Claude Bertrand *dit* Dauphine/, sergeant of the garrison.

236. MARIE FRANCOISE AVARE
January 11, 1744, baptism of Marie Francoise, legitimate daughter of Sieur Robert Avare (s) and Jeanne Picquery. Godparents: Julien Rondain (x) and Marie Francoise Bourdon (x), wife of Jacques le Vasseur, habitants.

237. PIERRE
January 16, 1744, baptism of Pierre, *négrillon* belonging to Mr. d'Herbanne. Godparents: Pierre Lauriat, officer of the garrison of this post, and Jeanne L'Abbe, wife of _____ /Illegible/ du Colet.

238. JEAN GAUTIER
January 28, 1744, baptism of Jean, son (according to the ordinances of the King) of Jean Gautier, absent from his wife for five years, and Marie André. Godparents: Jean Maderne (x), and Marie la Croix (x), wife of Sieur Francois Chagniaux.

239. MARIE FRANCOISE
February 17, 1744, baptism of Marie Francoise, infant Indian belonging to Madame Le Brun. Godparents: Gabriel Buart (x) and Marie Rousseau (s), his wife, habitants.

240. MARIE JEANNE BARBIER
February 17, 1744, baptism of Marie Jeanne, legitimate daughter of Etienne Barbier (x) and Louise Marguerite D'herbanne, habitants. Godparents: Gaspar Barbier (s), brother of the father of the infant, and Marie Jeanne Chaignaux (x), wife of Sieur Marion, habitants.

241. CECILE LE VASSEUR
February 19, 1744, baptism of Cecile, legitimate daughter of Jacques Le Vasseur and Marie Francoise Bourdon. Godparents: Etienne Barbier (x) and Marie Thily* (x), wife of Sieur Jean Mader.

*This name appears as Thily in the actual text; above it is written the name "Maderne."

242. JEANNE JOSEPH RICHER
March 16, 1744, baptism of Jeanne Joseph, legitimate daughter of Henri Richer and Marie Clermont. Godparents: Louis Riche of Pointe Coupée and Jeanne Joseph Picquery, wife of Sieur Robert /Avard/.

243. ATHANASE CHRISTOPHE FORTUNE
April 27, 1744, baptism of Athanase Christophe Fortune, *négrillon*, son of Marie and Cesar, slaves of Mr. Saint Denis, commandant. Godparents: Athanase Christophe Fortunat de Mezieres (s), *cadet* of the garrison of this post, and Marie Doleur Simon de St. Denis.

244. LOUIS FRANCOIS
June 15, 1744, baptism of Louis Francois, *négrillon*, son of Nanette, slave of Widow St. Denis, born June 13. Godparents: Louis Marion (s) and Victoire Margueritte Gonzal.

245. THERESE MALATIE
June 19, 1744, baptism of Therese, legitimate daughter of Louis Malatie and Jeanne Victoire /Garcia/. Godparents: Jacques Le Vasseur and Therese Barbier.

246. JEAN BAPTISTE CHARLES AVENAL
June 26, 1744, baptism of Jean Baptiste Charles, born June 24, legitimate son of George Avenel and Marie Francoise Larnoidier, habitants. Godparents: Charles Larnodier and Elisabeth Rachal.

247. MARIE POISOT
June 28, 1744, baptism of Marie, born June 26, legitimate

daughter of /Remy - text illegible/ Poisot and Anne Marie
Philippe. Godparents: /Illegible/ and Catherine Dupres.

248. JEAN PIERRE BESSON
July 22, 1744, baptism of Jean Pierre, born July 21, legitimate son of Jean Baptiste Besson and Louise Margueritte Gueÿdon. Godparents: Pierre Fosse and Jeanne Besson (s/ J. Robert Besson).

249. JEAN MADERNE
August 7, 1744, baptism of Jean, born August 6, legitimate son of Jean Maderne and Marie Thili. Godparents: Pierre Fosse, elder warden of this parish, and Margueritte Thily, wife of Thomas Leger, habitants of the parish of St. Pierre des Allemands, in whose absence Marie de La Croix (x), wife of Francois Chaniot, habitant, has served.

250. PIERRE GUILLEAUME ALORGE
August 17, 1744, baptism of Pierre Guilleaume, born that same day, legitimate son of Pierre Alorge, native of Andelis, province of Normandy, sergeant of the marines, and Catherine Meillier. Godparents: Guillaume Boissau (s), *cadet* in the company of Mr. Terpuÿ, and Marie Verger (s).

251. CHARLES TOUTIN
September 6, 1744, baptism of Charles, birthdate illegible, legitimate son of Charles Toutin, soldier, and Jeanne Gueÿdon. Godparents: Adrien Leger, habitant, and /illegible/, wife of Jacques Levasseur.

252. MARIE ANNE FAYARD
September 7, 1744, baptism of Marie Anne, legitimate daughter of Jean Fayard (s), soldier, and Francoise La Garrene, habitants. Godparents: Jean Maderne (x) and Marie La Croix, habitants.

253. BARNABÉ
September 11, 1744, baptism of Barnabé, born September 9, *négrillon*, son of Marie Francois and Francois, negro slaves of Madame Emmanuel Sanchez de Navarre, widow of deceased Mr. Jucherot St. Denis. Godparents: Pierre Antoin Jucherot de St. Denis and Marie Jucherot de St. Denis (s).

254. JOSEPH /LE/ DUC
September 13, 1744, baptism of Joseph, born September 12, legitimate son of Joseph /le/ Duc, soldier, and Marie Anne Gueÿdon, habitants. Godparents: Louis la Malathie and Louise Gueÿdon (s).

255. LOUIS BUART
September 15, 1744, baptism of Louis, born that same day,

legitimate son of Gabriel Buart and Marie Rouseau, habitants. Godparents: Louis Marion (s) and Anne Cheniot.

256. ILLEGIBLE
October 10, 1744, baptism of a *négrillon* born that same day of a *négresse* slave of Mr. De<u>cude?</u>, officer. Godparents: /illegibl<u>e</u>/ Avart, elder warden of this parish and *bourgeois* of this post, and Jeanne Abbé, wife of /illegibl<u>e</u>/.

257. LOUIS
November 10, 1744, baptism of Louis, born November 9, a *négrillon*, legitimate son of Louis and Marie Louise, slaves of Avare Robert (s), warden of this parish. Godparents. the owner and Elisabeth Rachal.

258. MARIE FRANCOISE
December 18, 1744, baptism of Marie Francoise, born December 17, *négritte* daughter of the *négresse* Angelique, slave of Widow Fisot. Godparents: Francois Vasseur and Marie Francois Vasseur.

259. ETIENNE VERGER
May 23, 1745, baptism of Etienne, born May 23, legitimate son of Joseph Verger (s) and Angelique Dumont. Godparents: Charle Jobart (x) and Therese Barbier.

260. ALEXIS
November 14, 1745, baptism of Alexis, born November 13, *négrillon* son of Louise *dit* Jocolone, slave of Gaspar Derbanne. Godparents: Alexis Grappe and Louise D'erbanne.

261. MARIE JEANNE
November 15, 1745, baptism of Marie Jeanne, *négritte*, legitimate daughter of Pierre and /illegibl<u>e</u>/, slaves of Pierre D'herbanne. Godparents: /illegibl<u>e</u>/ Prudhomme and Marie Anne Prevot de Guarre.

262. ETIENNE
November 26, 1745, baptism of Etienne, born November 24, *négrillon*, legitimate son of Jean Baptiste *dit* Flondor and Marie, both slaves of Widow Avard. Godparents: Etienne Barbier and Marie Francoise Bourdon.

263. JULIEN BESSON
March 24, 1746, baptism of Julien, legitimate son of Jean Baptiste Besson and Louise Marguerite Guedon. Godparents: Julien Francois Bideau (s/ Bidaux), sergeant, and Marie, wife of Mr. Dauphiné (s/ mark of Louise Dauphine).

264. PAULINE
March 26, 1746, baptism of Pauline, *négritte*, born of a

négresse belonging to Mr. Robert /Avar_d_7. Godparents: Monsieur LeCourt *cadet* (s/ Louis Mathias LeCourt de Prelle) and Madame Robert.

265. ELISABETH
March 26, 1746, baptism of Elisabeth, *négritte*, born of a *négresse* belonging to Mr. Robert /Avar_d_7. Godparents: Robert, "the son," and Mlle. Robert "the younger" (s/ Jeanne Robert).

266. PIERRE
May 12, 1746, baptism of Pierre, *négrillon*, born of a *négresse* belonging to Madame St. Denis. Godparents: Pierre Darbanne (x) and Mademoiselle Louise Etienne (x) /Louise Derbanne, wife of Etienne Barbie_r_7.

267. ATHANASE POISSOT
May 20, 1746, baptism of Athanase, legitimate son of Remis Poissot and Marie Philippe. Godparents: Athanase Fortuna de Mezieres and Marie de St. Denis.

268. LOUISE TOTAIN
June 10, 1746, baptism of Louise, legitimate daughter of Charle Totain and Jeanne Guedon. Godparents: Alexis Grappe (s), corporal, and Louise Derbanne (x).

269. JEANNE
June 25, 1746, baptism of Jeanne, *négritte*, born of a *négresse* belonging to Mde. St. Denis. Godparents: Nicolas Paul Bourdel and Jeanne /Le Roy *dit_e_7* Framboise.

270. LOUISE
September 12, 1746, baptism of Louise, *négritte*, born of a *négresse* belonging to Gaspard Darbanne. Godparents: Mr. LeCourt (s) and Louise Darbanne (x).

271. ELISABEHT MARIE FELICITÉ DE MEZIERES
September 13, 1746, baptism of Elisabeht /*sic*7 Marie Felicité, legitimate daughter of Mr. Athanase de Mezieres and Dame Marie Petronille Felicianc de St. Denis. Godparents: Cesar de Blanc (s), commandant, and Dame Emanuel Sanchez Navarre (s/ Emanuel Sanchez Navarro). Witness: Fr. Franciscus Ballejo.

272. MARIE LOUISE FAYART
September 27, 1746, baptism of Marie Louise, legitimate daughter of Jean Fallyar (s/ Jean Fayart) *dit* La Lamette, and Francoise Phizot. Godparents: Jean Louis Caesar *dit* Provencal (s/ Jean Louis Chesar Borme) and Marie Francoise Bourdon.

273. PIERRE ANTOINE
     December 2, 1746, baptism of Pierre Antoine, *mulâtre* born of a *négresse* belonging to Madame St. Denis. Godparents: Louis Antoine de St. Denis (s) and Marie Douleur Simon de St. Denis (s).

274. MARIE JEANNE CHAGNOT
     December 3, 1746, baptism of Marie Jeanne, legitimate daughter of Francois Chagnot (x) and Marie de la Croix. Godparents: Gabriel Buart (x) and Marie Maderne (x).

275. DANIEL LE DUC
     December 10, 1746, baptism of Daniel, legitimate son of Joseph Le Duc (x) *dit* Ville Franche and Marie Anne Guedon. Godparents: Daniel Pain (s), surgeon, and Elizabeth Rachal (x).

276. JEANNE /LA/ MALATHY
     January 17, 1747, baptism of Jeanne, legitimate daughter of Louis Malathy and Jeanne Victoire de Garcie. Godparents: Julien Rondin, habitant, and Jeanne Rioteau, his wife.

277. JEANNE MADER
     January 18, 1747, baptism of Jeanne, legitimate daughter of Jean Mader and Marie Thily. Godparents: Daniel Pain (s), surgeon, and Jeanne Chever.

278. MARCEL
     January 27, 1747, baptism of Marcel, *négrillon* born of a *négresse* belonging to Poissot, habitant. Godparents: Gabriel Buard (x) and Madame Le Brun (x).

279. MARIE LOUISE
     February 16, 1747, baptism of Marie Louise, *négritte* born of a *négresse* belonging to Mde. St. Denis. Godparents: Pierre Antoine de St. Denis (s) and Mademoiselle Marie des Nieges de St. Denis (s).

280. LOUISE PELAGIE GAUTIER
     May 11, 1747, baptism of Louise Pelagie, legitimate daughter of Renée Gautier *dit* La Fleure and Jeanne Lorand. Godparents: Julien Rondin (x) and Louise Darbanne (x).

281. GUILLAUME VERGER
     August 18, 1747, baptism of Guillaume, legitimate son of Joseph Verger and Angelique /Dumont/. Godparents: Guillaume Boisseau (s) and Jeanne /Chever *dite*/ Dufrene.

282. CLAUDE LE DUC
     August 31, 1747, baptism of Claude, legitimate son of Joseph

Le Duc (x) *dit* Ville Franche, soldier, and Marie Guedon. Godparents: Claude Bertrand *dit* Dauphine and Marie Louise (x), his wife. Witness: Jean Louis Chesar Bormé *dit* Provencal (s).

283. LOUIS
September 1, 1747, baptism of Louis, *mulâtre* born of a *négresse* belonging to Madame de St. Denis. Godparents: Daniel Pain, surgeon major (s) and Therese Barbier Dufrene (x).

284. GASPAR
January 12, 1747, baptism of Gaspar, *négrillon* born of a *négresse* belonging to Mr. Gaspar /Derbanne/. Godparents: Jacques LeVasseur, tenant on the place of Sieur Gaspar, and Marie Francoise Verger (x/ Marie Francoise Gaspar).

285. SUSANNE
September 13, 1747, baptism of Susanne, adult *négresse* belonging to the mission. Godparents: Claude Bertrand (x) and Marie Louise (x) his wife.

286. MARIE LOUISE L'ARNORDIERE
November 4, 1747, baptism of Marie Louise, legitimate daughter of Charle L'arnordiere and Jeanne de la Riviere. Godparents: Louis de St. Denis (s), officer, and Marie de St. Denis (s).

287. JEANNE MARIE LOUISE
December 11, 1747, baptism of Jeanne Marie Louise, *négritte* born of a *négresse* belonging to Madame St. Denis. Godparents: Mons. LeCourt, *cadet*(s) and Jeanne Chever (x).

288. JEANNE RONDAIN
January 8, 1748, baptism of Jeanne, legitimate daughter of Mesr. Julien Rondain, officer, and Jeanne du Pain. Godparents: Daniel Pain, surgeon major (s) and Jeanne Le Roy (x).

289. CATHERINE LEVASSEUR
/No month given/ 25, 1748, baptism of Catherine, legitimate daughter of Jacques Levasseur and Marie Francois Bourdon. Godparents: Pierre Fosse, elder warden, and Catherine Meillier (x).

290. PIERRE POISOT
June 4, 1748, baptism of Pierre, legitimate son of Remÿ Poisot (s) and Marie Philippe, habitants. Godparents: Pierre Bossier (s) and Marie LaCroix (x).

291. FRANCOIS
July 15, 1748, baptism of Francois, *négrillon* born of a *négresse* belonging to Sieur Poisot. Godparents: Francois Doucet (s) and Jeanne /Chever dit*e*/ Dufrene (x).

292. JEAN LOUIS (FEAUYRIED)
July 30, 1748, baptism of Jean Louis, *négrillon* born of a *négresse*, Jeanne, belonging to Fr. Eustache, infant of Jean Feauyried, soldier in the guards detached from the marines. Godparents: Jean Louis LeCourt (s) and Jeanne Roujot Pain (s). Also signed: "x/ mark of the father."

293. MARIE JEANNE RICHER
September 2, 1748, baptism of Marie Jeanne, born August 27, legitimate daughter of Henry Richer and Marie Joseph Clermont. Godparents: D. Pain (s) and Marie Jeanne Rougot (s), his wife.

294. JEAN BAPTISTE /LE/ DUC
September 15, 1748, baptism of Jean Baptiste, legitimate son of Joseph /le/ Duc *dit* Ville Franche, soldier, and Marie Anne Guedon. Godparents: Jean Baptiste Davion (x) and Marie Triche (s), his wife.

295. LOUIS CAESAR
October 12, 1748, baptism of Louis Caesar, *négrillon* born of a *négresse* belonging to Madame St. Denis. Godparents: Caesar de Blanc, commandant (s) and Marie de Neige de St. Denis (s).

296. MARIE JEANNE
October 27, 1748, baptism of Marie Jeanne, *négritte* born October 19 of a *négresse* belonging to Sr. Trichele. Godparents: Julien /Le Roy dit/ Framboise (s) and Marie Jeanne /Le Roy dit*e*/ Framboise.

297. PIERRE BOSSERON
November 28, 1748, baptism of Pierre, born November 20, legitimate son of Etienne Bosseron and Catherine Cheval. Godparents: Mr. Piquery, the son (x) and Marie Francoise /Le Vasseur dit*e*/ Jolibois (x).

298. JULIEN
December 26, 1748, baptism of Julien, *négrillon* born of a *négresse* belonging to Pierre Darbanne. Godparents: Julien Rondin, lieutenant (x) and Marie Francoise Le Vasseur (x).

299. MARIE LOUISE BUARD
December 31, 1748, baptism of Marie Louise, legitimate daughter of Gabriel Buard (x) and of Marie Anne Rousseau.

Godparents: Charle Dardenne (x) and Marie Louise Lage (s).

300. MARIE FRANCOISE LE BOEUF
January 3, 1749, baptism of Marie Francoise, legitimate daughter of Rene Le Boeuf and Emmanuel Duplessis. Godparents: Gille Francois (s) and Marie Anne Nanthe.*

*Written above this surname, between the lines, is the name "Guedon."

301. LOUIS TOUTAIN
January 23, 1749, baptism of Louis, legitimate son of Charle Toutain (x), soldier, and Jeanne Guedon. Godparents: Louis La Malathi, habitant (x) and Marie Francoise Levasseur (x).

302. PIERRE GUILLAUME CHEVER
January 26, 1749, baptism of Pierre Guillaume, legitimate son of Guillaume Chever (s), corporal, and Therese Barbier. Godparents: Pierre Alorge, sergeant (s) and Catherine Melier (x), his wife.

303. MARIE LOUISE VERGER
April 3, 1749, baptism of Marie Louise, legitimate daughter of Joseph Verger and Angelique /Dumont/. Godparents: Gaspard Derbanne (s/ Gaspar Derbanne) and Marie Francoise Verger (x).

304. PIERRE MICHEL
April 5, 1749, baptism of Pierre Michel, adult Indian belonging to Madame de St. Denis. Godparents: Pierre Fosse (x), habitant, and Marie des Neges de St. Denis (s).

305. LOUISE MARGUERITE
April 6, 1749, baptism of Louise Marguerite, *négritte* of Mdme. de St. Denis. Godparents: Claude Bertrand (s), first sergeant, and Louise Marguerite Duplecis.

306. EDMOND CHAGNOT
June 9, 1749, baptism of Edmond, legitimate son of Francois Chagnot, habitant, and Marie Anne LaCroix. Godparents: Edmond Thomas, soldier, and Anne Marie Philippe, wife of Remy Poissot.

307. MARIE FRANCOISE
September 19, 1749, baptism of Marie Francoise, *négritte* born that same day of a slave of Mr. Gaspard /Derbanne/. Godparents: Henry Trichle and Marie Francoise /Levasseur dite/ Jolybois.

308. MARIE JEANNE MADERE
September 22, 1749, baptism of Marie Jeanne, legitimate

daughter of Jean Madere, habitant, and Marie Thily. Godparents: Pierre Barrio, son of the governor of the Adayes, and Jeanne Rougot.

309. MARIE LOUISE DAVION
November 25, 1749, baptism of Marie Louise, legitimate daughter of Jean Baptiste Davion (x) and Marie Trichely. Godparents: Mr. Trichely(x) and Louise Francoise Gilote (x).

310. LOUIS ALEXANDRE
December 17, 1749, baptism of Louis Alexandre, *négrillon* born of a *négresse* belonging to Madame de St. Denis. Godparents: Louis de St. Denis, officer, and Marie des Neges de St. Denis.

311. GUILLAUME RENÉ GAUTIER
January 4, 1750, baptism of Guillaume René, legitimate son of René Gautier, soldier, and Jeanne Laurent. Godparents: Guillaume Chever (s) *dit* Dufrene, corporal, and Marie Jourdan (x).

312. JACQUES LEVASSEUR
February 20, 1750, baptism of Jacques, legitimate son of Jacques LeVasseur and Marie Francoise /Bourdon/. Godparents: Jean Louis Cesar Borme *dit* Provencal, soldier (s/ Jean Louis Cezere) and Therese Le Vasseur.

313. PIERRE POISSOT
March 9, 1750, baptism of Pierre, legitimate son of Remis Poisot (s), habitant, and Anne Marie Philippe Marthe. Godparents: Pierre Alorge (s), Sergeant, and Jeanne /Chever *dite*/ Dufrene (x).

314. JEANNE ELISABEH
March 28, 1750, baptism of Jeanne Elisabeh /sic/, adult Indian belonging to Madame Dominique /Monteche/. Godparents: Louis LeCourt (s) *cadet*, and Elisabh /sic/ Rachal Monet (s/ Elisabet Rachal Monet).

315. JEANNE
March 28, 1750, baptism of Jeanne, adult Indian belonging to Mr. Dauphine, sergeant. Godparents: Francois Manne (x), habitant of this post, and Jeanne Chever (x).

316. CESAR LARENAUDIERE
April 5, 1750, baptism of Cesar, legitimate son of Charle Larenaudiere and Jeanne La Riviere. Godparents: Cesar de Blanc, commandant (s), and Marie du Neges de St. Denis. Marginal note: infant died.

317. LOUIS ANTOINE
April 6, 1750, baptism of Louis Antoine, *négrillon* born of a *négresse* belonging to Madame St. Denis. Godparents: Messr. de St. Denis (s), officer, and Louise Etienne (x) ⟦Louise Marguerite Derbanne, wife of Etienne Barbier⟧.

318. MANUELLE RICHER
June 13, 1750, baptism of Manuelle, legitimate daughter of Henrÿ Richer and Marie Joseph Clermont. Godparents: Louis de St. Denis (s), officer, and Madame de St. Denis (x).

319. FRANCOIS GRAPPE
July 1, 1750, baptism of Francois, born December 4, 1747, legitimate son of Alexis Grappe and Margueritte Guedon. Godparents: Francois Hervé (s) and Jeanne Le Roy (x).

320. MARIE LOUISE GRAPPE
July 1, 1750, baptism of Marie Louise, born November 11, 1749, legitimate daughter of Alexis Grappe and Marguerite Guedon. Godparents: Dominique Monteche (x) and "Madame, his wife" (s/ Marie Francois de viel blet), both habitants.

321. GASPARD DERBANNE
July 7, 1750, baptism of Gaspard, legitimate son of Gaspard Derbanne (s) and Marie Francoise Verger. Godparents: Joseph Verger (s) and Jeanne Manne.

322. EDMOND THOMAS CHAGNOT
July 11, 1750, baptism of Edmond Thomas, legitimate son of François Chagnot and Marie Anne LaCroix. Godparents: Edmond Thomas *dit* Jourdain (x) and "Madame, his wife" (x).

323. LOUISE MARGUERITE
July 25, 1750, baptism of Louise Marguerite, a free child, daughter of Anne Marie, who is the daughter of Julien, a free *nègre*. Godparents: Louis de St. Denis (s), officer, and ⟦Marie Dolorit Simone Juchereau de St. Denis, wife of Cesar de Blanc⟧ (s/ Dolorit deblanc).

324. MARIE LOUISE
July 31, 1750, baptism of a *négritte* belonging to Mr. Trichely. Godparents: Mr. LeCourt (s), *cadet*, and Marie Louise Le Roy (x).

325. MARIE LOUISE
August 8, 1750, baptism of Marie Louise, born of an Indian belonging to Mr. ⟦Bertrand *dit*⟧ Dauphine. Godparents: Pierre Alorge (s), sergeant, and Marie Francoise Bourdon (x).

326. MARIE MADELEINE
August 15, 1750, baptism of Marie Madeleine, *négritte* born

of a *négresse* belonging to Madame de St. Denis. Godparents: Louis Gerard Pelerin (s) and Madame de Blanc (s).

327. DANIEL
September 13, 1750, baptism of Daniel, *négrillon* born of a *négresse* belonging to Sr. Poisot, habitant. Godparents: Daniel Pain (s), surgeon major, and Marie Joseph Clermont (s).

328. MARIE ANNE DARDENNE*
September 14, 1750, baptism of Marie Anne, born September 13, 1750, legitimate daughter of Charles Dardenne* *dit* Belle Rose and Louise Lager. Godparents: Gabriel Buard, habitant, and Marie Roussot.

*In both cases, the original spelling has been written over *incorrectly* as Derbanne -- an incidence which appears in each baptismal record of a Dardenne child. In one instance only (Entry 299), at which Sieur Dardenne served as a godfather, has his name been left with its original spelling. An examination of church and civil records for this period indicates that all adult male Derbannes who were contemporaries of Dardenne were sons of Sieur François Dion Despres Derbanne and the Sieur Derbanne's sons and heirs did not include any individual named Charles.

329. JEANNE ELISABETH /LE/ DUC
October 19, 1750, baptism of Jeanne Elisabeth, born October 19 also, legitimate daughter of Joseph /Le/ Duc *dit* Ville Franche, soldier, and of Marie Anne Guedon. Godparents: Pierre Antoine de St. Denis (s) and Madame Elisabht /sic/ Borme (s/ Marie Elisabet Denette).

330. MARIE ELEONARD
November 5, 1750, baptism of Marie Eleonard, daughter of Marie, property of Mde. de St. Denis. Godparents: Pierre Antoine de St. Denis (s) and Marie des Douleurs De Blanc (s).

331. MARGUERITTE
November 5, 1750, baptism of Margueritte, daughter of Margueritte, belonging to Madame de St. Denis. Godparents: Pierre Antoine de St. Denis (s) and Marie des Douleurs De Blanc (s).

332. MARIE ELEONORE DE ST. DENIS
November 5, 1750, baptism of Marie Eleonore, daughter of Marie des Neiges de St. Denis and a father unknown. Godparents: Cesar de Blanc, commandant, and Marie des Douleurs de St. Denis, his wife.

333. MARIE JEANNE
     November 22, 1750, baptism of Marie Jeanne, *négritte* born
     of a *négresse* belonging to Sr. Fosse *dit* Tourangeau, habi-
     tant of this post. Godparents: Louis de St. Denis (s),
     officer, and Marie Mader (x).

334. MARIE JEANNE NALER (VALER?)
     November 28, 1750, baptism of Marie Jeanne, legitimate
     daughter of Christophe Naler (Valer?) and Marie Jeanne de
     la Vez, both Spaniards. Godparents: Jean Baptiste Renaud
     dit de Rosier (s), soldier, and Marie Jeanne Riviere (x).

335. MARIE FRANCOISE BUARD
     December 9, 1750, baptism of Marie Francoise, legitimate
     daughter of Gabriel Buard (x) and Marie Anne Rousot. God-
     parents: Charles Toutin (x) *dit* Munier, habitant, and
     Marie Francoise Bourdon (x).

336. MARIE JEANNE
     January 4, 1751, baptism of Marie Jeanne, *négritte* born of
     a *négresse* belonging to the mission. Godparents: Jean
     Louis Cesar Borme (s), habitant, and Marie Jeanne Elisabeh
     Denes (s/ Marie Elisabeth Borme), his wife.

337. MARIE DE DOULEURS
     January 21, 1751, baptism of Marie de Douleurs, *négritte*
     born of a *négresse* belonging to Mde. de St. Denis. God-
     parents: Louis LeCourt (s) *cadet*, and Marie des Douleur
     de Blanc (s).

338. JEAN BAPTISTE
     February 24, 1751, baptism of Jean Baptiste, *négrillon*
     born of a *négresse* belonging to Pierre Derbanne. Godpar-
     ents: Jean Baptiste Davion St. Prix (x) and Jeanne le
     Roy (x).

339. RENE GAUTHIER *dit* LA FLEUR
     JEANNE LAURENT
     November 5, 1742, marriage of Rene Gauthier *dit* La Fleur
     (X), native of Moulines, diocese of Rouen, near Fougere
     in Bretagne, son of Michel Gauthier and Margueritte Pel-
     etier . . . and . . . Jeanne Laurent (x) of that parish,
     legitimate daughter of Pierre Laurent, native of Fougere,
     diocese of Rennes and Isabelle le Bos, native of Flanders,
     diocese of Gar. 3 bans. Witnesses: Julien Rondin (x),
     Rene Dubos, Pierre Alorge (s), Thomas Leger (s), Guil-
     laume Chever (s), and Jean Baptiste Brevel (s).

340. JOSEPH DUC *dit* VILLE FRANCHE
     MARIE ANNE GUEDON
     April 23, 1743, after publication of two bans, marriage of

Joseph Duc *dit* Ville Franche, soldier in the company of Monsieur de Terrepui, native of Memant in Dauphinois, bishopric of Valence, son of Claude Duc and Anne Favarre, of the same place. . . and . . . Marie Anne Guedon, native of this parish, daughter of Jaques Guedon *dit* Nantois and Marie Anne Therese, Indian *de la grande terre*. Witnesses: Guillaume Chever, Pierre Alorges /names of other witnesses illegible/.

341. PIERRE BERNARDIN *dit* LA BONTE
CATHERINE DUPRE
September 10, 1743, after three bans, marriage of Pierre Bernardin *dit* La Bonte (x), soldier of the company of Monsieur des Terrepui, native of Nannais in Switzerland, Canton of Berne, son of deceased Jean Bernardin and of Adrienne Martin, deceased at New Orleans . . . and . . . Catherine Dupre (x), native of this parish, daughter of deceased Jacques Dupres and Marie Philippe. Witnesses: Guillaume Schever (x), Jean Madere (x), Gabriel Buard (x), Guillaume Bargot (x), Poisot (x).

342. CHARLES TOUTAIN *dit* MEUNIER
JEANNE GAIDON
October 30, 1743, after three bans, marriage of Charles Toutain *dit* Meunier (x), soldier of the company of Terrepuy, resident of this post, native of the town of <u>Renne?</u> *en la* _____ /illegible/, diocese of Chartre, France, son of Jean Toutain and Marguerite La Motte. . . and . . . Jeanne Gaidon (x), native of this parish, daughter of deceased Jacques Gaidon and of Marie Theresse *de las grande terre*, deceased in this parish. Witnesses: Montaige (x), Jean Haiszes (x), Guillaume Chever, Verschiers de Terrepuy (s), and Jean Madere (x).

343. GASPAR
MARIE LOUISE
October 20, 1743, marriage of Gaspar and Marie Louise, negroes belonging to Sieur Robert Avare.

344. PIERRE
THERESE
October 28, 1743, marriage of Pierre and Therese, negroes belonging to Sieur Derbanne.

345. PIERRE *dit* PIEROT
MARIE DE NIEGES *dite* LA ROTTE
October 28, 1743, marriage of Pierre *dit* Pierot and Marie de Nieges *dite* la Rotte, slaves of Mde. St. Denis. No race given.

346. JEAN BAPTISTE DAVION *dit* ST. PRIX
MARIE TRICHE
November 13, 1745, after three bans, marriage of Jean
Baptiste Davion *dit* St. Prix (s), soldier of the regiment
of marines detached from the company of Mr. Verrier, commandant at Natchitoches, born at Natchitoches of the legitimate marriage of Charle d'Avion, deceased, and of the
living Francois Gilot . . . and . . . Marie Triche (s),
daughter of Henry Trichel and of deceased Marie Dumont.
Witnesses: Etienne Ha_____ /illegible/ (x), Henry Trichel
(x), Alorge (s) and Julien Davion (s).

347. ATHANASE CHRISTOPHE FORTUNA DE MEZIERES
MARIE PETRONILLA FELICIANA JUZAUD DE ST. DENIS
April 18, 1746, after one ban, marriage of Athanase Chris-
tophe Fortuna de Mezieres (s), native of Paris, parish of
St. Sulpice, legitimate son of deceased Monsieur Louis
Christophe Claude de Mezieres and of Dame Marie Joseph
Menard . . . and . . . Marie Petronilla Feliciane Juzaud
/Juchereau/ de St. Denis (s), native of this parish, le-
gitimate daughter of deceased Mons. Juzaud de St. Denis
and Dame Manuel Sanchez. Witnesses: De Blanc (s), Duco-
dere (s), Boisseau (s), LeCourt (s), Marie de St. Denis
(s), Pain, "Juzaud," and Fr. Eustache. Fr. Ildephonous
Joseph de Marmolejo, officiating.

348. ALEXIS GRAPPE
LOUISE MARGUERITE GUEDON
April 9, 1746, after three bans, marriage of Alexis Grappe,
corporal of a company detached from the marines, native of
Dolle in Franche Comté, bishopric of Besancon, legitimate
son of Pierre Grap, native of Dolle, and Catherine Benillot, native of the bishopric of Breze . . . and . . .
Louise Marguerite Guedon, widow of Jean Baptiste Besson,
legitimate daughter of Jacques Guedon *dit* Nantes, native
of Nantes, and Marie Therese, a native of Louisiana.
Witnesses: Mr. Dauphine (s/ Bertrant), Alorge (s), Munier /Charles Toutain/, Joseph /Le Duc *dit*/ Ville Franche
(x).

349. DOMINIQUE MONTECHE
MARIE FRANCOISE DE VILBLETTE
July 26, 1746, after three bans, marriage of Dominique
Monteche (s), soldier, native of St. Martin, parish of the
same name, duchy of Madene in Italy, legitimate son of Jean
Monteche, native of St. Martin, and Catherine Liÿonard,
native of same place . . . and . . . Marie Francoise de
Vilblette (s), native of Paris, parish of St. Paul, widow
of deceased Jean Es /Heszes/ *dit* La Machine, legitimate
daughter of Jean Baptiste de Vilblette, native of Chartres
in France, and Marie Therese Martancour, native of Paris.
Witnesses: Dufrene Guillaume (s/ Guillaume Chever),

Dauphine /Claude Bertrand/, Alorge (s), and Nicolas Paul
Bourdelle (s).

350. GASPARD DARBANNE
MARIE FRANCOISE VERGER
September 29, 1746, marriage of Gaspard Derbanne (s),
native of this parish, legitimate son of Francois Darbanne,
native of Canada, bishopric of Quebec, and of Jeanne de la
Grande Air . . . and . . . Marie Francoise Verger (x), a
native of this parish, legitimate daughter of Joseph Verger, native of Paris, and of Angelique Dumond, native of
Natchitoches. One ban. Witnesses: Joseph Verger (s),
Henry Triche (x), Rondain (x), Pierre Darbanne (x), Bisseau (s), Louise Derbanne (x), Blancpain (s) and two
illegible signatures.

351. LOUIS
SUSANNE
September 17, 1747, marriage of Louis and Susanne, negro
slaves of Fr. Eustache.

352. HENRY TRICHELELY
LOUISE FRANCOISE GILOT
October 21, 1747, after one ban, marriage of Henry Trichelely (x), native of Milbac, bishopric of Strasbourg, widower
of deceased Marie Dumont, son of Adam Trichely, native of
Strasbourg and of Jeanne Elisabeh /no last name/ of Berne
. . . and . . . Louise Francoise Gilot (x), native of Chalanton, bishopric of Paris, widow of deceased Etienne Roy
dit Franboise, daughter of Simon Gilot, native of Haffre
/Havre/ de Grace, bishopric of Normandy, and Agathe Gilot,
native of Chalanton, bishopric of Paris. Witnesses: De
Blanc (s), Rondin (x), Jean Baptiste Davion (x), Alorge
(s), and one illegible signature.

353. MATHIEU MONNET *dit* ST. MORICE
ELISABHET RACHAL
June 6, 1748, after three bans, marriage of Mathieu Monnet
dit St. Morice, soldier detached from the company of Benoit at this post, native of Paris, parish of St. Sulpice?,
legitimate son of Claude Monet, native of Paris, and of
/illegible/ . . . and . . . Elisabhet Rachal (s), native
of this parish, legitimate daughter of Pierre Rachal *dit*
St. Denis, soldier detached in this post, native of Isle
d'Oloron, and Marie Anne Benoit, native of Paris. Witnesses: De Blanc (s), Rondin (x), Alorge (s), Pain (s),
Verger (s), and Mr. Dominique /Monteche/ (x).

354. JOSEPH FRANCOIS VILDEC /PEREAU/
MARIE CATHERINE DUPRES
November 3, 1748, after three bans, marriage of Joseph

Francois Vildec, native of Quebec, parish of Notre Dame
de Leige, legitimate son of Joseph Francois Vildec, native
of L'isle d'Orleans, parish of Sainte Famille, bishopric
of Quebec, and Dorothé Brigon, native of Charle le bourg,
parish of St. Pierre, bishopric of Quebec. . . and . . .
Marie Catherine Depres, native of this parish, widow of
deceased Pierre Bernardin *dit* La Bonté, legitimate daughter of Jacques Depres, native of Paris, and Marie Philippe,
native of the Palantin. Witnesses: Sieur Bourgignon (s/
Poissot); Dufrene (s) /Guillaume Chever/, Gabriel /Buard/
(x), and Etienne /Barbier *dit*/ Marechal (x).

355. CAESAR DE BLANC
MARIE DES DOULEURS /DE ST. DENIS/
June 9, 1750, after one ban, marriage of Caesar de Blanc (s),
commandant for the King at the royal fort of St. Jean Baptiste, post of Natchitoches and of its dependencies, native
of Marseilles, parish and cathedral of the same diocese,
legitimate son of deceased noble Charle de Blanc, captain
of a regiment of Champagne, and of Dame Marguerite des
Pagnet . . . and . . . Marie des Douleurs, native of this
parish, legitimate daughter of deceased Mess. Jucheraud
de St. Denis, chevalier of the royal and military order of
St. Louis, commandant for the King during his life, at
this post, and Dame Manuel Sanchez Navarre (s), widow of
deceased St. Denis. Witnesses for groom: Pedro Barrio,
governor of Adays (s), Louis de St. Denis, Athanase de
Mezieres, officer; witnesses for bride: Madame /illegible/,
Mr. La rouble?, officer, and Mr. Pain. Fr. Eustache,
witness. Fr. Pedro "of Adays," officiating.

356. JEAN LOUIS CAESAR BORME *dit* PROVENCAL
MARIE ELISABETH DENES
August 17, 1750, after one ban, marriage of Jean Louis
Caesar Borme *dit* Provencal, soldier of the company of de
la Tour, native of Pignans in Provence, parish of St. Andre,
legitimate son of Jos. Borme and Anne Ronne. . . and . . .
Marie Elisabeth Denes (s/ Marie Anne Elisabeth), native of
Hennebout in Basse Bretagne /Lower Brittany/, bishopric of
Nanne, legitimate daughter of Jean Baptiste Denes and Marie
Elizabeth Dumont. Witnesses for groom: Louis de St. Denis
(s), officer, and Louis Pellerin du Cote (s); witnesses
for bride: Pierre de la Ronde (s) and Jean Louis LeCourt
(s), officers, and Marie de Blanc.

357. JEAN BOULET *dit* BRIM D'AMOUR
ANNE VERGER
October 12, 1750, after three bans, marriage of Jean Boulet
dit Brim d'Amour (x), soldier, native of Lesÿ in Autun,
duchy of Gascogne, parish of St. Julien, legitimate son of
François Boulet of Lesÿ and Milande Mies, native of St.

George . . . and . . . Anne Verger (x), native of this
parish, legitimate daughter of Joseph Verger (s), native
of Paris, parish of St. Benois, and Angelique Dumont, a
native of this parish. Witnesses for groom: Francois
Doucet *dit* Eustache (s), soldier, and Jean de Roblat *dit*
la R_____ /illegible/; witnesses for bride: Gaspard
Derbanne (s) and Henry Trichely (x).

358. JEAN BAPTISTE ETIENNE BARBIER
May 28, 1742, burial in parish cemetery, in presence of
godparents, Jean Baptiste Etienne Barbier, aged two days.

359. JOSEPH DOMINIQUE LEIBE
August 8, 1742, burial in parish cemetery of Joseph Dominique Leibe, a Spaniard, after receiving last rites.

360. MARIE JEANNE RONDIN
August 20, 1742, burial in parish cemetery, in presence
of the father and the mother, of Marie Jeanne Rondin, aged
one year.

361. FRANCOIS PERREAULT *dit* BELLEFLEUR
September 24, 1742, burial in parish cemetery of Francois
Perreault *dit* Bellefleur, soldier in the company of Terpuy, native of Paris.

362. REINE JEANNE /MADER/
April 4, 1743, burial in parish cemetery of Reine Jeanne,
in presence of father, aged three months.

363. ILLEGIBLE
?-17-1743. /Ink is almost completely faded./

364. PIERRE HENRY RICHER
April 8, 1743, burial in parish cemetery, in presence of
parents, Pierre Henry Richer, aged 7 months.

365. MARIE DUMONS
May 9, 1743, burial of Marie Dumons, in parish cemetery,
wife of Henri Triche.

366. JEAN FRANCOIS VIGNERON *dit* LA VIOLETTE
June 21, 1743, burial in parish cemetery of Jean Francois
Vigneron *dit* la Violette, native of Bruge in Flanders,
soldier in the company of Verchur de Terrepuy.

367. NICOLAS RENAULD *dit* LA VIDETTE
October 6, 1743, recording of the death and burial of Nicolas Renauld *dit* La Vidette, a soldier detached at the
Little Caddo village of Gros Nez, who was buried in that
village. Death reported by St. Denis and de la Chaise.

368. ANONYMOUS
   /Illegible/ 22, 1744, burial of a *négrillon* belonging to Sieur Marion, *endoyé*, in expectation of death, by Mme. Marion at her home. Witness: Besson (s).

369 LOUIS JUCHEROT DE ST. DENIS
   June 12, 1744, burial within the parish church of Louis Jucherot de St. Denis, aged 70 years, Chevalier of the Order of St. Louis, commandant of the Fort of Jean Baptiste, who died on the eleventh of the same month and year. Witnesses: Juero Bonet, Fr. Franco. Ballejo, and Verchus de Terrepuy.

370. EMMANUEL
   October 25, 1744, burial within the parish cemetery of an Indian slave, Emmanuel, belonging to Madame de St. Denis, aged nine years.

371. PIERRE
   January 23, 1745, burial in the parish cemetery of Pierre, an Indian of six years, slave of Madame St. Denis.

372. PIERRE JULIEN
   February 25, 1745, burial of Pierre Julien in the parish cemetery, a natural son of Julien, free *nègre*, a domestic of Madame Widow Jucherot de St. Denis, aged fifteen years.

373. PIERRE
   February 28, 1745, burial in parish cemetery of Pierre Noi_?_, aged eighteen years, died February 27, slave of Madame de Jucherot de St. Denis.

374. ILLEGIBLE
   May 12, 1745. /Remainder of entry illegible./

375. JEAN BAPTISTE BOSSIEE *dit* LE BRUN
   May 22, 1745, death and burial of Jean Baptiste Bossiee *dit* le Brun, aged 69 years, native of the parish of Notre Dame de Casselsagraf /Castelsagrat/ in France.

376. MARIE BARBE
   June 16, 1745, burial of Marie Barbe, Indian slave of Mme. St. Denis, widow of deceased Jucherot de St. Denis.

377. ROBERT AVARD
   October 24, 1745, burial of Robert Avard, aged 35 years, elder warden of this parish, in presence of several witnesses. Last rites were administered.

378. LOUIS /LOUISE/
   October 25, 1745, burial of Louis, *négritte* slave of

Madame de St. Denis, aged 3 years, <u>daughter</u> of Julien and Feliciane, Indian.

379. L'EVEILLE
 November 14, 1745, burial of L'Eveille, a male Indian, *en-doyé* at home of /̄Bertrand *di*t̲/ Dauphine, sergeant, in anticipation of death.

380. ILLEGIBLE
 November 24, 1745. /̄Remainder of entry illegible.̲/

381. RENE DUBOS
 January 30, 1745, certification by Fr. Eustache that two witnesses had reported to him the death of Rene Dubos, a habitant of this parish, and Dubos' burial in the parish cemetery by a Spanish priest during Fr. Eustache's absence.

382. JEAN BAPTISTE BESSON
 February 12, 1746, certification by Fr. Eustache that two witnesses had reported the death of Jean Baptiste Besson, a native of Paris, and Besson's burial in the parish cemetery during Fr. Eustache's absence.

383. TOUSSAINT
 April 29, 1746, burial of Toussaint, Indian of Mde. St. Denis.

384. PIERRE
 May 3, 1746, burial of Pierre, *négrillon* belonging to Mde. St. Denis.

385. LA BRYERE
 May 5, 1746, burial of La Bryere, chief of the Indian village of Na____, after having been baptized.

386. CYPRIEN JUZAUD
 August 15, 1746, certification by Fr. Eustache, that two witnesses had reported the death and burial of Cyprien Juzaud, *cadet*, in the Little Caddo village of Gros Nez where Juzaud was detached. Witnesses: LeCourt (s), *cadet*, and Aures, corporal.

387. ILLEGIBLE
 _____ 11, 1747, burial of a *négritte*. /̄Remainder of entry illegibl*e*/.

388. ILLEGIBLE

389. MARIE
 July 27, 1747, burial of Marie, property of Sieur St. Denis, soldier /̄Pierre Rachal *dit* St. Deni*s*/, after receiving last rites.

390. MARIE PETRONILLA FELICIANE DEMEZIERES
     February 2, 1748, burial in the church of Marie Petro-
     nilla Feliciane Demezieres, aged eighteen or about, after
     receiving last rites.

391. MARINETTE
     _____ 29, 1748, burial of Marinette, Indian belonging
     to Mr. Rondin, lieutenant.

392. BARNABE
     September 20, 1748, burial of Barnabe, *négrillon* belonging
     to Mde. St. Denis, aged five years.

393. ANONYMOUS
     March 24, 1749, burial of a *nègre* slave of Sieur Jean des
     Jean.

394. PIERRE /POISSOT/
     April 9, 1749, burial of Pierre, aged one year or about,
     child of Mr. Bourguignon /Remy Poissot/.

395. JEANNE RICHÉ
     April 16, 1749, burial of Jeanne, aged about one year,
     infant of Mr. Richer.

396. MARIE
     June 12, 1749, . . . Dauphine, sergeant of the guards.
     /Relationship of Marie to Bertrand *dit* Dauphine is totally
     illegible/

397. ILLEGIBLE
     June ?, 1749. /Remainder of entry illegible./

398. EMOND /CHAGNOT/
     June 19, 1749, burial of Emond, aged ten days, son of
     Francois /Chagnot -- page torn/.

399. ELISABETH GUYOL
     June 27, 1749, burial of Elisabeth Guyol, wife of Mr. de
     Blanc, commandant, about sixty years, died June 26 after
     receiving the last rites and was buried in the church.

400. ETIENNE CHAGNOT
     July 1, 1749, burial of Etienne Chagnot who died the eve-
     ning before at the age of 75 (45?) years.

401. LA ROSE
     June 15, 1750, burial of La Rose, habitant of this post,
     aged sixty years or about, who was drowned on the 14th
     and found on the 15th.

402. JEANNE RONDAIN
     July 14, 1750, burial of Jeanne Rondain, aged about 3 years.

403. MARGUERITE
___ 13, 1750, burial of an Indian belonging to Madame /torn/, aged eight years.

404. HENRY RICHER
___ 11, 1750, burial of Henry Richer who died the previous evening at the age of 45.

405. LOUIS FRANCOIS MARIE DE MEZIERES
January 25, 1760, baptism of Louis Francois Marie, son of Monsieur de Mezieres, *capitaine réformé* of the troops and Dame de Mezieres *ditte* Falsinte. Godparents: Louis de Kerlerecq, Chevalier de St. Louis, captain of the *Hauts Bois* and governor for his majesty of this province, represented by Sr. Atanase de Meziere (s), *cadet*, and Dame le Doux *ditte* Falsinthe (s). Witnesses: De Blanc, Le Doux (s), and Morire (s).

406. MARIE JOSEPHE DAMASENE DE SOTO BERMUDEZ
February 6, 1760, baptism of Marie Josephe Damasene de Soto Bermudez, legitimate daughter of Don Emmanuel de Soto and Marie des Neges de St. Denis. Godparents: Pierre Antoine de St. Denis, ensign (s), and Marie de Soto (x). Fr. Valentin, witness; Fr. Franciscus Caldes of Los Adaes, officiating.

407. MARIE JOSEPHE GRILLET
February 24, 1760, baptism of Marie Josephe, legitimate daughter of Marain Grille *dit* Sauterelle and Marie Louise Brevel. Godparents: Joseph du Pres (x) and Marie de l'Incarnation Derbanne (x).

408. JEAN BAPTISTE DUPREZ
March 1, 1760, baptism of Jean Baptiste, legitimate son of Jean Baptiste Dupres and Elisabeth Verge. Godparents: Louis Lamalaty *dit* Jobard (x) and Marie Francoise Poisot (x).

409. MARIE LOUISE GUEDON
March 3, 1760, baptism of Marie Louise, daughter of Marie Anne Guedon, widow of deceased Joseph le Duc Ville Franche, and a father unknown. Godparents: Louis Lamalati, represented by Francois /Levasseur *dit*/ Jolibois (x), and Marie Louise /Toutain *dite*/ Meunier (x).

410. MARIE LOUISE DU VIVIER
March 19, 1760, baptism of Marie Louise, daughter of Baptiste du Vivier and Jeanne Dupain. Godparents: Pierre Martier (x) and Louise La Renaudiere (x).

411. MARIE DUPRÉ
March 26, 1760, baptism of Marie, daughter of Josephe Duprés

and Marie de l'Incarnation Darbane. Godparents: Fr.
/Francois/ Vildaigre *dit* Pereau (s) and Marie Francoise
Poissot (x).

412. MARIE STRASE
April 8, 1760, baptism of Marie, daughter of /no given
name/ Strase and of Jeanne /no surname/, both Spaniards.
Godparents: Pierre Leveille (Sorelle?), (x), and Marie
Delincour.

413. MARIE THERESE
May 27, 1760, baptism of Marie Therese, Indian of Monsieur
de Mezieres, aged about 7 or 8 years. Godparents: Monsieur de Mezieres (s), officer, and Mme. de Mezieres (s).

414. ANDRÉ
/no date/, baptism of André, slave of Mr. LeCourt, officer.
Godparents: Andrés Rambin (s) and Jeanne Alorge (x).

415. THERESE
June 18, 1760, baptism of Therese, *négritte* of Mr. Pain.
Godparents: Antonio Vascocu (s) and Caterinne Mailier
(x).

416. MARIE ANNE VILDEC
July 3, 1760, baptism of Marie Anne, daughter of Fr. Barthelemie Perau* and Marie Caterinne Dupres. Godparents:
Jacques Lambre and Marie de l'Incarnation Derbanne, representé by Marie Anne Poiseau. Signed: Perau.

*The name "Vildec" is written over the name "Perau" in
the text of the entry.

417. MARIE ANORE
July 17, 1760, baptism of Marie Anore, daughter of Lisette,
Indian of Sr. Hervé. Godparents: André Rambin (s) and
Francoise Clermon (s).

418. JEAN FRANCOIS DUBOIS
August 10, 1760, baptism of Jean Francois, born August 6,
son of Jean Baptiste du Bois (s) and Marie Jeanne Clermont. Godparents: Francois Breton (s) and Marie Jeanne
Richy (x).

419. JULIEN RACHAL
August 31, 1760, baptism of Julien, son of Louis Rachal
and Marie LeRoy. Godparents: Jean Baptiste Davion
St. Prix (x) and Hiacinthe Triche (x), his wife.

420. PIERRE SEBASTIEN PRUDHOMME
September /blank/, 1760, baptism of Pierre Sebastien, son

of Sebastien Prudhomme and Jeanne Chever. Godparents: Jean Baptiste Trichele (s) and Margueritte Victoria Prudhomme (x).

421. MARIE VICTOIRE DERBANNE
October 8, 1760, baptism of Marie Victoire, daughter of Pierre Darbane and Marianne Le Clerc. Godparents: Dominique Monteche (x) and Marie Louise Manne (x).

422. MARIE LOUISE PRUDHOMME
October 9, 1760, baptism of Marie Louise, daughter of Jean Baptiste Prudhomme (s) and Marie Frse. Corentin. Godparents: Luis de St. Denis (s), officer, and Marie de Soto (x).

423. MARIE JEANNE
October 26, 1760, baptism of Marie Jeanne, *négritte* of Sr. Pierre Darbane. Godparents: Francois /Levasseur *dit*/ Jolibois (x) and Marie Jeanne Chagnot (x).

424. JEAN LAMBRE
November 20, 1760, baptism of Jean, son of Jean Lambre and Marie Jeanne Le Vasseur. Godparents: Jacques /illegible/ (x) and Cecile Le Vasseur (x).

425. MARIE JEANNE
November 23, 1760, baptism of Marie Jeanne, slave of Gabriel Buard. /No race given./ Godparents: Francois Carle and Marie Jeanne /Mader *dite*/ Jean des Jean.

426. MARIE HELENE
December 10, 1760, baptism of Marie Helene, *négritte* of Mr. de Blanc. Godparents: Charles Papilleau (s/ Papillault) and Marie Delincour (x).

427. PIERRE SORELLE
December 10, 1760, baptism of Pierre, son of Pierre Sorelle and Marie Rose Boisselier. Godparents: Jean Baptiste Trichle (s) and Marie Louise <u>Darbone?</u>.

428. AMBROIS /LE/ COMTE
December 30, 1760, baptism of Ambrois, son of Jean Baptiste le Conte (s/ Conte, *pere*) and Margueritte Le Roy. Godparents: Jean Francois Breton (s) and Marie Louise Davion.

429. LOUISE AGATHE LABERRY
January 20, 1761, baptism of Louise Agathe, daughter of Jean Labery (s) and Jeanne Guedon. Godparents: Sieur Borme (s), officer, and Louise Toutin (s).

430. MARIE FRANCOISE PAIN
February 18, 1761, baptism of Marie Francoise, born February

9, 1761, daughter of Daniel Pain (s) and Jeanne Rougot. Godparents: Francois Daniel Pain (s) and Marie Francois Dominique /Monteche/ (x).

431. REMY LAMBRE
February 20, 1761, baptism of Remy, son of Jacques Lambres (x) and Marie Anne Poisot. Godparents: Remy Poisot (s) and Caterinne Poisot (x).

432. MARIE ANGELIQUE
March 17, 1761, baptism of Marie Angelique, *nègritte* of Sr. Pierre Darbane. Godparents: Pierre du burdeau (s/ Pierre Huberdeau) and Marie Louise St. Prix (x).

433. MARIE DE L'ASSUMPTION
March 22, 1761, baptism of Marie de l'Assumption, *nègritte* of Sr. Buard. Godparents: Louis Buard (x) and Marie de l'Assumption Dupres (x).

434. PIERRE
March 22, 1761, baptism of Pierre, Indian of Mr. LaCourt. Godparents: Le Doux and Madame Borme (s).

435. ANTOINE
March 22, 1761, baptism of Antoine, *nègre* of Mr. LeCourt Godparents: Sieur Fazende (s), officer, and Madame Le Doux (s).

436. JEAN
March 22, 1761, baptism of Jean, *nègre* of H. Trichel. Godparents: Jean Lambre (x) and Theresa Lamalatie (x).

437. ETIENNE
March 22, 1761, baptism of Etienne, slave /race not given/ of Saint Prix. Godparents: Etienne Verge (x) and Cecile /Levasseur *dite*/ Jolibois.

438. ANTOINE
March 22, 1761, baptism of Antoine, slave /race not given/ of Sr. Pain. Godparents: Le Doux and Madame Pain (s/ Rougeau Pain).

439. MARIE ANTOINETTE BARBE RAMBIN
April 24, 1761, baptism of Marie Antoinette Barbe, daughter of Andres Rambin (s) and Francoise Clermont. Godparents: Pierre Dolet (s) and Marie Gertrude Hitta (x). Witness: Ant. Gil y Varvo /Barbo/ and Dubois, *oncle*.

440. JEAN BAPTISTE
May 3, 1761, baptism of Jean Baptiste. /No further identification/ Godparents: Alexis Grappe (s) and Marianne Vil Franche (x).

441. ANTOINE
May 3, 1761, baptism of Antoine. /No further identification./ Godparents: Pierre Besson (x) and Marie Louise Dolet (x).

442. HELENA
May 3, 1761, baptism of Helena. /No further identification./ Godparents: Jean Baptiste Vilfranche? and Fuelicite Vilfranche (x).

443. JEAN JOSEPH RŸSE
May 5, 1761, baptism of Jean Joseph, son of Jean Rÿse and Marie Jeanne Chagnot, by Fr. Joseph Diaz Infante, Spanish missionary of Los Adayes. Godparents: La Gase and Cecile Levasseur.

444. JEAN BAPTISTE
May 11, 1761, baptism of Jean Baptiste, *nègre* of Sr. Pain? Godparents: Jean Baptiste Samuel *dit* Leonet (x) and Mag--deleine Prudhomme (x).

445. JEAN BAPTISTE
May 11, 1761, baptism of Jean Baptiste, *nègre* of Sr. Jacques? Lambre. Godparents: Remÿs Poisot and Marianne Lambre.

446. MARIE MAGDELAINE
May 12, 1761, baptism of Marie Magdelaine, Indian of Mons. de Mezieres. Godparents: Ledoux (s), lieutenant, and Madame Fazende de Mezieres (s).

447. FELIX
May 12, 1761, baptism of Felix, Indian of de Mezieres. Godparents: Athanase de Meziere (x) and Mdelle. Marie Fazende le Doux (s).

448. LOUIS
May 12, 1761, baptism of Louis, Indian of de Mezieres. Godparents: Fazende (s), officer, and Fazende Le Doux (s).

449. MARIE FRANCOISE BREVELLE
June 14, 1761, baptism of Marie Francoise, daughter of Jean Baptiste Brevelle (x) and Marie Francoise Poisseau. Godparents: Remy Poissau (s/ Poisot) and Anne Marie Philippe -- represented by Catherinne Poisseau (x).

450. MARIANNE
July 9, 1761, baptism of Marianne, *négresse* of Chevalier de Jucherot de St. Denis, officer. Godparents: Emanuel de Soto (s) and Maria de Neges de St. Denis de Soto (s).

451. JEANNE
    July 19, 1761, baptism of Jeanne, Indian of about six years, property of Mons. Le Court (s). Godparents: Luis de Blanc and Francoise le Doux (s).

452. ELISABETH MALBORT
    July 22, 1761, baptism of Elisabeth, daughter of Jean Baptiste Malbort *dit* Sans Fason, soldier, and Jeanne Verge. Godparents: Pierre Darbane (x) and Elisabeth Verge (s).

453. ELISABETH JOSEPHE BUARD
    June 23, 1761, baptism of Elisabeth Josephe, daughter of Gabriel Buard and Marie Rousseau. Godparents: Louis Borme (s) and Elisabeth Borme (s).

    /Note: Part of this entry appears on the bottom of one page, the remainder on the top of another page. In the course of rebinding the registers, this entry was separated by two sheets (four pages) of marriage records, which follow./

454. JEAN LABERY
    JEANNE (ANNE?) GUEDON
    July 6, 1760, after publication of one ban, marriage of Jean Labery (s), legitimate son of Etienne LaBery and Isabelle Lestache, born at St. Paul, parish of the same name, on the frontier of Languidic /Languedoc/ . . . and . . . Jeanne (Anne?) Guedon (x), daughter of Jacques Guedon and Therese, Indian, a native of this parish. Witnesses: Dominique Monteche (x), Sieur Triche (x), Borme (s), Poisot (s), and Breton (s).

455. JEAN BAPTISTE BREVELLE
    MARIE FRANCOISE POISOT
    July 14, 1760, after publication of one ban, marriage of Jean Baptiste Brevelle, son of Jean Baptiste Brevelle and Marie Nanette, native of this parish . . . and . . . Marie Francoise Poisot (x), daughter of Remy Poisot and Anne Marie Philippe, native of this parish. Witnesses: Baptiste Dupres (x), Jacques Lambre (x), Gabrielle Buard (x) and Marin Grille (x).

456. VINCENT POYRIE
    JEANNE RICHÉ
    January 28, 1761, marriage of Vincent Poyrie (x), son of Guillaume Poyrie and Jeanne de visote, native of Mareisou, parish of the same name, bishopric of Turba___, dependency of Bygora . . . and . . . Jeanne Riché (x) daughter of Henry Riche and Marie Jeanne Clermon, native of this parish. 3 bans. Witnesses: Rambin (s), Dubois (s), St. Denis (s).

457. FRANCOIS CARLES
JEANNE MADERE
March 25, 1761, after publication of one ban, marriage of Francois Carles (x), son of Jean Carles and Marie Merles, native of Marceille /Marseille/, bishopric and parish of La Quaterne? . . . and . . . Jeanne Madere (x), daughter of Jean Madere and Marie Materne, native of this parish. Witnesses: Buard (x), Sieur Lambre, the younger (x), Sieur Lambre, the elder (x), Pain (s), and Sr. Monteche (x).

458. PIERRE DOLET
MARIE LOUISE TOTIN
March 30, 1761, after publication of one ban, marriage of Pierre Dolet, son of Albert Dolet and Therese Colin, native of Monte au honaux, diocese of Cambray, parish of St. Germain . . . and . . . Marie Louise Totin (s), daughter of Charles Totin and Jeanne Guedon, native of this parish. Witnesses: Jean Baptiste Trichele (s), Jean Labery (s), and Dominique Monteche (x).

459. JEAN BAPTISTE DUBARDEAU
MARIE JEANNE BARBIER
April 6, 1761, after publication of one ban, marriage of Jean Baptiste Dubardeau, son of Jean Baptiste duBardeau and Charlotte Rouleau, native of Montreal, diocese of Quebec . . . and . . . Marie Jeanne Barbier, daughter of Etienne Barbier and Louise Margueritte Darbane. No witnesses.

460. DOMINIQUE BARTHELEMIE RACHAL
August 2, 1761, baptism of Dominique Barthelemie, son of Barthelemie Rachalle and Marie Francoise Lamalathy *ditte* Jobard. Godparents: Dominique Monteche (x) and Cecile Levasseure (x).

461. DOMINIQUE FRANCOIS RONDIN
August 7, 1761, baptism of Dominique Francois, son of Louis Rondin (x) and Marie Berard. Godparents: Dominique Monteche (x) and La Thomas La Concepion (x).

462. THERESE
September 24, 1761, baptism of Therese, *négritte* of St. Denis. Godparents: Jacques Bunel, soldier, and Therese Lamalathy.

463. ANGE CHARLES FRANCOIS MARIE LEDOUX
October 2?, 1761, baptism of Ange Charles Francois Marie, legitimate son of Mons. Antoine Francois Ledoux, lieutenant, and Francoisse Falsinthe Ledoux. Godparents: Monsieur don Ungle, Governor of Adayes, and Charlotte de Boete Kerlerecq. Witnesses: St. Denis, Juan Prieto, and LeCourt. Fr. Josephe Calahora of Los Adayes, officiating.

464. LOUIS JOSEPH FIRMIN DE SOTO
     October 23, 1761, baptism of Louis Joseph Firmin, legitimate son of Don Manuel Soto and Dame Marie des Neges de St. Denis. Godparents: Louis Antoine de St. Denis, ensign (s) and Marie Soto (x). Fr. Valentin, witness. R. Joseph Diaz Infante, officiating.

465. THERESIA JACOBA
     December 1, 1761, baptism of Theresia Jacoba, natural daughter of Mariann, widow of Dominique Montes*. Godparents: Jacobus Levasion and Chatharina Voson. Certified in Latin, January 1, 1762, by Fr. Joseph Diaz Infante, from Los Adaes.

     *This should not be confused with Dominique Monteche.

466. MARIE ANTOINETTE LEROY /LE COURT7*
     January 11, 1762, baptism of Marie Antoinette, natural daughter of Jeanne Le Roy and a father unknown*. Godparents: Antoine Francois Ledoux, officer, represented by Louis Monette (x) and Marie Louise Le Roy.

     *See Entry No. 984.

467. JACQUES
     January 12, 1762, baptism of Jacques, born November 22, 1761, négrillon of Sr. Buard. Godparents: Jacques Bunel (s) and Marie Rousseau (s).

468. ANTOINE MARIE DE MEZIERES
     January 21, 1762, baptism of Antoine Marie de Mezieres, legitimate son of Mr. de Mezieres (s), captain, and Pelagie de Falsinthe. Godparents: Antoine Fazende (s), officer, and Marie des Neges St. Denis (s).

469. MARIE JEANNE URSULLE BOULET
     January 17, 1763, baptism of Maria Joanna Ursula, daughter of Joannis Bulai and Matea Anna Verges. Godparents: Dominicus Monteche and Maria Joanna Verges.

     Entered, in Latin, by Fr. Ignacio Laba of Los Adaes.

470. FRANCOIS ANTOINE SORELLE
     January 17, 1763, baptism of Franciscus Antonio, son of Petri Saurelle and Maria Rosa Boisselier. Godparents: Francus. Levasseur and Maria Catharena Dupre.

     Entered, in Latin, by Fr. Ignacio Laba of Los Adaes.

471. CATHERINE PRUDHOMME
     February 8, 1763, baptism of Catharena per Domo, daughter of Sebastianis per Domo and Joannis Dufren /Chever dite

Dufren_e_/. Godparents: Stephani Marichel /Etienne Barbier
dit Marecha_l_/ and Catharina Joliboa /Catherine Levasseur
dite Joliboi_s_/. Witnesses: Guillme Chever *dit* Dufrene (s).

Entered, in Latin, by "Pr Francus /illegibl_e_/ *a Concepcione
Bozeta*."

472. JEANNE MARIE PISEROT
May 23, 1763, baptism of Joanna Maria, legitimate daughter
of Joannis Pisserault and Cecilia Le Vassaux. Godparents:
Montexely /Montech_e_/ and Francisca Dubardaux.

Entered, in Latin, by Fr. Ignacio Maria Laba.

473. ANONYMOUS
/No date, no name, no parent_s_/. Godfather: Alexis Grappe
(s) and godmother: Louise Guedon (x), "uncle and aunt of
the infant." Baptized by Pere Infante, of Adailles.

474. MARIE LOUISE SILVIE DUBARDEAU
February 26, 1762,* baptism of Marie Louise Silvie, daughter
of Pierre Dubardeau and Marie Jeanne Barbier. Godparents:
Louis Antoine de St. Denis Jusserault (s) and Marie Baron
(s).   */This entry is recorded out of sequence./

475. IGNACE
May 24, 1763, baptism of Ygnacium, adult Indian. Godparents: Monzieur Cur (s/ LeCourt) and _____ /si_c_/
Prudhomme.

Entered, in Latin, by Fr. Ygnacio Franco. Laba.

476. MAGDELEINE JOSEPHE
May 24, 1763, baptism of Magdalena Josepha, adult Indian.
Godparents: Monzieur Cur (s/ LeCourt) and Luisa Alexis
/Grapp_e_/.

Entered, in Latin, by Fr. Ygnacio Franco. Laba.

477. MAGDELEINE
May 24, 1763, baptism of Magdelena, adult Indian. Godparents: Franciscus Pein and Magdalena Grappa.

Entered, in Latin, by Fr. Ygnacio Franco. Laba.

478. ETIENNE
May 24, 1763, baptism of Estephanus, Indian. Godparents:
Ludovicus Pein and Clemencia Larenaudiere.

Entered, in Latin, by Fr. Ygnacio Franco. Laba.

479. JEANNE
May 24, 1763, baptism of Juana, adult Indian. Godparents:

Ludovicus Andreas Borme and Pelagie Pain.***

480. CATHERINE
May 24, 1763, baptism of Catharina, adult Indian. Godparents: Estephanus Verger and Ludovicia Larenaudiere.***

481. ANTOINE FRANCOIS MARIE RACHAL
July 3, 1763, baptism of Antonio Franciscus Maria, legitimate son of Ludovici Rachal and Maria Franboirez /Marie Louise Le Roy *dite* Framboise_7. Godparents: Antonio Le du and Maria Fr^ca Le Du.***

482. MARIE JEANNE
July 8, 1763, baptism of Maria Joanna, daughter of Barthole and Maria Fran^ca. Godparents: Rap_____ /Illegible_7 and Joanna.***

483. CHARLES
July 8, 1763, baptism of Carolum, son of Caroli and Elisabeth. Godparents: Remigiuo /Poissot_7 and Ma. Phelipa.***

484. FRANCOISE
July 8, 1763, baptism of Fran^ca, daughter of Theresa and a father unknown. Godparents: Joannis Broi and Magdalena Traofar.***

485. JOSEPH FRANCOIS DE SOTO
September 19, 1763, baptism of Josephus Franciscus, legitimate son of Dn. Manuel de Soto and Ma. da Nieba de Sandeni. Godparents: Juan Prieto and Fca. Le bru.***

486. AUGUSTIN
September 20, 1763, baptism of Agustin, *négrito*, legitimate son of Margarita and Luiz. Godparents: Sargento Alexi /Sergeant Alexis Grappe_7 and Luis Margarita /Guedon_7.***

487. JACQUES
September 20, 1763, baptism of Jacob. Godparents: Frco. Grape and Ma. Magdalena Grape.***

488. BARTHELEMY LEROY /LECOURT_7*
September 20, 1763, baptism of Bartholome, son of Juana Roy, Godparents: Luis Monete and Marianna Villa Franca.***

    *See Entry No. 984.

489. MARIE STEPHANIE PELAGIE DE MEZIERES
September 20, 1763, baptism of Maria Estephania Pelagia,

*** Entered, in Latin, by Fr. Ygnacio Fran^co Laba of Los Adaes.

legitimate daughter of Atanacio Mezzer and Madama Mezzer. Godparents: Atanacio Pelagio de Mezzer and Fran^{ca} Le Doux. Infant was born that same day.

Entered, in Latin, by Fr. Ygnacio Fran^{co} Laba of Los Adaes.

490. EULALIE MARIE ANNE DE SOTO
December 22, 1763, baptism of Eulalia Maria Ana, legitimate daughter of Manuel de Zoto and Maria de Niebas /Marie des Nieges de St. Deni_s_/. Godparents: Gov. Angel de Marthos y Navarreti and Madama Borme.

Entered, in Latin, by Fr. Ygnacio Fran^{co} Laba of Los Adaes.

491. JEAN PIERRE DOLET
July 18, 176_2_ /sic/, baptism of Jean Pierre, born July 17, legitimate son of Pierre Dolet (s), habitant and Marie Louise Totin. Godparents: Jean Louis Borme (s), captain and commandant, and Jeanne Guedon (x).

492. ANTOINE FRANCOIS LEDOUX
March 20, 1764, burial of Antoine Francois Ledoux, native of Fresdiu, town of D'artois, son of Antoine Francois Le Doux, "/illegible/ *extraordinaire des guerre*," and Dame Marie Francoise; husband of Francoise Fassinde. Ledoux died the evening before, after receiving last rites.

493. CESAIRE DEBLANC
April 19, 1763, burial (in absence of priest, with the Spanish missionary from Los Adaes officiating) of Cesaire DeBlanc, commandant for the King of the royal fort of Natchitoches, Chevalier of the Royal and Military Order of St. Louis, native of Marseille, aged eighty years or about, who died the previous evening. Witnesses: LeCour (s)*; Pain (s), and de Mezieres.

*This was the signature of Pierre L_a_ Cour, soldier -- not that of LeCour_t_ de Prelle, officer, who signed so many previous entries.

494. MARIE LOUISE LABERRY
October 22, 1763, burial by Spanish priest, of Marie Louise, a child born September 22, legitimate daughter of Jean Baptiste Laberry.

495. DARBANNE
November 5, 1759, burial of an infant.

496. ANONYMOUS
November 23, 1759, burial of a small *métis* belonging to Officer Fassenthe.

497. ANONYMOUS
February 24, 1760, burial of a *nègre* of Sr. Buard.

498. ANONYMOUS
February 28, 1760, burial of a *négritte* of Fasinthe.

499. ANONYMOUS
May 10, 1760, burial of a small Indian of Mr. Meziere.

500. ANONYMOUS
June 5, 1760, burial of a small Indian of Sans Fason, soldier /Jean Baptiste Malbert/.

501. RONDIN
June 29, 1760, burial of a small daughter of Louis Rondin.

502. ANONYMOUS
September 29, 1760. Burial of an unidentified person who "drowned in this river and was found three days later."

503. ANONYMOUS
/no date/, 1760. Burial of an infant *métis* of Mr. Buard.

504. JOSEPHE CHRISTOPHE BALASTO
December 11, 1760, burial of a Spanish soldier.

505. MARGUERITTE
January 27, 1761, burial of an Indian slave of Sr. Buard.

506. CECILE MADER
February 5, 1761, burial of a small daughter of Sr. Jean des Jeans Mader.

507. JEANNE MATERNES
March 20, 1761, burial of the widow of Jean Mader, who died after receiving the last rites.

508. ANONYMOUS
August 2, 1761, burial of an Indian slave of Sr. La Riviere, sergeant.

509. ANONYMOUS
September 25, 1761, burial of an Indian slave of Joseph Dupres.

510. PIERRE JEAN DOLET
December 12, 1761, burial, in absence of priest, of Pierre Jean Dolet *dit* a Centienne, son of Albert Dolet and Therese Colin, native of Hen__, diocese of Cambray, parish of St. Germain. Burial performed by Jacques Bunel. S/ Jacques Bunel and Rubei, Sergeant at the post.

REGISTER 2

511. "For the year 1729: an act of marriage of Sieur VERGER, habitant of the post, and another act of baptism of JEAN FRANCOIS DECOUX, habitant of Pointe Coupee."

512. "2 Marriages for the year 1730
1 Death for 1729"   s/ R

513. PIERRE
May 15, 1729, baptism of Pierre, *négrillon*, born April 8, 1729, son of Ane?, *nègre*, and of Fanilian, *négresse*, belonging to Sieur Derbanne. Godparents: Pierre Coutaulas Duplessis (s/ P. Coutoleau Duplessis) and Jeanne Darbanne (x).

514. LOUISE
May 15, 1729, baptism of Louise, *négritte*, born April 12, 1729, daughter of Jasmin and Marie, negroes belonging to Mr. Darbanne. Godparents: Mr. Darbanne (s) and Mlle. Louise Marguerite De Juchereau (x).

515. JEANNE LE BEL
November 30, 1729, baptism of Jeanne, born November 25, 1729, legitimate daughter of Henry Le Bel and Anne Marie /no last name/. Godparents: René Du Bois (x) and Jeanne Chéniau (x).

516. LOUIS PIERRE
May 15, 1729, baptism of Louis Pierre, *négrillon*, property of Monsieur de St. Denis (s); commandant; son of Caton and Manon, negroes. Godparents: Mr. Pierre Coutoleau Duplessis, and Jeanne D'arbanne, *bourgeois*.

517. MARIE L'AVERGNE
/No date/. Baptism of Marie, born May 12, 1729, legitimate daughter of Jean Lavergne and Fanchette Tournedoe, habitants of Natchitoches. Godparents: Francois Viar (s/ Viard) and Marie Jeanne Bocques (x). Witness: Joseph Verger (s).

518. ELISABETH RACHAL
May 15, 1729, baptism of Elisabeth, born May 12, 1729,

legitimate daughter of Pierre Rachal and Marianne Benoist.
Godparents: Joseph Verger (s) and Elisabeth Dubois (x).

519. MARGUERITE
/No date/, baptism of Marguerite, born May 14, 1729, property of Sieur Duplessis (s) and Tourangeau, *bourgeois* of Natchitoches, legitimate daughter of Janot and Fanchon, negroes. Godparents: Pierre Fosse (x) and Louise Marguerite de Juchereaux de St. Denis (x).

520. MARIE LOUISE
May 20, 1729, baptism of Marie Louise, an Osage Indian of about 20 years, property of Francois Viard, *bourgeois* at Natchitoches. Godparents: Pierre Fossé (x) and Louise Marguerite de Juchero (x), wife of said Duplessis (s), *bourgeois* of same place.

521. MARIE
July 28, 1729, baptism of Marie, born July 26, property of Mr. de St. Denis, daughter of Cesar and Marie, negroes. Godparents: Henry Le Bel, *bourgeois* of Natchitoches (x) and Marianne Marchand (x) also of same place.

522. LOUISE LAGE
J_____ 30, 1730 /month illegible/, baptism of Louise, born 29th of same month, legitimate daughter of Jean Lagé and Francoise Buard, habitants of this place. Godparents: Jean Mader (x) and Louise Duplecis (x). "Perre Campo", missionary from the Adailles, officiating.

523. BONAVENTURE
April 8, 1751, baptism of Bonaventure, *négrillon* born of a *négresse* belonging to Madame de St. Denis. Godparents: Athanase Demezier (s) and Mademoiselle Marie Felicitie de Mezier (s).

524. ANTOINNE
June 10, 1751, baptism of Antoinne, *mulâtre* born of a *négresse* belonging to Mr. Demezier. Godparents: Chevalier de la Ronde, officer of a company of the marines (s), and Madame de Blanc (s/ St. Denis de blanc).

525. PIERRE LA RENAUDIERE
June 29, 1751, baptism of Pierre, legitimate son of Charles la Renaudiere and Jeanne la Riviere. Godparents: Chevalier de la Ronde (s) and Louise Derbanne (s).

526. FRANCOIS DANIEL PAIN
September 28, 1751, baptism of Francois Daniel, born September 27, legitimate son of Daniel Pain (s), surgeon major of this post, and Jeanne Roujot. Godparents:

Francois Roujot and Angelique Ch__tron /Illegible/, his wife, both absent and represented by Francois and Marie Jeanne Levasseur (x) (x).

527. LOUIS JOSEPH BLANPAIN
October 23, 1751, baptism of Louis Joseph, natural son of Joseph Blanpain (s) and of Margueritte, Indian. Godparents: Louis de St. Denis (s), officer of a company detached from the marines, and Mademoiselle Marie des Neiges de St. Denis (s/ Mari des nege de St. Deni). Witnesses: Pain (s).

528. MANUEL CLEMENT /CLEMENCE/ BORME
November 16, 1751, baptism of Manuel Clement, legitimate daughter of Jean Louis Cesar Borme and Marie Elisabeth Dénis. Godparents: Messre. Cesar de Blanc (s), chevalier and commandant, and Dame Emmanuel Sanche Navarre de St. Denis (x).

529. JULIEN POISOT
January 16, 1752, baptism of Julien, legitimate son of Remy Poisot *dit* Bourguignon (s) and Marie Philippe. Godparents: Mr. Rondin (x), lieutenant, and Jeanne Guedon (x).

530. JEAN LOUIS LE BOEUF
January 29, 1752, baptism of Jean Louis, legitimate son of René le Boeuf and Emmanuel Duplecis. Godparents: Pierre Louis Duplecis (x) and Jeanne le Roy (x).

531. LOUIS SEBASTIEN
April 20, 1752, baptism of Louis Sebastien, *négrillon* born April 17 of a *négresse* belonging to Madame de St. Denis. Godparents: Mr. Louis Cesar Borme (s), habitant, and Mademoiselle Marie de Neges de St. Denis (s/ Marie sint denis).

532. JEANNE DAVION
April 21, 1752, baptism of Jeanne, born April 18, legitimate daughter of Jean Baptiste Davion (x) and Marie Trichely. Godparents: Emanuel Trichely, *fils*(s) and Jeanne le Roy (s).

533. LOUIS ANTOINE _____
May 20, 1752, baptism of Louis Antoine, legitimate son of Joseph Antoine and Julienne*, Spaniards. Godparents: Pierre Antoine de St. Denis (s/ Ation de St. denis) and Madame de Blanc (s).

*It is not clear whether "Antoine" was the surname of the father and the surname of the mother was omitted, or whether the surnames of both father and mother are missing. Possibly this is the same family as that in Entry 688.

534. MARIE LOUISE
    May 23, 1752, baptism of Marie Louise, *négritte* born of
    a *négresse* belonging to Sieur Gaspard Derbanne (x). God-
    parents: Jean Derbanne and Marie Louise /le/ Roy (x).

535. LOUISE
    May 25, 1752, baptism of Louise, *négritte* born of a
    négresse belonging to M^{rs} Le Court and la Ronde, officers
    of a company detached from the marines. Godparents: Mr.
    Le Court (s) and Louise Derbanne (x).

536. ANTOINE PRUDHOMME
    June 2, 1752, baptism of Antoine, a son "according to the
    ordinances of the King," of Pierre Bastien Prudhomme and
    Jeanne Chever. Godparents: Antoine Janis (x) and Mdme.
    Chever (x).

537. MARIE RONDAIN
    June 18, 1752, baptism of Marie, legitimate daughter of
    Julien Rondain (x), lieutenant of the militia, and of
    Jeanne Riotord. Godparents: Louis Rondain (x) and Marie
    Le Roy (x).

538. CHRISTOPHE
    June 19, 1752, baptism of Christophe, *négrillon* born of a
    négresse belonging to Madame de St. Denis. Godparents:
    Louis de St. Denis (s) and "Mademoiselle, his wife" (s/
    Marie de·St. Denis).

    MARGINAL NOTE: Infant died on the fourth day after birth.

539. FRANCOISE DUBOIS
    July 13, 1752, baptism of Francoise, legitimate daughter
    of Jean Baptiste du Bois (s) and Marie Joseph Clermont,
    habitants of this post. Godparents: Pierre de la Ronde
    (s), officer, and Madame Rambin (s/ Francoise Clermont).

540. CLAUDE
    July 14, 1752, baptism of Claude, son of an Indian of Mr.
    Dauphine, sergeant. Godparents: Mr. de la Ronde (s) and
    Jeanne Alorge (s).

541. FRANCOIS BARTHELEMY VILDEC
    August 5, 1752, baptism of Francois Barthelemy, born
    August 2, legitimate son of Joseph Francois Vildec (s/
    Perro) and Marie Catherine Dupres. Godparents: Remy
    Poisot (s) and Madame, his wife (x).

542. MARIE MADELEINE
    August 22, 1752, baptism of Marie Madeleine, Indian of 6
    months, born of an Indian belonging to Francois Breton.
    Godparents: Jean Francois Breton (s) and Madame Borme
    (s/ Marie Elisabeth Borme).

543. MARIE LOUISE
September 3, 1752, baptism of Marie Louise, *négritte* born of a *négresse* belonging to Sieur Poisot. Godfather unnamed; godmother: Elisabeth Garein (x).

544. HYACINTH
September 24, 1752, baptism of Hyacinth, *négrillon*, son of a *négresse* belonging to Madame de St. Denis. Godparents: Louis Pellerin (s), officer, and Marie Rose /no last name/ (x).

545. JEANNE COULAS DE STA. THERESIA
October 2, 1752, baptism of Jeanne, legitimate daughter of Coulas de Sta. Theresia and Anne de Deos, Spaniards. Godparents: Messr. de St. Denis, officer (s/ Louis de St. Denis) and Dame Doloritte de Blanc (s/ Marie de Blanc).

546. JEAN JOSEPH BOULETTE
October 9, 1752, baptism of Jean Joseph, legitimate son of Jean Baptiste Boulet (x) and Anne Verger. Godparents: Joseph Verger, absent and represented by Etienne, his son (x), and Marie Verger (x).

547. ATHANASE DARDENNE
October 9, 1752, baptism of Athanase, born October 6, legitimate son of Charles Dardenne* (x) and Louise Lage. Godparents: Messire Demezier, officer (s) and Demoiselle Demeziere (s/ Felicité Demesieres).

*See note accompanying Entry 328.

548. JEAN BAPTISTE DERBANNE
November 4, 1752, baptism of Jean Baptiste, legitimate son of Gaspard Derbanne (s) and Marie Francoise Verger. Godparents: Jean Baptiste Derbanne, absent and represented by Etienne Verger, and Madame la Lime (x).

549. THERESE BUARD
November 5, 1752, baptism of Therese, legitimate daughter of Gabrier Buard (x) and Marie Rousot. Godparents: Francois Boseir, absent and represented by Gabriel Agée*, and Therese le Vasseur (x).   */Lagé/

550. JEAN PIERRE
November 9, 1752, baptism of Jean Pierre, *négrillon* born of a *négresse* belonging to Mr. de la Ronde, officer. Godparents: Mr. de la Ronde (s) and Mademoiselle Jeanne le Roy (s).

551. MARIE FRANCOISE LE DUC *dit* VILLEFRANCE
January 1, 1753, baptism of Marie Francoise, legitimate

daughter of Joseph le Duc *dit* Villefrange and Marie Anne
Guedon. Godparents: Louis malathy jobard, *fils* (s/ Loüis
Jobar), and Marie Francoise Chever (x).

552. FRANCOIS DANIEL MADER *dit* JEAN DES JEANS
January 6, 1753, baptism of Francois Daniel, legitimate
son of Jean Mader and Marie Materne*. Godparents: Francois Daniel Pain (s) and Manuel Clemence Borme, represented
by her mother (who s/ Marie Elisabeth Borme).

*Above this name, between the lines, is written in the
surname "Thily."

553. JEAN DANIEL
February 2, 1753, baptism of Jean Daniel, *négrillon* born
of a *négresse* of Mr. de Blanc, commandant. Godparents:
Mr. Pain (s) and Elisabeth Clemence Borme (s/ Marie Elisabeth Borme).

554. MARIE JOSEPH
March 1, 1753, baptism of Marie Joseph, *négritte* born of
a *négresse* belonging to Gaspard Derbanne. Godparents:
Joseph Verger, Jr. (x) and Jeanne Verger, absent and
represented by Marie Verger (x).

555. REMY EBUTRIN TOTAIN
March 25, 1753, baptism of Remy Ebutrin, born March 23,
legitimate son of Charles Totain and Jeanne Guedon. Godparents: Remy Poisot, habitant, absent and represented
by his son (x), and Marie Jeanne Levasseur (x).

556. MARIE LOUISE CHAGNOT
May 8, 1753, baptism of Marie Louise, born May 4, legitimate daughter of Francois Chagnot and Marie Anne la Croix.
Godparents: Pierre de St. Denis (s/ Chevalier de St.
Denis) and Marie des Neges de St. Denis (s).

557. LOUIS CHARLES DEBLANC
May 1, 1753, baptism of Louis Charles, born April 29,
1753, legitimate son of Cesaire de Blanc (s), chevalier
and commandant, and Marie des Douliers /de St. Denis/.
Godparents: Messrs. Louis de St. Denis, officer, absent
and represented by Pierre de St. Denis, his brother (s)
and Emmanuel Sanches Navarre de St. Denis (s). Witnesses: Grandmaison (s), Le Court (s), Mongot (s), and
one illegible signature.

558. JEAN PIERRE
June 23, 1753, baptism of Jean Pierre, *négrillon* born of
a *négresse* belonging to the mission. Godparents: Chevalier de la Ronde, officer (s), and Jeanne le Roy (x).

* 559. JACQUES
        June 23, 1753, baptism of Jacques, adult Indian belonging
        to the mission. Godparents: Jacques Lambre (x) and Marie
        Jeanne Levasseur (x).

* 560. AMBROISE
        June 23, 1753, baptism of Ambroise, adult Indian belong-
        ing to Hara (Herve?), soldier. Godparents: Ambroise le
        Comte (x) and Marie Delincour (x).

* 561. LOUISE
        June 23, 1753, baptism of Louise, adult *négresse* belonging
        to Marie Anne Benois. Godparents: Chevalier de la Ronde
        (s) and Louise Francoise Triche.

* ---   NOTE: The baptisms of these three slaves are recorded in
        one joint entry.

  562. LOUIS MONETTE
        June 26, 1753, baptism of Louis, legitimate son of Mathieu
        Monette and Elisabeth Rachal. Godparents: Louis Rachal,
        his uncle (x) and Marie Louise /Ie/ Roy (x).

  563. MARIE JOSEPH RAMBAIN
        July 23, 1753, baptism of Marie Joseph, legitimate daugh-
        ter of Andre Rambain and Francoise Clermont. Godparents:
        Paul Moro (s/ Paulle Moro) and Marie Joseph Clermont (s),
        habitant.

  564. LOUIS ANDRE BORME
        September 8, 1753, baptism of Louis Andre, born August 29,
        legitimate son of Jean Louis Caesar Borme (s) and Marie
        Elisabeth Denes. Godparents: Pierre de St. Denis (s) and
        Mlle. Marie des Neiges de St. Denis (s). Witness: De
        Blanc (s).

  565. ANNE HŸACINTHE
        September 13, 1753, baptism of Anne Hÿacinthe, *négritte*
        born of a *négresse* named Marie Francoise belonging to
        Madame de St. Denis. Godparents: Mr. Borme (s), church
        warden *en charge*, and Mademoiselle Marie Joseph (s/ marie
        joseph hanriet) /Marie Josephe Henriette Corantin/.

  566. JEANNE THERESE PRUDHOMME
        September 26, 1753, baptism of Jeanne Therese, legitimate
        daughter of Pierre Bastien Prudhomme (x) and Jeanne Che-
        ver. Godparents: Guillaume Chever (s) and Catherine
        Meiller, ill and represented by Jeanne, her daughter (s/
        jeanne alorge).

  567. MARIE LA RENAUDIERE
        September 26, 1753, baptism of Marie, legitimate daughter

Charles la Renaudiere (x) and Marie la Riviere. Godparents: Sr. Bordelle, soldier (s/ bourdelle), and "his wife"(s/ marrie delincourte).

568. MARIE THERESE
October 3, 1753, baptism of Marie Therese, *négritte* born of a *négresse* belonging to Mess. le Chevalier de la Ronde, officer. Godparents: Jean Baptiste /Davion di_t_7 St. Prix (x) and Jeanne le Roy (s).

569. MARIE HONORE
November 9, 1753, baptism of Marie Honore, *négritte* born November 8 of a *négresse* belonging to Mme. de St. Denis. Godparents: Mr. Pradier (s), surgeon-major at this post, and Mademoiselle de St. Denis (s/ Mari de St. denis).

570. MARIE MADELEINE LAMBRE
November 19, 1753, baptism of Marie Madeleine, born November 17, legitimate daughter of Jacques Lambre (x) and of Therese le Vasseur. Godparents: Jean Lambre (x) and Marie Jeanne Levasseur (x).

571. AUGUSTINE
December 9, 1753, baptism of a *négritte*, daughter of a *négresse* belonging to Sr. Borme, habitant. Godparents: Sr. Madere *dit* Jean des Jean and Madame Margueritte Vandal (x).

572. MARIE ANTOINITE PAGNOT
December 18, 1753, baptism of Marie Antoinite, born December 14, 1753, legitimate daughter of Antonne Pagnot and Marie Hÿnes, Spaniards. Godparents: Antoine de St. Denis (s/ Chevalier de St. Denis) and Marie de Nege de St. Denis (s).

573. MARIE ROSE
January 9, 1754, baptism of Marie Rose, *négritte* born of a *négresse* belonging to Madame de St. Denis. Godparents: Antoine Vandal (s) and Marie des Negis de St. Denis (s).

574. LOUIS ANTOINE
January 26, 1754, baptism of Louis Antoine, *négrillon* born of a *négresse* belonging to Mde. de St. Denis. Godparents: Pierre de St. Denis (s) and Madame de Blanc (s).
MARGINAL NOTE: Infant died fifth day after birth.

575. FRANCOISE VERONIQUE PRUDHOMME
March 2, 1754, baptism of Francoise Veronique, legitimate daughter of Pierre Prudhomme (x) and Madeline Bouchard. Godparents: Jacque Lambre (x) and Veronique Bouchard (x).

576. LOUISE REINE
    March 10, 1754, baptism of Louise Reine, born of a *négresse* belonging to Madame de St. Denis. Godparents: Louis Charles de Blanc, represented by Pierre Antoine de St. Denis (s), and Marie des Neiges de St. Denis (s).

577. MARIE LOUISE
    March 13, 1754, baptism of Marie Louise, Indian born of an Indian belonging to Mr. Dominique. Godparents: Pierre de la Ronde, officer (s) and Marie /Davion dit_e_/ St. Prix (s).

578. MARIE MADELEINE GRAPPE
    March 26, 1754, baptism of Marie Madeleine, legitimate daughter of Alexis Grappe and Marie Madeleine Guedon. Godparents: Chevalier de la Ronde (s) and Mademoiselle Trichely (s/ Jeanne Le Roy).

579. MANUEL MARIANNE
    November 11, 1754, baptism of Manuel Marianne, *négritte*, daughter of Nanette and Pierrot, negroes belonging to Madame de St. Denis. Godparents: Manuel de choto vermudes, Spaniard (s) /Manuel de Soto y Bermude_z_/ and Madame de Blanc (s).

580. MARIA JUANA
    May 30, 1754, baptism of Maria Juana, child of a father unknown.* Godparents: Daniel Pain (s) and Jeanne Pain (s). Baptized by the curé /name illegibl_e_/ of Los Adaes.

    *No mention was made of the child's mother. It is assumed that the infant was white, since the entry was numbered. Entries for blacks and Indians bear no numbers in this register.

581. MARIE LOUISE
    July 14, 1754, baptism of Marie Louise, *négritte* born the previous day of a *négresse* named Lisette belonging to Mr. Masse. Godparents: Manuel Bermudes, Spaniard (s/ M. Antone Soto Berm ez) and "Madame, his wife" (s/ Marie de St. denis).

582. GENEVIEVE
    August 4, 1754, baptism of Genevieve, *mulâttresse* born of a *négresse* named Marie Joseph, belonging to Mr. de Meziere. Godparents: Antoinne Janis (s/ Antoinne Janisse) and Cecile le Vasseur (x).

583. JEAN LOUIS
    August 7, 1754, baptism of Jean Louis, born of an Indian belonging to Mr. Dauphine, sergeant. Godparents: Jean Prudhomme (x) and Jeanne Rachal (x).

584. MARIE GENEVIEVE DUBOIS
     August 24, 1754, baptism of Marie Genevieve, legitimate
     daughter of Jean Baptiste Dubois (s) and Marie Joseph
     Clermont. Godparents: Jean Louis Cesaire Borme (s) and
     Marie Elisabh Denes (s).

585. MARIE JEANNE
     August 28, 1754, baptism of Marie Jeanne, free *mulâttresse*
     born of a free *mulâttresse* named Marie Anne. Godparents:
     Jean Leger (x) and Marie Jeanne Levasseur (x).

586. JEAN BAPTISTE DAVION
     September 12, 1754, baptism of Jean Baptiste, legitimate
     son of Jean Baptiste Davion and Marie Henry Triche. God-
     parents: Chevalier de la Ronde (s) and Marie Louise le
     Roy (x).

587. JEAN BAPTISTE MALBERT
     October 26, 1754, baptism of Jean Baptiste, legitimate
     son of Jean Baptiste Malbert, soldier, and Jeanne Verger.
     Godparents: Jean Baptiste Boulet (x), soldier, and Marie
     Francoise Verger (x).

588. LOUIS
     November 24, 1754, baptism of Louis, *négrillon* born Novem-
     ber 19 of a *négresse* belonging to Mr. Le Court, officer.
     Father unknown. Godparents: Le Court, represented by
     Manuel Triche (s/ Manuel Trichel) and Marie Louise le Roy
     (x).

589. MARIE LOUISE BOULET
     February 15, 1755, baptism of Marie Louise, legitimate
     daughter of Jean Baptise Boulet and Anne Verger. God-
     parents: Gaspard Derbanne (s) and Madame Trichely (x).

590. PELAGIE PAIN
     March 12, 1755, baptism of Pelagie, born February 25, le-
     gitimate daughter of Daniel Pain (s) and Marie Jeanne
     Rougot. Godparents: Chevalier de la Ronde (s) and Mde.
     Pelagie de Meziere (s).

591. MARIE CATHERINE BUARD
     March 11, 1755, baptism of Marie Catherine, born March 3,
     legitimate daughter of Gabriel Buard and Marie Anne Rou-
     saux. Godparents: Louis Rondin (x) and Catherine Dupres
     (s), both habitants.

592. MARIE ANNE
     March 11, 1755, baptism of Marie Anne, born of Marie Ju-
     lien, slave of Mde. de St. Denis, and a father unknown.
     /no race given/. Godparents: Emanuel Soto (s) and
     Doloritte de Blanc (s).

593. MARIE ANNE DOROTHE VILDEC /PEREAU/
March 20, 1755, baptism of Marie Anne Dorothe, legitimate daughter of Francois Vildec and Marie Catherine Dupre. Godparents: Baptiste Dupres, absent and represented by Robert Dupre, his brother (x), and Marie Anne Roussaux (s).

594. MARGUERITTE
March 28, 1755, baptism of Margueritte, *négresse* belonging to Gaspard Derbanne. Godparents: Jean Baptiste Trichely (s/ jeain beaitiste Trichele) and Margueritte le Roy (x).

595. MICHEL
March 30, 1755, baptism of Michel, *mulâtre* born of a *négresse* of Mde. de St. Denis. Godparents: Manuel Trichele (s) and Marie Jeanne Levasseur (x).

596. JEANNE MARGUERITE TOUTAIN
May 31, 1755, baptism of Jeanne Marguerite, born May 29, legitimate daughter of Charles Toutain and Jeanne Guedon. Godparents: Dominique Montaize (x) and Louise Marguerite Guedon (x).

597. LOUIS
June 8, 1755, baptism of Louis, *négrillon* born of a *négresse* belonging to Mr. Trichely. Godparents: Louis Rachal, soldier (x) and Margueritte le Roy (x).

598. MARIE FRANCOISE MADER
June 29, 1755, baptism of Jean Mader and Marie Maderne*. Godparents: Jacques Lambre (x) and Marie Francoise Bourdon (x).

*The surname "Maderne" has been written over with the name "Thily."

599. MARIE JEANNE
July 20, 1755, baptism of Marie Jeanne, *négritte* born the 19th of July to a *négresse* of Mr. de Blanc, commandant. Godparents: Jean Baptiste Prudhomme, *chirurgien pour le roy* (s/ Jean Baptiste) and Madame Pain.

600. JEAN FRANCOIS
August 12, 1755, baptism of Jean Francois, *négrillon* born of Louis and Susan, negroes belonging to the mission. Godparents: Jean Francois Breton (s) and Marie Malathie Jobard (x).

601. JULIEN RONDIN
August 13, 1755, baptism of Julien, legitimate son of Julien Rondin (x), officer, and Jeanne Riotor. Godparents: Sr. Pain, the son (s) and Clemence Borme, the daughter (s/ Marie Elisabeth Borme).

* 602. JEAN ANTOINE
        September 7, 1755, baptism of Jeanam Antonium, son of Lucretia and a father unknown.** Godparents: Domina Blan (s/ Marie de Blanc) and Emmanuel de Soto et Bermudez.

        **Jean Antoine and Lucretia obviously were not white since the entry was unnumbered. In this register only white entries bear numbers and accompanying marginal references to family names. Docs. 178 and 206, Natchitoches civil records, dated 1756, identify Lucreie and her infant Antoine as the slaves of Mme. de St. Denis.

* 603. BARTHELEMY RACHAL
        November 6, 1755, baptism of Bartholome, legitimate son of Ludovici Rachal and Marie Ludovice Ria /Ie Roy/. No godparents

* 604. ANDRE** FRANCOIS DERBANNE
        November 6, 1755, baptism of Antonio** Franciscus, legitimate son of Gaspario de Berban** and Anne Berger**. Godparents: Andres Rambin (s) and Anna Boulet.

        **The infant's given name is written "Andre" in the margin; in the text, however, it appears as "Antonio" which translates as "Antoine." The name "de Berban" has been written over, at a later date, with the name "Derbanne." Similarly, "Berger" has been changed to "Verger."

* ---   Entered, in Latin, by Fr. Anastasius, a visiting Jesuit.

  605. JEAN GABRIEL
        November 28, 1755, baptism of Jean Gabriel, *négrillon* of Gabriel Buard. Godparents: Gabriel Lage (x), M. Louise Buard.

  606. MARIE GENEVIEVE DUBOIS
        December 7, 1755, baptism of Marie Genevieve, legitimate daughter of Jean Baptiste du Bois and Marie Joseph Clarmont. Godparents: Andre Rambin (s) and Marie Jeanne Le Vasseur (s).

  607. MARGUERITTE
        December 7, 1755, baptism of Margueritte, *négritte* belonging to /Remy Poisot dit/ Bourguignon. Godparents: Jean Francois Bretton (s) and Marguerite le Roy.

  608. MARIE LOUISE GRILLET
        December 30, 1755, baptism of Marie Louise, legitimate daughter of Marin Grillet and Marie Louise Brevelle. Godparents: Gabriel Buard (x) and Marie Roussaux (s).

  609. MARIE ANNE
        January 6, 1756, baptism of Marie Anne, *négrillonne* of Mr. Triche. Godparents: Francoise Levasseur (x) and Margueritte Le Roy (x).

610. CREI? /LUCREI?/
     January 7, 1756, baptism of Crei?, négrillone slave of
     Dominique /Monteche/. Godparents: Louis Rachal (x) and
     Cecile Levasseur (x).

611. MARIE ANNE
     January 11, 1756, baptism of Marie Anne, négrillone of
     Md. de St. Denis. Godparents: Francois Longlois (s) and
     Marie Delincour (x).

612. MARIE JOSEPHE DUPREZ
     January 16, 1756, baptism of Marie Josephe, legitimate
     daughter of Jean Baptiste Dupres and Elisabeth Verger.
     Godparents: Gaspar D'erbane (s) and Anne Marie, wife of
     Sieur Louis Gignon (x).

613. FRANCOIS XAVIER BORME
     January 17, 1756, baptism of Francois Xavier, legitimate
     son of Cezar Borme (s) and Marie Elisabeth Denes. Godparents: "the undersigned" -- (s/ Chier de jucherau, by
     proxy) and Marie Doloris de St. Denis, Dame de Blanc (s).
     Fr. Joseph de Calahorra y Sarvos of the Los Adaes mission,
     officiating.

614. MARIE JEANNE
     March 8, 1756, baptism of Marie Jeanne, slave of Madame de
     St. Denis. Godparents: Jean Lambre (x) and Marie Francoise La Claire *dit* Robard.

615. MARIE MAGDELEINE LA RENAUDIERE
     April 10, 1756, baptism of Marie Magdeleine, legitimate
     daughter of Charles la Renaudiere and Jeanne del Rio*. Godparents: Guillaume Chever (x) and Jeanne Barbier (x).

     *Del Rio is the Spanish equivalent of de la Riviere, the
     name which is used elsewhere in these registers for Mme.
     la Renaudiere.

616. MARIE
     April 14, 1756, baptism of Marie, a slave of Mde. de St.
     Denis. Godparents: Dominique Monteche (x) and Therese le
     Vasseur (x).

617. ANONYMOUS
     April /blank/, 1756, baptism of a *métive*, born of a slave
     of Dominique Monteche. Godparents: Dominique Monteche
     (x) and Madame /illegible/ (x).

618. CATHERINE MARIE CASTRO
     February 6, 1756, baptism of Catherine Marie, legitimate
     daughter of Francois Castro and Marie Sta. Croix, Spaniards. Godparents: Cesard de Blanc, Chevalier and

commandant (s) and Marie Dolor de St. Denis de Blanc (s).

619. LOUIS
March 1, 1756, baptism of Louis, slave of Gabriel Buard. Godparents: Louis Buard (x) and Marie Louise /Grillet dite_7 Sauterelle (x).

620. PIERRE
April 5, 1756, baptism of Pierre, slave of Mde. de St. Denis. Godparents: Pierre Duplessis (x) and Marie Rose /no last name_7 (x).

621. MARIE JOSEPHE VÉRONIQUE DEBRANDÉ
April 10, 1756, baptism of Marie Josephe Veronique, legitimate daughter of Andre Debrande (s) and Francoise Veronique Bouchart. Godparents: Pierre Prudhomme (x) and Marie Joseph Clermont (s).

622. JULIENNE GAUTIER
May 12, 1756, baptism of Julienne, legitimate daughter of Rene Gautier and Jeanne Provatier. Godparents: Louis Rondin (x) and Julianne Provatier (x).

623. ELEANOR CHAGNOT
May 18, 1756, baptism of Eleanor, born May 15, legitimate daughter of Francois Chagnot and Marie Anne Lacroix. Godparents: Jean Louis Cesar Borme (s) and Elisabeth Rachale (s/ Elisabethe).

624. MARIE EMMANUEL DE SOTO
May 27, 1756, baptism of Marie Emmanuel, born May 11, legitimate daughter of Emmanuel Antonio Soto Bermudez (s) and Marie des Neges de St. Denis. Godparents: Pierre de la Ronde, officer (s) and Marie Emmanuela Sanchez Navarro de St. Denis (s).

625. ANTOINE
June 6, 1756, baptism of Antoine, *négrillon* of Mr. Trichele. Godparents: Antoine Fasinthe (s/ Antoinne Fazende) and Elisabeth Rachale (s).

626. FRANCOIS
June 6, 1756, baptism of Francois, *négrillon* of Mde. de St. Denis. Godparents: Francois Bontemps (x) and Cecile Levasseur (x).

627. JEAN BAPTISTE
January 6, 1756, baptism of Jean Baptiste, *naigre* of Mr. Buard. Godparents: Jean Mader (x) and Louise Lage (x).

628. JEAN BAPTISTE
    MARIE
June 6, 1756, marriage of two slaves of Gabriel Buard.

629. MARGUERITE PRUDHOMME
June 25, 1756, baptism of Marguerite, daughter of Pierre Prudhomme and Magdelaine darvalle? (Bouchard?). Godparents: Pierre Alorge (x) and Margueritte Prudhomme (x).

630. MARIE PELAGIE ATHANAISE DE MEZIERES
June 26, 1756, baptism of Marie Pelagie Athanaise, daughter of Monsieur Athanaise de Mezieres (s), officer of the troops, and Pelagie Fazende. Godparents: Antoine Le Doux, officer, represented by Antoine Fasinte (s) and Francoise Fasinte, represented by Francoise le Vasseur (x).

631. THERESE
July 6, 1756, baptism of Therese, daughter of Margueritte, Indian, belonging to Sr. Blanpain. Godparents: Paul Bourdele (s) and Therese Barbier (x).

632. JEAN FRANCOIS LAMBRE
July 13, 1756, baptism of Jean Francois, son of Jacob Lambre and Therese Le Vasseur. Godparents: Francois Levasseur (x) and Margueritte Dervin (x) /̄Derbanne/̄

633. JEAN FRANCOIS RAMBIN
July 18, 1756, baptism of Jean Francois, son of Andre Rambin and Marie Francoise la Clairmont. Godparents: Jean Francois le Breton (s) and Jeanne Rioter.

634. MARIE JEANNE DARDENNE
July 20, 1756, baptism of Marie Jeanne, daughter of Charles Dardenne* and Louise Lage. Godparents: Jean Baptiste Mongot (x) and Marie Jeanne Rougeot (s/ Jeann Pain).

*See note accompanying Entry 328.

635. GENEVIEVE
August 24, 1756, baptism of Genevieve, slave of Mr. Triche. /̄no race given/̄ Godparents: Emanuel Trichle (s) and Jeanne le Roy (s).

636. MARIE ELEONORE PRUDHOMME
September 7, 1756, baptism of Marie Eleonore, daughter of Bastien Prudhomme and Anne* Chever. Godparents: Guillaume Chever and Marie Jeanne Barbier (x). /̄*Jeanne/̄.

637. ANDRE MATHIEU
September 29, 1756, baptism of Andre Mathieu, *négrillon* born September 21, natural son of Matiane, *négresse* slave of Madame de St. Denis. Godparents: Louis Charles de Blanc, *fils de* Mr. de Blanc, commandant, and Marie Manuelle de Soto. Fr. Didier, a visiting priest, officiating.

638. JACQUES MAURICE DE BLANC
October 4, 1756, baptism of Jacques Maurice, born September 22, 1756, legitimate son of Cesaire de Blanc, chevalier and commandant, and Marie des Douleurs de St. Denis. Godparents: Jacques Didier, Jesuit, and Marie des Neges, wife of Emmanuel de Soto. Reverend Father Calahorra, witness. Fr. Valentin, *curé* at Natchitoches, officiating.

639. JEANNE MARIE BERARD DE LA GASE
October 25, 1756, baptism of Jeanne Marie, natural daughter of Marie Berard de la Gase and a father unknown. Godparents: /illegible/ Athanas Chagnon (x) and Marie Jeanne Chagnon (x).

640. FELICITE LE DUC
November 11, 1756, baptism of Felicite, daughter of Josephe Le Duc and Marianne Guedon. Godparents: Marie Athanase de Mezier, *cadet*, acting for Monsieur de Metzier, *capitaine*(s) and Jeanne Le Roy (s).

641. MARIE JEANNE BUARD
November __ /illegible/, 1756, baptism of Marie Jeanne, legitimate daughter of Gabriel Buard and Marie Rousseau. Godparents: Marain Grillet (x) and Marie Louise Brevelle (x).

642. JEAN BAPTISTE PRUDHOMME
January 8, 1757, baptism of Jean Baptiste, legitimate son of Jean Baptiste Prudhomme (s) and Marie Françoise Chever. Godparents: Guillaume Chever (s) and Catherinne Melier *ditte* Alorge (x).

643. JEAN DUPLESSIS
January 28, 1757, baptism of Jean, born January 8, natural son of Emmanuele Duplessis and a father unknown. Godparents: Jean Adrian Leger (x) and Marie Delincour, wife of Bourdelle (x).

644. DOMINIQUE DAVION
February 9, 1757, baptism of Dominique, son of Jean Baptiste Davion *dit* St. Prix and Marie Trichel. Godparents: Dominique Monteche (x) and Marie Francoise Vergé (x).

645. MARIE STÉPHANIE SORELLE
January 15, 1757, baptism of Marie Stephanie, daughter of Pierre Sorelle *dit* Marlie (s) and Rose Marie Boisselier. Godparents: Chevalier Pre. de Jucherot, officer (s) and Marie Stephanie de St. Denis *ditte* Sanche Navarre (s/ Manuela Sanche Navarre de St. Denis).

646. LOUISE CIRENA
February 8, 1757, baptism of Louise Cirena, *mulâttresse*

belonging to Monsieur de Blanc. Godparents: Emmanuel Soto (s) and Marie Soto *ditte* St. Denis (s).

647. FRANÇOIS TRISTANT
February 8, 1757, baptism of François, son of Pierre Tristant and Margueritte Victoire Prudhomme. Godparents: Francois Langlois (s) and Jeanne Le Roy (s).

648. MARIE FRANCOISE
March 9, 1757, baptism of Marie Francoise, *négrillone* of Mr. de Mezieres. Godparents: Francois Doucet (s) and Marie Theincour (x) /Marie Delincour/.

649. LOUIS PAIN
March 10, 1757, baptism of Louis, legitimate son of Daniel Pain (s) and Marie Jeanne Rougeot. Godparents: Louis Le Court, officer (s) and Madame de Blanc *ditte* de St. Denis.

650. MARIE ANTOINETTE RODRIGUE (STA. THERESIE)
April 13, 1756, baptism of Marie Antoinette, daughter of Jeanne Rodriguez, her mother, and /Illegible/ Sta. Theresie, her father, both Spanish. Godparents: Sieur Jucherot de St. Denis (s/ Le Chev. dejucheraud) and Marie Joseph Clermont (x).

651. LOUISE MARGUERITE LECOMTE
April 17, 1757, baptism of Louise Marguerite, daughter of Jean Baptiste LeComte and Marguerite Le Roy. Godparents: Henri Triche (x) and Marie Louise Le Roy (x).

652. PIERRE LAURENT LEROY (LE COURT)
April 17, 1757, baptism of Pierre Laurent, son of Jeanne le Roy and a father unknown*. Godparents: Laurent Rivoire (s) and Marie Louise Le Roy (x).

*See Entry 984.

653. FRANCOIS
April 24, 1757, baptism of Francois, *nègre* belonging to Mr. St. Pri. Godparents: Pierre Darbanne and Marie Francoise Dominique /Monteche/

654. CHARLOTTE FRANCOISE
April 24, 1757, baptism of Charlotte Francoise, *négresse* of Monsieur de Meziere. Godparents: Louis Le Court, officer, and Marie Francoise Rambin.

655. MARIE LOUISE
April 24, 1757, baptism of Marie Louise, Indian of Mr. Pain. Godparents: de la Ronde, officer, and Marie Louise le Roy.

656. JEAN BAPTISTE BOULET
June 24, 1757, baptism of Jean Baptiste, legitimate son of Jean Baptiste Boulet and Anne Verger. Godparents: Jean B. du Bois (s) and Anne Poisseau (x).

657. MARIE ANNE GRAPPE
June 26, 1757, baptism of Marie Anne, daughter of Lexis Grappe (s) and Louise Margueritte Guedon. Godparents: Charles Toutin and Marie Anne Rousseau (s/ Marie Rousaux).

658. ALEXIS MALBERT
June 26, 1757, baptism of Alexis, born December 8, 1756, son of Jean Baptiste Malbert (s) and Marie Jeanne Verger Godparents: Alexis Grappe (s) and Louise Marguerite Guedon (x).

659. FRANCOIS TOUTIN
June 26, 1757, baptism of Francois, born June 21, son of Charles Toutin and Jeanne Guedon. Godparents: Francois Grappe (x) and Marie Francoise Buard (x).

660. JEAN BAPTISTE DELASERT
July 3, 1757, baptism of Jean Baptiste, son of Joseph Michel de la Sert (x) and Anne Louisa Thawrete ?. Godparents: Louis Charles De Blanc (x) and Marie Josephe Clermont (x).

661. JEAN BAPTISTE
July 22, 1757, baptism of Jean Baptiste, slave of Mr. Borme. /no race given/ Godparents: Jean Baptiste Rougeot (s) and Marie Jeanne Rougeot (s), wife of Sr. Pain.

662. MARIE LOUISE TURPOT
August 20, 1757, baptism of Marie Louise, daughter of Jacques Turpot *dit* La France and Angelique /Dumont/. Godparents: Gaspare Darbane (s) and Marie Vergé.

663. JEAN BAPTISTE.
/no date/, baptism of Jean Baptiste, *nègre* of Monsieur Jean des Jeans. Godparents: Jean Baptiste Rougeau (s) and Marie Francoise Dominique (s) /Monteche/.

664. MARIE ANNE
/no date/, baptism of Marie Anne, *négresse* of Mr. Jean des Jeans. Godparents: Manuel Trichle (s) and Marie Anne Rousseau (s).

665. MARGUERITE VICTOIRE
/no date/, baptism of Marguerite Victoire, *négresse* of Mlle. Jeanne Le Roy. Godparents: Jean Fromantin(s) and Jeanne Alorges (s). Witnesses: Le Court (s), Chevalier de la Ronde (s), Gaspar Derbanne (s), Marie Louise Le Roy (x)

666. MARIE JOSEPHE DUPRES
     September 5, 1757, baptism of Marie Josephe, daughter of
     Jean Baptiste Dupres (x) and Elisabeth Verge. Godpar-
     ents: Remis Poissot (s/ Poisot) and Angelique Verge.

667. ELISABETH TERMETTE GRILLET
     September 27, 1757, baptism of Elisabeth Termette, daugh-
     ter of Marin Grillet and Marie Louise Brevelle. God-
     parents: Louis Buard (x) and Elisabeth Verge (s).

668. MARIE DE L'INCARNATION MARINNE
     October 10, 1757, baptism of Marie de l'Incarnation,
     daughter of Jean Marinne and Jeanne Josephe La Lanne*.
     Godparents: Martin Goutierre de Land (x) and Louise
     Marguerite Duplecis (x).

     *Above the name "La Lanne", written between the lines,
     appears the name "Dupre" which was apparently added at
     a later date. It is the editor's opinion that this
     addition is an error. A La Land-Dupre marriage did
     occur in 1770 (see Entry 1005), but this later La Land
     belonged to a different family from that in Entry 668
     above and in 1757 there was no connection between the
     Dupre family of Natchitoches and the Goutierre de Land/
     La Lanne family of Los Adayes.

669. MARIE JOSEPHE
     November 27, 1757, baptism of Marie Josephe, *négritte* of
     Sieur Bourgingnon *dit* Poisotte. Godparents: Julien
     Poisotte (x) and Marie Josephe du Verge (s/ Marie Joseph
     Dupres).

670. MARIE URSULLE
     January 5, 1758, baptism of Marie Ursulle, daughter of
     Lisette, Indian of Sieur Le Court?. Godparents: Jacque
     Rachal (x) and Jeanne Le Roy (s).

671. ANTOINE MARCEL DE SOTO
     February 3, 1758, baptism of Antoine Marcelle, born Jany. 16,
     son of Antoine Manuelle de Soto and Marie des Nege de
     St. Denis. Godparents: Pierre Antoine de Jucherot (s)
     and Marie Dolor de St. Denis De Blanc (s).

672. FRANCOIS DERBANNE
     February 4, 1758, baptism of Francois, son of Gaspar
     D'arbane and Marie Francoise Verger. Godparents: Jean
     Francois Breton (s) and Cecile Levasseur Jolibois.

673. VALENTIN JEAN BAPTISTE DUBOIS
     February 18, 1758, baptism of Valentin Jean Baptiste,
     son of Jean Baptiste du Bois (s) and Marie Josephe Cler-
     mont. Godparents: Dugue, represented by Pierre de St.

St. Denis (s) and Marie du Douleurs Simonne de Blanc (s/ Marie St. Denis de Blanc).

674. JOSEPH DUPRES
February 26, 1758, baptism of Joseph, born February 22, son of Joseph Dupres (x) and Marie de l'Incarnation Derbane. Godparents: Remis Poisotte (s/ Poisot), elder warden of the church, and Victoire Marguerite D'arbanne, represented by Marie Jeanne Derbane (x).

675. PIERRE JOSEPH CASTRE
March 9, 1758, baptism of Pierre Joseph, son of Francois de Castre and Marie de l'Incarnation de Ste. Croix. Godparents: Joseph Gallien, represented by Pierre Leveille (x) and Pierre Isabelle de la Aintelle (x).

676. JEAN PIERRE PRUDHOMME
April 17, 1758, baptism of Jean Pierre, son of Pierre Prudhomme (x) and Magdeleine Dorveille*. Godparents: Jean Borme (x) and Marie Jeanne Rougeau (s/ Mari Pain).

*Above the name "Dorveille," between the lines, is written the name "Bouchard."

677. FRANCOIS
April 21, 1758, baptism of Francois, son of Francois and Francoise, slaves of Mad. de St. Denis. Godparents: Joseph Sanches and Anne Louisiane (x) (x), Spaniards.

678. ALEXIS
May 10?, 1758, baptism of Alexis, son of Marianne, *négresse* slave of Mdme. de St. Denis. Godparents: Alexis Grappe, Sergeant (s) and Francoise? Margueritte Guedon (x).

679. CESAR MARIE DE MEZIERES
March 24, 1758, baptism of Cesar (Cesaire) Marie, son of Capt. de Mezieres and Pelagie Fasinth. Godparents: Cesaire de Blanc, chevalier and commandant (s) and Marie des Douleurs de Blanc *ditte* de St. Denis (s).

680. MARIE FELICITÉ DUPIN (DU PAIN)
June 4, 1758, baptism of Marie Felicité, daughter of Pierre Victor du Pain and Jeanne Catherine Alorge. Godparents: Capt. de Mezieres (s) and Dame de Blanc *ditte* de St. Denis (s).

681. MARIE ROSE LAMBRE
June 12, 1758, baptism of Marie Rose, daughter of Jean Lambre(x) and Marie Jeanne Le Vasseur. Godparents: Dominique Monteche (x) and Francoise Bourdon (x).

682. LOUIS RACHAL
June 12, 1758, baptism of Louis, son of Louis Rachal and

Marie Louise Le Roy. Godparents: Monsieur Le Court, officer (s) and Marie Elisabeth Borme (s).

683. ANNE MARIE
July 2, 1758, baptism of Anne Marie, Indian of Monsieur de Blanc (s). Godparents: Jean Baptiste Prudhomme (s) and Marie Josephe /Corantine/.

684. JEAN BAPTISTE RAMBIN
July 29, 1758, baptism of Jean Baptiste, son of Andre Rambin (s) and Marie Francoise Clermont. Godparents: Jean Baptiste du Bois (s) and Dame de Mezieres *ditte* Fazinthe.

685. EMMANUEL
July 30, 1758, baptism of Emmanuel, Indian of Sr. Dominique /Monteche/. Godparents: Emanuel Trichele (s) and Cecile Levasseur (x).

686. JACQUES
July 31, 1758, baptism of Jacques, *négrillon* of Monsieur de Blanc, commandant. Godparents: Louis de Blanc, his son (x) and Marie Josephe Prudhomme (x).

687. /TORN/
August ?, 1758, baptism of a *matise* belonging to la France, soldier. Godparents: Alexis Grappe (s) and Marie Jeanne Verger (s).

688. MARGUERITTE _____
August 25, 1758, baptism of Margueritte, daughter of Antoine _____ /sic/ and Jeanne Antoine, Spaniards. Godparents: Guillaume Chever (x) and Margueritte Prudhomme (x).

NOTE: Possibly this is the same family as that which appears in Entry 533.

689. MARIE LOUISE DERBANNE
September 2, 1758, baptism of Marie Louise, born at Avoyelles on February 5, 1758, daughter of Pierre Darbane and Marie Claire /le Clerc/. Godparents: Gaspare D'arbane (s) and Marie Louise D'arbane (x).

690. CHRISOSTOME PEREAU
September 25, 1758, baptism of Chrisostome, born May 31, 1757, son of Joseph Francois Pereau* and Marie Chatarinne De pres. Godparents: Sieur Lalande (x) and Marie Anne Bourquinnon Poisseau (x).

*The name "Pereau" has been written over with the name "Vildec", the *dit* of the Pereau family.

691. FATIN
October 22, 1758, baptism of Fatin, slave of M. de Meziere, officer. Godparents: Marie Pelagie Athanase de Mezieres, *cadet* (s), and Marie Josephe Prudhomme (x).

692. LOUIS RONDIN
October 22, 1758, baptism of Louis, son of Louis Rondin and Marie Berard. Godparents: Ignace de Noÿot (x) and Jeanne de Sotos (x).

693. MARIE LOUISE?
November 9, 1758, baptism of Marie <u>Louise?</u>, *mulâttresse* slave of Monsieur Le Court, officer. Godparents: Monsieur Pain, *garde magasin pour le roy* (s)* and "Mde., his wife" (s/ Jeanne Pain).

*This is the same signature as that affixed to earlier records by Daniel Pain, the former *chirurgien-major*.

694. CECILE ~~DEJEANS~~ MADER /*sic*/
December 1, 1758, baptism of Cecile, daughter of Jean des Jeans* and of Marie Maderne*. Godparents: Francois Le Vasseur (x) and Cecile le Vasseur (x).

*The name "des Jeans" is written over in the text with the name "Mader" and the name "Maderne" has been written over with the name "Thily." In the marginal reference, the name "Dejeans" has been lined through and replaced with "Mader."

695. JEANNE CHAGNOT
December 19, 1758, baptism of Jeanne, daughter of Francois Chagnot and Marie La Croix. Godparents: Monsieur de Mongeot (s), officer, and Jeanne Pain *ditte* Rougeau (s).

696. MARGUERITE MARLY (SORELLE)
December 24, 1758, baptism of Marguerite, daughter of Pierre Marly* and Marie Rose Boisselier. Godparents: Henry Triche (x) and Marie Francoise Bourdon *ditte* Monteche (x).

*The name "Marly" has been written over with the name "Sorelle."

* 697. FRANCOIS
February 25, 1759, baptism of Francois, *nègre* of Sieur Remy Poisseau. No godparents named.

* 698. MARIE
February 25, 1759, baptism of Marie, *négresse* of Sieur Remy Poisseau. No godparents named.

* --- A joint baptism

699. ANONYMOUS
February 25, 1759, baptism of a little *négritte* belonging to Gabriel Buard. Godparents: Louis La Malathy and Widow ⟨Toutain dit_e⟩ Meunier.

700. MAGDELEINE PRUDHOMME
February 25, 1759, baptism of Magdeleine, legitimate daughter of Bastien Prudhomme and Jeanne Chevere. Godparents: Louis La Malathie and Marianne Dorvalle.

701. GABRIEL
March ⟨day illegible⟩, 1759, baptism of Gabriel, slave of Monsieur de Mezieres. Godparents: Gabriel Fasindthe and Madame de Mezieres.

702. MARIE ANNE BUARD
March 11, 1759, baptism of Marie Anne, daughter of Gabriel Buard and Marie Rousseau. Godparents: Jacques Lambre (x) and Marie Anne Poisseau (x).

703. MARGUERITE
April 16, 1759, baptism of Marguerite, adult Indian belonging to Jeanne Le Roy. Godparents: Louis Rachal and Marguerite Le Roy.

704. MARIE ADELAIDE VICTOIRE PAIN
April 17, 1759, baptism of Marie Adelaide Victoire, daughter of Mr. Pain, *garde magasin*, and Marie Jeanne Rougeot. Godparents: Gabriel fasinthe (s) and Madame de Mezieres (s).

705. ISABELLE DAVION
April 24, 1759, baptism of Isabelle, daughter of Jean Baptiste Davion St. Prix and Marie Hiacinthe Triche. Godparents: Sr. Borme (s), elder warden of the church and officer of the militia, and Marie Elisabeth Borme (s), his wife.

706. JEAN BAPTISTE LA RENAUDIERE
May 2, 1759, baptism of Jean Baptiste, son of Charles de la Renaudiere (x) and Jeanne la Riviere. Godparents: Jean Baptiste la Rivier (s), sergeant, and Marie Jeanne Riche (s).

707. JEAN BAPTISTE LE ROY (LE COURT)
May 21, 1759, baptism of Jean Baptiste, son of Jeanne Le Roy and a father unknown.* Godparents: Jean Baptiste Davion (x) and Margarita le Roi (x). Entered, in Latin, by Fr. Anastasius, Roman Jesuit, on visit to Natchitoches.

*See Entry 984.

708. MARIE PELAGIE GRAPPE
July 6, 1759, baptism of Marie Pelagie, born October 3, 1758, daughter of Alexis Grappe and Louise Guedon (x). Godparents: Monsieur de Mezieres (s), Captain, and Dame Mezieres, his wife (s/ fazende Demeiziere).

709. ELEANORE
August 21, 1759, baptism of Eleanore, *négrillone* of Sr. Poisot *dit* Bourguignon. Godparents: Remy Poissot and Marie, wife of Marin Grillier (x).

710. JEAN BAPTISTE
August 23, 1759, baptism of Jean Baptiste, Indian of Mr. de Mezier. Godparents: Jean Baptiste B__abele? (s/ La riviera), and Marie Francoise Clermont, wife of Rambin (x).

711. MARIE FRANCOISE MALBERT
August 28, 1759, baptism of Marie Francoise, daughter of Sr. Jean B. Malbert and Jeanne Verge. Godparents: Sr. Bretan (s) and _____ la Simone? *ditte* Verge (x).

712. PERRINE ISABELLE LANGLOIS
August 31, 1759, baptism of Perrine Isabelle, daughter of Francois Langlois *dit* Sans Regret and Marie Gregoire de Sta. Crux. Godparents: Francois Ruis and Barbara Victoria Ruis.

713. MARIE LOUISE
September 8, 1759, baptism of Marie Louise, *négritte* of Mr. de St. Denis, the elder. Godparents: Jean Lage Pied ferme (x) and Marie Francois Vergé (x).

714. JEAN BAPTISTE PRUDHOMME
September 9, 1759, baptism of Jean Baptiste, son of Jean Baptiste Prudhomme (s) and of Marie Josephe Charlotte Corantin. Godparents: Louis de Blanc, the son, and Pelagie Pain.

715. MARGUERITTE
September 14, 1759, baptism of Margueritte, slave of Sieur Pierre Derbanne. Godparents: Henry Triche and Marie Riche.

716. LOUIS RACHAL
September 26, 1759, baptism of Louis, son of Barthelemie Rachal and Marie Francoise Lamalatie. Godparents: Louis Lamalatie (s/ Louis Jobar) and Marie Louise le Roy (x).

717. JEAN BAPTISTE DUBOIS
MARIE JOSEPH CLERMONT
June 7, 1751, marriage, after publication of one ban, of

Jean Baptiste Du Bois (s), native of Issoudun in Berry, parish of St. Cyr, archbishopric of Bourges, legitimate son of Philippe du Bois, native of the same Issodun, parish of St. Cyr, and of Genevieve Berger, native of Chateau Roux in Berry. . . and . . . Marie Joseph Clermont (s), native of Issoudun in Berry, parish of St. Cyr, archbishopric of Bourges, widow of deceased Henry Riche. Witnesses: Antoine Clermont (x), Remy Poisot (s), Jean Louis Cesar Borme (s), Jean Riche, Alorge (s) and Pain (s).

718. CHARLES PELLERIN *dit* LA LIME
MARIE VERGER
November 23, 1751, after three bans, marriage of Charles Pellerin *dit* la Lime (s), native of Moreuil in Picardie, Parish of St. Vast?, bishopric of Amiens, son of Charles Pellerin and Marie Francoise de la Porte, native of the same parish . . . and . . . Marie Verger (x), native of the parish of Natchitoches, daughter of Joseph Verger, a native of Paris, and of Angelique Dumont, native of this parish. Witnesses: Alorges (s), Bertrand (s) Joseph Verger (s) and Trichely.

719. ANDRE DEBRANTE *dit* CHAMPAGNE
VERONIQUE BOUCHARD
November 22, 1751, after three bans, marriage of Andre DeBrante *dit* Champagne, native of La Rochelle, "capital city" of the country of Aunis, parish of St. Jean de Prole, legitimate son of Francois Debrante, native of L'Andres in England and Susanne Lunot, native of La Rochelle. . . and . . . Francoise Veronique Bouchard (s), legitimate daughter of Antoine Bouchard, native of Fort Pontchartrain, parish of Notre Dame, bishopric of Quebec, and of Marie Francoise Hubert, native of Baptisquant /Batiscan/, parish of St. Paul, bishopric of Quebec in Canada. Witnesses: Rondin, Blanpain (s), Alorge (s), Provencal, Bertrant (s), and Louis Cesar Borme (s).

720. NICOLAS PAUL BOURDELLE *dit* ST. NICOLAS
MARIE DELINCOUR
November 22, 1751, after three bans, marriage of Nicolas Paul Bourdelle *dit* St. Nicolas (s), soldier of the company of Monette, native of Paris, parish of St. Germaine, son of Nicolas Bourdelle, native of Chartres, France, and of Nicole Vichÿ, native of the same parish. . . and . . . Marie Delincour (x), native of Sorberig in Germany, widow of deceased Adrien Leger *dit* Pied ferme, daughter of Cesar Delincour and of Ursulle de Salomee. Witnesses: Pierre Alorge (s), Claude Bertran *dit* Dauphiné (s), Joseph Blanpain, Henry Trichely (x) and M^{te} Monet.

721. PIERRE NOEL GALLIEN
MARIE RACHAL
January 8, 1752, after three bans, marriage of Pierre Noel Gallien (x), native of Quebec, parish of Beauport, bishopric of Quebec, legitimate son of Pierre Gallien, a native of Quebec and of Marie Morier, a native of the Isle d' Oriant . . . and . . . Marie Rachal (x), a native of Natchitoches, legitimate daughter of Pierre Rachal *dit* St. Denis, soldier, a native of the Isle d'Oléron, and Marie Anne Benoit, native of Paris. Witnesses: Alorge (s), Dominique /Monteche/ (x), Etienne, Antoine Bouchard (s).

722. PIERRE BASTIEN PRUDHOMME *dit* LA DOUCEUR
JEANNE CHEVER
January 8, 1752, after publication of two bans and dispensation with the third, and with the permission of the commandant under date of October 24, 1751, as well as that of the bishop who granted dispensation to the couple from the impediment of consanguinity in the third degree, was celebrated the marriage of Pierre Bastien Prudhomme *dit* la Douceur (x) soldier, native of this parish, legitimate son of Jean Prudhomme, a native of the province of Dauphinée, and Catherine Meillier, a native of Paris, parish of St. Sulpice . . . and . . . Jeanne Chever (x), native of this parish, legitimate daughter of Guillaume Chever and of Therese Barbier, a native of Dauphine. Witnesses: Guillaume Chever (s), Alorge (s), De Blanc (s), De la Ronde (s), Louis Cesar Borme (s), Pain (s), Rondin (x).

723. JEAN LOUIS GARIEN *dit* LA VERDURE
ELIZABETH DUPRES
June 19, 1752, after three bans, marriage of Jean Louis Garien *dit* la Verdure (x), native of St. Martin du l'aveque, parish of St. Martin, bishopric of Beauvais in Picardie, legitimate son of Luc Garein and Anne Petit, both natives of the same parish and bishopric as above . . . and . . . Elizabeth Dupres, native of this parish, legitimate daughter of Jacques Dupres, native of Paris, and of Anne Marie Philippe, a native of the Palatine. Witnesses: Poisot (s), Buard (x), Jean Baptiste Dubois (s) and Rambin (s). The bride also made her "x".

724. PIERRE TRISTANT *dit* LA JEUNESSE
MARGUERITTE VICTOIRE PRUDHOMME
November 8, 1752, after publication of two bans and dispensation with the third, was married Pierre Tristant *dit* la Jeunesse (s), soldier, native of Benneville in Lorraine parish of St. Remy, bishopric of Treves, legitimate son of deceased Louis Tristant, native of Damloup, bishopric of Verdun, and of Anne Bast____, native of Benneille? . . . and . . . Margueritte Victoire Prudhomme (x), native of this parish, bishopric of Quebec, legitimate daughter of

Jean Prudhomme, native of Romans in Dauphine, and of Catherine Meillier, a native of Paris, parish of St. Sulpice. Witnesses: Alorge (s), Pain (s), Guillaume Chever (s), Blanpain (s), Dominique /Monteche/ (x).

725. PIERRE PRUDHOMME
MARIE MADELEINE BOUCHARD
January 9, 1753, after publication of three bans, marriage of Pierre Prudhomme (x), native of this parish, legitimate son of Jean Prudhomme, native of Romans in Dauphine and of Catherine Meillier, native of Paris, parish of St. Sulpice . . . and . . . Marie Madeleine Bouchard (x), native of Kakacia /Kaskaskia/, canton of Illinois, parish of Notre Dame de la Immaculé Conception, bishopric of Quebec, legitimate daughter of Antoine Bouchard, native of Fort Pontchartrain, parish of Notre Dame, and of Marie Francoise Hubert, native of Baptisquant /Batiscan/, parish of St. Paul, in Canada. Witnesses: "the mother" (x), Alorge (s), Rambin (s), Borme (s), and one illegible signature.

726. JACQUES LAMBRE
THERESE LEVASSEUR
January 23, 1753, after three bans, marriage of Jacques Lambre (x), a native of Allemands /The German Coast of Louisiana/, parish of St. Louis, bishopric of Quebec, the legitimate son of deceased Martin Lambre native of Strasbourg in Alsace, bishopric of Cercle on the upper Rhine, and Marie Grandissa, a native of Alsace, province of the upper Rhine . . . and . . . Therese Levasseur (x), native of this parish, legitimate daughter of Jacques Levasseur, native of Paris, parish of St. Nicolas des Champs, and Marie Francoise Bourdon, native of Amiens in Picardie. Witnesses: Guillaume Chever (s) and Jobard (x).

727. LOUIS RACHAL *dit* BLONDAIN
MARIE /LE/ ROY
July 23, 1753, after three bans, marriage of Louis Rachal *dit* Blondain (x), soldier of the company of Montbrun, native of this parish, legitimate son of Pierre Rachal, a native of the Isle d'Oléron and of Marie Anne Benoist, a native of Paris . . . and . . . Marie /le/ Roy, native of this parish, legitimate daughter of deceased Etienne /le/ Roy and of Louise Francoise Gilot, a native of Chalanton. Witnesses: Bertran (s), Vandal (s), Rondin (x) Blanc (s), Bunel (s).

728. JEAN BAPTISTE MALBERT *dit* SANS FACON
JEANNE VERGER
July 18, 1753, after three bans, marriage of Jean Baptiste Malbert *dit* Sans Facon (s), soldier, native of Bouge in France, diocese of Vezon, legitimate son of Jean Baptiste Malbert and of Francoise Dormoy, natives of the same parish,

. . . and . . . Jeanne Verger, native of this parish, legitimate daughter of deceased /Joseph/ Verger, native of Paris, parish of St. B<u>e</u>noist?, and of Angelique Dumond. Witnesses: Gaspar Derbanne (s), Coutet (s), Antoine Despres (s), Trichely (x), du Fre____ (x). Bride also signed.

729. JEAN BAPTISTE DUPRES
ELIZABETH VERGER
June 4, 1754, after three bans, marriage of Jean Baptiste Dupres (x), native of Canne Brules, "parish of the Germans," bishopric of Quebec, legitimate son of Jacques Dupres, native of Paris, and of Anne Marie Philippe, native of the Palentine, archbishopric of Mayance /Mein<u>z</u>/ . . . and . . . Elisabeth Verger (s), native of this parish, legitimate daughter of deceased Joseph Verger, a native of Paris, and of Angelique Dumond, a native of this parish. Witnesses: Rondin (x), Vandal (s), Trichele (s).

730. CHARLES LEMOINE
ELISABETH DUPRES
June 4 1754, after three bans, marriage of Charles Le Moine, a native of Illinois, parish of Cascatia /K̲askaskia̲/ and bishopric of Quebec, legitimate son of deceased Michel le Moine a native of Bresses, and of Marie Guenard, a native of Nantes . . . and . . . Elisabeth Dupres (x), native of this parish, widow of deceased /Jean Louis Garien *dit*/ la Verdure, legitimate daughter of Jacques Dupres, a native of Paris, and of Anne Marie Philippe, a native of the Palatine. Witnesses: Dubois (s), Monet (s), Jobard (x), and Jean Francois Breton (s).

731. MANUEL ANTOINE BERMUDES /Y DE SOT<u>O</u>/
MARIE DES NEGES DE ST. DENIS
June 2, 1754, after publication of two bans and dispensation of third, marriage of Manuel Antoine Bermudes, a native of St. Jean /San Jua<u>n</u>/ Dorron, archbishopric of St. Jacques /Santiag<u>o</u>/ de Gritierce, Kingdom of Spain, legitimate son of Dominique Bermudes and of Marie Joseph de Suendu /de Sot<u>o</u>/ . . . and . . . Marie des Neges de St. Denis, native of this parish, legitimate daughter of deceased Louis Jucherot de St. Denis, chevalier and commandant of this post during his life, and Dame Manuel Sanche Navarre, widow of deceased St. Denis. Consent given by the Spanish Missionary, Father Pierre, who was sick and could not participate in the ceremony. Father Eustache, officiating. Also signed: Fr. Pedro Raminez. No other witnesses named.

732. MARIN GRILLET *dit* SAUTERELLE
MARIE LOUISE BREVEL
June 18, 1754, after publication of two bans and dispen-

sation with the third, marriage of Marin Grillet *dit* Sauterelle (x), soldier, native of town of Belleÿ, in Bugeÿ, bishopric of the same, legitimate son of deceased Antoine Grillet, native of the same, and of Termette Careb, a native of the parish of Contret, bishopric of Bugeÿ . . . and . . . Marie Louise Brevel (x), native of the Cadeaux dependency of Natchitoches, bishopric of Quebec, legitimate daughter of deceased Jean Baptiste Brevel, a native of Paris, and of deceased Anne, *Indienne*, a native of the Cadeaux dependency. Witnesses: Sr. gabriel /Buard/ (x), Bigot (s), Sr. Rondin (x), Sr. /Toutin *dit*/ Munier (x).

733. MANUEL Y VARVO
MANUELLE SEYENA
April 7, 1755, after three bans, marriage of Manuel y Varvo /Barbo/ (s), a native of the Adayes, legitimate son of Mathieu y Varvo, a native of Mexique, and of Jeanne Ernandes, a native of Adaye. . . and . . . Manuella Seyena (x), a native of Adays, legitimate daughter of deceased Joseph Seyena, a native of Mexique, and of Jeanne de dieu Rodrique. Witness: Manuel Soto (s).

734. CHARLES FRANÇOIS LEVEQUE
JEANNE RACHAL
April 7, 1755, after three bans, marriage of Charles François Leveque (x), a native of Canada, parish of St. Anne, bishopric of Quebec, legitimate son of deceased Maturin L'eveque, native of Canada, parish of St. Anne, and of deceased Marie Madeleine Morein, native of the parish of Baptisquant /Batiscan/ in Canada . . . and . . . Jeanne Rachal (x), native of this parish, legitimate daughter of Pierre Rachal (x), native of the Isle d'Oléron, parish of St. Denis, bishopric of ^{stes} /Saintes/, and of the deceased Marie Anne Benois, native of Paris, parish of St. Laurent. Witnesses: de la Ronde (s), Le Court (s), Borme (s), Trichely (x), and one illegible signature.

735. JOANNIS BAPTISTA DE SOREL
MARIA ROSA GOTIE
September 21, 1755, marriage of Joannis Baptista de Sorel, son of Petrus Sorel, of the French nation, and of Ludovice Delec, native of the province of Canada . . . and . . . Maria Rosa Gotie, daughter of Petrus Gotie and Marguerite Go_____, native of the parish of Natchitoches. Witnesses: Ludovicus Borme, Petrus Standeni (s/ Chevalier de St. Denis), Emmanuel de Soto (s). /Latin entry./

736. JACQUES TROUPART
ANGELIQUE DUMONT
May 3, 1756, after three bans, marriage of Jacques Troupart (x), legitimate son of Francois Troupart and of Michel Poupard, native of St. Lambert de Lattai /du Lattay/ in the

bishopric of Ange . . . and . . . Angelique Dumont (x), daughter of Charles Dumont and of Angelique, a native of this parish. Witnesses: Bertrand (s), Alexis Grappe (s), Malbert (s), and Breton (s).

737. JEAN BAPTISTE PRUDHOMME
MARIE FRANCOISE CHEVERT
May 5, 1756, after publication of one ban and dispensation of other two, marriage of Jean Baptiste Prudhomme, *cherugin pour la roy* at this post, son of Jean Prudhomme and of Catherine Meliere . . . and . . . Marie Francoise Chevert (s), daughter of Guillaume Chevert, soldier, and of Therese Barbier. Witnesses: Alorge (s), Jobard (x), and Pierre Prudhomme (x). Groom also signed.

738. JEAN BAPTISTE LECOMPTE
MARGUERITE LE ROY
July 3, 1756, after publication of one ban and dispensation of other two, marriage of Jean Baptiste Le Compte, son of Claude le Compte and Parine Combe, native of the parish of St. Martin de Vecin gua_inquence?_, diocese of St. Glavec (Glanse?) . . . and . . . Margueritte le Roy, daughter of Etienne le Roy and of Marie Louise Gillot, born in this parish. Witnesses: Antoine Desprez (s), de Mersier (x), Louet? (s), Dominique /Monteche/ (x), Bourdelle (s).

739. DOMINIQUE MONTECHE
MARIE FRANCOISE BOURDON
November 22, 1756, after publication of one ban and dispensation with other two, marriage of Dominique Monteche (x), son of Jean Monteche and Catherine Leonard, born in the principality of Modena, parish and bishopric of St. Martin in Italy, a soldier . . . and . . . Marie Francoise Bourdon, daughter of Francois Bourdon and of Marie Anne Beaupres of Amien in Picardy. Witnesses: /Mader *dit*/ Jean des Jean (x), /Lamalathie *dit*/ Jobard (x), Davion de St. Prix (x).

740. LOUIS RONDIN
MARIE BERARD (DE LA GACE)
February 6, 1757, after publication of one ban and dispensation with other two, marriage of Louis Rondin (x), son of Julien Rondin and Jeanne St. Louis? of this parish . . . and . . . Marie Berard (x), daughter of Ignace de la Gace and Aviette Remond, born in the port of La badie, dependency of Mexique. Witnesses: Breton (s), Poisot (s), Gaspar Derbanne (s), Longlois (s), Andre Debrande (s).

741. JOSEPH DUPRES
MARIE DE L'INCARNATION D'ARBANE
February 13, 1757, after publication of one ban and the dispensation of the other two, marriage of Joseph Dupres

(x), son of)-(* Dupres and of Marie Anne of this parish . . . and . . . Marie de l'Incarnation D'arbane (x), daughter of)-(D'arbane and of)-(Gonzale of the parish of Adailles. Witnesses: Rambin (s), Breton (s), Dubois (s), and one illegible signature.

*)-(is a symbol used on several occasions in this register by Father Eustache. The editor has not been able to determine that it is an abbreviation for any word in the French language -- the language used by Fr. Eustache. However, one common element exists in all cases in which this symbol was used: it appeared in the place of an omitted given name or surname.

742. JEAN LAMBRE
MARIE JEANNE LE VASSEUR
May 19, 1757, after three bans, marriage of Jean Lambre (x), son of Martin Lambre and of Eve Keniguinne*, native of the parish of Allemands /the German Coast/ . . . and . . . Marie Jeanne Le Vasseur, daughter of Jacques Le Vasseur and Marie Francoise Bourdon, born in this parish. Witnesses: Breton (s), /Lamalathie dit/ Jobard (x), /Mader dit/ Jean des Jeans (x).

*Above the name "Keniguinne", between the lines, is written the name "Le Roy".

743. PIERRE VICTOR DU PAIN
JEANNE CATHERINE ALORGE
July 9, 1757, after three bans, marriage of Pierre Victor du Pain (s), officer of the militia, son of Sieur Pierre du Pain and of Marie Therese Theré?, native of Paris, parish of St. Paul . . . and . . . Jeanne Catherine Alorge (x), daughter of Pierre Alorge and of Catherine Melier, a native of this parish. Witnesses: De Blanc (s), Lecourt (s), Pain (s), Borme (s), one illegible signature.

744. MARTIN GOUTIER DE LAND /GOUTIERREZ/
LOUISA /DE ST. DENIS/
January 30, 1758, after publication of one ban and dispensation of other two, marriage of Martin Goutier de Land (x), son of Joseph de Land and of Michele? Adevagar, a native of the port of Saltillis, in Spanish country . . . and . . . Louisa*(x), widow of Duplessis, native of this parish. Witnesses: Trichele (x), Charles (s), Bibo (s) Antoine Floriant (x).

*Entries 514, 519-520, and 522 identify Louisa as Louise Marguerite Juchereau de St. Denis, wife of Pierre Coutoleau Duplessis.

745. NICOLAS LAMB
ELISABETHE RACHAL
February 1, 1758, after three bans, marriage of Nicolas
Lamb (x), son of Antoine Lamb and of Marie Francoise Lomard, native of New Orleans . . . and . . . Elisabethe
Rachal (s), daughter of Pierre Rachal and of Marie Anne
Benoist, born in this parish. Witnesses: Breton (s),
Trichele (x), Dominique /Monteche/ (x), Rambin (s), and
Baptiste /Davion dit/ St. Prix (x).

746. JEAN RIESE
MARIE JEAN CHANGNOT
April 25, 1758, after three bans, marriage of Jean Riese
(s), son of /blank/ and /blank/ . . . and . . . Marie
Jean Changnot (x), daughter of Francois Chagnot and of
/blank/ of this parish. Witnesses: Gabriel Buard (x)
Poisot (s), Breton (s), Despres (s).

747. FRANCOIS LANGLOIS *dit* SANS REGRET
MARIE GREGOIRE DE SANTA CRUX
May 18, 1758, marriage of Francois Langlois *dit* Sans Regret (s), soldier, son of Jean Baptiste Langlois and of
Marie Catherine Moguet, native of Paris, parish of St.
Nicolas . . . and . . . Marie Gregoire de Santa Crux,
daughter of Jean Josephe de Santa Crux and of Ysabelle
Patrodille Castille, a native of Adayse, the Spanish post.
Witnesses: Trichele (x), Dominique /Monteche/ (x) /Lamalathie *dit*/ Jobard (x), and St. Prix?.

748. /BLANK/
MARIE
June 10, 1758, marriage of /blank/ and Marie, slaves of
Monsieur De Blanc, commandant.

749. JEAN BAPTISTE PRUDHOMME
JOSEPHE CHARLOTTE CORANTIN
July 13, 1758, after publication of one ban and dispensation with other two, marriage of Jean Baptiste Prudhomme
(s), born in this parish, son of Jean Prudhomme and of
Catherinne Milicre . . . and . . . Josephe Charlotte
Corantin (x), born in the parish of St. Louis at New
Orleans. Witnesses: De Blanc (s), Le Court (s), and
Pain (s).

750. LOUIS
JEANNE
July 29, 1758, marriage of Louis and Jeanne, slaves of Sr.
Triche, with the permission of their master.

751. JEAN BAPTISTE DU VIVIER
JEANNE DU PAIN
August 8, 1758, marriage of Jean Baptiste du Vivier (x)

son of Michel Rochelos de Vivier and Angelique le Fevre, native of the parish of Cap de la Magdeleine in Canada . . . and . . . Jeanne du Pain (x), daughter of Pierre du Pain and Martine Bonet, born in this parish. Witnesses: Borme (s), Poissot (s), Sr. /Lamalathie dit/ Jobar (x), Gabriel Buar (x).

752. BARTHELEMY RACHAL
MARIE LAMALATY
December 19, 1758, marriage of Barthelemy Rachal (x), son of Pierre Rachal and Marianne Benoit . . . and . . . Marie Lamalaty (x), daughter of Louis Lamalati and of Jeanne Victoire Garcie. Witnesses: "the father" (x), Sr. Dominique Monteche (x), Dupain (s), Jacques Lambre (x).

753. JACQUES LAMBRE
MARIE POISSEAU
February 26, 1759, marriage of Jacques Lambre (x), son of Martin Lambre and Eve Le Roy, native of the parish of Allemans /German Coast/ . . . and . . . Marie Poisseau (x), daughter of Remy Poisseau and Anne Marie Philippe, born in this parish. Witnesses: Borme (s), Poisot (s), Gabriel Buard (x), Dubois (s).

754. ETIENNE
ANGELIQUE
February /day illegible/, 1759, marriage of Etienne and Angelique, slaves of Sr. Remy Poissot.

755. FRANCOIS
MARIE
February /day illegible/, 1759, marriage of Francois and Marie, slaves of Sr. Poissot.

756. PIERRE BRASIER *dit* LA LIBERTÉ
June 8, 1751, burial of Pierre Brasier *dit* la Liberté, soldier, native of Lion in Picardy, thirty years or about.

757. JEAN CAMOIN BOSSŸ
August 16, 1751, burial of Jean Camoin Bossÿ, native of Marceille in Provence, parish of Cathedrale, about the age of 31. Died after receiving last rites.

758. ANONYMOUS
December 12, 1751, burial of an Indian infant, born of an Indian belonging to Mde. de St. Denis.

759. PIERRE FOSSE
June 3, 1752, burial of Pierre Fosse, native of Tours in Lourraine, about 70 years of age. Died after receiving last rites.

760. ST. PRIX INFANT
     June 8, 1752, burial of an infant of St. Prix, aged two
     months.

761. ANONYMOUS
     July 12, 1752, burial of an unnamed Indian woman, property
     of Madame St. Denis, aged about twenty years.

762. PIERRE BARON *dit* LA LIBERTE
     October 19, 1752, burial of Pierre Baron *dit* la Liberte,
     aged about 70, a soldier and native of Bretagne. Died
     after receiving last rites.

763. FRANCOIS CHAUZŸ
     October 30, 1752, burial of Francois Chauzÿ, a *nègre* of
     Mde. de St. Denis, aged about 20. Died with the sacra-
     ments.

764. JEAN BAPTISTE LA FONT
     September 30, 1752, burial of Jean Baptiste la Font, a
     soldier. Found the ninth day after drowning. About 30
     years of age.

765. JEAN PIERRE
     September 30, 1752, burial of Jean Pierre, *négrillon* of
     Mr. de la Ronde, nine days old.

766. JOSEPH VERGER
     April 20, 1753, burial of Joseph Verger, a native of
     Paris, about 55 years of age. Died after last rites.

767. CLEMENT BELLEOEIL *dit* DU BUISSON
     September 12, 1753, burial of Clement Belleoeil *dit* du
     Buisson, soldier, found the third day after drowning.
     Aged about forty.

768. DUVAL *dit* LA COURONNE
     September 14, 1753, burial of Duval *dit* la Couronne, a
     soldier of about 70 years; died after last rites.

769. FRANCOIS MONECUANT *dit* BEAUPRE
     September 27, 1753, burial of Francois Monecuant *dit*
     Beaupre, soldier, native of Dompierre, province of Aunis,
     bishopric of La Rochelle; after making a public renounce-
     ment of the heresy of Lutheranism on August 15, 1748,
     Monecuant "was sunk in the water and was drowned at the
     chute of the Lake a la Vase, the 20th of the same month
     and year as above." Testified to by Fr. Eustache in
     presence of Claude Bertrand *dit* Dauphine, sergeant and
     patron de la voiture, "and of all his detachement who
     have signed with me." [No other signatures appear.]

770. GABRIEL TOTAIN
    October 16, 1753, burial of Gabriel, aged two and a half years, son of Charles Totain, habitant.

771. JEAN LOUIS GAREIN *dit* LA VERDURE
    October 17, 1753, burial of Jean Louis Garein *dit* la Verdure, a native of St. Martin du Laveque, parish of St. Martin, bishopric of Beauvais in Picardie, aged about forty. Died on October 16 after receiving the sacraments.

772. FRANCOISE DUBOIS
    December 4, 1753, burial of Francoise, aged one year and five months, daughter of Jean Baptise Dubois, habitant.

773. JEAN BAPTISTE BREVEL
    January 25, 1754, burial of Jean Baptiste Brevel, a native of Paris, about seventy years.

774. MARTINNE BONNET
    July 31, 1754, burial of Martinne Bonnet, native of Tours in Tourain, about sixty years, found the same day that she was carried away by a whirlpool in the river.

775. JACQUE
    September 4, 1754, burial of Jacque, a Cannecy Indian of about eighteen years. Died after receiving last rites.

776. ANONYMOUS
    October 28, 1754, burial of the corpse of an Indian male, a *sauvege de la doute*, after first being baptized.

777. MARIE ANNE BENOIT
    November 7, 1754, burial of Marie Anne Benoit, a native of Paris, about seventy years of age. Died after last rites.

778. CHARLES TOTAIN
    November 20, 1754, burial of Charles, aged ten and a half, son of Charles Totain, habitant.

779. GENEVIEVE DUBOIS
    December 8, 1754, burial of Genevieve, aged three and a half months, daughter of Jean Baptiste Dubois, habitant.

780. ANTOINE ROY
    February 5, 1755, burial of Antoine Roy, a Spaniard of about 60 years. Died after last rites.

781. LA TETE PLATTE
    February 11, 1755, burial of La Tete Platte [the Flat Head], Indian of the "Nachitoches and old Chetdo village." Aged about 60 years. Baptized before death.

782. JEAN AURE
February 20, 1755, burial of Jean Aure, corporal, native of Auray in Lower Bretagne, about 65 years or about. Received last rites.

783. DACHANECTOC
April 22, 1755, burial of Dachanectoc, a Natchitoches Indian who was baptized before death. Aged about 30 years.

784. ANONYMOUS
May 16, 1755, burial of an infant slave of Don Manuel /̄de Sot_o_/ and Dame Marie des Neiges /̄de St. Deni_s_/.

785. CHRISTOPHE BATON
May 31, 1755, burial of Christophe Baton, soldier and drummer from the parish of St. Michel at Strasbourg. Aged about 35. Received last rites.

786. JEANNE ELISABETH LE DUC
June 28, 1755, burial of Jeanne Elisabeth, daughter of Joseph Le Duc, aged about four years and eight months.

787. MARIE ANNE
August 7, 1755, burial of Marie Anne, daughter of Marie Julien, a slave of Mde. St. Denis, aged about six months.

788. THOMAS *dit* LA CROIX
February 2, 1756, burial of Thomas *dit* La Croix, a native of /̄Illegibl_e_/ in Bretagne, soldier.

789. ANONYMOUS
March 15, 1756, burial of an infant slave, property of Mde. de St. Denis.

790. MARI JOSEPHE DUPRE
April 19, 1756, burial of Mari Josephe, daughter of Jean Baptiste Dupre.

791. MARGUERITE PRUDHOMME
June 16, 1756, burial of Marguerite, little daughter of Pierre Prudhomme and Magdelaine Dorvalle.

792. MARIE JOSEPHE LE DUC
August 19, 1756, burial of Marie Josephe, daughter of Joseph le Duc and Marie Anne Guedon.

793. /̄PIERRE/ RACHAL
April 18, 1756, "I have buried in the cemetery of our parish the named }+{ Rachal *dit* St. Denis, soldier."

NOTE: According to the General Roll of Louisiana Troops, Document D2c, 54:I in the Archives of the Colonies,

Archives Nationales at Paris, Pierre Rachal died at
Natchez on April 19, 1756. Obviously an error has been
made, either in the recording of his burial in these
registers of the church or in the recording of his
death on the general roll. It is also doubtful that he
died at Natchez, on the Mississippi River, and was buried
at Natchitoches, on the Red River. An explantation of
the symbol that prefaces Rachal's name in the burial
entry can be found in Entry 741.

794. MANON BLETTE /MARIE FRANCOISE VILLE BLETTE/
July 27, 1756, burial of Manon Blette, native of the parish of St. Paul in Paris. Died after receiving last rites.

795. FRANCOISE GILLOT*
October 19, 1756, burial of Francoise Gillot, born at Haldegras.

*Marginal note gives surname as Triche.

796. GASPARE BARBIER
October 28, 1756, burial of Gaspare Barbier, who died after receiving the last rites.

797. CLAUDE BERTRAND *dit* DAUFINE
October 28, 1756, burial of Claude Bertrand *dit* Daufine, a native of Grenoble, parish of St. Laurent.

798. JEAN MADER *dit* JEAN DES JEANS, *fils*
/No month and day/, 1756, burial of Jean Mader *dit* Jean des Jeans, *fils*.

799. JULIEN RONDIN
December 23, 1756, burial of Julien Rondin, officer, and senior warden of the church, died after displaying all the marks of a perfect Christian.

800. JEAN BAPTISTE PRUDHOMME
January 9, 1757, burial of Jean Baptiste, son of Jean Baptiste Prudhomme and Marie Francoise Chever.

801. MARIE BARBIER*
January 21, 1757, burial of Marie Barbier*, wife of Jean Baptiste Prudhomme, who died after receiving the last rites.

*This name should be Marie Francoise Chever, wife of Jean Baptiste Prudhomme and daughter of Therese Barbier.

802. JACQUES MAURICE DE BLANC
January 13, 1757, burial of Jacques Maurice, son of Commandant Cesaire de Blanc and Madame Marie des Douleurs.

803. THERESE BARBIER
   December 20, 1756, burial of Therese Barbier, wife of Dufresne, after receiving last rites.

804. JEAN FRANCOIS TRISTANT
   March 6, 1757, burial of Jean Francois, son of Pierre Tristant and Margueritte Victoire Prudhomme.

805. LA SERT /LA CERDA/ INFANT
   August 24, 1757, burial of a small daughter of Michel la Sert /Cerda/, Spaniard.

806. ANONYMOUS
   September 10, 1757, burial of a Negro slave, property of /Toutain dit/ Meunier.

807. ANONYMOUS
   September 18, 1757, burial of a Negro slave, property of Chagnot.

808. PIERRE ALORGE *dit* DIZANCOUR
   November 20, 1757, burial of Pierre Alorge *dit* Dizancour, born at Andelis in Normandy. Died after receiving last rites. Witnesses: Borme (s) and Dupain (s).

809. ANONYMOUS
   September 25, 1757, burial of a *métise* slave of Sieur Dominique /Monteche/.

810. LE ROY INFANT /LECOURT/*
   September 20, 1757, burial of a son of Jeanne Le Roy.

   *See Entries 652 and 984.

811. MATHIEU MONETTE
   January 1, 1758, burial of Mathieu Monette, born in the parish of St. Benoit.

812. /ILLEGIBLE/
   January 10, 1758, burial of a soldier.

813. GABRIEL
   March 4, 1758, burial of Gabriel /no last name, no indication of race or status/.

   NOTE: Apparently this individual was white, since his name is noted in the margin; marginal notations were made only on whites in this register. There also appears in the margin the symbol ////. This marginal symbol appears only one other time in the registers -- opposite the burial entry for Madame de St. Denis. See Entry 817.

814. MAGDELEINE LE VASSEUR
March 5, 1758, burial of Magdeleine le Vasseur.

815. MEUNIER
March 18, 1758, burial of Meunier /Charles Toutain *dit* Meunier, Sr.?/.

816. /ANGELIQUE/*
March 19, 1758, burial "of the corpse of an Indian, the grandmother of Madame St. Prix."

*Entry 346 identifies Madame St. Prix as Marie Triche, daughter of a German, Henry Trichel, and his wife Marie Dumont. Civil records of the parish identify Marie Dumont as a native of Natchitoches, and a sister of Angelique Dumont (Mme. Joseph Verger). Entry 736 identifies the mother of Angelique Dumont as Angelique, an Indian native of Natchitoches. Apparently it was Angelique whose burial entry is recorded above, since Madame St. Prix's paternal grandmother was not Indian.

817. MADAME DE ST. DENIS
March 16, 1758, burial of Madame de St. Denis.

NOTE: a marginal notation bears the symbol ⨯⨯⨯⨯⨯. See note for Entry 813.

818. ANONYMOUS
April 5?, 1758, burial of a Negro slave of Cesar Borme.

819. MME. MARIN
April 17, 1758, burial of the wife of Marin, a Spaniard.

820. FRANCOIS
FRANCOISE
April 19, 1758, burial of Francois and Francoise, a Negro slave couple of Mde. St. Denis.

NOTE: This was Francois and Marie Francoise, who were married in 1736 (see Entry 11). This slave couple were the parents of Natchitoches' legendary Marie Therese *dite* Coincoin whose baptism is recorded in Entry 225.

821. /JEAN MADER *dit*/ JEAN DES JEANS
April 21, 1758, burial of Jean des Jeans, elder warden of the church.

822. LA FLEUR
April 25, 1758, burial of la Fleur, soldier.

823. JACOB
May 1, 1758, burial of Jacob, *nègre* slave of Don Manuel /de Soto/.

824. ANONYMOUS
May 4, 1758, burial of an infant of Francoise.

825. ANONYMOUS
May 7, 1758, burial of a Negro slave of Sieur /Lamalathie dit/ Jobard.

826. GUERIN?
May 12, 1758, burial of <u>Guerin?</u>, *nègre* slave of Sr. St. Denis, *le chevalier*.

827. ANONYMOUS
May 13, 1758, burial of an infant slave of Sr. St. Denis.

828. JEAN RICHE
May 17, 1758, burial of Jean Riche.

829. _____ GAS
June 28, 1759, illegible burial entry.

830. MARIE
August 1, 1758, burial of Marie, *négresse* slave of Etienne Barbier.

831. DUPARD
September 1, 1758, burial of Dupard, a soldier who had converted to Catholicism and died as a true Catholic.

832. CATON
September 13, 1758, burial of Caton, a free *nègre*, formerly the property of St. Denis.

833. MARIE RAMBIN
September 16, 1758, burial.

834. LOUISON
November 10, 1758, burial of Louison, *négresse* of Chagnot.

835. /ILLEGIBLE/
November 27, 1758, burial.

836. JEAN BAPTISTE PRUDHOMME
April 11, 1765, baptism of Jean Baptiste, born April 10, legitimate son of Pierre Bastien Prudhomme and Jeanne Chever. Godparents: Jean Bte. Turpin (s) and Marie Jeanne Levasseur (x).

837. FRANCOIS DAVION
April 11, 1765, baptism of Francois, born April 10, legitimate son of Jean Baptiste Davion and Marie Trichel.

Godparents: Francois Grappe (x) and Marie Louise Davion (x).

838. VICTOIRE
May 21, 1765, baptism of Victoire, adult slave of Sieur Garonne, aged twenty years. /no race given/. Godparents: Louis Gabriel Buart (x) and Marie Jeanne Lamatti (x).

839. GILBERT CLOSOT
May /blank/, 1765, baptism of Gilbert, born November 14, 1764, legitimate son of Francois Closot and Marianne Reaubliu. Godparents: Gilbert Derancourt de St. Amand, (s), officer, and Pelagie Pain (s).

840. CATHERINE LATIE
June 17, 1765, baptism of Catherine, born June 17, legitimate daughter of Joseph Latie, corporal, and of Anne Verger. Godparents: Pierre LaCour (s), soldier, and Marie Catherine Baillot *dit* Poisot (x).

841. MARIE MAGDELEINE
July 21, 1765, baptism of Marie Magdeleine, born 20th of same month of Marie Louise, slave of Mr. Pain, *subdélégué*. Godparents: Louis Pain (s) and Pelagie Pain (s).

842. JEAN LOUIS VASCOCU
July 25, 1765, baptism of Jean Louis, born yesterday, legitimate son of Antoine Jean Vastcocu and Marie Barbe Toupse. Godparents: Jean Louis Toupse, uncle of the infant (x), and Marie _____ Cimolitte (x).

843. MARIE LOUISE RACHAL
July 30, 1765, baptism of Marie Louise, born June 9, legitimate daughter of Louis Rachal and of Marie Louise Le Roy. Godparents: Alexis Grappe (s) and Marie Louise Guedon (x).

844. MARIE FRANCOISE DE COSTE
August 16, 1765, baptism of Marie Francoise, born August 14, legitimate daughter of Francois de Coste, Spainard, and Marie de l'Assomption /no last name/. Godparents: Le Mée (s) and Marie Francoise Clermont (s).

845. LOUIS ANTOINE de la PERRIERE
October 2, 1765, baptism of Louis Antoine, born September 29, 1765, son of Louise /Bertrand *dite*/ Dauphine and natural son of Messire Louis George Monjonan de la Perriero, esquire and chevalier of St. Louis, captain and commandant of the post of Natchitoches. Godparents: Antoine Fazinde (s), Clemence Borme (s); s/ La Perriere.

846. REMY PEREAU*
September 20, 1765, baptism of Remy, born September 12, legitimate son of Francois Barthe Pereau* and Marie Catherine Dupres. Godparents: Remy Poisot and Barbe Elisabeth Dupre.

*The name "Pereau" has been written over with the name "Vildec" in both the marginal notation and in the text of the entry.

847. CLEMENCE RONDIN
October 27, 1765, baptism of Clemence, born October 25, legitimate daughter of Louis Rondin and Marie Berard. Godparents: Gaspar Filhiol, trader (x), and Clemence Bormé (s).

NOTE: Marginal notation indicates that the infant died.

848. MARIE ELISABETH ROSALIE PAIN
November 3, 1765, baptism of Marie Elisabeth Rosalie, born October 31, legitimate daughter of Daniel Pain, *garde magazin et subdélégué*, and Marie Rougeot. Godparents: Gilbert Derancourt de St. Amand (s), officer, and Elisabeth Borme (s). Witness: la Perier (s).

849. MARIE JEANNE CRETE
November ?, 1765, baptism of Marie Jeanne, born the day before, legitimate daughter of Pierre Crete and Marie Louise Verge. Godparents: Etienne Verge (x) and Marie Catherine Verge *dit* Malbert (x).

850. JEAN BAPTISTE
November 23, 1765, baptism of Jean Baptiste, slave of Jean Baptiste Dupres. Godparents: Athanase /Poissot *dit*/ Bourgnignon (x) and Elisabeth Verge (s).

851. LOUIS NICOLAS
December 8, 1765, baptism of Louis Nicolas, born December 1 of Marianne, a slave of Mr. Pain, and of a father unknown. Godparents: Louis Andre Borme (s) and Pelagie Pain (o).

852. CATHERINE MARIE JOSEPH
December 11, 1765, baptism of Catherine Marie Joseph, slave of Emmanuell Sotho. Father unknown. Godparents: Louis Andre Borme (s) and Clemence Borme (s).

853. MARIE JOSEPHE DUPRE
December 21, 1765, baptism of Marie Josephe, legitimate child of Joseph Dupre and Marie Derbanne, born on that same day. Godparents: Jean Baptiste Dubois (s) and Marie Joseph Clermon.

MARGINAL NOTE: The infant died.

854. ANTOINE LEMOIN
 December 29, 1765, baptism of Antoine, born December 14, legitimate son of Charles Lemoine and Elisabeth Dupre. Godparents: J. B. Gonite and Marie Anne Poisot (x).

855. THERESE RACHAL
 January 11, 1766, baptism of Therese, legitimate daughter of Jacques Rachal and Ursule Castelle, born January 10. Godparents: Pierre Darbanne (x) and Therese Lamaltie (x).

 MARGINAL NOTE: The infant died.

856. MARIE HELEINE BAILLIO
 January 20 (or 26?), 1766, baptism of Marie Heleine, born January 15, legitimate daughter of Pierre Baillot and Catherine Poissot. Godparents: Remy Poisot (x) and Marie Anne Poissot (x).

857. GENEVIEVE SOREL
 February 6, 1766, baptism of Genevieve, born February 4, legitimate daughter of Pierre Sorelle and Marie Bosselier. Godparents: Jean Laberry (s) and Marie Joseph Henry (x). Witness: Burelle (s).

858. MICHEL RICHER /RIS or JEAN-RIS/
 February 6, 1766, baptism of Michel, born February 4, legitimate son of Jean Richer and Marie Jeanne Chagniot. Godparents: Michel Bruno and Louise Chagniot.

859. FRANCOISE GRILLET
 February 13, 1766, baptism of Francoise, born February 12, legitimate daughter of Marin Grillet and Marie Louise Brevel. Godparents: Jean Gabriel Lagé *dit* La Rose and Francoise Buart.

860. SEVERINE ANTOINE GERTRUDE DE SOTO
 /no date/, 1766, baptism of Severine Antoine Gertrude, born 11th of same month, legitimate son of Dom Manuel de Soto, Spaniard, absent from this place, and Marie de Neiges de St. Denis. Godparents: Antoine Solis, secretary of Mr. /Illegible/ at Adailles, and Gertrude /Illegible/.

861. ANNE MARIE DUPRE
 March 11, 1766, baptism of Anne Marie, born February 23, legitimate daughter of Robert Dupre and Marie Jeanne Cavé. Godparents: Remy Poisot (s) and Anne Marie Poisot, grandmother of the infant (x).

862. JEAN JOSEPH
 March 29, 1766, baptism of Jean Joseph, born February 20,

child of Marie Therese, slave of Dom Manuel /̄de Soto/ and of a father unknown. Godparents: Jean Baptiste, slave of St. Denis, and Marie Louise, slave of Dom Manuel.

863. LOUIS JACQUES RENÉ
March 29, 1766, baptism of Louis Jacques René, twenty-year-old slave of Mr. Fazende. Godparents: Jacques Bunel, soldier (s) and Louise /̄Bertrand dite/ Dauphine.

864. ANDRE
March 29, 1766, baptism of Andre, slave of Mr. Antoine Fazende. Godparents: Louis, slave of Mr. Dreux, *fils*, and Marianne, slave of Mr. Borme.

865. NICOLAS
March 29, 1766, baptism of Nicolas, slave of Mr. Pain, *subdélégué*. Godparents. Jean Piserot (s) and Elisabeth Borme (s).

866. MARIANNE PELAGIE
March 29, 1766, baptism of Marianne Pelagie, slave of Mr. Bonapont. An Indian. Godparents: Andre Borme (s) and Pelagie Pain.(s).

867. AUGUSTIN
April 1, 1766, baptism of Augustin, slave of Mr. Fazende. Godparents: Antoine Fazende, officer, and Pelagie Pain.

868. THERESE
April 1, 1766, baptism of Therese, slave of Baptiste Prudhomme, *chirugien*. Godparents: Antoine _____ /̄Illegible/ and Therese Prudhomme.

869. CLEMENCE
April 1, 1766, baptism of Clemence, slave of Baptiste Prudhomme. Godparents: Daniel Pain and Clemence Borme.

870. THERESE
April 6, 1766, baptism of Therese, slave of Louis Rachal. Godparents: Guillaume Chevere and Therese Prudhomme.

871. MARIE ANNE
April 6, 1766, baptism of Marie Anne, slave of Louis Rachal. Godparents: Louis Rachal and Marianne Poisot.

872. JACQUES CHARLES NEGLE
April 6, 1766, baptism of Jacques Charles, born April 1, legitimate son of Jacques Negle of this post and Louise Larenaudiere. Godparents: Charles la Renaudiere and Marie Anne la Riviere, the grandparents.

873. MICHEL ANTOINE RAMBIN
April 14, 1766, baptism of Michel Antoine, born April 5, legitimate son of André Rambin (s), sergeant and habitant, and Marie Francoise Clermont. Godparents: Antoine Lemay (s/ Lémé), elder officer, and Francoise Buart (x).

874. MARIE HELEINE BREVELE
May 2, 1766, baptism of Marie Heleine, born May 1, legitimate daughter of Jean Baptiste Brevelle, habitant, and Marie Francoise Poisot. Godparents: Athanase Poisot (x), blood cousin of the infant, and Marie Darbane (x).

875. MARIE JEANNE MALBERT
June 8, 1766, baptism of Marie Jeanne, born June 6, legitimate daughter of Jean Baptiste Malbert and Jeanne Verge. Godparents: Jean Louis Cesaire Borme (s), captain, and Marie Jeanne Rougeot (s/ Jeanne Pain Rouisot).

876. THERESE DUPRE
June 25, 1766, baptism of Therese, born June 24, legitimate daughter of Baptiste Dupre, habitant, and Elisabeth /Verger/. Godparents: Ignace Anty (x), habitant, and Therese Lamalathy (x).

877. FRANCOIS ANTOINE GREGOIRE LANGLOIS
July 6, 1766, baptism of Francois Antoine Gregoire, born June 24, 1766, legitimate son of Francois Langlois, soldier of the company of Mr. Perriére, and Marie Gregoire de Ste. Croix. Godparents: Francois Antoine Solis (s), secretary of the governor of Adailles, and Marie des neiges de St. Denis (s).

878. MARIE JULIE
July 20, 1766, baptism of Marie Julie, born July 17, a slave of Sieur Pain, *garde magazin*. Godparents: Etienne Pavie, merchant (s) and Marie Pelagie Pain (s).

879. PIERRE DERBANNE
August ?, 1766, baptism of Pierre, born 4th of same month, legitimate son of Pierre Derbanne and Marie Louise Le Clerc. Godparents: Louis Jucheraud de St. Denis (s) elder lieutenant, and Louise Marguerite Derbanne (s/ Louise de St. Denis).

880. MARIE JEAN JACQUES DEMEZIERES
August 9, 1766, baptism of Marie Jean Jacques, born that same day, legitimate son of Messire Athanase de Mezieres (s) and Pelagie Fazende. Godparents: Jacque Fazende and Louise Guedon?.

881. MARIE PELAGIE
PIERRE
August 9, 1766, slaves of Sr. Demezieres. Remainder is

not legible.

882. HELEINE
August 21, 1766, baptism of Heleine, born August 1, slave of Mr. Pain, and daughter of Victoire and a father unknown. Godparents: Louis and Marie Louise, slaves of Mr. Pain.

883. JEAN BAPTISTE RACHAL
August 28, 1766, baptism of Jean Baptiste, born August 27, legitimate son of Barthelemy Rachal and Marie Francoise Lamalathy. Godparents. Jean Lambre and Marie Anne Poissot.

884. ANTOINE PHILIPPE DUBOIS
September 8, 1766, baptism of Antoine Philippe, born August 20, legitimate son of Jean Baptiste Dubois (s), habitant and of Marie Joseph Clermont. Godparents illegible.

885. JEAN FRANCOIS
September (or October?), 1766, baptism of Jean Francois, born the first of this month, son of Jeanne, a slave of Sieur de Mezieres, and of a father unknown. Godparents: Francois Grappe and Marie Magdeleine Grappe.

886. AGNES MORIN
November 9, 1766, baptism of Agnes, born October 25, legitimate daughter of Baptiste Morin and Catherine Levasseur. Godparents: Dominique Monteche and Marie Bourdon.

887. MARIE JOSEPH GONIT
November ?, 1766, baptism of Marie Joseph, born November 10, legitimate child of Jean Baptiste Gonit (s) and /Manuelle Rich_e_7. Godparents: Jean Baptiste DuBois (s) and Marie Joseph Clermont (s).

888. FRANCOIS AUGUSTIN BUARD
December 6, 1766, baptism of Francois Augustin, born October 23, 1766, legitimate son of Gabriel Buard and Marie Rousseau. Godparents: Louis Buard (x) and Marie Francoise Buard (x).

889. ANTOINE
December 27, 1766, baptism of Antoine, born that same month of a slave of Mr. Trichle and of a father unknown. Godparents not given.

890. MARIE FRANCOISE LABERRY
January 3, 1767, baptism of Marie Francoise, born January 1, 1767, legitimate daughter of Jean Bte. Laberry, habitant, and Jeanne Guedon. Godparents: Louis Toutin (x) and Marguerite Toutin (x).

891. LOUIS RONDIN
January 8, 1767, baptism of Louis, born that same day, legitimate son of Louis Rondin, habitant, and Marie Berard. Godparents: /illegible/ (x) and Marie _____ (x).

892. MARIE FRANCOISE CASTILLE
January 30, 1767, baptism of Marie Francoise Castille, born the 18th of that same month, of Marie Francoise Castille and a father unknown. Godparents: Pierre Poissot and Elisabeth Dupres.

893. MARIE LOUISE BEAUDIN
January 30, 1767, baptism of Marie Louise, born January 20, legitimate daughter of Laurent Beaudin and Michel St. Croix, habitants. Godparents: Etienne Bossan? (s), trader, and Marie Louise Grappe (s). Witness: Dubois (s).

894. MARIE THERESE TRISTANT
February ?, 1767, baptism of Marie Therese, born January 28, legitimate daughter of Pierre Tristant and Marguerite Prudhomme. Godparents: Francois /illegible/ (x) and Marie Therese /illegible/. MARGINAL NOTE: infant died.

895. AMBROISE
/Month and day illegible/, 1767, baptism of Ambrose, a slave of Mr. Grappe. Remainder illegible.

896. MARIE LOUISE
March 8, 1767, baptism of Marie Louise, born March 5, daughter of Elizabeth, slave of Mr. Poisot. /Godparents illegible./

897. DOMINIQUE PRUDHOMME
March 22, 1767, baptism of Dominique, born February 5, legitimate son of Jean Baptiste Prudhomme and Marie Francoise Corantine. Godparents: Dominique Monteche (x) and Marie Bourdon (x).

898. CATHERINE LAMBRE
March 27, 1767, baptism of Catherine, born February 20, legitimate daughter of Jean Lambre, merchant at this post, and of Marie Jeanne Levasseur. Godparents: /illegible/ and Catherine Levasseur.

899. MARIE JOSEPH
April 13, 1767, baptism of Marie Joseph, born April 4, daughter of Marie, Indian slave of Mr. Pain. Godparents: Louis Pain (s) and Marie /illegible/.

900. ROSE
/Illegible/ 8, 1767, baptism of Rose, born 2nd of same month of the legitimate marriage of Jean Louis and Marie Jeanne, slaves of Dominique Monteche. Godparents: Francois Grappe (x) and Marie Louise Grappe (x).

901. NOTE: At this point there appears one and a half pages of very abbreviated and almost totally illegible slave entries. Recognizable names of whites who were either the owners or served as godparents include:

Pierre Derbanne	Joseph Dupre	Marie Rose Lambre
Remy Poissot	Sieur Anty	Jacques Buard
Baptiste Dupre	Pierre Poissot	Alexis Grappe
Pierre Beson	Sieur Piserot	Louise Grappe
Jacques Le Vasseur		

902. MARIE HELEINE (CELEINE) BREVEL
/Month and day illegible/, 1767, baptism of Marie Heleine* Brevel, born on the 9th of same month, daughter of Jean Baptiste Brevel and Marie Francoise Poisot. Godparents: Pierre Gagney (x) and Marie Louise /illegible/ (x).

*The infant's name appears as "Celeine" in the text and as "Heleine" in the marginal notation.

903. MARIE ROSE DUPRE
June 18, 1767, baptism of Marie Rose, born June 7, legitimate daughter of Joseph Dupre and Marie l'Incarnation Derbanne. Godparents: Etienne Verge (x) and Marie Rose Lambre (x).

904. MARIE LOUISE
July 7, 1767, baptism of Marie Louise, born April 15, daughter of N_____tte?, Indian of Guillaume Lestache, a native of Dole? in Bourdeaux. Godparents: Alexis Grappe and Louise Guedon.

905. JOSEPH JACQUES LATTIE
July 16, 1767, baptism of Joseph Jacques, born July 15, legitimate son of Joseph Lattie, corporal, and Anne Verge. Godparents: Jacques Hebert (s), sergeant, and Marie Verge (x).

906. GENEVIEVE
August 5, 1767, baptism of Genevieve, born August 4, daughter of Marie J_____, slave of La Berry, and a father unknown. Godparents: Etienne and Justine, slaves of Remy Poissot.

907. MARIE FROSINE PELAGIE LE SAUSSAYE?
August 6, 1767, baptism of Marie Frosine Pelagie, born

September 15, 1766, legitimate daughter of Jacques Le Saussaye? and Marie Magdeleine Terri___?. Godparents: Jacques Fazende and /illegible/.

908. PIERRE
/Month and day illegible/, 1767, baptism of Pierre, a *mulâtre*, born June 1 of Jeanne, a slave of Jean Piserot. Godparents: Francois Levasseur and Jeanne Maderne.

909. ETIENNE
August 25, 1767, baptism of Etienne, born the 18th of /illegible/ of that same year, son of Agathe, slave of Mr. Demezieres, and of a father unknown. Godparents: Francois X. _____ /illegible/ and Marie /illegible/.

910. GUILLAUME
August 25, 1767, baptism of Guillaume, born May 25 of the same year, of Blette, a slave of Mr. Demezieres, and of a father unknown. Godparents: Julien Beson and Magdeleine Grappe.

911. MARIE JEANNE SOREL
September 9, 1767, baptism of Marie Jeanne, born September 8, legitimate daughter of Joseph Sorel, blacksmith, and Marie Rose Boisselier. Godparents: Jean /illegible/ and Jeanne Levasseur.

912. JEAN BAPTISTE DAVION
September ?, 1767, baptism of Jean Baptiste, born the 8th of the month, legitimate son of Jean Baptiste Davion and Marie Hiacinthe Trichle. Godparents: /illegible/.

913. PIERRE ETIENNE GAGNAY
October 19, 1767, baptism of Pierre Etienne, born October 7, legitimate son of Etienne Gagnay, miller, and Louise /Bertrand *dite*/ Dauphine. Godparents: Pierre Alorge and Pelagie Pain (s).

914. LOUIS FRANCOIS VASCOCU
October 19, 1767, baptism of Louis Francois, legitimate son of Antoine Vascocu and Marie Barbe Toups. Godparents: Andre Louis Bormé (s) and Pelagie Pain (s).

915. MARIE
October 25, 1767, baptism of Marie, a slave, born October 18. Owner and parents illegible.

916. MARIE FRANCOISE
November 1, 1767, baptism of Marie Francoise, born October 4, daughter of Marie Joseph, slave of Mr. Grappe. Godparents: Julien Besson and Marie Anne Grappe.

917. LOUIS PIERRE
    November 26, 1767, baptism of Louis Pierre, born /date
    illegibl_e_/, a slave of Francois Closot.

918. MARIE THERESE VALENTINE
    December 6, 1767, baptism of Marie Therese, born December
    4, daughter of Francois Valentine and Marie Louise Toutin.
    Godparents: Jean Baptiste La Berry (s) and Marguerite
    Guedon.

919. THEODORE ANTOINE
    January 3, 1768, baptism of Theodore Antoine, born January 1, son of Marguerite, a slave of Emanuel Soto. Godparents illegible.

920. LOUISE
    January 8, 1768, baptism of Louise, born December 20, 1767,
    of Marie Louise, a slave of Gabriel Buard. Godparents:
    Louis Gabriel Buard and Marie Louise Buard.

921. MARIE SUSANNE
    NICOLAS AUGUSTIN   /METOYE_R_/
    February 1, 1768, baptism of twins, born January 22, children of Therese, a slave of Sieur Sotho. Godparents:
    Nicolas Maraffret Laisard (s), godfather of both infants;
    Marie Louise Buard, godmother of Marie Susanne; Marie
    Francoise Buard, godmother of Nicolas Augustin.

922. MAGDELEINE
    February 14, 1768, baptism of Magdeleine, born January 24,
    daughter of Marie Therese, a slave of Mr. De Mezieres, and
    of a father unknown. Godparents: Mr. De Mezieres and
    Magdeleine Grappe.

923. JEAN
    March 2, 1768, baptism of Jean, born February 23, a slave
    of Mr. Pain. Mother's name illegible. Godfather:
    /Illegibl_e_/ Lémee (s), and Pelagie Pain (s).

924. FRANCOISE GENEVIEVE
    March 13, 1768, baptism of Francoise Genevieve, born March
    4, daughter of Marie Jeanne, a slave of Mr. Trichle, and
    of a father unknown. Godparents: Guillaume Chever and
    Marie Louise Grappe (s).

925. JEAN LOUIS
    March 23, 1768, baptism of Jean Louis, born March 15, son
    of Francoise, slave of Dominique Monteche, and of a father
    unknown. Godparents: <u>Baptiste?</u> Grappe and Marie Louise
    /Illegibl_e_/.

926. JEAN PIERRE GONIN
March 2_?, 1768, baptism of Jean Pierre, born yesterday of the legitimate marriage of Pierre Gonin, _____ /illegible/, and of Marie Louise _____ /illegible/. Godparents: Jean Baptiste? Gonin (s/ Gonit) and Marie Riche.

927. MARIE LOUISE LEVASSEUR
April 10, 1768, baptism of Marie Louise, born January 3, 1768, legitimate daughter of Francois Vasseure, habitant, and Marie Jeanne Mader. Godparents: "the grandfather" and Marie Bourdon.

928. JACQUES REMY RACHAL
April _?, 1768, baptism of Jacques Remy, born February 1, 1768, legitimate son of Jacques Rachal and Ursul Castel. Godparents: Remy Poisot (s) and Marie Francoise Bourdon.

929. THERESE GRILLET
April 23, 1768, baptism of Therese, born April 3, legitimate daughter of Marin Grillet and Marie Louise Brevel. Godparents: Pierre Poisot? and Therese Barbe? Grillet?.

930. JEAN BAPTISTE LEMOINE
May 22, 1768, baptism of Jean Baptiste, born May 19, legitimate son of Charles LeMoine and Elisabeth Dupré. Godparents: Jean Baptiste Dupré and Marie Derbanne, uncle and aunt of the infant.

931. ANTOINE POIRIER
June 18, 1768, baptism of Antoine, born June? 6?, 1767, son of Vincent Poirier, habitant of Rapides, and of Jeanne Richy. Godparents: Antoine Charbonnet (s) and Marie Genevieve Fontenele (s).

932. THERESE TOINETTE BAILOT
June 19, 1768, baptism of Therese Toinette, born May 8, daughter of Pierre Bailot and Catherine Poisot. Godparents: Athanase Poisot and /illegible/.

933. BARTHELEMY RACHAL
July 15, 1768, baptism of Barthelemy, born July 14, legitimate son of Barthelemy Rachal and Marie Francoise Lamalathi. Godparents: Jacob Lambre and Marie Jeanne Levasseur.

934. ANGELIQUE
July 18, 1768, baptism of Angelique, born July 4, 1768, daughter of Louise, slave of Remy Poissot. Godparents: /illegible/ and Angelique, slave of Remy Poissot.

935. CHARLES
August 7, 1768, baptism of Charles, born July 20, son of Therese, slave of Prudhomme, *chirugien*, and of a father unknown. Godparents: Joseph, slave of Mr. Menard, and Elisabeth, slave of Mr. Lamalathe.

936. MAGDELEINE BARTHE PEREAU
August 7, 1768, baptism of Magdeleine Barthe Pereau, born April 29, legitimate but posthumous daughter of Francois Barthe *dit* Pereau and of Catherine Dupre. Godparents: Athanase Poissot and Magdeleine Grappe.

937. MARIE NICOLAS ZOZIME DEMEZIERES
August 15, 1768, baptism of Marie Nicolas Zozime, born February 28, the legitimate son of Athanase Demezieres and of Marie Pelagie Fazende. Godparents: Francois Doucet (s) and Marie Francoise Clermont (s).

938. GENEVIEVE
August 15, 1768, baptism of Genevieve, born in June, the daughter of Therese, a slave of Mr. Demezieres, and of a father unknown. Godparents: Gabriel and Genevieve.

939. MARIE LOUISE
August 15, 1768, baptism of Marie Louise, born in July, daughter of Francoise, slave of Mr. Demezieres, and of a father unknown. Godparents: Marie Cesar Demezieres (s) and Marie Joseph Demezieres (s).

940. PIERRE GAGNE
October 3, 1768, baptism of Pierre, born October 1, legitimate son of Pierre Gagné and Marie Louise Davion. Godparents: Jean Baptiste Davion, grandfather, and Marie Verge.

941. MARIE JEANNE MORIN
November 1, 1768, baptism of Marie Jeanne, born October 10, legitimate daughter of Jean Baptiste Morin and Catherine LeVasseur. Godparents: Jean Baptiste Lambre and Marie Jeanne /no last name/, "cousin and blood-cousin" of the infant.

942. MARIE GENEVIEVE GONIN
November 3, 1768, baptism of Marie Genevieve, born October 23, legitimate daughter of Jean Baptiste Gonin and Emmanuel Riché. Godparents: Antoine Riché (x) and Genevieve Dubos (x).

943. MARIE GENEVIEVE CHARBONNET
December 25, 1768, baptism of Marie Genevieve, born November 28, legitimate daughter of Antoine Charbonnet (s) and

Antoinette Henoul de Livaudais. Godparents: Francois Coulon de Villiers (s), chevalier and commandant of this post, acting for Mr. Jacques Henoul de Livaudais, and Marie Genevieve Henoul de Livaudais de Villiers (s), acting for Madame Marie Genevieve Babin de Livaudais.

944. JEAN PIERRE DERBANNE
December 25, 1768, baptism of Jean Pierre, born December 10, legitimate son of Pierre Derbanne and Marie Louise Le Clerc. Godparents: Baptiste Trichle (s/ Jean Baptiste Trichele) and Marie Louise Grappe (s).

945. JEAN PIERRE PISEROT
December 26, 1768, baptism of Jean Pierre, born November 18, legitimate son of Jean Piserot, merchant, and Cecile Levasseur. Godparents: Jean Lambre (x) and Marie Jeanne Madere (x).

946. FELICITE
January 1, 1769, baptism of Felicite, born December 15, 1768, daughter of Marie Louise, slave of Mr. Trichle, and a father unknown. Godparents: Louis /Lamalathie *dit*/ Jobar (s) and Felicite Dupain (x).

947. MARIE MAGDELEINE
January 15, 1769, baptism of Marie Magdeleine, born January 14, daughter of Victoire Marguerite, slave of Mr. Le Comte, and of a father unknown. Godparents: Gaspar Fiol (x) and Marie Madeleine Grappe (x).

948. MARIE RACHAL
January 22, 1769, baptism of Marie, born November 24, 1768, legitimate daughter of Louis Rachal and Marie Louise Le Roy. Godparents: Jean Baptiste Buard (x) and Marie Le Roy (x).

949. ANNE PRUDHOMME
January 29, 1769, baptism of Anne, born December 17, 1768, daughter of Jean Baptiste Prudhomme, *chirugien du roy*, and Marie Josephe Corentin. Godparents: Jacques Bunel, sexton (s) and Jeanne Chever (x).

950. ANGELIQUE
January 29, 1769, baptism of Angelique, born January 8, daughter of Susanne, a slave of Remy Poisot, and a father unknown. Godparents: Etienne, *mulâtre*, and Angelique, slaves of Remy Poissot.

951. ANDRE
February 2, 1769, baptism of Andre, born January 28, 1769, son of Francoise, slave of Jean Lambre, and of a father unknown. Godparents: Francois Munier /Toutin/ (x) and Marie Rose Lambre (x).

952. BAPTISTE
February 2, 1769, baptism of Baptiste, born January 29, son of Jeanne, slave of Mr. Piserot, and a father unknown. Godparents: Jean Baptiste Lambre (x) and Marie Jeanne Piserot (x).

953. JACQUES
February 2, 1769, baptism of Jacques, born in November, 1768, son of Marie Jeanne, slave of Mr. Athanase de Mezieres, and a father unknown. Godparents: Jacques Fontenelle (s) and Francoise Le Doux (s).

954. ANTOINE MARTIN
February 27, 1769, baptism of Antoine Martin, born November 11, 1768, son of Marie Jeanne, slave of Baptiste Dupre, and a father unknown. Godparents: Antoine Baptiste Dupre and Suzaine, slave of Remy Poissot.

955. GASPARD BEAUDAIN
February 27, 1769, baptism of Gaspard, born the day before, legitimate son of Laurent Beaudain and Michel de Saint Croix. Godparents: Gaspar Fiol and Marie Louise Chagnot.

956. MARIE GENEVIEVE ROSALIE
March 5, 1769, baptism of Marie Genevieve, born February 20, daughter of Marie Leonore and of a father unknown, a slave of Jacob Lambre. Godparents: Louis Andre Borme (s) and Marie Genevieve Fontenette (s).

957. LOUIS DAVID
March 12, 1769, baptism of Louis, born January 2, legitimate son of Maturin David and Marie Jeanne Lamalathi. Godparents: Louis Lamalathi (s), uncle, and Marie Francoise Bourdon (x).

958. THERESE
March 26, 1769, baptism of Therese, born February 1769, daughter of Susanne, slave of Remy Poisot, and a father unknown. Godparents: Jacques Fontenette (s) and Therese Prudhomme.

959. JACQUES LAMBRE
March 28, 1769, baptism of Jacques, born February 2, legitimate son of Jacob Lambre and Marie Anne Poissot. Godparents: Dominique Monteche (x) and Marie Bourdon (x).

960. FRANCOIS
March 28, 1769, baptism of Francois, son of Marie Jeanne, slave of Mr. Trichle, and of a father unknown. Godparents: Louis Lamalathi (s) and Marie Manuel Soto (x).

961. JEAN BAPTISTE MALBERT
March 28, 1769, baptism of Jean Baptiste, born March 26, legitimate son of Jean Baptiste Malbert and Jeanne Verger. Godparents: Joseph Vergé (x) and Marie Louise Grappe (s).

962. THERESE
March 28, 1769, baptism of Therese, slave of Jean Baptiste Davion. Godparents: Manuel Trichele (s) and Marie Louise Grappe (s).

963. PELAGIE
March 28, 1769, baptism of Pelagie, slave of Mr. Morin. Godparents: Jean Baptiste Lambre (x) and Pelagie Lambre (x).

964. NICOLE LANGLOIS
July 24, 1769, baptism of Nicole, born July 20, legitimate daughter of Francois Langlois and Marie Gregoire de la Sta. Crux. Godparents: Henry Trichle (x) and Nicole Lambert (s).

965. THEODORE RAMBIN
August 25, 1769, baptism of Theodore, born August 12, legitimate son of André Rambin and Marie Francoise Clermont. Godparents: Theodore Dubois (s) and Marie Poisot (x).

966. JACQUES LEVASSEUR
August 25, 1769, baptism of Jacques, born August 20, legitimate son of Francoise Le Vassair and Marie Jeanne Gens des Gens. Godparents: Jacques LeVasseur (x) and Marie Anne LeVasseur (x), uncle and aunt of the infant.

967. MARIE FRANCOISE
August 25, 1769, baptism of Marie Francoise, born May 10, slave of Gabriel Buard, father unknown, /mother not named/. Godparents: Jean Baptiste Buard (x) and Marie Francoise /no last name/ (x).

968. PELAGIE BREVEL
September 10, 1769, baptism of Pelagie, born August 10, legitimate daughter of Baptiste Brevel and of Marie Francoise Poisot. Godparents: Etienne Vergé (x) and Magdeleine Grappe (x).

969. MARIE MAGDELEINE LABERRY
April 6, 1769, baptism of Marie Magdeleine, born April 4, legitimate daughter of Jean Baptiste LaBerry and Jeanne Guedon. Godparents: Pierre Besson (s) and Marie Magdeleine Grappe (x), "cousin and blood-cousin" of infant.

970. PIERRE DUPRÉ
June 4, 1769, baptism of Pierre, born May 25, legitimate
son of Joseph Dupré and Marie de L'Incarnation /Derbanne/.
Godparents: Pierre Poissot (x) and Marie Le Clerc (x).

971. PIERRE ANTOINE CARLE
June 4, 1769, baptism of Pierre Antoine, born June 2, 1769,
legitimate son of Francois Carle and Marie Louise la Renaudiere. Godparents: Pierre La Renaudiere (x) and Therese
Prudhomme (x).

972. JOSEPH PIERRE LALANE
/no date/, 1769, baptism of Joseph Pierre, born "6th of
same month", legitimate son of Joseph Antoine _____
/illegible/ LaLane, Spaniard, and Magdelaine Darbanne.
Godparents: Pierre Darbanne (x) and Marie Darbanne (x),
uncle and aunt of infant.

973. MARIE JEANNE CLAUDINE ANTOINETTE PELAGIE CHARBONNET
October 24, 1769, baptism of Marie Jeanne Claudine Antoinette Pelagie, born June 24 at 1:30 a.m., legitimate daughter of Jean Barthelemy Charbonnet, naval captain, and
Pelagie Pain. Godparents: Antoine Charbonnet (s) for
Sieur Claude Charbonnet, grandfather of the infant, and
Marie Jeanne Pain, grandmother (s).

974. JEAN BAPTISTE AUGUSTIN PAIN
October 24, 1769, baptism of Jean Baptiste Augustin, born
August 28 at 8 a.m., legitimate son of Sr. Daniel Pain,
subdélégué, and Marie Jeanne Roujot Pain. Godparents:
Jean Bte Roujot (s), juge et subdélégué at this post, and
Pelagie Pain Charbonnet (s).

975. MARIE JEANNE
October 28, 1769, baptism of Marie Jeanne, born September
15, daughter of Barbe, a slave of Mr. De Villiers, and of
a father unknown. Godparents: Charles and Marie Jeanne,
slaves of Mr. de Mezieres.

976. MARIE HYACINTHE GAGNE
December 24, 1769, baptism of Marie Hyacinthe, born December 5, legitimate daughter of Pierre Gagne and Marie Louise
Davion. Godparents: Dominique Davion (x) and Marie Louise
Gagne (x).

977. JEAN BAPTISTE LATIÉ
December 24, 1769, baptism of Jean Baptiste, born December 1, legitimate son of Joseph Latie and Anne Vergé.
Godparents: Jean Lambre (x) and Marie Anne Lavesseur (x).

978. JACQUES LAMBRE
December 24, 1769, baptism of Jacques, born November 20,

legitimate son of Jean Lambre and Marie Jeanne LeVasseur. Godparents: Jacques LeVassau (x) and Marie Anne Poisot (x).

979. JEAN LOUIS
December 27, 1769, baptism of Jean Louis, born December 20, of Therese, slave of Mr. Alexis Grappe, and a father unknown. Godparents: Julien Besson (s) and Marie Anne Grappe (x).

980. JACQUES NEGLE
MARIE LOUISE LA RENAUDIER
June 11, 1764, marriage, after one ban, of Jacques Negle (x), son of Jacques Negle and Anne Boyer, a native of the German Coast . . . and . . . Marie Louise La Renaudier (x), daughter of Charles Larenaudier and Marie Jeanne Louise Rivier. Witnesses: Pierre Derbanne (x), Rambin (s), Lecaze (s), Dufresne (s), Charles renaudiere (x).

981. JOSEPH LATIORE /LATTIER/
ANNE VERGE
June 20, 1764, after two bans, marriage of Joseph Latiore, corporal of a company under Sieur Makartis /Macarty/, son of Jean Latiore and of Francoise Riovoiranne, native of Roman in Dauphine, bishopric of Vienne, parish of St. Nicolas . . . and . . . Anne Verge (x), widow of Jean Boulet, daughter of Joseph Verge and Angelique Dumond, a native of this parish. Witnesses: Trichle (x), Poisot (s), Gonet (s), Dubois (s).

982. PIERRE CRETTE
MARIE LOUISE VERGE
August 22, 1764, after two bans, marriage of Pierre Crette (s), son of Pierre Crette and Angelique Rodriguez, parish of Beauport, bishopric of Quebec . . . and . . . Marie Louise Verge (x), daughter of Joseph Verge and of Angelique Dumon, a native of this parish. Witnesses: Gaspar Derbanne (s), Pierre Darbane (x), Rambin (s), Lecaze (s).

983. JEAN BAPTISTE MORIN
CATHERINE LEVASSEUR
February 12, 1765, after two bans, marriage of Jean Baptiste Morin (x), native of the parish of St. Francois de la Riviere Dessus, bishopric of Quebec, legitimate son of Jean Baptiste Morin and Agnes Mercier . . . and . . . Catherine Levassere (x), native of this parish, daughter of Jacques Le Vascere and Marie Francoise Bourdon. Witnesses: Piseros (s), Laberry (s), Hebert (s).

984. LOUIS LECOURT DE PRELLE
JEANNE LE ROY
March ?, 1765. No bans. Marriage of -- and legitimization of children of -- Louis LeCourt de Prelle (de Presle), *officier reformée*, native of Camaritte, bishopric of Kyrper /Quimper/ Corantin in Bretagne, son of Messire Josephe le Court, Seigneur de Presle, an ensign in the royal navy, and Demoiselle Jeanne de la Haye . . . and . . . Jeanne Le Roy, daughter of Sr. Etienne Le Roy and Demoiselle Louise Francoise Guillot, born in this parish of St. Francois des Natchitoches.

Ceremony performed by Fr. Valentin, Capucin missionary stationed at "the rapids on Red River", who discovered the couple living in the Riviere aux Cannes area without the benefit of a sanctioned marriage. The union was blessed in the presence of the bride's brother-in-law, Jean Baptiste LeComte (s).

Children legitimized at the time of this marriage were: Jean Baptiste, born June 21, 1759, and baptized by the Reverend Father Romero of the Spanish missions; /Marie Antoinette -- page is torn/, whose godfather was Messire Antoine Borme, captain, and whose godmother was Marie Louise LeRoy, born and baptized December 17, 1761; and Barthelemy, born September 18, 1763, whose godparents were Sieur Barthelemy Rachal and Demoiselle Margueritte le Compte, baptized by the Reverend Callahora, Superior of the Spanish mission. An earlier child, Pierre Laurent, born 1757, died in infancy.

This lengthy document was notarized by Daniel Pain upon Fr. Valentin's arrival at Natchitoches.

985. JEAN BAPTISTE GONAIN
MANUEL RICHE
March 19, 1765, marriage of Jean Baptiste Gonain (s/ Gonait), native of Lion, Canton of Switzerland, son of Abraham Gonain and Sara Demond . . . and . . . Manuel Riche (x), native of this parish, daughter of Henry Riche and Marie Joseph Clermont. 1 ban. Witnesses: Du Bois (s), Latie (x), Grillet (x).

986. PIERRE LA COUR
LOUISE CRETE /VERGER/
May 19, 1766, after three bans, marriage of Pierre La Cour, soldier of the company of Mr. de la Perriere, a native of the parish of Dissagne, bishopric of Perigueux, legitimate son of Pierre La Cour and Anne Augé . . . and . . . Louise Crete (x), widow of Pierre Crete. Witnesses: Bailliot (s), Baptiste Dupré (x), Henry Triche (x), and Joseph Latie (x).

987. ATHANASE
    LOUISE
    May 25, 1765, marriage of Athanase, *nègre*, and Louise, *sauvagesse*, slaves of Mr. St. Denis.

988. MICHEL BRUMOT
    MARIE RONDIN
    June 12, 1766, marriage of Michel Brumot, native of the parish of St. Martin, of the Isle de Roy, bishopric of Luçon, legitimate son of Michel Brumot and Louise Page . . . and . . . Marie Rondin, legitimate daughter of Julien Rondin and Marie Jeanne Riotor of this parish. 1 ban. Witnesses: Bossins (s), Le Clerc (s), Pierre Saurelle (s), and Ignace Anty (s).

989. ETIENNE GAGNYS   (GANIER)
    MARIE LOUISE BERTRAND
    October 27, 1766, marriage of Etienne Gagnys (Ganier) (x), native of *la haute ville de Quebec* in Canada, legitimate son of Baptiste Gagnys and Agathe Crevier . . . and . . . Marie Louise Bertrand (x), native of this parish, legitimate daughter of Claude Bertrand, elder sergeant of the troops, and Marie Elizabeth de Lisle. 1 ban. Witnesses: Villere (s), Berard (s), Hubert (s), La Perrier (s).

990. FRANCOIS VALENTIN
    MARIE LOUISE TOUTIN
    January 3, 1767, marriage of Francois Valentin (s), legitimate son of Jean Valentin and of Francoise? Geraygne? , native of Rochrayre /Roquevaire?7, bishopric of Marseilles . . . and . . . Marie Louise Toutin (s), widow of Pierre Dolis, native of this parish. 3 bans. Witnesses: Du Vivier (s), Durand (s), LaBerry (s), Bossan (s), and Dejarnul?.

991. REMY POISOT
    LOUISE CAVE
    July 4, 1767, marriage of Remy Poisot (x), legitimate son of Remy Poisot and Anne Marie Philippe, habitant and native of this parish . . . and . . . Louise Cavé, legitimate daughter of Francois Cavé and Marie Jeanne Brunet, native of New Orleans. 2 bans. Witnesses: Poisot (s) Bailliot (s), Robert Dupre (x), Josephe Verger (x), and Etienne Verger (x).

992. FRANCOIS CARLE
    MARIE LOUISE LARENAUDIERE
    /no date7, 1767, after publication of two bans -- one on the ninth Sunday after Pentecost, the second on the sixteenth of the same month, was married Francois Carlo (x), native of Marseille, parish of St. Lazare, legitimate son

of Jean Carle and Marie Merles . . . and . . . Marie
Louise Larenaudiere (x), widow of Jacques Naigle, legit-
imate daughter of Charles Larenaudiere and Marie Jeanne
Lariviere. Witnesses: La Berry (s), Le Clerc (s) and
Jean Lambre (x).

993. PIERRE GAGNAY
MARIE LOUISE DAVION
November 11, 1767, marriage of Pierre Gagnay, native of
St. Joachim, diocese of Quebec, legitimate son of Pierre
Gagnay and Marie Bruteau . . . and . . . Marie Louise
Davion, native of this parish, legitimate daughter of
Jean Baptiste Davion and Marie Hiacinthe Trichle. 1 ban.
Witnesses: Morin (s), "the grandfather" (x), Manuel
Trichele (s), Jean Baptiste Trichele (s).

994. JOSEPH MICHEL GOUTIERE
MARIE LOUISE LEBOEUF
February 1, 1768, marriage of Joseph Michel Goutiere (x),
legitimate son of Joseph Goutiere and of Michel de la
Ferrebeyre, Spaniards . . . and . . . Marie Louise Le
Boeuf (x), legitimate daughter of Henry Leboeuf and of
Emmanuel Duplecy, native of this parish. 1 ban. Wit-
nesses: Fazende (s), Maraffret (s).

995. ANTOINE CHARBONNET
MARIE ANTOINETTE HENOUL DE LIVAUDAIS
March 14, 1768, marriage of Antoine Charbonnet (s), native
of Thiers in Auvergne, parish of St. Genez, legitimate
son of Claude Charbonnet, wholesale merchant, and of Marie
Cusson . . . and . . . Marie Antoinette Henoul de Livaudais (s), native of New Orleans, legitimate daughter of
Jacques Henoul de Livaudais, elder captain of the post,
and of Marie Genevieve Babin La Source. 1 ban. Double-
wedding with couple below.

JEAN BAPTISTE CHARBONNET
MARIE PELAGIE PAIN
Same day. Marriage of Jean Baptiste Charbonnet (s), elder
captain of the Navy, brother of Antoine above . . . and
. . . Marie Pelagie Pain (s), native of this parish, legitimate daughter of Daniel Pain, *subdélégué et garde magazine du roy*, and Marie Jeanne Rougeot. 1 ban.

Witnesses to both marriages, all of whom signed this joint
entry, were: Jeanne Roujot Pain, Chevalier De Villiers,
Pain, Livaudais Villiers, De Mezieres, De St. Amand,
Poisot, Lemée, Poëy farré, and Fr. Joseph Marie de la
SS. Trinidad. Fr. Stanislas, officiating.

996. MATURIN DAVID
MARIE JEANNE LAMALATHY
March 20, 1768, marriage of Maturin David (x), native of Evrix /Evreux/, parish of St. Magdeleine, diocese of Angers, legitimate son of Pierre David and Anne Dupont. . . and . . . Marie Jeanne Lamalathy, native of this parish, legitimate daughter of Louis Lamalathy and Jeanne Victoire Garcie. 1 ban. Witnesses: Louis Lamalatie (s), Alexis Grappe (s), Francois Carle (s), Jean Baptiste Trichele (s).

997. JACQUES CHRISTILLIE
MARIE ANNE DOROTHÉE VILDEQUE /PEREAU dit VILDEC/
June 6, 1769, marriage of Jacques Christillie (s), native of the parish of St. Maurice /Bourg St. Maurice/ in Savoye /Savoie/, legitimate son of Jacques Antoine Christille and Marie Emperear . . . and . . . Marie Anne Dorothée Vildeque /Pereau dit Vildec/, legitimate daughter of Francois Vildeque and Marie Catherine Dupre, of this parish. 1 ban. Witnesses: Jean Lambre (x), Jacques Bunel (s), Hubert (s).

998. HONNORÉ VISIANT
MARIE LOUISE CHANIOT
July 25, 1769, marriage of Honnoré Visiant (x), native of Arle /Arles/ in Provence, legitimate son of Francois Visiant and Honnorée Sioucheppe . . . and . . . Marie Louise Chaniot (x), native of this parish, legitimate daughter of Francois Chaniot and Marie La Croix. 1 ban. Witnesses: Pierre Villard (s), Manuel Triche (s), Alexis Grappe (s), P. Lacoste (s).

999. JEAN BAPTISTE DUPRÉ
LOUISE MARGUERITE LECOMTE
September 11, 1769, marriage of Jean Baptiste Dupre (x), legitimate son of Jacques Dupre and of Marie Anne Philippe . . . and Louise Marguerite LeComte (x), native of this parish, legitimate daughter of Jean Baptiste Le Compte and Marguerite LeRoy. 1 ban. Double wedding with couple below.

MICHEL ROBIN
MARIE LOUISE BOULET
Same day. Marriage of Michel Robin (s), legitimate son of Michel Robin and Jeanne Bureau, parish of St. Martin, diocese of La Rochelle . . . and . . . Marie Louise Boulet (x), legitimate daughter of Jean Boulet and Anne Vergé, native of this parish. 1 ban.

Witnesses to both marriages, all of whom signed this joint entry, were: Poisot, Dupain, Baptiste Trichel, and Gr Derbanne.

1000. EMMANUEL TRICHLE
MARIE LOUISE GRAPPE
October 28, 1769, marriage of Emanuel Trichle (s), legitimate son of Henry Trichel and Marie Dumont, a native of this parish . . . and . . . Marie Louise Grappe (s), legitimate daughter of Alexis Grappe and Louise Marguerite Guedon, a native of the Cadeaux. 3 bans. Witnesses: Donato Bello (s), Gr Derbanne (s), LaBerry (s), Baptiste Trichel (s), Alexis Grappe (s), Mr. Trichle (x).

1001. ROMAIN DE LA FOSSE
MARIE ROSE BENOIT
December 26, 1769, marriage of Romain de la Fosse (s), native of Rouen in Normandy, legitimate son of Pierre de la Fosse and Jeanne Guilmain . . . and . . . Marie Rose Benoit, legitimate daughter of Jean Benoist and Anne Breau, native of the parish of Previditte ?, in the province of Acadie. 1 ban. Witnesses: Theodore Dubois (s), Prudhomme (s), Alexis Grappe (s), Roujot (s).

1002. JEAN BAPTISTE PIEDFERME /LEGER/
CLEMENCE LARENAUDIERE
January 14, 1770, marriage of Jean Baptiste /Legér dit/ Piedferme (x), native of /Illegible/, legitimate son of Adrien Léger and Marie Detincourt . . . and . . . Clemence Larenaudiere (x), native of this parish, legitimate daughter of Charles Larenaudiere and Jeanne la Riviere. 1 ban. Witnesses: Prudhomme (s), Gr Derbanne (s) and Lemée (s).

1003. NICOLAS LAIGNON
MARIE ANNE GUEDON
January 23, 1770, marriage of Nicolas Laignon, native of Pocharoinett?, diocese of Lombez in Gascogne, legitimate son of Jean Laignon and of Perrete La /Illegible/ . . . and . . . Marie Anne Guedon, native of this parish, widow of Joseph Le Duc. 1 ban. Witnesses: La Berry (s), Alexis Grappe (s), Pain (s), Piseros (s), Rambin (s).

1004. MATHIEU PLAISANCE
MARGUERITE TOUTIN
February 13, 1770, marriage of Mathieu Plaisance (x), native of Pot in Burre /Pau in Bearne?/, diocese of Lescar, legitimate son of Jean Plaisance and Jeanne Marcou . . . and . . . Marguerite Toutin (x), native of this parish, legitimate daughter of Charles Toutin and Jeanne Guedon. 3 bans. Witnesses: N. Laignon (s), Borme (s), Poisot (s), Dominique Monteche (x), La Berry (s), Alexis Grappe (s).

1005. JEAN LALANDE
CATHERINE DUPRE
February 26, 1770, marriage of Jean LaLande (s), native

of Dechou, diocese of Cominges /Comminges/, legitimate
son of Dominique La Lande and Marie David . . . and . . .
Catherine Dupre (x), widow of Francois Perot. 1 ban.
Witnesses: Jacques Bunel (s), Pierre Trudeau (s), Jean
David (x), Louis Ladé.

1006. JEAN BAPTISTE TRICHLE
MARIANNE DAUBLIN
March 5, 1770, marriage of Jean Baptiste Trichle (s), a
native of this parish, legitimate son of Henry Trichle
and Marie Dumon . . . and . . . Marianne Daublin (s/
Dobin), widow of François Closot, a native of New Orleans.
1 ban. Witnesses: Manuel Trichel (s), Labery (s),
Trichle, the father (x), Prudhomme (s).

1007. PAUL BOUËT LAFFITTE
MAGDELEINE GRAPPE
April 28, 1770, marriage of Paul Bouët Laffitte (s), legitimate son of Francois Bouët Laffitte and Marianne Laffitte,
native of the parish of Pouilleroque, diocese of Lectoure
in Gascogne . . . and . . . Magdeleine Grappe, legitimate
daughter of Alexis Grappe and Anne Guedon. 1 ban. Witnesses: N. Laignon (s), Louis De Blanc (s), Borme, *fils* (s),
Rambin (s).

1008. FRANCOIS LEMAITRE
LOUISE VILLE FRANCHE /LE DUC/
March 2, 1772, marriage of Francois Lemaitre (x), legitimate son of Francois Lemaitre and Anne Mairgay, native of
Nantes, parish of St. /illegible/. . . and . . . Louise
Ville Franche (x), legitimate daughter of Joseph Ville
franche and Marianne Guedon, a native of this parish. 1
ban. Witnesses: La Berry (x), N. Laignon (s), La Roche (s).

1009. LOUIS VERGER /VERCHER/
MARIE LOUISE GRILLET
March 3, 1772, marriage of Louis Verger /Vercher/, legitimate son of Jacques Verger and Catherine Dumont, native
of la Magdelaine in Canada . . . and . . . Marie Louise
Grillet, legitimate daughter of Marin Grillet and Marie
Louise Brevel, native of this parish. 1 ban. Witnesses:
Chauvin (s) and Latie (s).

1010. GUILLAUME HOUADRE (WILLIAM WARDEN)*
THERESE PRUDHOMME
April 2, 1772, marriage of Guillaume Houadre*, legitimate
son of Ridechelle Houadre and Marie Riber, native of
Philadelphia . . . and . . . Therese Prudhomme (x), legitimate daughter of Bastien Prudhomme and Jeanne Chever.
1 ban. Witnesses: /Jean Baptiste/ Prudhomme (s), Gagne
(x), Guillaume Chever (s), Metoyer (s).

*The signature of the groom appears on this document as "William Warden."

1011. ATHANASE POISOT
MARIE MANUEL DE SOTHO
April 12, 1773, marriage of Athanase Poisot, native of this parish, legitimate son of Remy Poisot, sub-lieutenant of the militia, and Marie Philippe . . . and . . . Marie Manuel de Sotho, legitimate daughter of Antoine Manuel de Sotho and Marie des Neiges de St. Denis (s). 1 ban. Witnesses: De la Chaise (s), Mª Soto (s), Remy Poisot (s), J. B. Dubois (s), Dupain (s).

1012. LOUIS FORTAIN
MARIE MAGDELEINE LA RENAUDIERE
April 24, 1773, marriage of Louis Fortain (x) native of Cap St. Ignace, diocese of Quebec, legitimate son of Louis Fortain and Magdeleine Langelier . . . and . . . Marie Magdeleine La Renaudiere (x), legitimate daughter of Charles La Renaudiere and Jeanne de la Rivierre, a native of this parish. 2 bans. Witnesses: Lamée (s), Francois D'la roche (s), Roujot (s), Borme (s).

1013. FRANCOIS HUGUES
JEANNE FELICITÉ LE DUC
June 1, 1773, marriage of Francois Hugues (x), legitimate son of Pierre Hugues and Francoise Bernard, native of Marceille . . . and . . . Jeanne Felicité Le Duc (s/ Jane Felicite), legitimate daughter of Joseph Le Duc and Marianne Guedon, native of this parish. 1 ban. Witnesses: N. Laignon (s) and Pierre La Coste.

1014. ELIE BERNARD
ELEONORE CHANIOT
March 7, 1774, marriage of Elie Bernard (x), native of La Rochelle, legitimate son of Jean Bernard and of Jeanne Eveque . . . and . . . Eleonore Chaniot (x), legitimate daughter of Francois Chaniot and of Marie Lacroix. 1 ban. Witnesses: Villard (s), Bormé (s), *Le Chv.* de Villiers (s), Villiere (s).

1015. JACQUES HUBERT
JEANNE DE LA RIVIERE
March 19, 1774, marriage of Jacques Hubert (s), native of Moret, parish of Notre Dame, legitimate son of Jean Baptiste Hubert and Anne Rose . . . and . . . Jeanne de la Riviere (x), widow of Charle La Renaudiere. 1 ban. Witnesses: Dubois (s), Bouet Laffitte (s), Laberry (s).

1016. PIERRE RAIMOND
FRANCOISE
March 20, 1774, marriage of Pierre Raimond (x), native of

Canada, legitimate son of Louis Raymond and Louise Jerome . . . and . . . Francoise, a free Indian (x). 1 ban. Witnesses: Alorge (s) and Jacques Ride (s).

1017. ESTEVAN VERGER
MARIA FRANCISCA DUPRES
June 17, 1775, marriage of Estevan Verger, native of this parish, legitimate son of Joseph Verger and Angelica Dumon . . . and . . . Maria Francisca Dupres, legitimate daughter of Joseph Dupres and Maria Darmand /Derbanne/, a native of this parish. 3 bans. Witnesses: Remigio Poissot, Sr. (s), Remigion Poissot, Jr., Gaspar Derbanne (s) and Bte. Trichel (s).

1018. LUIS GABRIEL BUART
MARIA ROSA LAMBRE
October 7, 1775, marriage of Luis Gabriel Buart (x), native of this post, legitimate son of deceased Gabriel Buart and Mariana Rousseau . . . and . . . Maria Rosa Lambre (s), native of this parish, legitimate daughter of Juan Lambre and Maria Juana Le Vasseur. 3 bans. Witnesses: Jacobo Lambre (x), Mr. Poison (s/ Poisot), Mr. Grillet (s/ Grillte), Domingo Monteje (x).

1019. JOSEPH VILLAREAL
MARIA FRANCISCA MORIN
December 31, 1775, marriage of Joseph Villareal, native of Monterey, legitimate son of Andres Villareal and Maria de la Creoz . . . and . . . Maria Francisca Morin, native of Natchitoches, legitimate daughter of Juan Morin and Juana Isabel Selinas? 3 bans. Witnesses: Antonio Vascocu, Ceser des Messiere (s/ Cesaire demezieres), Antonio Vascocu, Herman Castano de Castanare (s).

1020. JOSEPH POIRIER
FRANCISCA MARIA LE DOUX
February 20, 1776, marriage of Joseph Poirier, native of Isle Negra /Illinois/, legitimate son of Andres Poirier and Francisca Kintrie . . . and . . . Francisca Maria Le Doux (s), native of this post, legitimate daughter of Antonio Le Doux and Francisca Fazende. 2 bans. Witnesses: Mr. Roujot, Mr. Borme (s), A. Charbonnet (s), Mr. Dartigaux (s).

1021. PEDRO
MARIANA
May 18, 1776, marriage of Pedro and Mariana, negro slaves of Louis Burme, captain, both natives of Guinea. No bans. Witnesses: Hermano Donado; Juan Bautista, slave of Sr. St. Denis; Francisco, slave of Sr. St. Denis; Jean Luis, slave of Dominico Montes; Jean Pierre, slave of Widow Alexo Grappe; Fr. Casiano de Castanare (s).

1022. FRANCISCO
THERESA
May 25, 1776, marriage of Francisco and Theresa, negro slaves of St. Prix, both natives of Guinea. No bans. Witnesses: Antoine Vascocu (x), habitant, Augustin Lorence (x), habitant, and Pedro (x), Negro slave of Sieur Bormé.

1023. JUAN PEDRO
MARIA THERESA
June 15, 1776, marriage of Juan Pedro and Maria Theresa, negro slaves of the widow of Alexo Grappe. No bans. Witnesses: Juan Louis, slave of Dominico Montes; Juan Bautista, slave of Prudhomme; Augustin, slave of Grappe; Pedro Prince, slave of Borme.

Concurrent with this marriage was the legitimization of seven children previously born to Juan Pedro and Maria Theresa: Antonio, Juan Bautista, Juana, Paulo, Ambrosio, Juan Luis, Augustin.

1024. FRANCISCO LA ROCHE
MARIA FRANCESCA MALBERT
August 15, 1776, marriage of Francisco La Roche, native of Parish of San Francisco at Havre de Grace in Normandy, legitimate son of Pedro La Roche and Maria Juana La Roy, . . . and . . . Maria Francisca Malbert, native of this parish, legitimate daughter of Juan Bautisto Malbert and Juana Verger. 3 bans. Witnesses: Pedro Villard (x), Francisco Doucet (s), Andres Antonio Rambin (s), and Andre, slave (x).

1025. GUILLERMO LESTAGE
MANUELA TRICHE /RICHÉ/
September 4, 1776, marriage of Guillermo Lestage (x), legitimate son of Reynaldo Lestage and Maria Laquesane, native of Burdeos /Bordeaux/, parish of St. Projecto? . . . and . . . Manuela Triche (x), widow of Juan Bautista Gonin, native of this parish, legitimate daughter of Enrique Riche and Maria Josepha Clermont. 3 bans. Witnesses: Louis /Lamalathie dit/ Jobar (s), Manuel Trichele (s), Andre Rambin (s), Juan Bautista Dubois (s).

1026. BERNARDO ORTOLANT
MARIA ANA GRAPPE
October 9, 1776, marriage of Bernardo Ortolant (s), native of Burdeos /Bordeaux/, parish of St. Miguel, legitimate son of Reymundo Ortolant and Mariana Labattut. . . and . . . Maria Ana Grappe, native of this parish, legitimate daughter of Alexo Grappe and Margarita Luisa Guedon. 3 bans. Witnesses: Juan Bautista Labery (s), Nicolas Lagnon (s), Josef Poirier (s/ Le Chevalier Poirret), and Francois Doucet (s).

1027. FRANCISCO LE DOUX
MARGARITA ROUJOT
December 23, 1776, marriage of Francisco Le Doux (s),
native of Punta Contada /Pointe Coupée/, legitimate son
of Pedro le Doux and Cecilia Rondeau . . . and . . .
Margarita Roujot (s), native of Mobile, legitimate daughter of Juan Bautista Roujot and Margarita Demouy. Witnesses: Senor Borme (s), Sr. Cadet Lafitte (s/ Bouet
Laffitte), Sr. Chevalier de Villier (s), Roujot (s).

1028. JUAN
MARIA JUANA
January 18, 1777, marriage of Juan and Maria Juana, negro
slaves of Jacobo Lambre. No bans. Witnesses: Hº Casiano
de Castanores (s), Antonio Vascocu (s), Juan Luis and
Andre, slaves of Jacobo Lambre.

1029. PEDRO
VICTORIA
January 18, 1777, marriage of Pedro and Victoria, negro
slaves of Juan Labery. No bans. Witnesses: Antonio
Vascocu (s), Andres, *mulâtre* slave of Labery, Juan Bautista, *nègre* of Sr. St. Denis, and Herman Casiano (s).

1030. JUAN BAUTISTA MACIPE
MARIA LUISA LE MOINE
January 27, 1777, marriage of Juan Bautista Macipe, native
of Burdeos /Bordeaux/, legitimate son of Pedro Macipe,
and Juana Lafont . . . and . . . Maria Luisa Le Moine, a
native of Punta Contado /Pointe Coupée/, legitimate daughter of Carlos Le Moine and Isabel Dupres. 3 bans. Witnesses: Jacobo Lambre (x), Monsieur Bailio (s), Francisco Doucet (s), Antonio Vascocu (s).

1031. JULIAN BESSON
MARIA DE LA ENCARNACION VILDEQUE /PEREAU/
April 7, 1777, marriage of Julian Besson (s), native of
parish of Natchitoches, legitimate son of Juan Bautisto
Beson and Luisa Margarita Guedon. . . and . . . Maria de
la Encarnacion /Pereau *dite*/ Vildeque /or Vildec/ (x),
legitimate daughter of Pedro Vildeque and Maria Catalina
Dupres. 3 bans. Witnesses: Mr. Poissot (s), Manuel
Trichele (s), Bernardo D'ortolant (s), Jacobo Lambre (x).

1032. JUAN ADLET
MARIA GENOVEFA DUBOIS
April 18, 1777, marriage of Juan Adlet (s), native of
Mobile, legitimate son of Esteban Adlet and Genovefa
Fondelique . . . and . . . Maria Genovefa Dubois (s), native of this parish, legitimate daughter of Juan Bautista
DuBois and Maria Josepha Cleremont. Witnesses: Andres

Rambin (s), Mr. Dubois (s/ Dubois, *pere*), Francisco Rambin (s), and Mr. Lestage (x).

1033. ANDRES RAMBIN
MARIA CATALINA BUARD
April 23, 1777, marriage of Andres Rambin (s), native of New Orleans, legitimate son of Andres Rambin and Maria Francisca Clairmont . . . and . . . Maria Catalina Buard (s), native of this parish, legitimate daughter of Gabriel Buard and Maria Ana Roussot. 3 bans. Witnesses: Mr. Grillet (s), Mr. Adlet (s), Mr. Buart (x), J. B. Dubois (s).

1034. LORENZO
JUANA
April 26, 1777, marriage of Lorenzo and Juana, *negros* of Sr. Dn. Athanasio de Mezieres, Chevalier and Commandant. 3 bans. Witnesses: Athanasio de Mezieres (s) and Francois Doucet (s), Antonio Vascocu (s), Hermano Casiano (s).

1035. ANDRES DAVID
MARIA JUANA LAMALATY
May 2, 1777, marriage of Andres David, native of Nantes in Bretana, legitimate son of Andres David and Isabel Ana Morelle . . . and . . . Maria Juana Lamalathy, native of this parish, legitimate daughter of Luis Lamalaty and Juana victoria Garcia. 3 bans. Witnesses: Pedro La Coste (s), Juan Bautista Anty (s/ Antis), Antonio Vascocu (s), Hermano Casiano de Castonanes (s).

1036. CHRISTOVAL
MARIA ANA
June 21, 1777, marriage of Christoval and Maria Ana, slaves of Athanasio de Mezieres. 3 bans. No witnesses named.

NOTE: This entry was recorded, then X'd through.

1037. JUAN BAUTISTA DERBANNE
MARIA FELICIDAD DUPAIN
September 9, 1777, marriage of Juan Bautista Derbanne, native of this parish, legitimate son of Gaspar Derbanne and Maria Francisca Verger . . . and . . . Maria Felicidad Dupain, native of this parish, legitimate daughter of Pedro Dupain, officer of the militia, and of Juana Catalina Alorge. 2 bans.

NOTE: This entry was recorded, then X'd through. Apparently the marriage did not take place, since Marie Felicité was married to another the following June (Entry 1044) and Jean Baptiste married another in 1784 (Entry 1077).

1038. JUAN BAUTISTA LARENAUDIERE
MARIA LUISA DE COTON /DU VIVIER/
October 9, 1777, marriage of Juan Bautista Larenaudiere (s), native of this parish, legitimate son of Carlos La Renaudiere and Juana del Rio /de la Riviere/ . . . and

. . . Maria Luisa /⎯du Vivier dit_e_7 de Coton, native of this parish, legitimate daughter of Juan Bautista de Vivier de Coton and Juana Du Pain. 3 bans. Witnesses: Bernardo Ortolant (s/ B. Dortolant), Julian Besson (s), Francisco Grappe (s), Luis Lamalaty (s).

1039. SANTIAGO FORT
MARIA FRANCISCA MALBER
October 21, 1777, marriage of Santiago Fort, native of Agen, legitimate son of Pedro Fort and Maria _____ . . . and . . . Maria Francisca Malber, native of this parish, legitimate daughter of Juan Bautista Malbert and Juana Verger. 3 bans. Witnesses: Juan Lambre (x), Pablo Bouet Laffitte (s), Manuel Trichele (s), Andres Rambin (s).

1040. PEDRO BROSSET
MARIA JOSEPHA GRILLET
January 6, 1778, marriage of Pedro Bosset, native of Sainte, legitimate son of Juan Brosset and Juana Retint . . . and . . . Maria Josepha Grillet, native of this parish, legitimate daughter of Marino Grillet and Maria Luisa Brevel. 3 bans. Witnesses: Mr. Badin (s), Mr. Pavie (s/ E. Pavie), Luis Vercher (s), Luis Buart.

1041. JUAN BAUTISTA ANTY
MARIA CATHALINA GALIEN
January 24, 1778, marriage of Juan Bautista Anty (s), native of Nueva Orleans, legitimate son of Ignacio Anty and Cathalina Guerin. . . and . . . Maria Cathalina Galien, native of Punta Contada /⎯Pointe Coup_ée_7, legitimate daughter of Pedro Galien and Maria Rachal. 3 bans. Witnesses: Casiano de Castares (s), Donado Capuchino(s), Antonio Vascocu (s), Luis Rachal (s).

1042. PEDRO RAYMOND
MARGARITA BLANC PAIN
May 4, 1778, marriage of Pedro Raymond, native of Canada, legitimate son of Luis Raymond and Magdalena Jerome. . . and . . . Margarita Blanc Pain /⎯no parents or place of birth give_n_7. 3 bans. Witnesses: Casiano de Castanares (s), Antonio Vastcocu (s), Andre Vascocu (s).

1043. PEDRO BAILLIOT
MARIA ANA SCHELET
May 11, 1778, marriage of Pedro Bailliot (s), native of Negrepelis /⎯Negrepelisse in Tarn-et-Garonne, Franc_e_7, legitimate son of Juan Baillot and Catalina Lafont . . . and . . . Maria Ana Schelet (x), native of the German Coast on the Mississippi, legitimate daughter of Miguel Schelet and Ana Barbara Pomier. 3 bans. Witnesses:

Marino Grillet (s), Jacobo Lambre (s), Juan Bautista
Labery (s), Pedro Badin (s).

1044. JUAN BAUTISTA ARMANT
MARIA FELICITE DUPAIN
June 30, 1778, marriage of Juan Bautista Armant (s), a
native of Luisburg, bishopric of Quebec, legitimate son
of Maria Josef Armant and Cecilia Normant . . . and . . .
Maria Felicidad Dupain (s), native of this parish, legit-
imate daughter of Pedro Manuel Victor Dupain and Juana
Catalina Alorge. 3 bans. Witnesses: Senor Dartigaux
(s), Senor Pavie (s/ E. Pavie), Senor Metoyer (s), Senor
St. Anne (s/ Ailhaud Ste. Anne), Prudhomme (s), Pierre
Dupain (s).

1045. PEDRO DUPLAISIS
MARIA GREGORIA DE SANTA CRUX
July 6, 1778, marriage of Pedro Duplaisis, a native of
this parish, legitimate son of Pedro Duplaisis and of
Luisa Margarita /Juchereau de St. Denis/ . . . and . . .
Maria Gregoria de Santa Crux, native of Los Adays, legit-
imate daughter of Juan Josef de Santa Crux and of Petro-
nila Isabel /no last name/. 3 bans. Witnesses: Andres
Vascocu (s), Antonio Vascocu (s), Francisco Doucet (s),
Juan Luis Le Beuf (x).

1046. ANTONIO /LE/ NOIR
MARIA RONDIN
November 21, 1778, marriage of Antonio /le/ Noir, native
of Marsella /Marseille/, principal parish, legitimate
son of Francisco Noir and Ana Noir . . . and . . . Maria
Rondin, native of this parish, legitimate daughter of
Julian Rondin and Juana Dupain. 3 bans. Witnesses:
Antonio Vascocu (s), Andres Vascocu (s).

1047. GUILLERMO BARBE ROUGE /BARBEROUSSE/
MARIA JUANA CHAGNO
November 21, 1778, marriage of Guillermo Barbe Rouge, a
native of Marsella, parish of San Lorenzo, legitimate son
of Luis Barbe Rouge and Ana Teresa /no last name/ . . .
and . . . Maria Juana Chagno, native of this parish, legitimate daughter of Francisco Chagnot and Maria La Choix. 3
bans. Witnesses: Francisco Grappe (s/ Francois Grappe),
Juan Bautista Larenaudiere (s/ Baptiste La Renaudiere),
Esteban Derroven, Pedro Labride?.

1048. LUIS TOUTIN
MARIA SILVILLA HUBARDEAUX
November 21, 1778, marriage of Luis Toutin, native of
this parish, legitimate son of Carlos Toutin and Juana
Guedon . . . and . . . Maria Silvilla Hubardeaux, native

of this parish, legitimate daughter of Pedro Hubardeaux and Maria Juana Barbier. 3 bans. Witnesses: Jn. Bautista Lambre, Pedro Badin (s), Juan Bautista Labery (s), Manuel Trichele (s).

1049. JUAN SANTIAGO DAVID
MARIA ANA DARTIGAUX
January 19, 1779, marriage of Juan Santiago David, native of Dambierche, bishopric of Leon, legitimate son of Juan Bautista David and Maria Neurin . _ . . and . . . Maria Ana Dartigaux (s), native of Bayona /Bayonne/ in France, legitimate daughter of Pedro Dartigaux and Maria Monica Duthil (Duchil?). 3 bans. Witnesses: Antonio Charbonnet (s), Esteban Pavie (s), Francisco La Caze (s), Pedro Badin (s).

1050. FRANCISCO PIEVERT
MARIA JUANA CHAGNOT
May 11, 1779, marriage of Francisco Pievert, native of Naeche /Natchez/, legitimate son of Jn. Bauta. Pievert and Marion Duroche . . . and . . . Maria Juana Chagnot, native of this post, legitimate daughter of Francisco Chagnaut and Maria Lacroix; both of the betrothed have been widowed. 3 bans. Witnesses: Antonio Vascocu (s), Matheo LaBorde (s), Andres Vascocu (s), Antonio Negre /no signature or mark/.

1051. LUIS FONTENO
PELAGIE GRAPPE
June 19, 1779, marriage of Luis Fonteno, native of Opelousas, legitimate son of Felix Fonteno and Maria Briñac . . . and . . . Pelagie Grappe (s), native of this parish, legitimate daughter of Alexo Grappe and Luisa Guedon. 3 bans. Witnesses: Juan Bautista Trichele (s), Juan Bautista Labery (s), Nicolas Laignon (s), Juan Bautista Davion (x).

1052. ESTEBAN PAVIE
MARIA THERESA BUART
December 2, 1779, marriage of Esteban Pavie, native of La Rochela, parish of St. Bartolome, legitimate son of Joseph Pavie and Maria Juana Couse . . . and . . . Maria Theresa Buart (s), native of this parish, legitimate daughter of Gabriel Buart and Maria Ana Roussot. 3 bans. Witnesses: Joseph Pavie (s), Andres Rambin (s), Luis Gabriel Buart (x), Marino Grillet (s).

1053. MIGUEL ROBIN
MARIA LUISA BODIN
January 22, 1780, marriage of Miguel Robin, native of Sta. Onza /Saintonge, France/, parish of S. Martin, legitimate son of Miguel Robin and Juana Bureau . . . and . . .

Maria Luisa Bodin, native of this parish, legitimate
daughter of Lorenzo Bodin and Michaela Rosario Santa
Cruz. 3 bans. Witnesses: Antonio Vascocu (s), Andres
Vascocu (s), Francisco Doucet (s), Domingo Longuera (x).

1054. FELIPE FREDERIC
BARBARA CHELET
February 18, 1780, marriage of Felipe Frederic, native
of the German Coast, parish of S. Carlos, legitimate
son of Felipe Frederic and Catalina Antony . . . and. . .
Barbara Chelet, native of the same parish, legitimate
daughter of Miguel Chelet and Ana Barbara /Pommier/. 3
bans. Witnesses: La Berry (s), Grillet (s), Baillio
(s), Le Brun (s).

1055. JUAN BAUTISTA
THERESA
April 17, 1780, marriage of Juan Bautista and Theresa,
natives of Guinea, slaves of Franco. /Le/ Vasseur. 3
bans. Witnesses: Francisco Doucet (s), Antonio Vascocu
(s), Luis Gabriel Buart (x).

1056. FRANCISCO PRUDHOMME
MARIA BARBARA RAMBIN
May 9, 1780, marriage of Francisco Prudhomme, son of
Juan Bautista Prudhomme and Catalina Mellier, native of
this parish . . . and . . . Maria Barbara Rambin, native
of this parish, legitimate daughter of Andres Rambin and
Maria Francisca Clermont. 3 bans. Witnesses: Bautista
Dubois (s), Pedro Dupain (s), Bautista Prudhomme (s), and
Andres Rambin (s).

1057. FRANCISCO PABLO BOSSIE
CATALINA PELAGIA LAMBRE
May 18, 1780, marriage of Francisco Pablo Bossie, native
of the German Coast, legitimate son of Francisco Bossie
and Rosalia Barre . . . and . . . Catalina Pelagia Lambro,
native of this parish, legitimate daughter of Juan Lambre
and Maria Juana Levasseur. 3 bans. Witnesses: Juan
Bautista Bossie (s), Francisco Barre (s), Dominique Monteche (x), Jacob Lambre (x).

1058. JOSEPH DUPRES, *fils*
MARIA FRANCISCA LE COMPTE
May 18, 1780, marriage of Joseph Dupres, native of this
parish, legitimate son of Joseph Dupres and Maria Derbanne
. . . and . . . Maria Francisca Le Compte, native of this
parish, legitimate daughter of Juan Bta. Le Compte and
of Margarita Le Roy. 3 bans. Witnesses: Gaspar Derbanne (s), Gaspar Fiol (x), Esteban Verger (x), Juan
Bautista Davion (x).

1059. SANTIAGO
FRANCISCA *dite* SANGONETTE
May 20, 1780, marriage of two slaves of Santiago Lambre.
3 bans. Witnesses: Manuel Bas (x), Antonio Vascocu (s).

1060. JUAN POMIER
MARIA DUPRES
October 17, 1780, marriage of Juan Pomier, native of the
German Coast, legitimate son of Pedro Pomier and Maria
Barbara Masc /Metz/. . . and . . . Maria Dupres, native
of this parish, legitimate daughter of Robert Dupres and
Maria Cave. 3 bans. Witnesses: Joseph Dupre (x),
Bautista Dupres (x), Santiago Christille (s), Pedro
Bailliot (s).

1061. JUAN CHRISOSTOME PERAUT
MARIA LUISA SALVANT
September 25, 1781, marriage of Juan Chrisostome Peraut,
native of this parish, legitimate son of Francisco Peraut
and Maria Catalina Dupres . . . and . . . Maria Luisa
Salvant, native of Nueva Orleans, legitimate daughter of
Juan Salvant and Luisa Lambre. 3 bans. Witnesses:
Pedro Badin (s), Francisco Grappe (s), Francisco Le Vas-
seur, Remigio Lambre (s).

1062. LUIS BERTRAND
ISABEL DAVION
October 12, 1781, marriage of Luis Bertrand, native of
this parish, son of Pierre /Bertrand *dit*/ Dauphine and an
Indian named Juana . . . and . . . Isabel Davion, native
of this parish, legitimate daughter of Juan Bautista
Davion and Maria Jacinta Triche. 3 bans. Witnesses:
Juan Bautista Larenaudier (s), Luis Borme (s/ Borme, *fils*),
Juan Bautista Ste. Anne (s/ Ailhaud Ste. Anne), Pedro
Andres (s).

1063. FRANCISCO ROUQUIER
MARIA LUISA PRUDHOMME
May 5, 1782, marriage of Francisco Rouquier, native of
Puileveque /Puylaroque/, diocese of Cahors, legitimate
son of Marte Rouquier and Maria Rouquier. . . and . . .
Maria Luisa Prudhomme, native of this parish, legitimate
daughter of Juan Bautista Prudhomme (s) and Maria Josepha
Colentin. 3 bans. Witnesses: Esteban de Vaugine, com-
mandant (s), Juan Bautista Roujot (s), Pedro Dupain (s),
Pedro Alorge (s), Manuel Prudhomme (s).

1064. PEDRO DOLÉ
MARIA ROSE DUPRES
December 28, 1782, marriage of Pedro Dolé (s/ Dolet), a

native of this parish, legitimate son of Pedro Dole and
Maria Luisa Totin . . . and . . . Maria Rosa Dupres,
native of this parish, legitimate daughter of Joseph
Dupres and Maria de la Encarnacion Derban. 3 bans.
Witnesses: Juan Bautista Labery (s), Athanasio Poisot
(s), Juan Bautista Darban (s), Mauricio De Mouy (s).

1065. PEDRO DERBANNE
MARIA FRANCISCA BREVEL
February 13, 1783, marriage of Pedro Derbanne, native of
Punta Contada /Pointe Coupée/, legitimate son of Pedro
Derban and Maria Le Clert . . . and . . . Maria Francisca Brevel, native of this parish, legitimate daughter of
Juan Bautista Brevel and Francisca Poisot. 3 bans. Witnesses: Marino Grillet (s), Luis Verchaire (s), Juan
Bautista Derban (x), Gaspar Derban (x).

1066. GASPAR FIOL
TERESA LAMALATY
February 17, 1782, marriage of Gaspar Fiol, native of the
parish of Epifonia, bishopric of Tulon in France, legitimate son of Ponce Fiol and Juana Canne . . . and . . .
Teresa Lamalaty, widow of Ignacio Anty, legitimate daughter of Luis Lamalaty and Victoria Garcia. 1 ban. Witnesses: Remy Lambre (s), Andres David (s), Luis Rachal
(s/ Louis Bartelemi Rachal), Pedro Duplaisis (x).

1067. JULIAN RACHAL
MARIA LUISA BREVEL
April 29, 1783, marriage of Julian Rachal, native of this
parish, legitimate son of Luis Rachal and Maria Luisa
Le Roy. . . and . . . Maria Luisa Brevel (x), native of
this parish, legitimate daughter of Juan Bautista Brevel
and Maria Francisca Poisseau. 3 bans. Witnesses: Luis
Verger (s/ Verchair), Marino Grille (s), Luis Monet (s),
Luis Rachal, Jr. (s). Groom also X'd.

1068. ROBERTO MECHIM
FRANCISCA CASSEL (CASTEL?)
May 19, 1783, marriage of Roberto Mechim, native of Baltimore in the province of Pensilvania /sic/, legitimate
son of Guillermo Mechim and Maria Dever . . . and . . .
Francisca Cassel (Castel?), native of Nueva Orleans,
legitimate daughter of Gregorio Castel? and Cecilia
Castel? 3 bans. Witnesses: Luis Fortin, Antonio Le
Fevre, Pedro Broody, Francisco le Maistre. Signed with
four x's and one illegible signature.

1069. SANTIAGO LEVASSEUR
ROSALIA RAMBIN
June 5, 1783, marriage of Santiago Levasseur, native of

this parish, legitimate son of deceased Santiago le Vasseur and Maria Francisca Bourdant, deceased . . . and . . . Rosalia Rambin, native of this parish, legitimate daughter of deceased Andres Rambin and Francisca Clermont. 3 bans. Witnesses: Franco. Rambin (s), Joseph Besson? (s), Andre Borme, *fils* (s).

1070. JUAN BAUTISTA DENIS
MARIA ELIZABETH BEAUDOUIN
August 23, 1783, marriage of Juan Bautista Denis, native of the parish of St. Geneveva, living at Natchitoches for two years, legitimate son of Juan Bautista Denis, *vexsleux?*, and Maria Hubert. . . and . . . Maria Elizabeth Beaudouin, native of this parish, legitimate daughter of Francisco Beaudouin and Maria Anne Bontemps. 3 bans. Witnesses: Carolos Le Moine (x), Estevan Verger (x), Juan Pomier (x), Bernardo Pipe (x).

1071. REMIS TOUTIN
MARGARITA GRILLET
November 15, 1783, marriage of Remis Toutin, native of this parish, legitimate son of Carlos Toutin and Juana Guedon . . . and . . . Margarita Grillet, legitimate daughter of Marin Grillet and Maria Luisa Brevel, habitant of this same post. 3 bans. Witnesses: Juan Bauta. Laberi (s), Juan Bauta. Roujo (s), Mauricio du Muy (s), Estevan Pavie (s), Guillema Le Brun (s).

1072. AMBROSIO LE COMPTE
ELENA CLOUQUIE /CLOUTIER/
December 15, 1783, marriage of Ambrosio Le Compte (x), native and citizen of this parish, legitimate son of Juan Bauta. Le Compte and Margarita Le Roy . . . and . . . Elena Clouquie (x), native of Punta Contado /Pointe Coupée/, legitimate daughter of deceased Alexos Clouquie and Maria Rachal, residents of the same parish. 3 bans. Witnesses: Andres David (s), Santiago Rachal (x), Domingo Davion (x).

1073. MANUEL PRUDHOMME
CATHARINA LAMBRE
January 7, 1784, marriage of Manuel Prudhomme (s), native of this parish, legitimate son of Juan Bautista Prudhomme and Maria Josepha Colentin . . . and . . . Catharina Lambre (s), legitimate daughter of Jayme Lambre and Maria Poisseau, habitant of this post. 3 bans. Witnesses: Jean Lambre (x), Franco. Rouquire (s), Remigio Poisseau (s), Atanasio Poisseau (x), Remy Lambre (s).

1074. JUAN DE ARZE (ANZE?)
FRANCESCA LARENODIERE
January 13, 1784, marriage of Juan de Arze (Anze?), sergeant

of the first battalion of the regiment stationed in Louisiana, legitimate son of Juan de Arze and Leonor de <u>Arcaze</u>?, native of <u>Algeriza</u>? in Spain . . . and . . . Francesca Larenodiere (x), native of this parish, legitimate daughter of Carlos Larenodiere and Juana del Rio /̄de la Riviere_7, habitant of this post. 3 bans. Witnesses: Pedro Sorel (s), Domingo Noguerra (x), Josef Antonio del Castillo (x).

1075. LUIS THOMASINO
CATHARINA LATTIER
February 23, 1784, marriage of Luis Thomasino, native of Barcelona in Catalina, legitimate son of Luis Thomasino and Theresa Soles . . . and . . . Catharina Lattier, a native of this parish, legitimate daughter of Joseph Latie and Ana Verger. 3 bans. Witnesses: Gaspar Darbane (s), Pablo Baille (x), Juan Bautista Darban (x), La Cour (s).

1076. JOSEPH DELORNE
ANTONIA ISIDORA BOISSALIE
May 2, 1784, marriage of Joseph Delorme, native of Montreal in Canada, legitimate son of Joseph Delorne and of Madalena Mel<u>onne</u>? . . . and . . . Antonia Isidora Boissalie, widow of Guillelmo Boissalie. 3 bans. Witnesses: Ignacio Mayeux, Antonio Bascocie /̄Vascoc<u>u</u>_7, Luis Buart (x), Pedro Labery (x).

1077. JUAN BAUTISTA DARBANNE
MARIA ELENA BREVEL
May 13, 1784, marriage of Juan Bautista Darbanne (x), native of this parish, legitimate son of Gaspar Darbanne and Maria Francesca Verger . . . and . . . Maria Elena Brevel (x), native of this parish, legitimate daughter of Juan Bautista Brevel and Francesca Poissoi. 3 bans. Witnesses: Athanasio Poisoi (x), Remigio Poisot (s), Gaspar Darbanne (s), Pedro La Cour (s).

1078. JOSEPH LAURENT (LAURAN)
MARIA MORIN
May 15, 1784, marriage of Joseph Laurent (s/ Joseph Lauran), native of Nueva Orleans, legitimate son of Simon Laurent and Margarita Derban . . . and . . . Maria Morin, "native of the same town," legitimate daughter of Juan Bautista Morin and Catharina Le Vasseur. 3 bans. Witnesses: Juan Bauta. Lambre (x), Joseph Le Vasseur (x), Luis Buar (x), Juan Bautista Morin (x).

1079. JUAN MARCHANT
MARIA DARBAN
May 2<u>2</u>?, 1784, marriage of Juan Marchant, native of New Orleans, legitimate son of Bernardo Marchant and Cecilia Christophe . . . and . . . Maria Darban, widow of Joseph

Dupre, habitant of this post. 1 ban. Witnesses: Juan Vauchere and Antonio Lefevre.

1080. PEDRO LARENODIERE
JUANA LABERY
May 25, 1784, marriage of Pedro Larenodiere, native of this parish, legitimate son of deceased Carlos Larenodiere and Juana del Rio /de la Riviere/ . . . and . . . Juana Labery (s), legitimate daughter of Juan Bautista Labery and Juana Guedon, native of this parish. 3 bans. Witnesses: Juan Bautista Labery (s), Nicolas Lagneau (s), Juan Bautista Larenodiere (s), Franco. Grappe (s).

1081. GASPAR DARBANE
MARIA JOSEPHA PERO
July 26, 1784, marriage of Gaspar Darbane, native of this parish, legitimate son of Gaspar Darbane and Maria Francesca Verger . . . and . . . Maria Josepha Pero, native of this parish, legitimate daughter of deceased Francisco Pero and Chatarine Dupres. 3 bans. Witnesses: Estevan Verger, Franco. Perox, Pedro Darbane, Laland (s).

1082. GUILLELMO CHAVER
JUANA MARGARITA TOTIN
September 20, 1784, marriage of Guillelmo Chaver (x), legitimate son of Guillelmo Chaver and Theresa Barbie, native of this parish . . . and . . . Juana Margarita Totin, widow of Juan Bautista Plaisance. Witnesses: Pedro Du Plaisis (x), Francisco Langlois (x).

1083. PEDRO CHELETRE
MARGARITA REINE FEDERIQUE /FREDERIC/
October 9, 1784, marriage of Pedro Cheletre, native of the parish of S. Carlos on the German Coast of the Missippi, legitimate son of deceased Miguel Chelettre and Anna Barbara Pomie, habitant at this post . . . and . . . Margarita Reine Federique, legitimate daughter of Philipe Federique and Maria Catherina Sauvage, native of the parish of S. Carlos, and habitant of this post. 3 bans. Witnesses: Franco. Bossie (s), Franco. /Le/ Vasseur (x), Juan Bautista Denis (x), Joseph Latie (s/ Joseph).

1084. MICHEL BERNABE CHELETRE
MARIA JOSEPHA GONIN
October 25, 1784, marriage of Michel Bernabé Cheletre, native of the parish of S. Carlos on the German Coast of the Mississippi, legitimate son of deceased Miguel Chelettre and Anna Barbara Pomie . . . and . . . Maria Josepha Gonin, native of this parish, legitimate daughter of Juan Bautista Gonin and Manuela Riche. 3 bans. Witnesses: Juan Bautista du Bois, Phelipe Federique,

Franco. le Compte, Juan Adele (s).

1085. SANTIAGO LE VASSEUR
MARIA THERESA GRILLET
December 29, 1784, marriage of Santiago Le Vasseur (x), widower of Rosalia Rambin, legitimate son of Santiago Le Vasseur and Maria Francisca Bourdon . . . and . . . Maria Theresa Grillet (x), legitimate daughter of Marin Grillet and Maria Luisa Brevel. 3 bans. Witnesses: Remi Poisot (s), Juan Bautista Roujot (s), Andres David (s), Juan de Anze?

1086. JUAN BAUTISTA DE LOUCHE
URSULA BOULET
May 4, 1785, marriage of Juan Bautista de Louche (x), a native of Vernoy in Beie, province of Borgona /Bourgogne?/, legitimate son of Pedro de Louche and Maria Juana Boispoint. . . and . . . Ursula Boulet (x), native of this parish, legitimate daughter of Juan Bautista Boulet and Anna Verges. 3 bans. Witnesses: Pedro Lacour (s), Juan Massip (x), Estevan Verge (x), Antonio Imel (x).

1087. LUIS ENTI /ANTY/
MARIA JUANA CRETE
May 7, 1785, marriage of Luis Enti, native of Punta Contada /Pointe Coupée/, legitimate son of Ignacio Anti and Catharina Guerin, deceased . . . and . . . Maria Juana Crete, native of this parish, legitimate daughter of Pedro Crete and Maria Luisa Vergere, habitant of the same post. 3 bans. Witnesses: Juan Bautista Darbanne (x), Joseph Laurent (s), Luis Barthelemi Rachal (s), Estevan Verges (x).

1088. BARTHEMIO RACHAL
FRANCISCA LABERY
May 9, 1785, marriage of Barthemio Rachal, native of this parish, legitimate son of Luis Rachal and Maria Luisa Le Roy . . . and . . . Francisca Labery, legitimate daughter of Juan Bautista Labery and Juana Guedon, habitant of this parish. 3 bans. Witnesses: Juan Bautista Dartigos (s), Guillelemo Chever (x), Luis Toutin (x), Luis Rachal (x).

1089. PEDRO CHARPENTIER
MARIA RACHAL
May 30, 1785, marriage of Pedro Charpentier (x), native of Montreal, legitimate son of Joseph Charpentier, and Maria Saint Amour . . . and . . . Maria Rachal, widow of Alexos Cloutié, habitant of this parish. 3 bans. Witnesses: Juan Bautista Roujot (s), and Luis Rachal (s).

1090. JUAN BAUTISTA DU BOIS
JUANA RIS
May 31, 1785, marriage of Juan Bautista du Bois (x), native of this parish, legitimate son of Juan Bautista du Bois and Maria Josepha Clermont . . . and . . . Juana Ris (x), legitimate daughter of Miguel Juan Ris and Maria Juana Chagneau. 3 bans. Witnesses: Juan Bautista Du Bois, père (s), Andres Antonio Rambin (s), Antonio du Bois (s), Joseph Juan Ris (s).

1091. PEDRO GAÑON (GAGNON)
THERESA VALENTIN
October 3, 1785, marriage of Pedro Gañon (s/ Gagnon) a native of Chateaux Riche, bishopric of Quebec, legitimate son of Pedro Gañon and Maria Genoveva Rougere (<u>Roupre?</u>) . . . and . . . Theresa Valentin, native of this parish, legitimate daughter of Francisco Valentin and Maria Luis Totin. 3 bans. Witnesses: Juan Bautista du Bois (s), Juan Bautista Roujot (s), Guillaume Le Brun (s), Pedro Larenodiere (x), Andres David (s).

1092. FRANCISCO PEREAU
LUISA AGATHA LABERRY
October 6, 1785, marriage of Francisco Pereau, native of Natchitoches, legitimate son of Francisco Pereau and of Catharina de Pre . . . and . . . Luisa Agatha Laberry (s), native of this parish, legitimate daughter of Juan Bautista Laberi and Juana Guedon. 3 bans. Witnesses: Luis La Malathi (s), Joseph Verger (x), Pedro Larenodiere (x), Barthelemi Rachal (x).

1093. LUIS MONET
MARIA LUISA LE COMPTE
October 11, 1785, marriage of Luis Monet, native of this parish, legitimate son of Pedro Matheo Monet and Isabel Rachal . . . and . . . Maria Luisa Le Compte (x), widow of Juan Bautista De Pres. Witnesses: Estevan Pavie (s), Francisco Rouquire (s).

1094. BARTHOLOME RACHAL
MARIA FRANCISCA GRILLET
November 24, 1785, marriage of Bartholome Rachal, legitimate son of Bartholome Rachal and Maria Luisa Lamaty . . . and . . . Maria Francisca Grillet, native of this parish, legitimate daughter of Marin Grillet and Maria Francisca Brevel. 3 bans. Witnesses: Andres David (s), Santiago La Vesseur (x), Remigio Totin (s), Gaspar Fiol (x).

1095. DOMINGO NOGUERRA
MARIA FRANCISCA ORTIZ
December 5, 1785, marriage of Domingo Noguerra, native

of Sta. Maria de Moreinay in Galicia, soldier of the 2nd company of the regiment stationed in Louisiana, legitimate son of Juan Nogueira and Madalena Taborda . . . and . . . Maria Francisca Ortiz, native of Natchitoches, legitimate daughter of Joseph Maria Ortiz and Juana Hernandez. 3 bans. Witnesses: Pablo Bossie (x), Juan Bautista Saboye (x), Antonio Le Fevre (x).

1096. FRANCISCO LE VASSEUR
MARIA JUANA GRILLET
January 10, 1786, marriage of Francisco Le Vasseur (x), a native of this parish, widower of Maria Juana Madere* . . . and . . . Maria Juana Grillet (x), native of this parish, legitimate daughter of Marin Grillet and Maria Brevel. 3 bans. Witnesses: Louis Bertelmis Rachal (s), Gaspar Philibert (s), L. Verchair (s), Jayme Le Vasseur (x).

*For Le Vasseur-Madere marriage see St. Charles Parish, 1764.

1097. NICOLAS GALIEN
MARIA ANTONIA LECOUR
January 23, 1786, marriage of Nicolas Galien, native of Punta Contada /Pointe Coupée/, legitimate son of Noel Galien and Maria Rachal . . . and . . . Maria Antonia Le Cour, native of this parish, legitimate daughter of Sr. Mathias Le Cour and Juana Le Roy. 3 bans. Witnesses: Estevan de Vaugine, commandant (s), Juan Bautista Bartelemi /Rachal/ (x), Luis Enti (x), Franco. Langlois (s).

1098. EDUARDO MORPHI (MURPHY)
ELIZABETH JOSEPHA BUARD
February 1, 1786, marriage of Eduardo Morphi (s/ E. Murphy), native of the town of Navare in Ireland, legitimate son of Bernabé Morphi and Maria Eugenia Fleming . . . and . . . Elizabeth Josepha Buard (s), native of this parish, legitimate daughter of Gabriel Buard and Maria Ana Rousseau. 3 bans. Witnesses: Andres Antonio Rambin (s), Estevan Pavie (s), Franco. Bosie (s), Juan Bauta. Bosie (s).

1099. LUIS RACHAL
MARIA LABERY
February 27, 1786, marriage of Luis Rachal (x), legitimate son of Luis Rachal and Maria Luisa Le Roy . . . and . . . Maria Labery, legitimate daughter of Juan Bautista Labery and Juana Guedon. 3 bans. Witnesses: Pedro Monet (x), Guillelmo Chaver (x), Bartholome Rachal (x), Luis Rachal (x).

1100. LUIS DAVION
MARIA JOSEPHA GAGNE
April 25, 1786, marriage of Luis Davion (x), legitimate

son of Juan Bautista Davion and Maria Hyacinta Trichele
. . . and . . . Maria Josepha Gagne, legitimate daughter
of Estevan Gagne and Maria Luisa Bertrand. 3 bans. Witnesses: Francois Langlois (s), Gilbert Cloiseau (x),
Luis Bertrand (x), and Juan Bautista Davion (x).

1101. ANDRES BASTCOCU /VASCOCU/
MAGDALENA RAIMOND
June 26, 1786, marriage of Andres Bastcocu (x), son of
Antonio Bastcocu and Maria Barbara Toups . . . and . . .
Magdalena Raimond (x), daughter of Pedro Raimond and
Francisca Raimond. 1 ban. Witnesses: Franco. Prudhome
(x), Anto. Bastcocu (x), Andres Rambin, and Bta. La Re-
naudiere. Fr. Joseph d'Arazen of Opelousas, officiating.

1102. MARIA FRANCESCA FORT
June 25, 1786, baptism of Maria Francesca /birth date
illegible/, legitimate daughter of Jacques Fort and Francesca /Malbert/. Godparents: Phelipe Federico and Franca.
Chelatre. Fr. Joseph d'Arazen of Opelousas, officiating.

1103. PEDRO MAS (MAES)
MARIANA DE ARTIGO
June 27, 1786, marriage of Pedro Mas (s/ P. J. Maes) . . .
and . . . Madame Mariana de Artigo (s), legitimate daughter
of Mr. Pierre de Artigo and Madame Maria Monica de Artigo.
Witnesses: Pierre Dartigaux (s), Louis De Blanc (s),
Pierre Rousseau (s), J. B. Prudhomme (s), E. Pavie (s),
Jh. Capuran (s). Fr. Joseph d'Arazen of Opelousas, offi-
ciating.

1104. MENDOZA
/Month and day illegible/, 1775, burial of a Spaniard
named Mendoza.

1105. LANGLOIS
/Month and day illegible/, 1775, burial of a daughter of
Langlois.

1106. LANGLOIS
/Month and day illegible/, 1775, burial of /illegible/.

1107. JEAN RIS
/No date/, 1775, burial of Jean Ris by the church beadle
and chanter.

1108. ANONYMOUS
September 2?, 1775, burial of a nègre slave of Demezieres.

1109. BARETA
       September 15, 1775, burial of a child, the legitimate son of Bareta.

1110. MARGARITA ROUSAU /MARGUERITE DEMOUY ROUJOT/
       September 18, 1775, burial of the wife of <u>seno?</u> Rousau.

1111. ANONYMOUS
       September 21, 1775, burial of a *nègre* slave of Widow Buart.

1112. ANONYMOUS
       September 2_?, 1775, burial of a *négrite* of Widow Gabriel Buart.

1113. ANONYMOUS
       October 15, 1775, burial of a *nègre* slave of Sr. Piseros.

1114. ANONYMOUS
       October 28, 1775, burial of a *négrita* slave of Prudhomme.

1115. ANONYMOUS
       December 2, 1775, burial of a *nègre* slave of De Mezieres.

1116. ANONYMOUS
       January 13, 1776, burial of a *nègre* slave of Dartigaux.

1117. BODOINNE /BEAUDOIN?/
       February 2_?, 1776, burial of a two year old son of Bodoinne.

1118. BREVELLE
       March 7, 1776, burial of a two year old son of Brevelle.

1119. ANONYMOUS
       March 18, 1776, burial of a *négrito* of Remigio Poissot.

1120. ANONYMOUS
       April 4, 1776, burial of a *nègre* slave of Pavie.

1121. LACOUR
       May 15, 1776, burial of a legitimate son of Monsieur La Cour.

1122. ANONYMOUS
       May 15, 1776, burial of a *nègre* slave of Pedro Derbanne.

1123. GERONIMO MATULICHE
       May 21, 1776, burial of Geronimo Matuliches who died after receiving the last rites of the church.

1124. CHITO
       March? 8, 1776, burial of Chito, a free *nègre*.

1125. THERESA
       June 11, 1776, burial of Theresa, slave of Charbonnet.

1126. ANONYMOUS
       August 27, 1776, burial of a *négrito* of Bartolomé Rachal.

1127. IGNACIO ANTY *alias* LA FORME
       September 12, 1776, burial of Ignacio Anty *alias* La Forme, who died on September 11 after receiving the last rites.

1128. PHELIPE SANCHES
       November 10, 1776, burial of Phelipe Sanches, a native of /illegible/, who died after receiving the last rites.

1129. AUGUSTIN LAURENCE
       November 11, 1776, burial of Augustin Laurence who died after receiving the last rites.

1130. ANONYMOUS
       December 24, 1776, burial of a *nègre* slave of Bautista Trichele.

1131. ANONYMOUS
       December 28, 1776, burial of a *négrito* slave of Senor Mezieres.

1132. ANONYMOUS
       December 28, 1776, burial of a *négrito* slave of Bautista Prudhomme.

1133. PEDRO BESSON
       January 12, 1777, burial of Pedro Besson who died after receiving the last rites.

1134. JUAN MARIA BARGAS
       January 15, 1777, burial of Juan Maria Bargas.

1135. ANONYMOUS
       February 8, 1777, burial of a *nègre* slave of Enrique Trichele.

1136. MARIA ROSA VASCOCU
       February 27, 1777, burial of Maria Rosa, legitimate daughter of Antonio Vascocu.

1137. JUAN GAGNON
       February 29, 1777, burial of Juan Gagnon.

       NOTE: This is a long, involved, and practically illegible entry. It is definitely not an ordinary burial entry.

1138. ANONYMOUS
March 10, 1777, burial of a *nègre* of Gagne.

1139. ANONYMOUS
March 30, 1777, burial of a *mulâtre* belonging to Mr. la Cha____.

1140. MARIA JUANA VASCOCU
April (May?) 12, 1777, burial of Maria Juana, legitimate daughter of Antonio Vascocu, sacristan of this church.

1141. ELENA BAILLIO
June 25, 1777, burial of Elena, legitimate daughter of Baillio.

1142. LUIS GINAN
July 11, 1777, burial of Luis Ginan, native of Canada.

1143. ANONYMOUS
July 12, 1777, burial of an Indian of the house of Morier.

1144. ANONYMOUS
October 15, 1777, burial of a free adult Indian.

1145. TOUTIN
October 16, 1777, burial of a son of Toutin.

1146. BELLEHUNT
October 19, 1777, burial of the wife of Bellehunt.

1147. ROBLEAU?
October 19, 1777, burial of the wife of Miguel Ro<u>bleau?</u>.

1148. ANONYMOUS
October 21, 1777, /Illegible burial entry/.

1149. ANTONIO __ANA__
October 24, 1777, /Illegible burial entry/.

1150. ANONYMOUS
October 27, 1777, burial of a male slave of Bautista Dupres.

1151. ANONYMOUS
October 29, 1777, burial of a free Indian who was baptized before his death.

1152. ANONYMOUS
October 29, 1777, burial of an Indian slave of Jean Baptiste Dupres.

1153. MME. LE COUR
       November 3, 1777, burial of the wife of Monsieur le Cour
       /̄Le Court_/.

1154. ANONYMOUS
       November 4, 1777, burial of a *nègre* slave of Labery.

1155. ANONYMOUS
       November 8, 1777, burial of a *nègre* slave of Widow Grappe.

1156. ANONYMOUS
       November 11, 1777, burial of a *nègre* slave of Villard.

1157. MARIA GUETIERNEZ
       November 13, 1777, burial of the wife of Guetiernez.

1158. AUGUSTE LANGLOIS
       November 16, 1777, burial of Auguste Langlois.

1159. JEAN GUETIERNEZ
       November 17, 1777, burial of Jean, young son of Guetiernez.

1160. PRUDHOMME
       November 19, 1777, burial of a son of Prudhomme.

1161. LA RENAUDIERE
       November 20, 1777, burial of a small daughter of Widow
       La Renaudiere.

1162. MARTIN GUITIERNEZ
       November 20, 1777, burial of Martin Guitiernez.

1163. GUITIERNEZ
       November 22, 1777, burial of a son of Guitiernez.

1164. VILLAREAL
       November 22, 1777, burial of a son of Josef Villareal.

1165. CELICIGORA
       November 26, 1777, burial of Celicigora, a free Indian.

1166. MARIA ANA
       November 26, 1777, burial of a slave of de Mezieres.

1167. JULIAN
       November 29, 1777, burial of Julian, free *nègre*.

1168. ANONYMOUS
       November 30, 1777, burial of a *nègre* slave of Joseph Dupre.

1169. ANONYMOUS
       December 1, 1777, burial of a slave of Jacob Lambre.

1170. MME. TONANT (TENANT?)
December 3, 1777, burial of the wife of T<u>e</u>nant<u>?</u>.

1171. ANONYMOUS
December 3, 1777, burial of an Indian slave of de Mezieres.

1172. BRULOT
December 4, 1777, burial of "the one called Brulot."

1173. MME. BAILLIOT
December 8, 1777, burial of the wife of Bailliot.

1174. CARLOS LANGLOIS
December 8, 1777, burial of Carlos Langlois.

1175. ANONYMOUS
December 10, 1777, burial of a *negrito* of Widow Grappe.

1176. DOUCET
December 9, 1777, burial of "the one called Doucet."

1177. MARIA
December 11, 1777, burial of an Indian slave of de Mezieres.

1178. MARGARITA MARLIE (SOREL)
December 11, 1777, burial of Margarita, daughter of Marlie.

1179. ANONYMOUS
December 11, 1777, burial of a *negrito* of De Blanc.

1180. MME. DE MEZIERES
December 11, 1777, burial of the wife of Commandant de Mezieres.

1181. SANTIAGO
December 12, 1777, burial of Santiago, *negro* slave of St. Denis.

1182. ROCQUE
December ?, 1777, burial of Senor Rocque.

1183. CESAIRIO DE MEZIERES
December ?, 1777, burial of Cesairio de Mezieres.

1184. PEDRO
December ?, 1777, burial of a *negro* slave of de Mezieres.

1185. ANONYMOUS
December 15, 1777, burial of a *negro* of Widow Grappe.

1186. JUAN BAUTISTA LAMBRE
December 17, 1777, burial of Juan Bautista Lambre.

1187. MARIA DE MEZIERES
December 17, 1777, burial of Maria, daughter of Dn. Athanasio de Mezieres.

1188. CATALINA MORIN
December 18, 1777, burial of the wife of Morin.

1189. FAZANGA
December 19, 1777, burial of the young daughter of Senor Fazanga.

1190. MME. SANTIAGO RACHAL
December 23, 1777, burial of the wife of Santiago Rachal.

1191. MARIA GRO
December 23, 1777, burial of Maria Gro, free *negra*.

1192. ANGELICA
January 2, 1778, burial of Angelica, *negra* slave of Poisot.

1193. ENRIQUE TRICHELE
January 7, 1778, burial of Enrique Trichele.

1194. ANONYMOUS
January 7, 1778, burial of a *negro* of Bautista Trichele.

1195. ANONYMOUS
January 8, 1778, burial of a *negrito* belonging to St. Prix.

1196. ANONYMOUS
January 12, 1778, burial of a female Indian of __anant.

1197. ANONYMOUS
January 15, 1778, burial of a *negro* of Francisco Le Vasseur.

1198. FRANCISCA JEAN RIS
January 30, 1778, burial of Francisca Jean Ris.

1199. ANONYMOUS
February 3, 1778, burial of a *negrito* of Andres Esclavon.

1200. LUIS DE ST. DENIS
February 9, 1778, burial of Dn. Luis de St. Denis, who died on the seventh.

1201. ANONYMOUS
February 19, 1778, burial of a *negra* of Villard.

1202. ANTONIO
February 20, 1778, burial of a *negro* slave of Manuel Trichele.

1203. ANONYMOUS
February 22, 1778, burial of a *negrito* belonging to Pedro Derbanne.

1204. SANTIAGO RIDE *alias* LA BELLE FLEUR
March 30, 1778, burial of Santiago Ride *alias* la Belle Fleur.

1205. CESAR
April 10, 1778, burial of Cesar, free *negro*.

1206. ANONYMOUS
April 15, burial of a *negro* of Prudhomme.

1207. MME. DUPAIN
April 16, 1778, burial of the wife of Pedro Dupain.

1208. DUPRES
April 17, 1778, burial of a daughter of Juan Bautista Dupres.

1209. ANONYMOUS
April 21, 1778, burial of a *negrita* of Prudhomme.

1210. ANONYMOUS
April 22, 1778, burial of a *negro* of Joseph Dupres.

1211. /FREDERIC?/
June 9, 1778, burial of a small daughter of the one called Felipe /Frederic?/.

1212. ANONYMOUS
June 11, 1778, burial of a *negrito* of Santiago (Jacob) Lambre.

1213. MATONGE
June 8, 1778, burial of a niece (nephew?) of Matonge *alias* Chavenaut.

1214. ANONYMOUS
August 4, 1778, burial of a *negro* of Juan Lambre.

1215. ANONYMOUS
August 15, 1778, burial of a *negrito* of Luis Gabriel Buart.

1216. ILLEGIBLE
September 22, 1778, burial of a small daughter of Juan Luis? _____ /Illegible/.

1217. LUIS BARRÉTA
October 7, 1778, burial of Luis Barréta.

1218. ANONYMOUS
       October 25, 1778, burial of a *negrito* of Mezieres.

1219. RACHAL
       October 27, 1778, burial of a son of Bartolome Rachal.

1220. ANONYMOUS
       November 8, 1778, burial of a *negra* of Pedro Derbanne.

1221. ANTONIO RICHÉ
       December 17, 1778, burial of Antonio Riché, after the administration of the last rites.

1222. ANONYMOUS
       January 12, 1779, burial of a *negrita* of Widow Buart.

1223. MARIA TERESA ARMAND
       February 22, 1779, burial of Maria Teresa Armand.

1224. SANTIAGO FAZENDE *alias* MORIEN
       February 24, 1779, burial of Santiago Fazende *alias* Morien.

1225. ESTEBAN
       March 13, 1779, burial of a slave of Commandant de Mezieres.

1226. ANONYMOUS
       May? 12, 1779, burial of a *negro* of Bartolome Rachal.

1227. ANONYMOUS
       July 8, 1779, burial of a *mulato* of Labery.

1228. LE DOUX
       ?___ ?, 1779, burial of a son of Le Doux.

1229. MARIA LARENAUDIERE
       September 14, 1779, burial of Maria Larenaudiere who died after receiving the last rites.

1230. LE MOINE
       October 22, 1779, burial of a daughter of Carlos Le Moine.

1231. ANONYMOUS
       October 24, 1779, burial of the wife of a Spaniard of Nacogdoches.

1232. MARIA BARBARA TOUPS
       October 28, 1779, burial of Maria Barbara Toups, wife of Antonio Vascocu, who died after receiving the last rites.

1233. MARIA JUANA D'HUBARDEAU (BARDIER)
       November 20, 1779, burial of Maria Juana Barbier, widow of D'hubardeau.

1234. ANONYMOUS
November 29, 1779, burial of a *negrito* of Bautista Dupres.

1235. ANONYMOUS
December 11, 1779, burial of a *negrito* of Widow Buart.

1236. ANONYMOUS
December 13, 1779, burial of a *negrito* of Jacob Lambre.

1237. MME. CARLOS LEMOINE
January 1, 1780, burial of Mme. Carlos LeMoine, who died after receiving the last rites.

1238. ANONYMOUS
January 2, 1780, burial of a *negro* of Mons. Monteche.

1239. ANONYMOUS
January 3, 1780, burial of a *negra* of Mons. du Bois.

1240. ANONYMOUS
February 4, 1780, burial of a *negrito* of Bta. Dupres.

1241. MME. DOMINIQUE MONTECHE
February 8, 1780, burial of Mme. Dominique Monteche, who died after receiving the last rites.

1242. ANONYMOUS
July 4, 1780, burial of a *negrito* of Pavie.

1243. ANONYMOUS
July 25, 1780, burial of a *negro* of Mons. Prudhomme.

1244. PRUDHOMME
July 25, 1780, burial of a son of Jn. Bta. Prudhomme.

1245. ATANASIO
July 30, 1780, burial of Atanasio, a converted Indian.

1246. ANONYMOUS
September 13, 1780, burial of a *negrita* of Widow Buart.

1247. MARIA JUANA RIS
/‾Illegible‾/, 1780, burial of Maria Juana Ris.

1248. ANONYMOUS
October 18, 1780, burial of a *negrito* of Dn. Manuel Soto.

1249. ANONYMOUS
November 30, 1780, burial of a *negrito* of St. Prix.

1250. ANONYMOUS
December 3, 1780, burial of a *negrito* of Fontenot.

1251. ANONYMOUS
December 6, 1780, burial of a *negrito* of Badin.

1252. ANONYMOUS
December 12, 1780, burial of a white child, a foundling.

1253. TRICHÉ
December 21, 1780, burial of a son of Manuel Triché.

1254. CLAVIS
December 22, 1780, burial of a daughter of Clavis.

1255. ANONYMOUS
January 3, 1781, burial of a *negrito* of Bautista Dupres.

1256. LAFFITTE
January 3?, 1781, burial of a son of Laffitte.

1257. MME. LAFFITTE
January 12, 1781, burial of the wife of La Fitte.

1258. JUAN BAUTISTA DAVION ST. PRIX
February 6, 1781, burial of Juan Bautista Davion /alias/ St. Prix, who died the evening before after receiving the last rites.

1259. LUIS
February 11, 1781, burial of Luis, a converted Indian.

1260. GANIER
February 15, 1781, burial of a son of Ganier.

1261. ANONYMOUS
February 17, 1781, burial of a *negrito* of Mr. Poisot, Sr.

1262. ANONYMOUS
March 13, 1781, burial of a *negrito* of Remigio Poissot, Jr.

1263. ANONYMOUS
April 4, 1781, burial of a *negrito* of Joseph Duprés.

1264. ANONYMOUS
May 25, 1781, burial of a *negrito* of Bta. Dupres.

1265. FREDERIC
July 24, 1781, burial of a son of Francisco Frederic.

1266. ANONYMOUS
July 26, 1781, burial of a *negrito* of Poissot, Sr.

1267.   ANTONIO
        August 23, 1781, burial of Antonio, a converted Indian
        of the Adaise.

1268.   ROBLEAU
        August 25, 1781, burial of a son of Robleau.

1269.   JUAN BAUTISTA DUPRES
        September 1, 1781, burial of Juan Bautista Dupres, about
        fifty years of age, who died on August 31, after receiv-
        ing the last rites.

1270.   RACHAL
        September 9, 1781, burial of a son of Jacques Rachal.

1271.   ANA POISOT
        September 21, 1781, burial of the wife of Sr. Remigio
        Poisot, aged about 72 years, who died that same day after
        the last rites.

1272.   ANONYMOUS
        September 26, 1781, burial of /unknown/.

1273.   WIDOW ALORGE
        October 15, 1781, burial of Widow Alorge who died on the
        14th after receiving the last rites, aged about 70 years.

1274.   FORTIN
        October 15, 1781, burial of a son of Fortin.

1275.   DUPRES
        December 5, 1781, burial of a daughter of Joseph Dupres, Jr.

1276.   ANTONIO FREDERIC
        January 5, 1782, burial of Antonio Frederic.

1277.   ANONYMOUS
        February 13, 1782, burial of a *negrito* of Widow Buart.

1278.   ANONYMOUS
        March 13, 1782, burial of a *negro* slave of Juan Lambre.

1279.   JOSEPH DUPRES
        April 17, 1782, died on April 16, after receiving the last
        rites, aged about 45 years.

1280.   BOUILLIE
        April 25, 1782, burial of Bouillie, a free *negro* of about
        50? years, more or less. Died after receiving last rites.

1281.   DOMINGO MONTECHE
        May 13, 1782, burial of Domingo Monteche, a native of

Italy, about seventy years of age. Died after receiving the last rites.

1282. ANONYMOUS
May 13, 1782, burial of a *mulatillo* of Deblanc, in the "lower part of the cemetery."

1283. MARIA DUPRE
May 19, 1782, burial of Maria, daughter of deceased Joseph Dupre, aged about 7 years.

1284. ANONYMOUS
May 24, 1782, burial of a *negra* slave of Mr. Pavie.

1285. ANONYMOUS
July 7, 1782, burial of a *negrito* slave of Widow Triche.

1286. LAFFITTE
July 27, 1782, burial of a daughter of Bouet Laffitte.

1287. PEDRO BAILLIOT
July 29, 1782, burial of Pedro Bailliot, aged about 50 years, who died on the 28th after receiving the last rites.

1288. ANONYMOUS
August 7, 1782, burial of a *negra* slave of Dartigaux, who was killed on the 6th by lightning during a thunderstorm.

1289. MANDEVILLE
August 12, 1782, burial of Mandeville, a Canadian of about 70 years, who died after receiving the last rites.

1290. LE BRUN
August 15, 1782, burial of a son of Le Brun.

1291. MME. GUILLELMO /LE BRUN/
August 16, 1782, burial of Mme. Guillelmo, who died that same day after receiving last rites.

1292. CONSTANCIA
August 18, 1782, burial of Constancia, *negra* slave of de Mezieres who died after receiving the last rites.

1293. FREDERIC
September 7, 1782, burial of a son of Felipe Frederic.

1294. LA COUR
September 25, 1782, burial of a child of La Cour.

1295. BREVEL
September 29, 1782, burial of a daughter of Brevel.

1296. ANTONIO ST. DENIS
September 30, 1782, burial of Antonio St. Denis.

1297. ANONYMOUS
October 2, 1782, burial of a small slave of Metoyé.

1298. GANNIER
October 5, 1782, burial of a daughter of Gannier.

1299. ANONYMOUS
October 7, 1782, burial of a small Indian slave of Mr. Armant.

1300. POMIER
October 23, 1782, burial of a daughter of Pomier.

1301. FRANCISCO DOUCET
November 5, 1782, burial of Francisco Doucet, who died the same day at the age of 73 (43?), native of this parish. Received last rites.

1302. JACOBO LAMBRE
December 2, 1782, burial of Jacobo Lambre who died the preceding night, about 50 years of age.

1303. JOSEPH
December 6, burial of Joseph, who was baptized before his death.

1304. DORTOLANT
December 23, 1782, burial of a daughter of Dortolant.

1305. VAGAR
January 6, 1783, burial of a son of Gaspar Vagar.

1306. NOTE: The following entry is recorded out of sequence. Text is very blurred. A marginal note, recorded in a different handwriting, reads: *"Mulatillo de Deblanc a hugado. Nina de Dupres."* Roughly translated, the text itself reads:

"In the year 1782, the sixteenth of August, I, /illegible/, certify having buried in the cemetery of this parish of S. Fran^{co} of the post of Natchitoches, the corpse of Maria Luisa,*/illegible/, first /illegible/ with deceased Pedro D_____ /illegible/ and then /illegible/ with Sr. Guillelmo le Brun, after having received the sacraments of the Holy Church. In testimony of which I have signed the same day, month, and year above. Luis de Quintanilla."   */possibly "Totain"/

1307. JUAN BAUTISTA LECOMPTE
May 29, 1784, burial of Juan Bautista LeCompte, husband of Margarita Le Roy.

1308. MARCHAND
July 25, 1784, burial of a son of Jean Marchand and Maria Darban.

1309. MARIA ANTONIA?
August 18?, 1784, burial of a slave of /illegible/.

1310. MARIA ROSA BOISSALIE
August 31, 1784, burial of Maria Rosa Boissalie, wife of Pedro Sorel, who died after receiving the last rites.

1311. ANONYMOUS
December 12, 1784, burial of a *mulatillo* belonging to Mda. Gabriel /Buard/.

1312. ANONYMOUS
December 23, 1784, burial of a *negra* slave of Mr. Dartigo.

1313. ANONYMOUS
January 6, 1785, burial of a *negrito* slave of Mr. Grillet.

1314. MARIA JUANA LE VASSEUR
February 3, 1785, burial of Maria Juana Le Vasseur, wife of Juan Bautista Lambre.

NOTE: Entries 1315-1380 are bound out of sequence in this register.

1315. LUIS LE CLAIR /LE CLERC/
March 15, 1783, burial of Luis LeClair, a native of Paris, aged ninety years.

1316. ANONYMOUS
May 6, 1783, burial of a slave belonging to Mda. Triche.

1317. ANONYMOUS
May 15, 1783, burial of a slave belonging to Mr. Borme?.

1318. ANONYMOUS
May 20, 1783, burial of a *negrito* slave of Juan Lambre.

1319. ANONYMOUS
June 30, 1783, burial of a *negrito* slave of Franco. Le Vasseur.

1320. JUAN LUIS HUMEL /HIMEL/
July 30, 1783, burial of Juan Luis, aged about 7, son of Antonio Humel and Margarita Cheletre.

1321. URSULA DE _____ LECOMPTE
__?__ 1, 1783, burial of Ursula de _____, daughter of Franco. le Compte and Ursula Cha_____. /illegible/

1322. ANONYMOUS
April 7, 1785, burial of a *negra* slave of Julien Besson.

1323. ANONYMOUS
May 9, 1785, burial of a *negro* slave of Mr. Dartigos.

1324. ANONYMOUS
May 22, 1785, burial of a *mulatillo* belonging to Pedro Darban.

1325. GASPAR DARBANNE
June 24, 1785, burial of Gaspar Darbanne, who died after receiving the last rites.

1326. URSULA
July 4, 1785, burial of Ursula, a free *mulata*.

1327. THEOTISTA MASSIP
July 6, 1785, burial of Theotista, aged about three months, daughter of Juan Massip and Maria Le Moine.

1328. ANONYMOUS
August 13, 1785, burial of a *negrito* slave of Pedro Sorel.

1329. PEDRO SOREL
October 15, 1783, burial of Pedro, son of Pedro Sorel and Maria Rosa Boissalie, who died after receiving the last rites.

1330. LA LIME
October 19, 1783, burial of a son of Mr. La Lime.

1331. ANONYMOUS
October 22, 1783, burial of a *negrito* slave of Mr. Dartigo.

1332. JUAN LUIS LE BEUF
November 1, 1783, burial of Juan Luis le Beuf.

1333. LE VASSEUR
November 4, 1783, burial of a son of Franco. Le Vasseur.

1334. ROSALIA RAMBIN
November 8, 1783, burial of the wife of Santiago Le Vasseur.

1335. ANTONIO LA GRENADE
November 20, 1783, burial of Antonio la Grenade.

1336. ANONYMOUS
November 22, 1783, burial of a slave of Mr. Santiago Fort.

1337. ANONYMOUS
November 23, 1783, burial of a *negro* slave of Mr. Prudhomme.

1338. MARIA JUANA MADERE
December 29, 1783, burial of the wife of Fran^{co} Le Vasseur.

1339. PEDRO BROGDIS?
January 10, 1784, died after receiving last rites.

1340. ANONYMOUS
January 25, 1784, burial of a *negro* slave of Mda. Bapta. Triche.

1341. ANONYMOUS
January 28, 1784, burial of a *negro* slave of Mda. Bapta. Triche.

1342. GASPAR VAGAR
February 4, 1784, burial of Gaspar Vagar, husband of Bernarda Fran^{co}. Last rites administered before death.

1343. ANONYMOUS
May 16, 1784, burial of a slave child of Remigio Poissot.

1344. PAVIA
May 25, 1784, burial of a daughter of Mr. Pavia.

1345. BASTIEN PRUDHOMME
January ?, 1787, died "yesterday", in the fiftieth year of his life. Received last rites before death.

1346. ANONYMOUS
February 15, 1787, burial of a *negro* slave of Pierre Derbanne.

1347. ETIENNE PAVIE
June 1, 1787, burial of Etienne Pavie, a merchant at this post, aged about 45 years, a native of the parish of St. Barthelemy of La Rochelle, legitimate son of Joseph Pavie and Marie Jeanne Couze, who was killed on May ?, by an assassin, at his house on Red River. /remainder illegible/.

1348. MARIN?
On the same day as above, there was buried a male slave of Mr. Etienne Pavie, who was killed by an assassin on the same day as Mr. Pavie.

1349. ILLEGIBLE
On the same day as above, there was buried a *nègre* slave of Mr. Etienne Pavie, who was killed by an assassin on the same day as Mr. Pavie.

1350. ILLEGIBLE
/Same day as above; entry illegible./

1351. ANONYMOUS
August 23, 1787, burial of an infant slave, aged two years, property of Mr. Cha_____. The infant died the previous day.

1352. ANONYMOUS
September 15, 1787, burial of a *nègre* slave, who died the previous day, property of Widow Grappe.

1353. ANONYMOUS
November 4, 1787, burial of a *mulâtre* slave who died the previous day, property of Emmanuel Prudhomme.

1354. ANONYMOUS
November 5, 1787, burial of an infant slave of about two years, property of Mr. ___stage /Lestage/.

1355. BAILLIO
November 5, 1787, burial of Dlle. Baillio, who died on the 4th, at the age of twelve years.

1356. LESTAGE
November 6, 1787, burial of an infant of Mr. Lestage, about one year of age, who died the preceding day.

1357. JEAN BAPTISTE BOSSIE
November 9, 1787, burial of Jean Baptiste Bossie who died on November 8.

1358. JEAN BAPTISTE PRUDHOMME
October 21, 1786, burial of Jean Baptiste Prudhomme, *chirurgien*, aged about 50 years, who died after receiving the last rites.

1359. ANONYMOUS
October 22, 1786, "was buried in the place of interment of the community of the faithful, with the ordinary funeral ceremonies, a citizen who had lived with decency and who left behind him a very honest family."

1360. ANONYMOUS
October 23, 1786, burial of a female Indian who died the previous day.

1361. ANONYMOUS
 October 23, 1786, burial of a *nègre* slave of Mr. <u>Pomiles?</u>.

1362. ANONYMOUS
 November 1, 1786, burial of a slave infant of about three months, property of Mr. Rouquier.

1363. ANONYMOUS
 November 8, 1786, burial of slave infant of Mr. Morphil who died that same day.

1364. ANONYMOUS
 November 8, 1786, burial of a slave of Mr. Dolet who died on the seventh.

1365. ANONYMOUS
 November 8, 1786, burial of a slave of Mr. Deblanc, who died on the seventh.

1366. ANONYMOUS
 November 8, 1786, burial of a *nègre* slave of Monsieur Dartigaux.

1367. ANONYMOUS
 November 27, 1786, burial of a *nègre* slave of Widow Prudhomme, who died on November 26.

1368. ANONYMOUS
 November 29, 1786, burial of a slave who died on the 28th, property of Mr. DeBlanc, (a *nègre*).

1369. ANONYMOUS
 November 29, 1786, burial of a *nègre* slave of Mr. Capuran.

1370. ANONYMOUS
 November 30, 1786, burial of a *négresse* of Mde. De Blanc who died on the 29th.

1371. ANONYMOUS
 November 30, 1786, burial of a *négrillon* of Mr. De Blanc.

1372. ANONYMOUS
 December 1, 1787, burial of a *nègre* of Widow Prudhomme who had died the day before.

1373. ANONYMOUS
 December 7, 1787, burial of a *négresse* of Mr. Durand, the tailor; the slave died the day before.

1374. <u>THERESE?</u> TRICHE
 December 9, 1787, burial of <u>Therese?</u>, daughter of Widow B. Triche, who died the day before, aged 15 years.

1375. ANONYMOUS
December 10, 1787, burial of a *mulâtre* of Mr. Poissot.

1376. WIDOW CHAGNEAU
November 15, 1786, burial of Widow Chagneau who died the day before at the age of 55 years. Last rites administered.

1377. ANONYMOUS
November 16, 1786, burial of a slave child, aged one year, property of Mr. Gaspard Derbanne.

1378. ANONYMOUS
November 26, 1786, burial of a *négrillon*, a slave who died the day before, property of Etienne Pavie.

1379. ANONYMOUS
November ?, 1786, burial of a *nègre* slave of Mde. Widow Grappe.

1380. JEAN LOUIS CESAR BORME
January 29, 1787, burial of Jean Louis Cesar Borme, captain of the militia, son of Joseph and Anne <u>Rouvieres?</u> Borme, born at Pignans, diocese of /illegible/, on March 10, 1721; died after receiving the sacraments. "He had shown very Christian sentiments; he had confessed to us, the undersigned /illegible/ the 27th of the month /illegible/, has been buried on the 29th in the cemetery of the parish. Mr. /illegible/, commandant, the officers and the troops of the militia all accompanied by the /illegible/, have rendered the military honors that were due to his rank." Borme died January 28.

1381. RAMBIN
December 11, 1787, burial of a child of Mr. Rambin who died on December 10.

1382. ANONYMOUS
December 11, 1787, burial of a *négrillon* slave of Mr. Louis Buard.

1383. ANONYMOUS
December 11, 1787, burial of a *mulâtre* slave of Pierre Derbanne.

1384. RACHALLI?
December 12, 1787, burial of a child who died the day before, at the age of fourteen years. /Marginal note reads "<u>Rachalli?</u>" Name is totally illegible in text./

1385. ANONYMOUS
December 12, 1787, burial of a *mulâtresse* slave of Louis Buard.

1386. CHINO
December 12, 1787, burial of Chino, a free *mulâtre*, who died after receiving the sacraments of confession and extreme unction.

1387. GENEVIEVE NEBEL?
December 16, 1787, burial of Genevieve, who died the day before after receiving the last rites.

1388. DLLE. BARTHELEMY RACHAL?
December 17, 1787, burial of Dlle. Barthelemy Rachal?, who died "yesterday," at the age of 18.

1389. WIDOW BARTHELEMY RACHAL
December 17, 1787, burial of Widow Barthelemy Rachal.

1390. ANONYMOUS
December 21, 1787, burial of a slave child, aged about two years, who died the day before; property of Louis Bertrand.

1391. TOTIN
December 21, 1787, burial of a small infant of Louis Totin, who died the day before.

1392. GAGNE
December 22, 1787, burial of a small infant of Etienne Gagne; died December 21.

1393. ARMAND
December 28, 1787, burial of a small infant of Mr. Armand, died December 27.

1394. ANONYMOUS
December 28, 1787, burial of a *nègre* slave of Pierre Derbanne; died December 27.

1395. ILLEGIBLE (MARLY?)
December 28, 1787, burial of an infant or a slave of Marly, who died December 27.

1396. ILLEGIBLE
December 28, 1787, burial of [illegible], died December 27 at the age of forty years.

1397. ILLEGIBLE
December 28, 1787, burial of a small infant of Dame Jh. _____, died December 27, 1787.

1398. RAMBIN
December 29, 1787, burial of small infant of Andre Rambin, died December 28.

1399. MASSIP
       December 30, 1787, burial of a small infant of Jean Massip; died December 29.

1400. ANONYMOUS
       January 1, 1788, burial of a small *mulâtresse* slave of Mr. Armand; died December 31.

1401. ANONYMOUS
       January 1, 1788, burial of a *négresse* slave of Mr. Malige; died December 31.

1402. ANONYMOUS
       January 1, 1788, burial of an Indian slave, a female, who died December 31.

1403. ILLEGIBLE
       January 1, 1788, burial, /remainder of entry illegible/.

1404. CAVAILLEZ
       January ?, 1788, burial of Cavaillez, who died the day before, at the age of forty years, after receiving the last rites.

1405. ANONYMOUS
       January 5, 1788, burial of a *négrillon* slave of Gabriel Buard.

1406. ANTY
       January 11, 1788, burial of a small infant of Louis Anty; died January 10.

1407. ANONYMOUS
       January 11, 1788, burial of a *négresse* slave of Mr. Mas.

1408. ILLEGIBLE

1409. DUBOS
       January 23, 1788, burial of an infant of Francois Dubos; died January 22.

1410. ANONYMOUS
       January 23, 1788, burial of a *nègre* slave of Widow Grappe.

1411. ANONYMOUS
       February 3, 1788, burial of a *négrillon* slave of Widow J. B. Hubardeaux; died February 2.

1412. GRILLET
       February 7, 1788, burial of Monsieur Grillet with military honors; died February 6 after receiving last rites.

1413. ANONYMOUS
       February 7, 1788, burial of a *nègre* slave of Widow Grappe.

1414. SR. FREDERIC
       February 12, 1788, burial of Sr. Frederic who died February 11 after receiving the last rites, aged 43 years.

1415. RABALE
       February 12, 1788, burial of a small infant of Jh. Rabale.

1416. TOMASSIN
       February 13, 1788, burial of a small child, aged 4?, son of Louis Tomassin; died February 12.

1417. WIDOW JN. BTE. PRUDHOMME
       February 17, 1788, burial of Widow Jn. Bte. Prud'homme who died February 16 at her home, aged about fifty years, having displayed during her life all the grand sentiments of her religion.

1418. MAGNON
       March 1, 1788, burial of Magnon, who died the day before, after receiving the last rites.

1419. WIDOW ST. DENIS /LOUISE MARGUERITE DERBANNE/
       March 16, 1788, burial of the widow St. Denis, died March 15, about 80 years of age.

1420. ANONYMOUS
       March 25, 1788, burial of a small *mulâtre* slave of Sr. Metoyer who died March 24.

1421. DAME GAGNON
       July ?, 1788, burial of Dame Gagnon, who died the day before, with last rites; aged 33 years.

1422. ANONYMOUS
       August 8, burial of a small free *mulâtre*, son of /Illegible/, who died August 7 at the home of Mr. Badin.

1423. DAME LOUIS RACHAL
       ? 4, 1788, burial of Dame Louis Rachal, who died on the 3rd, at the age of fifty years or about.

1424. DAME BADIN
       October 8, 1788, burial of Dame Badin, who died October 7, at the age of about sixty years*.

       *This entry is broken by a full page that is bound out of sequence. Only one entry (No. 1425 which follows) is recorded on the misbound page.

1425. PIERRE DARTIGAUX
May 15, 1788, death of Pierre Dartigaux, merchant, native of the province of Gascogne and the environs of T<u>asbe</u>? (T<u>arbe</u>?), in France; aged about fifty years. "In his illness he had shown true Christian sentiments." Dartigaux was buried May 16 "with the funeral services due a Christian who has lived with decency and left a very honorable family."

1426. DAME DORTOLAND
November 1, 1788, burial of Dame Dortoland who died the day before, after receiving last rites; aged 35 years.

1427. FRANCOIS LE VASSEUR
January 4, 1789, burial of Francois Le Vasseur, who died the day before, at the age of eighteen years, after receiving the last rites.

1428. ANONYMOUS
January 5, 1789, burial of an Indian living with Sr. Remy Totin; died January 4.

1429. ANTOINE GUILHARD
January 6, 1789, burial of Antoine Guilhard, who died January 5, at the age of fifty years, after receiving the last rites.

1430. MARIE JEANNE BUARD
January 10, 1789, burial of Marie Jeanne Buard who died the night before after receiving last rites.

1431. BOSSIE
January ?, 1789, burial of a child of Silvestre Bossie, aged 1 year, who died the day before.

1432. PIERROT
January 19, 1789, burial of Pierrot, *nègre* of Dubös, who died January 18.

1433. ANONYMOUS
January 20, 1789, burial of a *négrillon* slave of Baptiste Dartigaux; died January 19.

1434. ANONYMOUS
January 21, 1789, burial of a free *mulâtre*, small child of Agnes, free *mulâtresse*.

1435. ANTOINE PAVIA
January 25, 1789, burial of Antoine Pavia, who died on the 24th.

1436. ANONYMOUS
January 25, 1789, burial of a small slave girl of two months, property of Sr. /Illegible/, deceased.

1437. DURAND CHARPENTIER /DURAND, *charpentier*?/
January 25, 1789, burial of Durand Charpentier /possibly "Durand, *charpentier*" (carpenter)/, who died January 24 at the age of fifty years or about.

1438. ILLEGIBLE
February 26, 1789, burial of a small child who died the previous day.

1439. A_____ LANGLOIS *dit* FIFI
May 15, 1789, burial of A_____ Langlois, who died the previous evening.

1440. ANONYMOUS
June 9, 1789, burial of a slave child of Etienne Verger.

1441. ANONYMOUS
September 4, 1789, burial of a slave child of one year, who died September 3 /owner illegible/.

1442. ANONYMOUS
September 4, 1789, burial of a *négrillon* slave of Sr. Pierre Derbanne; died September 3.

1443. ANONYMOUS
January 11, 1790, burial of a *négrillon* slave of Remy Lambre; died January 10.

1444. ANONYMOUS
January 15, 1790, burial of a *nègre* slave of Louis Rachal, died January 15.

1445. ANONYMOUS
/Illegible/, 1790, burial of a *nègre* slave of Buard.

1446. DUBOI
April 15?, 1790, burial of Mr. Duboi, who died the previous day.

1447. ANONYMOUS
April 18, 1790, burial of a *nègre* slave of Francisco Prudhomme; died April 17.

1448. SOREL *dit* MARLY
July 21, 1790, burial of Sorel *dit* Marly; died July 20 at his home.

1449. ANONYMOUS
August 12, 1790, burial of a *négrillon* slave of Mr. Metoyer,

who died August 11.

1450. ANONYMOUS
Septembre 8, 1790, burial of a *négrillon* slave of Remy Lambre.

1451. ANONYMOUS
September 8, 1790, burial of a slave of Widow Gabriel Buard; died September 7.

1452. ANONYMOUS
October 1, 1790, burial of a *nègre* slave of Widow Grappe; died September 30.

1453. ANONYMOUS
October 15, 1790, burial of a *nègre* slave of Widow Gabriel Buard; died October 14.

1454. ANONYMOUS
October 17, 1790, burial of a *nègre* slave of Manuel Prudhomme; died October 16.

1455. ANONYMOUS
October 20, 1790, burial of a *mulâtre* belonging to Pierre Derbanne; died October 19.

1456. ILLEGIBLE
November 9, 1790, burial of an infant who died November 8; /name of father illegible/.

1457. DUBOI
November 11, 1790, burial of an infant of Francois Duboi; died November 10.

1458. ANONYMOUS
December 13, 1790, burial of a *négritte* of Remy Lambre; died December 12.

1459. ANONYMOUS
December 19, 1790, burial of a *négrillon* of Pierre Derbanne.

1460. /ENTRY TORN/
December 20, 1790, burial of an infant of Baptiste /torn/; died December 19.

1461. ANONYMOUS
December 31, 1790, burial of a *négrillon* of Louis Buard; died December 30, 1790.

1462. DERBANNE
February 4, 1791, burial of an infant of Baptiste Derbanne; died February 3.

1463. ANONYMOUS
February 6, 1791, burial of a *négrillon* of Mr. Rouquier.

1464. CUPIDON
February 22, 1791, burial of Cupidon, *nègre* of Mr. Monette; died February 21.

1465. SUSANNE
April 12, 1791, burial of Susanne, Indian; died April 11.

1466. AUGUSTIN
April 15, 1791, burial of a *négrillon* of Widow Jacob Lambre.

1467. ANONYMOUS
April 20, 1791, burial of an unknown person who died on the 19th in the house of Mr. Badin.

1468. ANONYMOUS
April 23, 1791, burial of a *nègre* of Widow Trichel?.

1469. GONZALES
April 25, 1791, burial of Gonzales, a traveller.

1470. JEAN BAPTISTE MORIN
May 11, 1791, burial of Jean Baptiste Morin; died May 10.

1471. JEAN LOUIS
May 12, 1791, burial of Jean Louis, *nègre* of Widow Jacob Lambre.

1472. CHALER
May 27, 1791, burial of a daughter of Pierre Chaler.

1473. CHELETRE
June 7, 1791, burial of an infant of Barnabe Cheletre, a son, who died June 6 at the age of twelve days.

1474. ANONYMOUS
June 21, 1791, burial of a *négrillon*, aged nine days, property of Mr. Brevel.

1475. ANONYMOUS
June 23, 1791, burial of a *négrillon*, slave of Manuel Prudhomme.

REGISTER 3

1476. JEAN BAPTISTE GAGNÉ
September 8, 1786, baptism of Jean Baptiste, born August 30, legitimate son of Etienne Gagné, joiner and carpenter, and Louise Bertrand, his wife. Godparents: Louis Davion, habitant (x), and Marie l'Incarnation /Pereau/ (x).

1477. JEANNE
September 8, 1786, burial of a *négresse* of Mr. Derbanne, who died September 7 at the age of 45, after receiving the last rites.

1478. PIERRE CAZEAUX *dit* FAULEVANT
MARIANNE BONTON
September 5, 1786, marriage of Pierre Cazeaux *dit* Faulevant, son of Pierre Cazeaux and Thereze Christophe . . . and . . . Marianne Bonton, daughter of Pierre Bonton and of Fanchon Botson, widow of Francois Beaudouan, hunter; both habitants of this parish. One ban. Witnesses: Pierre Charpentier (x), Joseph Latier (s/ Joseph), farmer.

1479. JEAN BAPTISTE
September 6, 1786, baptism of Jean Baptiste, born August 15, son of Agnes, free *mulâtresse*. Godparents: Silvester Bossié (s), *orfèvre* /goldsmith or silversmith/, and Marie Louise Dupree.

1480. PIERRE CHALER
*/MARIE VICTOIRE/ DERBANNE
September 6, 1786, after publication of one ban, marriage of Pierre Chaler, son of Francois Chaler and of Marie Louise /torn/ . . . and . . . /torn/* Derbanne, daughter of /torn/.* Witnesses: Pierre Derbanne, Sr.; Pierre Derbanne, *fils* (s), Edouard Morphy (s), Francois Bossié (s), Jean Baptiste Bossié (s). Also signed by Pierre Chaler and one X.

*According to a Chaler-Derbanne marital dispensation reprinted in *The Louisiana Genealogical Register*, XVIII (September 1971), 210, the first wife of Pierre Chaler was Marie Victoire Derbanne, daughter of Pierre.

NOTE: In rebinding this register, pages 1 and 2 were reversed. As bound, Entry 1480 begins at the bottom of page 2 and is finished at the top of page 1.

1481. JEAN
September 9, 1786, burial of Jean, *nègre* of about 30 years, property of Mr. Pomie, habitant. Deceased drowned on September 8.

1482. ETIENNE MASSIPE
September 10, 1786, baptism of Etienne, born "about the first of August last," legitimate son of Jean Massip and Marie Lemoine, his wife, habitants. Godparents: Etienne Pavie (s), merchant, and Dame Therese Pavie (s).

1483. JEAN BAPTISTE VILDEC *dit* PEROT
September 10, 1786, baptism of Jean Baptiste, born December 11, 1785, legitimate son of Francois Barthelemy Pereau and Agate Labayrie, his wife. Godparents: Jean Baptiste Labayrie (s/ Laberry) and Jeane Guedon (x), both habitants.

1484. CATHERINE ANNE TOMAZIN
September 10, 1786, baptism of Catherine Anne, born August 28, 1786, legitimate daughter of Louis Tomazin and Catherine Latier. Godparents: Joseph Latier (x) and Anne Robin (x), both habitants. (f)

1485. MARIE LOUISE GAGNON
September 10, 1786, baptism of Marie Louise, born August 29, 1786, legitimate daughter of Piere Gagnon and Marie Thereze Valentin. Godparents: Guilhaumme Chever (x) and Marguerite Totin.

1486. ATHANAS
September 10, 1786, baptism of Athanas, born May 22, son of _____, *nègre,* belonging to Messire Pierre Rousseau, commandant of this post, and of Marie Louise, *nègresse* belonging to Madame St. Denis. Godparents: Dominique Davion (x) and Marie Antoine (s).

1487. CHARLES
September 10, 1786, baptism of Charles, born April 30, 1786, son of Pierran, *nègre,* belonging to Jean Labayrie, and of Catherine, property of the same. Godparents: Jean Baptiste, *nègre* of Pierre Rousseau, commandant, and Augustine, *nègresse* of Mr. Labayrie.

1488. MARIE FRANCOISE
September 10, 1786, baptism of Marie Francoise, born July 13, 1786, daughter of Jean Baptiste, *nègre* of Mr. Maytaye, and Jeane, *nègresse* of Dame Widow Buart. Godparents: Louis Alexandre, *nègre* of Louis Buard, and Ursulle, *nègresse* of Demoiselle Buard.

1489. AUGUSTIN
September 10, 1786, baptism of Augustin, son of ____ Baptiste

nègre of Mr. Dartigaux, and of _____, *négresse* of the same. Godparents: Nicolas Augustin, *nègre* of Mr. Metaye, and Marie Louise, *négresse* of Mr. Dartigaux.

1490. AGATHE LESTAGE
September 17, 1786, baptism of Agathe, born August 7, legitimate daughter of Guillhaumme Lestage and Manuelle Richet, habitants. Godparents: Pierre Metoyer (s) and Genevieve Gonin (x).

1491. JEAN BAPTISTE LECOMPTE
September 17, 1786, baptism of Jean Baptiste, born June 13, legitimate son of /Ambroise/ Lecompte and Helene /Cloutier/. Godparents: Alexis Cloutier (x) and Marie Louise Lecompte (x), habitants.

1492. STANISLAS
September 24, 1786, baptism of Stanislas, born July 26, son of Marie Francoise, *négresse* of Mr. Derbanne. Godparents: Remi Poissot, *fils* (x) and Marie Antoine Bastien (s) /same signature as that of Marie Antoine, Entry 1406/.

1493. MARIE FROZINE
October 1, 1786, baptism of Marie Frozine, born September 16, daughter of Louis, *nègre* of Mr. Derbanne, and of Genevieve, *négresse* of the same. Godparents: Joseph Marcel Soto (s) and Marie Louise Lecompte Monet (x).

1494. MARIE JEANNE RABALÉ
October 15, 1786, baptism of Marie Jeanne, legitimate daughter of Joseph Rabalé and Marie Louise Malbert, habitants of Avoyelles. Godparents: Joseph Vergé (x) and Marie Jeane Vergé Malbert (s). (f)

1495. MARIE LUCE RACHAL
November 5, 1786, baptism of Marie Luce, born October 17, legitimate daughter of Louis Barthelemi Rachal and Marie Francoise Grillé, habitants. Godparents: Louis Lamalaty (s) and Marie Louise Rachal (x).

1496. JEAN BAPTISTE AILHAUD STE. ANNE
MARIE LOUISE BUARD
December 7, 1786, after publication of one ban, marriage of Jean Baptiste Ailhaud Ste. Anne (s), native of /le/ Poet, diocese of Gap in province of Dauphine . . . and . . . Marie Louise Buard (s), native of this parish. Witnesses: Etienne Marafret Layssard (s), commandant of Rapides; Louis Charles Deblanc (s), captain of the cavalry forces at this place; Etienne Pavie (s), merchant at this place; Pierre Metoyer (s), habitant at this place; François Monginot (s), *medecin*; and Remi Lambre (s), habitant.

1497. CHARLES DURET
MARIE ELEONORE BASTIEN PRUD'HOMME
December 12, 1786, marriage of Charles Duret (x), native of the town of Quebec . . . and . . . Marie Eleonore Bastien Prud'homme (x), native of this parish. 2 bans. Witnesses: Pierre Gagnon (s), carpenter; François Rambint (s), tailor; and Emmanuel Prud'homme (s) and Guilhaumme Chever (x), both habitants.

1498. JEAN BAPTISTE MAURIN
JEANE RACHAL
December 12, 1786, after publication of one ban, marriage of Jean Baptiste Morin (s/ Maurin), native of Bordeaux . . . and . . . Jeane Rachal, widow of deceased Mr. Rompré. Witnesses: Etienne de Vaugine (s), Francois Monginot, doctor (s), Jean Massip, and Charles le Moine, all habitants.

1499. MARIE AGATHE TOTIN
December 17, 1786, baptism of Marie Agathe, born November 20, 1786, legitimate daughter of Remy Totin and Margueritte Grillet. Godparents: Gaspard Filibert (s/ Luc Gaspard Philibert) and Rosalie Vercher (x).

1500. ATHANASE DE MEZIERES
December 18, 1786, recording by Fr. Juan Delvaux, under orders of Commandant Pierre Rousseau, of an "Extract from the Registers of the Parish of St. Antoine de Bexar."

"I certify that . . . the following was recorded in Folio 94: 'In the parish church of the town of Sn. Fernand, Presidio de Sn. Antonio de Bexar, on the third day of the month of November, in the year 1779, I buried Dn. Athanazio de Mezieres, Chevalier of the Order of St. Louis and Commandant of the post of Natchitoches, province of Louisiana, widower in second nuptials of Da. Pelagia Fazende, with last rites.' s/ A. Bx Pedro Fuenta."

1501. MARIE JOSEPH FRANCOISE RACHAL
December 25, 1786, baptism of Marie Joseph Francoise, born October 24, 1786, legitimate daughter of Louis Rachal and Marie Joseph Labayrie. Godparents: Mr. Monginot, doctor (s), and Marie Louise Leroy (x). (f)

1502. JEAN BAPTISTE TIMOTHÉE ADLÉ
December 31, 1786, baptism of Jean Baptiste Timothée, born October 20, legitimate son of Jean Adelay and Marie Genevieve Dubös. Godparents: Jean Baptiste Larenaudiere (s) and Marie Francoise Grappe (s). (f)

1503. MARIE URSULLE /LE/ VASSEUR
January 1, 1787, baptism of Marie Ursulle, born October 21,

1786, legitimate daughter of Francois Vasseur and Marie Jeanne Grillet. Godparents: Jacques Le Vasseur (s) and Marie Jeanne Lambre (s).

1504. JEAN PIERRE FRANCOIS SEVERIN LARENAUDIERE
January 6, 1787, baptism of Jean Pierre Francois Severin, born December 6, 1786, legitimate son of Pierre Larenaudiere and Jeane Labayrie. Godparents: Barthelemy Chabais, merchant (s), and Magdelaine Labayrie (x).

1505. ANTOINE RACHALLE
MARIE LOUISE LEMOINE
January 6, 1787, after two bans, marriage of Antoine Rachalle, son of Louis Rachalle and Marie Louise Leroy, a native of this parish . . . and . . . Marie Louise Lemoine, daughter of Charles Le Moine and Ysabelle Dupre. Witnesses: Mr. Morin (s), Joseph Sauvage (s), Jean Massip.

1506. MARIE PELAGIE MELANIE BOSSIÉ
January 21, 1787, baptism of Marie Pelagie Melanie, born December 31, 1786, legitimate daughter of Jean Baptiste Bossié, gold and silver smith, and Marie Ste. Geme. Godparents: Joseph Ste. Geme (s/ joseph Saindem) and Pelagie Lambre (s).

1507. MARIE PELAGIE MODESTE BERTRAND
January 21, 1787, baptism of Marie Pelagie Modeste, born December 31, 1786, legitimate daughter of Louis Bertrand and Ysabelle Davion. Godparents: Louis Davion (x) and Ursule Gagne (x).

1508. PAUL ALEXANDRE DERBANNE
January 31, 1787, at 10 o'clock A. M., baptism of Paul Alexandre, born January 25, legitimate son of Baptiste Derbanne and Magdelaine Brevel. Godparents: Emmanuel Prud'homme (s) and Pelagie Brevel.

1509. LOUIS CESAR ANTY
February 4, 1787, at one o'clock P.M., baptism of Louis Cesar, born January 4, 1787, legitimate son of Louis Anty and Marie Jeanne Crete. Godparents: Pierre Lacour (x) and Therese Lamalaty Gaspard /Fiol/ (x).

1510. JACQUES DANIEL BERRIER
MARIE FRANCOISE VASCOCU
February 11, 1787, after publication of one ban, marriage of Jacques Daniel Berrier (s), native of St. Martin d' Arosa, diocese of Man /Mon?/, habitant of this parish . . . and . . . Marie Francoise Vascocu (x). Witnesses: Francois Prudhomme (x) and Louis Combas (s).

1511. MARIE LOUISE MAŸOU
March 3, 1787, at 11 a.m., baptism of Marie Louise, born February 7, legitimate daughter of Ignace Maÿou and Therese Flibot. Godparents: Antoine le Noir (x) and Marie Rondin (x). (f)

1512. MARIE ANNE ROUQUIER
March 6, 1787, at 3 p.m., baptism of Marie Anne, born July 21, 1786, legitimate daughter of François Rouquier (s), merchant of this post, and Dame Marie Louise Prud'homme (s). Godparents: Pedro Rousseau (s), captain and commandant, and Catherine Milhet Rousseau (s).

1513. JEAN PIERRE CHELETRE
March 11, 1787, at 1 p.m., baptism of Jean Pierre, born February 21, 1787, legitimate son of Pierre Chelet and of Margueritte Frederic, habitants. Godparents: Philippe Frederic (x) and Anne Barbe Pommier (x). (f)

1514. FRANCOIS ISIDORE DUBOË
March 13, 1787, at six p.m., baptism of Francois Isidore, born February 22, legitimate son of Francois Duboë and of Eleonore Jeanne Ryse. Godparents: Jean Baptiste Duboe (s/ Bte Dubois *g. père*) and Marie Jeanne Chagne.

1515. LOUIS CESAR
March 27, 1787, at 10 a.m., baptism of Louis Cesar, born March 11, legitimate son of Bernard, a free *négresse*. Godparents: Etienne de Vaugine, *fils* (s) and Marie Lambre (s).

1516. BERNARD RENOY
March 28, 1787, baptism of Bernard, born March 14, legitimate son of Joseph Renoy and Marie Mercier. Godparents: Bernard Dortolant, lieutenant of the cavalry (s), and Marianne Dortolant (x).

1517. MARIE EMILIE ARMANT
April 1, 1787, at 3 p.m., baptism of Marie Emilie, born January 14, legitimate daughter of Joseph Marie Armant, merchant, and Marie Therese Le Gro. Godparents: Pierre Joseph Maes, merchant (s), and Marie Serpante Badin (s).

1518. FRANCOIS LAVESPERE
MARIE LOUISE DERBANNE
April 20, 1787, at 4 p.m., after 1 ban, marriage of Francois Lavespere (s), native of Bordeaux, legitimate son of Jean Lavespere and Magdelaine Angevais . . . and . . . Marie Louise Derbanne (x), native of this parish, legitimate daughter of Pierre Derbanne and Marie Lecler. Witnesses: François Rouquier (s), merchant; François Bossic (s), merchant; François Chabus (s), merchant, and François Marie Monginot (s), doctor.

1519. LOUIS NEUVILLE DOLET
April 28, 1787, at 4 p.m., baptism of Louis Neuville, born April 7, legitimate son of Pierre Dolet and Marie Ane Dupre. Godparents: Louis Lambre (s) and Marie Francoise Vergé.

1520. FRANCOIS AUGUSTIN BUARD
May 6, 1787, at 10 a.m., baptism of François, born April 20, legitimate son of Louis Buard and Marie Lambre. Godparents: François Augustin Buard (x) and Marie Jeanne Lambre (s).

1521. MARIE JEANNE FROSINE (PHROSINE) GALIEN
May 27, 1787, baptism of Marie Jeanne Frosine (Phrosine), born November 2, 1786, legitimate daughter of Nicolas Galien and Marie Ana Lecour. Godparents: Pierre Charpentier (x) and Francoise Le Cour (x). (f)

1522. DENIS COVECHI
June 24, 1787, at 10 a.m., baptism of Denis, born October 12, 1784, legitimate son of Jean Covechi and Nency Hochel. Godparents: Jean Lambre (x) and Marie Lambre (s).

1523. JULIEN GAGNÉ
July 22, 1787, at 8 a.m., baptism of Julien, born July 10, legitimate son of Pierre Gagné and Marie Louise Davion, habitants. Godparents: P. Gagné (x) and M. Josephe Gagné (x).

1524. JOSEPH MARIE CESAR LAFFITTE
August 19, 1787, at 10 a.m., baptism of Joseph Marie Cesar, born August 9, legitimate son of Bouët Lafitte, merchant, and Marianne de Soto. Godparents: Marcel de Soto (s) and Francoise Grappe (s).

1525. MARIE SERAPHIE CHALER
August 25, 1787, baptism, at 10 a.m., of Marie Seraphie, born August 4, legitimate daughter of Pierre Chaler and Marie Derbanne. Godparents: Francois Lavespere (s) and Marie Francoise Brevel (x).

1526. MARIE CELESTE
August 25, 1787, at 10 a.m., baptism of Marie Celeste, born July ?, 1787, daughter of /torn/ Perrine, a free *mulâtresse*. Godparents: Jean Marie Armant (s), merchant /Illegible/ New Orleans, and Susanne Prudhomme (s).

1527. JEAN JOSEPH MARTIANEAU
MAGDALINE LABAYRIE
September 6, 1787, at 11 a.m., after publication of one ban, marriage of Jean Joseph Martianeau, legitimate son of Guillaume Mar___?___ and Jeanne ___?___, native of Bordeaux? and now a merchant at this post . . . and . . .

Magdaline Labayrie, legitimate daughter of Jean Baptiste Labayrie and Jeanne Guedon (s). Witnesses: François Bossié (s), habitant; Louis Durand (s); François Barthelemi Chabus (s); and Jean Baptiste Grappe (s), all residents of this post.

1528. MICHEL ARNAND /ERNANDEZ/
MARIE OLIVIER
September 11, 1787, at 9 a.m., after publication of three bans, marriage of Michel Arnand, legitimate son of Michel Arnand and Josephe Joue, native of post Ste. Marie . . . and . . . Marie Olivier, widow of Jean Couty, legitimate daughter of Michel Olivier and <u>Minanette?</u> Robert, native of Pointe Coupée. Witnesses: Pierre Lacour (s), Remi Poissot (x), and Louis Totin (s), habitants of this post.

1529. VALENTIN DUBOË
ROSE CHELATRE
October 8, 1787, at 9 a.m., after three bans, marriage of Valentin Duboë, native of this parish, legitimate son of Jean Baptiste Duboë (s/ Bte. Dubois) and Marie Josephe Clermont (s) . . . and . . . Rose Chelatre, native of the parish of Allemands, legitimate daughter of Michel Chelatre and Anne Pomier, habitants of this parish. Witnesses: Joseph Latier (s), Philippe Frederic, and Bernabé Cheletre.

1530. BARTHELEMY RUBEN RACHAL
January 22, 1788, at 9 a.m., baptism of Barthelemy Ruben, born December 29, 1787, legitimate son of Barthelemy Rachal and Francoise Labayrie. Godparents: Louis Rachal (x) and Marie Labayrie (x). (f)

1531. ANTOINE
January 23, 1788, at 10 a.m., baptism of Antoine, an adult Indian of about 20 years. Godparents: Valentin Layssard (s), Marie Louise Marte De Blanc (s/ Marie Marthe).

1532. PHILIPPE FREDERIC
November 29, 1787, at 1 p.m., baptism of Philippe, born October 20, 1787, legitimate son of Philippe Frederic and Marie Barbe Cheletre. Godparents: Antoine Imil (x) and Marie Louise Buard Ailhot (s).

1533. MARIE FELICITÉ LAVESPERE
January 3, 1788, at 10 a.m., baptism of Marie Felicité, born December 16, 1787, legitimate daughter of François Lavespere (s) and Marie Derban. Godparents: Etienne Verger (x) and Marie Francoise Dupré Verger (x).

1534. PIERRE RAMIS
MARIANNE NICOLLE LANGLOIS
February 27, 1788, at 9 a.m., after 1 ban, marriage of

Pierre Ramis (s), corporal, legitimate son of Antoine
/Ramis/ and Magdeline Leven?, native of the village of
Olbena in Spain . . . and . . . Marianne Nicolle Langlois,
legitimate daughter of François Langlois and Marie Gregoire, native of this parish. Witnesses: Louis Borme
(s) and Francois Le Maitre (x).

1535. MARIE MODISTE VASCOCU
April 6, 1788, at 10 a.m., baptism of Marie Modiste, born
March 18, legitimate daughter of Andres Vascueul and Magdeliene Raimond. Godparents: Louis Vasicoueul (x) and
Eulalie Vascocu (x). (f)

1536. FRANCOIS AUGUSTIN RAMBIN
April 6, 1788, at 10 a.m., baptism of Francois Augustin,
born February 5, legitimate son of Andre Rambin, churchwarden, and Marie Catherine Buard. Godparents: Francois
Augustin Buard (x) and Marie Rose Lambre Buard (s).

1537. LOUIS RACHAL
April 13, 1788, at 10 a.m., baptism of Louis, born March
22, legitimate son of Julien Rachal and Marie Louise Brevel, habitants. Godparents: Louis Monet (s) and Dame
Monet (x). (f)

1538. BENOIT MONTANARY
FRANCOISE GRAPPE
April 23, 1788, at 4 p.m., after 3 bans, marriage of Benoit Montanary (s), legitimate son of Jean Baptiste Montanari and Margueritte Tottan, native of New Orleans . . .
and . . . Francoise Grappe (s), legitimate daughter of
Alexis Grappe and Marie Louise Guedon, native of this parish. Witnesses: Bernard Dortolant (s), officer; Marc
Aulay (s/ Marcollay); François Rambin (s); and Badin (s);
all habitants of this post.

1539. JACQUES LACASE
MARIE LOUISE DUPRE
May 7, 1788, at 10 a.m., after 2 bans, marriage of Jacques
Lacase, legitimate son of Charles Lacase and Fillis Langloi, native of the parish of Opelousas . . . and . . .
Marie Louise Dupre (x), legitimate daughter of Joseph Dupre and Marie de la Incarnation Derbanne, native of this
parish. Witnesses: Pierrite Derbanne (s), Francois
Lavesper (s), J. Baptiste Buard (s), and Louis Derbanne
(s), all habitants of this post. Jacques Lacase made his
"X".

1540. LOUIS CELESTIEN PLOCHER
May 18, 1788, baptism of Louis Celestien, born April 11, legitimate son of Antoine Plocher and Marie Therese Vascocu.
Godparents: Antoine Vascocu, uncle of the infant, and

Marie Francoise Vascocu, widow Daniel /Berrier/.

1541. ANNE BARBE DUBOË
June 8, 1788, baptism of Anne Barbe, born May 15, legitimate daughter of Valentin Duboë and Rose Cheletre. Godparents. Jean Baptiste Duboë (s/ Bte. Dubois, *grandpère*) and Anne Barbe Pomier, widow Cheletre (x).

1542. JACOB HOOPOK
MARIE SALVAN
July 6, 1788, request to marry, filed by Jacob Hoopok, a native of "Wirgine or Virginie", province of North America, who seeks to be married in the Catholic Church to Marie Salvan, legitimate daughter of Jean Salvan and Marie Louise Lambre, a native of New Orleans.

Hoopok's faith had been questioned, prior to the application by several individuals. Bouet Laffite, merchant at the post and François Bossie, habitant, testify that Hoopok signed the following profession of faith when they requested him to do so:

"I Jacob Houpok believe from firm faith and confess all and each article contained in the symbol of the faith of /illegible/ of holy romain Church: to wit: I believe in one god almighty, creator of heaven and earth and all /illegible/ visible and invisible, and in his only son, jesus christ, born, etc. etc."

The future groom then cited all of the sacraments, swore that he believed Jesus Christ was present in both the bread and the wine, that he revered all the relics, that he respected the images of Jesus Christ and the Virgin Mary and all the saints, that he believed in the Church's power of excommunication, that he believed the Holy Catholic and Roman Church was the mother and mistress of all other churches, that he believed the Pope of Rome to be the successor to St. Peter and vicar of Jesus Christ in all things and to be deserving of obedience. He then renounced, rejected, and abjured all the heresies that were rejected by the Catholic Church. S/ Jacob Hooppock.

1543. JEAN BAPTISTE FONTENEAU (f)
July 14, 1788, baptism of Jean Baptiste, born May 5, legitimate son of Louis Fonteneau and Pelagie Grappe. Godparents: Jean Baptiste Grappe (s) and Genevieve Sorel (x).

1544. JACOB HOPOK
MARIE SALVAN
July 23, 1788, after publication of three bans, marriage of Jacob Hopok (s), son of George Hopok and Margueritte Rosoe (Rofee?), native of Virginia . . . and . . . Marie Salvan,

legitimate daughter of Jean Salvan and Marie Louise Lambre, a native of New Orleans. Witnesses: Francois Bossié (s), Louis Buard (x), Silvestre Bossié (s), and Soulange Bossié (s).

1545. FRANCINE BODOUIN /MARIE FROZINE DENIS/*
August 12, 1788, baptism of Francine, legitimate daughter of P. Bodouin and M. Elizabeth Beaudouin. Godparents: Nicolas Beaudouin and Marianne Depres. */See Entry 1959/ (f).

1546. ALEXIS CLOUTIER
MARIE FRANCOISE LECOMPTE
August 18, 1788, after publication of two bans, marriage of Alexis Cloutier, legitimate son of Jean Baptiste Cloutier and Marie Rachal, native of the post of Pointe Coupée . . . and . . . Marie Francoise Lecompte, widow Dupré, legitimate daughter of Jean Baptiste Lecompte and Marguerite Le Roy, a native of this parish. Witnesses: Pierre Sorel *dit* Marly (s) and Jean Baptiste Anty (s), habitants.

1547. PIERRE NAGSAN GAGNON
August 17, 1788, baptism of Pierre Nagsan, born July 28, legitimate son of Pierre Gagnon (s) and Marie Therese Valentin, native of this parish. Godparents: Julien Besson (s) and Marie Jeanne Chagneau, widow Frederic (x).

1548. FRANCOIS PILIO /CHRISTOPHE/
August 24, 1788, baptism of Francois Pilio, born October 11, 1787, son of Marie de l'Ascension and of Pierre Christophe. Godparents: Francois Hugues *dit* Tonan (x) and Francois Lecour (x).

1549. LOUIS EPINETTE
SUSANNE ARLLIVEAUX /OLIVO/
September 10, 1788, after publication of one ban, marriage of Louis Epinette (s/ Louis Epinet), native of Marenne in St. Onge /Marinnes, located at base of Ile d'Oléron/, the legitimate son of Guillaumme Epinette and Anne Doussaint . . . and . . . Susanne Arlliveaux, native of Pointe Coupée, legitimate daughter of Pierre Aullivaux and Marianne Riché. Witnesses: André Rambin (s), church warden; Pierre Duboe (x); Pierre and Bastien Aulliveaux (x) (x).

1550. MAGDELEINE EUPHEMIE FREDERIC
September 14, 1788, baptism of Magdeleine Euphemie, born August 13, 1788, legitimate daughter of Philippe Frederic and Marie Catherine Sauvage. Godparents: Jean Francois Frederic (x) and Marie Catherine Bardon (s).

1551. LOUIS NAMISEE /NARCISSE/ PRUDHOMME
September 20, 1788, baptism of Louis Namisee, born August

24, legitimate son of Emmanuel Prudhomme (s) and Catherine Lambre (s). Godparents: Francois Rouquier (s), merchant, and Marie Lambre (s).

1552. CLAUDE THOMAS PIERRE METOYER
THERESE BUARD
October 13, 1788, after publication of one ban, marriage of Claude Thomas Pierre Metoyer (s), legitimate son of Nicolas Francois Metoyer and Marianne Dupron . . . and . . . Therese Buard (s), widow of Etienne Pavie, native of this parish, legitimate daughter of Gabriel Buard and of Marianne Rousseau. Witnesses: André Rambin (s), church warden; Louis Buard (x); Bouet Lafitte; Ailhaud Ste. Anne.

1553. REMY CAZIMIR PERRAU
November 1, 1788, baptism of Remy Cazimir, born March 4, legitimate son of Christophe Perrau and Marie Louise Salvan. Godparents: Remy Pereau (x) and Marie Jeanne Sorel (x).

1554. JEAN BAPTISTE DERBANNE
November 1, 1788, baptism of Jean Baptiste, born December 22, 1787, legitimate son of Gaspar Derbanne and Marie Josephe Perau. Godparents: Jean Lalande (x) and Marie Le Clerc (x).

1555. MARIE MELANIE RACHAL
November 1, 1788, baptism of Marie Melanie, born September 9, 1788, legitimate daughter of Louis Rachal and Marie Joseph Labayrie. Godparents: Fr. Delvaux and Jeanne Guedon (x).

1556. MARIE CATHERINE PEREAU
November 1, 1788, baptism of Marie Catherine, born May 12, 1787, legitimate daughter of Francois Pereau and Marie Agathe Labayrie. Godparents: Jean Lalande (x) and Catherine Dupre.

1557. MARIE LOUISE MASSIP
November 2, 1788, baptism of Marie Louise, born July 30, legitimate daughter of Jean Massip and Marie Le Moine. Godparents: Louis Monette (s) and Marie Louise Lecompte Monette (x).

1558. MARIE ANTOINE TAURÉ /Torres/
November 4, 1788, baptism of Marie Antoine, born "toward the end of October of the year past," legitimate son of Joseph Tauré, habitant of Riviere aux Cannes, and Jeanne des Rois /de los Reyes/. Godparents: Ambroise Le Compte (x) and Marie Antoine St. Denis (s).

1559. JEAN BAPTISTE CHELETRE
November 16, 1788, baptism of Jean Baptiste, born "toward the end of the month of September last," legitimate son of Pierre Cheletre and Margueritte Frederic. Godparents: J. Baptiste Latier (x) and Marie Rosalie Frederic (x).

1560. MARIANNE ARTEMISE LE MAITRE
November 22, 1788, baptism of Marianne Artemise, born about three days earlier, legitimate daughter of Francois Le Maitre *dit* La lime and Marie Louise Ville Franche. Godparents: Nicolas Le Maitre and Constance Victoire Le Maistre.

1561. ANTOINE ADELAIS
November 23, 1788, baptism of Antoine, born September 17, legitimate son of Etienne Adelais and Marie Genevieve du Bös. Godparents: Antoine du Bös (x) and Marie Genevieve Fond'lik (Frederic?) (x).

1562. MARIE FRANCOISE CHELETRE
November 23, 1788, baptism of Marie Francoise, born October 24, legitimate daughter of Barnabé Cheletre and Marie Joseph Gonin. Godparents: Francois Gonin(x) and Genevieve Gonin (x).

1563. MARIE FELICITE DE LOUCH
November 23, 1788, baptism of Marie Felicite, born October 27, legitimate daughter of Jean de Louch and Ursulle* Boulet. Godparents: Pierre Beaudouin (x) and Anne Robin (x).

*Penned in above and before the name Ursulle is the name Marie Jeanne. The name Boulet is changed, in the same writing, to Boulette.

1564. JOSEPH ANDRE RENOI
December 4, 1788, baptism of Joseph Andre, born November 30, legitimate son of Joseph Renoi and Marie Joseph Mercier. Godparents: Joseph Jean ris (x) and Genevieve Sorelle (x).

1565. JACQUES ROSMOND CHAMARD
December 16, 1788, baptism of Jacques Rosmond, born October 14, legitimate son of Mr. Chamard, merchant, and of Catherine Bardon. Godparents: Jacques Constant, merchant (s) and Marie Chamard (s).

1566. MARIE ASPASIE BOSSIE
January 11, 1789, baptism of Marie Aspasie, born December 7, 1788, legitimate daughter of Francois Bossie and Catherine Pelagie Lambre. Godparents: Louis Lambre (s) and Marie Lambre (s), habitants.

1567. MARIE STASIE DERBANE
       January 18, 1789, baptism of Marie Stasie, born January 11, legitimate daughter of Jean Baptiste Derbane and Marie Helene Brevel. Godparents: Athanas Poissot, *fils* and Marie Louise Antoine St. Denis (s/ Marie Antoine).

1568. JOSEPH JEAN RIS
       MARIE FRANCOISE VASCOCU
       January 28, 1789, after publication of two bans, marriage of Joseph Jean Ris, native of this parish, legitimate son of Jean Ris and Marie Jeanne Chagneau . . . and . . . Marie Francoise Vascocu, widow Daniel /Berrier/, legitimate daughter of Antoine Vascocu and Marie Barbe Toups, a native of this parish. Witnesses: Francois Rambin (s), Guillaumme Barberoux (s), Jean Louis Vascocu (s) and André Vascocu (s), habitants.

1569. MARIE JOSEPHE MODERN?
       February 2, 1789, baptism of Marie Josephe, about seven years of age, daughter of Francois Modern? and Nanette, an Indian. Godparents: Pierre Dolet (s) and Dame Marianne de Soto Bouet Lafitte (s).

1570. PIERRE MODERN?
       February 2, 1789, baptism of Pierre, about four years of age, son of Nanette, an Indian. Godparents: Pierre Paul Bouet Laffitte (s) and Catherine Raimond Bardon (s).

1571. MICHEL MODERN?
       February 2, 1789, baptism of Michel, aged about one year, son of Nanette, Indian. Godparents: Gaspar Fiolle (x) and Therese Lamalaty Fiolle (x).

1572. CHARLES PHILIPPE LARENAUDIERE
       February 4, 1789, baptism of Charles Philippe, born January 1, 1789, legitimate son of Pierre Larenaudiere and Jeanne Labayrie. Godparents: J. B. Pie Ferme (Leger) (x) and Marie Clemence Larenaudiere (x).

1573. MARIE MODESTE ANTY
       February 8, 1789, baptism of Marie Modeste, born January 7, legitimate daughter of Louis Anty and Marie Jeanne Crete. Godparents: Pierre La Cour (s) and Marie Celeste Verger (x).

1574. PIERRE FORT
       February 10, 1789, baptism of Pierre, born December 13, 1788, legitimate son of Jacques Fort and Marie Francoise Malbert. Godparents: Pierre Michel (x) and Marie Pelagrie Frederic (x).

1575. PAUL _____
February 11, 1789, baptism of Paul, born February 9, "son of Dlle. Francoise, living at this post." Godparents: Bouett Laffitte (s) and Marianne de Soto Laffitte (s).

1576. MARIE CELESTE CHALER
February 14, 1789, baptism of Marie Celeste, born January 15, 1789, legitimate daughter of Pierre Chaler and Marie Derbanne. Godparents: Louis Derbanne (s) and Marie Francoise Barthelemy Rachal (x).

1577. MARIE LOUISE DOLET
February 22, 1789, baptism of Marie Louise, born November 11, 1788, legitimate daughter of Pierre Dolet and Rose Dupre. Godparents: Pierre Dupre (x) and Marianne Dupre (x).

1578. THERESE OZITE TOMASSINE
February 22, 1789, baptism of Therese Ozite Tomassine, born January 27, legitimate daughter of Louis Tomassine and Catherine Latier. Godparents: Francois Latier (x) and Marie Robin (x).

1579. MARIE EUPHROSINE RACHAL
February 25, 1789, baptism of Marie Euphrosine, born December 1, 1788, legitimate daughter of Louis Barthelemy Rachal and Marie Francoise Grillet. Godparents: Jean Baptiste Theodore Grillet (x) and Marie Adelaide Vercher (x).

1580. BERNARD SIMEON GAGNE
March 21, 1789, baptism of Bernard Simeon, born February 17, legitimate son of Etienne Gagne and Marie Louise Bertrand. Godparents: Bernard D'ortolant (s) and Marie Louise Rouquier (s/ Prudhomme Rouquier).

1581. EMANUEL _____
March 22, 1789, baptism of Emanuel, born March 14, son of Francoise, widow of Joseph Lange?. Godparents: Manuel Gonzales, soldier (x) and Marie Therese Langlois (x).

1582. JEAN POMIER
April 1, 1789, baptism of Jean, born March 20, legitimate son of Jean Pomier and Marie Robert Dupre. Godparents: Philippe Frederic (x) and Anne Barbe Pomier, widow Cheletre (x).

1583. MARIE HORTENCE BERTRAND
April 5, 1789, baptism of Marie Hortence, born December 28, 1788, legitimate daughter of Louis Bertrand and Isabelle Davion. Godparents: Francois Grappe (x) and Marie

Louise Grappe Triché (x).

1584. MARIE JOSEPH HENOEL? TOTIN
April 12, 1789, baptism of Marie Joseph Henoel?, born January 19, 1789, legitimate daughter of Remy Totin and of Margueritte Grillet. Godparents: Henri Triche and Marie Joseph Triche.

1585. PIERRE SIRIAC LEVASSEUR
April 12, 1789, baptism of Pierre Siriac, born January 31, legitimate son of Joseph Levasseur and Therese Grillet. Godparents: Pier__ Beilland? and Marie Barbe Grillet.

1586. FELICITE MODEST TRICHE
April 13, 1789, baptism of Felicite Modest, born September 30?, 1787, legitimate daughter of Manuel Triche and Marie Louise Grappe. Godparents: Julien Besson and Francoise Grappe Benoit /Montenary/.

1587. CASSE (CASER?) DUBOË
April 14, 1789, baptism of Casse (Caser?) du Boë, born January 26, legitimate son of Francois du Boë and Eleonore Jean ris. Godparents: Joseph Jean ris and Marie Joseph Clermont Duboë.

1588. MARIE AIME LAVESPERE
April 19, 1789, baptism of Marie Aime, born March 31, legitimate daughter of Francois Lavespere and Marie Louise Derbanne. Godparents: Louis Derbanne and Marie Baillane.

1589. ANDRÉ ST. ANDRÉ
MARIE RACHAL
April 20, 1789, after two bans, marriage of André St. André, native of Montreal in Canada, son of Jacques St. André and Marianne Picard . . . and . . . Marie Rachal, native of this parish, legitimate daughter of Jacques Rachal and Ursulle Castel. Witnesses: Etienne Vergé (x), Louis Rachal (x) and Baptiste Barthelemy Rachal (x), all habitants.

1590. LOUIS LAMBRE
MARIANNE DUPRE
April 22, 1789, after two bans, marriage of Louis Lambre (s), native of this parish, legitimate son of Jean Baptiste Lambre and Marie Jeanne Levasseur . . . and . . . Marianne Dupré, native of this parish, legitimate daughter of Joseph Dupre and Marie Derbanne. Witnesses: Pierre Chaler (s), Pierre Baillio (s) and Louis Bartelemis Rachal (s).

1591. REMI JACQUES CHRISTI
August 25, 1789, baptism of Remi Jacques, born December 1,

1788, legitimate son of Jacques Christi and Dorothée Perau. Godparents: Remy Perau and Genevieve ⟨illegible⟩.

1592. LOUIS ETIEN DERBANNE
August 25, 1789, baptism of Louis Etien, born July 6, legitimate son of Pierre Derbanne, *fils*, and Marie Francoise Brevel. Godparents: Balthasar Brevel and Widow St. Denis.

1593. MARIE DENIS
August 25, 1789, baptism of Marie, about five months of age, legitimate daughter of Jean Baptiste Denis and Marie Beaudouin. Godparents: Francois Davion and Marie Therese Beaudouin.

1594. SILVESTRE RACHAL
August 31, 1789, baptism of Silvestre, born August 2, legitimate son of Antoine Rachal and Marie Louise Le Moine. Godparents: Charles Le Moine and Marie Louise Dupre La Casse.

1595. MARIE ELISABETH SAIDEK
August 31, 1789, baptism of Marie Elisabeth, born December 5, 1788, legitimate daughter of Pierre Clavis Saidek and Ursulle Cheletre. Godparents: Mr. Morphil and Elizabeth Buard, his wife. (f)

1596. PIERRE BEAUDOUIN
NANETTE ROBIN
September 19, 1789, after 3 bans, marriage of Pierre Beaudouin, native of the ⟨illegible⟩, legitimate son of Francois Beaudouin and Marianne Bontems . . . and . . . Nanette Robin, legitimate daughter of Michel Robin and Marie Louise Boulé, native of this parish. Witnesses: Joseph Latier (s), Pierre Cajou (x), Pierre Lacour (s).

1597. RICHARD SYMIS
MARIE LA CONCESSION PEREZ
September 22, 1789, after 3 bans, marriage of Richard Symis, son of Jean Symis and Margueritte Chisley, native of the town of Bristol in Great Britain . . . and . . . Marie la Concession Perez, legitimate daughter of Joseph Christophe Perez and Marie Josephe Pelone, native of San Antonio, province of Texas. Witnesses: Andre David (s) and Pierre Sorel (s), Bouet Lafitte, *fils* (s).

1598. PIERRE VICTORIN METOYER
September 26, 1789, baptism of Pierre Victorin, born September 5, legitimate son of Claude Thomas Pierre Metoyer, merchant (s), and Dame Therese Buard (s). Godparents: Jean Baptiste Ailhaud Ste. Anne (s), captain, and Marie

Louise Buard St. Anne (s).

1599. MARIE THERESE VICTOIRE AILHAUD ST. ANNE
September 26, 1789, baptism of Marie Therese Victoire, born July 17, legitimate daughter of Jean Baptiste Ailhaud St. Anne (s), captain, and Marie Louise Buard (s). Godparents: Jean Antoine Ailhaud St. Anne, absent, but represented by Mr. Metoyer (s) and Therese Buard Metoyer (s).

1600. REMY LAMBRE
SUZETTE PRUDHOMME
September 26, 1789, after 1 ban, marriage of Remy Lambre (s), legitimate son of Jacob Lambre and Marianne Poissot . . . and . . . Suzette Prudhomme (s), native of this parish, legitimate daughter of Jean Baptiste Prud'homme and Marie Josephe Collantin. Godparents: Francois Rouquier (s), merchant; Gaspar Fiolle (s), merchant; Manuel Prudhomme (s), habitant.

1601. ANTOINE SOULANGE FREDERIC
September 27, 1789, baptism of Antoine Soulange, born August 30, 1789, legitimate son of Philippe Frederic, *fils*, and Barbe Cheletre. Godparents: Antoine Ymel, *fils*, and Barbe Halock.

1601. MARGUERITTE RABALÉ
(bis) September 27, 1789, baptism of Margueritte, born August 12, legitimate daughter of Joseph Rabalé and Marie Louise Malbert. Godparents: Jean Baptiste Bossier and Marie des Neiges. (f)

1602. IGNACE MAÏOU
October 4, 1789, baptism of Ignace, born August 15, legitimate son of Ignace Maiou, blacksmith, and Marie Therese Filibot. Godparents: Michel Rambin and Marie Louise Euphrasie Rambin.

1603. MARIE EMMANUEL LESTAGE
November 1, 1789, baptism of Marie Emmanuel, born November 1, 1788, legitimate daughter of Guilhaumme Lestage and Emmanuel Riche. Godparents: Jean Baptiste Lestage and Emmanuel de Soto Poissot.

1604. JOHN HORN
MARIE LOUISE BEAUDIN
November 10, 1789, after 3 bans, marriage of John Horn, a native of York in Great Britain, son of Jean Horn and of Josephe Bencois? . . . and . . . Marie Louise Beaudin, native of this parish, widow Robin, legitimate daughter of Laurens Beaudin and Marie Michel St. Croix. Witnesses:

André David, *chantre* /singer or lay clerk in the church/ (s) and Louis Chamard, merchant (s).

1605. JEAN SILVESTRE HOPOK
December 26, 1789, baptism of Jean Silvestre, born April 21, legitimate son of Jacob Hopak and Marie Salvan. Godparents: Athanas Poissot and Ulalie Bossié.

1606. JEAN BAPTISTE MAES
December 27, 1789, baptism of Jean Baptiste, born September 22, 1789, legitimate son of Pierre Joseph Maes (s) and Marianne Dartigaux (s). Godparents: Baptiste Dartigaux (s) and Marie Victoire Maes, represented by Dame Therese Le gros Armant (s).

1607. JOSEPH NOEL MALIGE
January 6, 1790, baptism of Joseph Noel, born December 25, 1789, legitimate son of Joseph Malige and Marianne Bardon. Godparents: Joseph Tozin (s/ Tauzin) and Marianne Poissot, widow Jacob Lambre.

1608. MARIE SUZETE GAGNE
January 6, 1790, baptism of Marie Suzete, born August 11, 1789, legitimate daughter of Pierre Gagne and Marie Louise Davion. Godparents: Joseph Gagne and Hyacinthe Gagne.

1609. JOSEPH ANTOINE MARCEL DE SOTO
MARIE BAILLIO
January 30, 1790, after 2 bans, marriage of Joseph Antoine Marcel de Soto, native of this parish, legitimate son of Manuel de Soto and Marie de St. Denis . . . and . . . Marie Baillio, native of this parish, legitimate daughter of Pierre Baillio and Catherine Poissot. Godparents: Ailhaud St. Anne (s), captain, Emanuel Prudhomme (s), Remy Lambre (s), Athanas Poissot (s), and de Blanc, *fils* (s). (f)

1610. ALEXANDRE SOULANGE BOSSIE
MARIE IMEL
February 6, 1790, after 2 bans, marriage of Alexandre Soulange Bossie, native of the parish of St. Charles, post des Allemands, legitimate son of Francois Bossie and of Rosalie Charlotte Barre . . . and . . . Marie Imel, native of this parish, legitimate daughter of Antoine Imel and Marguerite Cheletre. Witnesses: Francois Bossié (s), Barthelemy Campanelle (s/ Canpanel), Paul Cheletre (x), and Antoine Lambre (s).

1611. MARIE POMPOSE LAFFITE
February 7, 1790, baptism of Marie Pompose, about one month of age, legitimate daughter of Bouet Laffitte and Marie de Soto. Godparents: Pierre D_____ and Dame Fonteneau.

1612. ANDRÉ FREDERIC
MARIANNE CHELETRE BAILLIO
February 16, 1790, after 1 ban, marriage of André Frederic, native of St. Charles parish, post of les Allemands, legitimate son of Philippe Frederic and Catherine Bernard . . . and . . . Marianne Cheletre, widow Baillio, native of the same parish of St. Charles, legitimate daughter of Michel Cheletre and Barbe Pomier. Witnesses: Guillaumme Lestage (x), Bernabé Chelette (x), Pierre Chelette (x), Francois Lecompte (x).

1613. PIERRE JOSEPH ALMAN
MARIE THERESE LANGLOIS
February 16, 1790, after 2 bans, marriage of Pierre Joseph Alman (x), native of Baroli in New Galice, legitimate son of deceased Don Joseph Alman and deceased Marie Gertrude Gôme . . . and . . . Marie Therese Langlois (s), native of this parish, legitimate daughter of François Langlois and Marie Gregoire Sta. Crux. Witnesses: Benoit Pessyo (s/ Benoit Pescio), soldier; Jean Joseph St. Anne (x); Francois Le Maitre (x); Pierre Ramis (s/ Pedro Ramiz), corporal.

1614. PIERRE CESAR BROSSET
February 21, 1790, baptism of Pierre Cesar, born December 29, 1789, legitimate son of Pierre Brosset and Marie Josephe Grillet. Godparents: Antoine Grillet and M. Barbe Grillet.

1615. MARIE ADRIENNE ST. ANDRE
February 23, 1790, baptism of Marie Adrienne, about one month of age, legitimate daughter of Andre St. Andre and Marie Rachal. Godparents: Mr. Monet and Celeste Verger.

1616. LOUIS GALIEN
February 28, 1790, baptism of Louis, aged about two months, legitimate son of Nicolas Galien and Marie Le Cour. Godparents: Louis Monet and Marie Louise LeCompte Monet. (f)

1617. MARIE DES _____ DERBANNE
April 4, 1790, baptism of Marie des _____ /illegible/, legitimate daughter of Gaspard Derbanne and Marie Joseph Pereau. Godparents: Francois Monginot and Dame Massip.

1618. JEAN PIERRE BEAUDOUIN
April 13, 1790, baptism of Jean Pierre, born March 8, legitimate son of Pierre Beaudouin and Anne Robin. Godparents: Pierre Baudouin and Marie Robin.

1619. MARIE THERESE VASCOCU
April 25, 1790, baptism of Marie Therese, aged about one month, legitimate daughter of André Vascocu and Magdeline Raymond. Godparents: Francois Vascocu and /illegible/.

1620. SILVESTRE CESAR BOSSIE
May 4, 1790, baptism of Silvestre Cesar, born February 25, legitimate son of Silvestre Bossie and Marie Jeanne Lambre. Godparents: Antoine Lambre and Eulalie Bossie.

1621. JEAN BAPTISTE PRUDHOMME
May 9, 1790, baptism of Jean Baptiste, about three months of age, legitimate son of Francois Prudhomme and Marie Rambin. Godparents: Michel Rambin and Dame Rambin.

1622. BAPTISTE BALTHASAR PLOCHER
May 23, 1790, baptism of Baptiste Balthasar, about one month of age, legitimate son of Antoine Plocher and Marie Therese Vascocu. Godparents: Guilhaume Barberaux and Marie Jeanne Chagneau.

1623. JOSEPH CELESTIN BERNARD
June 1, 1790, baptism of Joseph Celestin, about six months of age, legitimate son of Elie Bernard and Eleonore Chagneau. Godparents: Michel Chagneau and Marie Jean-ris.

1624. JEAN JOSEPH RACHAL
June 5, 1790, baptism of Jean Joseph, born May 22, legitimate son of Louis Rachal and Marie Joseph Labayrie. Godparents: M. Martineau and Marie Louise Martineau.

1625. JACQUES ISAAC PEJOBSANS
GUILHAUMME PEJOBSANS /ROBINSON/
JEAN BAPTISTE PEJOBSONS
June 6, 1790, baptism of Jacques Isaac, aged about five years, Guilhaumme, aged about three years, and Jean Baptiste, aged about one year, legitimate children of Elie Pejobsans and Marie Matin. Godparents: Francois Cheletre, Bernabe Cheletre, and Baptiste Ch___ /torn/, Francoise Cheletre, Marie Joseph Gonin, and Marie /torn/.

1626. FRANCOIS DORCIEN RACHAL
July 4, 1790, baptism of Francois Dorcien, aged one month, legitimate son of Barthelemy Rachal and Francois Labayrie. Godparents: François Totin and Dame Guillaume /Chever dit/ Du Frene.

1627. DOMINIQUE DAVION
PELAGIE GAGNÉ
July 21, 1790, after 3 bans, marriage of Dominique Davion (x), native of this parish, legitimate son of Jean Baptiste Davion and Marie Hyacinthe Trichel (x) . . . and . . . Pelagie Gagné, native of this parish, legitimate daughter of Etienne Gagné and Marie Louise Bertrand. Witnesses: Jean Baptiste Davion (x), Louis Davion (x), Louis Bertrand (x), and Bernard Dortolant (s), corporal.

1628. LOUIS JOSEPH STE. GERMAINE
July 21, 1790, baptism of Louis Joseph, aged about four years, native of the parish of Acatopa /Attakapas/, legitimate son of Louis St. Germaine and Marie La Pointe. Godparents: de Blanc, commandant, and Dame Marie de Soto.

1629. CHARLES ETIENNE ST. GERMAINE
July 21, 1790, baptism of Charles Etienne, aged about two years, native of the parish of Opelousas, legitimate son of Louis St. Germaine and Marie La pointe. Godparents: de Blanc and Mme. de Blanc.

1630. JEAN LOUIS HOPPOCK
July 24, 1790, baptism of Jean Louis, born July 3, legitimate son of Jean Jac___ Hopock and Marie Salvan. Godparents: Jean Louis Buard and Dlle. Eugenie Buard.

1631. LOUIS RACHAL
August 1, 1790, baptism of Louis, born June 16, legitimate son of Bmy. Rachal and Françoise Grillet. Godparents: /torn/ Rachal, *fils*, and Dlle. Levasseur.

1632. DENIS ONEZIME BUARD
August 1, 1790, baptism of Denis Onezime, born July 13, legitimate son of Louis Buard and Marie Rose Lambre. Godparents: Jean Louis Buard and Marie Catherine Buard.

1633. MARIE JOSEPHE ROUQUIER
August 24, 1790, baptism of Marie Josephe, born November 25, 1789, legitimate daughter of Francois Rouquier, merchant, and Marie Louise Prudhomme. Godparents: Mr. Dupain, merchant, and Dame Remy Lambre.

1634. AUGUSTIN FREDIEU
MARIE JEANNE SOREL
September 15, 1790, after 1 ban, marriage of Augustin Fredieu (x), merchant at this post, native of Toscane in Italy, legitimate son of Fr. Fredieu and Angelique Claive . . . and . . . Marie Jeanne Sorel (s), native of this parish, legitimate daughter of Pierre Sorel and Marie Rose Boissilier. Witnesses: André Rambin (s), church warden, Louis Buard (x), Luc Sorel.

1635. MARIE BALTILE DUBOË
September 19, 1790, baptism of Marie Baltile, born August 1, legitimate daughter of Valentin Duboë and Rose Cheletre. Godparents: François Cheletre and Françoise Cheletre.

1636. SALVADOR REMIS
MARIE IGNE? REOBLEAU
September 20, 1790, after 1 ban, marriage of Salvador Remis,

legitimate son of Andre Remis and Marie Nicole Per____, "a native of the place called *peuple St.* _____ *de la passe*" in the Kingdom of Mexico . . . and . . . Marie Igne Robleau, native of Adayes, legitimate daughter of Guilhaume Robleau and Marie Isidore Separda. Witnesses: Pedro Ramis (s), Francois Fibles, Benoist Pescio (s).

1637. MARIE ASPASIE DEBLANC
August 20, 1788, baptism of Marie Aspasie, born March 12, 1788, daughter of M. Louis Charles Deblanc (s), lieutenant of the army and commandant, and Dame Elisabeth Pompone Derneville (s). Godparents: Athanas Poissot (x), habitant, and Marie De Soto (s), spouse of Athanas Poissot. (f)

1638. SILVESTER BOSSIER
MARIE JEANNE LAMBRE
October 17, 1787, after 1 ban, marriage of Silvester Bossier (s), son of M. Francois Bossier and Dame Rosalie Charlotte Barré, native of the parish of St. Charles on the German Coast . . . and . . . Marie Jeanne Lambre, a native of this parish, legitimate daughter of deceased Jean Baptiste Lambre and deceased Marie Jeanne Levasseur. Witnesses: François Bossié (s) and Louis Buard (x).

1639. FRANCOIS MONGINOT
MARIE FRANCOISE BUARD
April 24, 1788, after 1 ban, marriage of François Monginot (s), doctor, son of Francois Marie Monginot and Dame Marie Agen . . . and . . . Marie Francoise Buard (s), legitimate daughter of Gabriel Buard and Marianne Rousseau, native of this parish. Witnesses: André Rambin (s), church warden; Francois Bossié (s); Baptiste Buard (s); Remy Lambre (s).

1640. JEAN BAPTISTE ANTY
MARIE FRANCOISE LEVASSEUR
June 24, 1788, at 3 p.m., after 2 bans, marriage of Jean Baptiste Anty, legitimate son of Ignace Anty and Catherine Guerine, native of New Orleans, now a habitant of this post,. . . and . . . Marie Francoise Levasseur, daughter of Francois Le Vasseur and Marie Madern, native of this post. Witnesses: Pierre Sorel *dit* Marly (s) and Jacques Le Vasseur (s).

1641. MARIE CHARLOTTE MODESTE PRUDHOMME
September 25, 1787, at 6 p.m., baptism of Marie Charlotte Modeste, aged about one month, legitimate daughter of François Prudhomme and Marie Rambin. Godparents: Mr. Monginot, doctor (s) and Marie Charlotte Capuran (s).

1642. PIERRE JOSEPH MAES
February 1, 1788, at 10 a.m., baptism of Joseph, born

December 31, 1787, legitimate son of Pierre Joseph Maes (s), merchant, and Dame Marianne Dartigaux (s). Godparents: Pierre Dartigaux (s), merchant, and Dame Marie Monique Dutihl (s/ Marie Duthile Dartigaux).

1643. LOUIS GUILHAUMME DUPARE
September 28, 1790, baptism of Louis Guillaume, born October 10, 1789, legitimate son of Mr. Guilhaumme Dupare (s), lieutenant, and Anne Nanette Prudhomme (s). Godparents: Victor Dupain (s), merchant, and Dame Prudhomme Rouquier (s).

1644. NOTE: Entries 1637-1643 have been bound out of sequence. Correct chronological sequence resumes with Entry 1644, which is only a partial marriage entry at the top of the page, bearing the signatures: Ls. Tomasino (x); David, *temoins*; and Remy Poisot (x).

1645. ELISABETH MARCELLITE DEBLANC
June 5, 1791, baptism of Elisabeth Marcellite, born April 14, 1790, legitimate daughter of Louis Charles de Blanc, commandant of this post, and Dame Elisabeth Derneville. Godparents: Marcel de Soto and Celeste Mathie de Blanc.

1646. MARIE ROSELIE LARENADIERE
June 23, 1791, baptism of Marie Roselie, born May 18, legitimate daughter of Pierre Larenaudiere and Jeanne Labayrie. Godparents: Bouet Lafitte and Marie Rosalie Vercher.

1647. PIERRE DUPRE
FRANCOISE LECOURT
July 2, 1791, after 3 bans, marriage of Pierre Dupre, native of this parish, legitimate son of Joseph Dupre and Marie Derbanne . . . and . . . Francoise LeCourt, native of this parish, legitimate daughter of /Jean Louis Matthias/ Le Court and Jeanne /Le Roy/. Witnesses: Manuel Sompoy? (s), Athanase Poissot (x), Vergé (x) and Buard (s).

1648. MARIE EUPHRASIE BERNARD
July 9, 1791, baptism of Marie Euphrasie, born June 29, legitimate daughter of Elie Bernard and Eleonore Chagneau. Godparents: Sr. Barberou (x) and Dame Larenaudiere.

1649. LOUIS FORT
July 17, 1791, baptism of Louis, born May 3, 1791, son of Louis Jacques Fort and Marie Francoise Malbert. Godparents: Mr. Monet and Dlle. Barthelemy Rachal.

1650. MARIE MELANIE LAVESPERE
July 17, 1791, baptism of Marie Melanie, born _____ 29,

legitimate daughter of Sr. Francois Lavespere and Marie
Louise Derbanne. Godparents: Joseph /illegible/ and
Marie Verge.

1651. LOUIS GAGNE
July 17, 1791, baptism of Louis, born /illegible/, legitimate son of Pierre Gagne and /Marie Louise Davion/.
Godparents: /illegible/.

1652. UNKNOWN
1791. /Entry is almost completely torn away./

1653. MARIE LOLITTE RACHAL
April 10, 1791, baptism of Marie Lolitte, born January 6,
legitimate daughter of Julien Rachal and Marie Louise
Brevel. Godparents: Louis /illegible/ and Marie Dupre.

1654. NANETTE DENIS
April 10, 1791, baptism of Nanette, born September 3, 1790,
legitimate daughter of Jean Baptiste Denis and Marie Isabelle Baudoin. Godparents: Athanase Le Court and Nanette
Robin.

1655. BRUNO TOTIN
April 29, 1791, baptism of Bruno, born the 11th of that
month, legitimate son of Remy Totin and Marguerite Grillet.
Godparents: Gaspar Filibert and Genevieve Levasseur.

1656. MARIE DES DOULEURS DE SOTO
May 1, 1791, baptism of Marie des Douleurs, born March 5,
legitimate daughter of Marcel de Soto and Marie Baillo.
Godparents: Athanase Poissot and /illegible/.

1657. ANTOINE VASCOCU
GENEVIEVE GONIN
/date torn/, after 3 bans, marriage of /torn/ Vascocu, a
native of this parish, legitimate son of Antoine Vascocu
(x) and Marie Toups . . . and . . . Genevieve Gonin, native of this parish, legitimate daughter of /Jean Baptiste/
Gonin and Manuel Riché. Witnesses: Antoine Ploché (s/
Antoine Plauché), Louis Vascocu, Barnabé Cheletre, Jean
Baptiste Duboë (x), and Louis Vascocu (s).

1658. JEAN BAPTISTE LATTIER
MARIE PELAGIE FREDERIC
May 31, 1791, after 2 bans, marriage of Jean Baptiste
Lattier, native of this parish, legitimate son of Joseph
Lattier and Anne Verger . . . and . . . Marie Pelagie
Frederic, native of the parish of St. Charles, post des
Allemands, legitimate daughter of Philippe Frederic and
Marie Catherine Sauvage.

NOTE: no signatures; the entry is apparently continued

on the following page which is missing or out of place. Chronological sequence seems to indicate that this is the first part of the entry recorded as No. 1644.

1659. ETIENNE DUCHET
CATHERINE SALVAN
July 26, 1791, marriage, after 3 bans, of Etienne Duchet, native of Canada, son of Sr. Basile Duchet and Marie Louise Senecal . . . and . . . Catherine Salvan, native of the environs of New Orleans, legitimate daughter of Jean Salvan and Marie Louise Lambre. Witnesses: Louis Buard (x), Remy Lambre (s), Augustin Fredieu (x), Chrisostome Peraut (x).

1660. FREDIEU
July 26?, 1791, baptism of /illegible/, born May 10, legitimate daughter of Augustin Fredieu and Marie Jeanne Sorel. Godparents: Remy Lambre (s) and Marie Genevieve Sorel (s).

1661. DAVID ROBINSON
July 25, 1791, baptism of David, born the 25th of /illegible/, son of the one called Robinson and of Anne, his wife. Godparents: Andre David and /illegible/.

1662. LOUIS LEVASSEUR
October 9, 1791, baptism of Louis, born August 2, legitimate son of Jacques Levasseur and Therese Grillet. Godparents: Louis Lambre and Dame Louis Lambre.

1663. JOSEPH AIMABLE PEREAU (VILDEC)
October 13, 1791, baptism of Joseph Aimable, born December 1, 1790, legitimate son of Chrisostome Perau* and Marie Louise Salvat. Godparents: Julien Besson and Dame Widow Grappe.
*Above this name is written "Vildec."

1664. MARIE EUPHRASIE POMMIER
October 16, 1791, baptism of Marie Euphrasie, born September 15, legitimate daughter of Jean Pommier and Marie Robert Dupre. Godparents: Francois Cheletre and Cecile Robert /Dupre/.

1665. IGNACE LE MAITRE
November 4, 1791, baptism of Ignace, born August 2, 1791, legitimate son of Francois Le Maitre and Louise /le Duc/, his wife. Godparents: Baptiste Grappe and Marie /illegible/.

1666. MARIE CELESTE JEAN-RIS
November 4, 1791, baptism of Marie Celeste, born September 17, legitimate daughter of Joseph Jean-ris and of

Francoise Vascocu. Godparents: Antoine Vascocu and /illegible/.

1667. JEAN BAPTISTE DAVION
MARIE ULALIE VASCOCU
November 3, 1791, after 3 bans, marriage of Jean Baptiste Davion, native of this parish, legitimate son of Jean Baptiste Davion and Marie Hyacinthe Triche . . . and . . . Marie Ulalie Vascocu, native of this parish, legitimate daughter of Antoine Vascocu and Marie Barbe Toups. Witnesses: J. Bapt. Davion (s), Antoine Vascocu (x), Henry Trichet (s), and Andre Vascocu (s).

1668. JOSEPH TAUZIN
MARIE CHAMARD
November 8, 1791, after 3 bans, marriage of Joseph Tauzin, native of the town of /illegible/ in Auch, France, legitimate son of Gerard Tauzin and Jeanne Berthau . . . and . . . Marie Chamard, native of New Orleans, legitimate daughter of Louis Chamard and Dame Marie Catherine Bardon. Witnesses: Francois Rambin (s), Ailhaud Ste. Anne (s), Francois Lacaze (s), Marie Chagneau, Jh. Malige (s) and Marie Chagneau.

1669. MARIE CELESTINE BASTIEN /PRUDHOMME/
December 5, 1791, baptism of Marie Celestine Bastien, born August 27, daughter of Dlle. Marie Louise Bastien /Prudhomme/. Godparents: Guilhaume Valdeck and Dame Guilhaume Chever.

1670. JEAN BAPTISTE GAGNE
July ?, 1791, baptism of Jean Baptiste, born the 12th of /illegible/, legitimate son of Etienne Gagne and Marie Louise Bertrand. Godparents: /illegible/ and Marie Louise Gagne.

1671. PIERRE BEAULIEU
MARIE THERESE BEAUDOIN
December 12, 1791, after 3 bans, marriage of Pierre Beaulieu, native of St. Genevieve in Illinois, habitant of this post, son of Pierre Beaulieu and Genevieve /illegible/ . . . and . . . Marie Therese Beaudoin, daughter of Francois Beaudouin and Marianne Bontan. Witnesses: Andre Frederic (x), J. B. Dubois (x), P. Cheletre (x).

1672. JEAN BAPTISTE BARTHELEMY RACHAL
MARIE PELAGIE BREVELLE
December 19, 1791, after 2 bans, marriage of Jean Baptiste Barthelemy Rachal, native of this parish, legitimate son of Barthelemy Rachal and Marie Lamalaty . . . and . . . Marie Pelagie Brevelle, legitimate daughter of Jean Baptiste Brevel and Marie Françoise Poissot, a native of this

parish. Witnesses: Guerboi (s), La Verdalay (s), Gaspar Fiolle (x), Louis Barthelemy Rachal (s).

1673. MARIE AGATHA MAES
/torn/, 1791, baptism of Marie Agatha, born January 18, daughter of Joseph Maes (s) and Marianne Dartigeaux (s). Godparents: Pierre Joseph Mes, *fils*, and Marie Anne Conan Dartigaux (s).

1674. FRANCOIS ANTOINE CARLE /LE NOIR/*
January 1, 1792, baptism of Francois Antoine, born December 20, 1791, son of Marie Ulalie Carle. Godparents: Francois Feble, soldier, and Marie Louise Langlois.

*Book 11 of the Natchitoches Registers, under dates of May 30, 1831, and June 1, 1835, records the second and third marriages of Francois Antoine Carle Le Noir. The record of the second marriage identifies him as the "natural son of Lally /Eulalie/ Carle," while the record of the third marriage identifies him as "legitimate son of Antoine Lenoir and Eulalie Carle." *American State Papers - Public Lands*, III (38 vols., Washington, D.C.: Gales & Seaton, 1832-1861), p. 82, yields testimony relating to Antoine Lenoir, Sr. "his wife, and a child he had brought up" during the late 1790s. In 1778 Antoine Lenoir, Sr., married Marie Rondain (see Entry 1046). The editor has not found record of a subsequent marriage to Eulalie Carle. The identity of his wife in the late 1790s is not known.

1675. MARIE DES NEIGES BROM /BROWN/
January 15, 1792, baptism of Marie des Neiges, aged eleven months, legitimate daughter of Thomas Brom and Marie Tiel /Teal/. Godparents: Jean Baptiste David and Dame Gaspar Fiolle.

1676. MARIE THERESE BERTRAND
January 22, 1792, baptism of Marie Therese, born November 22, 1791, daughter of Louis Bertrand and Ysabelle Davion. Godparents: Louis Clauso and Dlle. Marie Gagné.

1677. JOSEPH DE L'EPIPHENIE BOSSIER
February 19, 1792, baptism of Joseph de L'Epiphenie, born January ?, 1792, legitimate son of François Bossie and Dame Catherine Pelagie Lambre. Godparents: Joseph Lambre and Marie Therese Eugenie Buard.

1678. MARIE POMPOSE
February 19, 1792, baptism of Marie Pompose, aged one year or about, daughter of Nanette, Indian. Godparents: Francois Monginot and Marie Genevieve Jean-ris.

1679. JEAN BAPTISTE LEMOINE
FELICITE LACAZE
February 21, 1792, after one ban, marriage of Jean Baptiste
Lemoine, native of this parish, son of Charles Lemoine and
Isabelle Dupre . . . and . . . Felicité Lacaze, native of
the parish of Opelousas, daughter of Charles Lacaze and
Felicité Langlois. Witnesses: Charles Lacaze (x), Antoine
Lemoine (x), Etienne Verge (x), Jacques Lacaze (x).

1680. VALENTIN
February 27, 1792, baptism of /illegible/, legitimate son
of Andre Francois Vallentin and Marie Malige. Godparents:
Mr. Malige and Dame Labayrie.

1681. MARIE GENEVIEVE EUPHRASIE ANTY
March 4, 1792, baptism of Marie Genevieve Euphrasie, born
January 20, daughter of Jean Baptiste Anty and Marie François Levasseur. Godparents: François Levasseur and
Genevieve Levasseur.

1682. MARIE ZEMISE BEAUDOIN
April 7, 1792, baptism of Marie Zemise, born February 5,
daughter of Pierre Beaudoin and Anne Robin. Godparents:
Jean Nicolas Beaudoin and Marie Elisabeth Beaudoin.

1683. MARIE LOUISE EUPHRASIE PRUDHOMME
April 8, 1792, baptism of Marie Louise Euphrasie, born
January _?_, 1792, legitimate daughter of Francois Prudhomme
and Marie Barbe Rambin. Godparents: Pierre Ternier and
Euphrasie Rambin.

1684. MARIE FRANCOISE MORALES
April 14, 1792, baptism of Marie Francoise, legitimate
daughter of Joseph Manuel Morales and Marie Pologne. Godparents: Etienne Vergé and Mme. Etienne Vergé.

1685. ANGELIQUE DOMICILE RABALÉ
April 15, 1792, baptism of Angelique Domicile, born January 15, legitimate daughter of Joseph Rabalé and Marie
Louise Malbert. Godparents: Etienne Vergé and Angelique
Malbert.

1686. JEAN BAPTISTE DENIS RAMBIN
April 15, 1792, baptism of Jean Baptiste Denis, born June
5, 1791, legitimate son of Andre Rambin and Marie Catherine /Buard/. Godparents: Louis Buard and Marie Anne
Gabriel /Buard née Rousseau/.

1687. JEAN BAPTISTE DORCIN MAÏOU
April 15, 1792, baptism of Jean Baptiste Dorcin, born March
3, 1791, son of Ignace Maïou and Marie Louise? (Therese?)
Tibau /Flibot?/. Godparents: J. Babt. Dortolant and

/‾Illegible_7 Maïou.

1688. MICHEL RAMBINT
       MARIE THERESE MAILLIOUX
       May 22?, 1792, after 1 ban, marriage of Michel Rambint,
       native of this parish, legitimate son of deceased Andre
       Rambint and Francoise Clermont . . . and . . . Marie
       Therese Maillioux, native of this post, legitimate daugh-
       ter of Ignace Maillioux and Marie Therese Filibote, his
       spouse. Witnesses: Louis Chamard, Luis Marli (s/ Louis
       Sorel Marli X), Laurent Maillouxe, Francois Rambin.

1689. MARIE MATHILDE /‾STA. CRU_Z_7*
       July 15, 1792, baptism of Marie Mathilde, aged one month,
       daughter of an Indian and a father unknown.* Godparents:
       Benoit Pascio, soldier, and Dame Ramis.

       *See Entry 2092.

1690. MARIE BOSSIER
       July 15, 1792, baptism of Marie, born April 15, legitimate
       daughter of Silvestre Bossier and Marie Lambre. Godpar-
       ents: Jean Louis Lambre and Marie Therese Eugenie Lambre.

1691. MARIE ROSE LATTIER
       /‾Illegible_7, 1792, baptism of Marie Rose, legitimate daugh-
       ter of Jean Baptiste Latie and Marie Pelagie Frederic.
       Godparents: Joseph Latie and Dame Frederic.

1692. HELOÏSE SERAPHINE MALIGE
       July 30, 1792, baptism of Heloïse Seraphine, born July 15,
       daughter of M. Malige and Marie Anne Bardon. Godparents:
       Remi Lambre (s) and Dame Armant (s/ Therese Armant).

1693. JEAN BAPTISTE BELONI VERCHER
       August 25, 1792, baptism of Jean Baptiste, born April 22,
       legitimate son of Louis Vercher and Marie Louise Grillet.
       Godparents: Jean Pierre Vercher and Elizabeth David.

REGISTER 4

1694. UNKNOWN
/Partial entry, bearing only the signatures: Louis de Blanc, Marie de St. Denis, Elizabeth Derneville, and Le Chv. Coulon de Villiers.

1695. LUIS BASILIO GAGNE
June 17, 1776, baptism of Luis Basilio, born June 15, legitimate son of Esteban Gagne and Maria Luisa Dauphine.*
Godparents: Luis Beteran /Bertrand/ (x) and Mariana Grappe (x).

*Above this name is written the name "Bertrand."

1696. JUAN BAUTISTA FRANCISCO LAFFITTE
July 2, 1776, baptism of Juan Bautista Francisco, born June 24, 1776, legitimate son of *Cadet* Beouet La Fitte and Magdalena Grappe. Godparents: Juan Bautista Grappe (s) and Mariana Grappe (x).

1697. AITHANASIO MARIA POISSOT
July 29, 1776, baptism of Aithanasio Maria, legitimate son of Athanasio Poissot and Maria de Soto. Godparents: Remigio Poissot (s) and Maria de Nieves (s/ Marie de St. denis).

1698. JOSEF MARIA FELIX ARMANT
August 4, 1776, baptism of Josef Maria Felix, born July 10, legitimate son of Joseph Armant Maria and Theresa le Gros. Godparents: Athanasio de Mezieres (s) and Maria Genovefa /Illegible/ (s).

1699. JACOBO LA LANDE
September 1, 1776, baptism of Jacobo, born July 8, legitimate son of Juan La Lande and Catalina de Pret. Godparents: Remigio Poissot (s) and Maria Luisa Dupres.

1700. PELAGIA BAILLIO
September 8, 1776, baptism of Pelagia, born August 18, legitimate daughter of Pedro Baillio and Catalina Poissot. Godparents: Jacobo Lambre (x) and Maria Luisa Derbanne (x).

1701. MARIA JOSEFA GAGNE
September 22, 1776, baptism of Maria Josefa, born August 23, legitimate child of Pedro Gagné and Maria Luisa Davion. Godparents: Nicolas Tibot, absent, and represented by Ignacio Mayoux (s/ Ignace Maillioux) and Maria Theresa Thilibou.

1702. MARIA JOSEPH POIRIER
October 17, 1776, baptism of Maria Joseph, born July 6, legitimate son of Joseph Poirier and Maria Francisca Le Doux (s). Godparents: Gabriel Antonio Le Doux (s) and Francisca Fazende. Witnesses: J. Chevalier.

1703. LUIS
January 16, 1777, baptism of Luis, born 1770, an Apalacho Indian, already *endoyé*, legitimate son of Joseph Manuel, Apalacho, and Maria Lorensa, also an Indian. Godparents: Martin Gutierrez de Lana and Maria Gregoria de Sta. Cruz.

1704. JUAN BAUTISTA CASTEL
January 19, 1777, baptism of Juan Bautista, born January 16 and *endoyé*, son of Maria Castel and a father unknown. Godparents: Juan Bautista Derbanne (s) and Maria Felicidad Dupain (s/ Felicité Dupain).

1705. JACOBO CASTEL
January 19, 1777, baptism of Jacobo, born January 16 and *endoyé*, a twin of Juan Bautista /Entry 1704/ and son of Maria Castel by a father unknown. Godparents: Josef Duprès and Maria Ana Deroie.

1706. MARIA ROSA VASCOCU
January 27, 1777, baptism of Maria Rosa, born January 24 and *endoyée*, legitimate daughter of Antonio Vascocu and Maria Barbara Tups, and a twin of Maria Juana /Entry 1707/. Godparents: Juan Bautista Roujot and Maria Isabel Demouy (s/ Elizabeth).

1707. MARIA JUANA VASCOCU
January 27, 1777, baptism of Maria Juana, born January 24, legitimate daughter of Antonio Vascocu and Maria Barbara Tups, and a twin of Maria Rosa /Entry 1706/. Godparents: Francisco Rambin (s) and Maria Ana Dartigaux (s).

1708. PEDRO RACHAL
January 30, 1777, baptism of Pedro, born January 21, legitimate son of Bartolome Rachal and Maria Francesca La Malaty. Godparents: Pedro La Cour (s) and Maria Luisa Prudhomme (s).

1709. FRANCISCO DUPRES
February 9, 1777, baptism of Francisco, born February 3, legitimate son of Josef Dupres and Maria Derbanne. Godparents: Athanasio de Mezieres (s) and Maria Genovefa Fontenette (s).

1710. CATALINA SALVAGE
/illegible dates of baptism and birth/, legitimate daughter of Luis Salvage, Apalaty, and Maria Juana /illegible/. Godparents: /illegible/.

1711. MARIA LA COUR
March 7, 1777, baptism of Maria, born March 3, legitimate daughter of Pedro Lacour (s) and Maria Luisa Vergaire. Godparents: Josef Boulet and Maria Dupres.

1712. ANGELA MALVER
March 9, 1777, baptism of Angela, born March 6, legitimate daughter of Juan Bautista Malver and Juana Verger. Godparents: Juan Bautista Derbanne and Francisca Malver.

1713. MARIA PAULA DE LOS DOLORES TORRES
March 31, 1777, baptism of Maria Paula de los Dolores, born March 22, legitimate daughter of Josef Torres and Juana de los Reyes, residents of Los Adais. Godparents: Nicolas de la Motte and Maria Josefa de Soto.

1714. MARIA ISABEL BREVELLE
April 27, 1777, baptism of Maria Isabel, born April 26, legitimate daughter of Juan Bautista Brevel and Maria Francesca Poissot. Godparents: Josef Dupres and Maria Isabel Demouy.

1715. FRANCISCO PRUDHOMME
May 18, 1777, baptism of Francisco, born May 15, legitimate son of Juan Bautista Prudhomme and Enriqua /Corantine/. Godparents: Francisco Prudhomme (x) and Maria Genovefa Fontenette (s).

1716. PABLO COUTY
May 25, 1777, baptism of Pablo, born May 23, legitimate son of Juan Couty and Maria Francesca _____ /sic/. Godparents: Pablo Bouet Lafitte (s) and Magdalena Grappe.

1717. MARIA LUISA LANGLOIS
June 13, 1777, baptism of Maria Luisa, born November 29, 1776, legitimate daughter of Luis Augusto Langlois (s) and Maria Luisa Richèe. Godparents: Luis Coulong, Chevalier de Villier (s) and Maria Theresa Le gros (s).

1718. JOSEPH DOMINGO VILLAREAL
September 7, 1777, baptism of Joseph Domingo, born August 31, legitimate son of Joseph Villareal and Maria Francisca /Morin7. Godparents: Martin Gutierrez and Maria Andres Chisilo.

1719. JUAN ESTEBAN LESTAGE
September 15, 1777, baptism of Juan Esteban, born August 24, legitimate son of Guillelmo Lestage and Manuela Riché. Godparents: Juan Adlee (s/ Jean Adle) and Isabel Demouy (s/ Elizabeth).

1720. JUAN ANTONIO FORTIN
September 19, 1777, baptism of Juan Antonio, born September 6, 1777, legitimate son of Luis Fortin and Magdalena La Renaudiere. Godparents: Juan Bautista Pieferme and Maria Larenaudiere.

1721. DOMINGO RACHAL
September 21, 1777, baptism of Domingo, born July 18 and endoyé, legitimate son of Santiago Rachal and Ursula Castel. Godparents: Domingo Montege (x) and Maria Juana Le Vasseur (x).

1722. MARIA LUISA MARTA DEBLANC
October 19, 1777, baptism of Maria Luisa Marta, born July 30, legitimate daughter of Dn. Luis Carlos Deblanc and Isabel Ponponne Derneville. Godparents: Luis Antonio de St. Denis and Luisa Margarita de St. Denis.

1723. NICOLAS LEMAITRE
November 5, 1777, baptism of Nicolas, born November 3, legitimate son of Francesco Le Maitre and Maria Luisa /le Duc dit7 Ville franche. Godparents: Nicolas Laignon (s) and Luisa Guedon.

1724. MARIA TERESA MALLOUX
November 15, 1777, baptism of Maria Teresa, born October 30, 1777, legitimate daughter of Ignacio Malloux and Teresa Fibote. Godparents: Santiago Ride (s) and Maria Juana Chagnon.

1725. JUAN BAUTISTA FRANCISCO LE DOUX
November 20, 1777, baptism of Juan Bautista Francisco, born September 8 and endoyé, legitimate son of Francisco Le Doux (s) and Margarita Roujot (s). Godparents: Juan Bautista Roujot (s) and Isabel Demouy (s).

1726. ISABEL DAVID
November 22, 1777, baptism of Isabel, born November 20, legitimate daughter of Andres David and Maria Juana La Malaty. Godparents: Pedro Lacosta (s) and Theresa La Malaty (x).

1727. MARIA BANDICHON /BONTEMPS/
December 8, 1777, baptism of Maria, born the preceeding month, natural daughter of the wife of Baudouin*. Godparents: Manuel Prudhomme (s) and Maria Ana Dartigaux (s).

*At this point are inserted the words "Marie Anne Bandichon." This is a poor phoenetic spelling of the actual name of Mme. Baudouin -- Bontemps.

1728. JUAN BAUTISTA ORTOLANT
December 26, 1777, baptism of Juan Bautista, *endoyé*, the legitimate son of Bernardo Ortolant and Maria Ana Grappe. Godparents: Juan Bautista Grappe (s) and Margarita Guedon.

1729. LUIS LE VASSEUR
January 20, 1778, baptism of Luis, born December 27, 1777, legitimate son of Francisco Le Vasseur and Maria Juana Mader. Godparents: Luis Jobar, represented by Luis Vascocu who states that Jobar is absent, and Maria Theresa Trichele.

1730. DELETTA VERGER (DELEITA VERCHAIRE)*
February 8, 1778, baptism of Deleita,* born February 3, legitimate daughter of Luis Verchaire and Maria Luisa Grillet. Godparents: Pedro Scheletre and Barbara Schelete.

*This name is written in the text as Deleita Verchaire and incorrectly in the margin as Deletta Verger. "Deleita" is probably an abbreviated version of "Adelaida."

1731. MANUEL TRICHELE
February 22, 1778, baptism of Manuel, born February 4, legitimate son of Juan Bautista Trichele and Maria Ana Daublin. Godparents: Manuel Trichele (s) and Maria Ana Dartigaux (s).

1732. JUAN BAUTISTA ADLET
February 23, 1778, baptism of Juan Bautista, born January 23 and *endoyé*, legitimate son of Juan Bautista Adlet and Maria Genovefa Dubois. Godparents: Juan Bautista Dubois and Maria Josepha Clairmont.

1733. MARIA LUISA EUFRASIE RAMBIN
March 1, 1778, baptism of Maria Luisa Eufrasie, born February 24, legitimate daughter of Andres Rambin and Maria Catalina Buard. Godparents: Francisco Rambin (s) and Maria Luisa Buart (s).

1734. MARIA FRANCISCA HELENA POIRIER
March 8, 1778, baptism of Maria Francesca Helena, born November 15, 1777, and *endoyée*, legitimate daughter of

Josef Poirier and Maria Francisca Le Doux. Godparents: Angel Carlos Le Doux (s/ Charles Le Doux) and Maria Francesca Poirier, represented by Clemencia Borme (s/ Clemense Borme).

1735. FRANCISCO TRICHELE
March 11, 1778, baptism of Francisco, born March 4, legitimate daughter of Manuel Trichele and Maria Luisa Grappe. Godparents: Francisco Grappe (s) and Pelagia Grappe (s).

1736. JUAN BAUTISTA MARINO ADLEE
February 23, 1778, baptism of Juan Bautista Marino, born January 23, 1778 and *endoyé*, legitimate son of Juan Bautista Adlee and Maria Genovefa Dubois. Godparents: Juan Bautista Dubois (s) and Maria Josepha Clairemont (s).

1737. MARIA BAUTISTA ARMANT
March 25, 1778, baptism of Maria Bautista, born February 19, 1778, legitimate son of Maria Joseph Armant (s) and Theresa Le Gros. Godparents: Juan Bautista St. Anne Aillhaud (s/ Ailhaud Ste. Anne) and Maria Ana Dartigaux (s).

1738. JUAN BAUTISTA ARMAND
April 10, 1778, baptism of Juan Bautista, born February 18, 1778, a natural son of Juan Bautista Armand and of Felicite Du Pain. Godparents: Juan Bautista LeComte and Maria Le Court.

1739. MARIA FRANCISCA ROSALIA GAGNE
May 20, 1778, baptism of Maria Francisca Rosalia, born May 19, legitimate daughter of Esteban Gagne and Maria Luisa /Bertrand/. Godparents: Pedro Bertran and Maria Francisca Grappe.

1740. MARIA CELESTIA VERGER
June 25, 1778, baptism of Maria Celestia, born June 23, legitimate daughter of Esteban Verger and Maria Francisca Dupres. Godparents: Josef Dupres, represented by Joseph Dupres, *fils*, and /illegible/ Verger.

1741. JUAN LUIS BUART
March 20, 1778, baptism of Juan Luis, born February 16, legitimate son of Luis Gabriel Buart and Maria Rosa Lambre. Godparents: Juan Lambre (x), his grandfather, and Maria Francisca Buart (s).

1742. MARIA POMIER
September 29, 1778, baptism of Maria, born September 5 and *endoyée*, legitimate daughter of Juan Pomier and Maria Dupres. Godparents: Juan Bautista Denis and Margarita Frederic.

1743. MARIA FRANCISCA CLARA CHARRON
September 20, 1778, baptism of Maria Francisca Clara, born June 15, legitimate daughter of Pedro Esteban Charron (s) and Maria Ana Olivaut. Godparents: Francisco Grappe (s) and Maria Francesca Grappe.

1744. HELENA ROBLAU
September 21, 1778, baptism of Helena, born September 11, legitimate daughter of Guillermo Roblau and Antonio Zedora de Zepeda. Godparents: Luis Gabriel Buart and Pelagie Lambre (s).

1745. MARIA CATALINA BROSSET
September 29, 1778, baptism of Maria Catalina, born September 29, legitimate daughter of Pedro Brosset and Maria Josefa Grillet. Godparents: Josef Dupres and Maria Catalina Lambre (s).

1746. MARIA MARTA FORT
October 7, 1778, baptism of Maria Marta, born September 29, legitimate daughter of Santiago Fort and Francisca Malber. Godparents: Gaspar Derbanne (s) and Maria Juana Verger (s).

1747. MARIA TERESA ROSALIA JACINTA LAFITTE
October 7, 1778, baptism of Maria Teresa Rosalia Jacinta, born October 6, legitimate daughter of Pablo Blouet la Fitte and Maria Madalena Grappe. Godparents: Manuel Trichele and Maria Teresa Trichele.

1748. DOROTEA MASIPE
October 11, 1778, baptism of Dorotea, born October 8 and *endoyée*, legitimate daughter of Juan Masipe and Maria Le Moine. Godparents: Carlos Le Moine and Dorotea Vildec.

1749. GENOVEFA BODIN
October 18, baptism of Genovefa, who was born "the current month," legitimate daughter of Lorenzo Bodin and Micaela Rosalia Santa Cruz. Godparents: Felipe Frederic and Barbara Schelet.

1750. MARIA JULIANA SENTION?* TORRES
January 25, 1779, baptism of Maria Juliana, born January 9, legitimate daughter of Josef Torres and Juana de los Reyes. Godparents: M_____ /illegible/ Demouy and Maria Josepha Soto.

*The name "<u>Sention?</u>" appears in the margin but not in the text. Perhaps "Sention" is a phoenetic spelling of the Spanish given name "de l'Ascension".

1751. ESTEBAN RACHAL
February 8, 1779, baptism of Esteban, born January 24, legitimate son of Bartolome Rachal and Maria Francisca Lamalaty. Godparents: Esteban Pavie and Maria Teresa Buart.

1752. JUAN BAUTISTA DUPRES
February 15, 1779, baptism of Juan Bautista, born January 31, legitimate son of Josef Dupres and Maria Encarnacion Derbanne. Godparents: Pedro Derbanne, represented by Pedro Derbanne, Jr., and Maria Luisa Derbanne.

1753. JUAN BAUTISTA FREDERIC
January 20, 1779, baptism of Juan Bautista Frederic, born January 18, legitimate son of Felipe Federic and Maria Catalina Sauvage. Godparents: Juan Bautista Dartigaux (s) and Maria Catalina Lambre (s).

1754. MARIA TERESA ARMAND
February 22, 1779, baptism of Maria Teresa, born February 10, legitimate daughter of Juan Bautista Armand and Maria Felicidad Dupain. Godparents: Juan Bautista Prudhomme (s) and Therese Le gros (s). Also signed: Jean Marie Armant.

1755. JUAN BAUTISTA LESTAGE
March 7, 1779, baptism of Juan Bautista, born February 15, legitimate son of Guillermo Lestage and Manuele Riche. Godparents: Juan Bautista Labery (s) and Pelagia Grappe.

1756. JUAN BAUTISTA PLAISANCE
March 7, 1779, baptism of Juan Bautista, born February 15, legitimate son of Juan Bautista Plaisance and Marguerita Toutin. Godparents: Francisco Toutin and Juana Guedon.

1757. HELENA BAILLIOT
April 20, 1779, baptism of Helena, born February 27, legitimate daughter of Pedro Bailliot (s) and Mariana Schelet. Godparents: Joseph Dupres and Barbara Schelet.

1758. JUAN BAUTISTA BREVELLE
April 26, 1779, baptism of Juan Bautista, born April 15, legitimate son of Juan Bautista Brevelle and Francisca Poisot. Godparents: Juan Bautista Dupres and Maria Luisa Lecompte.

1759. DIEGO ANTONIO BACA
May 3, 1779, baptism of Diego Antonio, born December of 1778 and endoyó, legitimate son of Diego Antonio Baca, native of Lugur de Tomé and Maria Antonia Sanchez, native of the same place. Godparents: Antonio Noir and Francesca Larenaudiere.

1760. MANUEL GAGNE
June 3, 1779, baptism of Manuel, born May 20 and *endoyé*, legitimate son of Pedro Gañe and Maria Luisa Davion. Godparents: Manuel Davion and Teresa Prudhomme.

1761. BAUTISTA LE MAITRE
June 3, 1779, baptism of Bautista, born June 2, legitimate son of Francisco le Maitre and Maria Luisa /le Duc/. Godparents: Guillermo le Brun and Juana Guedon.

1762. MARIA MAGDALENA GRILLET
June 13, 1779, baptism of Maria Magdalena, born June 8, legitimate daughter of Marino Grillet (s) and Maria Luisa Brevel. Godparents: Pedro Baillot and Ana Barbara Pomier.

1763. ESTEBAN VALERIO LE DOUX
July 8, 1779, baptism of Esteban Valerio, born July 5, legitimate son of Francisco Le Doux and Margarita Roujot. Godparents: Esteban Pavie (s) and Clemencia Borme (s).

1764. ANDRES VILLAREAL
August ?, 1779, baptism of Andres, born August 1, legitimate son of Josef Villareal and Francisca /Morin/. Godparents: Andre Vascocu (s) and Maria Ana Guedon.

1765. IGNACIO ANTY
September 5, 1779, baptism of Ignacio, born June 19, legitimate son of Juan Bautista Anty and Catalina Galien. Godparents: Luis Anty (s) and Theresa Lamalaty (s).

1766. PABLO POISSOT
September 27, 1779, baptism of Pablo, born September 13, legitimate son of Remigio Poisot, Jr., and Luisa Cavé. Godparents: Gaspar Derbanne and Maria Luisa Derbanne.

1767. MARIA VICTORIA POISSOT
September 27, 1779, baptism of Maria Victoria, born September 13, twin of Pablo /Entry 1766/, legitimate daughter of Remigio Poisot, Jr., and Luisa Cavé. Godparents: Francisco Le Vasseur and Maria Victoria Derbanne.

1768. MARIA LUIS CESARIO DEBLANC
October 2, 1779, baptism of Maria Luis Cesario, born September 7, 1779, legitimate son of Luis Carlos Deblanc and Isabel Ponpona Derneville. Godparents: Joseph Maria Carlos Deblanc and Maria Luisa Marta Deblanc.

1769. LUIS ANDRES RAMBIN
October 2, 1779, baptism of Luis Andres, born September 25, legitimate son of Andres Rambin (s) and Maria Catalina Buart. Godparents: Luis Gabriel Buart (x) and

Maria Barbara Rambin.

1770. VALENTIN ADLET
November 17, 1779, baptism of Valentin, born November 15 and *endoyé*, legitimate son of Juan Adlet (s) and Maria Genovefa /Dubois/. Godparents: Juan Bautista Valentin Dubois and Maria Francisca Clermont.

1771. MARIA FELICIDAD DELEIDA ARMANT
January 8, 1780, baptism of Maria Felicidad Deleida, born December 9, 1779, legitimate daughter of Josef Maria Armant and Maria Theresa Gros. Godparents: Juan Bautista Dartiguax (s) and Maria Felicidad Dupain (s/ Felicite Armant).

1772. JUAN BAUTISTA BUART
February 19, 1780, baptism of Juan Bautista, born February 17, legitimate son of Luis Gabriel Buart and Maria Rosa Lambre. Godparents: Juan Bautista Buart and Pelagia Lambre (s/ Catherine Pelagie Lambre).

1773. MANUEL SIMEON /LE/ VASSEUR
March 2, 1780, baptism of Manuel Simeon, born February 23, legitimate son of Francisco Vasseur and Maria Juana Mader. Godparents: Luis Gabriel Buart and Catalina Pelagia Lambre.

1774. ESTEBAN TRICHE
March 15, 1780, baptism of Esteban, born February 25, legitimate son of Bautista Triche, deceased, and Mariana Doblin (s). Godparents: Esteban Pavie and Enriquita Prudhomme.

1775. JUAN PEDRO VERCHAIRE
March 22, 1780, baptism of Juan Pedro, born February 20, legitimate son of Luis Verchaire and Maria Luisa Grillet. Godparents: Antonio Grillet and Maria Juana Grillet.

1776. MARIA LUISA CLAVIS (SAIDET)
May 13, 1780, baptism of Maria Luisa, born July 11, 1779, daughter of Pedro Clavis Saidet and Ursula Schelet, his wife. Godparents: Pedro Schelet and Maria Ana Schelet.

1777. MARIA FRANCISCO LUIS FONTENOT
May 16, 1780, baptism of Maria Francisco Luis, born April 16 and *endoyé*, legitimate son of Luis Fontenot and Pelagia Grappe. Godparents: Francisco Grappe (s) and Maria Luisa Guedon.

1778. ESTEBAN VERGER
June 8, 1780, baptism of Esteban, born May 30, legitimate

son of Esteban Verger and Maria Francisca Dupres. Godparents: Atanasio Poisot and Maria Manuela de Soto.

1779. JUAN BAUTISTA BROSSET
June 11, 1780, baptism of Juan Bautista, born May 19, legitimate son of Pedro Brosset and Maria Josefa Grillet. Godparents: Andres Frederic and Maria Juana Grillet.

1780. MARIA ISABEL BOUSSER *dit* LE BRUN
August 11, 1780, baptism of Maria Isabel Bousser, born August 10, legitimate daughter of Guillermo le Brun (s) (Bousser) and Maria Luisa Totin. Godparents: Juan Bautista Labery (s) and Juana Guedon.

1781. AUGUSTO BAILLIOT
August 12, 1780, baptism of Augusto, born July 22, legitimate son of Pedro Bailliot and Maria Ana Schelet. Godparents: Bernabé Schelet and Maria Victoria Derbanne.

1782. JUAN PEDRO JULIAN RAYMUNDO ORTOLANT
September 30, 1780, baptism of Juan Pedro Julian Raymundo, born September 21, legitimate son of Bernardo Ortolant and Maria Ana Grappe. Godparents: Julian Besson (s) and Maria Francisca Grappe.

1783. MARIA ISABEL GANNIER (GAGNE)
September 30, 1780, baptism of Maria Isabel, born September 27, legitimate daughter of Esteban Gagne and Luisa Bertrand. Godparents: Julien Besson (s) and Maria Isabel Davion.

1784. JOSEPH LUIS LAMBRE
October 2, 1780, baptism of Joseph Luis, born September 4, 1780, legitimate son of Juan Lambre and Maria Juana Le Vasseur. Godparents: Luis Gabriel Buart and Maria Catalina Lambre (s).

1785. MARIA TERESA BREVEL
November 1, 1780, baptism of Maria Teresa, born October 24 and *endoyée*, legitimate daughter of Juan Bautista Brevelle and Maria Francisca Poissot. Godparents: Francisco Merier and Maria Soto.

1786. MARIA JOSEFA PAVIE
November 19, 1780, baptism of Maria Josefa, born August 15 and *endoyée*, legitimate daughter of Esteban Pavie and Theresa Buart. Godparents: Luis Buart and Maria Juana Buart.

1787. MARIA SELEUSIA JACINTA TRICHE
November 27, 1780, baptism of Maria Seleusia Jacinta,

born October 20, legitimate daughter of Manuel Triche and Maria Luisa Grappe. Godparents: Pedro Pablo Laffitte and Maria Francisca Grappe.

1788. MARIA ISIDORA ROBLEAU
November 30, 1780, baptism of Maria Isidora, born November 20, legitimate daughter of Guillelmo Robleau and Antonio Isidora Zepeda. Godparents: Bertrand Plaisence and Madalena Labery.

1789. JOSEF MARIA _____
December 8, 1780, baptism of Josef Maria, born in November and *endoyé*, son of a white father and mother "unknown."

1790. MARIA FRANCISCA CLAVIS SAIDET
December 17, 1780, baptism of Maria Francisca Clavis, born December 8, legitimate daughter of Pedro Clavis Saidet and Ursula Chelete. Godparents: Pedro Bailliot, represented by Andres Frederic, and Francisca Chelete.

1791. GUILLELMO JUAN MIGUEL BARBEROUSSE
December 17, 1780, baptism of Guillelmo Juan Miguel, born December 6, legitimate son of Guillelmo Barberousse (s/ Barbaroux) and Maria Juana Chainiot. Godparents: Miguel Chainiot, represented by Josef Jeanris, and Maria Juana Chainiot.

1792. MARIA FRANCISCA IMEL
February 24, 1781, baptism of Maria Francisca, born January 20, legitimate daughter of Antonio Imel and Margarita Shelete. Godparents: Francisco /Le/ Vasseur and Francisca Chelete.

1793. ANDRES FREDERIC
February 25, 1781, baptism of Andres, born January 12, 1780, legitimate son of Felipe Frederic and Barbara Chelete. Godparents: Andres Frederic and Francisca Chelete.

1794. JUAN DAVID DUPRES
March 19, 1781, baptism of Juan David, born February 27, legitimate son of Josef Dupre and Maria Derbanne. Godparents: Atanasio Poissot and Maria Luisa Dupres.

1795. ANTONIO RACHAL
April 8, 1781, baptism of Antonio, born March 29, legitimate son of Bartolome Rachal and Maria Lamalaty. Godparents: Antonio Grillet and Maria Lambre.

1796. FRANCISCO PRUDHOMME
May 6, 1781, baptism of Francisco, born April 30,

legitimate son of Francisco Prudhomme and Maria Rambin.
Godparents: Andre Rambin (s) and Maria Luisa Prudhomme.

1797. MARIA FRANCISCA ADELAIDE RAMBIN
May 6, 1781, baptism of Maria Francisco, born April 10, legitimate daughter of Andres Rambin and Catalina Buart. Godparents: Francisco Prudhomme and Isabel Josephe (s/ Elizabeth Joseph Buard).

1798. MARIA CATALINA FREDERIC
June 3, 1781, baptism of Maria Catalina, born May 15, legitimate daughter of Felipe Frederic and Maria Catalina Sauvage (s). Godparents: Andres Frederic and Margarita Grillet.

1799. FRANCISCO LESTAGE
June 10, 1781, baptism of Francisco, born May 25, legitimate son of Guillermo Lestage and Manuela Riche. Godparents: Francisco Dubois and Ana Barbara Pomier.

1800. FRANCISCO ENRIQUE FREDERIC
July 23, 1781, baptism of Francisco Enrique, born July 15 and *endoyé*, legitimate son of Francisco Frederic and Maria Juana Chainion. Godparents: Joseph Aise (s/ Janris) and Eleonor, his sister.

1801. PEDRO MAZIPE
August 5, 1781, baptism of Pedro, born July 24, legitimate son of Juan Masipe and Maria le Moine. Godparents: Carlos Le Moine and Maria Ana Dartigaux (s/ Marianne David).

1802. VICTORIA CONSTANCIA LE MAITRE
August 5, 1781, baptism of Victoria Constancia, born August 3, legitimate daughter of Francois Le Maitre and Maria Luisa /Le Duc/. Godparents: Remigio Toutin and Maria Luisa Labery (s/ Louise Agathe Laberry).

1803. MARIA JACINTA ANASTASIA MAYOUX
August 31, 1781, baptism of Maria Jacinta Anastasia, born August 27, legitimate daughter of Ignacio Mayoux (s/ Ignace Maillioux) and Maria Teresa Fhelipot. Godparents: Miguel Chainniot and Juana Chainiot.

1804. MARIA LUISA ANTY
September 8, 1781, baptism of Maria Luisa, born May 26, legitimate daughter of Juan Bautista Anty and Catalina Galien. Godparents: Ambrosio Le Compte and Maria Luisa Dupres.

1805.   PEDRO ANDRES TRICHE
        December 25, 1781, baptism of Pedro Andres, born November 30, legitimate son of Manuel Triche and Maria Luisa
        Grappe. Godparents: Juan Bautista Grappe (s) and
        Maria Teresa Triche (s), sister of the infant.

1806.   MARGARITA MODESTIA /LE/ VASSEUR
        February 7, 1782, baptism of Margarita Modestia, born
        January 15, legitimate daughter of Francisco Vasseur
        and Maria Juana Mader. Godparents: Juan Bautista Buart
        and Catalina Lambre (s).

1807.   FRANCISCO ADLET
        February 8, 1782, baptism of Francisco, born January 15,
        legitimate son of Juan Esteban Adlet and Maria Genovefa
        Dubois. Godparents: Francisco Rouquier (s) and Luisa
        Rambin.

1808.   MARIA JOSEFA MADELENA ISIDORA CHRISTILLE
        February 17, 1782, baptism of Maria Josefa Madelena Isidora, born January 26 and *endoyée*, legitimate daughter
        of Jacques Christille and Maria Ana Dorotea Vildeque.
        Godparents: Pedro Baillot and Maria Josefa Vildegue.

1809.   JULIAN BODIN
        April 1, 1782, baptism of Julian, born April 1, 1781,
        legitimate son of Lorenzo Bodin and Micaela Crux. Godparents: Julian Rachal and Maria Luisa Brevel.

1810.   FELICIDAD RACHAL
        April 7, 1782, baptism of Felicidad, born February 21,
        legitimate daughter of Luis Rachal and Maria Luisa Le
        Roy. Godparents: Remigio Lambre (s/ Remy Lambre) and
        Widow Jn. Bta. Dupres.

1811.   JUAN BAUTISTA DEBLANC
        April 7, 1782, baptism of Juan Bautista, born January
        20 and *endoyé*, legitimate son of Luis Deblanc and Isabel
        Derneville. Godparents: Juan Bautista Florien and
        Juana Helena Florien, represented by Cesario Deblanc and
        Maria Luisa Prudhomme (s/ Marie Loüise Rouquier).

1812.   JUAN LUIS BAILLIOT
        April 12, 1782, baptism of Juan Luis, born March 10,
        legitimate son of Pedro Bailliot and Maria Ana Chelete.
        Godparents: Pedro Bailliot and Rosa Chelete.

1813.   SANTIAGO ZUIRINO* VERCHAIRE
        April 14, 1782, baptism of Santiago Zuirino, born March
        30, legitimate son of Luis Verchaire and Maria Luisa
        Grillet. Godparents: Luis Rachal (s) and Maria Luisa

Brevel.

*Numerous, subsequent, church and civil records give this individual's name as Jacques <u>Therin</u> rather than Zuirin or Zuirino.

1814. JUAN BAUTISTA GRILLET
April 21, 1782, baptism of Juan Bautista, born April 1, legitimate son of Marino Grillet and Maria Luisa Brevel. Godparents: Juan Bautista Rachal and Maria Silvilla D'hubardeau.

1815. MARIA ROSA CLAVIS /SAIDEK/
May 30, 1782, baptism of Maria Rosa, born May 3, legitimate daughter of Pedro Clavis Aedec /Saidek/ and Ursula Chelete. Godparents: Juan Pomier and Rosa Chelete.

1816. JUAN BAUTISTA BONNET
June 2, 1782, baptism of Juan Bautista, born March 24, legitimate son of Juan Bonnet and Antonia Garcia, Spaniards. Godparents: Juan Bautista Buart and Maria Luisa Buart (s/ Marie Loüise Buard).

1817. SANTIAGO* SILVESTRE BUART
June 2, 1782, baptism of Santiago Silvestre, born May 20, legitimate son of Luis Gabriel Buart and Maria Rosa Lambre. Godparents: Jacob Lambre, represented by Remigio Lambre (s), his son, and Maria Luis Buart (s).

*This name appears as "Santiago" in the text and as "Jacob" in the margin.

1818. MARIA JOSEFA ENRIQUETA GANIER
June 17, 1782, baptism of Maria Josefa Enriqueta, born May 30, legitimate daughter of Pedro Gannier and Maria Luisa Davion. Godparents: Luis Davion and Margarita Totin.

1819. JUAN JACOBO JOSEPH ARMAND
June 24, 1782, baptism of Juan Jacobo Joseph, born March 19, legitimate son of Joseph Maria Arman and Theresa Le Gros. Godparents: Juan Jacobo David (s) and Monica Dutil (s/ Duttile Dartigaux).

1820. MARIA FELICIDAD BREVEL
July 25, 1782, baptism of Maria Felicidad, born June 27, legitimate daughter of Juan Bautista Brevel and Maria Francisca Poisot. Godparents: Bartolome Rachal and Maria Helena Brevel.

1821. JUAN IGNACIO MÀXIMILIANO LARENAUDIERE
July 4, 1782, baptism of Juan Ignacio Maximiliano, born

July 1, 1782, natural son of Francisca Larenaudiere and a father who has not declared himself. Godparents: Juan Ignacio Pieferme and Magdalena Larenaudiere.

1822. MARIA LUISA HELENA EUFROSINA PAVIE
August 25, 1782, baptism of Maria Luisa Helena Eufrosina, born August 21, 1782, legitimate daughter of Esteban Pavie and Theresa Buart. Godparents: Dionisio Buart and Maria Luisa Eufrosia Rambin.

1823. ROQUE REMIGIO SILVESTRE POISOT
August 27, 1782, baptism of Roque Remigio Silvestre, born August 17, 1782, legitimate son of Atanasio Poisot and Maria de Soto St. Denis. Godparents: Remigio Lambre (s) and Catalina Lambre (s).

1824. MARIA BARBARA JOSEPHA
September 2, 1782, baptism of Maria Barbara Josepha, born in October of the previous year, daughter of Luisa, an Apalacho Indian of Rapides. Godparents: Remigio Lambre (s) and Maria Luisa Dupre.

1825. JUAN BAUTISTA TODOS SANTOS BESSON
October 2, 1782, baptism of Juan Bautista Todos Santos, born that same day, legitimate son of Julian Besson and Maria Peraut. Godparents: Juan Lalande (s) and Francisca Gappe (s).

1826. JUAN FRANCISCO MARIA ROUQUIER
December 4, 1782, baptism of Juan Francisco Maria, born November 4, legitimate son of Francisco Rouquier (s) and Maria Luise Prudhomme. Godparents: Juan Bautista Prudhomme (s) and Maria Josefa, his wife (s).

1827. MARIA BARBARA FREDERIC
December 9, 1782, baptism of Maria Barbara, born November 13, legitimate daughter of Felipe Frederic and Barbara Chelete. Godparents: Barnabe Chelete and Rosa Chelete.

1828. ANTONIO ROBLEAU
December 27, 1782, baptism of Antonio, born December 18, legitimate son of Guillermo Robleau and Isidora /de Zepeda/. Godparents: Antonio Lambre (s) and Maria Rosa Lambre (s).

1829. VALERIE ANTY
December 29, 1782, baptism of Valerie, born November 9, legitimate son of Juan Bautista Anty (s) and Maria Catalina Galien. Godparents: Nicolas Galien and Maria Le Court.

1830. ANA GANNIER /GAGNE/
February 7, 1783, baptism of Ana, born January 15, legitimate daughter of Esteban Gannier and Luisa Bertrand. Godparents: Juan Bautista Armand and Ana Prudhomme (s).

1831. BARTOLOME LESTAGE
February 12, 1783, baptism of Bartolome, born January 15, legitimate son of /Guillelmo/ Lestage and Manuela Riche. Godparents: Bartolome Rachal and Maria Josefa Laforet.

1832. JUAN BAUTISTA FREDERIQUE
April 9, 1783, baptism of Juan Bautista, born March 27, legitimate son of Felipe Frederique and Maria Chatarina Sauvage. Godparents: Juan Bautista Delousche and Margarita Frederique.

1833. JUAN FONTENEAU
April 20, 1783, baptism of Juan, born March 21, legitimate son of Luis Fonteneau and Pelagia Grave.* Godparents: Simon Fonteneau and Maria Josepha Laberhi. *_Gagne_/

1834. ELISABETH MASSIP
June 21, 1783, baptism of Elisabeth, born May 20, legitimate daughter of Juan Massip and Maria Luisa Lemoine. Godparents: Juan Baut. Lemoine and Maria Rosa Dolè.

1835. FELICITY JACINTA BERTRAN
June 24, 1783, baptism of Felicity Jacinta, born June 12, legitimate daughter of Luis Bertran and Elisabeth Davion. Godparents: Juan Bautista Davion and Maria Josepha Gagñe.

1836. MARIA EMMANUEL CESARIO PRUDHOMME
July 6, 1783, baptism of Maria Manuel Cesario, born May 22, legitimate son of Francisco Prudhomme and Maria Barbara Rambin. Godparents: Manuel Prudhomme and Rosalie Rambin.

1837. JOSEPH NICOLAS TOMPSON
August 10, 1783, baptism of Joseph Nicolas, born January 24, 1783, legitimate son of Carlos Tompson and Maria Bron?, natives of Charles-town. Godparents: Nicolas L'agneau and Luisa Ville franche.

1838. MARIA MARIA-ANNA ROSALIA BARBE-ROUGE /BARBEROUSSE/
August 11, 1783, baptism of Maria Maria-Anna Rosalia Barbe-Rouge, born May 28, legitimate daughter of Guillelmo Barbe-Rouge and Maria Juana Chagneau. Godparents: Franco. Pieverd and Leonore Chagneau.

1839. JUAN BAUTISTA RAMBIN
       August 25, 1783, baptism of Juan Bautista, born August
       16, legitimate son of Andres Antonio Rambin and Catha-
       rina Buar. Godparents: Juan Bautista Buart and Rosalia
       Rambin.

1840. JOSEPH DUPRÉ
       October 7, 1783, baptism of Joseph, born July 18, legit-
       imate son of Joseph du Prés and Franca. le Compte. God-
       parents: Ambroisio le Compte and Maria Luisa du Prés.

1841. JUAN BAUTISTA FRANCISCO BOSIÉ
       October 12, 1783, baptism of Juan Bautista, born Septem-
       ber 11, legitimate son of Francisco Bosié and Catharina
       Pelagia Lambre. Godparents: Juan Bautista Bosié and
       Maria Rosa Lambre.

1842. JUAN BAUTISTA DOLÉ /ADLE/
       October 21, 1783, baptism of Juan Bautista, born Septem-
       ber 13, legitimate son of Juan Dolé and Maria Genovefa
       du Bois. Godparents: Juan Bautista Clom and Maria
       Juana Changneau.

1843. MARIA CATHERINA FELICITY VILDEQUE /PEREAU/
       November 1, 1783, baptism of Maria Catherina Felicity,
       born June 27, legitimate daughter of Juan Chrystosimo
       Vildegue and Maria Luisa Salvan. Godparents: J_____
       /illegible/ Lambre and Catharina du Pres.

1844. FRANCISCO CHRISTI
       November 1, 1783, baptism of Francisco, born August 2,
       legitimate son of Jayme Christi and Maana Vildegue.
       Godparents: Franco. Vildegue and Maria Luisa LeCompte.

1845. CELESTE METHILDY DEBLANC
       November 2, 1783, baptism of Celeste Methildy, born June
       15, legitimate daughter of Don Luis de Blanc and Isabel
       Pompom Derneville. Godparents: Joseph Maria Carlos De
       Blanc, representing Estevan Miro, governor of Province
       of Louisiana, and Maria Luisa Martha de Blan, acting for
       Celeste Miro y Macarti.

1846. JUAN BAUTISTA LEMAITRE
       December 1, 1783, baptism of Juan Bautista, born Novem-
       ber 19, legitimate son of Francisco Le Maitre and Luisa
       Villefranche. Godparents: Juan Bautista Ailhaud Sainte
       Anne and Francisca LeBeuf.

1847. MARIA JOSEPHA LAFITTE
       February 14, 1784, baptism of Maria Josepha, born Decem-
       ber 15, 1783, daughter of Pablo Bouet LaFitte and Mari-
       anna de Soto. Godparents: Athanasio Poisoi and Maria
       Soto.

1848. MARIA ATHANASIO ORTOLON
February 19, 1784, baptism of Maria Athanasio, born January 28, legitimate son of Don Bernardo Ortolon and Maria Grappe. Godparents: Juan Bautista Ailhaud Sainte Anne and Theresa Valentin.

1849. JUAN BAUTISTA RACHAL
April 25, 1784, baptism of Juan Bautista, born April 1, legitimate son of Julian Rachal and Maria Luisa Brevel. Godparents: Juan Bautista Brevel and Maria Luisa Le Roux? /Le Roy?/.

1850. FRANCISCO PORIÈ
April 25, 1784, baptism of Francisco, born January 1, 1783, legitimate son of Vincenze Poiriè and Maria Juana Richè. Godparents: Juan Bautista Poriè and Francisca Grille.

1851. JUAN PEDRO ARZE
April 28, 1784, baptism of Juan Pedro, born February 26, son of Juan de Arce, sergeant, and Francisca Larenodiere. Godparents: Pedro Larenodiere and Madalena Larenodiere.

1852. MARIA JOSEPHA ADELAIDE MERCIER
April 30, 1784, baptism of Maria Josepha Adelaide, born October 24, 1783, legitimate daughter of Luis Mercier and Maria Luisa Lefevre. Godparents: Gilbert Clariso and Maria Silvia Barbie.

1853. CECILIA MAYOUX
June 21, 1784, baptism of Cecilia, born May 31, 1784, legitimate daughter of Ignacio Mayoux and Teresa Philipot. Godparents: Lorenzo Mayoux and Maria Theresa Mayoux.

1854. REMIGIO ROBERT
June 24, 1784, baptism of Remigio, born November 22, 1783, son of Luis Robert and Juana Robert. Godparents: Remigio Pereaux and Maria Josepha Pereaux.

1855. MARGARITA DENIS
July 21, 1784, baptism of Margarita, born July 3, daughter of Juan Bautista Denis and Maria Isabel Boduin, his wife. Godparents: Pedro Cheletre and Margarita Frederique.

1856. MARIA TERESA EUGENIA BUAR
August 24, 1784, baptism of Maria Teresa Eugenia, born August 7, legitimate daughter of Luis Buar and Maria Rosa Lambre. Godparents: Franco. Bozié and Theresa Buar.

1857. MARIA VICTORIA BREVEL
       September 12, 1784, baptism of Maria Victoria, born
       September 1, legitimate daughter of Juan Bautista Bre-
       vel and Francisca Poisot. Godparents: Pedro Versally*
       and Maria Victoria Darban.   */Chaler *dit* Versailles/

1858. ALEXOS HILARIO DE LERI TRICHE
       September 19, 1784, baptism of Alexos Hilario de Leri
       Triche, born July 25, legitimate son of Manuel Triche
       and Maria Luisa Grappe. Godparents: Luis La Malaty and
       Theresa la Malaty.

1859. MARIA JUANA PIEVERT
       October 10, 1784, baptism of Maria Juana, born October 7,
       legitimate daughter of Francisco Pievert and Maria Juana
       Chagñeaux. Godparents. Elias Bernard and Genovefa Ris.

1860. MARIA ROUQUIER
       October 11, 1784, baptism of Maria, born September 17,
       legitimate daughter of Franco. Rouquier and Maria Luisa
       Prudhomme. Godparents: Manuel Prudhomme and Catharina
       Lambre.

1861. LUIS BLANC (LE BLANC)
       October 21, 1784, baptism of Luis, born November 29,
       1781, legitimate son of Luis Le Blanc and Catharina Olivo,
       habitants of Guachita. Godparents: Juan Bautista Grappe
       and Roselia Olivo.

1862. MARIA LUCILLA DEBLANC (LE BLANC)
       October 21, 1784, baptism of Maria Lucilla, born Febru-
       ary 5, 1784, legitimate daughter of Luis Le Blanc and
       Catharina Olivo, habitants of Rachita. Godparents: Juan
       Bautista Grappe and Maria Theresa Triche.

1863. PEDRO CLAVIS SAYDEK
       November 14, 1784, baptism of Pedro, born September 20,
       legitimate son of Pedro Clavis Saydek and Ursula Che-
       lete. Godparents: Pedro La Cour and Maria Juana Crete.

1864. JOSEPH ANGE BONET
       November 22, 1784, baptism of Joseph Ange, born November
       21, 1784, son of Juan Bonnet and Maria Antonia Raymund.
       Godparents: Juan Bautista Le Duc and Maria Theresa
       Valentin.

1865. MARIA LUISA MODESTA FORT
       December 5, 1784, baptism of Maria Luisa Modesta, born
       October 3, legitimate daughter of Santiago Fort and
       Maria Franca. Malbert. Godparents: Juan Bautista Ra-
       chal and Maria Luisa Lecompte.

1866. JUAN BAUTISTA THOMAS DEBLANC
December 5, 1784, baptism of Juan Bautista Thomas, born September 18, legitimate son of Luis De Blanc and Elisabeth Derneville. Godparents: Joseph Antonio Marcello Soto, representing Bautista de Macarti, and Maria Luisa Martha de Blanc representing Brigida de Reggio.

1867. LUIS JOSEPH THOMASINO
December 15, 1784, baptism of Luis Joseph, born November 28, son of Luis Thomasino and Catharina Latie. Godparents: Joseph Latie and Monica Dartigos.

1868. BERNABE LESTAGE
December 29, 1784, baptism of Bernabe, born November 24, legitimate son of Guillelmo Lestage and Manuela Riche. Godparents: Bernabe Cheletre and Maria Luisa du Prés.

1869. REMIGIO TOTIN
January 16, 1785, baptism of Remigio, born December 20, 1784, legitimate son of Remigio Totin and Margarita Grillet. Godparents: Antonio Grillet and Maria Barbara Grillet.

1870. MARIA GERTRUDE VAUCHERE
February 7, 1785, baptism of Maria Gertrude, born January 10, legitimate daughter of Juan Vauchere and Margarita Lestage. Godparents: Pedro Dartigos, represented by Rda. P. F. Franco. de Caldes, and /Illegible/.

1871. MARIA LUISA LARENODIERE
February 15, 1785, baptism of Maria Luisa, born February 9 of Pedro Larenodiere and Juana Labery. Godparents: Juan Bautista Larenodiere and Juana Guedon.

1872. JUAN PEDRO DOLÉ
February 18, 1785, baptism of Juan Pedro, born January 1 of Juan Pedro Dolé and Maria Rosa du Pre. Godparents: Estevan Vercher and Maria Luisa Dupre.

1873. MARIA JUANA MASSIP
February 27, 1785, baptism of Maria Juana, born February 2, legitimate daughter of Juan Massip and Maria Le Moine. Godparents: Antonio Lemoine and Maria Labery.

1874. JUAN BAUTISTA DERBAN
February 27, 1785, baptism of Juan Bautista, born February 17, of Juan Bautista Darban and Maria Elena Brevel. Godparents: Juan Bautista Brevel and Luisa Margarita Darban.

1875. PEDRO IGNACE JOSEPH ARMAND
March 7, 1785, baptism of Pedro Ignace Joseph, born

February 1, legitimate son of Joseph Maria Armand and
Teresa legros. Godparents: Pedro Dartigos and Adelaida
Armand.

1876. MARIA LUISA BERTRAND
March 10, 1785, baptism of Maria Luisa, born March 3,
legitimate daughter of Luis Bertrand and Elisabeth Davion. Godparents: Domingo Davion and Maria Josepha
Triche.

1877. JOSEPH VERCHER
May 7, 1785, baptism of Joseph, born April 15 of Luis
Vercher and Maria Luisa Grillet. Godparents: Juan Luis
Vercher and Maria Rosalia Vercher.

1878. MARIA DE LA NEIGES PRUDHOMME
May 8, 1785, baptism of Maria de los Nieves, born April
24 of Franco. Prudhomme and Maria Rambin. Godparents:
Franco. Rambin and Anna Prudhomme.

1879. MARIE FRANCOISE LAURENT
May 20, 1785, baptism of Maria Franca. born May 8, legitimate daughter of Joseph Laurent and Maria Morin. Godparents: Franco. Le Vasseur and Juan Bautista Morin.

1880. JUAN PEDRO MANUEL PRUDHOMME
July 21, 1785, baptism of Juan Pedro Manuel, born June
23 of Pedro Manuel Prudhomme and Catharina Lambre. Godparents: Remigio Lambre and Anna Prudhomme.

1881. MARIE DERBANNE
August 25, 1785, baptism of Maria, born May 12 of Gaspar
Darban and Maria Josepha Peraux. Godparents: Joseph
Vercher and Madalena Peraux.

1882. FRANCOIS ROBIN
September 18, 1785, baptism of Franco. born September 23,
1784, legitimate son of Miguel Robin and Maria Luisa
Baudin. Godparents: Franco. Davion and Maria Luisa
Rachal.

1883. JEAN JACQUES CHRISTI
September 25, 1785, baptism of Juan Santiago, born June
19, 1785, legitimate son of Santiago Christi and Maria
Anna Derotée /Pereau/. Godparents: Julian Besseau
/Besson/ and Maria Luisa Lemoine.

1884. MARIE PELAGIE CHELETRE
September 25, 1785, baptism of Maria Pelagia, born August 4, 1785, legitimate daughter of Pedro Cheletre and
Margarita Federique. Godparents: Francisco Cheletre
and Maria Federique.

1885. MARIE LOUISE MODESTE POISSOT
October 10, 1785, baptism of Maria Luisa Modesta, born September 17, 1785, legitimate daughter of Remigio Poissot and Luisa Cavè. Godparents: Joseph Verger and Maria Luisa La Compte.

1886. JEAN BAPTISTE GAGNE
October 31, 1785, baptism of Juan Bautista, born October 22, legitimate son of Pedro Gagnè and Maria Luisa Davion. Godparents: Juan Bautista Davion and Maria Josephe Triche.

1887. JEAN CHRISOSTOME FAUSTINE VILDEC *dit* PERAUT
November 1, 1785, baptism of Juan Chrysostome Faustino, born June 2, legitimate son of Juan Chrysostomo Peraux and Maria Luisa Salvan. Godparents: Juan Pedro Lalande and Marianne Du Pres.

1888. MARIE HORTENSE ANASTHASIE ROUSSEAU
November 4, 1785, baptism of Maria Ortancia Anasthasis, born October 1785, legitimate daughter of Pedro Jorge Rousseau, captain and Commandant of this post, and Maria Margarita Catharino Milhet. Godparents: Juan Bautista Dartigos, represented by Nicolas Rouseau, and Maria Dartigo.

1889. MARIE MODESTE FONTENEAU
November 25, 1785, baptism of Maria Modesta, born November 12, 1785, legitimate daughter of Luis Fonteneau and Maria Pelagia Grappe. Godparents: Juan Bautista Ailhaud St. Anne and Francisca Grappe.

1890. MARIE DES NEIGES HYACINTHE LAFITTE
December 25, 1785, baptism of Maria des los Nivies Jacinta, born December 1, legitimate daughter of Pablo Bouet La Fite and Maria Anna de Soto. Godparents: Pedro Pablo Bouet le Fite and Luisa Margarita Guedon.

1891. FELICITE MERCIER
December 27, 1785, baptism of Felicity, born December 2, daughter of Luis Mercier and Maria Luisa le Feuvre. Godparents: Juan Bautista Morin and Maria Josepha Gagne.

1892. SUSANNE _____
January 3, 1786, baptism of Susanne /no last name/, natural daughter of Solomon and Maria Barbara, habitants of Rapides. Godparents: Francisco La Casse and Maria Catharina Lambre. Infant born in February of 1785.

1893. MARIE CYPRIANNE DERBANNE
February 2, 1786, baptism of Maria Cypriana, born December

26, 1785, legitimate daughter of Pedro Darban and Maria Franca. Brevel. Godparents: Athanasio Poissot and Maria LeClerc.

1894. MARIA JOSEPHA BERNARD
February 7, 1786, baptism of Maria Josepha, born January 22, 1786, legitimate daughter of Elias Bernard and of Leonore Chagneaux. Godparents: Joseph Martin and Maria Juana Chagneau.

1895. PIERRE GEORGE CESAR DEBLANC
February 11, 1786, baptism of Pedro Jorge Cesario, born January 14, 1786, legitimate son of Luis de Blanc and of Elisabeth Pompon Derneville. Godparents: Pedro Rousseau, captain and commandant, and Maria Catharina Millet.

1896. MARIA JOSEFA CHELETTRE
February 17, 1786, baptism of Maria Josefa, born January 31, 1786, daughter of Bernabe Cheletre and Maria Josefa Gonin. Godparents: Guillelmo L'estage and Anna Barbara Pomié.

1897. JUAN LOUIS DELOUCHE
March 21, 1786, baptism of Juan Luis, born March 8, legitimate son of Juan Bautista de Louche and Ursula Boulé. Godparents: Luis Thomasino and Catharina Lattiè.

1898. MARIA PELAGIA FEDERIK
March 21, 1786, baptism of Maria Pelagia, born February 24, legitimate daughter of Philipe Federik and Barbara Cheletre. Godparents: Franco. Humel and Maria Federik.

1899. JEAN BAPTISTE ETIENNE PAVIE
March 23, 1786, baptism of Juan Bautista Estevan, born February 19, 1786, legitimate son of Estevan Pavia and Theresa Buard. Godparents: Juan Bauta. Bozie and Maria Francisca Buard.

1900. ISABEL RACHAL
March 25, 1786, baptism of Isabel, born February 28, 1786, legitimate daughter of Bartholome Rachal and Franca. Laberi. Godparents: Luis Rachal and Juana Guedon.

1901. MARIA THERESA ZITE /OZITE/ RAMBIN
March 26, 1786, baptism of Maria Theresa Zite, born November 30, 1785, legitimate daughter of Andres Rambin and Catharina Buard. Godparents: Miguel Rambin and Theresa Buard.

1902. FRANCISCO ORTHOLAN
April 2, 1786, baptism of Francisco, born February 25,

1786, legitimate son of Bernardo Ortholan and Maria Anna Grappe. Godparents: Francisco Grappe and Pelagia Grappe.

1903. REMIGIO VICTORIANO LE VASSEUR
April 9, 1786, baptism of Remigio Victoriano, born March 24?, legitimate son of Santiago Le Vasseur and Maria Theresa Grillet. Godparents: Remigio Lambre and Maria Lambre.

1904. MARIA DE LOS DOLORES
April 16, 1786, baptism of Maria de los Dolores, born April 26, 1785, daughter of Luisa, slave of Mde. Le Compte and a father unknown. Godparents: Luis, free *mulato*, and Genoveva, slave of Gaspar Fiol.

1905. JULIAN RACHAL
April 16, 1786, baptism of Julian, born March 8, 1786, legitimate son of Julian Rachal and Maria Luisa Brevel. Godparents: Antonio Rachal and Maria Pelagia Brevel.

1906. BENJAMIN WALLECE
April 19, 1786, baptism of Benjamin, born April 27, 1782, legitimate son of Josue Wallece and Elena Milston. Godparents: Eduardo Morphi and Maria Juana Buard.

1907. MARIA JOSEPHA PRUDHOMME
April 25, 1786, baptism of Maria Josepha, born May 24, 1785, natural daughter of Catharina Prudhomme and a father unknown. Godparents: Santiago Prudhomme and Theresa Prudhomme.

1908. JUAN BAUTISTA CHRISTILLE
April 26, 1786, baptism of Juan Bautista, born March 12, legitimate son of Juan Christille and Maria Darban. Godparents: Augustin Buard and Maria Luisa Dupres.

1909. JUAN BAUTISTA DENIS
June 28, 1786, baptism of Juan Bautista, born December 22, 1785, legitimate son of Juan Bautista Denis and of Maria Elisabeth /Beaudouin/. Godparents: Juan Pedro Roquer and Margarita Rouquer. Baptism performed by the *curé* from Opelousas.

1910. PEDRO
June 28, 1786, baptism of Pedro, *negrito* of Commdt. Pedro Rousseau, natural son of Maria Luisa, a slave. Godparents: Luis Alexandro, free *negro*, and M. Congo.

1911. ELEONORE CLAVIS SAIDET
June 29, 1786, baptism of Leonor, born June 10, daughter

of Pedro Clavis Saidet and Ursula Slet /Chelette/. Godparents: Franco. Schelet and Leonor Himel.

1912. MARIA JUANA
June 29, 1786, baptism of Maria Juana, born May 22, *mulata* slave of Manl. Triche, daughter of Maria Juana and a father unknown. Godparents: Marin, *negro*, and Conga, *negra* of Mr. Prudhomme.

1913. JUAN PEDRO
June 29, 1786, baptism of Juan Pedro, "aged about five," *cuarterón* slave of Monsieur Jooyon? Capuran, son of Pauline, *mulatta*, and a father unknown. Godparents: Nicolas Renaud and Madame Charlota Capuran.

1914. ALEXANDRO HILDEBERT BOSSIE
June 29, 1786, baptism of Alexandro Hildebert, born May 6, legitimate son of Franco. Bossie and Pelagia Lambre. Godparents: Soulange Bossiè and Maria Juana Lambre.

1915. MARIA EUPHROSINE LE MAITRE
June 29, 1786, baptism of Maria Euphrosine, born May 3?, legitimate daughter of Francisco Le Maitre and Marisa Luisa Le Duc. Godparents: Juan Bautista Le Duc and Sussana Livo /Olivo/.

1916. JUAN BAUTISTA GAGNÉ
September 8, 1786, baptism of Juan Bautista, born August 30, legitimate son of Estevan Gagné and Luisa Bertrand. Godparents: Luis Davion and Marie de la Incarnation Perau.

1917. ESTEVAN MASSIPE
September 10, 1786, baptism of Estevan, born August 15, legitimate son of Juan Massipe and Maria Lemoine. Godparents: Estevan Pavie and Theresa Pavie.

1918. JUAN BAUTISTA VILDEC
September 10, 1786, baptism of Juan Bautista, born December 11, 1785, legitimate son of Francois Perau Vildec and Luisa Labayrie, natives of this parish. Godparents: Juan Bautista Labayrie and Juana Guedon.

1919. CATALINA ANNA THOMASSIN
September 10, 1786, baptism of Catalina Anna, born October 28, 1785, legitimate daughter of Luis Thomassino, native of Spain, and Catalina Latie, native of this parish. Godparents: Joseph Latie and Anna Robin.

1920. MARIA LUISA GAGNON
September 10, 1786, baptism of Maria Luisa, born August

29, legitimate daughter of Pedro Gagnon and Theresa Valentin, natives of this parish. Godparents: Guillermo Chever and Margarita Totin.

1921. AGATA LESTAGE
September 17, 1786, baptism of Agata, born August 7, legitimate daughter of Guillermo Lestage and Manuela Richet, natives of this parish. Godparents: Pedro Metoyer and Genoveva Gonin.

1922. JUAN BAUTISTA LECOMPTE
September 17, 1786, baptism of Juan Bautista, born June 13, 1786, legitimate son of Ambroisio Lecompte and Helena Cloutié, natives of this parish. Godparents: Alexis Cloutié and Maria Luisa Lecompte.

1923. MARIA ANNA RABALÉ (f)
November 5, 1786, baptism of Maria Anna, born in March last, legitimate daughter of Joseph Rabalé and Maria Luisa Malbert, natives of the parish and post of Avoyelles. Godparents: Josephe Vergé and Maria Anna Vergé.

1924. MARIA LUISA RACHAL
November 5, 1786, baptism of Maria Luisa, born October 11, 1786, legitimate daughter of Luis Bartolomé Rachal and Maria Francisca Grillet, natives of this parish. Godparents: Luis Lamalaty and Maria Luisa Rachal.

1925. MARIA AGATA TOTIN
December 17, 1786, baptism of Maria Agata, born November 20 last, legitimate daughter of Remy Totin and Margarita Grillet, natives of this parish. Godparents: Luis Gaspar Filibert and Rosalia Vercher.

1926. MARIA JOSEPHA FRANCISCA RACHAL
December 25, 1786, baptism of Maria Josepha Francisca Rachal, born November 24, 1786, legitimate daughter of Luis Rachal and Maria Josepha Labery, natives of this parish. Godparents: Francois Monginot and Maria Luisa Leroy. (f)

1927. JUAN BAUTISTA TIMOTHEO ADELAY
December 31, 1786, baptism of Juan Bautista Timotheo, born October 21, legitimate son of Juan Adelay and Maria Genoveva Duboë, natives of this parish. Godparents: Juan Bautista Larenaudiere and Maria Francisca Grappe. (f)

1928. MARIA URSULA /LE/ VASSEUR
January 1, 1787, baptism of Maria Ursula, born October 21, 1786, legitimate daughter of Francisco Vasseur and Maria Juana Grillet of this parish. Godparents: Iago Vasseur and Maria Juana Lambre.

1929. JUAN PEDRO FRANCISCO SEVERIO LARENAUDIERE
January 6, 1787, baptism of Juan Pedro Francisco Severio, born December 6, 1786, legitimate son of Pedro Larenaudiere and Juana LaBery, natives of this parish. Godparents: Francisco Bartolome Chabus and Madelina Labery.

1930. MARIA PELAGIA MELANIA BOSSIE
January 21, 1787, baptism of Maria Pelagia Melania, born December 31, 1786, legitimate daughter of Juan Bautista Bossie, native of the parish of Jean Baptiste de los Allemands, and Maria St. Geme, native of New Orleans. Godparents: Joseph St. Geme and Pelagia Lambre.

1931. MARIA PELAGIA MODESTA BERTRAND
January 21, 1787, baptism of Maria Pelagia Modesta, born December 31, 1786, legitimate daughter of Luis Bertrand and Isabel Davion, natives of this parish. Godparents: Luis Davion and Ursula Gagné.

1932. PABLO ALEXANDRO DERBANNE
January 31, 1787, baptism of Pablo Alexandro, born January 25, 1787, legitimate son of Juan Bautista Derbanne and Maria Madelena Brevel, natives of this parish. Godparents: Manuel Prudhomme and Pelagia Brevel.

1933. LOUIS CESARIO ANTY
February 4, 1787, baptism of Louis Cesar, born January 4, legitimate son of Luis Anty and Maria Juana Crete, natives of this parish. Godparents: Pedro Lacour and Teresa Lamalaty.

1934. MARIA LUISA MAIOU
March 3, 1787, baptism of Maria Luisa, born April 7, 1786, legitimate daughter of Ignace Maiou, native of the province of Canada, and Teresa Flibot, native of this parish. Godparents: Antonio Le Noir and Maria Rondin. (f)

1935. MARIA ANA ROUQUIER
March 6, 1787, baptism of Maria Ana, born July 21, 1786, legitimate daughter of Francisco Rouquier, native of France, and Maria Luisa Prudhomme, native of this parish. Godparents: Pedro Roussau, commandant of this post, and Catalina Millet Rousseau.

1936. JUAN PEDRO CHELETRE
March 11, 1787, baptism of Juan Pedro, born April 21, 1786, legitimate son of Pedro Cheletre and Margarita Frederic, natives of this parish. Godparents: Felipe Froderic and Ana Barba Pomier. (f)

1937. FRANCISCO ISIDORO DUBOI
March 13, 1787, baptism of Francisco Isidoro, born 22nd

February, legitimate son of Francisco Duboë and Leonora Jeanris, natives of this parish. Godparents: Juan Bautista Duboë and Maria Juana Chagnau.

1938. BERNARD RENOY
March 28, 1787, baptism of Bernard, born March 14, legitimate son of Joseph Renoy and Marie Mercie, natives of this parish. Godparents: Bernard Dortolant and Dame Dortolant.

1939. MARIE EMILIA ARMANT
April 1, 1787, baptism of Marie Emilia, born January 14, legitimate daughter of Joseph Maria Armant, native of France and Maria Teresa Le Gros, native of Punta Contada. Godparents: Pedro Joseph Maes and Maria Badin.

1940. LUIS NEUVILLE DOLET
April 28, 1787, baptism of Luis Neuville, born April 7, 1787, legitimate son of Pedro Dolet and Maria Rose Dupré, native of this parish. Godparents: Luis Lambre and Maria Francesca Vergé.

1941. FRANCISCO AGUSTIN BUAR
May 6, 1787, baptism of Francisco Agustin, born April 20, legitimate son of Luis Buar and Maria Rosa Lambre. Godparents: Francisco Agustin Buar and Maria Juana Lambre.

1942. MARIA ANA FROSINA GALLIEN
May 27, 1787, baptism of Maria Juana /sic/ Frosina, born November 20, 1786, legitimate daughter of Nicolas Gallien and Maria Le Court, natives of this parish. Godparents: Pedro Charpentier and Francisca Le Court. (f)

1943. DIONISIO COVECHI
June 24, 1787, baptism of Dionisio, born October 12, 1784, legitimate son of Juan Covechi and Nancy Hochel, natives of the province of English North America. Godparents: Juan Lambre and Maria Lambre.

1944. JULIAN GAGNÉ
July 22, 1787, baptism of Julian, born July 10, legitimate son of Pedro Gagné and Maria Luisa Davion, natives of this parish. Godparents: Pedro Gagné and Maria Josepha Gagné.

1945. JOSEPH MARIA CESARIO LAFITTE
August 19, 1787, baptism of Joseph Maria Ceserio, born August 9, legitimate son of Bouet de laffitte, a native of the province of Leaguadoca /Languedoc/ in France. Godparents: Don Marcel De Soto and Francisca Grappe.

1946. MARIA SERAPHIA CHALER
August 25, 1787, baptism of Maria Seraphia, born August 4, legitimate daughter of Pedro Chaler and Maria Derbanne, a native of this parish. Godparents: Francisco Lavespere and Maria Francesca Brevel.

1947. BARTOLOME RUBEN RACHAL
January 2, 1788, baptism of Bartolome Ruben, born December 9, 1787, legitimate son of Bartolome Rachal and Francisca Labery. Godparents: Luis Rachal and Maria Labery. (f)

1948. ANTONIO
January 23, 1788, baptism of Antonio, adult Indian of some 20 years. Godparents: Valentine Layssard and Maria Luisa Marta De Blanc.

1949. FELIPE FREDERIC
November 29, 1787, baptism of Felipe, born October 20, 1787, legitimate son of Felipe Frederic and Maria Barba Cheletre, native of this parish. Godparents: Antonio Imel and Maria Luisa Buar.

1950. MARIA FELICIDAD LAVESPERE
January 3, 1788, baptism of Maria Felicidad, born December 16, 1787, the legitimate daughter of Francisco Lavespere, native of France, and Maria Derbanne, native of this parish. Godparents: Estevan Verge and Maria Francisca Dupre.

1951. MARIA CARLOTTA MODESTA PRUDHOMME
September 25, 1787, baptism of Maria Carlotta Modesta, born about two months earlier, legitimate daughter of Francisco Prudhomme and Maria Rambint, natives of this Parish. Godparents: Francisco Monginot and Maria Carlos Capuran. (f)

1952. PEDRO JOSEPH MAES
February 1, 1788, baptism of Pedro Joseph, born December 31, 1787, legitimate son of Pedro Joseph Maes and Maria Ana Dartigaux, natives of France. Godparents: Pedro Dartigaux and Dame Maria Monica Dartigaux.

1953. MARIA MODESTA VASCOCU
April 6, 1788, baptism of Maria Modesta, born February 8, legitimate daughter of Andres Vascocu and Madelena Raymond, natives of this parish. Godparents: Luis Vascocu and Ulalia Vascocu. (f)

1954. FRANCISCO AGUSTIN RAMBINT
April 6, 1788, baptism of Francisco Agustin, born February 5, the legitimate son of Andres Rambint and Maria

Catalina Buard, natives of this parish. Godparents: Francisco Agustin Buard and Maria Rosa Lambre.

1955. LUIS RACHAL
April 13, 1788, baptism of Luis, born February 22, legitimate son of Julian and Maria Luisa Brevel, natives of this parish. Godparents: Luis Monet and Dame Monet. (f)

1956. LUIS CELESTINO PLOCHER
May 18, 1788, baptism of Luis Celestino, born April 11, legitimate son of Antoine Ploche and Maria Teresa Vascocu. Godparents: Antonio Vascocu and Maria Francisca Vascocu.

1957. ANA BARBA DUBOË
June 8, 1788, baptism of Ana Barba, born May 15, legitimate daughter of Valentino Duboë and Rosa Cheletre, natives of this parish. Godparents: Juan Bautista Duboë and Widow Chelette.

1958. JUAN BAUTISTA FONTENAU
July 14, 1788, baptism of Juan Bautista, born March 5, 1788, legitimate son of Luis Fontenau, native of the *puerto de alebamonds*, and Pelagia Grappe, native of this parish. Godparents: Juan Bautista Grappe and Geneveva Sorel. (f)

1959. MARIA FROZINA DENIS
August 12, 1788, baptism of Maria Frozina, born about the end of April last, legitimate daughter of Juan Bautista Denis and Isabel Beaudouin, natives of this parish. Godparents: Juan Nicolas Beaudouin and Maria Ana Dupre. (f)

1960. PEDRO NAGSAN GAGNON
August 17, 1788, baptism of Pedro Nagsan, born July 28, son of Pedro Gagnon, native of Canada, and Maria Teresa Valentin, native of this parish. Godparents: Julian Besson and Maria Juana Chagnau.

1961. MARIA ASPASIA DEBLANC
August 25, 1788, baptism of Maria Aspasia, born March 12, legitimate daughter of Luis Carlos Deblanc, commandant of this post, native of this parish, and Isabel Pompona Derneville, native of New Orleans. Godparents: Don Athanasio Poissot and Maria de Soto, wife of Poissot. (f)

1962. FRANCISCO PILAR CHRISTOBAL
August 24, 1788, baptism of Francisco Pilar, born October 11, 1787, legitimate son of Pedro Christobal and Maria de la Ascension, native of *pueblo de los Nacochdoches*. Godparents: Francisco Hugues and Francisca Lecour.

1963. MARIA MADELENA FREDERIC
September 14, 1788, baptism of Maria Madelena, born August 13, 1788, legitimate daughter of Felipe Frederic and Maria Catalina Sauvage, native of this parish. Godparents: Juan Francisco Frederic and Maria Catalina Bardon.

1964. LUIS NARCISSO PRUDHOMME
September 20, 1788, baptism of Luis Narcisso, born 24th of August, legitimate son of Manuel Prudhomme and Catalina Lambre, natives of this parish. Godparents: Francisco Rouquier and Maria Lambre.

1965. REMI CASIMIR PEREAU (VILDEC)
November 1, 1788, baptism of Remi Casimir, born March 4, legitimate son of Crisostomo Pereau (Vildec) and Maria Luisa Salvan, natives of this parish. Godparents: Remi Perau and Maria Juana Sorel.

1966. JUAN BAUTISTA DERBANNE
November 1, 1788, baptism of Juan Bautista, born December 22, 1787, son of Gaspard Derbanne and Maria Josephe Pereau, natives of this parish. Godparents: Juan La Lande and Maria Le Clerc.

1967. MARIA MELANIE RACHAL
November 1, 1788, baptism of Maria Melanie, born September 9, legitimate daughter of Luis Rachal and Maria Josepha Labery, natives of this parish. Godfather: /none given/. Godmother: Juanna Guedon.

1968. MARIA CATALINA PEREAU (VILDEC)
November 1, 1788, baptism of Maria Catalina, born May 12, 1788, legitimate daughter of Francesco Pereau (Vildec) and Maria Agatha LaBery, natives of this parish. Godparents: Juan Lalande and Catalina Dupre.

1969. MARIA LUISA MASSIP
November 2, 1788, baptism of Maria Luisa, born July 30, legitimate daughter of Juan Massip, native of France, and Maria Lemoine, native of this parish. Godparents: Luis Monet and Maria Luisa LeCompte.

1970. MARIA ANTONIA TORRES
November 4, 1788, baptism of Maria Antonia, born at the end of October last, legitimate daughter of Joseph Torres, native of Natchitoches, and Juanna de los Reyes, a native of the same place. Godparents: Ambrosio Lecompte and Maria Antonia /no last name given/.

1971. JUAN BAUTISTA CHELETRE
November 16, 1788, baptism of Juan Bautista, born about the end of September, legitimate son of Pedro Cheletre and Margarita Frederic, natives of this parish. Godparents: Juan Bautista Latie and Maria Rosalia Frederic.

1972. MARIA ANA ARTEMISA LEMAITRE
November 22, 1788, baptism of Maria Ana Artemisa, born November 19, legitimate daughter of Francisco Lemaitre and Maria Luisa Villefrance, natives of this parish. Godparents: Nicolas Lemaitre and Constancia Victoria Lemaitre.

1973. ANTONIO ADELAY
November 23, 1788, baptism of Antonio, born September 17, legitimate son of Juan Estevan Adelay and Marie Genoveva Duboë. Godparents: Antonio Duboë and Maria Genoveva Frederic.

1974. MARIA FRANCISCA CHELETRE
November 23, 1788, baptism of Maria Francisca, born October 24, 1788, legitimate daughter of Bernabe Cheletre, native of the parish of Juan Bautista de los Alemanes, and Maria Josepha Gonin, native of this parish. Godparents: Francisco Gonin and Genoveva Gonin.

1975. MARIA FELICIDAD DELOUCHE
November 23, 1788, baptism of Maria Felicidad, born October 27, legitimate daughter of Juan Delouch and Ursula Boulé, natives of this parish. Godparents: Pedro Beaudouin and Maria Ana Robin.

1976. JOSEPH ANDRES RENOY
December 4, 1788, baptism of Joseph Andres, born November 30, legitimate son of Joseph Renoy and Maria Josepha Mercie. Godparents: Joseph Juan-Ris and Genoveva Sorel.

1977. IAGO ROSMON CHAMARRE
December 16, 1788, baptism of Iago Rosmon, born October 14, legitimate son of Ives Chamarre, native of France, and Catalina Bardon, native of New Orleans. Godparents: Iago Coustiel? and Maria Chamarre.

1978. MARIA ASPASIE BOSSIE
January 11, 1789, baptism of Maria Aspasie, born December 7, 1788, legitimate daughter of Francisco Bossie and Catalina Pelagia Lambre. Godparents: Luis Lambre and Maria Lambre.

1979. MARIA ANASTASIA DERBANNE
January 18, 1789, baptism of Maria Stasia Derbanne, born

January 11, 1789, legitimate daughter of Juan Bautista Derbanne and Maria Helena Brevel, natives of this parish. Godparents: Athanasio Poissot and Maria Antonia /no last name/.

1980. MARIA FROZINA
February 2, 1789, baptism of Maria Frozina, about seven years of age, daughter of an Indian named Nanette and a father unknown. Godparents: Pedro Dolet and Dna. Laffitte.

1981. MIGUEL
February 2, 1789, baptism of Miguel, about one year of age, son of an Indian named Nanette and a father unknown. Godparents: Gaspar Fiolle and Dna. Fiolle.

1982. PEDRO
February 2, 1789, baptism of Pedro, about 4 years of age, son of an Indian named Nanette and a father unknown. Godparents: Pedro Laffitte and Maria Catalina Bardon.

1983. CARLOS FELIPE LARENAUDIERE
February 4, 1789, baptism of Carlos Felipe, born January 1, 1789, legitimate son of Pedro Larenaudiere and Juana Labery, natives of this parish. Godparents: Juan Bautista Pie'ferme (Leger) and Maria Clemence Larenaudiere.

1984. MARIA MODESTA ANTY
February 8, 1789, baptism of Maria Modesta, born January 7, 1789, legitimate daughter of Luis Anty and Maria Juana Crete, natives of this parish. Godparents: Pedro La Cour and Maria Celeste Vergé.

1985. PEDRO FORT
February 10, 1789, baptism of Pedro, born December 13, 1788, legitimate son of Iago Fort, native of France, and Maria Francisca Malbert, native of this parish. Godparents: Pedro Miguel and Maria Pelagia Frederic.

1986. PABLO
February 11, 1789, baptism of Pablo, born February 9, son of a *senorita* named Francisca, native of this parish, and of a father unknown. Godparents: Bouet Laffitte and Dna. Laffitte.

1987. MARIA CELESTE CHALER
February 14, 1789, baptism of Maria Celeste, born January 15, legitimate daughter of Pedro Chaler, native of New Orleans, and Maria Derbanne, native of this parish. Godparents: Luis Derbanne and Maria Francesca Bartolome Rachal.

1988. MARIA DIONISIA DOLET
February 22, 1789, baptism of Maria Dionisia, born November 11, 1788, legitimate daughter of Pedro Dolet and Maria Rosa Dupre, native of this parish. Godparents: Pedro Dupre and Maria Ana Dupres.

1989. THERESA OSITA THOMASSIN
February 22, 1789, baptism of Theresa Osita, born January 27, legitimate daughter of Luis Tomassin, native of Catalina, and Catalina Latie, native of this parish. Godparents: Francisco Latie and Maria Robin.

1990. MARIA UFROSINA RACHAL
February 25, 1789, baptism of Maria Ufrosina, born December 1, 1788, legitimate daughter of Luis Bartolome Rachal and Maria Francisca Grillet. Godparents: Juan Bautista Theodora Grillet and Maria Adelaida Vercher.

1991. BERNARDO SIMEON GAGNE
March 21, 1789, baptism of Bernardo Simeon, born February 17, 1789, legitimate son of Estevan Gagne and Maria Luisa Bertrand, natives of this parish. Godparents: Bernardo Dortolant and Maria Luisa Dna. Rouquier.

1992. MANUEL _____
March 22, 1789, baptism of Manuel, born March 14, son of Francisca, widow of Joseph Langes, and a father unknown. Godparents: Manuel Gonzales and Maria Theresa Langlois.

1993. JUAN POMIER
April 1, 1789, baptism of Juan, born March 20, legitimate son of Juan Pomier, native of France, and Maria Robert Dupre, native of this parish. Godparents: Felipe Frederic and Ana Barba Pomier.

1994. MARIA HORTENSIA BERTRAND
April 5, 1789, baptism of Maria Hortensia, born December 28, 1788, legitimate daughter of Luis Bertrand and Izabel Davion, native of this parish. Godparents: Francisco Grappe and Dame Triche.

1995. MARIA JOSEPHA HONORIA TOTIN
April 12, 1789, baptism of Maria Josepha Honoria, born January 19, legitimate daughter of Remy Totin and Margarita Grillet. Godparents: Enrique Triche and Maria Josepha Triche.

1996. PEDRO SIRIAC LEVASSEUR
April 12, 1789, baptism of Pedro Siriac, born January 31, legitimate son of Iago Levasseur and Teresa Grillet, natives of this parish. Godparents: Pedro Bailliou and Barbe Grillet.

1997. FELICIDAD MODESTA TRICHE
April 13, 1789, baptism of Felicidad Modesta, born September 30, 1788, legitimate daughter of Manuel Triche and Maria Luisa Grappe, natives of this parish. Godparents: Julian Besson and Francisca Grappe Benoit /Montenary/.

1998. CESAR DUBOË
April 14, 1789, baptism of Cesar, born January 26, legitimate son of Francisco Duboë and Leonora Juan-ris, natives of this parish. Godparents: Joseph Jean-ris and Dme. Duboë.

1999. MARIA AIME LAVISPERE
April 19, 1789, baptism of Maria Aime, born March 31, legitimate daughter of Francois Lavispere, native of France, and Maria Luisa Derbanne. Godparents. Luis Derbanne and Maria Baillot.

2000. IAGO REMY CHRISTI
August 25, 1789, baptism of Iago Remy, born December 1, 1788, legitimate son of Iago Christi and Dorothea Pereau (Vildec), natives of this parish. Godparents: Remy Pereau and Genoveva Sorel.

2001. LUIS OLIER? DERBANNE
August 25, 1789, baptism of Louis <u>Olier?</u>, born July 6, legitimate son of Pedro Derbanne and Maria Francesca Brevel, natives of this parish. Godparents: Balthasar Brevel and Widow St. Denis.

2002. MARIA DENIS
August 25, 1789, baptism of Maria, about 5 months of age, legitimate daughter of Juan Bautista Denis and Maria Beaudouin, natives of this parish. Godparents: Francisco Davion and Maria Teresa Beaudouin.

2003. SILVESTRE RACHAL
August 31, 1789, baptism of Silvestre, born August 2, legitimate son of Antonio Rachal and Maria Luisa Lemoine, natives of this parish. Godparents: Carlos Lemoine and Maria Luisa Dupre Lacase.

2004. MARIA ISABEL SAIDEK
August 31, 1789, baptism of Maria Isabel, born December 5, 1788, legitimate daughter of Pedro Clavis Saidek and Ursula Cheletre. Godparents: Carlos Lemoine and Isabel Buard. (f)

2005. PEDRO VICTORINO METOYER
September 26, 1789, baptism of Pedro Victorino, born

September 5, legitimate son of Mr. Claudio Thomas Pedro Metoyer, native of La Rochela in France, and Dme. Teresa Buard, native of this parish. Godparents: Juan Bautista Ailhaud St. Anne and Dna. St. Anne.

2006. MARIA TERESA VICTORIA AILHAUD ST. ANNE
September 26, 1789, baptism of Maria Teresa Victoria, born July 17, 1789, legitimate daughter of Juan Bautista Ailhaud St. Anne, native of the province of Dauphine, captain of the militia, and Dna. Maria Luisa Buard, a native of this parish. Godparents: Juan Antonio Ailhaud St. Anne, represented by Mr. Metoyer, and Dna. Metoyer.

2007. ANTONIO SOULANGE FREDERIC
September 27, 1789, baptism of Antonio Soulange, born August 30, legitimate son of Felipe Frederic and Barba Cheletre, natives of this parish. Godparents: Antonio Ymel and Barba Reyna Vildek.

2008. MARGARITA RABALÉ
September 27, 1789, baptism of Margarita, born June 12, legitimate daughter of Joseph Rabalé and Maria Luisa Malbert, natives of this parish. Godparents: Juan Bautista Tessier and Maria de Niebes /no last name/. (f)

2009. IGNACIO MAYOU
October 4, 1789, baptism of Ignacio Mayou, born August 15, legitimate son of Ignacio Mayou and Maria Teresa Filibot. Godparents: Miguel Rambint and Maria Luisa Rambint.

2010. MARIA MANUEL LESTAGE
November 1, 1789, baptism of Maria Manuel, born November 1, 1788, legitimate daughter of Guillermo Lestage and Manuel Riche. Godparents: Juan Bautista Lestage and Dna. de Soto Poissot.

2011. JUAN SILVESTRE HOPOK
December 26, 1789, baptism of Juan Silvestre, born April 21, legitimate son of Iago Hopok and Maria Salvant. Godparents: Athanasio Poissot and Ulalia Bossie.

2012. JUAN BAUTISTA MAES
December 27, 1789, baptism of Juan Bautista, born September 22, 1788, legitimate son of Pedro Joseph Maes, native of France, and Maria Ana Dartigaux, a native of the same. Godparents: Juan Bautista Dartigaux and Maria Victoria Maes.

2013. JOSEPH NOEL MALIGE
January 6, 1790, baptism of Joseph Noel, born December 25,

1789, legitimate son of Joseph Malige and Maria Ana Bardon. Godparents: Joseph Tauzin and Maria Ana Poissot.

2014. MARIA ANGELA GAGNE
January 6, 1790, baptism of Maria Angela, born August 11, 1789, legitimate daughter of Pedro Gagne and Maria Luisa Davion, natives of this parish. Godparents: Joseph Gagnes and Hiacinta Gagne.

2015. MARIA POMPOSA LAFITTE
February 7, 1790, baptism of Maria Pomposa, born January 6, 1790, legitimate daughter of Bouet Lafitte, native of the province of Languedoca in France and Maria Ana de Soto, native of the parish of Opelousas. Godparents: Pedro Dolet and Dna. Fonteneau.

2016. PEDRO CESARIO BROSSET
February 21, 1790, baptism of Pedro Cesario, born December 29, 1789, legitimate son of Pedro Brosset and M. Josepha Grillet. Godparents: Antonio Grillet and Maria Barba Grillet.

2017. MARIA ADRIANA ST. ANDRE
February 23, 1790, baptism of Maria Adriana, about one month of age, legitimate daughter of Andres St. André and Maria Rachal. Godparents: Luis Monet and Celeste Vergé.

2018. LUIS GALLIEN
February 28, 1790, baptism of Luis, born about a year ago, legitimate son of Nicolas Gallien and Maria Lecour, natives of this parish. Godparents: Luis Monet and Luisa Lecompte Monet. (f)

2019. MARIA DE NIEGES DERBANNE
April 4, 1790, baptism of Maria de Nieves, about one month of age, legitimate daughter of Gaspard Derbanne and Maria Josepha Pereau (Vildec). Godparents: Francisco Monginot and Dna. Massip.

2020. JUAN PEDRO BEAUDOIN
April 15, 1790, baptism of Juan Pedro, born March 8, 1790, legitimate son of Juan Pedro Beaudoin and Ana Robin, natives of this parish. Godparents: Pedro Beaudouin and Maria Robin.

2021. MARIA TERESA VASCOCU
April 25, 1790, baptism of Maria Teresa, born March 25, legitimate daughter of Andres Vascocu and Madelena Raymond, natives of this parish. Godparents: Francisco Vascocu and Dna. Ploché.

2022.   CESERIO BOSSIE
        May 4, 1790, baptism of Ceserio, born February 25, legitimate son of Silvestre Bossie and Maria Juanna Lambre. Godparents: Antonio Lambre and Ulalia Bossie.

2023.   JUAN BAUTISTA PRUDHOMME
        May 9, 1790, baptism of Juan Bautista, about 3 months of age, legitimate son of Francisco Prudhomme and Maria Rambint, natives of this parish. Godparents: Miguel Rambint and Dna. Rambint.

2024.   JUAN BAUTISTA BALTAZAR PLOCHER
        May 23, 1790, baptism of Juan Bautista Baltazar, about one month of age, legitimate son of Antonio Plocher and Maria Teresa Vascocu. Godparents: Guillermo Barberou and Maria Juanna Chagneau.

2025.   JOSEPH CELESTIN BERNARD
        June 1, 1790, baptism of Joseph Celestin, about six months of age, legitimate son of Elias Bernard and Leonora Chagneau. Godparents: Miguel Chagneau and Maria Juan-ris.

2026.   JUAN JOSEPH RACHAL
        June 5, 1790, baptism of Juan Joseph, born May 22, 1790, legitimate son of Luis Rachal and Maria LaBerry, natives of this parish. Godparents: Mr. Martinau and Dna. Martinau.

2027.   IAGO ISAAC RAJOBSON /ROBINSON/
        June 6, 1790, baptism of Iago Isaac, aged about five years, legitimate son of *Llit? Pajobson and Maria Martin, natives of New England. Godparents: Francesca Cheletre and Genoveva Gonin.   */Elie in Entry 1625/

2028.   GUILLERMO PAJOBSON /Robinson/
        June 6, 1790, baptism of Guillermo, aged about 3 years, legitimate son of Llit? Pajobson and Maria Martin, natives of New England. Godparents: Bernabé Cheletre and Maria Josepha Gonin.

2029.   JUAN BAUTISTA RAJOBSON /Robinson/
        June 6, 1790, baptism of Juan Bautista, aged about one year, legitimate son of Llit? Rajobson and Maria Martin, natives of New England. Godparents: Bautista Lestage and Maria Josepha Gonin.

2030.   FRANCISCO DORCINO RACHAL
        July 4, 1790, baptism of Francisco Dorcino, aged about one month, legitimate son of Bartolome Rachal and Francesca LaBery, natives of this parish. Godparents: Francisco Totin and Guillerma /Chever dit/ Dufrene.

2031. LUIS JOSEPHE ST. GERMAINE
July 21, 1790, baptism of Luis Josephe, about four years of age, legitimate son of Luis St. Germaine and Maria La Pointe. Godparents: Luis Carlos De Blanc and Dna. Marcel De Soto.

2032. CARLOS ESTEVAN ST. GERMAINE
July 21, 1790, baptism of Carlos Estevan, aged about two years, legitimate son of Luis St. Germaine and Maria La Pointe. Godparents: Luis C. De Blanc and Dna. De Blanc.

2033. JUAN LUIS HOPOCK
July 24, 1790, baptism of Juan Luis, born July 3, legitimate son of Jacob Hopok, native of New England, and Maria Salvan, native of this parish. Godparents: Juan Luis Buard and Eugenia Buard.

2034. LUIS RACHAL
August 1, 1790, baptism of Luis, born June 16, 1790, legitimate son of Bartholome Rachal and Francisca Grillet. Godparents: Bartholome Rachal and Dna. Lavesseur.

2035. DIONISIO ONESIN BUARD
August 1, 1790, baptism of Dionisio Onesin, born July 13, legitimate son of Luis Buard and Maria Rosa Lambre. Godparents: Juan Luis Buard and Maria Catalina Buard.

2036. MARIA JOSEPHA ROUQUIER
August 24, 1790, baptism of Maria Josepha, born November 25, 1789, legitimate daughter of Francois Rouquier, steward of this church and a native of France, and Maria Luisa Prudhomme. Godparents: Mr. Dupain and Dna. Lambre.

2037. MARIA BATILDE DUBOË
September 19, 1790, baptism of Maria Batilde, born August 1, legitimate daughter of Valentino Duboë and Rosa Chelettre. Godparents: Francisco Chelettre and Francisca Chelettre.

2038. SILVESTRE ANTY
September 26, baptism of Silvestre, about one month of age, legitimate son of Luis Anty and Maria Ana Cheletre*. Godparents: Gaspard La Cour and Ulalia Bossié.

*This name is recorded in error. The wife of Louis Anty and mother of Silvestre was Marie Jeanne Crete.

2039. LUIS NICOLAS MERCIER
September 26, 1790, baptism of Luis Nicolas, born June 8, legitimate son of Luis Mercier and Maria Luisa Levevre. Godparents: Nicolas Mercier and Teresa Mayou.

2040. LUIS GUILLERMO DUPARE
September 28, 1790, baptism of Luis Guillermo, born October 10, 1789, legitimate son of Guillermo Dupare, native of Normandy in France, and Ana Naneta Prudhomme, native of this parish. Godparents: Victor Dupain and Dna. Rouquier.

2041. ANTONIO PAKSAN MASSIP
November 1, 1790, baptism of Antonio Paksan, born October 23, 1790, legitimate son of Juan Massip and Maria Lemoine. Godparents: Antonio Rachal and Maria Pelagia Frederic.

2042. MARIA HORTENSIA RICHARD
November 7, 1790, baptism of Maria Hortensia, born August 2, legitimate daughter of <u>Mestre?</u> Richard and Maria de la Conception. Godparents: Pedro Ramis and Maria Langlois.

2043. JUANNA CHELETRE
November 14, 1790, baptism of Juanna, born October 6, legitimate daughter of Pedro Cheletre and Margarita Frederic. Godparents: Augustin Fredieu and Maria Juana Sorel.

2044. JUAN BAUTISTA SAIDEK
November 14, 1790, baptism of Juan Bautista, born October 8, legitimate son of Pedro Clavis Saidek and Ursula Cheletre. Godparents: Juan Bautista Duboë and Maria Ana Cheletre.

2045. LUIS PEREAU (VILDEC)
November 21, 1790, baptism of Luis, born August 19, legitimate son of Francisco Pereaut (Vildec) and Maria Luisa Labery. Godparents: Juan Bautista Duboë and Maria Ana Cheletre.

2046. MARIA CILESIA LOLETTE TRICHE
November 21, 1790, baptism of Maria Celesia Lolette, born March 8, 1790, legitimate daughter of Manuel Triche and Maria Luisa Grappe, natives of this parish. Godparents: Don Bouet de Laffitte and Dna. Laffitte.

2047. MARIA HELENA POMPOSA MONTANARY
November 21, 1790, baptism of Maria Helena Pomposa, born August 18, legitimate daughter of Benito Montanary of New Orleans and Francisca Grappe, native of this parish. Godparents: Francisco Grappe and Luisa Guedon.

2048. MARIA PELAGIA DE NIEVES ADELAY
November 21, 1790, baptism of Maria Pelagia de Nieves,

born August 5, legitimate daughter of Juan Adelay and Maria Genoveva Duboë. Godparents: Francisco Rambint and Pelagia Grappe.

2049. MARIA UFROISINA FONTENAU
November 21, 1790, baptism of Maria Ufrosina, born October 2, legitimate daughter of Luis Fontenau and Pelagia Grappe. Godparents: Manuel Prudhomme and Maria Lambre.

2050. JUAN FOSTEN SOULANGE BOSSIE
November 28, 1790, baptism of Juan Fosten Soulange, born November 6, legitimate son of Soulange Bossie and Leonora Ymel. Godparents: Francisco Bossie and Dna. Bossie.

2051. MARIA TERESA ISABEL METOYER
December 28, 1790, baptism of Maria Teresa Isabel, born November 14, legitimate daughter of Mr. Claudio Thomas Metoyer, native of La Rochelle, and Dna. Teresa Buard, native of this parish. Godparents: Andres Rambint and Dna. Rambint.

2052. EDUARDO CESAR MORPHIL
February 13, 1791, baptism of Eduardo Cesar, born September, 1790, legitimate son of Eduardo Morphil, native of Ireland, and Ysabel Josepha Buard, native of this parish. Godparents: Cesar Archeval and Dna. Ysabel Archeval.

2053. MARIA PELAGIA TOMASSIN
March 9, 1791, baptism of Maria Pelagia, born February 2, legitimate daughter of Luis Tomassin and Catalina Latié. Godparents: Bautista Latié and Pelagia Felipe /Frederic/.

2054. THEOTIS POISSOT
March 16, 1791, baptism of Theotis, born August 9, 1790, legitimate son of Remy Poissot and Luisa Cave. Godparents: Pedro Derbanne and Dna. Derbanne.

2055. MARIA JUSTA ALEMAN
March 20, 1791, baptism of Maria Justa, born November 10, 1790, legitimate daughter of Pedro Joseph Aleman and Maria Teresa Langlois. Godparents: Pedro Ramis and Dna. Ramis.

2056. PEDRO URSIN CHALER
April 2, 1791, baptism of Pedro Ursin, born January 20, legitimate son of Pedro Chaler and Maria Derbanne. Godparents: Pedro Derbanne and Juana Lebrun?

2057. MARIA LOLETA RACHAL
April 10, 1791, baptism of Maria Loleta, born January 6, legitimate daughter of Julien and Maria Luisa Brevel. Godparents: Luis Lambre and Maria Dupre.

2058. MARIA NANETA DENIS
April 10, 1791, baptism of Maria Naneta, born September 3, 1790, legitimate daughter of Juan Bautista Denis and Maria Ysabel Beaudouin. Godparents: Atanasio Lecour and Naneta Robin.

2059. LEON BRUNO TOTIN
April 29, 1791, baptism of Leon Bruno, born April 11, legitimate son of Remy Totin and Margarita Grillet. Godparents: Gaspar Filibert and Genoveva Levasseur.

2060. MARIA DE DOLORES DE SOTO
May 1, 1791, baptism of Maria de Dolores de Soto, born March 5, legitimate daughter of Marcel De Soto and Maria Baillot. Godparents: Atanasio Poissot and Dna. Poissot.

2061. YSABEL MARCELLITA DEBLANC
June 5, 1791, baptism of Ysabel Marcellita, born April 14, 1790, legitimate daughter of Luis Carlos Deblanc, commandant of this post, and Dna. Ysabel Pompano Derneville. Godparents: Marcel De Soto and Celeste Matilde Deblanc.

2062. MARIA ROSALIA LARENAUDIERE
June 23, 1791, baptism of Maria Roselia, born May 18, legitimate daughter of Pedro Larenaudiere and Juanna LaBery. Godparents: Bouet Laffitte and Rosalia Vercher.

2063. LUISA EUFROSIA BERNARD
July 9, 1791, baptism of Luisa Eufrosia, born June 29, legitimate daughter of Elias Bernard and Leonora Chagneau. Godparents: Barberoux and Dna. Larenaudiere.

2064. LOUIS FORT
July 17, 1791, baptism of Louis, born May 3, legitimate son of Iago Fort and Maria Francisca Malbert. Godparents: Mr. Monet and Dna. Bartolome Rachal.

2065. MARIA MELANIA LAVISPERE
July 17, 1791, baptism of Maria Melania, born May 28, legitimate daughter of Francisco Lavispere and Maria Luisa Derbanne. Godparents: Joseph Derbanne and Maria Vergé.

2066. LUIS GAGNÉ
July 17, 1791, baptism of Luis, born June 23, legitimate son of Pedro Gagné and Maria Luisa Davion. Godparents:

Luis Clauso and Pelagia Gagné.

2067. JUAN BAUTISTA GAGNE
July 17, 1791, baptism of Juan Bautista, born May 12, legitimate son of Estevan Gagne and Maria Luisa Bertrand. Godparents: Pedro Gagné and Maria Luisa Gagné.

2068. ANASTASIA FREDIER
July 26, 1791, baptism of Anastasia, born July 10, legitimate daughter of Agustin Fredieu and Maria Juanna Sorel. Godparents: Remy Lambre and Maria Genoveva Sorel.

2069. JUAN BAUTISTA JOSUE DUBOË
July 31, 1791, baptism of Juan Bautista Josue, born December 7, 1790, legitimate son of Francois Duboe and Maria Leonora Juan-ris. Godparents: Antonio Duboë and Maria Juan-ris.

2070. ANTONIO NARCISSE RACHAL
August 25, 1791, baptism of Antonio Narcisse, born June 2, 1791, legitimate son of Antoine Rachal and Maria Luisa Lemoine. Godparents: Bartolome Rachal and Dna. Massip.

2071. ANDRE DAVID ROBINSON
September 25, 1791, baptism of Andre David, born August 25, legitimate son of Martie Robinson, native of New England, and Marie Martin of the same. Godparents: Andre David and Dna. Rambint.

2072. LUIS LEVASSEUR
October 9, 1791, baptism of Luis, born August 2, legitimate son of Jacques Francois Levasseur and Teresa Grillet. Godparents: Luis Lambre and Dna. Lambre.

2073. JOSEPH AMABLE PEREAU (VILDEC)
October 13, 1791, baptism of Joseph Amable, born December 1, 1790, legitimate son of Chrisostome Pereau and Maria Luisa Salvan. Godparents: Julian Besson and Widow Grappe.

2074. MARIA EUFROSIN POMIER
October 16, 1791, baptism of Maria Eufrosin, born September 15, legitimate daughter of Juan Pomier and Maria Robert /Dupre/. Godparents: Francois Cheletre and Cecilia Robert /Dupre/.

2075. IGNACIO LEMAITRE
November 4, 1791, baptism of Ignacio, born August 2, legitimate son of Francisco Lemaitre and Luisa /Ic Duc/. Godparents: Bautista Grappe and Maria Juana Goutiere.

2076. MARIA CELESTE JEAN-RIS
November 4, 1791, baptism of Maria Celeste, born October 17, legitimate daughter of Joseph Jean-Ris and Francisca Vascocu. Godparents: Antonio Vascocu and Dna. Juan-ris.

2077. MARIA CELESTINA SEBASTIEN _____
November 5, 1791, baptism of Maria Celestina, born August 27, a white child, daughter of a father and mother unknown*. Godparents: Francisco Guillermo Veldek and Guillerma Chever.

*The French entry of this baptism, recorded in Book 3 (Entry 1669) identifies the infant's mother as "Dlle. Marie Louise Bastien /no last name/."

2078. MARIA GENOVEVA AGATA MAES
November 28, 1791, baptism of Maria Genoveva Agata, born January 18, 1791, legitimate daughter of Mr. Pedro Joseph Maes and Maria Ana Dartigaux, natives of France. Godparents: Joseph Maes and Maria Ana Conan Dartigaux.

2079. FRANCISCO ANTONIO CARLE /LE NOIR/
January 1, 1792, baptism of Francisco Antonio Carle, born December 20, a white child, son of a father and a mother unknown*. Godparents: Francisco Feble and Maria Luisa Langlois.

*The French entry of this baptism, recorded in Book 3 (Entry 1674) identifies the mother of the infant as Marie Ulalie Carle. See note accompanying Entry 1674.

2080. MARIA DE NIEVES BROM /BROWN/
January 15, 1792, baptism of Maria de Nieves, about 11 months, legitimate daughter of Thomas Brom and Maria Teal. Godparents: Juan Bautista David and Teresa La Malaty.

2081. MARIA TERESA BERTRAND
January 22, 1792, baptism of Maria Teresa, born November 22, 1791, legitimate daughter of Luis Bertrand and Isabel Davlon, natives of this parish. Godparents: Luis Clauso and Maria Gagné.

2082. JOSEPH DE EPIFANIA BOSSIE
February 19, 1792, baptism of Joseph de Epifania, born January 6, legitimate son of Francisco Bossier and Catalina Pelagia Lambre. Godparents: Louis Joseph Lambre and Maria Teresa Eugenia Buard.

2083. MARIA POMPOSA
February 19, 1792, baptism of Maria Pomposa, aged about one year, daughter of an Indian named Nanette. Godparents: Francisco Monginot and Maria Genoveva Jean-ris.

2084. JOSEPH VALENTIN
February 23, 1792, baptism of Joseph, born December 3, 1791, legitimate son of Andres Francisco Valentin and Angelique Malige. Godparents: Mr. Malige and Dna. Labery.

2085. GENOVEVA EUFRASIA ANTY
March 4, 1792, baptism of Genoveva Eufrasia, born January 20, legitimate daughter of Juan Bautista Anty and Maria Francisca Levasseur, natives of this parish. Godparents: Francisco Levasseur and Genoveva Levasseur.

2086. MARIA LUISA ZÉMIRE BEAUDOUIN
April 7, 1792, baptism of Maria Luisa, born February 5, 1792, legitimate daughter of Pedro Beaudouin and Ana Robin, natives of this post. Godparents: Nicolas Beaudouin and Ysabel Beaudouin.

2087. LUISA EUFRASIA PRUDHOMME
April 8, 1792, baptism of Luisa Eufrasia, born January 19, 1792, daughter of Francisco Prudhomme and Maria Barba Rambint. Godparents: Pedro /illegible/ and Eufrasia Rambint.

2088. MARIA FRANCISCA MORALES
April 14, 1792, baptism of Maria Francisca, about five months of age, daughter of Joseph Manuel Morales and of Maria Pologna. Godparents: Estevan Vergé and Dna. Vergé.

2089. JUAN BAUTISTA DIONISIO RAMBINT
April 15, 1792, baptism of Juan Bautista Dionisio, born June 5, 1791, legitimate son of Andres Rambint and Maria Catalina Buard. Godparents: Dionisio Buard and Maria Ana Gabriel /Buard née Rousseau/

2090. JUAN BAUTISTA DORCIN MAYOU
April 15, 1792, baptism of Juan Bautista Dorcin, born March 3, 1792, son of Ignacio Mayou and Maria Terese Tibaud. Godparents: Juan Bautista Dortolant and Anastasia Mayou.

2091. ANGELICA DOMICILA RABALÉ
April 15, 1792, baptism of Angelica Domicila, born January 15, 1792, legitimate daughter of Joseph Rabalé and Maria Luisa Malbert. Godparents: Estevan Vergé and Angelica Malbert.

2092. MARIA MATILDA STA. CRUZ
July 15, 1792, baptism of Maria Matilda Sta. Cruz, aged about one month, a white child, father and mother unknown.*
Godparents: Benito Pescio and Dna. Ramis.

*The French entry of this baptism, recorded in Book 3 (Entry 1689) identifies the infant as child of "an Indian and a father unknown."

2093. MARIA BOSSIE
July 15, 1792, baptism of Maria Bossie, born April 15, legitimate daughter of Silvestre Bossie and Maria Lambre. Godparents: Juan Luis Lambre and Maria Teresa Eugenia Lambre.

2094. MARIA ROSA BERGITA LATIE
July 16, 1792, baptism of Maria Rosa Bergita, born May 8, daughter of Juan Bautista Latié and Maria Pelagia Frederic. Godparents: Joseph Latie and Dna. Frederic.

2095. ELOISA SERAPHINA MALIGE
July 30, 1792, baptism of Eloisa Seraphina, born July 15, legitimate daughter of Mr. Malige and Maria Ana Bardon. Godparents: Remy Lambre and Dna. Armant.

2096. JUAN BAUTISTA BELONI VERCHER
August 25, 1792, baptism of Juan Bautista Beloni, born April 22, son of Luis Vercher and Maria Luisa Grillet. Godparents: Juan Pedro Vercher and Isabel David.

2097. MARIA JOSEPHA CONSTANCIA DEBLANC
August 29, 1792, baptism of Maria Josepha Constancia, born October 26, 1791, legitimate daughter of Luis Carlos de Blanc, native of this parish, and Isabel Pompona Derneville, native of New Orleans. Godparents: Joseph Loppes de la Peña, chevalier and captain of the Spanish Regiment and *alcade* of New Orleans, and Dna. Maria Azun?, widow of deceased Don _____ _____ /blanks in text are not filled in/ Dreux.

2098. MARIA HELENA CHELETTRE
MARIA EMMANUEL CHELETTE
September 2, 1792, baptism of Maria Helena and Maria Emmanuel, born the past June, twin daughters of Barnabe Chelettre and Maria Josepha Gonin. Godparents of the first: Bautista Lestage and Helena Baillot; godparents of the second: Juan Bautista duboë and Ulalia Bossie.

2099. MARIA LOCADIA BOSSIE
October 8, 1792, baptism of Maria Locadia, born March 8, 1792, daughter of Soulange Bossie and Leonora Ymel. Godparents: Placide Bossier and Francisca Ymel.

2100. LOUIS JOSEPH TAUZIN
October 8, 1792, baptism of Louis Joseph, born August 11, 1792, son of Joseph Tauzin and Maria Chamarre. Godparents: Luis Chamarre and Catalina Bardon.

2101. MARIA ROSALIA BERGITA LESTAGE
October 9, 1792, baptism of Maria Rosalia Bergita, born July 10, 1792, daughter of *Cadet* Lestage and Manuella Riche. Godparents: Francisco Gonin and Maria Rosalia Frederic.

2102. MARIA MARCELLITA DUPRES
October 10, 1792, baptism of Maria Marcellita, born May 2, daughter of Pedro Dupre and Francisca Le Cour. Godparents: Bartholome Le Cour and Maria Luisa? Dupres.

2103. JUAN BAUTISTA DAVION
October 10, 1792, baptism of Juan Bautista, born May 24, son of Francisco Davion and Margarita Cloutie, natives of this parish. Godparents: Juan Bautista Davion and Helena Cloutie.

2104. MARIA TEOTIS MASSIPE
October 14, 1792, baptism of Maria Teotis, born June 7, daughter of Juan Massip and Maria Lemoine. Godparents: Bautista Dartigaux and Dorotea Massip.

2105. FELICIDAD PALVADOS
October 14, 1792, baptism of Felicidad, born September 4, 1792, legitimate daughter of Juan Palvados and Leonora Tessié. Godparents: Joseph Tessié and Maria Francisca Triche.

2106. MARIA LUISA CILESIA DESOTO
October 14, 1792, baptism of Maria Luisa Cilesia, born August? 24, daughter of Joseph Marcel de Soto and Maria Baillot. Godparents: Luis Carlos de Blanc and Maria Ana de Soto.

2107. CELESTIA MARTIN
October 24, 1792, baptism of Celestia, about seven years, daughter of deceased Zacharias Martin and Celestia Teal. Godparents: Christobal Teal and Maria Frozina Martin.

2108. JUAN MARTIN
October 24, 1792, baptism of Juan, about three years, son of deceased Zacharias Martin and Celestia Teal. Godparents: Bautista /illegible/ and Dna. Rouquier.

2109. ZACHARIAS MARTIN
October 24, 1792, baptism of Zacharias, born about two years earlier, son of deceased Zacharias Martin and Celestia Teal. Godparents: Iago Teal and Teresa Lamalaty.

2110. JUANINA ANESIA PEREAU (VILDEC)
November 4, 1792, baptism of Juanina Anesia, born February 20, legitimate daughter of Francisco Pereau and Luisa Laberry. Godparents: Francisco Grappe and Maria Juanna Lalande.

2111. MARIA EUSEBIA CHELETTRE
November 4, 1792, baptism of Maria Eusebia, born September 30, 1792, legitimate daughter of Pedro Chelettre and Margarita Frederic. Godparents: Andres Frederic and Cecilia Robert /Dupre̲/.

2112. MARIA CELESTE _____
November 12, 1792, baptism of Maria Celeste, born January 1792, white, of a father and mother unknown. Godparents: Benito Pescio and Maria Polonia.

2113. PEDRO DELOUCHE
November 25, 1792, baptism of Pedro, born August 16, 1790, legitimate son of Juan Delouche and Maria Ursula Boulé. Godparents: Miguel Jory and Maria Marta Fort.

2114. JULIAN DELOUCHE
November 25, 1792, baptism of Julian, born April 12, 1792, son of Juan De louche and Maria Ursula Boulé. Godparents: Gil /i̲llegible̲/ and Cecilia Robert /Dupre̲/.

2115. JUAN BAUTISTA DAVION
December 9, 1792, baptism of Juan Bautista, born October 8, 1792, son of Domingo Davion and Pelagia Gagne. Godparents: Juan Bautista Davion and Ursula Gagne.

2116. JUAN BAUTISTA BARTOLOME RACHAL
December 25, 1792, baptism of Juan Bautista Bartolome, born August 30, 1792, son of Juan Bautista Bartolome Rachal and Maria Pelagia Brevel. Godparents: Baltasar Brevel and Theresa Lamalaty Fiolle.

2117. AUGUSTIN CESERIO FREDIEU
December 28, 1792, baptism of Augustin Ceserio, born December 8, 1792, legitimate son of Augustin Fredier and Maria Juanna Sorel. Godparents: Lucas Sorel and Maria Josepha Triche.

2118. LUIS SAIDEK
December 29, 1792, baptism of Luis, born November 15, son of Pedro Clavis Saidek and Ursula Cheletre. Godparents: Luis Monet and Maria Luisa Lecompte.

2119. CARLOS CELESTINO TOTIN
January 12, 1793, baptism of Carlos Celestino, born December 6, 1792, son of Remo Totin and Margarita Grillet. Godparents: Luis Levasseur and Elena Grillet.

2120. MARIA YSABEL ASPASIA MORPHIL
January 20, 1793, baptism of Maria Ysabel Aspasia, born December 13, 1792, daughter of Eduardo Morphil, native of Ireland, and Josepha Isabel Buard, native of this parish.

Godparents. Luis Buard and Dna. St. Anne.

2121. MARIA REYNA TOMASSIN
January 27, 1793, baptism of Maria Reyna, born January 6, daughter of Luis Tomassin, native of Spain, and Catalina Latié, native of this parish. Godparents: Miguel Ernande and Maria Olivier.

2122. ANTONIO FRANCISCO VASCOCU
January 27, 1793, baptism of Antonio Francisco, born December 5, 1792, son of Antonio Vascocu, native of New Orleans and Geneva Gonin, native of this parish. Godparents: Francisco Gonin and Maria Francisca Vascocu.

2123. ROSA MATILDA ALEMAN
February 10, 1793, baptism of Rosa Matilda, born January 30, daughter of Don Pedro Joseph Aleman and Maria Teresa Langlois. Godparents: Benito Pescio and Nicolosa Langlois.

2124. MIGUEL LORENZO RAMBINT
February 24, 1793, baptism of Miguel Lorenzo, born January 15, son of Antonio Miguel Rambint and Maria Teresa Mayou, natives of this parish. Godparents: Lorenzo Mayou and Maria Rambint.

2125. LUIS ADELAY
March 20, 1793, baptism of Luis, born November 6, 1792, son of Juan Adelay and Genoveva Duboë. Godparents: Luis Fonteneau and Maria Luisa Grappe.

2126. MARIA FRANCISCA POMPOSA ANTY
March 30, 1793, baptism of Maria Francisca Pomposa, born March 2, daughter of Luis Anty, native of Pointe Coupee, and Maria Juanna Crete, native of this parish. Godparents: Bautista Anty and Maria Francesca Levasseur.

2127. ASPASIA DUBOË
March 31, 1793, baptism of Aspasia, born January 9, daughter of Francisco Duboë and Leonora Jean-Ris, natives of this parish. Godparents: Joseph Michel Chagneau and Genoveva Jean-Ris.

2128. MARIA ANA CEPHALIDA LAMBRE
March 31, 1793, baptism of Maria Ana Cephalida, born March 16, *endoyée* in home of Sr. Andres Verdalay, legitimate daughter of Remy Lambre and Susanna Prudhomme, natives of this parish. Godparents: Francisco Rouquier, *mayor domo* /Chief Warden/ of this parish, and Maria Ana de Soto Poiccot.

2129. JUAN BAUTISTA LEMOINE
April 1, 1793, baptism of Juan Bautista, born February 15,

legitimate son of Juan Bautista Lemoine and Felicidad Lecase, natives of this parish, *endoyée* in home of Maria Ana Poissot. Godparents: Carlos Lemoine and Maria Catalina Sauvage.

2130. MARIA MODESTA NICOLAS AGUSTIN /METOYER/
April 22, 1793, baptism of Maria Modesta Nicolas Agustin, about six months of age, legitimate daughter of Augustin, free *mulato*, and Agnes, free *mulata*, natives of this parish. Godparents: Dominique, free *mulato*, and Maria Teresa, free *negra*.

2131. REMY RACHAL
April 22, 1793, baptism of Remy, born January 30, legitimate son of Bartolome Rachal and Francisca Laberry, natives of this parish. Godparents: Bautista Rachal and Francisca Rachal.

2132. MARIA LUISA MERCIER
April 27, 1793, baptism of Maria Luisa, born January 31, legitimate daughter of Luis Mercier and Maria Luisa Levevre, natives of this parish. Godparents: Francisco Mercier and Helena Robleau.

2133. JUAN VITAL VASCOCU
April 29, 1793, baptism of Juan Vital, born November 27, 1792, legitimate son of Luis Vascocu and Maria Madelena Pereau (Vildec). Godparents: Francisco Vascocu and Maria Juanna Lambre.

2134. MARIA FRANCISCA ARTEMISA RACHAL
April 29, 1793, baptism of Maria Francisca Artemisa, born December 20, 1792, legitimate daughter of Luis Rachal and Maria Francesca Grillet. Godparents: Domingo Rachal and Francisca Rachal.

2135. MARIA JOSEPHA HENRIQUE ROUQUIER
April 30, 1793, baptism of Maria Josepha Henrique, born July 9, 1792, legitimate daughter of Francisco Rouquier, chief warden of this church, and Maria Luisa Prudhomme. Godparents: Juan Silvestre Sarpy, represented by Juan Maria Francisco Rouquier, and Dna. Margarita Sanche, represented by Dame Rouquier.

2136. MARINO BROSSET
May 5, 1793, baptism of Marino, born March 29, legitimate son of Pedro Brosset and Maria Josepha Grillet, native of this parish. Godparents: Juan Bautista Brosset and Ysabel Lebrun.

2137.   JOSEF AUGUSTIN BUARD
        ANTONIO EVARISTE BUARD
        May 5, 1793, baptism of Josef Augustin and Antonio Evariste, born March 17, twin sons of Luis Buard and Maria Rosa Lambre, natives of this parish. Godparents of the first: Francisco Agustin Buard and Maria Ana Buard; godparents of the second: Josef Lambre and Maria Teresa Eugenia Buard.

2138.   MARIA JOSEPHA FROSINA RACHAL
        May 5, 1793, baptism of Maria Josepha Frosina, born 16th of March, daughter of Luis Rachal and Maria Josepha La Bery. Godparents: Mr. Monginot and Madame Monginot.

2139.   MARTIN ERLD
        June 10, 1793, baptism at Rapides of Martin, born December 5, 1783, legitimate son of Ricardo Erld and Maria Gray of the American nation. Godparents: Carlos Huoot and Felicite Etie, both Catholics.

2140.   DAVID ERLD
        June 10, 1793, baptism at Rapides of David, born April 17, 1787, legitimate son of Ricardo Erld and Maria Gray of the American Nation. Godparents: Carlos Huoot and Felicite Etie, both Catholics.

2141.   MARIA NOEMY ERLD
        June 10, 1793, baptism at Rapides of Maria Noemy, born August 3, 1781, legitimate daughter of Ricardo Erld and Maria Gray of the American nation. Godparents: Carlos Huoot and Felicite Etie, both Catholics.

2142.   ISAAC DEIL /TEAL?/
        June 10, 1793, baptism at Rapides of Isaac, born February 24, 1782, legitimate son of Juan Deil and Leticia /no surname given/, Americans. Godparents: Carlos Huoot and Felicite Etie, both Catholics.

2143.   ANTONIO
        June 11, 1793, baptism at the Apalache village at the place of Dionesio *el Gefe*, of Antonio, aged two years, son of Bautisto, Apalache, and Magdalena la Movilien, Indian. Godparents: Antonio and Francesca, Christian Indians.

2144.   ESTEBAN
        June 11, 1793, baptism at the Apalache village of Estevan, four days old, son of Antonio and Mariana. Godparents: Estevan and Margarita, both of the same nation.

2145.   ESTEVAN
        June 11, 1793, baptism at the Apalache village of

Estevan, aged four years, son of Luis and Hamaicta. Godparents: Jacobo, of the same nation, and Maria Barbara /no last name/, a white.

2146. ESTEVAN
June 11, 1793, baptism at the Apalache village of Estevan, aged three years, legitimate son of Estevan and of Franca. Godparents: Luis Fonteno and Maria Barbara /no last name/, whites.

2147. ANASTASIA
June 11, 1793, baptism at the Apalache village of Anastasia, aged seven years, daughter of Thomas and Catharina. Godparents: Luis Fontenot and Catharina, of the tribe.

2148. MARGARITA
June 11, 1793, baptism at the Apalache village of Margarita, aged two years, daughter of Nicolas and Franca. Godparents: Luis Fonteno and Catharina, of the tribe.

2149. CATHARINA
June 11, 1793, baptism at the Apalache village of Catharina, aged two and a half years, daughter of Thomas and Catharina. Godparents: Solomon and Catharina of the tribe.

2150. LUISA
HELENA
June 11, 1793, baptism at the Apalache village of Luisa and Helena, aged eighteen months, twin daughters of Nicolas and Genoveva. Godparents: Luis Fontenot and Maria Barbara /no last name/, whites.

2151. FRANCA.
June 11, 1793, baptism at the Apalache village of Franca., aged three years, daughter of Nicolas and Magdalena. Godparents: Estevan and Franca., both of the tribe.

2152. CLARISA
June 11, 1793, baptism at the Apalache village of Clarisa, aged two years, daughter of Estevan and Franca. Godparents: Juan Bautista and Catharina, both of the nation.

2153. FELICITE
June 11, 1793, baptism of Felicite at the Apalache village, aged six years, daughter of Juan and Maria Juana. Godparents: Carlos Huoot and Felicite Etië, whites.

2154. MAXIAMA
June 11, 1793, baptism at the Apalache village of Maxiama,

aged three days, son of Thomas and Catharina. Godparents: Luis and Victoria of the nation.

2155. DIONESIOS
June 11, 1793, baptism at the Apalache village of Dionesios, aged five years, son of Thomas and Catharina. Godparents: Dionesio *el gete* and Franca.

2156. LUIS
June 11, 1793, baptism of Luis at the Apalache village, aged about ten years, son of Chopé and Franca. Godparents: Luis Fonteno and Catharina, of the tribe.

2157. MARIA DEL PILAR RACHAL
June 15, 1793, baptism of Maria del Pilar, aged about six years, daughter of Maria Rechel and a father unknown. Godparents: Francisco Davion and Maria Jpha. de Torres.

2158. LUIS
June 15, 1793, baptism of Luis, born December 12, 1792, son of Luisa, a Christian Indian, and a father unknown. Godparents: Juan Bautista and Genoveva.

2159. FRANCISCO ESTEVAN DUGUE (DUCHET)
June 26, 1793, baptism of Francisco Estevan, born November 14, 1792, legitimate son of Estevan Dugue and Catharina Salvan. Godparents: Franco. Bosie and Maria Salvan.

/NO ENTRIES FOR 1794/

2160. LUISA JOSEPHINA MAES
January 11?, 1795, baptism of Luisa Josephina, born April 10, 1794, legitimate daughter of Pedro Joseph Maes and Maria Ana Dartigaux. Godparents: Juan Bautista Ailhaud St. Anne and Francesca Lorenza.

2161. FRANCISCO PEREAU (VILDEC)
January 12, 1795, baptism of Francisco, born December 14, legitimate son of Francisco Pereau (Vildec) and Luisa Agata Labayrie, natives of this parish. Godparents: Francisco Coupalon and Dna. Andres Vascocu.

2162. MARIA MARGARITA FREDERIC
January 17, 1795, baptism of Maria Margarita, born June 20, 1793, daughter of Felipe Frederic and Barba Cheletre. Godparents: Andres Frederic and Anna Margarita Cheletre.

2163. LUIS BOUET LAFITTE
January 18, 1795, baptism of Luis, born November 30, 1794, son of Don Pablo Bouet Laffitte, native of France, and

Maria Ana Desoto, native of this parish; *endoyé* in the home of Don Luis Jobard. Godparents: Luis Jobard and Dna. Marcel de Soto.

2164. JOSEPH MARCEL DE SOTO
January 18, 1795, baptism of Joseph Marcel, born July 10, 1794 of Joseph Marcel de Soto and Maria Baillio, natives of this parish. Godparents: Silvestre Poissot and Dna. Celeste Matilde de Blanc.

2165. LUIS BERTRAND
January 18, 1795, baptism of Luis, born November 23, 1795 /sic/, legitimate son of Luis Bertrand and Ysabel Davion, natives of this parish. Godparents: Gilbert Closo and Pelagia Gagné.

2166. LUIS VASCOCU
January 18, 1795, baptism of Luis, born August 31, 1794, legitimate son of Luis Vascocu and Madelena Perau, natives of this parish. Godparents: Remigio Perau and Francisca Vascocu.

2167. FRANCISCO PLACIDE BOSSIER
January 19, 1795, baptism of Francisco Claude, born October 4, 1794, legitimate son of Francisco Bossie, native of the parish of St. Charles on the German Coast, and Catalina Pelagia Lambre, native of this parish. Godparents: Placide Bossier and Ulalia Bossie.

2168. MARIA LUISA CHELETTRE
January 20, 1795, baptism of Maria Luisa, born November 15, 1794, daughter of Pedro Chelettre and Margarita Frederic. Godparents: Juan Francisco Frederic and Maria Luisa Lecompte.

2169. JUAN BAUTISTA LATIE
January 25, 1795, baptism of Juan Bautista, born July 16, 1794, son of Juan Bautista Latié and Maria Pelagia Frederic. Godparents: Francisco Latié and Maria Rosalia Frederic.

2170. JUAN DENIS IAGO FORT
January 25, 1795, baptism of Juan Iago Denis, born October 19, 1794, son of Don Iago Fort and Maria Francisca Malbert. Godparents: Denis Buard and Maria Marta Iago Fort.

2171. LUIS POMIER
February 1, 1795, baptism of Luis, born February 11, 1794, legitimate son of Juan Pomier and Maria Dupre. Godparents: Iago Lacaza and Maria Luisa Dupré.

2172. JUAN PEDRO TORRES /STA. CRUX7
February 8, 1795, baptism of Juan Pedro, born October 14, 1794, legitimate son of Maria Juan Santa Crux and Maria Anna Torres, natives of the post of Los Adayes. Godparents: Francisco Lemaitre and Dna. Nicola Langlois.

2173. HILAIRE LAVISPERE
February 8, 1795, baptism of Hilaire, born June 22, 1793, legitimate son of Francisco Lavispere and Maria Luisa Derbanne. Godparents: Manuel Derbanne and Francisca Rachal.

2174. MARIA PELAGIA BELAZIN JUAN-RIS
March 1, 1795, baptism of Pelagia Bolazin, born December 10, 1794, legitimate daughter of Joseph Juan-Ris and Francisca Vascocu. Godparents: Joseph Michel Chagnau and Maria Eulalia Vascocu.

2175. MARIA MARGARITA PRUD'HOMME
March 14, 1795, baptism of Maria Margarita, born May 18, 1794, legitimate daughter of Iago Prudhomme and Maria Luisa Antonia /de St. Denis7*. Godparents: Bautista Prudhomme and Widow St. Denis.

*Entry 3395 identifies the wife of Iago Sebastian Prudhomme as "Maria Luisa Antonia, daughter of a father and mother unknown." In the civil records of the parish, District Court Suit No. 130, Bundle 4, Marie Louise *vs.* David Case, Mme. Jacques Prudhomme is further identified as the godchild of the widow of Louis Antoine St. Denis (Louise Marguerite Derbanne Barbier). In all probability she is the same Marie Louise Antoine Bastien who frequently appears as a godmother in Register III and is identified in two of those records as Marie Louise Antoine de St. Denis.

2176. MARIA MELANIA DEBLANC
March 22, 1795, baptism of Maria Melania, born October 4, 1793, daughter of Luis Carlos de Blanc and Ysabel Pompona Derneville, a native of New Orleans. Godparents: Luis Cesairio de Blanc, her brother, and Dna. Maria Melania De Blanc, represented by Dna. Aspasie De Blanc.

2177. MAXIMILIANO DEBLANC
March 22, 1795, baptism of Maximiliano, born October 12, 1794, son of Luis Carlos De Blanc and Ysabel Pompona Derneville. Godparents: Juan Valentin Dufosset and Maria Pavi? La Cour.

2178. ADELAIDE TAUZIN
March 22, 1795, baptism of Adelaide, born September 16, 1793, daughter of Joseph Tauzin, of the diocese of Auray in France, and Maria Chamarre, native of the Illinois country. Godparents: Miguel Chamarre and Adelaide Armant.

2179. EULALIE EMILIE BOSSIE
March 29, 1795, baptism of Eulalie Emilie Bossie, born January 19, 1794, daughter of Soulange Bossie and Eleonore Ymel, native of this parish. Godparents: Antonio Ymel and Ulalie Bossie.

2180. FRANCISCO BENJAMIN METOYER
April 10, 1795, baptism of Francisco Benjamin, born July 11, 1794, legitimate son of Claudio Thomas Metoyer, a native of La Rochela, and Teresa Buard, native of this parish. Godparents: Francisco Monginot and Dna. Luis Buard.

2181. MARIA ANA DESIDERADA PRUD'HOMME
April 5, 1795, baptism of Maria Ana Desiderada, born July 28, 1794, legitimate daughter of Antonio Prud'homme and Maria Lambre, natives of this parish. Godparents: Atanasio Poissot and Maria Anna Lambre.

2182. MARIA OZITE /AUSITE/ RACHAL
April 5, 1795, baptism of Maria Ozite, born April 4, 1792, daughter of Julian Rachal and Maria Luisa Brevel. Godparents: Baltasar Brevel and Dna. Lambre.

2183. MARIA ASPASIA DERBANNE
April 5, 1795, baptism of Maria Aspasia, born March 20, 1793, daughter of Pedro Derbanne and Maria Francisca Brevel, natives of this parish. Godparents: Domingo Prudhomme and Francisca Rachal.

2184. MARIA DIONISIA CHALER
April 5, 1795, baptism of Maria Dionisia, born September 25, 1794, daughter of Pedro Chaler and Maria Derbanne. Godparents: Pablo Couty and Maria Poissot.

2185. ROSALIA VINCENT
April 5, 1795, baptism of Rosalia, born November 29, 1794, daughter of Miguel Vincent and Helena Roublot. Godparents: Pedro Roublot and Rosalia Gagné.

2186. FELICIANA THEOPHILA LEMAITRE
April 12, 1795, baptism of Feliciana Theophila, born May 8, 1794, daughter of Francisco Lemaitre and Luisa /le Duc dit/ Villefranche. Godparents: Joseph Teissier and Nicolassa Langlois.

2187. REMIGIO SILVESTRE MASSIP
April 14, 1795, baptism of Remigio Silvestre, born January 15, 1794, son of Juan Massip and Maria Luisa Lemoine. Godparents: Remigio Pereau and Juanna le Brun.

2188. MARIA DE LOS NIEVES _____
April 18, 1795, baptism of Maria de los Nieves, born
March 3 "of a father unknown," /mother not named/. God-
parents: Chevalier de Blanc and Nicolassa Langlois.

2189. JUAN BAUTISTA LARENAUDIERE
April 30, 1795, baptism of Juan Bautista, born October
10, 1794, son of Pedro Larenaudiere and Juanna Labayrie,
natives of this parish. Godparents: Miguel Ernandes and
Maria Olivier.

2190. GENOVEVA CELESTE
May 9, 1795, baptism of Genoveva Celeste, born October
20, 1794, daughter of Susanna, free Indian, and a father
unknown. Godparents: Joseph Locovis and Genoveva Juan-
Ris.

2191. MIGUEL DELOUCHE
IAGO DELOUCHE
May 16, 1795, baptism of Miguel and Iago, twins born May
25, 1794, sons of Juan Delouch and Ursula Boule. Godparents: Miguel Ernandes and Maria Olivier and Iago _____
and Maria Luisa Dupre.

2192. LUIS LASTI /SOLASTIE/ DERBANNE
May 17, 1795, baptism of Luis Lasti, born February 18,
1794, son of Juan Bautista Derbanne and Maria Helena
Brevel. Godparents: Bautista Brevel and Maria de Soto.

2193. LUIS BERNADO MALIGE
May 23, 1795, baptism of Luis Bernado, born April 19, son
of Joseph Malige and Maria Anna Bardon. Godparents:
Bernardo Ortolant and Maria Luisa De Blanc.

2194. MARIA ASTASIA DAVION
May 24, 1795, baptism of Maria Destasia /Astasia/, born
December 10, 1793, daughter of Francisco Davion and Mar-
garita Cloutie. Godparents: Juan Pedro Cloutie and
Susanna Gagné.

2195. MARIA AGATHE RACHAL
May 24, 1795, baptism of Maria Agatha, born December 6,
1794, daughter of Bartolome Rachal and Maria Francisca
Grillet. Godparents: Juan Bautista Brosset and Ufrosina
David.

2196. MANUEL ILARIO RACHAL
May 24, 1795, baptism of Manuel Ilario, born July 28,
1794, son of Juan Bautista Bartolome Rachal and Maria
Pelagia Brevel. Godparents: Manuel Rachal and Francisca
Rachal.

2197. MARIA PLACIDA DERBANNE
May 24, 1795, baptism of Maria Placida, born February 10, daughter of Gaspar Derbanne and Maria Josepha Perau, natives of this parish. Godparents: Placide Bossie and Maria LaLande.

2198. ADALAIDE LOCADIE DUBOË
June 3, 1795, baptism of Adalaide Locadie, born January 12 of Francisco Duboë and Leousa Juan-ris, natives of this parish. Godparents: Joseph Martin and Adelaide Rambint.

2199. MARIA FELICIDAD TORRES
June 4, 1795, baptism of Maria Felicidad, aged four years, daughter of Gabriel Torres, a native of Los Adayes, and of Maria Rachal, a native of Natchitoches. Godparents: Simeon Rachal and Maria Gertrudes /no last name/.

2200. LUIS EVRIE DENIS
JUAN PEDRO DENIS
June 7, 1795, baptism of Luis Evrie and Juan Pedro, born February 17, 1794, twin sons of Juan Bautista Denis and Anna Robin*. Godparents of the first: Luis Evrie and Maria Luisa Larenaudiere; godparents of the second: Pedro Beaudouin and Maria Dupre.

*This is obviously an error. Entries before and after 1795 show the wife of Jean Baptiste Denis to be Marie Elisabeth Beaudouin, while Anne Robin was married to Pierre Beaudouin.

2201. JUAN PLACIDE PLOCHÉR
June 22, 1795, baptism of Juan Placide, born September 4, 1793, son of Antonio Plochér, native of Provenca province, and Maria Teresa Vascocu, native of this parish. Godparents: Estevan Henrique Ploché and Maria Ecué Ploché.

2202. MANUEL ATANASIO MORALES
July 5, 1795, baptism of Manuel Atanasio, born April 29, 1794, son of Manuel Morales, native of Los Adayes, and Maria Polonia, native of Los Adayes Godparents: Atanasio Poissot and Maria De Soto.

2203. MARIE LUCILE PLAISANT
August 9, 1795, baptism of Marie Lucile, born July 23, daughter of Bertrand Plaisante and Marie Barbe Grillet, natives of this parish. Godparents: Baptiste Plaisant and Honorine Toutin.

2204. MARIE CLAIRE
August 6, 1795, baptism of Marie Claire, aged 15 months, daughter of an Indian named La Camite, and Etienne, Indian. Godparents: Louis Clauseau and Francoise Rachal.

2205. ELISABETH ST. GERMAINE (LA FORRÉ)
       August 25, 1795, baptism of Elisabeth, born at Ouchouitos,
       daughter of Marie Louise St. Germaine, who declares Jo-
       seph La Forré to be the father of the infant. Godparents:
       Joseph Lucovisi and Maria Celeste Leconte.

2206. JOSEPH ETIENNE
       August 30, 1795, baptism of Joseph Etienne, aged fifteen
       months, . . . "act carried over to the register of the
       blacks and slaves."

2207. JOSEPH AUGUSTIN ARAGON
       September 6, 1795, baptism of Joseph Augustin, aged five
       months, legitimate son of Jean Aragon and Claire Marie
       Barbon. Godparents: Benoist Montanari and Francoise
       Grape.

2208. MARC MAXIMILIAN MALDONAT
       September 6, 1795, baptism of Marc Maximilian, aged six
       months or about, son of Joseph Louis Maldonat and Jeanne
       Marie Barbo. Godparents: Joseph Triche and Marie
       Theresé Triche.

2209. MARIE THERESE ROSALIE PRUDHOMME
       September 10, 1795, baptism of Marie Therese Rosalie,
       born August 22, daughter of Francois Prudhomme and Marie
       Barbe Rambin. Godparents: Francois Rouquier and Therese
       Mayoux.

2210. MARIE AIMÉE PERAU (VILDEC)
       September 13, 1795, baptism of Marie Aimée Perau, aged
       three and a half, *endoyée* by Sieur Vascocu, daughter of
       Jean Chrisostome Perau (Vildec) and Marie Louise Salvant.
       Godparents: Francois Grape and Marie Perau.

2211. MARIE JOSEPH PALVADO
       September 13, 1795, baptism of Marie Joseph, born Novem-
       ber 2, 1793, daughter of Jean Palvado and Leonor Tessier,
       endoyée by Pierre Tessier, her uncle. Godparents: Jean
       Baptiste Tessier and Marie Perau.

2212. EUGENE LEBEUF
       September 20, 1795, baptism of Eugene LeBeuf, born May 29,
       son of Francois LeBeuf and Genevieve <u>Dubie?</u>, living at the
       post of Ouachitas. Godparents: Simon Lebeuf, uncle of
       the infant, and Elisabeth Olivau.

2213. ANDRÉ RAMBIN
       September 20, 1795, baptism of André, born October 11,
       1794, son of Michel Rambin and Therese Maiou of this par-
       ish. Godparents: André Antoine Rambin and Geneviève
       Rysse /Jean-Ris/.

2214. ANTOINE RACHAL
September 21, 1795, baptism of Antoine, aged 46 months, *endoyé* by Charles Lemoine, son of Antoine Rachal and Marie Louise Lemoine, natives of this parish. Godparents: Charles Lemoine and Jeanne Lebrun.

2215. ANDRÉ ADELÉ
September 22, 1795, baptism of André, born February 18, son of Jean Adelé and Marie Genovieve Dubois. Godparents: Antoine Rambin and Marie Baiou.

2216. MARIE CELESTE BEAUDOIN
September 27, 1795, baptism of Marie Celeste, born August 18, daughter of Pierre Baudouin and Anne Robin, natives of this parish. Godparents: Athanase LeCour and Marie Robin.

2217. MARIE FRANCOISE MERCIER
September 27, 1795, baptism of Marie Francoise, born September 19, daughter of Francois Mercier and Marie Louise Bastien Prudhomme. Godparents: Joseph Cantal<u>ois?</u> and Marie Adelaide Bautiste /no surname give<u>n</u>/, both residents of this parish.

2218. MARIE FRANCOISE BEAUDOIN
September 27, 1795, baptism of Marie Francoise, born May 3, 1793, daughter of Pierre Baudouin and Anne Robin. Godparents: Francois Lattier and Marie Francoise Le Maitre, all residents of this parish.

2219. MARIE DENIS CHRISTI
October 4, 1795, baptism of Marie Denis, about 8 months old, daughter of Jacques Christi and Marie Anne Deroté /Pereau/. Godparents: Laurent Maiou and Marie Magdeleine Perau.

2220. ANDRE JEAN BAPTISTE VASCOCU
October 18, 1795, baptism of Andre Jean Baptiste, born September 28, son of André Vascocu and Magdeleine Remond. Godparents: Jean Baptiste <u>Davion?</u> and Marie Francoise Vascocu.

2221. MARIE ANNE RACHAL
October 20, 1795, baptism of Marie Anne, born July 12, daughter of Julien Rachal and Marie Louise Brevel. Godparents: Jean Baptiste Dupré and Sophie Lattie.

2222. MARIE FELICITE TRISTANT *dit* LAJEUNESSE
October 20, 1795, baptism of Marie Felicite, born May 11, daughter of Jean Baptiste Lajeunesse (Tristant) and Elizabeth Brevel. Godparents: Louis Cavet and Marie Ollivier.

2223. JEAN PIERRE BAUDOIN
October 25, 1795, baptism of Jean Baptiste, born April 3, son of Nicolas Baudouin and Marie Denege Malbert. Godparents: Pierre Baudouin and Marie Anne Vergé.

2224. MARIE CELESTE POISSAU
November 1, 1795, baptism of Marie Celeste, born September 5, child of Antoine Poissau and Marie Civile Goutier, residents of this parish. Godparents: Jean Baptiste Davion and Francoise Grap.

2225. JEAN TOMCIN
November 3, 1795, baptism of Jean, aged eight years, a native of the post of Natechée /Natchez/, living at Ouachitas, son of deceased Tomcin, name of mother not known by the godfather. Godparents: Jean Poiret and Marie Silvie Dubardeau.

2226. JACQUES LAMONTAGNE
November 3, 1795, baptism of Jacques, aged five years, son of Francois Lamontagne and Marie Huguefoy, residents of Ouchitas. The infant, an *endoyé*, was taken to the church at Natchitoches by his godparents: Jean Poiret and Marie Silvie Hubardeau.

2227. MARIE OSITE DUPRE
November 18, 1795, baptism of Marie Osite, born March 6, 1794, daughter of Pierre Dupre and Francoise LeCour. Godparents: Athanase Dupré and Cecile LeCour.

2228. ANTOINE DUBOIS
November 24, 1795, baptism of Antoine, born October 30 "at the coast of Grand Lecore," son of Antoine Dubois and Marie Joseph Malige. Godparents: Joseph Malige, grandfather of the infant, and Heleonore Jean-rit.

2229. MARIE JUDITH LEVASSEUR
November 25, 1795, baptism of Marie Judith, born September 15, daughter of Jacques Levasseur and Marie Therese Grillet. Godparents: Antoine Grillet and Marie Celeste Vergé.

2230. LOUIS GABRIEL TOMMASIN
December 2, 1795, baptism of Louis Gabriel, born September 17, son of Louis Toumasin and Catherine Latié. Godparents: Gabriel Rousot and Marie Adelaide Vercher.

2231. MARIE ROSALIE GOUEL /GOUÉ/
December 4, 1795, baptism of Marie Rosalie, born September 3, daughter of Simon Gouel? and Genevieve Bodin. Godparents: Jean Pierre Bodin and Rosalie Santa Crux.

2232. MARIE REBECCA MILKAIN (TILLE)
January 1, 1796, baptism of Marie Rebecca, born April 5, 1795, daughter of Marie Tille and of Noble Milkain, who declares himself to be the father of the infant. Godparents: Daniel Filk? and Marie Joseph Malige.

2233. ANNE EULALIA QUERK
January 3, 1796, baptism of Anne Eulalia, aged four years, born in the nation of the "Jactas" /Choctaws/, daughter of Edmond Querk and Anne Olsup, now living at this post. Godparents: Placilde Bosquet /Bossie?/ and Eulalie Bosquet /Bossie?/.

2234. MARIE LOUISE LEMOINE
January 8, 1796, baptism of Marie Louise, born November 3, 1795, daughter of Charles Lemoine and Jeanne LeBrun. Godparents: Guillaume Lebrun and Elisabeth LeBrun.

2235. VICTOIRE MATILDE TAUZIN
January 10, 1796, baptism of Victoire Matilde, born December 23, 1795, daughter of Joseph Tauzin and Marie Chamart of this parish. Godparents: André Chamard and Celeste Matilde DeBlan.

2236. FRANCOIS CHARLES MASSIP
February 12, 1796, baptism of Francois, born December 7, 1795, son of Jean Massip and Marie Lemoine. Godparents: Augustin Fraidieu and Marie Jeanne Saurel.

2237. ATHANASE BROUTÉ /BROSSET/
March 12, 1796, baptism of Athanase, born April 30, 1795, son of Pierre Brouté /Brosset/ and Marie Joseph Grillet, residents of this parish. Godparents: Athanasse Poissot and Maria Dupre.

2238. MARIE DENISE LEMOINE
March 20, 1796, baptism of Marie Denise, born March 29, 1795, daughter of Jean Baptiste Lemoine and Felicite Lacaze*, residents of this parish. Godparents: Jacques Lacaze* and Marie Lemoine.

*In both cases, this name has been written over with the name "LaCour" so heavily that the original name is no longer legible. According to Entry 3385, Jean Baptiste Lemoine married Felicite Lacaze, and numerous baptisms for their children, as well as civil records, corroborate Felicite's identity as Lacaze. Since Felicite had a brother named Jacques Lacaze, and there was no Jacques LaCour in the parish at that time, it may be assumed that the godfather's name also was Lacaze rather than LaCour.

2239. MARIE THERESE DAVION
March 27, 1796, baptism of Marie Therese, born December 30, 1795, daughter of Dominique Davion and Pelagie Gagné, residents of this parish. Godparents: Louis Davion and Jeanne Gagné.

2240. MARIE OLIVIER FRAIDIEU
March 27, 1796, baptism of Marie Olivier, born August 4, 1795, daughter of Augustin Fraidieu and Marie Jeanne Sorel. Godparents: Dominique Sorel and Marie Magdeleine Perau, all residents of this parish.

2241. JOSEPH VINCENT MICHEL
April 25, 1796, baptism of Joseph, born November 25, 1794 at Ouachitas Post. Parents: Vincent Michel and deceased Helen Roublet. Godparents: Joseph Lucoviq and Elisabeth Pompone Derneville.

2242. JEAN JACQUES LAMBRE
May 1, 1796, baptism of Jean Jacques, born February 20, son of Remi Lambre (s) and Susanne Prudhomme (s). Godparents: Manuel Prudhomme (s) and Marie Louise Prudhomme (s).

2243. MARIE MARTIN
May 9, 1796, baptism of Marie, aged about seven years, daughter of deceased Zacharie de Martin and Rebeca Teel. Godparents: Jean Quingelte and Elisabeth Denet, widow Borme.

2244. JOSEPH BUARD
May 15, 1796, baptism of Joseph, born January 24, son of Louis Buard and Marie Rose Lambre. Godparents: Francois Marie Monginot and Elisabeth Joseph Buart, all residents of this parish.

2245. MAGDELEINE BASTIEN PRUDHOMME
May 15, 1796, baptism of Magdeleine, aged twelve years or about, daughter of Naillois, a *sauvagesse*, and Bastien Prudhomme, who certifies that he is the father of the child, in the presence of Pierre Maillou and Rose Gagne, godparents. All are residents of this parish.

2246. MARIE DAMASILA DESAUTO
May 20, 1796, baptism of Marie Domasila, born April 6, daughter of Marcel De Sauto and Marie Baiou. Godparents: Marie Louis Cesar Deblanc and Marie Louise Euphrasie Rambin.

2247. JEAN BAPTISTE DUBOIS
June 12, 1796, baptism of Jean Baptiste, born June 6, 1795 at the post of Rapides, son of Jean Baptiste DuBois

and Rose Chelet, residents of this parish. Godparents: Jean Louis Baiou and Manuel Triche.

2248. JOSEPH FRANCOIS LATIÉ
June 12, 1796, baptism of Joseph Francois, born June 20, 1795, at the Post of Rapides, son of Joseph Latié and Francois Chelet. Godparents: Francois Chelet and Catherine Latié.

2249. MARIE HELEINE ANTY
June 12, 1796, baptism of Marie Heleine, born January 29, daughter of Louis Anti and Maria Jeanne Crete. Godparents: Pierre LaCour and Heleine Cloutier.

2250. *LESIME ONESIME ST. ANDRE
June 21, 1796, baptism of Onesime, born January 28, 1793, son of André St. André and Marie Rachal. Godparents: Etienne Francois Rachal and Francoise Rachal, all residents of the parish.

*The infant's name appears in the text only as "Onesime;" in the margin it is written as "Lesime Onesime." For those not familiar with French names it should be noted that "Lesime" was the usual pronunciation of the name "Onesime."

2251. MARIE VICTOIRE ST. ANDRE
June 21, 1796, baptism of Marie Victoire, born July 26, 1795, daughter of Andre Saint Andre and Marie Rachal. Godparents: Jean Baptiste Dupré and Victoire Poissot. All are residents of this parish.

2252. MARIE MAGDELEINE LARENAUDIERE
July 3, 1796, baptism of Marie Magdeleine, born May 23, daughter of Pierre Larenaudiere and Jeane Laberi. Godparents: Louis Rachal and Marie Josephe Laberi.

2253. LOUIS MANUELLE GALLIEN
July 6, 1796, baptism of Louis Manuel, aged about thirteen months, son of Nicolas Gallien and Marie LeCourt. Godparents: Barthelemi LeCour and Marie Robin. All are residents of this parish.

2254. LOUIS NEUVILLE GALLIEN
July 6, 1796, baptism of Louis Neuville, about four years and three months of age, son of Nicolas Gallien and Marie LeCourt. Godparents: Alexis Cloutier and Cecile LeCour. All are residents of this parish.

2255. MARIE LOUISE /LE COURT/*
July 6, 1796, baptism of Marie Louise, Indian, aged three and a half years, daughter of Marie Ursulle, Indian of

the Caddo nation, and of a father unknown.* Godparents: Barthelemi Rachal and Cecile LeCour.

*The record of this infant's later marriage, dated October 30, 1813, and recorded in Register 5, identifies her as Marie Louise LeCour, daughter of Barthelemy LeCour/t/ and "Marie Suil." Her subsequent succession, which was filed at Natchitoches in 1822 (Succession No. 15, Office of the Clerk of Court) and similar records on her brothers and sister (Cesair, Jean Baptiste Athanase, Neuville, Joseph Valleri, Jacques Eloy, and Marie Barbe LeCour) offer further proof that Barthelemy LeCourt was the common-law husband of the Caddo Indian, Marie Ursulle.

2256. JEAN JACQUES LEMAITRE
August 4, 1796, baptism of Jean Baptiste, born July 7, son of Louis Lemaitre and Louise Villefranche (Le Duc). Godparents: Jacques Meziere and Sophie Lattir.

2257. MARIE ARCENE CHELET
August 21, 1796, baptism of Marie Arcene, born June 4, daughter of Bernabe Chelet and Marie Joseph Gonier. Godparents: Joseph Tauzin and Marie Conand.

2258. MICHEL CYPRIEN MALIGE
August 25, 1796, baptism of Michel Cyprien, born December 1, 1794, son of Joseph Malige and Marie Anne Bardon. Godparents: Michel Chamar and Marie Jeanne Anne Malige.

2259. MICHEL DERBANE
September 11, 1796, baptism of Michel, born June 15, 1795, son of Pierre Derbanne and Marie Francoise Brevel. Godparents: Michel Ernandes and Marie Olivier.

2260. MARIE HIACINTHE BAULIEU
September 18, 1796, baptism of Marie Hiacinthe, aged about five months, daughter of Pierre Baulieu and Therese Baudouin. Godparents: Louis <u>Coutin?</u> and Marie Louise La Renaudiere.

2261. MARIE JUDITH BAULIEU
September 18, 1796, baptism of Marie Judith, aged about three years, daughter of Pierre Baulieu and Therese Baudouin. Godparents: Laurent Maillou and Marie Anne Baudouin.

2262. ANDRE FORT
September 19, 1796, baptism of Andre, born June 28, legitimate son of Jacques Fort and Marie Francoise Malbert. Godparents: Andre Frederic and Marie Barbe /no last name/.

2263. MARIE ROSE JARRI
October 2, 1796, baptism of Marie Rose, aged seven weeks, daughter of Pierre Jarri and Cecile Dupre, native of this parish. Godparents: Jean Pomier and Marie Fort.

2264. JEAN BAPTISTE GRAPE
October 23, 1796, baptism of Jean Baptiste, born August 9, son of Jean Baptiste Grape and Genevieve Sorel. Godparents: Dominique Sorel and Marie Jeanne Sorel.

2265. PIERRE HIPOLITE RAMBIN
October 29, 1796, baptism of Pierre Hipolite, aged twenty days, son of Michel Rambin and Therese Maiou. Godparents: Pierre Maiou and Marie Joseph Trichel.

2266. FRANCOIS DONATIEN VASCOCU
October 29, 1796, baptism of Francois Donatien, twenty days old, son of Antoine Vascocu and Genevieve Bonin /Gonin/. Godparents: Francois Vascocu and Marie Joseph Chelet.

2267. MARIE AIMÉE RACHAL
November 1, 1796, baptism of Marie Aimée, born August 6, daughter of Dominique Rachal and Rosalie Vercher. Godparents: Manuel Rachal and Adelaide Rachal.

2268. MARIA LUISA
August 3, 1775, baptism of Maria Luisa, slave of Sr. Mezieres. Godfather: Atanasio, slave of Mezieres and the brother of the child, and Maria Luisa, slave of Prudhomme.

2269. SANTIAGO
August 3, 1775, baptism of Santiago, born July 25, slave of Noiyan. Godparents: Luis Armand and Maria Ana Dartigaux.

2270. GENOVEFA
August 26, 1775, baptism of Genovefa, *negrita* slave of Prudhomme. Godparents: Francisco Borme and Maria Magdelena Lernodier.

2271. ATANASIO
September 17, 1775, baptism of Atanasio, born September 15, slave of Mr. Buhart. Godparents: Francisco, *negro*, and Maria Luisa, *negra*.

2272. SEBASTIEN
September 24, 1775, baptism of Sebastien, born September 12, slave of Sr. Bayon Lavery /La Berry *dit* Bayonne/. Godparents: Antonio Vascocu and Margarita Totin.

2273.   MARIANA
        October 29, 1775, baptism of Mariana, *negrita* slave of
        Sr. Saintpris /̄Davion *dit* St. Prix̄/. Godparents: Juan
        Bautista, slave of St. Denis, and Mariana, slave of Sr.
        Borme.

2274.   JUAN LUIS
        November 12, 1775, baptism of Juan Luis, *negrito* slave
        of Jacobo Lambre. Godparents: Juan Luis and Maria,
        negra, both slaves.

2275.   CATALINA
        December 7, 1775, baptism of Catalina, born November 13,
        slave of Pierre Darbanne. Godparents: Andres Vascocu
        (s) and Maria Victoria Darbanne.

2276.   ROMANO
        December 29, 1775, baptism of Romano, two years old, slave
        of El Cour /̄Louis Mathias Le Court̄/. Godparents: Bar-
        tolome and Francisca, the child's sister, both slaves of
        El Cour. s/ LeCourt.

2277.   HELENA
        December 29, 1775, baptism of Helena, aged about three
        years, slave of El Cour /̄Louis Mathias Le Court̄/. God-
        parents: Francisco Doucet (s) and Theresa.

2278.   DOROTHEA
        December 29, 1775, baptism of Dorothea, aged about one
        year, slave of El Cour /̄Louis Mathias Le Court̄/. God-
        parents: Ar. Athanasio de Mezieres (s) and Modesta Rou-
        jot (s).

2279.   MARIA SUSANA
        December 19, 1775, baptism of Maria Susana, aged about
        four years, slave of El Cour /̄Louis Mathias Le Court̄/.
        Godparents: Luis el Cour and Maria el Cour.

2280.   SUSANNA
        January 1, 1776, baptism of Susanna, born December 9,
        1775, slave of Trichele. Godparents: Luis Borme (s/
        Borme *fils*) and Maria Luisa Prudhomme (s).

2281.   MARIA DENEISE
        January 6, 1776, baptism of Maria Deneise, born December
        7, 1775, slave of Widow Alexis /̄Grappē/. Godparents:
        Alexandro and Maria Deneve, "both of this parish."

2282.   JOSEPH
        January 28, 1776, baptism of Joseph, born January 13,
        father unknown. Godparents: Francisco, slave of Sr.

Le Blanc, and Victoria, slave of Sr. Bayonne.

2283. MARIA EULALIA /METOYER/
January 28, 1776, baptism of Maria Eulalia, born January 15, father unknown, slave of Dn. Manuel /de Soto/*.
Godparents: Louis Bormé (s) and Clemencia Bormé (s).

*This name is erased in the text and in the marginal note, a circumstance which appears in this register at all entries pertaining to mulatto slaves owned by Sr. de Soto. The examination of other parish records reveal this infant to be the child of Marie Therese *ditte* Coincoin, a Negro slave, who was between 1767 and 1786 the mistress of Claude Thomas Pierre Metoyer. See, for example, Rex *vs*. de Soto, Doc. 1227, French Archives, Office of the Clerk of Court, Natchitoches.

2284. MARGARITA
February 15, 1776, baptism of Margarita, born February 4, father unknown, slave of Enrique Trichle. Godparents: Luis La Malaty (s) and Mariana Dartigaux (s).

2285. LUIS
February 15, 1776, baptism of Luis, born January 25, slave of Manuel Trichle. Godparents: Luis Borme (s/ Borme *fils*) and Mariana Grappe.

2286. MARIA FRANCISCA
March 10, 1776, baptism of Maria Francisca, born February 10, slave of Joseph Dupre and natural daughter of Francisca. Godparents: Francisco, slave of St. Denis, and Maria, slave of Sr. Mezieres.

2287. FELIPE
March 20, 1776, baptism of Felipe, adult slave of Poisson, the elder /Remy Poissot/. Godparents: /Jean Baptiste La Berry *dit*/ Bayon and Mme. Poisson.

2288. THERESA
March 23, 1776, baptism of Theresa, born . . . /entry not completed/.

2289. MARIA JUANA
March 24, 1776, baptism of Maria Juana, born September 8, 1775, natural daughter of Julia, slave of Le Compte. Godparents: Pedro, *negro* slave of Juan La Bery, and Genoveva, slave of Le Comte.

2290. SILVANO
March 31, 1776, baptism of Silvano, born February 11, natural son of the *negra* Angelica, slave of Pedro Derbanne. Godparents: Jacobo (x) and Maria (x).

2291. HELENA
April 21, 1776, baptism of Helena, natural daughter of Margarita, *negra* slave of Bartolome Rachal. Godparents: Luis, *negro* of Dominique Montes, and Helena, representing Maria Juana, slave of Bautista Brevelle.

2292. SUSANNA
May 28, 1776, baptism of Susanna, born May 19, *negrita*, natural daughter of Margarita, slave of Widow Buart. Godparents: Andre Vascocu (s) and Elisabeth Joseph Buart (s).

2293. JUAN
May 28, 1776, baptism of Juan, born May 20, natural son of the *negra* Cecilia, slave of Badin. Godparents: Juan Bautista Lambre (s) and Catalina Lambre (s).

2294. JUAN BAUTISTA
June 2, 1776, baptism of Juan Bautista, born May 26, *negro*, natural son of the *negra* Margarita, slave of Mr. Poissot. Godparents: Juan Bautista Dartigaux (s) and Luisa Agueda Bayonne (s/ Louise Agathe Laberry).

2295. JACINTO
June 7, 1776, baptism of Jacinto, born May 24, natural son of Coleta, *negra* slave of Sr. Mezieres. Godparents: Zosimo de Mezieres and Maria Genoveva Fontenette (s).

2296. ANDRES
September 1, 1776, baptism of Andres, born August 24, natural son of Maria Luisa, slave of Widow Buart. Godparents: Andres Rambin (s) and Catalina Buart (s).

2297. JACOBO
September 20, 1776, baptism of Jacobo, born May 7, natural son of Theresa, Indian slave of Mr. Kindrie. Godparents: Jacobo Le Vasseur (x) and Magdelena Raymond (x).

2298. JOSEPH
CATALINA
December 21, 1776, baptism of Joseph and Catalina, born December 3, twin slaves of Bautista Trichele. Godparents of the first: Pedro, *negra* slave of Sr. Borme, and Maria Theresa, slave of Widow Grappe; godparents of the second: Juan Pedro, slave of Widow Grappe, representing Pedro de Borme, and Juana, slave of Dominigo Montes.

2299. MARIA
January 19, 1777, baptism of Maria, *endoyée*, daughter of Francisca, *negra* slave of Juan Bautista Prudhomme. Godparents: Luis, slave of Montez, and Maria, slave of le Blanc.

2300. MARIA THERESA
January 21, 1777, baptism of Maria Theresa, born December 31, 1776, daughter of Maria Luisa, slave of Remigio Poisot, Sr., and of a father unknown. Godparents: Pedro, *negro* slave of Borme, and Maria Theresa, slave of Widow Alexis Grappe.

2301. JUAN LUIS
January 26, 1777, baptism of Juan Luis, born October 13, 1776, son of Maria, *negra* slave of Widow Buart. Godparents: Juan Luis Lambre (s) and Maria Anna Buart (s).

2302. JUAN PEDRO
January 27, 1777, baptism of Juan Pedro, son of a slave of Trichele named Maria Juana. Godparents: Maria Antonio Mezieres (s) and Maria Genovefa Fontenette (s).

2303. JOSEF MARIA JACINTO
February 8, 1777, baptism of Josef Maria Jacinto, born January 20, natural son of Maria Elena, slave of Le Blanc /de Blanc/. Godparents: Josef Maria Carlos Le Blanc /de Blanc/ and Enrique Laisar?.

2304. NICOLAS AUGUSTIN
February 9, 1777, baptism of Nicolas Augustin, born February 5, natural son of Juana, *negra* slave of Sr. Mezieres. Godparents: Nicolas Augustin /Metoyer/, free *mulato*, and Maria Susana /Metoyer/, free *mulata*.

2305. MONICA
March 30, 1777, baptism of Monica, Indian, aged about four years, father unknown, property of Mr. Dartigaux (s). Godparents: Juan Bautista Dartigeux (s) and Maria Ana Dartigeaux (s).

2306. ZOSIMO
April 19, 1777, baptism of Zosimo, aged about three months, Indian son of an Indian named Maria Luisa, father unknown. Godparents: Zosimo Mezieres and Maria Genovefa Fontenette (s).

2307. MARIA THERESA
April 19, 1777, baptism of Maria Theresa, aged about two years, natural daughter of a *negra* slave of Jacobo Lambre. Godparents: Francisco Vascocu and Clemencia Borme (s).

2308. PELAGIA
May 11, 1777, baptism of Pelagia, born May 7, natural daughter of Margarita, *negra* slave of Bartolomé Rachal. Godparents: Nicolas and Pelagia, slaves of Bautista Dupres

2309. MARIA ROSA
       May 14, 1777, baptism of Maria Rosa, born May 12, natural daughter of Cecilia, *negra* slave of Pedro Villard. Godparents: Miguel Oliver (x) and Luisa Agueta Labery (s/ Louise Agathe Laberry).

2310. FRANCISCO MIGUEL
       May 18, 1777, baptism of Francisco Miguel, <u>adult?</u>, *negrito*? slave of Athanasio Mezieres. Godparents: Francisco Doucet (s) and Juana, slave of Mezieres.

2311. SANTIAGO
       May 18, 1777, baptism of Santiago, adult slave of A. Demezieres. Godparents: Santiago Mezieres and Genovefa.

2312. AUGUSTINO
       May 18, 1777, baptism of Augustino, slave of A. Demezieres. Godparents: Athanasio de Mezieres and Maria Genovefa Fontenette (s).

2313. MARIANA
       May 18, 1777, baptism of Mariana, slave of A. Demezieres. Godparents: Chevalier de Villiet (s/ Louis Le Chv. de Villiers) and Maria Felicidad de Mezieres (s).

2314. MARIA ESTER
       May 18, 1777, baptism of Maria Ester, slave of A. Demezieres. Godparents: Chev. de Villiet (s) and Maria Josepha de Mezieres.

2315. ROSA
       May 18, 1777, baptism of Rosa, slave of A. Demezieres. Godparents: Athanasio de Mezieres and Maria Genovefa Fontenette (s).

2316. LUIS
       June 22, 1777, baptism of Luis, born June 9, natural son of Francisca, *negra* slave of Pedro Derbanne. Godparents: Luis Toutin (x) and Maria Victoria Derbanne (x).

2317. LUIS
       June 26, 1777, baptism of Luis, born June 24, *negrito*, natural son of Maria Josefa, *negra* slave of Widow Buard. Godparents: Luis Vascocu and Maria Isabel Buart (s/ Elisabeth Buard).

2318. URSULA
       September 8, 1777, baptism of Ursula, born August 29, natural daughter of Theresa, *negra* slave of Le Vasseur. Godparents: Gaspar Derbanne and Felicidad Dupain (s).

2319. MARIA GENOVEFA
September 14, 1777, baptism of Maria Genovefa, born August 8, natural daughter of Maria Juana, slave of Bernardo Ortolant. Godparents: Maria Cesario Messieres (s) and Maria Genovefa Fontenette (s).

2320. JUAN LUIS
September 14, 1777, baptism of Juan Luis, born September 8, legitimate son of Juan Luis, *negro*, and Maria Juana, slaves of Domingo Montes. Godparents: Pedro Josef and Juana, *negro* slaves of Sr. Messieres.

2321. LUIS
October 12, 1777, baptism of Luis, born October 11, *mulato* son of Carlota, *mulata* slave of Jacobo Lambre. Godparents: Luis Toutin and Maria de la Encarnacion Perot.

2322. MARIA JACINTA
December 8, 1777, baptism of Maria Jacinta, born December 4, legitimate daughter of Pedro and Teresa, *negros* of Widow Grappe. Godparents: Luis Bertran and Maria Davion.

2323. GENOVEFA
December 8, 1777, baptism of Genovefa, born December 4, natural daughter of Cecilia, slave of Juan Mazipe. Godparents: Andres Vascocu (s) and Maria Le Moine.

2324. JOSEF ANTONIO /METOYER/
February 8, 1778, baptism of Josef Antonio, born January 26, natural son of Maria Theresa Qoinquin, slave of Dn. Manuel /de Soto/*. Godparents: Marcelo /de Soto/* and Maria Ana /de Soto/*.

*See note accompanying Entry 2283.

2325. ATANASIO
March 1, 1778, baptism of Atanasio, born January 20, natural son of Theresa, slave of Juan Bautista Dupres. Godparents: Bautista Denis and Maria Luisa LeCompte.

2326. DOROTEA /MONET/*
March 1, 1778, baptism of Dorotea, born October 31, 1777, natural daughter of Margarita, a slave of Juan Bautista Dupres. Godparents: Joseph Dupre and Dorotea Peraut.

*Upon the death of Jean Baptiste Dupre, and the remarriage of his widow to Louis Monet (see Doc. 1839, French Archives, Office of the Clerk of Court, Natchitoches), the child Dorothée (Dorotea) became part of the Monet household. She used the surname Monet even prior to her manumission. See Entry 2699 for example.

2327. MARIA GENOVEFA
March 22, 1778, baptism of Maria Genovefa, born March 7 of Maria Luisa, slave of Davion. Godparents: Baltasar, free *mulato*, and Maria Genovefa Fontenette (s).

2328. MARIA ANA
March 26, 1778, baptism of Maria Ana, born March 17, natural daughter of Juana, *negra* slave of Widow Buart. Godparents: Dionisio Buart and Maria Ana Buart.

2329. JOSEPH SANTIAGO
May 15, 1778, baptism of Joseph Santiago, a free child of about two and a half years, natural son of Maria, a free *mulata*. Godparents: Santiago Mezieres and Margarita La Chaise.

2330. ATANASIO
May 26, 1778, baptism of Atanasio, born May 25, natural son of Augustina, *negra* slave of Labery. Godparents: Francisco Toutin and Juana Labery (s).

2331. JOSEF
May 28, 1778, baptism of Josef, born May 19, natural son Maria Juana, *negra* slave of Bautista Trichele. Godparents: Luis Toutin and Margarita Toutin.

2332. SANTIAGO
May 31, 1778, baptism of Santiago, aged about one and a years, natural son of Francisca, Indian slave of Samuel *alias* Lionnois. Godparents: Andres Vascocu (s) and Maria Francisca Grappe.

2333. HELENA
June 6, 1778, baptism of Helena, adult slave of Villard, father and mother unknown. Godparents: Francisco Le Doux (s) and Modestia Roujot, his wife (s).

2334. MARIA FRANCISCA
June 7, 1778, baptism of Maria Francisca, born June 2, natural daughter of a Banta *negra* who is unbaptized, a slave of Santiago Lambre. Godparents: Francisco Le Vasseur and Maria Francesca Le Vasseur.

2335. JUAN BAUTISTA LUIS
June 22, 1778, baptism of Juan Bautista Luis, born June 18, natural son of Julia, a Banta *negra* and slave of Andres Rambin. Godparents: Luis Vascocu and Maria Barbara Rambin.

2336. MARIA ROSA
June 28, 1778, baptism of Maria Rosa, born June 21, natural daughter of Francisca, *negra* of Josef Dupre. Godparents: Juan Bauta. Derbanne and Maria Louisa Dupres.

2337. ANTONIO CELESTINO
July 5, 1778, baptism of Antonio Celestino, born June 25,

natural son of Maria, *negra* slave of Wd. Alexis Grappe.
Godparents: Antonio Vascocu and Maria Francesca Grappe.

2338. MARIA FRANCISCA
July 12, 1778, baptism of Maria Francisca, born July 9, natural daughter of Juana, *negra* slave of Juan Lambre. Godparents: Luis Vascocu and Ynez Morin.

2339. ANDRES
October 4, 1778, baptism of Andres, born September 19, natural son of Margarita, *negra* slave of Poissot. Godparents: Andre Vascocu (s) and Maria Dupres.

2340. MARIA JUANA
November 24, 1778, baptism of Maria Juana, born November 16, natural daughter of a Bozal *negra* called Diciz. Godparents: Santiago David (s) and Maria Ana Dartigaux.

2341. MARIA LUISA
November 29, 1778, baptism of Maria Luisa, born November 14, natural daughter of Cecilia, slave of Badin. Godparents: Luis Gabriel Buart and Maria Luisa Buart (s).

2342. CARLOS
December 26, 1778, baptism of Carlos, aged about one year. slave of Le Court. Godparents: Jn. Bta. Dupres and Francisca Le Compte.

2343. ROSALIA
December 26, 1778, baptism of Rosalia, aged about two years, slave of Le Court. Godparents: Luis Anty (s) and Maria Catalina Gallien.

2344. HELENA
December 26, 1778, baptism of Helena, aged about one and a half years. Godparents: Jn. Bta. Anty and Elena Cloutié.

2345. PEDRO
January 24, 1779, baptism of Pedro, born January 15, natural son of Francisca, slave of Bte. Trichele. Godparents: Pedro, slave of La Bery, and Mariana, slave of Sr. Borme.

2346. JOSEF
February 14, 1779, baptism of Josef, born February 7, natural son of Francisca, *negra* slave of Jacob Lambre. Godparents: Juan and Isabel, slaves of Lambre.

2347. JOSEF
March 6, 1779, baptism of Josef, born March 31, natural *mulato* son of Babel, "a free *mulata* of the Sr. Demezieres."

Godparents: Zosimo Meziere and Margarita La Chaise.

2348. MARIA FRANCISCA
March 25, 1779, baptism of Maria Francisca, born March 4, natural daughter of Maria Juana, slave of Manuel Trichele. Godparents: Remigio Toutin and Maria Francisca Grappe.

2349. LUIS
May 9, 1779, baptism of Luis, aged about ten to twelve years, an Indian slave of Dartigaux. Godparents: Juan Baut. Dartigaux (s) and Maria Luisa Prudhomme (s).

2350. ISABEL
May 9, 1779, baptism of Isabel, born that same day, the natural daughter of Isabel, a slave of Bartolome Rachal. Godparents: Juan and Isabel, slaves of Jacobo Lambre.

2351. PEDRO JUAN
MARIA SIRINA
May 11, 1779, baptism of Pedro Juan and Maria Sirina, born May 9, twins of Francisca, slave of Prudhomme. Godparents of the first: Dominico Prudhomme and Maria Ana Dartigaux (s); godparents of the second: Andre Vascocu (s) and Maria Barbara Rambin.

2352. BALTASAR
May 23, 1779, baptism of Baltasar, born May 20, natural son of Maria Ana, *negra* slave of Juan Lambre. Godparents: Francisco Vascocu and Ines Morin.

2353. MARIA JACINTA
May 25, 1779, baptism of Maria Jacinta, born May 10, natural daughter of a Bosal *negra* of Rambin. Godparents: Juan Bautista Dartigaux (s) and Luisa Rosa Rambin.

2354. MARIA TERESA
May 30, 1779, baptism of Maria Teresa, born April 1779, legitimate daughter of Luis, a Christian Indian, and of Carlota, a Christian Indian. Godparents: Juan Bautista Ailhaud Ste. Anne (s) and Maria Luisa Prudhomme (s).

2355. ISABEL
July 18, 1779, baptism of Isable, born about fourteen or fifteen months earlier, slave of Monsr. Dupain. Godparents: Sr. Marcolet (s/ Marcollay) and Maria Luisa Prudhomme (s).

2356. ANTONIO
July 18, 1779, baptism of Antonio, born July 3, *negrillo*

slave of Pedro Derbanne. Godparents: Antonio des Mezieres (s) and Maria Barbara Rambin.

2357. THERESA
August 22, 1779, baptism of Theresa, born August 7, the natural daughter of Maria, *negra* slave of Pedro Dartigaux. Godparents: Luis Vascocu and Maria Luisa Prudhomme (s).

2358. BERNARDO
August 29, 1779, baptism of Bernardo, born August 15, natural son of Maria Theresa, slave of Poisot. Godparents. Bernardo Ryse and Maria Ana Soto.

2359. MARIA JUANA
September 19, 1779, baptism of Maria Juana, born September 9, natural daughter of Maria, *negra* slave of Sr. de Mezieres. Godparents: Zosimo Mezieres (s/ Zosime de Mezieres) and Maria Damascena de Soto, represented by Maria Josepha Mezieres (s).

2360. JUANA
September 26, 1779, baptism of Juana, aged about one and a half years, natural daughter of a Bozal *negra* of Jacob Lambre. Godparents: Luis Vascocu and Juana Labery.

2361. JUAN
November 7, 1779, baptism of Juan, born October 24, natural son of Luisa, slave of Poisot, Sr. Godparents: Juan and Isabel, slaves of Jacob Lambre.

2362. REMIGIO
November 14, 1779, baptism of Remigio, born in the month of October, natural son of Francisca, slave of Bautista Dupres. Godparents: Pedro Dupres and Maria Francisca Le Compte.

2363. HELENA MAGDALENA
January 30, 1780, baptism of Helena, born January 15, natural daughter of Theresa, slave of Santiago Le Vasseur. Godparents: Juan and Isabel, slaves of Francisco Le Vasseur.

2364. JOSEPH ANTONIO
March 18, 1780, baptism of Joseph Antonio, born March 3, natural son of Maria, slave of Widow Buart. Godparents: Nanette, free *negra* and Francisco Doucet (s).

2365. SANTIAGO
March 26, 1780, baptism of Santiago, born March 2, natural son of Maria Juana, slave of Ortolant*. Godparents:

Juan Bautista Grappe (s) and Maria La Renaudiere.
*Marginal note reads: "Santiago, slave of Garcon."

2366. MARIA
March 26, 1780, baptism of Maria, aged about one year, natural daughter of a Bozal *negra* and Cashetumena, slave of Tostajos?, property of Roberto Dupre. Godparents: Juan Pedro, slave of Widow Grappe, and Isabel, slave of Santiago Lambre.

2367. ATANASIO
March 26, 1780, baptism of Atanasio, born March 2, legitimate son of Francisco and Teresa, slaves of St. Prix. Godparents: Chrisostome Perot and Maria Davion.

2368. JACINTA
April 12, 1780, baptism of Jacinta, born April 10, *mulato* natural son of Helena, *mulata* slave of Luis Deblanc. Godparents: Josef Maria Carlos De Blanc and Maria Luisa Martha DeBlanc.

2369. MARIA HELENA
April 16, 1780, baptism of Maria Helena, born March 28, natural daughter of Margarita, slave of Widow Buart. Godparents: Luis Vascocu and Maria Ana Buart.

2370. THERESA
April 16, 1780, baptism of Theresa, adult slave of Francisco LeVasseur. Godparents: Luis Buart and Maria Juana Crete.

2371. SANTIAGO
April 21, 1780, baptism of Santiago, born April 10, legitimate son of Lorenzo and Juana, *negro* slaves of de Mezieres. Godparents: Santiago de Mezieres (s) and Francisca Larenaudiere.

2372. JOSEF LUIS
May 9, 1780, baptism of Josef Luis, born August 1, 1779, natural son of Theresa, slave of Widow Cloutié. Godparents: Juan Luis Vascocu and Catalina Lambre (s).

2373. PEDRO
MARIA ANA
May 13, 1780, baptism of Pedro and Maria Ana, aged about six or seven years, slaves of Marin Grillet. Godparents of the first: Pedro Schelet and Margarita Grillet; godparents of the second: Felipe Frederic and Francisca Schelet.

2374. FRANCISCO THOMAS
May 21, 1780, baptism of Francisco Thomas, born about the

first of this month, natural son of a Bozal *negra* slave
of Jacob Lambre. Godparents: Agustin and Maria Juana
Buart.

2375. REMIGIO
May 28, 1780, baptism of Remigio, born May 15, natural
son of Francisca, slave of Pedro Derbanne. Godparents:
Esteban Verger and Maria Luisa Dupres.

2376. GUILLERMO
June 11, 1780, baptism of Guillermo, born June 3, legitimate son of Juan Luis and Maria Juana, slaves of Monteche.
Godparents: Guillermo Barberousse and Francisca Larenaudiere.

2377. FRANCISCO
July 30, 1780, baptism of Francisco, born June 9, natural son of Maria Juana, slave of Widow Triche. Godparents:
Juan Bautista Derbanne and Therese Prudhomme.

2378. CARLOS
August 6, 1780, baptism of Carlos, born August 4, natural
son of a Bozal *negra* slave of Jacob Lambre. Godparents:
Antonio, free *mulato*, and Carlota, *mulata* slave of Jacob
Lambre.

2379. LORRINA
August 12, 1780, baptism of Lorrina, born July 7, natural son of Francisca, slave of Pedro Bailliot. Godparents: Andres Frederic and Francisca Schelet.

2380. SANTIAGO
September 17, 1780, baptism of Santiago, born September
2, natural son of Maria Josefa, slave of Atanasio Poisot.
Godparents: Santiago de Mezieres (s) and Maria Ana Soto.

2381. BALTASAR
October 1, 1780, baptism of Baltasar, born September 16,
natural son of Maria Luisa, slave of Davion. Godparents:
Juan Bautista Grappe (s) and Maria La encarnation Peraut.

2382. MARIA LUISA
November 6, 1780, baptism of Maria Luisa, born October
12, natural daughter of Maria Ana, slave of Bautista
Dupre. Godparents: Bautista Anty (s) and Maria Luisa
Salveron.

2383. MARIA FRANCISCA ROSALIA /METOYER/
December 24, 1780, baptism of Maria Francisca Rosalia,
born December 9, 1780, natural daughter of Maria Teresa,
slave of Metoyé.* Godparents: Pablo Bouet Laffitte (s)

and Maria Francisca Grappe (s).

*Marie Therese *dite* Coincoin was purchased by Claude Thomas Pierre Metoyer in 1778 from Mme. de Soto (Doc. 1312, French Archives, Office of the Clerk of Court, Natchitoches). See note accompanying Entry 2283.

2384. MARIA JOSEFA
January 15, 1781, baptism of Maria Josefa, born January 12, natural daughter of a Bozal *negra* of Jacob Lambre. Godparents: Bautista Rachal and Maria Luisa Salvant.

2385. GENOVEFA
January 28, 1781, baptism of Genovefa, born January 15, natural daughter of Isabel, slave of Remigio Poisot. Godparents: Pedro Bailliot and Maria Poisot.

2386. INES
February 8, 1781, baptism of Ines, born January 19, the natural daughter of Francisca, slave of Widow Bta. Triche. Godparents: Juan Ris (s/ Janris) and Eleonor Rise.

2387. LUIS TOMAS
February 25, 1781, baptism of Luis Tomas, born December 20, 1780, natural son of Maria Juana, slave of Luis Buart. Godparents: Juan Luis Buart and Maria Lambre.

2388. MARIA DELEISA
March 4, 1781, baptism of Maria Deleisa, born December 28, 1780, natural daughter of Maria Luisa, slave of the Widow Buart. Godparents: Antonio de Mezieres (s) and Luisa Rambin.

2389. MARGARITA
March 4, 1781, baptism of Margarita, born in the month of May, 1780, natural daughter of Maria, slave of Josef Triche. Godparents: Atanasio, slave of Juan Bautista LeCompte, and Victoria, slave of Juan Bautista Labery.

2390. ESTEBAN
March 6, 1781, baptism of Esteban, born February 20, natural son of Julia, slave of Juan Lambre. Godparents: Luis Lambre and Maria Juana Crete.

2391. MARIA MODESTIA
April 17, 1781, baptism of Maria Modestia, *endoyée*, slave of Le Court and daughter of Madelena, an Indian. Godparents: Pedro Derbane and Maria Le Court.

2392. MARIA CELESTINE
April 17, 1781, baptism of Maria Celestine, *endoyéo*, a slave of Le Court and daughter of Teresa, an Indian.

Godparents: Nicolas Augustin /Metoyer/ and Maria Susana /Metoyer/.

2393. AUGUSTIN
April 22, 1781, baptism of Augustin, born April 6, natural son of Maria Ana, slave of Pedro Derbanne. Godparents: Remigio Lambre and Maria Luisa Derbanne.

2394. MARIA EUGENIA
May 11, 1781, baptism of Maria Eugenia, born April 30, natural daughter of Genovefa, free *mulata*. Godparents: Atanasio de Meziere, represented by his brother Santiago (s) and Maria Josefa Mezieres (s).

2395. ANTONIO
May 13, 1781, baptism of Antonio, born April 4, natural son of a *mulata* of Manuel Triche. Godparents: Domingo Rachal and Theresa Lamalaty.

2396. JUAN FRANCISCO
May 20, 1781, baptism of Juan Francisco, born April 24, natural son of a Bozal *negra* slave of Dartigaux. Godparents: Juan Santiago David (s) and Francisca de Vaugine (s).

2397. ANDRES
June 5, 1781, baptism of Andres, *endoyé* by Madme. Grillet, natural son of Enriqueta, slave of Bartolome Rachal. Godparents: André Rambin (s) and Catalina Lambre (s).

2398. JUAN
June 12, 1781, baptism of Juan an adult of about 45 years, slave of Dartigaux. Godparents: Juan Bautista Dartigaux (s) and Francisca Larernaudiere.

2399. MARIA MARGARITA
August 12, 1781, baptism of Maria Margarita, born August 7, natural daughter of Carlota, slave of Jacob Lambre. Godparents: Luis Rachal (s/ Louis Bertelmis) and Serpanda Badin (s/ Serpande Badin).

2400. ANDRES
September 1, 1781, baptism of Andres, born August 30, natural son of Victoria, slave of Ganier. Godparents: Andres Valentin and Francisca Larenaudiere.

2401. MAGDALENA
September 12, 1781, baptism of Magdalena, born in the month of December, 1780, natural daughter of Cecilia, a slave of Pedro Badin. Godparents: Pedro Badin and Maria Luisa Salvant.

2402. MARIA SUSANA
October 14, 1781, baptism of Maria Susana, born September 24, natural daughter of Maria Juana, slave of Pedro Derban. Godparents: Guillelmo Baberousse (s/ Barbarroux) and Leonor Ris.

2403. ANA
November 1, 1781, baptism of Ana, born October 15, natural daughter of a *negra* named Therese, slave of the Widow of Bta. Dupre.

2404. MARIA LUISA /LECOMPTE/*
December 15, 1781, baptism of Maria Luisa, born November 26, natural daughter of Francisca,* slave of Widow Bta. Dupre. Godparents: Domingo Rachal and Maria Luisa Brevel.

*This Francesca, mother of the infant, is the same Francoise whose baptism is recorded in Entry 484. Civil records of the parish reveal that she was sold in 1772 to de Lissard Jouannis and resold to Jean Baptiste Dupre (Docs. 765 and 771, French Archives, Office of the Clerk of Court, Natchitoches). Upon the marriage of Dupre's widow to Louis Monet in 1785 (Doc. 1839, *ibid*) she became a servant in the Monet household. Subsequent records identify her daughter Marie Louise, baptized in Entry 2404, as a *mulattresse* who used the surname "LeCompte." (See baptism of Louis, April 10, 1803, Register 5; Petition to manumit Louis Monet, *La. Senate Journal, 7th Leg., 1st Sess.*, pp. 25, 27, 46, and *La. House Journal, 7th Leg., 1st Sess.*, pp. 39, 71, 75, 83; and Marriage of Louis Monette to Marie Louise Cottonmais, July 23, 1829, Register 11.

2405. MARIA LUISA
December 30, 1781, baptism of Maria Luisa, born December 14, natural daughter of Maria Luisa, slave of Jn Lambre. Godparents: Luis Lambre (s) and Maria Francisca /le/ Vasseur.

2406. VICTORIA
January 21, 1782, baptism of Victoria, born January 6, natural daughter of Luisa, slave of Brevel. Godparents: Antonio Brevel and Maria Francisca Brevel.

2407. PEDRO
February 3, 1782, baptism of Pedro, born January 16, natural son of Margarita, slave of Bartolome Rachal. Godparents: Juan Bautista and Ysabel, slaves of Le Vasseur and Jacob Lambre, respectively.

2408. MANUEL
February 3, 1782, baptism of Manuel, born January 20,

natural son of Pelagia, slave of Jacob Lambre. Godparents: Jacob, slave of Lambre, and Madelena, slave of the same.

2409. JOSEF
February 17, 1782, baptism of Josef, born November 20, 1781, *endoyé*, natural son of Catalina, slave of Pedro Badin. Godparents: Antonio, free *mulato*, and Ana, free *negra*.

2410. JOSEF ANTONIO
February 25, 1782, baptism of Josef Antonio, born January 25, natural son of Maria, slave of de Mezieres. Godparents: Luis Do<u>llet?</u> and Francisca Gutierrez.

2411. JUAN BAUTISTA ATANASIO HILARIO
March 31, 1782, baptism of Juan Bautista Atanasio Hilario, born December 15, 1781, natural son of Maria, slave of Juan Bautista Lecomte. Godparents: Juan Bta. Davion and Francisca Grappe (s).

2412. MAGDALENA
April 12, 1782, baptism of Magdalena, born March 2, natural daughter of Francisca, slave of Jacob Lambre. Godparents: Josef, free *mulato*, and Maria Magdalena, slave of Fr. Quintanilla.

2413. MARIA OCTANCIA
April 7, 1782, baptism of Maria Octancia, a *mulata* born March 12, natural daughter of Helena, *mulata* slave of M. De Blanc. Godparents: Antonio Prudhomme (s) and Maria Prudhomme (s/ Maria Luisa Rouquier).

2414. VICTORIA
April 14, 1782, baptism of Victoria, born March 29, natural daughter of Maria Juana, slave of Widow Triche. Godparents: Pedro and Victoria, slaves of Labery.

2415. CLEMENCIA
May 12, 1782, baptism of Clemencia, born April 20, natural daughter of Isabel, slave of Mr. Pavie. Godparents: Joseph Pavie (s) and Clemencia Borme (s).

2416. MARIA
May 19, 1782, baptism of Maria, born May 1, natural daughter of Maria, slave of Maria Francisca Buart (s). Godparents: Juan Bta. Buart and Maria Francisca Buart (s).

2417. MARIA
May 19, 1782, baptism of Maria, born March 23, natural daughter of Maria, slave of Luis Fontenot. Godparents:

Bautista Dortolant and Rosalia Jacinta /ño last name/.

2418. FELICIDAD
June 23, 1782, baptism of Felicidad, born April 15, legitimate daughter of Francisco and Maria Luisa, *negro* slaves of Monsieur Dartigaux. Godparents: Bautista Dartigaux and Ana Prudhomme.

2419. MARIA HELENA
July 21, 1782, baptism of Maria Helena, born July 19, natural daughter of Francisca, slave of Juan Bautista Prudhomme. Godparents: Antonio Prudhomme (s) and Luisa Rambin.

2420. MARIA ANA
July 28, 1782, baptism of Maria Ana, born July 27, natural daughter of Maria, *mulata* slave of Le Brun. Godparents: Francisco Rambin (s) and Ana Prudhomme.

2421. MARIA JUANA
August 4, 1782, baptism of Maria Juana, natural daughter of Ester, slave of Dartigaux. Godparents: Pedro and Victoria, *negros*, married slaves of Labery.

2422. MARIA JUANA FRANCISCA
September 7, 1782, baptism of Maria Juana Francisca, born September 3, natural daughter of Maria Juana, slave of Dortolant. Godparents: Pedro Pablo Bouet /Laffitte/ (s) and Marie Francisca /no last name/.

2423. JUDIT
September 15, 1782, baptism of Judit, born September 5, natural daughter of Maria Josefa, slave of Marino Grillet. Godparents: Antonio Prudhomme (s) and Juana Labery.

2424. MARIA
October 1, 1782, baptism of Maria, adult of about 40, a *negra* of Guinea, slave of Dartigaux. Godparents: Luis Langlois and Monica Duthil Dartigaux (s/ Mari Monique dartigaux).

2425. MARIA JOSEFA MADELENA
November 10, 1782, baptism of Maria Josefa Madelena, *endoyée*, legitimate daughter of Luis Robert and Ana Carlota, free Indians. Godparents: Julian Besson (s) and Maria Josefa Peraut.

2426. PEDRO TODOS SANTOS /METOYER/*
November 10, 1782, baptism of Pedro Todos Santos, born October 31, 1782, natural son of Maria Theresa, slave of Metoyé. Godparents: Pedro and Maria Ana, his wife,

negro slaves of Sr. Borme.

*See note accompanying Entry 2283.

2427. MARIA LUISA
December 26, 1782, baptism of Maria Luisa, born January 23, natural daughter of Theresa, Indian slave of Widow Cloutier. Godparents: Luis Galien and Maria Rachal.

2428. GENOVEFA
December 27, 1782, baptism of Genovefa, born December 6, natural daughter of Julia, slave of Juan Lambre. Godparents: Pedro and Victoria, his wife, slaves of Labery.

2429. CELESTINO
January 12, 1783, baptism of Celestino, born December 22, 1782, natural son of Maria Luisa, slave of Remigio Poisot. Godparents: Pedro Dolé (s/ Pierre Dolet) and Maria Ana Dupres.

2430. JOSEPH
April 14, 1783, baptism of Joseph, born February 28, slave of Mda. Baptista Trichel, son of Franca., *negra* slave of Maria Ana /Illegible/ and a father unknown. Godparents: Joseph Bizot and Maria Josepha Laberiy.

2431. DOMINGO
April 20, 1783, baptism of Domingo, born January 11, son of Maria Luisa, slave, a *negra* of Widow Alexis /Grappe/ and a father unknown. Godparents: Josephe, slave of Mr. Borme, and Pelagia, *mulata* slave of Mr. Manuel /Trichel/.

2432. JULIAN
April 8, 1783, baptism of Julian, born March 7, slave of Mdm. Gabriel /Buard/, son of Margarita, slave, and a father unknown. Godparents: Julian and Maria, *negro* slaves of Pedro Derban.

2433. DOMINGO
May 1, 1783, baptism of Domingo, born April 21, *negrito* son of Maria, *negra* slave of Pedro Dartigos, and a father unknown. Godparents: Franco. /Langlois dit/ Sans Regret and Juana /Sorel ditte/ Marli.

2434. JUAN BAUTISTA AUGUSTIN
June 22, 1783, baptism of Juan Bautista Augustin, born May 1, *negrito* son of Juana, slave of Mda. Gabriel /Buard/, and of a father unknown. Godparents: Augustin /Metoyer/ and Maria Susanna /Metoyer/, free *mulatos*.

2435. MARIA
June 22, 1783, baptism of Maria, born May 11, *negrita*

daughter of Juana, slave of Luis Buar, and of a father unknown. Godparents: Santiago, slave of Mr. Le Blanc, and Maria, slave of Jacob Lambre.

2436. HIPOLITO
September 7, 1783, baptism of Hipolito, born about twelve years before, an Indian slave of Mr. de Vaugine. Godparents: Joseph Vauchere and Silesia de Vaugine.

2437. JUAN BAUTISTA
September 7, 1783, baptsm of Juan Bautista, slave of Mr. Dartigos. Godparents: Juan Bautista Antonio Garcia Raymundo and /godmother not named/.

2438. NICOLAS
September 7, 1783, baptism of Nicolas, slave of Mr. Dartigos. Godparents: Pedro Joseph, slave of Mr. Borme, and Ursula, slave of Rdo. P. F. Franco. de Caldes.

2439. LUIS
September 7, 1783, baptism of Luis, Congo slave of Sr. Athanasio de Mezieres. Godparents: Sr. Jorin? and Maria Josepha de Mezieres.

2440. SANTIAGO
September 7, 1783, baptism of Santiago, *mulato* slave of Mda. Jacob Lambre. Godparents: Juan Luis and Maria Juana, slaves of the same lady.

2441. NICOLAS
September 7, 1783, baptism of Nicolas, slave of Mde. du Pres. Godparents: Franco., slave of Athanasio Poisoi, and Maria Luisa, slave of the same.

2442. PEDRO
September 7, 1783, baptism of Pedro, slave of Mr. /Grillet *dit*/ Sauterelle. Godparents: Juan, slave of Mr. Juan Lambre, and Maria Juana, slave of Mr. de Vaugine.

2443. LOUIS JOSEPH
December 1, 1783, baptism of Louis Joseph, *mulato* son of Pelagia, *mulata* slave of Manuel Triche, and of a father unknown. Godparents: Luis, *mulato* slave of the same, and Maria Theresa, slave of Mda. Alexis /Grappe/.

2444. MARIE HELENE ADELAIDE
November 28, 1783, baptism of Maria Elena Adelaida, born November 26, daughter of Maria Luisa, *negra* slave of Mda S. Denis, and of a father unknown. Godparents: Juan Luis, slave of Mde. St. Denis, and Cecilia, slave of Mr. Badin.

2445.   JUAN BAUTISTA
        December 7, 1783, baptism of Juan Bautista, *negrito*, son
        of a *negra* named Babe, slave of Mr. Pavie, and of a fa-
        ther unknown, born November 25. Godparents: Juan Bau-
        tista, slave of Pedro Darban, and Maria Luisa, slave of
        Estevan de Vaugine.

2446.   ANONYMOUS
        December 20, 1783, baptism of a slave child, born May 25,
        son of Theresa, slave of Mr. LeCourt, and a father unknown.
        Godparents: Parents: Pedro and Magdalena, slaves of Le
        Court.

2447.   MARIA THERESA /LECOMTE/*
        December 26, 1783, baptism of Maria Theresa, daughter of
        Theresa, slave of Mr. LeCourt, and of a father unknown.
        Godparents: Francois Langlois and Maria Nicolosa Lang-
        lois.

        *This infant's surname appears in numerous later records
        of the parish, i.e.: Widow Louis Metoyer to Theophile
        Metoyer, Donations Book 30, p. 52, Office of the Clerk
        of Court, Natchitoches. See Entry 3448 for Marie The-
        rese's marriage to Louis Metoyer.

2448.   MARIA DE LOS NIEVES Y MARIA ANNA*
        December 28, 1783, baptism of Maria de los Nieves y Maria
        Anna, born December 17, *cartrona* daughter of Genoveva, a
        mulata, and a father unknown. Godparents: Franco. He-
        berd and Maria Juana Ris.

        *Although this infant's name seems to indicate that TWO
        infants were baptized, such does not appear to be the
        case. All words describing the infant were written in the
        singular person and only one set of godparents was named.

2449.   MARIA SILESIA
        February 5, 1784, baptism of Maria Silesia, born December
        27, 1783, *cartrona* daughter of Maria Luisa, a *mulata* slave
        of Mr. Pavie, and of a father unknown. Godparents: Juan
        Bautista Allnaud Saint Anne and Dna. Sylesa de Vaugine.

2450.   MARIA JOSEPHA
        February 8, 1784, baptism of Maria Joseph, born December
        20, 1783, daughter of Theresa, slave of Mda. du Pres. God-
        parents: Luis, *mulato*, and Maria Luisa, slave of Athanasio
        Poisot.

2451.   PABLO
        February 15, 1784, baptism of Pablo, born January 10, son
        of Genoveva, slave of Pedro Darban, and a father unknown.
        Godparents: Franco. Langlois and Agnes, free *mulata*.

2452. ANDRES
February 15, 1784, baptism of Andres, born January 15, son of Theresa, slave of Pedro Darban, and of a father unknown. Godparents: Francisco Langlois and Agnes, a free *mulata*.

2453. CELESTE
March 21, 1784, baptism of Celeste, born March 17, *mulata* daughter of Judith, *negra* slave of Mr. Rambin, and a father unknown. Godparents: Franco. Rambin and Catharina Vauchere.

2454. CARLOS
March 21, 1784, baptism of Carlos, born December 26, 1783, *negrito*, son of Franca., *negra* slave of Mda. Du Pres and of a father unknown. Godparents: Nicolas and Juana Antonia, slaves of Mda. Du Pres.

2455. MARIA
March 25, 1784, baptism of Maria, born September 30, 1783, *mulata* daughter of Chatarina, slave of Mr. Badin, and a father unknown. Godparents: Guillelmo and Cecilia, slaves of the same.

2456. PEDRO
April 10, 1784, baptism of Pedro, about 25 years old, a slave of Franco. LeVasseur. Godparents: Santiago Le Vasseur and Genoveva LeVasseur.

2457. JUAN BAUTISTA
April 10, 1784, baptism of Juan Bautista, about 25 years old, slave of Mda. Jacob Lambre. Godparents: Juan Bautista Darban and Maria Juana Crete.

2458. PEDRO
April 10, 1784, baptism of Pedro, about 30 years, slave of Mr. Badin. Godparents: Pedro, slave of Mr. Borme, and Maria Luisa, slave of Mr. Prudhomme.

2459. JAYMÉ
April 10, 1784, baptism of Jaymé, about 16 years, slave of Mr. Labery. Godparents: Pedro Larenodiere and Franca. Labery.

2460. ESTEVAN
April 10, 1784, baptism of Estevan, about 28 years, slave of Mr. Labery. Godparents: Luis Toutin and Juana Labery.

2461. JUAN BAUTISTA
April 10, 1784, baptism of Juan Bautista, about 16 years,

slave of Mr. Vauchere /Vercher/. Godparents: Juan Bautista Alliaud Sainte Anne and Margarita L'estage.

2462. SANTIAGO
April 10, 1784, baptism of Santiago, about 30 years, slave of Mr. Juan Lambre. Godparents: Gaspar Darban and Maria Juana Crete.

2463. PEDRO
April 10, 1784, baptism of Pedro, about 15 years, Indian slave of Mr. Gaspar Fiol. Godparents: Juan Vauchere /Vercher/ and Margarita L'estage.

2464. FRANCO.
April 10, 1784, baptism of Franco., about 25 years, a slave of Gaspar Fiol. Godparents: Franco. Nuisman de Vaugine and Madalena Labery.

2465. JOSEPH
April 10, 1784, baptism of Joseph, about 18 years, slave of Mr. Grillet. Godparents: Remigio Toutin and Margarita Grillet.

2466. REMIGIO
April 10, 1784, baptism of Remigio, slave of Mda. Jacob Lambre. Godparents: Remigio Toutin and Margarita Grillet.

2467. MARIA JUANA
April 10, 1784, baptism of Maria Juana, about 30 years, slave of Mr. Pomier. Godparents: Pedro La Cour and Maria Juana Crete.

2468. MARIA
April 10, 1784, baptism of Maria, about 35 years, slave of Mda. du Pres. Godparents: Diego de Mezieres and Magdalena Labery.

2469. ISABEL
April 10, 1784, baptism of Isabel, about 15 years, Indian of Gaspar Fiol. Godparents: Pedro Larenodiere and Juana Labery.

2470. AGNES
April 10, 1784, baptism of Agnes, about 20 years, slave of Pedro Sorel. Godparents: Franco. Nuisman de Vaugine and Silesia de Vaugine.

2471. MARIA FRANCA.
April 10, 1784, baptism of Maria Franca., about 28 years, slave of Mr. Vaugine. Godparents: Juan Bautista Roujot and Silesia de Vaugine.

2472. MARIA LUISA
April 10, 1784, baptism of Maria Luisa, about 18 years, slave of Mr. Armand. Godparents: Joseph Vauchere and Maria Juana Sorel.

2473. MARGARITA
April 10, 1784, baptism of Margarita, about 20 years, slave of Juan Lambre. Godparents: Juan Bautista Darban and Franca. Labery.

2474. GENOVEVA
April 10, 1784, baptism of Genoveva, about 18 years, Indian slave of Mr. Armant. Godparents: Pedro Larnodiere and Genoveva Saurel.

2475. MARIA FRANCA.
April 10, 1784, baptism of Maria Franca., about 25 years, slave of Mr. Pavie. Godparents: Pedro Larenodiere and Maria Franca. Gutierrez.

2476. CHARLOTA
April 10, baptism of Charlota, *mulata* slave of Mda. Jacob Lambre. Godparents: Carlos, slave of the same, and Ursula, slave of Mda. Gabriel /Buard/.

2477. ROSA
April 10, 1784, baptism of Rosa, slave of Luis Rachal. Godparents: Carlos, slave of Mda. Jacob Lambre, and Margarita, slave of Mr. Pavie.

2478. ATHANASIO
April 12, 1784, baptism of Athanasio, born February 26, *negrito* son of Maria Juana, slave of Mda. Jacob Lambre, and a father unknown. Godparents: Luis Alexandro, slave of Luis Buar, and Anna, slave of Mr. Vaugine.

2479. JUAN PEDRO
May 2, 1784, baptism of Juan Pedro, born January 26, *negrito* son of Enrieta, slave of Mda. Barthelemi /no last name/ and a father unknown. Godparents: Juan Pedro and Genoveva, *mulatos*, "the first free, the second a slave."

2480. MADGALENA
May 9, 1784, baptism of Madgalena, born April 24, *negrita* daughter of Francisca, slave of Pedro Darban, and a father unknown. Godparents: Agustin /Metoyer/, *mulato*, and Marianna, slave of Mda. de Pres.

2481. JUAN BAUTISTA
June 20, 1784, baptism of Juan Bautista, born June 5,

mulato son of Angelica, slave of Remy Poissot, and a father unknown. Godparents: Franco. and Maria Luisa, slaves of Athanasio Poissot.

2482. PELAGIA /LECOURT/
July 22, 1784, baptism of Pelagia, born April 12, 1783, daughter of Madalena, slave of Mde. Lecomte. Godparents: Athanasio Le Cour and /Illegible/ Le Cour.

2483. FELICIDAD
July 22, 1784, baptism of Felicidad, born April 5, daughter of Luisa, Indian, and of a father unknown. Godparents: Athanasio Le Cour and Cecilia Le Cour.

2484. FRANCO.
July 22, 1784, baptism of Franco., born December 14, 1783, son of Maria, *negra*, and a father unknown. Godparents: Francisco Davion and Francisca Le Cour.

2485. ATHANASIO
August 1, 1784, baptism of Athanasio, born July 24, *mulato* son of Maria Juana, slave of Pedro Darban, and of a father unknown. Godparents: Juan Bautista and Angelica, slaves of the same.

2486. ANDRES
September 19, 1784, baptism of Andres, born September 9, *negrito* son of Luisa, slave of Juan Bautista Brevel, and of a father unknown. Godparents: Luis, slave of Remigio Poissot and Maria Juana, slave of Juan Bautista Brevel.

2487. MARIA LUISA
September 19, 1784, baptism of Maria Luisa, born August 23, *negrita* daughter of Angelica, slave of Mr. Dartigo, and a father unknown. Godparents: Athanasio Poissot and Esther, slave of Mr. Dartigos.

2488. MARIA BARBARA
September 26, 1784, baptism of Maria Barbara, born September 18, *negrita* daughter of Pelagia, slave of Mda. Jacob Lambre, and a father unknown. Godparents: Pedro and Maria, slaves of Mr. Borme.

2489. FRANCO. /METOYER/*
October 4, 1784, baptism of Franco., born September 26, a free *mulato*, son of Theresa, free *negra*, and a father unknown. Godparents: Juan Bautista, slave of Mr. Le Blanc /De Blanc/, and Maria Luisa, slave of Mr. Prudhomme.

*See note accompanying Entry 2283.

2490. FRANCA.
January 1, 1785, baptism of Franca., born October 21, 1784, *negrita* of Maria, slave of Mr. Fonteneau, and of a father unknown. Godparents: Jayme Enrique, slave of Mr. le Blanc, and Elena, slave of Mr. Fonteneau.

2491. DOMINGO
January 1, 1785, baptism of Domingo, born December 20, 1784, *negrito* son of Maria Josepha, slave of Marin Grillet, and a father unknown. Godparents: Juan Luis Vercher and Maria Rosalia Vercher.

2492. JUAN LUIS
January 22, 1785, baptism of Juan Luis, born January 8, *mulato* son of Julia, *mulata* slave of Juan Lambre, and a father unknown. Godparents: Juan Bautista Morin and Maria Lambra.

2493. MARIA
February 13, 1785, baptism of Maria, born December 27, 1784, *negrita* daughter of Margarita, slave of Mda. Gabriel Buar, and of a father unknown. Godparents: Bartholomé Rachal and Maria Pomier.

2494. MARIA JUANA
March 6, 1785, baptism of Maria Juana, born February 13, *negrita*, legitimate daughter of Juan Bautista and Theresa, slaves of Franco. Le Vasseur. Godparents: Andres David and Maria Francisca le Vasseur.

2495. MARIA JOSEPHA
March 12, 1785, baptism of Maria Josepha, about 2 years of age, natural daughter of Vicense and Catherina, Indian habitants of Rapides. Godparents: Dionisio, *Gefe* of the Apalache nation, and Elizabeth Derneville.

2496. MARIA JUANA
March 13, 1785, baptism of Maria Juana, born January 4, *mulata* daughter of Maria, slave of Maria Franca. Buar. Godparents: Juan Pedro, free *mulato*, and Maria Juana, slave of Mr. Vaugine, the son.

2497. MANUEL
March 26, 1785, baptism of Manuel, born March 14, *mulato* son of Maria Luisa, slave of Mr. Armand, and a father unknown. Godparents: Juan Bauta. Armand and Maria Luisa Martha le Blanc /de Blanc/.

2498. ANTONIO
March 28, 1785, baptism of Antonio, born March 17, *mulato* son of Catharina, slave of Mr. Badin. Godparents: Antonio Lambra and Maria Lambra.

2499. MARIA ROSA
       May 5, 1785, baptism of Maria Rosa, born May 3, *mulata* daughter of Maria, slave of Mr. Athanas de Mezieres, and a father unknown. Godparents: Athanasio Armand and Maria Josepha de Mezieres.

2500. JUAN FRANCISCO
       May 14, 1785, baptism of Juan Francisco, *negro* adult, slave of Mr. Juan Lambre. Godparents: Alexandro, slave of Luis Gabriel /Buard/, and Martha, slave of Mr. le Blanc /de Blanc/.

2501. JUAN BAUTISTA
       May 14, 1785, baptism of Juan Bautista, *negro* adult, slave of Mr. Le Blanc /de Blanc/. Godparents: Sebastien, slave of Juan Lambra, and Marta, slave of Mr. Le Blanc /De Blanc/.

2502. MARIA-MARTHA
       May 14, 1785, baptism of Maria-Martha, *negra* adult, slave of Mda. Jacob Lambra. Godparents: Sebastian, slave of Juan Lambra, and Maria, slave of Mda. Jacob Lambra.

2503. JUAN BAUTISTA
       May 16, 1785, baptism of Juan Bautista, born April 29, *negrito* son of Celeste, slave of Mr. Labery, and a father unknown. Godparents: Juan Bautista, slave of Mda. du Pres, and Angelica, slave of Mr. Vaugine.

2504. ANTONIO ISIDORO
       June 5, 1785, baptism of Antonio Isidoro, born May 16, *negrito*, legitimate son of Iaco amd Maria Franca., slaves of Mda. Jacob Lambra. Godparents: Guillelmo, slave of Mr. Badin, and Pelagia, slave of Mda. Jacobo /Lambre/.

2505. GABRIEL
       June 5, 1785, baptism of Gabriel, born June 1, *negrito* son of Rosalia, *negra* slave of Mda. Jacob /Lambre/, and a father unknown. Godparents: Alexandro, slave of Luis Buar, and Maria Elonor, slave of Mda. Jacob /Lambre/.

2506. HONORIO
       June 26, 1785, baptism of Honorio, born May 8, *mulato* son of Maria Luisa, slave of Franco. Grappe, and a father unknown. Godparents: Juan Bautista Davion and Franca. Grappe.

2507. SUSANNA
       June 26, 1785, baptism of Susanna, born June 8, *negrita* daughter of Maria Juana, slave of Mr. Labery, and a father unknown. Godparents: Juan Bauta. Dartigo and Maria Agatha Labery.

2508. URSULA BERNARDA
July 3, 1785, baptism of Ursula Bernarda, born June 25, free *mulata*, daughter of Margarita, slave of Mda. Jacob /Lambre/. Godparents: Franco. Antonio and Bernarda, free *negros*.

2509. PEDRO
July 10, 1785, baptism of Pedro, born June 20, *negrito* son of Maria, slave of Mr. Dartigos, and a father unknown. Godparents: Luis Carlos Le Blanc /De Blanc/ and Maria Anna Dartigaux.

2510. MARIA ADELAIDA
August 7, 1785, baptism of Maria Adelaida, born July 18, daughter of Maria Juana, slave of Mda. Gascon, and a father unknown. Godparents: Gregorio, slave of Mda. Alexis /Grappe/, and Maria-Anna, slave of Luis Le Blanc /De Blanc/.

2511. FRANCO.
August 15, 1785, baptism of Franco., born August 1, *mulato* son of Carlota, *mulata* slave of Mda. Jacob Lambre. Godparents: Franco. Antonio, free *negro*, and Maria-Anna, slave of Mda. Jacob /Lambre/.

2512. MANUEL
August 28, 1785, baptism of Manuel, born August 14, *negrito* son of Marianna, slave of Mr. Juan Lambra, and a father unknown. Godparents: Juan Luis, slave of Mda. S. Denis, and Luisa, slave of Juan Lambra.

2513. ANTONIO JOSEPH FRANCISCO
August 29, 1785, baptism of Antonio Joseph Francisco, born May 23, *mulato* son of Elena, *mulata* slave of Mr. Le Blanc /De Blanc/, and a father unknown. Godfather: /not named/; godmother: Celeste le Blanc /De Blanc//

2514. MARIA LUISA
September 25, 1785, baptism of Maria Luisa, born September 3, daughter of Angelica, slave of Mda. Jacob Lambra, and a father unknown. Godparents: Franco., slave of the same, and Ursula, slave of Rdo. P. F. Francco. de Caldez.

2515. MARIA ANNA
September 25, 1785, baptism of Maria Anna, born September 10, *negrita* daughter of Catharina, slave of Pedro Gagne, and a father unknown. Godparents: Guillelmo, slave of Mr. Badin, and Maria Luisa, slave of Mr. Prudhomme.

2516. ANONYMOUS
September 26, 1785, baptism of an Indian, aged about two years, son of Jaquatzin of the Apalache nation, living at Rapides. Godparents: Athanasio Le Cour and Maria Rachal.

2517. ANTONIO
September 30, 1785, baptism of Antonio, about six years of age, legitimate son of Bautista and Rescua, Indians of the Apelache nation living at Rapides. Godparents: Dionesio, *gefe* of that nation, and Elizabeth Derneville.

2518. MARGARITA
September 30, 1785, baptism of Margarita, about six years of age, legitimate daughter of Bautista and Rescua, Indians of the Apelache nation living at Rapides. Godparents: Luis le Blanc /de Blanc/ and Manuela, an Apelache Indian.

2519. FRANCA.
October 2, 1785, baptism of Franca., born May 20, daughter of Maria, slave of Mda. Jph. des Pres, and of a father unknown. Godparents: Francisco Langlois and Michaela Rosalia Sta. Cruz.

2520. FRANCA.
October 2, 1785, baptism of Franca., born May 1, daughter of Veney (Vency?), slave of Michel Robin, and of a father unknown. Godparents: Pedro Moreau and Nicolossa Langlois.

2521. MARGARITA
October 2, 1785, baptism of Margarita, about one and a half years, *negrita* daughter of Veney (Vency?), slave of Michel Robin, and a father unknown. Godparents: Pablo Bouette /Laffitte/ and Michaela Rosalia Sta. Cruz.

2522. JUAN BAUTISTA
November 13, 1785, baptism of Juan Bautista, born October 24, son of Maria Luisa, *mulata* slave of Mr. Pavia, and a father unknown. Godparents: Juan Bautista Maturin David and Maria Eufrasia Maturin David.

2523. ANONYMOUS
November 4, 1785, baptism of a slave infant, born October 20, daughter of Pelagia, slave of Mr. Pomié, and a father unknown. Godparents: Juan Bautista, slave of Mda. Baranga, and Bernarda, free *negra*.

2524. URSULA
January 12, 1786, baptism of Ursula, born November 1, 1785, Indian, legitimate daughter of Luis Robert and

Charlota, both Indians. Godparents: Luis Fonteneau and
Maria Juana Gutierrez.

2525. JUAN FRANCO.
January 27, 1786, baptism of Juan Franco., born December
27, 1785, son of Genoveva, free *mulata*, and a father unknown. Godparents: Juan Franco. Rambin and Maria Juan
Ris.

2526. FRANCA.
February 5, 1786, baptism of Franca., born January 14,
mulata daughter of Maria Luisa, slave of Pedro Dartigos,
and a father unknown. Godparents: Bernabé Cheletre and
Rose Cheletre.

2527. JULIANA
March 1, 1786, baptism of Juliana, born January? 17, 1786,
negrita daughter of Franca., slave of Mda. Bapta. Triche,
and a father unknown. Godparents: Juan Pedro, free *negro*, and Margarita, slave of Mda. Jacob /Lambre/.

2528. JUAN BAUTISTA
March 25, 1786, baptism of Juan Bautista, born March 12,
negrito son of Maria-Anna, *negra* slave of Mda. Jacob
/Lambre/. Godparents: Juan Bauta., slave of Mda. Jacob
and Maria Juana, slave of Mr. Vaugine.

2529. BASILIO
April 20, 1786, baptism of Basilio, born March 24, son of
Theresa, slave of Pedro Derban, and a father unknown.
Godparents: Pedro /Laberry dit/ Bayon and Maria du Pres.

2530. MARIA FRANCISCA
April 26, 1786, baptism of Maria Francisca, born March 3,
negrita daughter of Angelica, slave of Mr. Remi Poisot,
and a father unknown. Godparents: Augustin Buard and
Maria Rachal.

2531. JUAN BAUTISTA
September 6, 1786, baptism of Juan Bautista, born August
15, son of Agnes, *mulata*, and a father unknown. Godparents: Silvestre Bossie and Maria Luisa Dupre.

2532. ATHANASIO
September 10, 1786, baptism of Athanasio, born May 22,
son of Maria Luisa, slave (*negra*) of Dna. Widow St. Denis,
and a father unknown. Godparents: Domingo Davion and
Maria Antonia /de St. Denis/.

2533. CARLOS
September 10, 1786, baptism of Carlos, born April 30, son

of Catalina, *negra* slave of Mr. Labery, and a father unknown. Godparents: Juan Bautista, *negro*, and Augustina, *negra*.

2534. MARIA FRANCISCA
September 10, 1786, baptism of Maria Francisca, born July 12, a daughter of Juanna, *negra* of Widow Buart, and a father unknown. Godparents: Luis Alexandro, *negro*, and Ursula, *negra*.

2535. AUGUSTIN
September 10, 1786, baptism of Augustin, born June 29, son of Angela, *negra* slave of Mr. Dartigaux, and a father unknown. Godparents: Augustin, *negro*, and Maria Luisa, *negra*.

2536. STANISLAS
September 24, 1786, baptism of Stanislas, born July 26, son of Maria Francisca, *negra* slave of Mr. Pedro Darban, and a father unknown. Godparents: Remi Poissot and Maria Antonia Bastien /de St. Denis/.

2537. MARIA FROZINA
October 1, 1786, baptism of Maria Frozina, born September 16, daughter of Genovefa, *negra* slave of Pedro Dervanne, and a father unknown. Godparents: Joseph Marcel de Soto and Maria Luisa Lecomte, Dna. Monet.

2538. LUIS CESAR
March 27, 1787, baptism of Luis Cesar, born March 12, son of Bernarda, free *negra*, and a father unknown. Godparents: Estevan Vaugine and Maria Lambre.

2539. MARIA FRANCISCA DE DOLORES
April 4, 1787, baptism of Maria Francisca de Dolores, aged about three months, daughter of a *negra* slave of Dna. Widow LeComte, and a father unknown. Godparents: Antonio Joseph /Metoyer/, *mulato*, and Francisca, *negra*.

2540. ATHANASIO
April 25, 1787, baptism of Athanasio, aged about four months, Indian, father and mother unknown. Godparents: Iago, *negro*, and Maria Juana, *mulata*.

2541. LUIS ZENON
April 25, 1787, baptism of Luis Zenon, a *pardo* of about five months, son of a *mulata* slave of Widow LeCompte, and a father unknown. Godparents: Antonio, *mulato*, and Maria Luisa, *negra*.

2542. MARIA FRANCISCA DE DOLORES
May 1, 1787, baptism of Maria Francisca de Dolores, born

April 17, daughter of Maria Luisa, *negra* slave of Dna. Widow St. Denis, and a father unknown. Godparents: Andre, *negro*, and Maria Madelena.

2543. PEDRO
May 20, 1787, baptism of Pedro, born the first of the month, son of a *negra* slave of Francisco /Le/ Vasseur, and a father unknown. Godparents: Pedro, *negro*, and Maria Ana, *negra*.

2544. SEBASTIAN
May 30, 1787, baptism of Sebastian, born May 15, son of Juliana, *negra* slave of Luis Buard, and a father unknown. Godparents: Juan Luis Buar and Teresa Eugenia Buar.

2545. MARIA FELICIDAD
June 20, 1787, baptism of Maria Felicidad, born the first of the month, child of Maria Luisa, *negra* slave of Mr. Dartigo, and a father unknown. Godparents: Miguel Chamarre and Catalina Bardon.

2546. DOMINGO
July 1, 1787, baptism of Domingo, born June 27, son of Madelena, *negra* slave of Widow Buar, and a father unknown. Godparents: "a *negro* called Choera"* and Maria Luisa, *negra*.

*François *dit* Choera, son of François and Maria Françoise, and a slave of the St. Denis family. See Entry 111, in Register 1, and Doc. 178, Succession of St. Denys, French Archives, Office of the Clerk of Court, Natchitoches.

2547. MARIA LUISA
July 1, 1787, baptism of Maria Luisa, born June 8, 1787, *negrita* daughter of Francisca, *negra* slave of Widow Buart, and a father unknown. Godparents: Luis, *negro*, and Maria Luisa, *negra*.

2548. MARIA HORTENSIA
July 8, 1787, baptism of Maria Hortensia, born May 15, daughter of a *mulata* called Pelagia, slave of Widow Grappe, and a father unknown. Godparents: Baltasar, *mulato*, and Felicidad, *mulata*.

2549. MARIA CELESTIA
August 5, 1787, baptism of Maria Celestia, born July 8, daughter of a free *mulata* named Perrine and a father unknown. Godparents: Juan Maria Armant and Susanne Prudhomme.

2550. PEDRO
September 25, 1787, baptism of Pedro, born September 4,

"*negro* son of a father unknown," property of Mr. Dartigaux. Godparents: Pedro, *negro*, and Maria, *negra*.

2551. ANONYMOUS
September 29, 1787, baptism of a child of an unmarried Indian and a father unknown. Godparents: Mr. Monet and Dna. Lambre.

2552. LUIS
November 1, 1787, baptism of Luis, *negro*, father and mother unknown, property of Widow Grappe. Godparents: Luis, *negro*, and Teresa, *negra*.

2553. HENRIQUE
November 8, 1787, baptism of Henrique, born October 20, "parents are *negros*", property of Mr. Monet. Godparents: Eugenio, *negro*, and Pelagia, *negra*.

2554. LUIS
November 20, 1787, baptism of Luis, *negro*, son of a father unknown, property of Mr. Rousseau. Godparents: Pedro and Maria, *negros*.

2555. MARIA FROSINNA
November 25, 1787, baptism of Maria Frosinna, a *pardo*, daughter of a father unknown. Godparents: Juan Luis, *negro*, and Maria Luisa, *negra*.

2556. MARIA LUISA
December 4, 1787, baptism of Maria Luisa, born about one month before, *negra* child of a father unknown, property of Mr. Metoyer. Godparents: Valerio Armant and Eufrosina Rambint.

2557. MARIA
December 11, 1787, baptism of Maria, aged about one month, *negra* child of a father unknown, property of Widow Le Comte. Godparents: Athanasio and Maria, *negros*.

2558. ALEXANDRO
January 4, 1788, baptism of Alexandro, *negro*, father unknown, property of Mr. Fonteneau. Godparents: Augustin and Margarita, *negros*.

2559. MARIA SUSANNA
January 11, 1788, baptism of Maria Susanna, aged about one year, *pardo* daughter of a father unknown, property of Widow LeComte. Godparents: Pedro and Susanna /Metoyer/, *mulatos*.

2560. AGUSTIN
January 25, 1788, baptism of Agustin, born January 1, *negro*, father unknown, property of Mr. St. Anne. Godparents: Nicolas Agustin /Metoye_r_7, *mulato*, and "a *negra* named Contine."

2561. JUAN LUIS
January 25, 1788, baptism of Juan Luis, aged about one month, *negro*, father unknown, property of Mr. De Blanc. Godparents: Juan Luis and Maria Ana, *negros*.

2562. ALEXANDRO
February 15, 1788, baptism of Alexandro, adult *negro* of about 15 years, father unknown, property of Mr. De Blanc. Godparents: Athanasio, *negro*, and Maria Ana, *negra*.

2563. SOPHIA
February 22, 1788, baptism of Sophia, about one month old, *negra*, slave of Widow Buard, father unknown. Godparents: Juan and Sophia, *negros*.

2564. MARIA
February 22, 1788, baptism of Maria, born February 5, daughter of an Indian and a father unknown. Godparents: Luis, Indian, and Maria, *mulata*.

2565. LUIS CESERIO
March 11, 1788, baptism of Luis Ceserio, born February 8, *pardo*, father unknown, property of Widow Lecomte. Godparents: Luis and Francisca, *mulatos*.

2566. BAUTISTA
March 24, 1788, baptism of Bautista, *negro* adult of 30 years, parents unknown, property of Mr. St. Anne. Godparents: Mr. Rambin and Dna. Metoyer.

2567. JOSEPH
March 24, 1788, baptism of Joseph, adult *negro*, about 20 years old, parents unknown, property of Gaspar Fiolle. Godparents: Luis Anti and Dna. Maturin /David7.

2568. JUAN LUIS
March 24, 1788, baptism of Juan Luis, adult *negro*, about twenty years, father unknown, property of Remy Lambre. Godparents: Manuel and Maria Luisa, *negros*.

2569. MARIA AUGUSTINA
March 27, 1788, baptism of Maria Augustina, born March 8, *pardo*, daughter of a father unknown, property of Widow Lecomte. Godparents: Augustin and Francisca, *mulatos*.

2570. FRANCISCA
April 8, 1788, baptism of Francisca, born March 20, *negra*, property of Manuel Prudhomme. Godparents: Juan, *negro*, and Francisca, *negra*.

2571. LUISA
April 30, 1788, baptism of Luisa, born April 10, *negra*, property of Mme. Badin. Godparents: Guillermo and Luisa, *negros*.

2572. LUIS ALEXANDRO
May 21, 1788, baptism of Luis Alexandro, born May 1, *negro*, property of Mr. Luis Buard. Godparents: Alexandro, *negro*, and Juanna, *mulata*.

2573. JUAN LUIS
May 21, 1788, baptism of Juan Luis, born April 15, *negro*, property of Mr. Badin. Godparents: Juan Luis and Juanna, *negros*.

2574. JUAN BAUTISTA
June 4, 1788, baptism of Juan Bautista, born June 1, *negro*, property of Dna. Maria Lambre. Godparents: Antonio Prudhomme and Maria Bailio.

2575. GABRIEL
/illegible/, 1788, baptism of Gabriel, born June 15, *negro*, father unknown, property of Remy Lambre. Godparents: Miguel and Catalina, *negros*.

2576. MANUEL
July 5, 1788, baptism of Manuel, born June 8, *negro*, father unknown, property of Manuel Prudhomme. Godparents: Manuel, *negro*, and Cecilia, *negra*.

2577. CECILIA
July 12, 1788, baptism of Cecilia, about one month old, *negra*, father unknown, property of Widow Lambre. Godparents: Christobal and Cecilia, *negros*.

2578. FRANCISCA
September 1, 1788, baptism of Francisca, born the first of the month, *negra*, father unknown, property of Widow Buard. Godparents: Manuel and Juanna, *negros*.

2579. JOSEPH
September 7, 1788, baptism of Joseph, born August 15, *negra*, father unknown, property of Remy Lambre. Godparents: Joseph and Maria Ana, *negros*.

2580. LUISA
September 29, 1788, baptism of Luisa, about 15 days old,

parda, father unknown, property of Mr. Monet. Godparents: Antonio, *negro*, and Maria Luisa, *mulata*.

2581. RAPHAEL
October 9, 1788, baptism of Raphael, aged about one month, *negro*, father unknown, property of Mr. Dortolant. Godparents: Iago, *negro*, and Margarita, *negra*.

2582. JUAN LUIS
October 16, 1788, baptism of Juan Luis, born October 4, *negro*, father unknown, property of Mr. Badin. Godparents: Juan Luis and Juanna, *negros*.

2583. MARGARITA
October 23, 1788, baptism of Margarita, born October 1, *parda*, father unknown, property of Pedro Derbanne. Godparents: Joseph Derbanne and Guillerma Valdek.

2584. PEDRO
October 30, 1788, baptism of Pedro, aged about one month, *negro*, father unknown, property of Francisco Levasseur. Godparents: Pedro and Maria Ana, *negros*.

2585. LUCIA
November 1, 1788, baptism of Lucia, about three days old, Indian, father unknown. Godparents: Christobal and Lucia, *negros*.

2586. SEBASTIAN
December 12, 1788, baptism of Sebastian, about one month old, *negro*, property of Luis Buard. Godparents: Luis Buard and Teresa Eugenia Buard.

2587. MARIA FELICIDAD
December 12, 1788, baptism of Maria Felicidad, several days old, father unknown, property of Dna. Dartigaux. Godparents: Miguel Chamarre and Catalina Bardon.

2588. DOMINGO
December 21, 1788, baptism of Domingo, about 15 days old, *negra*, father unknown, property of Widow Buard. Godparents: Luis and Maria Luisa, *negros*.

2589. MARGARITA
December 31, 1788, baptism of Margarita, *negra*, father unknown. Godparents: Joseph and Margarita, *negros*.

2590. MARIA LUISA
January 15, 1789, baptism of Maria Luisa, about one month old, *negra*, father unknown, property of Widow Buard. Godparents: "the *negro* called Choura"* and Maria Luisa,

negra.

*See note accompanying Entry 2546.

2591. JUAN BAUTISTA
February 1, 1789, baptism of Juan Bautista, adult *negro*. Godparents: Juan and Maria Ana, *negros*.

2592. MANUEL
February 1, 1789, baptism of Manuel, adult *negro*, property of Mr. Prudhomme. Godparents: Manuel and Maria Celeste, *negros*.

2593. LUIS
February 4, 1789, baptism of Luis, born September 15, 1788, *negro*, father unknown, property of Dna. Maria Lambre. Godparents: Antonio Prudhomme and Dna. Baillo.

2594. JOSEPH
March 5, 1789, baptism of Joseph, adult *negro*, father unknown. Godparents: Domingo Prudhomme and Dna. Lambre.

2595. ISIDORE
March 12, 1789, baptism of Isidore, born April 26, <u>1788?</u>, *negro*, father unknown, property of Pedro Derbanne. Godparents: Francisco and Francisca, *negros*.

2596. CONSTANCIA CELESTINE*
March 21, 1789, baptism of Constancia,* about one month old, *negra*, father unknown, property of Mr. Metoyer*. Godparents: Estevan and Teresa, *negros*.

*The marginal note identifies this slave as "Celestin, slave of Marie Metoyer." The text identifies her as "Constancia, slave of Mr. Metoyer."

2597. MARIA FRANCISCA
March 21, 1789, baptism of Maria Francisca, *negra*, father unknown, property of Mr. Metoyer. Godparents: Pedro and Maria Juana, *negros*.

2598. MARIA ADELAIDA
April 3, 1789, baptism of Maria Adelaida, about one month old, *negra*, father unknown, property of Mr. Morphil. Godparents: Pedro Baillo and Adelaide Rambint.

2599. PERRINA
April 19, 1789, baptism of Perrina, aged about two months, *negra*, father unknown, property of Mr. Deblanc. Godparents: Juan Louis and Cecilia, *negros*.

2600. MARIA
April 19, 1789, baptism of Maria, about 15 days old,

parda, father unknown, property of Mr. Labery. Godparents: Sebastian, *negro*, and Pablina, *mulata*.

2601. MARIA HELENA
September 1, 1789, baptism of Maria Helena, about two months old, *negra*, father unknown, property of Mr. Mezieres. Godparents: Juan Francisco LeVasseur and Maria Juana Sorel.

2602. MARIA LUISA
September 1, 1789, baptism of Maria Luisa, aged about one month, *parda*, father unknown, property of Mr. Monet. Godparents: Mr. Monet and Dna. Monet.

2603. SUZANNA
September 15, 1789, baptism of Suzanna, born September 8, *negra*, father unknown, property of Dame Remy Poissot. Godparents: Manuel and Maria Juana, *negros*.

2604. MARIA ANA
October 2, 1789, baptism of Maria Ana, about one month old, *negra*, father unknown, property of Mr. Remy Poissot. Godparents: Manuel and Maria Ana, *negros*.

2605. PELAGIA
October 31, 1789, baptism of Pelagia, born October 11, *negra*, father unknown, property of Remy Lambre.

2606. DOMINGO
December 4, 1789, baptism of Domingo, about one month of age, *negro*, father unknown, property of Widow Lambre. Godparents: Domingo Prudhomme and Dna. Malige.

2607. AGUSTIN
December 4, 1789, baptism of Agustin, about one month old, *negro*, father unknown, property of Mr. Rouquier. Godparents: Manual Rachal and Maria Francisca Rachal.

2608. MARIA EDÉ
December 18, 1789, baptism of Maria Edé, aged one and a half years, *negra*, father unknown, property of Luis Jobard. Godparents: Ante. Rascou /Antoine Vascocu_/ and Dna. Fiolle.

2609. MARIA CELESTE
January 1, 1790, baptism of Maria Celeste, aged about one month, *negra*, father unknown, property of Mr. Mezieres. Godparents: Valeri Armant and Sophie, *negra*.

2610. MARIA CELESTE
January 8, 1790, baptism of Maria Celeste, born December

20, 1789, *negra*, father unknown, property of Widow Bartholome Rachal. Godparents: Bartolome Rachal and Francisca Rachal.

2611. MARIA ANITA
January 31, 1790, baptism of Maria Anita, about 15 days old, *negra*, father unknown, property of Dna. Badin. Godparents: "the *negro* called Prince" and Maria Ana, *negra*.

2612. FRANCOIS
February 10, 1790, baptism of Francois, *pardo*, father unknown, property of Mr. Monginot. Godparents: Carlos and Maria, *negros*.

2613. ANTONIO
February 17, 1790, baptism of Antonio, about one month old, *pardo*, property of Mr. LaCase. Godparents: Francisco Chiq, *negro*, and Juanna, *mulatta*.

2614. PELAGIA
March 9, 1790, baptism of Pelagia, about one month old, *negra*, father unknown, property of Mr. Bossie. Godparents: Alexandro and Maria Luisa, *negros*.

2615. MARIA FRANCISCA
April 3, 1790, baptism of Maria Francisca, about 15 days old, *parda*, father unknown, property of Mr. Malige. Godparents: Remy Posau /Poisot/ and Guillerma Dufrene /Chever ditte Dufrene/.

2616. ANGELICA
April 3, 1790, baptism of Angelica, about one month old, *negra*, father unknown, property of Mr. Grillet. Godparents: Francisco Rambint and Genoveva Sorel.

2617. CARLOS
April 3, 1790, baptism of Carlos, adult *negro*, father unknown, property of Mr. Remy Lambre. Godparents: Guillermo and Maria Luisa, *negros*.

2618. FRANCISCO
April 3, 1790, baptism of Francisco, adult *negro*, father unknown, property of Mr. Remy Lambre. Godparents: Manuel and Maria Luisa, *negros*.

2619. JOSEPH
May 27, 1790, baptism of Joseph, *negro*, father unknown, property of Mr. Labery. Godparents: Juan and Maria Ana, *negros*.

2620. LUIS
May 27, 1790, baptism of Luis, about 15 days old, *negro*, father unknown, property of Mr. /Grillet *dit*/ Sauterelle. Godparents: Pedro and Francisca, *negros*.

2621. SUSANNA
June 15, 1790, baptism of Susanna, about one month old, Indian, father unknown, property of Mr. Remy Lambre. Godparents: Remy Lambre and Dna. Lambre.

2622. JOSEPH
June 31, 1790, baptism of Joseph, about eight days old, *pardo*, father unknown, property of Luis Rachal. Godparents: Joseph and Maria, *negros*.

2623. MARIA LUISA CATICHE /METOYER/*
August 6, 1790, baptism of Maria Luisa Catiche, about one month old, *parda*, father unknown*, property of Widow LeCompte. Godparents: Augustin /Metoyer/ and Susanna /Metoyer/, *mulatos*.

*According to the Metoyer family genealogy compiled circa 1880 by the late Rev. A. Dupre, pastor of St. Augustine Parish on Isle Brevelle (now on file in the St. Augustine Parish archives, Melrose, Louisiana), Catiche was the natural daughter of Louis Metoyer, who was the mulatto son of the black Marie Therese *ditte* Coincoin. For Coincoin's purchase and manumission of Catiche see Docs. 2550 and 2552, French Archives, Office of the Clerk of Court, Natchitoches.

2624. MARIA
August 13, 1790, baptism of Maria, about one month old, *negra*, father unknown, property of Luis Buard. Godparents: Alexandro, *negro*, and Maria Luisa, *negra*.

2625. FRANCISCO
September 15, 1790, baptism of Francisco, about one month old, *negro*, father unknown, property of Pedro Gagné.

2626. SUZANNA
October 9, 1790, baptism of Suzanna, about four months old, *negra*, father unknown, property of Mr. De Blanc. Godparents: Agustin, *negro*, and Juanna, *negra*.

2627. ANDRES
October 23, 1790, baptism of Andres, about 15 days old, *negra*, father unknown, property of Francisco Bossié. Godparents: Andres and Juanna, *negros*.

2628. PEDRO JOSEPH
November 13, 1790, baptism of Pedro Joseph, about 15 days

old, *negro*, father unknown, property of Mr. Fonteneau. Godparents: "the *negro* called Peruce" and Catiche, *mulata*.

2629. MARIA SUSANNA
November 30, 1790, baptism of Maria Susanna, Indian, father unknown, property of Widow Dartigaux. Godparents: Juan and Susanna, *mulatos*.

2630. JOSEPH
December 7, 1790, baptism of Joseph, about two months old, *negro*, father unknown, property of Luis Buard. Godparents: Joseph and Catalina, *negros*.

2631. MARIA FRANCISCA
December 26, 1790, baptism of Maria Francisca, about one month old, *negra*, father unknown, property of Mr. Mezieres. Godparents: Mr. Lacaze and Coleta Mezieres.

2632. MARIA TERESA LOUISE*
December 26, 1790, baptism of Maria Teresa*, about 15 years old, adult *negra*, father unknown, property of Mr. Remy Lambre. Godparents: Manuel and Maria Luisa, *negros*.

*This name is given in the text as "Maria Teresa" and in the margin as "Marie Louise".

2633. MARIA LUISA
January 7, 1791, baptism of Maria Luisa, *negro* adult, property of Mr. Buard. Godparents: Juan Bautista and Maria Ana, *negros*.

2634. PEDRO
January 6, 1791, baptism of Pedro, adult *negro*, property of Widow Dartigaux.

2635. MARIA FANCONETA
January 12, 1791, baptism of Maria Fanconeta, born August 25, 1790, *negra*, father unknown, property of Dna Varraque. Godparents: Juan Bautista and Maria Juanna, *negros*.

2636. MARIA JUANNA
February 1, 1791, baptism of Maria Juanna, born January 19, father unknown, property of Widow Buard. Godparents: Andres David and Dna. Vercher.

2637. MIGUEL
February 25, 1791, baptism of Miguel, adult *negro*, father unknown, property of Mr. Remy Lambre. Godparents: Luis, *mulato*, and Rosalia, *negra*.

2638. MONICA
June 23, 1791, baptism of Monica, *negra* adult, father unknown, property of Manuel Prudhomme. Godparents: Manuel and Naneta, *negros*.

2639. JUAN BAUTISTA
July 17, 1791, baptism of Juan Bautista, born June 25, *negro*, father unknown, property of Mr. Dolet. Godparents: Juan Bautista Chever and Dna. Malige.

2640. MARIA SUSETA
July 17, 1791, baptism of Maria Suseta, about three months of age, *negra*, father unknown, property of Mr. Fonteneau. Godparents: Guillermo and Rosalia, *negros*.

2641. LUIS CESAIRE /LE COURT/*
July 17, 1791, baptism of Luis Cesaire, several days old, Indian, father unknown*, property of Le Cour. Godparents: Atanasio Le Cour and Dna. Monet.

*See note accompanying Entry 2255 and the marriage of Cesair LeCour to Marie Gertrude Maurine, July 23, 1829, Register 11.

2642. JOSEPH
August 7, 1791, baptism of Joseph, about one month old, *mulato*, father unknown, property of Maria Juanna, a free *negra*. Godparents: Agustin /Metoyer/ and Maria Susanna /Metoyer/, *mulatos*.

2643. MARIA CATICHA
August 25, 1791, baptism of Maria Caticha, born June 25, *negra*, father unknown, property of Mr. Metoyer. Godparents: Domingo /Metoyer/, *mulato*, and Francisca, *negra*.

2644. JOSEPH ATANASIO
August 25, 1791, baptism of Joseph Atanasio, born June 27, *pardo*, father unknown, property of Mr. Metoyer. Godparents: Francisco and Maria, *negros*.

2645. LUIS BARNABE
August 25, 1791, baptism of Luis Barnabe, about 11 months old, *negra*, father unknown, property of Widow Buard. Godparents: Domingo /Metoyer/, *mulato*, and Maria Luisa, *negra*.

2646. JUAN PEDRO
September 25, 1791, baptism of Juan Pedro, born August 24, *negro*, father unknown, property of Andres Felipe.* Godparents: Pedro and Helena, *negros*.

*/Frederic/

2647. ESTEVAN NOEL
October 14, 1791, baptism of Estevan Noel, born December 26, 1790, *pardo*, father unknown, property of Julian Besson. Godparents: Julian Besson and Dna. Chrisostome Pereau.

2648. MARIA DE LA ASSOMPTION
November 2, 1791, baptism of Maria de la Assomption, about one month old, Indian, father unknown. Godparents: Mr. Dortolant and Dna. Montenari.

2649. CELESTINO
December 11, 1791, baptism of Celestino, about two months old, *negro*, father unknown, property of Agustin Fredieu. Godparents: Pedro, *negro*, and the *negra* called Contine.

2650. FLORENTINO
December 18, 1791, baptism of Florentino, *pardo*, father unknown, property of Mr. Monet who declares him to be free. Godparents: Baltasar /Jean Baptiste Baltasar *dit* Baltasar Monet/, *mulato*, and Susana /Metoyer/, *mulata*.

2651. ROSALIA
January 28, 1792, baptism of Rosalia, born January 15, *negra*, father unknown, property of Mr. Ramis. Godparents: Benito Pescio and Margarita Langloy.

2652. YSABEL
March 7, 1792, baptism of Ysabel, *negra* adult, father unknown, property of Mr. Ailhaud St. Anne. Godparents: "a son of Mr. Deblanc" and Adelaida Armant.

2653. MARIA HELENA
March 7, 1792, baptism of Maria Helena, *negra* adult, father unknown, property of Ailhaud St. Anne. Godparents: Andres Rambint and Eufrasia Rambint.

2654. LUIS ANDRES
March 7, 1792, baptism of Luis Andres, aged about three months, *negro*, father unknown, property of Ailhaud St. Anne. Godparents: Bautista Armant and Adelaide Rambint.

2655. LUIS THOMAS
March 11, 1792, baptism of Luis Thomas, about three months old, *negro*, father unknown, property of Widow Buard. Godparents: Andres Rambint and Eufrasia Rambint.

2656. ROSALIA
March 31, 1792, baptism of Rosalia, born September 6, 1791, *parda*, father unknown, property of Widow Grappe. Godparents: Bautista Grappe and Geneveva Jean-ris.

2657. LUIS
April 3, 1792, baptism of Luis, *negro* adult, father unknown, property of Remy Lambre. Godparents: Joseph and Juanna, *negros*.

2658. MARIA FRANCISCA
April 3, 1792, baptism of Maria Francisca, *negra* adult, father unknown, property of Remy Lambre. Godparents: Carlos, *negro*, and Maria Francisca.

2659. MARIA SALY FELIX*
April 3, 1792, baptism of Maria Saly, adult *negra*, father unknown, property of Remy Lambre. Godparents: Bastian and Maria, *mulatos*.

*This name is given in the text as "Maria Saly" and in the margin as "Maria Felix."

2660. ATANASIO
April 3, 1792, baptism of Atanasio, about three months old, *negro*, father unknown, property of Remy Lambre. Godparents: Atanasio, *negro*, and Consancia, *mulata*.

2661. JUAN PEDRO NOLBERT
April 8, 1792, baptism of Juan Pedro Nolbert, born March 31, *pardo*, father unknown, property of Mr. Labery. Godparents: Pedro and Victoria, *negros*.

2662. JUAN FRANCOIS
April 8, 1792, baptism of Juan Francois, about three months old, *negro*, father unknown, property of Mr. Metoyer. Godparents: Luis Alexandro and Maria Rosa, *negros*.

2663. ANDRÉ
April 8, 1792, baptism of André, about 1 month old, *pardo*, father unknown, property of Mr. Metoyer. Godparents: Juan and Pelagia, *negros*.

2664. MARIA ANA
April 8, 1792, baptism of Maria Ana, *negra* adult, father unknown, property of Mr. Metoyer. Godparents: Alexandro and Maria Josepha, *negros*.

2665. MARIA MARTA
April 8, 1792, baptism of Maria Marta, *negra* adult, father unknown, property of Manuel Prudhomme. Godparents: Guillermo and Maria Elana Leonora, *negros*.

2666. MARIA LEONORA
April 8, 1792, baptism of Maria Leonora, *negra* adult, father unknown, property of Agustin Fredieu. Godparents: Alexandro and Maria Luisa, *negros*.

2667. JOSEPH
April 8, 1792, baptism of Joseph, *negro* adult, father unknown, property of Ailhaud St. Anne. Godparents: Pedro Ternier and Maria Ana Buard.

2668. LUIS ALEXANDRO
April 8, 1792, baptism of Luis Alexandro, *negro* adult, father unknown, property of Mr. Rouquier. Godparents: Alexandro and Catalina, *negros*.

2669. IAGO
April 8, 1792, baptism of Iago, adult *negro*, father unknown, property of Mr. Rouquier. Godparents: Estevan Pavie, *fils*, and Maria Helena Pavie.

2670. JULIAN
April 8, 1792, baptism of Julian, *negro* adult, father unknown, property of Mme. Widow Dartigaux. Godparents: Francisco, *mulato*, and Margarita, *negra*.

2671. JUAN BAUTISTA
April 8, 1792, baptism of Juan Bautista, adult *negra*, father unknown, property of Mr. Badin. Godparents: Sebastian and Leonora, *negros*.

2672. JUAN
April 8, 1792, baptism of Juan, adult *negro*, father unknown, property of Pedro Derbanne. Godparents: Juan and Maria Juana, *negros*.

2673. FRANCISCO
April 8, 1792, baptism of Francisco, adult *negro*, father unknown, property of Mr. Rouquier. Godparents: Francisco and Teresa, *negros*.

2674. AGUSTINO
April 8, 1792, baptism of Agustino, adult *negro*, property of Mr. Rouquier. Godparents: Agustino and Maria Ana, *negros*.

2675. ESTHER
April 8, 1792, baptism of Esther, about three months old, *negra*, father unknown, property of Widow Triche. Godparents: Iago, *negro*, and Dorotea, *negra*.

2676. MADELENA
July 15, 1792, baptism of Madelena, about 13 months old, *parda*, father unknown, property of Widow Triche. Godparents: Iago, *mulato*, and Madelena, *mulata*.

2677. SILVESTRE
July 15, 1792, baptism of Silvestre, born June 20, *negro*, father unknown, property of Widow Triche. Godparents: Luis and Madelena, *negros*.

2678. FRANCISCO
July 16, 1792, baptism of Francisco, about 11 months old, *pardo*, father unknown, property of Widow Grappe. Godparents: Francisco Rambint and Widow Grappe.

2679. FRANCISCA
July 29, 1792, baptism of Francisca, born June 8, *parda*, father unknown, property of Mr. Monet. Godparents: Bautista, *mulato*, and Maria Juanna, *negra*.

2680. CESERIO
August 12, 1792, baptism of Ceserio, about four months old, *negro*, father unknown, property of Dna. Lambre. Godparents: Mauricio, *negro*, and "the *negra* called Contine."

2681. JUAN
August 26, 1792, baptism of Juan, about 5 months old, *negro*, father unknown, property of Mr. Labayrie. Godparents: Juan and Catalina, *negros*.

2682. PABLO
August 26, 1792, baptism of Pablo, about 7 months, *negro* father unknown, property of Remy Lambre. Godparents: Miguel, *negro*, and "the *negra* called La Fille."

2683. JUAN BAUTISTA
August 30, 1792, baptism of Juan Bautista, born August 1, *negro*, father unknown, property of Mr. Rouquier. Godparents: Bautista and Maria, *negros*.

2684. JORGE
August 30, 1792, baptism of Jorge, born at the end of July, *negro*, father unknown, property of Pedro Derbanne. Godparents: Joseph, *mulato*, and Maria Josepha, *negra*.

2685. MADELENA
August 30, 1792, baptism of Madelena, about five months old, *negra*, father unknown, property of Mr. Rouquier. Godparents: Iago, *negro*, and Pabla, *mulata*.

2686. ANTONIO
August 30, 1792, baptism of Antonio, about one month old, *negro*, father unknown, property of Mr. *Cadet* Lestage. Godparents: "the *mulato* called Regis" and Bergita, *mulata*.

2687. ALEXANDRO SEVERIN?
September 23, 1792, baptism of Alexandro Severin?, born about August 6, *negro*, father unknown, property of Mr. Levasseur. Godparents: Luis Levasseur and Genoveva Levasseur.

2688. ANDRES
October 7, 1792, baptism of Andres, aged about 1 month, *negro*, father unknown, property of Mr. Tauzin. Godparents: Andres Chamarre and Adelaida Armant.

2689. ESTEVAN
October 14, 1792, baptism of Estevan, several months old, an Indian, father unknown, property of Bertrand Plaisance. Godparents: Bertrand Plaisance and Dna. Luis Totin.

2690. MARIA LUISA
October 14, 1792, baptism of Maria Luisa, about six months old, *negra*, father unknown, property of Dna. Varangue. Godparents: Estevan, *mulato*, and Genoveva, *negra*.

2691. JUAN BAUTISTA
October 21, 1792, baptism of Juan Bautista, about three months old, *pardo*, father unknown, property of Julian Besson. Godparents: Juan Bautista Besson and Genoveva Sorel.

2692. ESTHER
November 4, 1792, baptism of Esther, about 15 days old, *parda*, father unknown, property of Mr. De Blanc. Godparents: Juan Luis, *negro*, and Marta, *mulata*.

2693. ANTONIO
November 4, 1792, baptism of Antonio, *negro*, father unknown, property of Luis Buard. Godparents: Luis, *negro*, and Juanna, *mulata*.

2694. FRANCISCO ZENON
December 23, 1792, baptism of Francisco Zenon, about two months old, *negro*, father unknown, property of Antonio Prudhomme. Godparents: Juan Bautista, *mulato*, and Maria Luisa, *negra*.

2695. FRANCISCO
December 23, 1792, baptism of Francisco, about two months old, *negro*, father unknown, property of Pedro Badin. Godparents: Francisco, *negro*, and Maria Luisa, *negra*.

2696. MARIA FROZINA
January 20, 1793, baptism of Maria Frozina, born November 30, 1792, *negra*, father unknown, property of Mr. Morphil.

Godparents: Dionisio Buard and Maria Ana Buard.

2697. FRANCISCO
January 27, 1793, baptism of Francisco, about one year old, *negro*, father unknown, property of Mr. Mezieres. Godparents: Francisco Florio and Maria Juana, *negra*.

2698. MIGUEL
January 27, 1793, baptism of Miguel, *negro* adult, father unknown, property of Juan Delouch. Godparents: Gil *inguiendo?* and Cecilia Robert /Dupre/.

2699. DOROTEA
February 6, 1793, baptism of Dorotea, born December 26, 1792, *negra*, father unknown, property of Pedro Derbanne. Godparents: Manuel Bartolome Rachal and Dorotea Monet.

2700. GENOVEVA TERESA
February 24, 1793, baptism of Genoveva Teresa, adult *negra*, father unknown, property of Fr. Delvaux. Godparents: Luis Alexandro Guerbois and Theresa Lamalaty Fiolle.

2701. MARIA FRANCISCA ADELAIDA
March 23, 1793, baptism of Maria Francisca Adelaida, born March 18, *parda*, father unknown, property of Fr. Delvaux. Godparents: Juan Marin Francisco Rouquier and Maria Ana Rouquier.

2702. MARIA
March 31, 1793, baptism of Maria, born February 28, *parda*, father unknown, property of Widow Dartigaux. Godparents: Nicolas /Augustin Metoyer/, *mulato*, and Sophia, *negra*.

2703. ULALIA
March 31, 1793, baptism of Ulalia, born June 1, 1792, a *parda*, father unknown, property of Mr. St. Anne. Godparents: Domingo /Metoyer/ and Susanna /Metoyer/, *mulatos*.

2704. MARIA FRANCISCA
March 31, 1793, baptism of Maria Francisca, about three months old, *negra*, father unknown, property of Mr. Metoyer. Godparents: Pedro Mayou and Adelaida Rambint.

2705. FRANCISCO HONORÉ
March 31, 1793, baptism of Francisco Honoré, about four months old, *negro*, father unknown, property of Mr. Monginot. Godparents: Joseph and Juanna, *negros*.

2706. MARIA JUANNA
March 31, 1793, baptism of Maria Juanna, about one year old, *negra*, father unknown, property of Mr. Metoyor. Godparents: Juan Bautista and Cecilia, *negros*.

2707. MARIA CONSTANCIA
March 31, 1793, baptism of Maria Constancia, about eight months old, *negra*, father unknown, property of Widow Dartigaux. Godparents: Francisco Florio and Monica, Indian.

2708. MARTA
March 31, 1793, baptism of Marta, about one year old, *negra*, father unknown, property of Athanasio Poissot. Godparents: Francisco and Maria Ana, *negros*.

2709. MADELENA
March 31, 1793, baptism of Madelena, slave of Metoyer. Godparents: Francisco Florio and Monica, Indian.

2710. MARIA JUANA BABÉ
March 31, 1793, baptism of Maria Juana Babé, slave of Mr. Metoyer. Godparents: Sebastian and Maria Juanna, *negros*.

2711. MARGARITA
March 31, 1793, baptism of Margarita, slave of Mr. Metoyer. Godparents: Bautista and Maria, *negros*.

2712. MARIA LUISA
March 31, 1793, baptism of Maria Luisa, slave of Mr. Labery. Godparents: Carlos and Maria Ana, *negros*.

2713. LUIS
March 31, 1793, baptism of Luis, slave of Mr. Labery. Godparents: Francisco and Juanna, *negros*.

2714. MARIA ANGELICA
March 31, 1793, baptism of Maria Angelica, slave of Mr. De Blanc. Godparents: Domingo /Metoyer/ and Juanna, *mulatos*.

2715. CECILIA GENIA
March 31, 1793, baptism of Cecilia Genia, slave of Mr. De Blanc. Godparents: Francisco and Cecilia, *negros*.

2716. URSULA
March 31, 1793, baptism of Ursula, slave of Athanasio Poissot. Godparents: Juan and Ursula, *negros*.

2717. JUAN
March 31, 1793, baptism of Juan, slave of Athanasio Poissot. Godparents: Juan and Margarita, *negros*.

2718. IAGO
March 31, 1793, baptism of Juan, slave of Athanasio Poissot. Godparents: Domingo and Maria, *negros*.

2719. MARIA ANA
March 30, 1793, baptism of Maria Ana, slave of Widow Dartigaux. Godparents: Juan Bautista and Maria, *negros*.

2720. MARIA
March 31, 1793, baptism of Maria, slave of Widow Dartigaux. Godparents: Andres and Maria, *negros*.

2721. MARIA FRANCISCA
March 31, 1793, baptism of Maria Francisca, slave of Mr. St. Anne. Godparents: Juan Luis and Francisca, *negros*.

2722. MARIA VICTORIA
March 31, 1793, baptism of Maria Victoria, slave of Widow Dartigaux. Godparents: Andres and Victoria, *negros*.

2723. ALEXANDRO
March 31, 1793, baptism of Alexandro, slave of Maria Ana Buard. Godparents: Francisca Flores and Maria Francisca.

2724. FRANCISCA
March 31, 1793, baptism of Francisca, slave of Mr. Grillet. Godparents: Juan Francisco and Angelica, *negros*.

2725. MARGARITA
March 31, 1793, baptism of Margarita, slave of Mr. Morphil. Godparents: Francisco and Margarita, *negros*.

2726. PEDRO
March 31, 1793, baptism of Pedro, slave of Mr. Morphil. Godparents: Antonio Prudhomme and Adelaida Rambint.

2727. PABLO
March 31, 1793, baptism of Pablo, slave of Mr. Morphil. Godparents: Marcel de Soto and Theresa Maÿou.

2728. IAGO
March 31, 1793, baptism of Iago, slave of Mr. Morphil. Godparents: Marcel de Soto and Maria Frozina Rambint.

2729. PEDRO
March 31, 1793, baptism of Pedro, slave of Mr. Morphil. Godparents: Juan and Maria Juana, *negros*.

2730. JOSEPH
March 31, 1793, baptism of Joseph, slave of Mr. Morphil. Godparents: Francisco and Francisca, *negros*.

2731. FRANCISCO
March 31, 1793, baptism of Francisco, slave of Athanasio Poisot. Godparents: Bautista and Maria Ana, *negros*.

2732. FRANCISCA
March 31, 1793, baptism of Francisca, slave of Athanasio Poisot. Godparents: Pedro and Juanna, *negros*.

2733. JUAN
March 31, 1793, baptism of Juan, slave of Mr. Monginot. Godparents: Juan and Maria, *negros*.

2734. SUSANNA
March 31, 1793, baptism of Susanna, slave of Mr. Monginot. Godparents: Juan Luis and Maria, *negros*.

2735. MARIA JUANNA
March 31, 1793, baptism of Maria Juanna, slave of Mr. Monginot. Godparents: Antonio and Marta, *negros*.

2736. MARIA ANA
April 7, 1793, baptism of Maria Ana, adult *negra*, property of Fr. Delvaux. Godparents: Agustin /Metoyer/, *mulato*, and Genoveva, *mulata*.

2737. SUSANNA
April 7, 1793, baptism of Susanna, about three years old, daughter of an Indian and a father unknown. Godparents: Pedro /Metoyer/, free *mulato*, and Susanna /Metoyer/, free *mulata*.

2738. MARIA LUISA
April 7, 1793, baptism of Maria Luisa, about five years old, daughter of an Indian and a father unknown. Godparents: Athanasio Armant and Genoveva Sorel.

2739. ISABEL
June 10, 1793, baptism at Rapides of Isabel, *negrita*, born March 22, 1789, daughter of Felicité, a *negra* of Martin Gray. Godparents: Charlos Hago? and Felicité Etie.

2740. PELAGIA
June 11, 1793, baptism at post of Dionisio *el Gefe Apalache*, of Pelagia, about one year, a *negra*, daughter of Hace, slave of Dionisio *el Gefe*. Godparents: Bautista and Susana.

2741. FRANCA.
June 11, 1793, baptism at the Apalache of Franca., about 12 years old, daughter of "the same *negra* of Dionisio." Godparents: Bautista and Franca.

2742. DOMINIQUE
June 15, 1793, baptism of Dominique, about three and a

half months, son of Franca., slave of Ambrosio Lecomte. Godparents: Franco. and Margarita.

2743. JOSEF
June 15, 1793, baptism of Josef, about 26 months, *negro* son of Maria, slave of Alexo Rutie /Cloutier/. Godparents: Luis and Genoveva.

2744. MARIA DE LOS NIEVES
June 15, 1793, baptism of Maria de los Nieves, born March 12, *negra*, daughter of Maria, slave of Mdme. Lecomt. Godparents: Juan Luis and Magdalena.

2745. MARGARITA
June 15, 1793, baptism of Margarita, born March 19, *cuarterona*, daughter of Magdalena, *mulata* of Mde. Lecomte. Godparents: Dominique /Metoyer/ and Margarita.

2746. MARIA
June 15, 1793, baptism of Maria, born May 2, 1791, *negra* daughter of Barbara, slave of Ambrosio LeComte. Godparents: Juan Bautista and Clemencia.

2747. MARIA SUSANA
June 15, 1793, baptism of Maria Susana, about three years old, *negra* daughter of Maria, slave of Madame LeComte. Godparents: Jacobo and Mariana.

2748. MARIA LUISA
June 15, 1793, baptism of Maria Luisa, born February 30, 1792, *negra* daughter of Maria Juana, slave of Widow Le Comte. Godparents: Juan Bautista and Elena Cloutie.

2749. MARIA ROSA /METOYER/*
June 15, 1793, baptism of Maria Rosa, about eleven months old, *mulata* daughter of Franca., a *mulata* slave of Madame LeComte. Godparents: Josef and Maria Luisa Marta.

*According to Dupre, "Metoyer Family Genealogy" (see note accompanying Entry 2623) Maria Rosa was the natural daughter of Louis Metoyer, *mulato*. This infant was purchased and manumitted in 1800 by Louis' older brother Augustin Metoyer (see Widow LeComte to Nicolas Augustin, *Old Natchitoches Data*, Doc. 279, Cammie G. Henry Collection, Northwestern State University Library, Natchitoches).

2750. MANUEL
June 15, 1793, baptism of Manuel, born December 25, 1792, *mulato* son of Maria, *negra* of Alexo Cloutié. Godparents: Pedro and Maria.

2751. TODOS SANTOS
June 30, 1793, baptism of Todos Santos, born October 31, 1792, a *griffe*, son of Febi, a *negra* of Guinea, belonging to Dn. Juan Bautista LaBery. Godparents: Jacobo and Mariana.

2752. CASIMIRO
July 13, 1793, baptism of Casimiro, about 20 days old, *negro* son of Pelagia, slave of Mr. Dulé /Dolet/. Godparents: Nicolas Lemetre and Maria Juana Le Beuf.

2753. ALEXIS
January 1, 1795, baptism of Alexis, born July 17, 1794, son of Maria Josepha, *negra* slave of Mr. /Grillet dit/ Sauterelle. Godparents: Juan Bautista Plaisance and Maria Barba Grillet. Father unknown.

2754. FRANCISCO
January 12, 1795, baptism of Francisco, born December 22, 1794, *mulato* son of Genoveva, slave of Widow Labayrie, and a father unknown. Godparents: Francisco /Illegible/ and Widow LeCompte.

2755. FRANCISCO JOSEPH MARIA
January 12, 1795, baptism of Francisco Joseph Maria, born February 15, 1794, a free *mulato*, son of Catalina, free *negra*, and a father unknown. Godparents: Francisco Monginot and Maria Josepha Malige.

2756. JUAN PEDRO
January 18, 1795, baptism of Juan Pedro, about one and a half years of age, *negro* son of Rosa, *negra* of Agustino Fredieu, and of a father unknown. Godparents: Luis Buard and Madelena Perau.

2757. MARCELLINO
January 25, 1795, baptism of Marcellino, born April 20, 1794, *negro* son of Genovefa, *negra* slave of Widow Triche, and of a father unknown. Godparents: Bautista Plaisance and Maria Josepha Totin.

2758. ATANASIO
February 1, 1795, baptism of Atanasio, about six months old, *negro* son of Margarita, *negra* slave of Eduardo Morphy. Godparents: Iago and Maria Josepha.

2759. PELAGIA
February 2, 1795, baptism of Pelagia, born January 15, *negra* daughter of Madelena, slave of Andrés Rambin, and a father unknown. Godparents: Francisco Agustin Rambin and Adelaide Rambin.

2760. GREGORIO SILVESTRE
February 8, 1795, baptism of Gregorio Silvestre, born May 8, 1794, *negrito* son of Catalina, *negra* slave of Luis Jobar, and a father unknown. Godparents: Francisco, *negro*, and Genoveva, *mulata*.

2761. MANUEL
February 8, 1795, baptism of Manuel, about 10 months old, *mulato* son of Juliana, *mulata* slave of Luis Buard. Godparents: Iago, *negro*, and Bergita, *mulata*.

2762. FRANCISCO
February 8, 1795, baptism of Francisco, about six months old, *negro* son of Maria, *negra* slave of Francisco Lacase, and a father unknown. Godparents: Agustin /Metoyer/. *mulato*, and Dorotea, *negra*.

2763. MARIA
February 23, 1795, baptism of Maria, about one and a half years old, *negra* daughter of Maria Luisa, *negra* slave of Iago Lacase, and a father unknown. Godparents: Roc, *negro*, and Francisca Maria, *negra*.

2764. JUAN FRANCISCO FLORENTINO /CONANT/
March 1, 1795, baptism of Juan Francisco Florentino, born "the sixth or seventh of January, 1794," a free *mulato*, son of Susanna /Metoyer/, free *mulata*, and a father unknown. Godparents: Luis /Metoyer/, free *mulato*, and Maria Teresa /ditte Coincoin/, free *negra*.

*Numerous subsequent records identify this son of Marie Susanne Metoyer as Florentin <u>Conant</u>. For example, see Succession of Suzanne Metoyer, #355, Office of the Clerk of Court, Natchitoches.

2765. MARIA TERESA EMELIA
March 1, 1795, baptism of Maria Teresa Emelia, born October 15, 1794, *negrita* daughter of Catalina, *negra* slave of Francisco Levasseur, and a father unknown. Godparents: Juan Bautista Teodoro Grillet and Maria Luisa Gagnon.

2766. MARIA TERESA
March 15, 1795, baptism of Maria Teresa, about one and a half years, *mulata* daughter of Maria Luisa, *mulata* slave of Mr. Metoyer, and a father unknown. Godparents: Luis /Metoyer/, *mulato*, and /illegible/, *negra*.

2767. MARIA LUISA
March 15, 1795, baptism of Maria Luisa, about 10 months old, *negra* daughter of Maria, *negra* slave of Mr. Metoyer, and a father unknown. Godparents: Juan Luis, *negro*, and Teresa, *negra*.

2768. MARIA CECILIA
March 15, 1795, baptism of Maria Cecilia, about one and a half years of age, *negra* daughter of Madelena, *negra* slave of Mr. Metoyer, and a father unknown. Godparents: Juan Luis, *negro*, and Maria Silesia, *mulata*.

2769. JUAN LUIS
March 15, 1795, baptism of Juan Luis, aged three months, *negro* son of Pelagia, *negra* slave of Mr. Francisco Bossier, and a father unknown. Godparents: Juan Luis, and Monica, an Indian.

2770. CRISTOBAL
April 4, 1795, baptism of Cristobal, about 30 years old, *negro* slave of Mr. Metoyer, native of the Moco nation. Godparents: Luis and Genoveva, *mulata*.

2771. IAGO
April 4, 1795, baptism of Iago, about 30 years of age, *negro* slave of Metoyer, native of the Moco nation. Godparents: Luis and Genoveva, *mulattos*.

2772. FRANCISCA
April 4, 1795, baptism of Francisca, about 30 years old, *negra* of the Jamba nation, property of Mr. Metoyer. Godparents: Luis and Genoveva, *mulattos*.

2773. FRANCISCA
April 4, 1795, baptism of Francisca, about 20 years of age, native of the Adid? nation, *negra* slave of Antonio Prudhomme. Godparents: Luis and Teresa, *negros*.

2774. MARIA
April 4, 1795, baptism of Maria, aged about 30 years, a native of Jamaica, *negra* slave of Remigio Lambre. Godparents: Pedro and Teresa, *negros*.

2775. PEDRO
April 4, 1795, baptism of Pedro, about thirty years, a native of Jamaica, *negro* slave of Metoyer. Godparents: Pedro and Teresa, *negros*.

2776. MARIA
April 4, 1795, baptism of Maria, about 20 years old, a native of the Conga nation, *negra* slave of Marcel de Soto. Godparents: Joseph and Angelica, *negros*.

2777. IAGO
April 4, 1795, baptism of Iago, about 20 years, native of the Conga nation, *negro* slave of Manuel Prudhomme. Godparents: Iago and Maria Anna, *negros*.

2778. ANGELICA
April 4, 1795, baptism of Angelica, aged about 20 years, native of the Uar (Nar?) nation, *negra* slave of Andres Rambint. Godparents: /illegible/ De Blanc and Dna. Metoyer.

2779. PEDRO
April 4, 1795, baptism of Pedro, aged about 20 years, of the Congo nation, *negro* slave of Marcel de Soto. Godparents: Joseph and Madelena, *negros*.

2780. FRANCISCO
April 4, 1795, baptism of Francisco, about 20 years of age, native of the Congo nation, *negro* slave of Marcel de Soto. Godparents: Juan and Victoria, *negros*.

2781. ANTONIO
April 4, 1795, baptism of Antonio, about thirty years old, of the Jamba nation, slave of Marcel de Soto. Godparents: Juan and Victoria, *negros*.

2782. JUAN
April 4, 1795, baptism of Juan, about 30 years old, native of the Nago nation, *negro* slave of Andres Rambint. Godparents: Bautista Le Vasseur and Adelaida Rambint.

2783. CLARISSA
April 4, 1795, baptism of Clarissa, about 20 years, of the Congo nation, *negra* slave of Mr. Metoyer. Godparents: Luis Buard and Ulalia Bossie.

2784. ANTONIO
April 4, 1795, baptism of Antonio, about 20 years, of the Maraba nation, *negro* slave of Luis Closo. Godparents: Manuel Triche and Francisca Triche.

2785. ATANASIO
April 4, 1795, baptism of Atanasio, about 30 years of age, of the Maniga nation, *negro* slave of Jiliberto Closo. Godparents: Bautista Triche and Genoveva Gonin.

2786. MADELENA
April ?, 1795, baptism of Madelena, about two months old, *negrita* daughter of Juanna, *negra* slave of Manuel Prudhomme. Godparents: Pedro and Maria Luisa, *negros*.

2787. ANNA
April ?, 1795, baptism of Anna, about one and a half years, *mulata*, native of this parish, daughter of Maria Luisa, *negra* slave of Manuel Prud'homme, and a father unknown. Godparents: Agustin and Dorotea, *negros*.

2788. HONORE
April ?, 1795, baptism of Honore, about one year of age, *negrito*, native of this parish, son of Maria, *negra* slave of Remigio Lambre, and of a father unknown. Godparents: Pedro, *negro*, and Maria Luisa, *negra*.

2789. JOSEPH
April ?, 1795, baptism of Joseph, about two months old, *negrito*, native of this parish, son of Maria, *negra* slave of Remigio Lambre, and of a father unknown. Godparents: Atanasio and Bergita, *mulatos*.

2790. ATANASIO
April ?, 1795, baptism of Atanasio, about three months old, *negro* son of Francisca, *negra* slave of Antonio Prudhomme, and of a father unknown. Godparents: Francisco and Cicilia, *negros*.

2791. JUAN BAUTISTA HONORE
April ?, 1795, baptism of Juan Bautista Honore, *mulato* son of Maria, *negra* slave of Mr. Metoyer, and of a father unknown. Godparents: Joseph /Metoyer/, *mulato*, and Theresa /ditte Coincoin/, *negra*.

2792. YSABEL
April ?, 1795, baptism of Ysabel, about one year, *negrita* daughter of Maria Luisa, *negra* slave of Remigio Poissot and a father unknown. Godparents: Pedro and Genoveva, *negros*.

2793. PEDRO
April ?, 1795, baptism of Pedro, about one year old, *negrito* son of Angelica, *negra* slave of Remigio Poissot, and of a father unknown. Godparents: Pedro and Genoveva, *negros*.

2794. CELESTE
April ?, 1795, baptism of Celeste, about two years old, *negrita* daughter of Angelica, *negra* slave of Remigio Poissot. Godparents: Juan Bautista Buard and Victoria Poissot.

2795. HONORE
April ?, 1795, baptism of Honore, about two years old, *negrito* son of Maria Juanna, *negra* slave of Marcel de Soto, and of a father unknown. Godparents: Joseph, *mulato*, and Bergita, *mulata*.

2796. JUAN BAUTISTA
April ?, 1795, baptism of Juan Bautista, about one year old, *negrito* son of Maria Juanna, *negra* slave of Mr.

Metoyer, and of a father unknown. Godparents: Juan Bautista Buard and Helena Pavie.

2797. PELAGIA
April ?, 1795, baptism of Pelagia, about one year old, *negrita* daughter of Esther, *negra* slave of Mr. Metoyer, and a father unknown. Godparents: Andres Rambint and Helena Pavie.

2798. ANTONIO
April ?, 1795, baptism of Antonio, about four years old, *negrito* son of Maria Juana, *negra* slave of Marcel de Soto, and a father unknown. Godparents: Estevan Pavie and Frozina Rambint.

2799. HELENA
April ?, 1795, baptism of Helena, about eight months old, *negrita* daughter of Sophia, *negra* slave of Antonio Prud-'homme, and of a father unknown. Godparents: Pedro and Margarita, *negros*.

2800. MARIA JUANNA
April ?, 1795, baptism of Maria Juanna, born March 2, *mulata* daughter of Maria Anna, free *negra* "who was the property of Mr. Badin," and of a father unknown. Godparents: Joseph Langlois, *mulato*, and Bergita, *mulata*.

2801. MODESTA
April ?, 1795, baptism of Modesta, about 18 months of age, *negrita* daughter of Margarita, *negra* slave of Bautista Buard, and of a father unknown. Godparents: Moricio and Juanna, *negros*.

2802. ZENON
April ?, 1795, baptism of Zenon, about 16 months of age *negrite* son of Henriqua, *negra* slave of Widow Bartholome Rachal, and a father unknown. Godparents: Andre and Isabel, *negros*.

2803. AGUSTIN
April ?, 1795, baptism of Agustin, about one year old, *mulatto* son of Maria Juanna, *negra* slave of Silvestre Bossié, and of a father unknown. Godparents: Juan Bautista and Pelagia, *negros*.

2804. SUSANA
April ?, 1795, baptism of Susana, about one year old, *negrita* daughter of Maria Anna, *negra* slave of Maria Anna Buard, and of a father unknown. Godparents: Iago and Helena, *negros*.

2805. HONORE
April ?, 1795, baptism of Honore, five months of age, *negrito* son of Pelagia, *negra* slave of Antonio Prud-'homme, and of a father unknown. Godparents: Iago and Catalina, *negros*.

2806. MARIA LEONORA
April ?, 1795, baptism of Maria Leonora, eighteen months old, *mulata* daughter of Rosa, *negra* slave of Remigio Lambre, and of a father unknown. Godparents: Miguel and Catalina, *negros*.

2807. JUAN PEDRO
April ?, 1795, baptism of Juan Pedro, eighteen months old, *negrito* son of Maria Ana, a *negra* slave of Luis Davion. Godparents: Pedro Gagne and Rosalia Gagne.

2808. JUAN BAUTISTA
April ?, 1795, baptism of Juan Bautista, eleven months old, *mulato* son of Margarita, slave of Francisco Grappe, and a father unknown. Godparents: Luis David and Frosina David.

2809. ALEXANDRO
April ?, 1795, baptism of Alexandro, *negrito* son of Maria, *negra* slave of Bautista Dartigaux, and of a father unknown, aged one year. Godparents: Juan Luis and Maria Luisa, *negros*.

2810. MELANIA
April ?, 1795, baptism of Melania, about eight months old, *mulata* daughter of Rosa, *negra* slave of Francisco Rouquier, and a father unknown.

NOTE: At this point there is a skip in the pagination of the register, from 428 to 433. Apparently, several pages of baptismal entries have been lost.

2811. JUAN BAUTISTA
/no date/, baptism of Juan Bautista, about 30 years, of the Conga nation, *negro* slave of Atanasio de Mezieres. Godparents: Augustin /Metoyer/, *mulata*, and Maria, *negro*.

2812. ANTONIO
/no date/, baptism of Antonio, about 30 years old, of the Sami? nation, *negro* slave of Bernabé Cheletre. Godparents: Francisco G_____ /illegible/ and Maria Marta Fort.

2813. VERONICA
/no date/, baptism of Veronica, about three months of age, *negrita* of <u>Marianna?</u>, *negra* slave of Henrique Triche. Godparents: Nicolas, *mulato*, and Catalina, *negra*.

2814. PEDRO
/no date/, baptism of Pedro, aged about two years, *negro* slave of Henrique Triche, son of Maria Anna. Godparents: Nicolas, *mulato*, and Maria Juana, *negra*.

2815. MARGARITA
/no date/, baptism of Margarita, 15 years old, a native of the Minan nation, *negra* slave of Henrique Triche. Godparents: Bautista, *mulato*, and Maria Juanna.

REGISTER 4-B

NOTE: Unlike the previous volumes, this register has not been rebound and stamped with an identifying number. For identification purposes only it is usually referred to by researchers as Book 4-B. Its cover bears the faded heading: *Baptêmes des blancs et des Indiens depuis le 8'obre 1796 au 11 7bre 1801; Il y a aussi des Mariages 1786-1801.*

2816. November 8, 1796. Visit of the Bishop to Natchitoches.

2817. ATANASIO RACHAL
November 11, 1796, baptism of Atanasio, born September 20, 1796, legitimate son of Juan Bautista Rachal and Pelagia Brevel, natives of this post. Grandparents: Bartolome Rachal and Maria Lamalatie, natives of this parish; Juan Bautista Brevel and Maria Franca. Poissot, natives of this parish. Godparents: Bartolome Rachal and Maria Brevel.

2818. JEAN LOUIS CESER BOSSIÉ
November 13, 1796, baptism of Jean Louis Ceser, born December 28, 1795, legitimate son of Soulange Bossier and Heleonor Himel, natives of this parish. Grandparents: Francois Bossié and Antoine Himel. Godparents: Louis Buart and Marie Bossié.

2819. PIERRE LANDRI BERNARD
November 13, 1796, baptism of Pierre Landri, born March 10, legitimate son of Elie Bernar and Heleonor Chagnau, residents of this parish. Grandparents: Elie Bernard and Jeanne Leveque; Francois Chagnau and Marie LaCroix. Godparents: Pierre Elie and Francoise Grape.

2820. ANTOINE LEMOINE
February 19, 1797, baptism of Antoine, aged two and a half years, legitimate son of Antoine Lemoine and Genevieve Bellegarde. Grandparents: Charles Lemoine and Elisabeth Dupre; Jn. Babptiste Bellegarde and Magdelaine Montpierre. Godparents: Charles Lemoine, represented by Sieur Valentin Delessart?, and Marie Louise Lemoine, represented by Marie Francoise Chevailler Poiret.

2821. REMI LEMOINE
February 19, 1797, baptism of Remi, born July 4, 1796,

legitimate son of Antoine Lemoine and Genevieve Bellegarde. Grandparents: Charles Lemoine and Elisabeth Dupre; Jn. Baptiste Bellegarde and Magdeleine Montpierre. Godparents: Jean Baptiste Bellegarde and Marie Bellegarde.

2822. FORTUNE
February 21, 1797, baptism of Fortune, Indian infant of the Apalaches nation, aged three months, son of Catherinne, an Indian of the Apalaches, and a father unknown. Godparents: Louis Toutin and Susanne.

2823. ANTOINE
February 21, 1797, baptism of Antoine, Indian infant of the Apalaches village, aged ten years, legitimate son of deceased Joseph, Indian, and Marie, Indian, of the Apaches /sic/. Godparents: Louis Toutin and Marguerite.

2824. VICTOIRE
February 21, 1797, baptism of Victoire, aged three months, Indian of the Apalaches village, daughter of Marie Anne, Indian of the Apalaches, and a father unknown. Godparents: Antoine and Margueritte, Indians of the Apalaches.

2825. MARGUERITTE
February 21, 1797, baptism of Margueritte, Indian girl of the Apalaches village, aged one year, daughter of Marie Anne, Indian of the Apalaches, and a father unknown. Godparents: Antoine, *capitaine* of the Apalaches, and Janneton, Indian of the Apalaches.

2826. FRANCOISE JEAN BAPTISTE*
February 22, 1797, baptism of Jean Baptiste, aged nine months, son of Francoise, Indian of Natchitoches, and a father unknown. Godparents: Louis /Metoyer/, free *mulâtre*, and Brigitte, a *mulâtress* slave of Barthelemi Rachal.

*The infant's name is given in the text as Jean Baptiste, but appears in the margin as Francoise.

2827. ADELAIDE
March 17, 1797, baptism of Adelaide, aged four years, the daughter of Marie, an Indian of Natchitoches, and a father unknown. Godparents: Manuel Derban and Cidonie Derbane.

2828. CATHERINNE CLAIRE HOUFEROGUE
April 13, 1797, baptism of Catherinne Claire, born March 22, legitimate daughter of Pierre Houferogue and Margueritte Detuile. Grandparents: /paternal grandparents not given/ and Jacques Detull and Marie Leger. Godparents:

Jacques Meziere and Catherinne Clair Detuile.

2829.   BENOIST BERTRAND
April 14, 1797, baptism of Benoist, *endoyé* at his home, legitimate son of Louis Bertrand and Elisabeth Davion. Grandparents: Louis Bertrand and Jeanne Dauphiné; Jean Baptiste Davion and Marie Hiacinthe Triche. Godparents: Benoist Montanari and Eulalie Vascocu.

2830.   MARIE DENISE BUART
April 16, 1797, baptism of Marie Denis, legitimate daughter of Jean Denis Buart and Marie Victoir Poissot. Grandparents: Gabriel Buart and Marie Anne Roussau; Jean Baptiste Remis Poissot and Marie Cavé. Godparents: Francois Marie Monginot and Marie Francoise Buart.

2831.   EUPHRASIE CATHERINNE TAUSIN
May 15, 1797, baptism of Euphrasie Catherinne, born April 30, legitimate daughter of Joseph Tausin and Marie Chamart. Grandparents: Girard Tausin and Jeanne Bartheau; Louis Charles Chamart and Catherinne Bardon. Godparents: Rosemond Chamard and Marie Louise Euphrasie Rambin.

2832.   MARIE CELESTE VILDEC *dit* PERAU
June 2, 1797, baptism of Marie Celeste, born May 17, *endoyée*, legitimate daughter of Francois Perau and Marie Louise Agathe Laberi. Grandparents: Barthelemi Perau and Marie Catherinne Dupre; Jean Baptiste Laberi and Susanne Guedon. Godparents: Francois Rouquié and Jeanne Margueritte Totin.

2833.   DENISE POMIER
June 4, 1797, baptism of Denise, born December 6, 1796, legitimate daughter of Jean Pomier and Marie Robert Dupré. Grandparents: Nicolas Pomier and Anne Bar; Robert Dupré and Manon Cavé. Godparents: Pierre Jarri and Marie Dupré.

2834.   MARIE CARMELITE BAUDOUIN
June 11, 1797, baptism of Marie Carmelite, born December 23, 1796, legitimate daughter of Jean Nicolas Baudouin and Marie Denege Malbert. Godparents: Joseph Rabalai and Marie Poissot. Grandparents: Pierre Baudouin and Marie Bontems; Jean Baptiste Malbert and Jeanne Vergér.

2835.   PIERRE JEAN BAPTISTE BOSSIÉ
June 11, 1797, baptism of Pierre Jean Baptiste, born March 22, 1797, legitimate son of Francois Paul Bossié and Catherinne Pelagie Lambre. Grandparents: Francois Bossie and Rosalie Charlotte Boré; Jean Baptiste Lambre and Marie Jeanne Levasseur. Godparents: Joseph Dartigau and Marie Genevieve Agathe Maes.

2836. JEAN BAPTISTE ISAAC FRAIDIEU
June 15, 1797, baptism of Jean Baptiste Isaac, born December 11, 1796, legitimate son of Augustin Fraidieu and Marie Jeanne Saurel. Grandparents: /paternal side not given7; Pierre Saurel and Marie Rose Boisselier. Godparents: Jean Baptiste Grape and Marie Jacques Fort.

2837. JOSEPH VALERI /LECOURT7*
June 21, 1797, baptism of Joseph Valeri, born in the month of February last, son of Marie Ursule, free *mulatresse**, and a father unknown*. Godparents: Antoine Joseph /Metoyer7, free *mulato*, and Margueritte, free *mulata*.

*See Entry 2255 for parental information. This entry above, 2837, is partially in error. It must be noted that Entry 2255, and most other records on Marie Ursulle, identify her as "an Indian of the Caddo tribe." Her identification as a *mulatresse* in Entry 2837 above is apparently a careless error on the part of the priest who recorded the entry above without accompanying information on the child's grandparents as is provided in the other baptismal records of this period

Further indication that Entry 2837 is in error is provided by the marriage of Marie Ursulle's oldest daughter, Marie Louise LeCourt to Pierre César Brosset, October 30, 1813, *op. cit*. Intermarriage between whites and those who bore Negro blood was illegal in this period, and the LeCourt-Brosset marriage enjoyed the sanction of both the law and the church. It is further noted that the records filed in the succession of Marie Louise LeCourt Brosset, *op. cit.*, also identify her and the other children of Marie Ursulle as "white."

2838. JEANNE RACHAL
June 25, 1797, baptism of Jeanne, born December 13, 1796, legitimate child of Barthelemi Rachal and Francoise Laberi. Grandparents: Louis Rachal and Marie Leroi; Jean Baptiste Laberi and Jeanne Guedon. Godparents: Joseph Martinau and Marie Magdeleine Laberi.

2839. EDOUARD OCTAVE* RACHAL
LOUIS JOSEPH BERNARD RACHAL
August 15, 1797, baptism of twins, born June 6, 1797, the legitimate sons of Louis Rachal and Marie Joseph Laberi. Grandparents: Louis Rachal and Marie Louise Des Rois /Le Roy7; Jean Baptiste Laberi and Jeanne Guedon. Godparents of the first infant: Jean Baptiste Dartigau and Marie Anne Colar; godparents of the second: Bernard Hitchoura and Margueritte Totin.

*The name of the first infant appears in the text as Edouard and in the margin as Octave; the name of the second infant appears in the text as Louis Bernard and in the margin as Joseph Bernard.

2840. MARIE LOUISE BAUDOUIN
September 23, 1797, baptism of Marie Louise, born February 1, legitimate daughter of Pierre Baudouin and Anne Robin. Grandparents: Francois Baudouin and Marie Anne Bontemps; Michel Robin and Marie Louise Boulai. Godparents: Pierre LaCour and Elisabeth Lebrun.

2841. JEAN BAPTISTE RACHAL
September 23, 1797, baptism of Jean Baptiste aged 18 months, legitimate son of Antoine Rachal and Marie Louise Lemoine. Grandparents: Louis Rachal and Marie Louise /Le/ Roi; Charles Lemoine and Elisabeth Dupre. Godparents: Jean Baptiste Lemoine and Francoise Laberi.

2842. MARIE ASPASIE RIS
October 1, 1797, baptism of Marie Aspasie, born September 17, legitimate daughter of Joseph Jean Ris and Marie Francoise Vascocu. Grandparents: Jean Ris and Marie Jeanne Chagnau; Antoine Vascocu and Marie Barbe Toups. Godparents: André Vascocu and Magdeleine Raimond.

2843. REMI POISSOT
October 1, 1797, baptism of Remi, born April 24, legitimate son of Antoin Poissot and Marie Silvie Goutier. Godparents: Jean Baptiste Dartigau and Eulalie Bossié. Grandparents: Remi Poissot and Marie Louise Cave; Michel Goutier /Goutierrez/ and Marie Duplessis.

2844. MARIE FELICITÉ BOUET LAFITE
October 1, 1797, baptism of Marie Felicite, born September 16, 1797 in this post, legitimate daughter of Paul Bouel Lafite and Marie Anne Sautau /de Soto/, living at *baillou au pierre* /Bayou Pierre/, province of Thecle?* Grandparents: /paternal side not given/; Manuel Sautau /de Soto/ and Marie Denege /de St. Denis/. Godparents: Marie Athanase Poissot and Marie Felicité Demezieres. *Texas?

2845. MARIE ROSE DERBANE
October 1, 1797, baptism of Marie Rose, aged one year, legitimate daughter of Gaspar Derbanne and Marie Joseph Perau. Grandparents: Gaspart Derbane and Francoise Verger; Francois Perau and Catherine Dupre. Godparents: Julien Besson and Marie Anne Perau.

2846. FRANCOIS JULIEN BESSON
October 1, 1797, baptism of Francois Julien, born March 9, legitimate son of Julien Besson and Marie l'Incarnation Perau. Grandparents: Jean Baptiste Besson and Louise Guedon; Francois Barthelemi Perau and Catherinne Dupre. Godparents: Benoist Montanari and Marie Anne Dorothée Perau.

2847. MARIE THERESE MAGDELEINE
October 2, 1797, baptism of Marie Therese Magdeleine, born July 22, *mulâtresse* infant of Magdeleine, a free *mulâtresse*, and a father unknown. Godparents: Pierre /Metoyer/, free *mulâtre*, and Marie Jeanne, slave of Athanase Demesiere.

2848. JEAN BAPTISTE SEVERE CLOUTIER
October 8, 1797, baptism of Jean Baptiste Severe, aged one year, legitimate son of Alexis Cloutier and Francoise Lecomte. Grandparents: Alexis Cloutier and Marie Rachal; Jean Baptiste Lecomte and Margueritte /Le/ Roi. Godparents: Nicolas Gallien and Margueritte /Le/ Roi.

2849. MARIE SUSANNE LEMOINE
October 8, 1797, baptism of Marie Susanne, born April 4, 1797, legitimate daughter of Charles Lemoine and Jeanne Lebrun. Godparents: Charles Lemoine and Catherinne Brossé. Grandparents: Charles Lemoine and Elisabeth Dupre; Guillaume Lebrun and Marie Louise Totin.

2850. JEAN CHRISOSTOME PERAU
October 15, 1797, baptism of Jean Chrisostome, about three years old, legitimate son of Jean Chrisostome Perau and Marie Louise Salvant. Grandparents: Barthelemi Perau and Catherine Dupre; Jean Salvant and Marie Louise Lambre. Godparents: Joseph Chagnau and Marie Salvant.

2851. JEAN LOUIS PIERRE PERAU
October 15, 1797, baptism of Jean Louis Pierre, about one and a half years old, legitimate son of Jean Chrisostome Perau and Marie Louise Salvant. Grandparents: Barthelemi Perau and Catherine Dupre; Jean Salvant and Marie Louise Lambre. Godparents: Louis Fontenau and Marie Lalande.

2852. JULIEN LEANDRE DUBOË
October 17, 1797, baptism of Julien Leandre, born October 14, legitimate son of Antoine Duboës and Marie Joseph Malige, living at Biou au pierre /Bayou Pierre/. Grandparents: Jean Baptiste Duboës and Marie Jeanne Clermont; Joseph Malige and Marie Antoine Lebrun. Godparents: Julien Besson and Marie Genevieve Duboë.

2853. MARIE DELOISE LATIÉ
November 11, 1797, baptism of Marie Deloise, born April 3, legitimate daughter of Jean Baptiste Latié and Marie Pelagie Frederik. Grandparents: Joseph Latié and Anne Vergé; Philippo Frederik and Marie Catherinne Sauvage. Godparents: Francois Frederik and Marie Catherinne Frederik, uncle and aunt of the infant.

2854. JEAN BAPTISTE GOUÉ
November 16, 1797, baptism of Jean Baptiste, born July 2, legitimate son of Simon Goué and Genevieve Bodin. Grandparents: Joachim Goué and Narcise /no last name/; Laurens Bodin and Marie Rosalie Michel Santa Crouse. Godparents: Jean Baptiste Brosset and Catherinne Brosset.

2855. BERNARD HISSOURA
November 23, 1797, baptism of Bernard, born October 9, legitimate son of Bernard Hissoura and Margueritte Grillé. Grandparents: Jen? Hissoura and Bernard Daitchou; Marin Grillé and Marie Louise Brevel. Godparents: Jean Baptiste Theodor Grillé and Marie Jean Grillé.

2856. ETIENNE CESAIR OUALES /WALLACE/
January 8, 1798, baptism of Etienne Cesair, born September 22, 1797, legitimate son of Jacques /Jacob/ Ouales and Marie Hiacinthe Gagne, a native of this post. Grandparents: Joseph Oualis and Onée Bultrong; Etienne Gagne and Marie Louise Bertrand. Godparents: Louis Gagne and Ursule Gagne, uncle and aunt of the infant.

2857. PIERRE LAVESPER
March 4, 1798, baptism of Pierre, born November 7, 1797, legitimate son of Francois Lavespere and Margueritte Derbanne. Grandparents: Jean Francois Lavespere and /paternal grandmother not named/; Pierre Derbane and Marie Claire /Le Clerc/. Godparents: Pierre Chaler and Marie Louise Dupre.

2858. AGATHE DORTHINE MERCIÉ
March 16, 1798, baptism of Agathe Dorthine, born March 4, legitimate daughter of Francois Mercie and Marie Louise Prudhomme. Grandparents: Francois Mercie and Margueritte Barbet; Sebastien Prudhomme and Jeanne Chever. Godparents: Sebastien Prudhomme and Louise Agathe Laberi.

2859. MARIE POMPONE PRUDHOMME
March 16, 1798, baptism of Marie Pompone, born December 20, 1797, at Baiou au Pierre, province of Teche /Texas/, legitimate daughter of Francois Prudhomme and Marie Rambin, living at Baiou au Pierre. Grandparents: /paternal side not given/; Andre Rambin and Francoise Clermon. Godparents: Pierre Dolé and Marie Rose Dupré.

2860. MARIE DAVION
March 18, 1798, baptism of Marie, born February 10, 1798 legitimate daughter of Dominique Davion and Pelagie Gagné. Grandparents: Jean Baptiste Davion and Marie Hiacinthe Triche; Etienne Gagné and Marie Louise Bertrand. Godparents: Louis Gagné and Marie Joseph Gagné.

2861. DENIS ETIENNE CASSENAVE
March 18, 1798, baptism of Denis Etienne, born June 9, 1797, at Rapides, legitimate son of Michel Denis Cassenave and Marie Jean Ris, habitants of this post. Grandparents: Bernard Cassenave and Felicité Clavau; Jean Ris and Marie Jeanne Chagnau. Godparents: Jean Baptiste Etienne _____ /illegible/ and Marie Thereze Elizabeth Metoie.

2862. MARIE DELAIDE DUPRÉ
/illegible/, 1798, baptism of Marie Delaide, born February 2, 1796, legitimate daughter of Pierre Dupré and Marie Francoise DeCourt /LeCourt/. Grandparents: Joseph Dupré and Marie Derbanne; Louis LeCourt and Jeanne Leroi. Godparents: Athanase Decour /LeCourt/ and Rose Dupré.

2863. MARIE GUILLARI
April 7, 1798, baptism of Marie Guillari, aged four months, legitimate daughter of Louis Guillari, Indian of the Aidaie nation, and Rosalie, a free *métive*. Grandparents: unknown. Godparents: Manuel Derbane and Dorothée, a free *métive* living at this post.

2864. JOSEPH MICHEL ACOSTA
April 8, 1798, baptism of Joseph Michel, aged three months, legitimate son of Me__?__ Acosta and Marie Paule Torres. Grandparents: Manuel Acosta and Jeanne Cirose?; Joseph Torres and Juanna Leroi*. Godparents: Michel _rmende? /Ernandes?/ and Marie Jeanne Bebé.   */de los Reyes/

2865. JOSEPH MARCEL CHRISTIE
April 8, 1798, baptism of Joseph Marcel, born March 6, legitimate son of Jacques Christie and Marie Anne Dorothee Perau. Grandparents: /paternal side not given/; Francois Perau and Catharinne Dupre. Godparents: Joseph Marcel /de Soto?/ and Marie de l'Incarnation Perau.

2866. MARIE CHARLOTTE LANGLOIS
April 8, 1798, baptism of Marie Charlotte, born December 24, 1797, daughter of Marie Langlois and a father unknown. Grandparents: /not given/. Godparents: Marie Charlotte Capuran and Francois Lacase.

2867. MARIE MARCELLITE POISSOT
April 15, 1798, baptism of Marie Marcellite, born September 4, 1796, legitimate child of Remi Poissot and Louise Cavé. Grandparents: Remi Poissot and Marie Felipe; Francois Cavé and Marie Jeanne Brunet. Godparents: Athanase Poissot and Marie Soto.

2868. DOMINIQUE /METOYER/*
May 29, 1798, baptism of Dominique, legitimate son of

Dominique /̄Metoye̱r/, a free *mulâto*, and Margueritte /̄Le Compte̱/, a free *mulâtresse*. Godparents: Jean Baptiste LeCompte /̄white̱/, and Marie Francoise Imel.

2869. REMI EUPH_____ MARCEL /̄DE SOTO̱/
May 13, 1798, baptism of Remi Euph____ Marcel, born March 23, legitimate son of Joseph Antoine Marcel /̄de Soto̱/ and Marie Baiou. Grandparents: Manuel Marcel /̄de Soto̱/ and Marie Denege St. Denis; Pierre Baiou and Catherinne Poissot. Godparents: Remi Perau and Marie des Douleurs Marcel /̄de Soto̱/.

2870. JUSTINE ADELAIDE SANTA CRUZ
May 17, 1798, baptism of Justine Adelaide, born May 10, legitimate child of Marie Torres and Ouane /̄Jua̱n/ Marie Saneta Crux. Grandparents: Joseph Torres and Marie Jeanne Desrois*, Pierre Crux and **Etroied?** Hernandes. Godparents: Michel Chamart and Marie Francoise Adelaide Rambin.   */̄de los Reye̱s/

2871. MARIE SUZANNE RACHAL
May 27, 1798, baptism of Marie Suzanne, born March 11, legitimate daughter of Dominique Rachal and Marie Vercher, habitants. Grandparents: Barthelemi Rachal and Marie Louise Lamalatie; Louis Vercher and Marie Louise Grillé. Godparents: Jacques Vercher and Silvie Brosset.

2872. LOUIS ANTI
June 17, 1798, baptism of Louis, born December 19, 1797, legitimate son of Louis Anti and Marie Jeanne Creq /̄Crete̱/. Grandparents: Ignace Anti and Catherine Guerin; Pierre Creq and Marie Louise Vergé.

2873. FRANCOIS DERBANE
June 17, 1798, baptism of Francois, born December 19, 1797, legitimate child of Jean Baptiste Derbane and Marie Heleine Brevel. Grandparents: Gaspart Derbanne and Manon Verge; Jean Baptiste Brevel and Francoise Poissot. Godparents: Gaspar Lacour and Felicite Brevel.

2874. JEAN BAPTISTE COUTI
/̄Illegible̱/, 1798, baptism of Jean Baptiste, legitimate son of Jean Paul Couti and Marie Josephe Torres. Grandparents: /̄paternal side not give̱n/; Joseph Torres and Marie Jeanne /̄Illegible̱/. Godparents: Jean Baptiste David and Marie /̄Illegible̱/ Rouquier.

2875. CESAIRE THOMASSIN
August 2, 1798, baptism of Cesaire, born February 23, legitimate son of Louis Tomacine and Catherinne Latié. Grandparents: Louis Tomacine and Therese Soulé; Joseph Latié

and Anne Verger. Godparents: Bernard Lissoura and Marie Therese Victoire Aillot.

2876. JEAN BAPTISTE BAUDIN
August 23, 1798, baptism of Jean Baptiste, born March 15, 1797, legitimate son of Jean Laurent Baudin and Marie Modeste. Grandparents: Laurent Baudin and Marie Michel Rosalie La Croix /Sta. Crux7; /maternal grandfather unnamed7 and Marie Magdaleine, Indian of the Canneti /Canneci7 nation. Godparents: Gaspart Bodin and Marie Magdeleine, the grandmother.

2877. JACQUES BROSSET
September 9, 1798, baptism of Jacques, born May 28, 1798, legitimate son of Pierre Brosset and Marie Joseph Grillé. Grandparents: Jean Brosset and Jeanne Rutin; Marin Grillé and Marie Louise Brevel. Godparents: Jean Baptiste Theodore Grillet and Catherine Brosset, uncle and sister of infant.

2878. HELEINE VASCOCU
September 23, 1798, baptism of Heleine, born August 20, legitimate daughter of Antoine Vascocu and Genevieve Gonin. Grandparents: Antoine Vascocu and Marie Barbe /Toups7 Jean Baptiste Gonin and Manuel Riche. Godparents: Louis Vascocu and Francois Triché.

2879. FRANCOISE DETUI
October 6, 1798, baptism of Francoise, born August 5, 1798, legitimate daughter of Guillaume Jacob Detui and Marie Ottemare (Ottemane?). Grandparents: Jacob Detui and Marie Leger; David Ottemane and Elisabeth Kiava. Godparents: David Ottemane and Julie Ofenogue.

2880. MARIE LOUISE
October 14, 1798, baptism of Marie Louise, born May 28, daughter of Pelagie /LeCourt7, a free *mulâtresse*, and a father unknown. Godparents: Joseph Chagneau and Margueritte, a free *mulâtresse*.

2881. MARIE LAMBRE
October 15, 1798, baptism of Marie, born July 4, legitimate daughter of Remi Lambre and Susanne Prudhomme. Grandparents: Jacques Lambre and Marie Anne Poissot; Jean Baptiste Prudhomme and Henriette Crontain. Godparents: Athanase Poissot and Catharinne Lambre.

2882. PIERRE JARRI
October 21, 1798, baptism of Pierre, born August 8, 1798, legitimate son of Pierre Jarri and Cecile Dupre. Grandparents: Michel Jarri and Marie Demien; Robert Dupre and Marie Cave. Godparents: Jacques Fort and Marie Dupre.

2883. MARIE SUSANNE PLAISANCE
November 4, 1798, baptism of Marie Susanne, born October 12, legitimate daughter of Bertrand Plaisance and Marie Barbe Grillé. Grandparents: Jean Baptiste Plaisance and Margueritte Totin; Marin Grillé and Marie Louise Brevel. Godparents: Manuel Triche and Marie Joseph Triche.

2884. MARIE DES ANGES THIERRY
November 18, 1798, baptism of Marie des Anges, born October 23, legitimate daughter of Pierre Tierri and Marie Rosalie Frederik, living at this post. Grandparents: Antoine Tierri and Francoise Bequet; Philippe Frederik and Marie Catherinne Sauvage. Godparents: Pierre Chelatre and Marie Catherine Sauvage.

2885. JEAN BAPTISTE LEMOINE
December 2, 1798, baptism of Jean Baptiste, born May 30, legitimate son of Jean Baptiste Lemoine and Felicité Lacase. Grandparents: Charles Lemoine and Elisabeth Dupre; Charles Lacase and Felicité Langlois. Godparents: Paul Poissot and Elizabeth David.

2886. HENRI EVARISTE? TAUSIN
December 27, 1798, baptism of Henri <u>Evariste?</u>, born October 11, 1798, legitimate son of Joseph Tausin and Marie Chamart. Grandparents: Girard Tausin and Jeanne /no last name/; Louis Chamart and Catherinne Bardon. Godparents: Nicolas Henri Lauve and Marie Anne Bardon.

2887. PIERRE ETIENNE POISSOT
January 28, 1799, baptism of Pierre Etienne, born November 14, 1797, *endoyé*, legitimate son of Athanase Poissot and Marie Louise Heleine Euphrosine Pavie. Grandparents: Athanase Poissot and Marie Soto; Etienne Pavie and Thérèse Buart. Godparents: Pierre Pavie, uncle of infant, and Thérèse Buart, grandmother of infant.

2888. FRANCOIS OLIVER BÉBÈ
February 4, 1799, baptism of Francois Oliver, born December 24, 1798, son of Julia Bébè, and a father unknown. Godparents: Francois Durci and Modeste Fontenau.

2889. AMELIE BAIOU /BAILLIO/
March 29, 1799, baptism of Amelie, born February 23, 1798, at the post of Rapides, legitimate daughter of Pierre Baiou and Emelie Lacour, residents of the post of Rapides. Grandparents: Pierre Baiou and Catherinne Poissot; Jean Baptiste Lacour and Marie Anne Leonard. Godparents: Manuel Prudhomme and Catherinne Lambre.

2890. MARIE ADELAIDE LARENAUDIERE
March 23, 1799, baptism of Marie Adelaide, born November

20, 1798, legitimate daughter of Pierre Larenaudiere and Jeanne Laberi. Grandparents: Charles Larenaudiere and Jeanne La Riviere; Jean Baptiste Laberi and Jeanne Guedon. Godparents: Athanase Dupre and Marie Louise Larenaudiere.

2891. NARCIS RACHAL
March 24, 1799, baptism of Narcis, born December 17, 1798, legitimate son of Louis Barthelemi Rachal and Francoise Grillé. Grandparents: Barthelemi Rachal and Marie Lamathie; Marin Grillé and Marie Louise Brevel. Godparents: Narcisse Prudhomme and Marie Therese Elisabeth Metoier.

2892. MARIE EUPHROSINE CHRISTI
March 23, 1799, baptism of Marie Euphrosine, born June 12, 1798, at Tapaltaque, dependency of Nacodoche, natural daughter of Marie Magdeleine Christi and a father unknown. Infant is baptized with the consent of *Père* Baillot, *curé* of that place. Godparents: Jounne Morvant and Marie Euphrosine Morvant.

2893. MARIE LOUISE LANGLOIS
April 3, 1799, baptism of Marie Louise, born September 1, 1798, legitimate daughter of Louis Langlois and Marie Celeste Verger. Grandparents: Augustin Langlois and Marie Louise Riche; Etienne Vergé and Francoise Dupre. Godparents: Pierre Dolet and Francoise Dupre.

2894. MARIE CELESTE LACASE
May 5, 1799, baptism of Marie Celeste, aged six months, legitimate daughter of Etienne Lacase and Dorothée Massip. Grandparents: Charles Lacase and Felicité Langlois; Jean Massip and Marie Lemoine. Godparents: Jean Massip and Marie Louise Dupré.

2895. VICTOIRE CONSTANCE ROQUE (DU ROQUE)
May 6, 1799, baptism of Victoire Constance, born April 16, legitimate daughter of Nicolas Du Roque and Marie Manuel Rasse, living on the *vacherie* of Mr. Prudhomme. Grandparents: Pierre du Roque and Marie Durbanes; Joseph Rassé and Barbe Corde. Godparents: Marianne Torre and Victoire Constanc Lemaitre.

2896. MARIE CONSTANCE LUGUE
May 12, 1799, baptism of Marie Constance, seven years old, native of the post of Ouachita and a resident of that place, legitimate daughter of Jean Lugue and Anne Olivier. Grandparents: Michel Olivier and Anne Robert; /paternal side not given/. Godparents: Francois Rouquié and Marie Olivier.

2897. JEAN BAPTISTE AUGUSTIN /METOYER/
May 12, 1799, baptism of Jean Baptiste Augustin, born

September 7, legitimate son of Nicolas Augustin /Metoyer/, free *mulâtre*, and Marie Agnes, free *mulâtresse*. Grandparents: Marie Therese /ditte Coincoin/ and Francoise. Godparents: Daniel, *mulâtre*, and Marie Modeste.

2898. MARIE SUSANE BOSSIÉ
August 4, 1799, baptism of Marie Susane, born March 8, 1798, legitimate daughter of Soulange Bossié and Heleonore Himle. Grandparents: Francois Bossie and Charlotte Baré; Antoine Himle and Margueritte Cheletre. Godparents: Alexandre Hildever Bossié and Marie Aspasie Bossié.

2899. JEAN BAPTISTE AZENOR RAMBIN
August 6, 1799, baptism of Jean Baptiste Azenor, born October 17, 1798, legitimate son of Michel Rambin and Marie Therese Maiou. Grandparents: Andre Rambin and Francoise Clermon; Ignace Maiou and Therese Felibot. Godparents: Jean Baptiste Larenaudiere and Anastasie Maiou.

2900. FRANCOIS EMERAND DUBOIS
September 2, 1799, baptism of Francois Emerand, born March 24, legitimate son of Antoine Dubois and Marie Joseph Malige, living at Biou au Pierre; infant was born in the post. Grandparents: Jean Baptiste Dubois and Marie Joseph Clermon; Joseph Malige and Marie Antoine Lebrun. Godparents: Francois Dubois and Marie Anne Malige, uncle and aunt of infant.

2901. JOSEPH ANDRÉ VASCOCU
September 29, 1799, baptism of Joseph André, born August 28, legitimate son of André Vascocu and Marie Magdeleine Remond. Grandparents: Antoine Vascocu and Marie Barbe Toups; Pierre Remond and Marie /no last name/. Godparents: Joseph Jean Ris and Marie Modeste Vascocu.

2902. MARIE AMELIE LACOUR
September 29, 1799, baptism of Marie Amelie, born December 1, 1798, legitimate daughter of Gaspar Lacour and Marie Felicité Brevel. Grandparents: Pierre Lacour and Marie Louise Verger; Jean Baptiste Brevel and Francoise Poissot. Godparents: Nicolas Lauve and Marie Victoire Brevel.

2903. JACQUES
October 17, 1799, baptism of Jacques, aged two years, at the Apalaches village, son of Joseph and Marie Louise. Grandparents: (maternal) Thomas and Catherinne. Godparents: Etienne, chief of the Apalache, and Roi Cheletre.

2904. ETIENNE
October 17, 1799, baptism of Etienne, aged seven years, at the Apalaches village, son of Joseph and Marguerite, both

Indians. Godparents: Ouin and Etienne, both Indians.

2905. JEAN BAPTISTE
October 17, 1799, baptism of Jean Baptiste, aged two years, at the Apalaches village, child of Joseph and Marguerite, both Indians. Godparents: Jean Baptiste Dubois and Marie Anne Gracien Couiaque.

2906. JEAN BAPTISTE
October 17, 1799, baptism of Jean Baptiste, aged five months, at the Apalaches village, child of Chrisostome and Marguerite, both Indians. Godparents: Jean Baptiste Porrié and Anastasie, living in the Apalaches village.

2907. ANTOINE
October 17, 1799, baptism at the Apalaches village, of Antoine, aged three years, child of Henriette and a father unknown. Godparents: Jean Baptiste Porrié and Catherinne, Indian.

2908. MARIE LOUISE
October 17, 1799, baptism at the Apalaches village, of Marie Louise, aged two months, daughter of Antoine, a native of the Apalaches, and Marie Anne. Godparents: Jean Baptiste Duboi and Marie Louise, Indian.

2909. MARIE LOUISE
October 17, 1799, baptism at the Apalaches village, of Marie Louise, aged four years, daughter of Joseph and Margueritte of the Apalaches nation. Godparents: Antoine Tinsa and Marie Louise Courtin.

2910. SUSANNE
October 19, 1799, baptism at the Apalaches village, of Susanne, aged two years, daughter of Michel and Claris. Godparents: Jean Baptiste Valleri and Anne Barbe Duboi.

2911. MARIE JOSEPH
October 17, 1799, baptism at the Apalaches village, of Marie Joseph, about one year old, daughter of Saccalé and Victoire. Godparents: Jean Baptiste Valleri and Marie Joseph.

2912. VALENTIN DUBOIS
October 17, 1799, baptism at the Apalaches village, of Valentin, a native of Couteil /Cotile/, legitimate son of Jean Baptiste Duboi and Rose Cheletre. Grandparents: Jean Baptiste Dubois and Marie Joseph Clermon; Michel Cheletre and Anne Barbe Pommie. Godparents: Valentin Adelet and Marie Pierre Cheletre.

2913. MARIE ROSE DUBOIS
October 17, 1799, baptism at the Apalaches village of Marie Rose, aged two years, native of Couteille /Cotile7, legitimate daughter of Jean Baptiste Dubois and Rose Cheletre. Grandparents: Jean Baptiste Dubois and Marie Joseph Clermon; Michel Cheletre and Anne Barbe Pommie. Godparents: Jean Baptiste Porrié and Marie Batilde Dubois.

2914. JOSEPH
October 17, 1799, baptism of Joseph, aged seven years, at the Apalaches village, son of Touaa and Francoise, both Indians. Godparents: Joseph Morin and Genevieve Gracien.

2915. LOUIS
October 17, 1799, baptism of Louis, aged 5 years, at the Apalaches village, son of Touaa and Francoise, both Indians. Godparents: Nicolas and Marie Joseph.

2916. FRANCOISE
October 17, 1799, baptism at the Apalaches village of Francoise, aged 3 years, daughter of Touaa and Francoise, both Indians. Godparents: Nicolas and Francoise.

2917. CATHERINNE
October 17, 1799, baptism at the Apalaches village of Catherinne, aged four years, daughter of Touaa and Francoise, both Indians. Godparents: Etienne, chief of the Apalaches, and Catherinne, Indian.

2918. ANNE
October 17, 1799, baptism at the Apalaches village of Anne, daughter of Touaa and Francoise. Godparents: Jean Baptiste Poirié and Anne Poirié.

2919. PIERRE VALLERI
October 17, 1799, baptism of Pierre Valleri at the Apalaches village, aged twenty five, son of Carode and Marianne. Godparents: Valleri and Marie Joseph.

2920. FRANCOISE
October 18, 1799, baptism of Francoise, aged six years, at the Apalaches village, daughter of Macti and Anne. Godparents: Ouen and Francoise.

2921. ANASTASIE
October 18, 1799, baptism at the Apalaches village of Anastasie, aged four years, daughter of Macti and Anne. Godparents: Etienne, chief of the Apalaches, and Anastasie.

2922. PIERRE
October 18, 1799, baptism at the Apalaches village of Pierre aged one year, son of Macti and Anne. Godparents: Pierre

Valeri and Marie Louise.

2923. LOUIS RACHAL
October 18, 1799, baptism, at the home of Mr. Monet*, of Louis, about 22 months of age, legitimate son of Antoine Rachal and Marie Louise Lemoine. Grandparents: Louis Rachal and Marie Louise Leroi; Charles Lemoine and Elisabeth Dupre. Godparents: Simeon Rachal and Marie Rachal.

2924. CHARLES LEMOINE
October 18, 1799, baptism, at the home of Mr. Monet*, of Charles, about one year, legitimate son of Antoine Lemoine and Genevieve Bellegarde. Grandparents: Charles Lemoine and Elisabeth Dupre; Jean Baptiste Bellegarde and Magdeleine Monpierre. Godparents: Pierre Massip and Margueritte Massip.

2925. ATHANASE DENIS
October 18, 1799, baptism, at the home of Mr. Monet*, of Athanase, aged three years, legitimate son of Jean Baptiste Denis and Marie Elisabeth Baudouin. Grandparents: Jean Baptiste Denis and Marthe Hubert; Francois Baudouin and Marie Bontems. Godparents: Louis Lambre and Margueritte Denis.

2926. MARIE DENIEGE DENIS
October 18, 1799, baptism, at the home of Mr. Monet*, of Marie Deniege, aged two years, legitimate daughter of Jean Baptiste Denis and Marie Elisabeth Baudouin. Grandparents: Jean Baptiste Denis and Marthe Hubert; Francois Baudouin and Marie Bontems. Godparents: Antoine Rachal and Marie Louise Lemoine.

2927. FRANCOISE RACHAL
October 18, 1799, baptism of Francoise, at the home of Mr. Monet*, aged one year or about, legitimate daughter of Barthelemi Rachal and Francoise Laberi. Grandparents: Louis Rachal and Marie Louise LeRoi; Jean Baptiste Laberi and Jeanne Guedon. Godparents: Louis Totin and Elisabeth Rachal.

2928. MARIE LOUISE OSITE SAINT ANDRE
October 18, 1799, baptism at the home of Mr. Monet*, of Marie Louise Osite, aged 23 months, legitimate daughter of

---

*Louis Monet and the other families who convened at his home during this pastoral visit were residents of the Rivière aux Cannes community. Roughly speaking, this settlement stretched from the juncture of present Cane River with present Red River to the foot of Isle Brevelle, just above Derry, where present Old River branches from the Cane.

André Saint André and Marie Rachal. Godparents: Jacques St. André and Marie Louise Lecomte. Grandparents: Jacques Botien *dit* St. André and Marie Anne Picart; Jacques Rachal and Ursule Christophe.

2929. JEAN BAPTISTE
October 18, 1799, baptism at the home of Mr. Monet*, of Jean Baptiste, aged twenty months, a free *mulâtre*, son of Cecile, a free *mulâtresse*, and a father unknown. Godparents: Antoine and Marie Anne, slave of Mr. Monet.

*See note on preceding page.

2930. MARIE MODESTE BAUDOUIN
October 20, 1799, baptism at home of Widow Lecomte,** of Marie Modeste, aged seven months, legitimate daughter of Pierre Baudouin and Anne Robin. Grandparents: Francois Baudouin and Marie Bontemps; Michel Robin and Marie Louise Boulet. Godparents: /Illegible/ Bergean and Heleine Cloutié.

2931. MARIE URSULLE GALLIEN
October 20, 1799, baptism at home of Widow Lecomte,** of Marie Ursulle, legitimate daughter of Nicolas Gallien and Marie LeCour, aged about 2 years. Grandparents: Noel Gallien and Marie Rachal; Louis Lecour /LeCourt/ and Marguerite Leroi. Godparents: Jean Baptiste Lecour and Margueritte Cloutier. /This entry errs - should be Jeanne/

2932. JEAN BAPTISTE ATHANASE /LECOUR/*
October 20, 1799, baptism at home of Widow Lecomte,** of Jean Baptiste Athanase, aged eight months, son of Ursulle, and a father unknown.* Godparents: Jean Baptiste LeCour and Marie Jeanne Euphrosine Gallien.

*See note accompanying Entry 2255.

2933. JEAN BAPTISTE BAUDOUIN
October 20, 1799, baptism at home of Widow Lecomte,** of Jean Baptiste, aged five months, son of Jean Nicolas Baudouin and Marie Deneige Malbert. Godparents: Jean Baptiste Tessier and Marie Therese Brevel. Grandparents: Francois Baudouin and Marie Bontemps; Jean Malbert and Marie Jeanne Vergé.

2934. MARIE ANGEL BAUDOUIN
October 20, 1799, baptism at home of Widow Lecomte,** of

**Mme. Lecomte, the Baudouins, Cloutiers, Galliens, Lecours, and Delouches lived at the upper end of the Rivière aux Cannes community. See also the note on the preceding page.

Marie Angel, two years old, daughter of Jean Nicolas Baudouin and Marie Deneige Malbert. Grandparents: Francois Baudouin and Marie Bontemp; Jean Malbert and Marie Jeanne Vergé. Godparents: Jean Baptiste Agen and Anne Baudouin.

2935. ANNE DELOUCHE
October 20, 1799, baptism at the home of Widow Lecomte,** of Anne, three year old daughter of Jean Baptiste Delouche and Ursule Boulet. Grandparents: Pierre Delouche and Marie Jeanne Baujouin; Joseph Boulet and Anne Vergé. Godparents: Jean Louis Brosset and Catherine Brosset.

**See note at end of preceding page.

2936. CYPRIEN RACHAL
October 22, 1799, baptism at Isle a Brevel of Cyprien Rachal, twenty months old, legitimate son of Julien Rachal and Marie Louise Brevel. Grandparents: Louis Rachal and Marie /Le/ Roi; Jean Baptiste Brevel and Marie Francoise Poissot. Godparents: Jean Baptiste Leconte and Cyprienne Derbanne.

2937. JOSEPH FRANCOIS MARTINAU
November 12, 1799, baptism of Joseph Francois, born May 20, legitimate son of Joseph Martinau, deceased, and Marie Magdeleine Laberi. Godparents: Francois Chabuche and Elizabeth Rachal. Grandparents: Guillaume Martinau and Jeanne Lemoine, natives of Bordeau in France /maternal grandparents not named/.

2938. MARIE MELANIDE TRICHE
November 22, 1799, baptism of Marie Melanide, born February 2, 1798, legitimate daughter of Henri Triché and Genevieve Jean Ris. Grandparents: Manuel Triche and Marie Louise Grape; Jean Ris and Marie Jeanne Chagnau. Godparents: Joseph Jean Ris and Marie There Triche.

2939. PIERRE LEANDRE GRAPE
November 22, 1799, baptism of Pierre Leandre, born October 12, 1798? legitimate son of Jean Baptiste Grape and Genevieve Sorel. Grandparents: Alexis Grape and Louise Guedon; Pierre Sorel and Rose Bosselie. Godparents: Julien Besson and Pelagie Grape.

2940. MARIE ONESIME GRAPPE
November 22, 1799, baptism of Marie Onesime, born April 13, 1799, legitimate daughter of Jean Baptiste Grape and Genevieve Sorel. Grandparents: Alexis Grape and Louise Guedon; Pierre Sorel and Rose Bosselie. Godparents: Jean Baptiste Davion and Francoise Grape.

2941. JOSEPH HYPOLITE BORDELON
November 22, 1799, baptism of Joseph Hypolite, born December 13, 1798, legitimate son of Hypolite Bordelon and Marie Therese Trichel. Grandparents: Nicolas Bordelon and Adrienne Rondeau; Manuel Trichel and Marie Louise Grape. Godparents: Francois Grape and Adrienne Rondeau, represented by Genevieve Jean Ris.

2942. PIERRE MANUEL LEVASSEUR
December 2, 1799, baptism of Pierre Manuel, born July 1, 1798, legitimate son of Jacques LeVasseur and Marie Therese Grillet. Grandparents: Jacques LeVasseur and Marie Francoise Bourdon; Marin Grillet and Marie Louise Brevel. Godparents: Manuel LeVasseur and Marie Magdeleine Grillet.

2943. MARIE THERESE LEMAITRE
December 6, 1799, baptism of Marie Therese, born November 16, legitimate daughter of Francois Lemaitre *dit* La Lime and Louise (Le Duc *dit*) Villefranche. Grandparents: Francois Lemaitre and Francois Mingui; Jean Baptiste Villefranche and Marie Anne Guedon. Godparents: Joseph Foriente, corporal in the Louisiana Regiment, and Marie Therese Langlois.

2944. ADELAIDE BUART
December 8, 1799, baptism of Adelaide, born July 2, legitimate daughter of Jean Denis Buart and Marie Victoire Poissot. Grandparents: Gabriel Buart and Marie Anne Rousseau; Remi Poissot and Louison Cavé. Godparents: Jean Baptiste Buart and Marie Poissot, uncle and aunt.

2945. JACQUES TIEL /TEAL/
December 15, 1799, baptism of Jacques, born July 28, 1798, legitimate son of Jacques Teal and Marie Rose Seideik. Grandparents: Edouard Teel and Rebecca Dejones; Pierre Clavis Seideik and Ursule Cheletre. Godparents: Philippe Frederik and Marie Barbe Frederik.

2946. JEAN BAPTISTE CASSENAVE
December 15, 1799, baptism of Jean Baptiste, born April 15, legitimate son of Michel Cassenave, native of the town of La Rochelle in France, and Marie Jeanne Ris. Grandparents: Bernard Cassenave and Renée Clavau; Jean Ris and Marie Jeanne Chagnau. Godparents: Paul Marcolet and Adelaide Rambin.

2947. MARIE HONORINE PALVADOS
December 17, 1799, baptism of Marie Honorine, born March 21, 1798, legitimate daughter of Jean Palvados, native of the Isle Dieu in France, and of Heleonore Texier. Grandparents: Francois Palvados and Jeanne Bernard; Pierre

Texier and Magdeleine Turpin. Godparents: Antoine Grille and Marie Honorine Totin.

2948. MARIE MARGUERITE ZELINE CLOUTIÉ
December 26, 1799, baptism of Marie Marguerite Zeline, born January 26, legitimate daughter of Jean Pierre Cloutier and Marie Salvan. Grandparents: Alexis Cloutier and Marie Rachal; Jean Salvan and Marie Louise Lambre. Godparents: Nicolas Gallien and Margueritte Cloutié, represented by Marie Aspasie Bossié.

2949. MARIE DELISSE HISSOURA
December 31, 1799, baptism of Marie Delisse, born December 4, legitimate daughter of Bernard Hissoura, native of Navarre, and Marguerite Grillé. Grandparents: Jean Hissoura and Bernard Delche; Marin Grillé and Marie Louise Brevel. Godparents: Marie Francois Rouquier, represented by Lenure Fontenau, and Marcelitte Rouquier.

2950. LOUIS FRANCOIS XAVIER BERTRAND
January 4, 1800, baptism of Louis Francois Xavier, born January 2, legitimate son of Louis Bertrand and Elisabeth Davion. Grandparents: Louis Bertrand and Jeanne Dauphiné; Jean Baptiste Davion and Marie Hiacinte Triche. Godparents: Louis Fonteneau and Marie Baiou /Baillio/.

2951. JEAN BAPTISTE VASCOCU
January 26, 1800, baptism of Jean Baptiste, five months old, legitimate son of Louis Vascocu and Magdeleine Perau. Grandparents: Antoine Vascocu and Marie Barbe /Toups/; Francois Perau and Marie Catherine Dupre. Godparents: Antoine Vascocu and Marie Baiou /Baillio/.

2952. JACQUES UUALIS /WALLACE/
February 23, 1800, baptism of Jacques, eight months old, legitimate son of Jacques Uualis and Hiacinthe Gagne. Grandparents: Joseph Uualis and /Illegible/ Bulstrong; Etienne Gagne and Marie Louise Bertrand. Godparents: Dominique Davion and Marie Joseph Gagne.

2953. PIERRE NEUVILLE UUALIS /WALLACE/
February 23, 1800, baptism of Pierre Neuville, eight months old, legitimate son of Jacques Uualis and Hiacinthe Gagne. Grandparents: Joseph Uualis and /Illegible/ Bulstrong; Etienne Gagne and Marie Louise Bertrand. Godparents: Pierre Paul Boete Lafite and Marie Denegie Lafite.

2954. JEAN BAPTISTE FERRIER
March 2, 1800, baptism of Jean Baptiste, born March 16, 1799, legitimate son of Joseph Ferrie, native of Marcel (Marcet?, Maral?) in Provence, and Elisabeth Lebrun.

Grandparents: Jean Baptiste Ferrié and Margueritte Caiote Ducoté; Guillaume Lebrun and Marie Louise Toutin. Godparents: Charles Lemoine, represented by Jean Baptiste Plaisance, and Jeanne Margueritte Totin.

2955. FRANCOIS MERCIER
March 6, 1800, baptism of Francois, born December 11, 1799, legitimate son of Louis Mercié and Marie Louise Lefevre. Grandparents: Joseph Marie Mercié and Catherinne Degagne; Pierre Lefevre and Marie Louise Savarin. Godparents: Francois Roi and Marie Joseph Mercié.

2956. HELEINE LEMOINE
March 16, 1800, baptism of Heleine, born June 29, 1799, legitimate daughter of Charles Lemoine and Jeanne Lebrun. Grandparents: Charles Lemoine and Elisabeth Dupré; Guillaume Lebrun and Marie Louise Totin. Godparents: Jean Baptiste Lemoine and Silvie Brosset.

2957. FRANCOIS MANUEL BOETE LAFITTE
March 28, 1800, baptism of Francois Manuel Boete, about one year old, native of Baiou au Pierre, legitimate son of Paul Boete Lafitte and Marie Anne Desoto, living at Baiou au Pierre. Grandparents: paternal, unknown; maternal: Manel Soto and Marie Denege St. Denis. Godparents: Francois Chabuche and Sophie Holié.

2958. JEAN PIERRE BASIL GUERI (THIERRY)*
April 6, 1800, baptism of Jean Pierre Basil, born February 6, legitimate son of Pierre Gueri* and Marie Rosalie Frederick. Grandparents: Antoine Gueri and Francoise Bequet; Philippe Frederick and Catherinne Sauvage. Godparents: Jean Baptiste Frederik and Marie Pelagie Cheletre.

*The family surname appears as Gueri in the text and as Thierry in the margin.

2959. MARIE MASSIP
April 12, 1800, baptism of Marie, born September 2, legitimate daughter of Juan Massip and Marie Louise LeMoine. Grandparents: Pierre Massip and Jeanne Lafont; Charles Lemoine and Elisabeth Dupre. Godparents: Pierre Massip and Marie Conan.

2960. MARIE EUGENIE LUGUE
April 13, 1800, baptism of Marie Eugenia, about four years old, born at post du Ouachita, living in this post for five months, legitimate daughter of deceased Jean Lugue and deceased Anne Olivier. Grandparents: /Paternal side not given/; Michel Olivié and Anne Robert. Godparents: Michel Ernande and Marie Olivier, aunt of the infant.

2961. MARIE CHELAITRE
April 14, 1800, baptism of Marie, born January 4, 1800, legitimate daughter of Barnabé Chelaitre and Marie Joseph Gonin. Grandparents: Michel Chelaitre and Anne Barbe Pommier; Jean Baptiste Gonin and Manuel Riche. Godparents: Barthelemi Lestage and Marie Francoise Himel.

2962. MARIE FANNI ARMAND
April 28, 1800, baptism of Marie Fanni, born March 17, legitimate daughter of Jean Baptiste Armand and Marie Catherine Frederik. Grandparents: Joseph Marie Armand and Therese Legros; Philippe Frederik and Marie Catherinne Sauvage. Godparents: Joseph Marie Armand and Marie Catherinne Sauvage.

2963. JACQUES POMMIER
FELICITÉ POMMIER
April 27, 1800, baptism of Jacques and Felicité, born April 4, 1799, legitimate, twin infants of Jean Pommié and Marie Dupré. Grandparents: Pierre Pomié, native of the German Coast, and Marie Barbe Mase; Robert Dupré and Marie Cavé. Godparents of the first: Jacques Fort and Marie Jeanne /̲Sorel dit/̲ Marli; godparents of the second: Antoin Himel and Felicité Lavespere. Infants had been *endoyé*.

2964. MARIE OSITE
April 27, 1800, baptism of Marie Osite, born July 30, 1799, *quarteronne* daughter of a free *mulâtresse*, Magdeleine, living at the home of Francois Grape, and a father unknown. Godparents: Jean Baptiste David and Therese Lamalathie.

2965. LOUIS DAMAS BOSSIÉ
May 4, 1800, baptism of Louis Damas, born October 29, 1799, legitimate son of Francois Paul Bossié and Catherinne Pelagie Lambre, living in this post. Godparents: Louis Joseph Lambre and Marie Therese Eugenie Buart. Grandparents: Francois Bossié and Rosalie Barré; Jean Baptiste Lambre and Marie Jeanne Levasseur.

2966. MARIE LOUISE CLAIRE
May 11, 1800, baptism of Marie Louise Claire, born September 22, 1799, *quarteronne* daughter of Felicite, a free *mulâtresse*, and a father unknown. Godparents: Joseph Triche and Euphrasine Rambin.

2967. MARIE THERESE FONTENEAU
May 15, 1800, baptism of Marie Therese, born March 15, 1795, legitimate daughter of Louis Fonteneau and Pelagie Grape. Grandparents: Philippe Fonteneau and Marie Briniac; Alexis Grape and Louise Guedon. Godparents: Philippe Fonteneau and Marie Briniac, grandparents, represented by Louis Fonteneau and Therese Lamalatie.

2968. MARIE SUSANNE DERBANE
June 25, 1800, baptism of Marie Susanne, born October 17, 1799, legitimate daughter of Gaspart Derbanne and Marie Joseph Perau. Grandparents: Gaspart Derbanne and Marie Vergé; Francois Perau and Catherinne Dupre. Godparents: Jean Baptiste Davion and Adelaide Verché.

2969. BERTRAND ISAAC PLAISANCE
July 6, 1800, baptism of Bertrand Isaac, born June 22, legitimate son of Bertrand Plaisance and Marie Barbe Grillé. Grandparents: Jean Baptiste Plaisance and Margueritte Toutin; Marin Grillé and Marie Louise Brevel. Godparents: Nicolas Henri Lauve and Sophie Holie.

2970. CHRISTOPHE TEEL
August 12, 1800, baptism of Christophe, born December 4, 1798, legitimate son of Christofe Teel, native of the Carolinas in America, living at this post for several years, and Marie Louise Seideik. Grandparents: Edouard Teel and Rebecca Jones, natives of the Carolinas; and Pierre Clavis Seidek and Ursule Cheletre. Godparents: Edouard Morphie, represented by Bernabé Cheletre, and Elisabeth Buard.

2971. JEAN BAPTISTE TEEL
August 12, 1800, baptism of Jean Baptiste, born March 20, legitimate son of Christofe Teel, native of the Carolinas in America, living at this post for several years, and Marie Louise Seideik. Grandparents: Edouard Teel and Rebecca Jones, natives of the Carolinas; and Pierre Clavis Seidek and Ursule Cheletre. Godparents: Bernabé Cheletre and Agathe Maës.

2972. MARIE ADELAIDE RACHAL
August 24, 1800, baptism of Marie Adelaide, born July 2, legitimate daughter of Louis Rachal and Marie Joseph Laberi. Grandparents: Louis Rachal and Marie Louise Leroi; Jean Baptiste Laberi and Marie Jeanne Guedon. Godparents: Francois Rouquié and Thereze Lamalathie.

2973. MARIE THERESE BODIN
August 25, 1800, baptism of Marie Therese, born March 11, legitimate daughter of Jean Laurent Bodin and Marie Modeste, an Indian of the Canneci nation. Grandparents: Laurent Bodin and Marie Michele Rosalie Croux; Marie Magdeleine, Indian of the Canneci nation. Godparents: Jacques Lecour and Marie Therese Langlois.

2974. REMI POISSOT
September 11, 1800, baptism of Remi, about one year old, legitimate son of Paul Poissot and Marie Louise Anti.

Grandparents: Remi Poissot and Marie Louise Cavé; Jean Baptiste Anti and Catherine Gallien. Godparents: Jean Baptiste Anti, grandfather, represented by Valeri Anti, and Marie Louise Cavé, grandmother.

2975. LOUIS GEROME RACHAL
September 21, 1800, baptism of Louis Gerome, about five months old, *endoyé*, legitimate son of Dominique Rachal and Rosalie Vercher. Grandparents: Barthelemi Rachal and Francoise Lamalati; Louis Vercher and Marie Louise Grillé. Godparents: Pierre Vercher, uncle of infant, and Francoise Rachal.

2976. MARIE MAGDELEINE BOUET LAFITE
September 25, 1800, baptism of Marie Magdeleine at Baiou au Pierre, with consent of Reverend Father Moreno, *curé* of Nacogdoche; infant born November 17, 1799?, legitimate daughter of Louis Pierre Paul Lafitte and /illegible/ Gagne, living at Baio au Pierre in the parish of Nacogdoche Grandparents: Paul Bouet Lafitte and Magdeleine Grape; Etienne Gagne and Louise Bertrand. Godparents: Paul Bouet Lafite and Marie Joseph Gagné.

2977. MANUEL BOSSIÉ
October 5, 1800, baptism of Manuel, about three months of age, legitimate son of Soulange Bossié and Heleonor Himlle. Grandparents: Francois Bossié and Charlotte Barré; Antoine Himlle and Marguerite Cheletre. Godparents: Manuel Grenau and Victoire Bossié, represented by Joseph Lambre and Ulalie Bossié.

2978. MARIE EUPHROSINE DUBOIS
October 12, 1800, baptism of Marie Euphrosine, about one year old, legitimate daughter of Francois Dubois and Heleonor Jean Ris. Grandparents: Jean Baptiste Dubois and Marie Joseph Clermont; Jean Ris and Marie Jeanne Chagneau. Godparents: Henri Triche and Marie Euphrosine Rambin.

2979. MARIE MODESTE PERAU
November 2, 1800, baptism of Marie Modeste, born January 15, 1799, legitimate daughter of Jean Chrisostome Perau and Margueritte Salvant. Grandparents: Francois Perau and Catherinne Dupre; Jean Salvant and Margueritte Louise Lambre. Godparents: Jean Fonteneau and Modeste Fonteneau.

2980. ABRAHAM EDOUARD VILERET
November 5, 1800, baptism of Abraham Edouard, born May 18, 1799, at the post of Baton Rouge, legitimate son of Abraham Vileret, native of America, and Tebité Russ, native of America, living for five months in this post. Grandparents: Louis Vilerel and Catherinne Anglois; Isecaie

Russ and Rebecca Elbé. Godparents: Edouard Morphil and Elisabeth Buart.

2981. JOSEPH JEROME TOMACINE
November 9, 1800, baptism of Joseph Jerome, born September 13, legitimate son of Louis Tomacine, native of Barcelona, and of Catherinne Latié, a native of this parish. Grandparents: Louis Tomcine and Therese Soulé; Joseph Latié and Anne Vergé. Godparents: Joseph Cantalogue and Therese Tomacine.

2982. JEAN FRANCOIS ANTOINE GONSALES
November 9, 1800, baptism of Jean Francois Antoine, born October 28, legitimate son of Francois Gonsale, native of Mexico, and Marie Apolonie Deragon, native of the Adaies, living now in this post. Grandparents: Joseph Antoin Gonsales and Marie Chandelarie; Simon Deragon and Marie Anne Morille. Godparents: Francois Levasseur and Marie Jeanne Grillé.

2983. ANTOINE CHRISTIAN HESSER
December 8, 1800, baptism of Antoine Christian Hesser, born September 27, legitimate son of Christian Hesser and Marie Francoise Adelaide Rambin. Godparents: Andres Antoine Rambin and Elisabeth Buart. Grandparents: Frederick Hesser and Catherine Bull, native of Philadelphia; Andre Antoine Rambin and Marie Catherinne Buart.

2984. AUGUSTIN /METOYER/
December 25, 1800, baptism of Augustin, born April 6, a free *mulâtre*, legitimate son of Nicolas Augustin, free *mulâtre*, and Marie Agnes /Poissot/, free *mulâtresse*.. Grandparents: Marie Therese /dit Coincoin/, free *négresse*, and Francoise, free *mulâtresse*. Godparents: Antoine Joseph /Metoyer/, *mulâtre*, and Marie Ursule.

2985. MARIE AUREILE
December 25, 1800, baptism of Marie Aureile, aged two years, *mulatresse* daughter of Marie Elisabeth, a free *mulâtresse*. Grandparents: Marie Anne, a free *mulâtresse*. Godparents: Pierre /Metoyer/, free *mulâtre*, and Marie Ursulle.

2986. MARIE ADELIA GALLIEN
November 24, 1800, baptism of Marie Adelia, born December 8, 1799, legitimate daughter of Nicolas Gallien and Marie LeCour. Grandparents: Noël Gallien and Marie Rachal; Louis LeCour and Jeanne Leroi. Godparents: Jean Baptiste LeCompte, representing Jean Baptiste Prudhomme, and Marie Rouquié.

2987. PIERRE RACHAL
       November 30, 1800, baptism of Pierre, born August 4, legitimate son of Julien Rachal and Marie Louise Brevel. Grandparents: Louis Rachal and Marie Louise Leroi; Jean Baptiste Brevel and Marie Francoise Poissot. Godparents: Pierre LaCour and Marie Therese Brevel.

2988. MARIE DE NEIGES DERBANE
       December 7, 1800, baptism of Marie de Neiges, born April 19, legitimate daughter of Jean Baptsite Derbane and Henriette Brevel. Grandparents: Gaspart Derbanne and Marie Vergé; Jean Baptiste Brevel and Marie Francoise Poissot. Godparents: Baltasar Brevel and Marie Francoise Brevel.

2989. MARIE AIMÉE PERAU
       December 7, 1800, baptism of Marie Aimée, born September 19, legitimate daughter of Francois Perau and Marie Louise Agathe Laberi. Grandparents: Francois Barthelemi Perau and Catherinne Dupre; Jean Baptiste Laberi and Jeanne Guedon. Godparents: Remi Lambre and Marie Aimee Rouquié.

2990. LAURENT MAIOU
       December 8, 1800, baptism of Laurent, born October 5, 1800, legitimate son of Laurent Maiou and Margueritte Duval. Grandparents: Ignace Maiou and Therese Filibot, living in this post; Francois Duval and Therese Blanpan, habitants of the post of Ouachita. Godparents: Ignace Maiou and Marie Louise Maiou, uncle and aunt of the infant.

2991. ANDRE RAMBIN
       January 18, 1801, baptism of Andre, born December 12, 1800, legitimate son of Michel Rambin and Therese Maiou. Grandparents: Andre Rambin and Francoise Clermont; Ignace Maiou and Therese Flibot. Godparents: Andre Rambin and Marie Catherinne Perau.

2992. JEAN BAPTISTE /METOYER/
       February 9, 1801, baptism of Jean Baptiste, born October 10, 1800, legitimate son of Louis /Metoyer/, a free *mulâtre*, and Therese /Lecompte/, who have presented the infant to be baptized on the day of their marriage. Grandparents: Marie Therese /dit Coincoin/, free *négresse*, and Therese, an Indian of the Canneci nation; "grandfathers unknown." Godparents: Dominique /Metoyer/, free *mulâtre*, and Margueritte /Lecompte/, free *mulâtresse*.

2993. JOSEPH /METOYER/
       February 9, 1801, baptism of Joseph, born July 22, 1799, legitimate son of Dominique /Metoyer/, free *mulâtre*, and Margueritte /Lecompte/, free *mulâtresse*. Grandparents: Marie Therese /dit Coincoin/, free *négresse*, and Marie,

négresse slave of Madame Widow Lecompte; "grandfathers unknown." Godparents: Jacques, natural son of an Indian of the Canneci nation, and Marie Susanne /Metoyer/, *mulâtresse* slave of Mr. Metoyer.

2994. MARIE OLIVE RACHAL
February 10, 1801, baptism of Marie Olive, born December 20, 1800, legitimate daughter of Barthelemi Rachal and Marie Magdeleine Grillé. Grandparents: Barthelemi Rachal and Marie Lamalati; Marin Grillé and Louise Brevel. Godparents: Antoin Grillé and Margueritte Grillé.

2995. MANUEL RACHAL
March 8, 1801, baptism of Manuel, born December 24, 1799, legitimate son of Antoine Rachal and Marie Louise Lemoine. Grandparents: Louis Rachal and Marie Louise Leroi; Charles Lemoine and Elisabeth Dupre. Godparents: Louis Rachal and Marie Laberi.

2996. MARIE CAROLINE LEMOINE
March 8, 1801, baptism of Marie Caroline, born July 2, 1800, legitimate daughter of Jean Baptiste Lemoine and Felicité Lacase. Grandparents: Charles Lemoine and Elisabeth Dupre; Charles Lacase and Felicité Langlois. Godparents: Antoine Rachal and Marie Louise Lemoine.

2997. ANTOINE FRAIDIEU
March 9, 1801, baptism of Antoine, born December 19, 1799, legitimate son of Augustin Fraidieu and Marie Jeanne Sorel. Grandparents: Pierre Saurel and Marie Rose Boisselie; /paternal grandparents not named/. Godparents: Denis Buart and Marie Francoise Malbert.

2998. MARIE ROSALIE
April 12, 1801, baptism of Marie Rosalie, aged three years, a small Indian girl of the Cadots, living at the home of Mr. Poissot, father and mother unknown. Godparents: Jean Francois, free *mulâtre*, and Marie Jeanne, slave of Mr. Badin.

2999. JOSEPH LATIE
April 19, 1801, baptism of Joseph, born August 5, 1800, legitimate son of Jean Baptiste Latie and Marie Pelagie Frederik. Godparents: Pierre LaCour and Marie Therese Brevel.

3000. MARIE ADELAIDE DAVION
May 5, 1801, baptism of Marie Adelaide, born May 9, 1800, legitimate daughter of Dominique Davion and Pelagie Gagné. Grandparents: Jean Baptiste Davion and Marie Hiacinthe Triche; Etienne Gagné and Marie Louise Bertrand. Godparents: Francois Davion and Rose Gagné.

3001. FRANCOIS ISAAC RACHAL
May 10, 1801, baptism of Francois Isaac, born June 25, 1800, legitimate son of Jean Baptiste Rachal and Marie Pelagie Brevel. Grandparents: Barthelemi Rachal and Marie Lamalathie; Jean Baptiste Brevel and Marie Francoise Poissot. Godparents: Jean Baptiste Brevel and Marie Victoire Brevel.

3002. PELAGIE POISSOT
May 31, 1801, baptism of Pelagie, about 18 months, born in this post, legitimate daughter of Antoine Poissot and Marie Silvie Gautier /Goutierrez/. Grandparents: Remi Poissot and Marie Louise Cavé; Michel Goutier /Goutierrez/ and Marie Duplessis. Godparents: Pierre Triche and Victoire Constance Lemaitre.

3003. MARIE DENEIGE MANUEL GONIN
June 7, 1801, baptism of Marie Deneige Manuel, born May 6, legitimate daughter of Francois Gonin and Marie Barbe Frederik. Grandparents: Jean Baptiste Gonin and Manuel Riché; Philippe Frederik and Barbe Cheletre. Godparents: Philippe Frederik and Genevieve Gonin.

3004. MARIE EUPHROSINE LANGLOIS
June 26, 1801, baptism of Marie Euphrosine, born June 8 and *endoié*, legitimate daughter of Marie Langlois and a father unknown. Grandparents: Francois Langlois and Marie Gregoire De La Croix. Godparents: Francois Robin and Margueritte Duval, wife of Laurent Maiou.

3005. ANDRÉ PAUL COUTI
July 4, 1801, baptism of André Paul, born November 2, 1800, legitimate son of Paul Couti and Marie Joseph Corretant /Torres/. Grandparents: Paul Couti and Marie Michel Olivier; Joseph Correntant /Torres/ and Marie Jeanne Deroi /de los Reyes/. Godparents: André Chamart and Marie Catherine Bardon.

3006. PIERRE BERNARD GUISARNAT
July 25, 1801, baptism of Pierre Bernard, born May 13, legitimate son of Bernard Guisarnat and Marie Louise Larenaudiere. Grandparents: Jean Guisarnat and Catherinne Borde; Pierre Larenaudiere and Jeanne Laberi. Godparents: Pierre Larenaudiere and Jeanne Laberi.

3007. MARIE ASPASIE LARENAUDIERE
July 25, 1801, baptism of Marie Aspasie, born November 1, 1800, legitimate daughter of Pierre Larenaudiere and Jeanne Laberi. Grandparents: Charles Larenaudiere and Jeanne Lariviere; Jean Baptiste Laberi and Jeanne Guedon. Godparents: Bernard Guisarnat and Marie Rosalie Larenaudiere.

3008. FRANCOIS CELESTIN RACHAL
August 2, 1801, baptism of Francois Celestin, born October 1, 1800, legitimate son of Barthelemi Rachal and Francoise Laberi. Grandparents: Louis Rachal and Marie Louise Deroi /Le Roy/; Jean Baptiste Laberi and Jeanne Guedon. Godparents: Francois Chabuche and Marie Rouquié.

3009. MARIE JOSEPH THERESE GONSALES
August 9, 1801, baptism of Marie Joseph Therese, born July 11, legitimate daughter of Pierre Gonsales and Catherinne Bonnet. Grandparents: Bernard Gonsales and Catherinne Lamoure; Jean Bonnet and Antoinette Remande Gassile.* Godparents: Jean Bonnet and Marie Joseph Gonin.   */Garcia/

3010. PIERRE LACOUR
August 10, 1801, baptism of Pierre, born December 4, 1800, legitimate son of Gaspait Lacour and Marie Felicité Brevel. Grandparents: Pierre Lacour and Marie Louise Vergé; Jean Baptiste Brevel and Marie Francoise Poissot. Godparents: Pierre Lacour and Marie Therese Brevel.

3011. MARIE MONET /DE SOTO/ *
August 23, 1801, baptism of Marie Monet, born October 28, 1800, at Baiou au Pierre; consent for baptism given by Father Caitan, *curé* of Nacoddoche. Infant is the legitimate daughter of Mr. Marcel Soto and Marie Baiou /Baillio/, living at Baiou au Pierre. Grandparents: Manuel /Soto/* and Marie St. Denis; Pierre Baiou /Baillio/ and Catherinne Poissot. Godparents: Francois Perau and Marie Monet Delacise.

*As in Register 4 (see note accompanying Entry 2283) the surname "de Soto" has been erased from those entries which deal with this family.

3012. LOUIS EUGENE TAUSIN
August 23, 1801, baptism of Louis Eugene, born July 13, legitimate son of Joseph Tausin and Marie Chamart. Grandparents: Girard Tausin and Jeanne Bartheau; Louis Chamart and Catherinne Bardon. Godparents: Louis Joseph Tausin and Adelaide Tausin, brother and sister of the infant.

3013. MARIE FELICITE GUILLORI
August 23, 1801, baptism of Marie Felicite, born February 11, legitimate daughter of Louis Guillori, Indian of the Opelousas nation, and Marie Rosalie, Indian of the Caneci nation. Grandparents: unknown. Godparents: Barthelemi Lecour and Marie Jeanne Euphrosine Gallien.

3014. ANNE CASSENAVE
August 25, 1801, baptism of Anne, born June 16, legitimate daughter of Michel Denis Cassenave and Marie Ris. Grand-

parents: Bernard Cassenave and Felicité Deforge; Jean Ris and Marie Jeanne Chagneau. Godparents: Jean Baptiste David and Anne Gagne.

3015. MARIE ANNE BUART
August 30, 1801, baptism of Marie Anne, born May 24, 1801, legitimate daughter of Jean Baptiste Buart and Marie Poissot. Grandparents: Jean Baptiste Gabriel Buart and Marie Anne Rousseau; Remi Poissot and Louise Cavé. Godparents: Francois Rouquier and Marie Anne Buart.

3016. FRANCOIS VASCOCU
August 30, 1801, baptism of Francois, born July 4, 1801, legitimate child of Louis Vascocu and Magdeleine Perot. Grandparents: Antoine Vascocu and Marie Barbe Toups; Francois Perot and Catherinne Dupré. Godparents: Francois Perot /Jr./ and Ulalie Vascocu.

3017. MARIE HELEINE LAVESPERE
August 30, 1801, baptism of Marie Heleine, born June 1, legitimate daughter of Francois Lavespere and Marie Louise Derbanne. Grandparents: Jean Lavespere and Magdeleine Angerau; Pierre Derbanne and Marie Le Clerc. Godparents: Pierre Derbanne and Heleine Brevel.

3018. JEAN JACQUES PRUDHOMME
September 5, 1801, baptism of Jean Jacques, born July 9, legitimate son of Antoine Prudhomme and Marie Lambre. Grandparents: Jean Baptiste Prudhomme and Henriette Colantin; Jacques Lambre and Marie Poissot. Godparents: Remi Lambre and Marie Louise Prudhomme.

3019. SUSANNE PRUDHOMME
September 5, 1801, baptism of Susanne, born May 11, 1799, legitimate daughter of Antoine Prudhomme and Marie Lambre. Grandparents: Jean Baptiste Prudhomme and Henriette Colantin; Jacques Lambre and Marie Poissot. Godparents: Pierre Dupain, represented by Francois Rouquié, and Catherinne Lambre.

3020. MARIE LAMBRE
September 5, 1801, baptism of Marie, born April 22, 1801, legitimate daughter of Remis Lambre and Suanne Prudhomme. Grandparents: Jacques Lambre and Marie Anne Poissot; Jean Baptiste Prudhomme and Henriette Colantin. Godparents: Antoine Prudhomme and Sophie Hautié.

3021. MARIE FRANCOISE EUGENIE MORPHY
September 7, 1801, baptism of Marie Francoise Eugenie, born July 6, legitimate daughter of Edouard Morphy and Marie Elisabeth Joseph Buart. Grandparents: Bernabig Morphi and

Eugenie Fleming; Gabriel Buart and Marie Anne Rousseau.
Godparents: Jean Baptiste Buart and Marie Francoise
Buart.

3022. FRANCOISE ELISABETH MIGLAANE /MCCLAIN/
September 12, 1801, baptism of Francoise Elisabeth, born
March 22, legitimate daughter of Jacques Miglaane and
Marthe Tampson. Grandparents: Maurice Miglaane and
Rebecca Cotes; Charles Tompson and Parthe Roche. Godparents: Pierre Joseph Mais and Marie Louise Euphrosine
Rambin.

3023. MARIN GRILLÉ
November 14, 1796, burial of Marin Grillé who accidentally
drowned the day before at the age of 67 years, husband of
Marie Jeanne Brevel. Last rites not administered.

3024. MANUEL LAFITE
November 22, 1796, burial of Manuel who died the day before
at the age of 5 months, son of Paul Bouet Lafite and Marie
Anne Sautau /de Soto/.

3025. DOMINIQUE /METOYER/
November 22, 1796, burial of Dominique, born October 5,
endoié at his home before his death, son of Dominique /Metoyer/, free *mulâtre*, and Margueritte /LeComte/, free *mulâtresse*.

3026. PIERRE DERBANNE
November 22, 1796, burial of Pierre Derbanne who died the
day before at the age of 65 years, after receiving the
last rites of the church, spouse of Marie Claire /LeClerc/.

3027. FRANCOIS RODRIGUES
November 22, 1796, burial of Francois Rodrigues, soldier
of the Louisiana Regiment, company of Mr. Favrot, aged
thirty years, legitimate son of André Rodrigues and Marie
Marinero (Marmero?), native of la Corogne. Rodrigues had
accidentally drowned, dying without the last rites.

3028. ROUQUIER
January 1, 1797, burial of an infant son of Francois Rouquier and Marie Buart /sic/, eight days old, *endoié*.

3029. DEBLAN
January 6, 1797, burial of an infant of Joseph Charles
Deblanc and Magdelaine LaCour, who died the day before at
the age of eight days, *endoié*.

3030. REMI POISSOT
January 6, 1797, burial of Remi Poissot, who died the day

before after receiving the last rites, husband of Louise Cavé.

3031. NICOLAS NAIONS /LAIGNON/
February 20, 1797, burial of Nicolas Naions, husband of Marie Guedon, who died the day before, at the age of 75, after receiving the last rites.

3032. MARIE ANNE DARTIGAU
February 27, 1797, burial of Marie Anne, aged thirty-five years, wife of Pierre Joseph Maes, who died suddenly.

3033. VISENTE FONCECA
April 30, 1797, burial of Visente Fonceca, aged 42 years, soldier of Louisiana Regiment and a native of Guadalaxara /Guadalajara/ in New Spain, who died the day before after receiving the last rites.

3034. ETIENNE GAGNÉ
April 30, 1797, burial of Etienne Gagné, aged 75 years, husband of Marie Louise Bertran, who died the day before after receiving the last rites.

3035. MARIE VICTOIRE DERBANE
June 10, 1797, burial of Marie Victoire Derbane, aged 35, wife of Pierre Chalais; no last rites were administered since Mme. Chalais was "hardly sick" and the priest was called too late. Death occurred on June 9.

3036. DENISE POMIER
July 19, 1797, burial of Denise, who died the day before at the age of 7 months, daughter of Jean Pommier and Marie Robert Dupre.

3037. DENOIÉ
August 10, 1797, burial of _____ Denoié, who drowned at the age of 38 years, a native of Pointe Blanche district in the government of Montreal, Canada. Baptismal name of the deceased was not known by the priest.

3038. JOSEPH NASSARIO
August 21, 1797, burial of Joseph Nassario, who died the day before after receiving the last rites. Deceased was said to be "from the *provinces internes*" but it was not known the exact place.

3039. LOUIS FOUENTE
September 10, 1797, burial of Louis Fouente, aged thirty years, a native of Grenada, who died at the home of Athanas Poissot after receiving the last rites.

3040. MARIE ROSE LAMBRE
November 10, 1797, burial of Marie Rose who died the day before at the age of 39, after receiving the last rites. Deceased was wife of Louis Buart.

3041. HENRI MOUNOIR
December 29, 1797, burial of Henri Mounoir, son of Michel Mounoir and Jeanne Lucas, "a book-binder of Bretagne;" Mounoir died the day before at the age of 32, after receiving the last rites.

3042. GUILLAUME LESTAGE
December 29, 1797, baptism of Guillaume Lestage, who died the day before, at the age of 65 years, after receiving the last rites. Husband of Manuelle Riche.

3043. PIERRE GAGNE
April 2, 1798, burial of Pierre Gagne, who died the day before, at the age of about sixty years, husband of Marie Louise Davion. Received the last rites before his death.

3044. LOUIS PLAISANCE
July 14, 1798, burial of Louis, aged 16 months, son of Pierre Plaisance and Marie Barbe Grille; infant died the previous day.

3045. FRAIDIEU
July 29, 1798, burial of an infant son of Augustin Fraidieu and Marie Jeanne Sorel, who died on the day of his birth after receiving the last rites.

3046. FRANCOIS MONGINOT
August 20, 1798, burial of Francois Monginot, a native of Lambek, a town in Provence. Deceased was a master surgeon, the son of Sieur Francois Marie Monginot and Marie Agar, and husband of Marie Francoise Buart; he died the day before, without warning, and without the last rites.

3047. MARIE CLAIR [LE CLERC]
August 31, 1798, burial of Marie Clair, aged 60 years or about, wife of deceased Pierre Derbanne. Mme. Derbanne died the day before, after receiving the last rites.

3048. DUBOE
September 5, 1798, burial of an infant son of Francois Duboé and Heleonor Jean Ris. Infant had received the last rites, but had not been taken to church for baptism.

3049. MARIE BLAC SAMUL
September 18, 1798, burial of Marie Blac Samul, aged eight years, native of Lauvanie (Sauvanie?), son of Jean Baptiste

Samul and Jeanne, an Indian of the Canneci nation.

3050. MICHEL JOSEPH ACOSTA
September 28, 1798, burial of Michel Joseph, aged eight months, legitimate son of <u>Maireced?</u> Acosta and Marie Paule Torres.

3051. CHARLES LEMOINE
September 29, 1798, burial of Charles Lemoine, aged 70, a native of Illinois, who died the day before after receiving the last rites. Lemoine was the widower of Elisabeth Dupre, and son of deceased Michel LeMoine; mother's name not known.

3052. JOSEPH DARTIGAU
October 14, 1798, burial of Joseph, aged eight years, son of deceased Pierre Dartigau and Marie Caunan. The child died the day before without the last rites.

3053. NICOLAS SMITH
October 16, 1798, burial of Nicolas Smith, who died the day before, without warning and without the last rites; aged 30 years or about.

3054. LOUIS BERTRAND
November 18, 1798, burial of Louis, aged four years, legitimate son of Louis Bertrand and Elisabeth Simpré /St. Prix/.

3055. PRUDHOMME
November 29, 1798, burial of a son of Manuel Prudhomme and Catherine Lambre, *endoié*.

3056. ST. CIRE
January 29, 1799, burial of a free *mulâtre*, son of Cecile, a free *mulâtresse*, and a father unknown. Child died the day before, at the age of five years; was living at the home of Mr. Metoier.

3057. PIERRE
April 19, 1799, burial of Pierre, a free *nègre*, aged 97 years, a native of Guinée; died without last rites.

3058. JULIE DETUIL
June 5, 1799, burial of Julie, daughter of Jacob Detuile and Marie Richard, died the day before at the age of 16 years.

3059. AUGUSTIN BUART
June 22, 1799, burial of Augustin Buart during Fr. Pavie's journey to "the capitol." Buart died the preceding day, at the age of thirty years, was a native of the Natchitoches

post, died after making a confession, but did not receive the last rites.

3060. MARIE RICHART
July 2, 1799, burial of Marie Richart, widow of Jacob Detuil, who died at the age of 50 years without receiving the last rites. Fr. Pavie was absent at New Orleans.

3061. ANTOINE FREDERIK
July 8, 1799, burial of Antoine, five year old son of Felix Frederik and Barbe Cheletre, who died in the absence of Fr. Pavie.

3062. RACHAL
July 15, 1799, burial, in Father Pavie's absence, of an infant of Jean Baptiste Rachal and Pelagie Brevel. *Endoié*.

3063. SAMUEL BARRE
December 20, 1799, burial of Samuel Barre, a native of Ireland, who died suddenly at the home of Mr. Morphil. The deceased was about thirty years; Morphil did not know the names of his parents.

3064. LOUIS DAVION
December 28, 1799, burial of Louis Davion who died the day before, after receiving the last rites. Deceased was 35 years of age, and the husband of Marie Joseph Gagne.

3065. MARIE DELISSE HISSOURA
December 31, 1799, baptism of Marie Delisse, who had been born on December 4, legitimate daughter of Bernard Hissoura and Marguerite Grillé. Grandparents: Jean Hissoura and Bernard Delche; Marin Grillé and Marie Louise Brevel. Godparents: Marie Francois Rouquier, represented by Lesure Fontenau, and Marcelitte Rouquié.

3066. FRANCES LEMAITRE
February 2, 1800, burial of Frances LeMaitre *dit* La Lime, who died the day before, with last rites, at the age of 72 years. Husband of Louise Villefranche.

3067. FRANCOISE CLERMON
February 28, 1800, burial of Francoise Clermon, who died the day before at the age of 79, widow of deceased André Rambin. Mme. Rambin received the last rites but made no confession.

3068. ETIENNE RACHAL
March 6, 1800, burial of Etienne Rachal who died the day before at the age of 20 years, a native of this post, son of deceased Barthelemi Rachal and Marie Francoise La

Malathi. Rachal died after receiving the last rites, but made no confession.

3069. LOUIS LEQUINTE
May 25, 1800, burial of Louis Lequinte who died the day before after receiving the last rites, although he made no confession. Deceased was twenty-five years old, an Indian of the Canneci nation.

3070. TAUSIN
June 20, 1800, burial of a two-day-old infant of Joseph Tausin and his wife Marie Chamart, *endoié*, died the preceding day.

3071. ANDRE DAVID
July 4, 1800, burial of Andre David, a native of France, widower of Marie Jeanne Lamalatie. David died the day before, aged fifty years; received the last rites but made no confession.

3072. MARIE THERESE LEMAITRE
July 14, 1800, burial of Marie Therese, eight-month-old daughter of deceased Francois LeMaitre *dit* La Lime, and Louise Ville Franche; infant died the preceding day.

3073. MARIE FRANCOISE FORT
August 11, 1800, burial of Marie Francoise, fourteen year old daughter of Jacques Fort and Francoise Malbert, his wife; Marie Francoise died the preceding day after receiving the last rites, but made no confession.

3074. MARIE FRANCOISE POISSOT
September 7, 1800, burial of Marie Francoise Poissot, wife of Jean Baptiste Brevel. Mme. Brevel died the preceding day at the age of 56 years. She made no confession but received the last rites.

3075. JARRI
September 13, 1800, burial of an infant, *endoié*, aged seven days, legitimate son of Pierre Jarri and Cecile Dupré.

3076. MARIE MONIQUE
September 25, 1800, burial of Marie Monique, an Indian of the Canneci nation, who died before at the age of twenty-seven; deceased had been very sick and received the last rites.

3077. JEAN FRANCOIS GONSALE
November 9, 1800, baptism of Jean Francois, born October 28, legitimate son of Francois Gonsale, a native of Mexico, and Marie Apolonie Deragon, native of Adaie. Grandparents:

Antoine Gonsale and Marie Chandelarie; Simon Deragon and Marianne Morille. Godparents: Francois Levasseur and Marie Jeanne Grillet.

3078. MARIE ANNE GUEDON
November 10, 1800, burial of Marie Anne Guedon, a native of this post who died the preceding day at the age of 76 years, widow of Nicolas Noions /Laignon/. Deceased received the last rites, but made no confession.

3079. JACQUES CADET FORT
April 2, 1801, burial of Jacques Cadet Fort, a native of Bordeau, France, aged 35 years, husband of Marie Francoise Malbert, who died the day before after receiving the last rites, but without confession.

3080. ETIENNE VERGÉ
June 11, 1801, burial of Etienne Vergé, who died the preceding day after receiving the last rites, but without making his last confession. Vergé was 56 years of age, a native of this parish, and husband of Marie Francoise Dupre.

3081. PELAGIA
July 19, 1795, baptism of Pelagia, born July 4, *negrita* daughter of Catalina, *negra* slave of Widow Triche, and a father unknown. Godparents: Joseph Triche and Maria Luisa Gagne.

3082. HELENA
July 26, 1795, baptism of Helena, aged 13 months, *mulata* daughter of Maria Luisa, *negra* slave of Francois Grappe, and a father unknown. Godparents: Zozine de Mezieres and Maria David.

3083. JOSEPH
July 26, 1795, baptism of Joseph, aged fifteen months, the *mulato* son of Felicidad, *mulata* slave of Francois Grappe, and a father unknown. Godparents: Luis David and Teresa Triche.

3084. CELESTE
July 26, 1795, baptism of Celeste, born May 8, 1793, *mulata* daughter of Pelagia, *mulata* of the succession of Dto. Manuel Triche, and a father unknown. Godparents: Bautista Grappe and Da. Duforet.

3085. THOMAS
July 26, 1795, baptism of Thomas, aged twenty-five years, an adult *negro* of Congo, belonging to the succession of Dto. Manuel Triche. Godparents: Iago, *mulato*, and Pelagia, *mulata*.

3086. LUIS
August 16, 1795, baptism of Luis, aged eight months, son of Charlotte, slave of Mr. Saint Anne, and a father unknown. Godparents: Auguste Biou /Baillio7 and Reine Pierre Clavis Saidec.

3087. DOMINIQUE
August 16, 1795, baptism of Dominique, aged eleven months, son of Heleine, slave of Mr. Saint Anne. Godparents: Jean Renau and Elizabeth David.

3088. JOSEPH ETIENNE
August 30, 1795, baptism of Joseph Etienne, 15 months old, son of Elisabeth, slave of Mr. Saint Anne. Godparents: Joseph Valery and Euphrasie Rambin.

3089. JEAN BAPTISTE AUGUSTIN /METOYER7
August 30, 1795, baptism of Jean Baptiste Augustin, aged three years, a free *mulâtre*, legitimate son of Nicolas Augustin /Metoyer7, a free *mulâtre*, and Agnes /Poissot7, also free. Godparents: Louis /Metoyer7 and Marie Susanne /Metoyer7.

3090. PIERRE
September 6, 1795, baptism of Pierre, son of Celeste, slave of Mr. Titis Perau. Godparents: Prince and Marguerite.

3091. JOSEPH CESAIRE
September 13, 1795, baptism of Joseph Cesaire, born July 23, son of Stasie, slave of Julien Besson. Godparents: Augustin, *nègre* of Sieur Julien Besson, and Genevieve, slave of Mr. Gaspart.

3092. CILESIE
September 13, 1795, baptism of Cilesie, born June 27, son of Susanne, slave of Sieur Jean Baptiste Buart. Godparents: Jean Baptiste and Margueritte.

3093. HONORE
September 27, 1795, baptism of Honore, born August 10, 1794, son of Marie, slave of Monsieur Le Blan /Deblanc7, commandant of this post. Godparents: Jacques and Marie Jeanne, slaves of the commandant.

3094. JOSEPH PLACIDE
October 18, 1795, baptism of Joseph Placide, born June 8, son of Therese, slave of Jean Baptiste Brevel. Godparents: Gilbert Claudau /Closot_7 and Marie Louise Antoine /de St. Denis7.

3095. FRANCOISE
October 18, 1795, baptism of Francoise, aged four years, a

daughter of Louise, slave of Jean Baptiste Brevel. Godparents: ⟨Illegible⟩ Renau and Marie Silvie Hubardau.

3096. MARIE BARBE ⟨LECOURT⟩*
November 1, 1795, baptism of Marie Barbe, born April 2, 1795, daughter of Marie Ursule, a free *metive*, and a father unknown*. Godparents: Jacques Lecomte and Marie Silvie Hubardeau.

*See note accompanying Entry 2255.

3097. JEAN BAPTISTE
November 22, 1795, baptism of Jean Baptiste, born November 7, son of Marie Anne, slave of Louis Davion. Godparents: Jean Baptiste and Marie Louise, slaves.

3098. CHARLES JACQUES*
December 2, 1795, baptism of Jacques*, born June 9, 1794, son of Susanne, slave of Sieur Louis Rachal. Godparents: Jacques Vercher and Marie Rachal.

*The infant's name appears as Jacques in the text and as Charles in the margin.

3099. TOUSSAINT
December 20, 1795, baptism of Toussaint, born October 12, son of Francoise, slave of Sieur Derbanne. Godparents: Silvestre, slave of said Derbanne, and Angelique, slave of Sr. Ramis.

3100. FRANCOISE ROSALIE*
December 20, 1795, baptism of Rosalie*, born August 3, the daughter of Marie Jeanne, slave of Sieur Derbanne. Godparents: Etienne, slave of Sr. Derbanne, and Marie Louise, slave of Sieur Badin.

*The infant's name appears as Rosalie in the text and as Francoise in the margin.

3101. MARIE JUDITH
December 21, 1795, baptism of Marie Judith, born in May, daughter of Angelique, slave of Sieur Mace ⟨Maes⟩. Godparents: Jean Baptiste Thomas Deblan and Celeste Martilde Deblan.

3102. MARIE BARBE
January 1, 1796, baptism of Marie Barbe, aged three months, daughter of Julie, slave of Louis Gabriel Buart. Godparents: Joseph and Genevieve, slaves of Louis Gabriel Buart.

3103. MARIE MARTHE
January 3, 1796, baptism of Marie Marthe, born November 10, 1795, daughter of Marie Jeanne, slave of Monsieur Marcel

/̄de Sot_o_7*. Godparents: Jean Baptiste Dartigau and Marie Marthe Deblanc, spouse of Mr. Dufores.

*See note accompanying Entries 2283 and 3011.

3104. MARIE MARGUERITTE
January 24, 1796, baptism of Marie Margueritte, born January 1, daughter of Marie Louise, slave of Madame St. Denis. Godparents: Guillaume and Marie Heleonore.

3105. FELICITÉ
February 14, 1796, baptism of Felicité, born December 28, 1795, slave of Monsieur Sauterel /̄Grillet_7, daughter of Marie Joseph. Godparents: Jacques Vercher and Magdeleine /̄Grillet *dit*_7 Sauterelle.

3106. JEAN BAPTISTE
February 14, 1796, baptism of Jean Baptiste, aged five months *mulâtre* son of Francoise, slave of Marguerite Dupre. Godparents: Prince and Marie.

3107. JEAN BAPTISTE
March 20, 1796, baptism of Jean Baptiste, born January 15, son of Magdeleine, slave of Pierre Ternié. Godparents: Louis Clausot and Eulalie Vastcocu.

3108. JEAN BAPTISTE
March 26, 1796, baptism of Jean Baptiste, born January 20, slave of Mr. Morphil. Godparents: Pierre and Marie Joseph.

3109. MARGUERITTE
March 26, 1796, baptism of Margueritte, aged three months, daughter of Magdeleine, slave of Mr. Metoyer. Godparents: André and Margueritte.

3110. MICHEL
March 26, 1796, baptism of Michel, born October 4, 1792, son of deceased Rosalie, slave of Mr. Metoyer. Godparents: Nicolas Augustin /̄Metoye_r_7 and Marie Cilesie.

3111. JEAN NOEL
March 26, 1796, baptism of Jean Noel, born October 27, 1795, son of Marie Jeanne, slave of Mr. Metoyer. Godparents: Manuel and Marie Therese.

3112. PAUL
March 27, 1796, baptism of Paul, aged three months, son of Marie Jeanne, slave of Silvestre Bosquié /̄Bossi_é_7. Godparents: Francois Gaunet and Reine Clavis.

3113. MARIE ANGELIQUE
March 27, 1796, baptism of Marie Angelique, born October 30,

1795, daughter of Marie Louise, slave of Mr. Metoyer.
Godparents: Antoine Himel and Marie Marthe Fort.

3114. AGATHE
March 27, 1796, baptism of Agathe, born February 20, 1796, daughter of Felicité, slave of Sieur Antoine Prudhomme. Godparents: Baptiste and Catherinne.

3115. VICTOIRE
March 27, 1796, baptism of Victoire, about eight years old, slave of Mr. Dartigau. Godparents: Joseph and Victoire, slaves.

3116. MARIE VICTOIRE
March 27, 1796, baptism of Marie Victoire, aged one year, daughter of Marie Fani, slave of Mr. Morphil. Godparents: Hidoire Cesair Morphil and Elisabeth Haspasie Morphil.

3117. MARGUERITTE
March 28, 1796, baptism of Margueritte, born January 30, daughter of Elisabeth, slave of Widow Barthelemi /Rachal7. Godparents: Silvestre Poissot and Marie Louise Rachal.

3118. ONSTANCE /Constance7
March 28, 1796, baptism of Onstance, born January 9, daughter of Pelagie, slave of Widow Barthelemi /Rachal7. Godparents: Jean Baptiste Grape and Elisabeth David.

3119. MARIE ROSE
April 10, 1796, baptism of Marie Rose, aged six months, daughter of Marie, slave of Remi Poissot. Godparents: Antoine and Marie, slaves of Pierre Derbane.

3120. JEAN
April 10, 1796, baptism of Jean, aged seven months, son of Marie, slave of Francois Rouquie. Godparents: Augustin, slave of Guillaume Chevert, and Marianne, slave of Manuel Prudhomme.

3121. VALERI
May 15, 1796, baptism of Valeri, born January 23, son of Pelagie, slave of Francois Grape. Godparents: Joseph Triche and Adelaide Rambin.

3122. ATHANASE
May 15, 1796, baptism of Athanase, about twenty years old, slave of Louis Simpri /St. Prix, *dit* of Davion7. Godparents: Louis Levasseur and Victoire Constance LeMaitre.

3123. SILVESTRE
June 25, 1796, baptism of Silvestre, give months old, son

of Marie, slave of Jean Baptiste Grape, living in this post. Godparents: Auguste, slave of Mr. Grape, and Catherinne, slave of Mr. Badin.

3124. MARIE ANNE FANNI
July 5, 1796, baptism of Marie Anne Fanni, born May 12, the legitimate daughter of Marie Anne, slave of Louis Lamalati. Godparents: Fontenel Fonteneau and Marianne Rouquier.

3125. JEAN
August 13, 1796, baptism of Jean, born April 1, son of Marie Lassentian /l'Ascenscion/, slave of Monsieur Monginot. Godparents: Jacques, slave of Sieur Morphi, and Ursule, slave of Sieur Alliot de St. Anne.

3126. MARIE GENEVIEVE ADELAIDE
September 11, 1796, baptism of Marie Genevieve Adelaide, aged three months, *mulâtresse* daughter of Marie, *négresse* slave of Monsieur Deblanc, captain and commandant of the post of Okatapas /Attakapas/. Godparents: André Bernard Chamar and Marie Francoise Adelaide Rambin.

3127. MAGDELEINE
October 9, 1796, baptism of Magdeleine, aged one month, daughter of Marie Francoise, slave of Louis Gabriel Buart, and a father unknown. Godparents: Gaspart and Marie Louise.

3128. CYPRIEN
October 29, 1796, baptism of Cyprien, aged two months, son of Pelargie, *négresse* of Athanase de Meziere, and a father unknown. Godparents: Manuel Triche and Therese Maiou.

3129. FELICITE
October 29, 1796, baptism of Felicite, aged one month, daughter of Helen, slave of Louis Buart. Godparents: Andre, slave of Louis Buart, and Margueritte, slave of Baptiste Buart.

3130. MARIE THERESE
November 15, 1796, baptism of Marie Therese, aged three months and eleven days, *mulâtresse* daughter of Jeanne, a slave of Mr. Benoist /Montenary/, and a father unknown. Godparents: Jean Baptiste, slave of Mr. Lafite, and Therese slave of Mr. Benoist.

3131. MARIE JUDITH
November 6, 1796, baptism of Marie Judith, aged two and a half months, daughter of Marie Anne, slave of Mr. Dartigau, and a father unknown. Godparents: Joseph, slave of Mr. Dartigau, and Marie Louise, slave of Mr. Monginot.

3132. FELICITÉ
November 13, 1796, baptism of Felicité, born September 17, *mulâtresse* daughter of Cecile, a free *mulâtresse*, and a father unknown. Godparents: Joseph /Metoyer/, free *mulatre*, and Marie Susanne /Metoyer/, free *mulatresse*.

3133. MARIE
November 13, 179*3*, baptism of Marie, aged three months, daughter of Catherine, slave of Francois Grape. Godparents: Jean Louis, slave of Beçon /Besson/, and Felicité, slave of Francois Grape. */An apparent error in the record/

3134. LOUIS
November 19, 1796, baptism of Louis, aged seven years, son of Ursule, slave of Manuel Prudhomme and a father unknown. Godparents: Francois, slave of Mr. Prudhomme, and Marie Louise, slave of Mr. Cadet Marion.

3135. HONORE
November 19, 1796, baptism of Honore, one year old, *négrillon* son of Marthe, slave of Manuel Prudhomme. Godparents: Louis Alexandre, slave of Louis Buart, and Marie, slave of Guillaume Ertase.

3136. MARIE
November 19, 1796, baptism of Marie, aged three, *négresse* daughter of Marthe, slave of Manuel Prudhomme, and a father unknown. Godparents: Francois Antoine, free *nègre*, and Marie, slave of Guillaume Ertase.

3137. JEAN LOUIS
December 4, 1796, baptism of Jean Louis, aged nineteen days, *mulâtre* son of Catherinne, slave of Pierre Gagné, and a father unknown. Godparents: Jean Louis and Catherinne, slaves of Mr. Badin.

3138. MARIE
December 11, 1796, baptism of Marie, *négresse* daughter of Marie Joseph, a slave of Antoine Prudhomme, and of a father unknown. Godparents: Francois, slave of Mr. Dolar, and Marie Louise, slave of Manuel Prudhomme.

3139. MARIE ANNE
December 11, 1796, baptism of Marie Anne, *négresse* daughter of Francoise, slave of Antoine Prudhomme, and a father unknown. Godparents: Alexandre, slave of Denis Buart, and Marie Anne, slave of Mr. Badin.

3140. JEAN BAPTISTE FORTUNÉ
February 3, 1796, baptism of Jean Baptiste Fortuné, aged 16 months, a free *mulâtre*, son of Margueritte, *négresse*

slave of Charles Peytavin Duriblon (s/ Charles Peytavin Daublonc) who has declared that he gave liberty to the child. Godparents: Jean Baptiste Peytavin Dubond, represented by Joseph Tausin (s) and Adelaide Tausin (s).

3141. BERNARD
February 5, 1797, baptism of Bernard, aged two months, son of Louison, *négresse* slave of Mr. Pavie, merchant, and of a father unknown. Godparents: Bernard Guicherand and Elisabeth, *mulâtresse* slave of Mr. Trudo, commandant.

3142. ST. CIRE
February 22, 1797, baptism of St. Cire, aged three years, a free *mulâtre*, son of Cecile, a free *griffe*, and a father unknown. Godparents: Louis Monet and Margueritte Lecompte.

3143. JEAN BAPTISTE
February 22, 1797, baptism of Jean Baptiste, aged two years, *mulâtre* son of Dorothée /Monet/, *mulâtres* slave of Mr. Monet, and a father unknown. Godparents: Louis Rachal, represented by Louis Monet, and Margueritte Leroi, Widow Lecompte, represented by Margueritte Lecompte, her daughter.

3144. HENRIETTE /CLOUTIER/*
February 22, 1797, baptism of Henriette, aged two months, *quarteronne* daughter of Dorothée /Monet/, *mulâtresse* slave of Mr. Monet, and a father unknown. Godparents: Louis, a free *mulâtre*, and Marie Louise, a free *mulâtresse*.

*This infant's surname appears in such later records as "Quittance of Heirs of Deceased Pierre Metoyer to Jn. Bte. Louis Metoyer, Administrator," Succession of Pierre Metoyer, No. 193, Office of the Clerk of Court, Natchitoches, under date of April 20, 1837.

3145. NICOLAS
February 22, 1797, baptism of Nicolas, aged seventeen months, a *grif*, son of Francoise, *négresse* slave of Mr. Monet, and a father unknown. Godparents: Charles, *nègre*, slave of Mr. Monet, and Marie Louise, a free *mulâtresse*.

3146. ROMUAL
April 2, 1797, baptism of Romual, aged two months, the *mulâtre* son of Magdeleine, slave of Madame Baptiste Riche, and a father unknown. Godparents: Jean Baptiste Theodore Grillé and Genevieve Bonin /Gonin/.

3147. JULIEN
April 16, 1797, baptism of Julien, aged one month, son of Magdeleine, slave of Mr. Demesiere, and a father unknown. Godparents: Athanase, slave of Louis Simpré /St. Prix, *dit* of Davion/, and Magdeleine, slave of Mr. Grenoble.

3148. JOSEPH
April 16, 1797, baptism of Joseph, nine months old, *nègre* son of Margueritte, slave of Marie Therese /ditte Coincoin/, free *négra*, and a father unknown. Godparents: Augustin, slave of Mr. Antoine Prudhomme, and Marie Anne, slave of Manuel Prudhomme.

3149. JACQUES
April 16, 1797, baptism of Jacques, one year old *nègre* of Mr. St. Anne, son of Susanne, his slave, and a father unknown. Godparents: Nicolas Augustin /Metoyer/, a free *mulâtre*, and Marie Agnes, a free *négresse*.

3150. LOUIS
April 16, 1797, baptism of Louis, aged seven months, *nègre* son of Margueritte, slave of Mr. Morphil, and a father unknown. Godparents: Joseph, slave of Remi Lambre, and Susanne, slave of Mr. Morphil.

3151. MARIE FRANCOISE
April 16, 1797, baptism of Marie Francoise, born April 16, 1796, daughter of Pauline, *négresse* of Mr. Cuparan, and a father unknown. Godparents: Marie Poissot and Francoise Rachal.

3152. THERESE
April 23, 1797, baptism of Therese, aged three months, the *négra* daughter of Susanne, slave of Louis /Rachal dit/ Rat, and a father unknown. Godparents: Alexis, slave of Remi Lambre, and Victoire, slave of Louis Rat.

3153. MARIE LOUISE
April 17, 1797, baptism of Marie Louise, aged three months, *négra* daughter of Francoise, slave of Widow Triche, and a father unknown. Godparents: Francois and Marie, slaves of Widow Triche.

3154. MARIE HELEINE ADELAIDE
April 17, 1797, baptism of Marie Heleine Adelaide, born March 27, 1796?, daughter of Genevieve, slave of Md. Triche. Godparents: Pierre and Agnes, slaves of Mr. Triche.

3155. FANNI
April 20, 1797, baptism of Fanni, aged one year, *négresse* daughter of Marie, slave of Mr. Metoier, and a father unknown. Godparents: Jean Baptiste Buart and Marie Adelaide Rambin.

3156. MARIE MARTH
June 20, 1797, baptism of Marie Marth, born June 14, 1796, *négresse* daughter of Clarisse, slave of Mr. Metoier, and a

father unknown. Godparents: Jean, slave of Mr. Athanase Poissot, and Marie Heleonore, free *négresse*.

3157. MARIE LALIE
June 4, 1797, baptism of Marie Lalie, *mulâtresse* daughter of Marie Francoise, slave of Mr. Buart, and a father unknown. Godparents: Rock, slave of Mr. Bossié, and Marie Heleonore, free *négresse*.

3158. MICHEL
June 4, 1797, baptism of Michel, aged three months, son of Catherinne, slave of Francois Levasseur, and a father unknown. Godparents: Louis, slave of Joseph Lambre and Catherinne, slave of Francois Levasseur.

3159. MARIE BARBE
June 15, 1797, baptism of Marie Barbe, aged one month, *négresse* daughter of Venus, slave of Mr. Marcel /de Soto/* and a father unknown. Godparents: Cassé Cointe, soldier, and Marie Louise, *négresse* slave of Mr. Armant.

*See notes accompanying Entries 2283 and 3011.

3160. MARIE FRANCOISE
June 15, 1797, baptism of Marie Francoise, aged three months, *négresse* daughter of Rosette, slave of Mr. Rouquier, and a father unknown. Godparents: Pierre, *nègre* slave of Jean Pierre Lalande, and Francoise, slave of Mr. Colin.

3161. JACQUES
July 2, 1797, baptism of Jacques, aged one month, *nègre* son of Sophie, slave of Antoine Prudhomme. Godparents: Eugene, slave of Mr. La Renaudiere, and Monique, a free *mulâtresse*.

3162. MARIE FRANCOISE
July 2, 1797, baptism of Marie Francoise, aged two months, *mulâtresse* slave of Antoine Prudhomme, "daughter of Pelagie, daughter of Pelagie," and a father unknown. Godparents: Joseph and Marie Louise, slaves of Mr. Badin.

3163. MARIE ANNE
July 2, 1797, baptism of Marie Anne, aged one month, the *négresse* daughter of Margueritte, slave of Jacob Lamber, and a father unknown. Godparents: Cesair and Marie, slaves of Mr. Poissot.

3164. HENRI EUSEBE
July 23, 1797, baptism of Henri Eusebe, born July 10, *nègre* son of Magdeleine, slave of André Rambin, and a father unknown. Godparents: Louis Tausin and Pamela Bossié.

3165. FANNI
August 13, 1797, baptism of Fanni, born April 22, *négresse* daughter of Fanni, slave of Mr. Morphil, and a father unknown. Godparents: Diego Marie, soldier, and Genevieve, slave of Athanase Poissot.

3166. ANNE
August 20, 1797, baptism of Anne, born June 24, *négresse* daughter of Henriette, slave of Widow Barthelemi Rachal, and a father unknown. Godparents: Joseph, slave of Mr. Gaspar /Derbanne?/, and Margueritte, slave of Mr. Bossié.

3167. MARIE SUSANNE
September 17, 1797, baptism of Marie Susanne, aged 15 months*, *mulâtresse* daughter of Marie Louise, slave of Francois Grappe, and a father unknown. Godparents: Marie Lassis and Francois Dubois.

*Within the margin, in a different handwriting and a more modern ink, appears the notation: "born June 7, 1795."

3168. REMIS
October 15, 1797, baptism of Remis, born February, *quarteron* slave of Sieur Julien Besson, son of the *mulâtresse* Astasie. Godparents: Andre Bernard Chamart and Helene Roubleau.

3169. MARIE JEANNE
November 21, 1797, baptism of Marie Jeanne, born March, *négresse* daughter of Marie, slave of Jacques Fort, and of a father unknown. Godparents: Andres Frederik and Marie Francoise Fort.

3170. JEAN BAPTISTE
December 4, 1797, baptism of Jean Baptiste, aged four months, *nègre* son of Rosalie, slave of Mr. Fontenau, and a father unknown. Godparents: Jean Sever Fontenau and Marie Pompone Dubois.

3171. AUGUSTIN
December ?, 1797, baptism of Augustin, born October 14, *nègre* son of Laurine, slave of Sieur Lavespere. Godparents: Joseph, slave of Mr. Remi Lambre, and Margueritte, slave of Mr. Derbane.

3172. CESIR
January 28, 1798, baptism of Cesir, aged two months, son of Celeste, *négresse* slave of Titi? Perau, and of a father unknown. Godparents: Jean Baptiste, *nègre* slave of Mr. Pantaleon, and Therese, slave of Ailhot St. Anne.

3173. JOSEPH MICHEL
February 3, 1798, baptism of Joseph Michel, aged one year, *nègre* son of Genevieve, slave of Widow Poissot, native of this parish, father unknown. Godparents: Guillaume, slave of Mr. Badin, and Heleonore, free *négresse*.

3174. JACQUES
March 24, 1798, baptism of Jacques, aged two years, *mulâtre* son of Marie Anne, slave of deceased Guillaume Lestage, and a father unknown. Godparents: Francois Gonin and Adelaide Rambin.

3175. FRANCOISE
March 24, 1798, baptism of Francoise, born October 7, 1797, *négresse* daughter of Marie, *négresse* slave of deceased Guillaume Lestage, and a father unknown. Godparents: Baptiste, slave of Louis Gabriel Buart, and Louise, slave of deceased Guillaume Lestage.

3176. GABRIEL
April 6, 1798, baptism of Gabriel, two years old, *nègre* son of Marie Jeanne, slave of Mr. Ambroise Lecomte, and a father unknown. Godparents: Joseph Michel, slave of Remi Lambre, and Genevieve, slave of Mr. Lambre.

3177. LOUIS
April 8, 1798, baptism of Louis, aged <u>sixteen?</u> months, son of Marie Jeanne, slave of Mr. <u>Metoyer?</u>. Godparents: Jean Louis, slave of Julien Besson, and /illegible/.

3178. MARIE CATHERINE
April 22, 1798, baptism of Marie Catherine, *negresse* daughter of Magdeleine, slave of Mr. <u>Ternier?</u>, and a father unknown. Godparents: Guillaume Barberou and Marie Catherine Mar___.

3179. MARIE SUSANNE /ANTY/*
April 29, 1798, baptism of Marie Susanne, born October 30, 1797, *quarterone* daughter of Marie Susanne, *mulâtresse* slave of Mr. Metoier, and a father unknown. Godparents: Louis /Metoyer/ and Agness /Poissot/, free *mulâttos*.

*This infant's surname appears in such later records as: Baptism of Marie Barbe Metoyer, August 28, 1822, Baptismal Register I, St. John the Baptist Catholic Church, Cloutierville, Louisiana.

3180. MARIE JEANNE
April 29, 1798, baptism of Marie Jeanne, born April 17, daughter of Catherinne, a *négresse* slave of Marie Louise, Widow Gagné. Godparents: Francois, slave of M. Baptiste Riche, and Marie, slave of Mr. Badin.

3181. MARCELIN
May 12, 1798, baptism of Marcelin, born March 10, *nègre* son of Catherinne, slave of Monsieur Levaseur, and a father unknown. Godparents: Guillaume, slave of Mr. Badin, and Magdeleine, slave of Mr. Badin.

3182. ONESIME
May 17, 1798, baptism of Onesime, aged five years, *nègre* slave of Charles Peytavin Duriblon, Jr., son of Angelique, a slave of Mr. Duriblon, and of a father unknown. Godparents: Antoine Joseph /Metoyer_7, *mulâtre*, and Margueritte, *négresse*.

3183. CELESTIN
May 28, 1798, baptism of Celestin, born April 1, *nègre* son of Marie, slave of Mr. Metoie, and a father unknown. Godparents: Pierre, slave of Mr. Morphil, and Marie, slave of Widow Cadet Lestage.

3184. MARIE JEANNE
July 1, 1798, baptism of Marie Jeanne, born August, 1797, *négresse* daughter of Isabel, slave of Monsieur Ailhaud St. Anne, and a father unknown. Godparents: Jean Baptiste Etienne Pavie and Marie Therese Victoire Ailhaud St. Anne.

3185. MARGUERITTE
July 8, 1798, baptism of Margueritte, born June 10, *négresse* daughter of Marie Joseph, slave of Widow /Grillet di_t_7 Sauterel, and a father unknown. Godparents: Jacques, slave of Mr. Morphil, and Margueritte, slave of Widow Derbane.

3186. MARIE LOUISE
November 11, 1798, baptism of Marie Louise, born May 15, *négresse* daughter of Marianne, slave of Louis Fontenau, and a father unknown. Godparents: Augustin, slave of Julien Besson, and Marie Joseph, slave of Louis Fontenau.

3187. JOSEPH
December 30, 1798, baptism of Joseph, born October 22, *nègre* son of Margueritte, slave of Mr. Morphil, and a father unknown. Godparents: Joseph, *mulâtre* slave of Mr. Badin, and Marie Heleonore, a free *négresse*.

3188. FRANCOIS BARTHELEMI
December 30, 1798, baptism of Francois Barthelemi, born August 24, *nègre* son of Catherinne, slave of widow Baptiste Triche, and a father unknown. Godparents: Francois, *mulâtre* slave of Mr. Badin, and Heleine, slave of Mr. Badin.

3189. JEANNE
December 30, 1798, baptism of Jeanne, born June 28, a small *négresse*, daughter of Marie Anne, slave of Baptiste Triche

and a father unknown. Godparents: Francois, slave of
Mr. Badin, and Catherinne, slave of Mme. Widow Grape.

3190. MARIE
/Date of baptism, date of birth, name of mother, and name
of owner are illegible./ Godparents: Antoine, slave of
/Illegible/, and Francoise, slave of Mr. Hypolite B ? .

3191. MARIE
April 8, 1798, baptism of Marie, aged three months, a
négresse, daughter of Felicité, slave of Antoine Prudhomme,
and a father unknown. Godparents: Jean, slave of /Illeg-
ible/, and Marie Jeanne, slave of Mr. Poissot.

3192. MARIE MELANIE
April 8, 1798, baptism of Marie Melanie, aged six weeks,
négresse daughter of Marie Louise, slave of Mr. Rambin.
Godparents: Guillaume, slave of Mr. Badin, and Marie
Louise, slave of Mr. Rambin.

3193. CATHERINNE
April 8, 1798, baptism of Catherinne, aged six weeks, the
mulâtresse daughter of Marie Francoise, slave of Mr. Rouquié. Godparents: Barnabé, a free *nègre*, and Marie, a
free *mulâtresse*.

3194. CELESTE
April 9, 1798, baptism of Celeste, born October 4, 1797,
a free *mulâtresse*, daughter of Margueritte, a slave of
Charles Peytavin Duriblon, and of a father unknown. Mr.
Duriblon gives the child its freedom. Godparents: Vale-
ri Armand and Euphrasie Rambin.

3195. MARIE
April 15, 1798, baptism of Marie, born February 14?, daughter of Jeanne, slave of Athanase Poissot, and a father unknown. Godparents: Joseph, free *mulâtre*, and Genovieve,
slave.

3196. AUGUSTIN
January 13, 1799, baptism of Augustin, aged two? weeks,
son of Marie Anne, slave of Felix Trudeau, commandant, and
a father unknown. Godparents: Hiacinthe, a free *mulâtre*,
and Marie Louise, slave of Mr. Armand.

3197. MARIE JEANNE
January 27, 1799, baptism of Marie Jeanne, aged four
months, *négresse* daughter of Cecile, slave of Pierre Cha-
lais *dit* Versaille, and a father unknown. Godparents:
Michel, slave of Remi Lambre, and Therese, slave of Mr.
Ailhot de St. Anne.

3198. JEAN
March 23, 1799, baptism of Jean, born May 24, 1798, son of Marie Louise *dite* Clorise, slave of Mr. Metoier. Godparents: Maurice, slave of Augustin Buart, and Marie Louise, slave of Widow Lestase.

3199. PERINE
MARIE
March 23, 1799, baptism of Perine and Marie, born August 12, 1798, twin *négresses*, natural daughters of Magdeleine, slave of Mr. Metoier. Godparents of the first: Louis, slave of Mr. Metoier, and Henriette, slave of Mr. Prudhomme; godparents of the second: Louis, slave of Mr. Metoier, and Marie Francoise, slave of Mr. Metoier.

3200. MARIE JEANNE
March 23, 1799, baptism of Marie Jeanne, born July 13, 1798, *négresse*, natural daughter of Esther, slave of Mr. Metoier. Godparents: Joseph Torres and Marie Jeanne Cheletre.

3201. JEAN BAPTISTE
March 23, 1799, baptism of Jean Baptiste, born January 24, son of Genevieve, *mulâtresse* slave of Louis Toutin. Godparents: Andre Chamart and Marie Felicite Torres.

3202. MARIE ANNE
March 24, 1799, baptism of Marie Anne, born April 7, 1798, *quarterone* daughter of Marie /Adelaide7, *mulâtresse* slave of Marie Louise Mariotte, her mother. Godparents: Francois Rouquiere and Marie Buart.

3203. MARIE REINE DES ANGES
March 24, 1799, baptism of Marie Reine des Anges, born October 12, 1798, *négresse* daughter of Charlotte, slave of Mr. Aillot de St. Anne. Godparents: Joseph Michel, slave of Louis Lambre, and Marie DeNeige, slave of Aillot de St. Anne.

3204. MARIE THERESE
March 24, 1799, baptism of Marie Therese, born March 30, 1798, *mulâtresse* daughter of Marie Jeanne, slave of Louis Rachal. Godparents: Louis Rambin* and Marie Louise.*

*Above the name Louis, in a darker ink and a different handwriting, is written the name Andre; above the name Marie Louise, in that same handwriting and ink, is added the name Rachal.

3205. CESAIR
March 24, 1799, baptism of Cesair, born April 9, 1798, son of Pelagie, slave of Barthelemi Rachal. Godparents: André,

slave of Barthelemi Rachal, and Susanne, slave of Jean
Baptiste Buart.

3206. MARCELIN
March 24, 1799, baptism of Marcelin, born September 22,
1798, *nègre* son of Marie Francoise, slave of Louis Buart.
Godparents: Joseph and Marie, slaves of Mr. Badin.

3207. MARIE THERESE
March 24, 1799, baptism of Marie Therese, aged nine months,
négresse daughter of Susanne, slave of Louis Buart. Godparents: Louis Alexandre and Heleine, slaves of Louis
Buart.

3208. RAPHAËL
March 24, 1799, baptism of Raphaël, born February 15, 1798,
son of Marie Therese, slave of Mr. Maes. Godparents: Jean
Francois, slave of Mr. Dartigau, and Marie Louise, slave of
Me. Widow Monginot.

3209. JEAN FRANCOIS
March 25, 1799, baptism of Jean Francois, native of Guinée,
aged eighteen years or about, father and mother unknown,
slave of Mr. Metoier. Godparents: Jean Francois, slave
of Mr. Badin, and Louison, slave of Mr. Pavie.

3210. CELESTIN
May 12, 1799, baptism of Celestin, aged one year, *nègre*
son of Marie, slave of Remi Lambre. Godparents: Eugene,
slave of Mr. Larenaudiere, and Marie, slave of Mr. Badin.

3211. MARIE CELESTE
May 12, 1799, baptism of Marie Celeste, aged three weeks,
négresse daughter of Jeanne, slave of Dominique Davion.
Godparents: Francois, slave of Mr. Gilbert Clausau, and
Marie Celeste, slave of Mr. Rambin.

3212. GENEVIEVE
May 12, 1799, baptism of Genevieve, slave of Remi Lambre,
négresse daughter of Marie Therese. Godparents: Jean
Baptiste, slave of Remi Lambre, and Francoise, slave of
Mr. /illegible/.

3213. MARIE ANASELITE
August 11, 1799, baptism of Marie Anaselite, born September
15, 1798, *mulâtresse* daughter of Fanie Venus, *négresse* slave
of Mr. St. Marcel. Godparents: Silvestre Poissot and
Adelaide Rambin.

3214. EULALIE
August 25, 1799, baptism of Eulalie, aged eight months,

négresse daughter of Heleine, slave of Mr. de St. Anne. Godparents: Jean Baptiste and Ursulle, slaves of Mr. de St. Anne.

3215. MARIE FRANCOISE JOSEPHINE
September 1, 1799, baptism of Marie Francoise Josephine, aged four months, *mulâtresse* daughter of Louison, *négresse* slave of Joseph Pavie, merchant at New Orleans; the *négresse* lives at this post. Godparents: Joseph and Marie Francoise, *nègres* slaves of Mr. Rouquier.

3216. ETIENNE
September 15, 1799, baptism of Etienne, born March 24, *nègre* son of Victoire, slave of Mr. Maes. Godparents: Bastien, slave of Mr. Maes, and Francoise, slave of Francois Rouquié.

3217. REMI
October 18, 1799, baptism of Remi, aged thirteen months, *nègre* son of Anne, *négresse* slave of Mr. Monet, and a father unknown. Baptism occurred at the home of Mr. Monet. Godparents: Marie Jeanne and Jean Baptiste, slaves of Mr. Monet.

3218. MARIE FRANCOISE
October 18, 1799, baptism of Marie Francoise, aged seven months, *mulâtresse* daughter of Marie Louise, *mulâtresse* slave of Mr. Monet, and a father unknown. Godparents: Jacques Lecomte and Dorothée /Monet_7.

3219. THEOTISE
October 18, 1799, baptism at home of Mr. Monet, with permission of Monsignor Leveque, of a four-day-old infant named Theotise, *négresse* daughter of Marie Joseph, *négresse* slave of Mr. Monet, and a father unknown. Godparents: Jean Baptiste Baltasar /Monet_7, a free *mulâtre*, and Marie Louise, a free *mulâtresse*.

3220. MARIE JEANNE
October 18, 1799, baptism of Marie Jeanne, aged two years, with permission of Msgr. Leveque of New Orleans to perform the baptism in the home of Mr. Monet, *négresse* daughter of Francoise, *négresse* slave of Mr. Monet, and a father unknown. Godparents: Athanase, slave of Mr. Monet, and Jeanne Chatonai, slave of deceased Martinau.

3221. JEANNE
October 18, 1799, baptism in the home of Mr. Monet, with permission of Msgr. Leveque, of an infant born April 20, 1799, named Jeanne, the *négresse* daughter of Susanne, a slave of deceased Martinau. Godparents: Joseph Bissonet

and Dorothée /Monet/.

3222. MARIE THERESE
October 18, 1799, baptism at the home of Mr. Monet, with permission of Monsignor Leveque, of Marie Therese, born August 20, *négresse* daughter of Francoise, slave of Mr. Monet, and a father unknown. Godparents: Simeon Rachal and Dorothée /Monet/.

3223. NARCIS
October 20, 1799, baptism of Narcis, aged six years, *endoié* by Mr. Delvau, the prior *curé*. Baptism performed at the home of Widow Lecomte; infant was the *négrillon* son of Marie Jeanne, a slave of Me. Widow Lecompte. Godparents: Ambroise Lecompte and Marie Lecour.

3224. SILVIN
October 20, 1799, baptism of Silvin, aged two years, *endoié* by Mr. Delvau, prior *curé* of this post. Infant was the *négrillon* son of deceased Marie, a slave of Widow Lecompte. Godparents: Athanase, *nègre* slave of Widow Lecompte, and Margueritte, a free *mulâtresse*.

3225. CYPRIEN
October 20, 1799, baptism of Cyprien, *mulâtre* son of Magdeleine, *mulâtresse* slave of Widow Lecomte, and a father unknown. Ceremonies performed at the home of Widow Lecomte. Godparents: Louis, *mulâtre*, and Francoise, *mulâtresse*, slaves of Mr. Lecomte.

3226. MARIE
October 20, 1799, baptism at the home of Widow Lecomte, of Marie, aged two years, *mulâtresse* daughter of Magdeleine, *mulâtresse* slave of Widow Lecompte and a father unknown. Godparents: Louis Cesair and Pelagie, free *mulâtres*.

3227. CATHERINNE
October 20, 1799, baptism at the home of Widow Lecomte, of Catherinne, *négresse* daughter of deceased Marie, slave of Widow Lecomte, and a father unknown. Godparents: Athanase, slave of Mr. Lecompt and Louison, Indian.

3228. ADELAIDE
October 20, 1799, baptism at home of Widow Lecomt, of Adelaide, *mulâtresse* daughter of Francoise, slave of Widow Lecomte. Godparents: Athanase Lecour and Francoise Le Compte.

3229. ALEXIS
October 20, 1799, baptism at home of Widow Lecomte, of Alexis, aged five years, *endoié* by Mr. Delvau, *nègre* son of

Marie Jeanne, slave of Joseph Dupre, *fils*, and a father unknown. Godparents: Athanase, slave of Me. Lecomte, and Marie Jeanne.

3230. ATHANASE
October 20, 1799, baptism at the home of Widow Lecomte, of Athanase, *endoié*, *nègre* son of Marie Jeanne, slave of Joseph Dupre, *fils*, and a father unknown. Godparents: Etienne and Clemence, slaves of Mr. Ambroise Lecomte.

3231. JACQUES
October 20, 1799, baptism at the home of Widow Lecomte, with consent of Msgr. Leveque, of a *nègre*, aged 25 years, born in Jamaique, father and mother unknown, a slave of Mr. Ambroise Lecompte. Godparents: Athanase Lecour and Marie Rose Robin.

3232. JOSEPH
October 20, 1799, baptism at the home of Me. Widow Lecomte, of a *nègre* of the age of twenty-five years or about, a native of the coast of Guinee, father and mother unknown, slave of Mr. Ambroise Lecompte. Godparents: Barthelemi Lecour and Cecile Lecour.

3233. MARIE CILESIE
October 20, 1799, baptism at the home of Me. Widow Lecompte, of Marie Cilesie, an infant of four years who had been previously *endoié* by Mr. Delvau, *curé* of this parish, daughter of Elisabeth, slave of Ambroise Lecompte. Godparents: Athanase, slave of Mr. Lecompte, and Genevieve, slave of Mr. Simpré [Davion *dit* St. Prix].

3234. FELICITÉ
October 20, 1799, baptism at the home of Me. Lecomte, of Felicité, a *négresse* of three years, daughter of Elisabeth, slave of Ambroise Lecompte, and a father unknown. Godparents: Athanase and Felicite, both Indians.

3235. JACQUES
October 20, 1799, baptism at the home of Widow Lecompte, of a *négrillon* of three years, *endoié*, son of Celeste, a slave of Nicolas Gallien. Godparents: Athanase and Marie Jeanne, slaves of Me. Lecompte.

3236. JEAN BAPTISTE
October 20, 1799, baptism at the home of Me. Widow Lecompte, of Jean Baptiste, a *nègre* aged sixty years, native of Maringa, father and mother unknown, slave of Pierre Baudouin. Godparents: Louis Monet and Marie Rose Robin.

3237. JEAN BAPTISTE
October 20, 1799, baptism at the home of Me. Widow Lecompte,

of Jean Baptiste, a free *quarteron* of two years, *endoié*, son of Francoise *mulâtresse* slave of Me. Widow Lecompte. Godparents: Louis Cesair and Pierre, slaves of Joseph Dupré, *fils*.

3238. MARIE CELESTE
October 20, 1799, baptism at the home of Nicolas Gallien, with permission of Msgr. Leveque of New Orleans, of a *négresse* who was sick, 20 years old, a native of Cenegal, mother and father unknown. Godparents: Jean Baptiste Gallien and Marie Rose Robin.

3239. MARIE
October 20, 1799, baptism at the home of Etienne Vergé on Isle a Brevel, of a small *mulâtresse* slave, aged one year, daughter of deceased Marie, slave of Mr. Etienne Vergé, and a father unknown. Godparents: Narcis Prudhomme and Cyprienne Derbanne.

3240. FRANCOIS ALEXANDRE
November 17, 1799, baptism of Francois, *nègre* infant of seven months, son of Marie Louise, *négresse* slave of Denis Buart, and a father unknown. Godparents: Louis Alexandre and Marie, slave of Me. Cadet Magnon, living at this post.

3241. MARIE LOUISE
December 2, 1799, baptism of Marie Louise, a *négresse* born September 2, 1792, daughter of Rosalie, slave of Mr. Fontenau, and a father unknown. Godparents: Francois Mulon, free *mulâtre*, and Marie Louise, slave of Mr. Badin.

3242. EULALIE
December 8, 1799, baptism of Eulalie, *négritte*, born June 3, daughter of Fanni, *négresse* slave of Mr. Morphil, living in this post, and a father unknown. Godparents: Pierre Quieri and Marie Victoire Poissot.

3243. JEAN PIERRE
December 15, 1799, baptism of Jean Pierre, aged seven years, *nègre* son of deceased Marie, slave of Fonteneau, living in this post, and a father unknown. Godparents: Joseph, slave of Me. Widow Gaspart, and Victoire, slave of Me. Widow Gagné.

3244. HONORÉ
February 23, 1800, baptism of Honoré, *négrillon* of four months, native of this post, son of Magdeleine, *négresse* slave of Pierre Ternié /dit/ Grenoble, and a father unknown. Godparents: François, slave of Mr. Channian?, and Victoire, *négresse* slave of Widow Etienne Gagné.

3245. JEAN BAPTISTE
March 2, 1800, baptism of Jean Baptiste, *mulâtre* of the age of two years, native of this post, son of Marie, the *négresse* slave of Mr. Varange, and a father unknown. Godparents: Nicolas, a free *mulâtre*, and Marie, slave of Mr. Badin.

3246. MARIE
April 13, 1800, baptism of Marie, an infant *grif* of four months, daughter of Ursule, slave of Manuel Prudhomme. Godparents: Louis, a free *mulâtre*, and Marie Celeste, a slave of Manuel Prudhomme.

3247. LOUIS
April 13, 1800, baptism of Louis, a *négrillon* born February 1, son of Pelagie, *négresse* slave of Antoine Prudhomme. Godparents: Louis, free *mulâtre*, and Francoise, slave of Mr. Colin.

3248. FELICITÉ
April 13, 1800, baptism of Felicité, a *négresse* born March 16, daughter of Sali, *négresse* slave of Mr. Metoyer, and a father unknown. Godparents: Louis /Metoyer/, a free *mulâtre*, and Susanne /Metoyer/, free *mulâtresse*.

3249. FELICITÉ
April 13, 1800, baptism of Felicité, a *négresse* of six months, daughter of Margueritte, *négresse* slave of Me. Jacob Lambre, and a father unknown. Godparents: Francois, slave of Louis Gabriel /Buard/, and Francoise, slave of Mr. Colin.

3250. GENEVIEVE
April 13, 1800, baptism of Genevieve, a *négresse* born February 15, daughter of Marie, slave of Mr. Metoier, living at this post, and a father unknown. Godparents: Antoine, slave of Me. Destase?, and Anne, slave of Mr. Metoyer.

3251. MARIE ADELAIDE
April 13, 1800, baptism of Marie Adelaide, a *négresse* of 16 months, daughter of Felicite, slave of Antoine Prudhomme, and of a father unknown. Godparents: Charles, *nègre* of Manuel Prudhomme, and Marie Adelaide, slave of Me. St. Denis.

3252. MARIE FRANCOISE
April 13, 1800, baptism of Marie Francoise, a *négresse* born July 25, 1798, in the post, daughter of Margueritte, *négresse* slave of Marie Therese, a free *mulâtresse*, and a father unknown. Godparents: Antoine, slave of Mr. Badin, and Marie Francoise, slave of Mr. Rouquie.

3253. ETIENNE
April 13, 1800, baptism of Etienne, *nègre*, aged eighteen months, son of Elisabeth, *négresse* slave of Pierrit Derbane. Godparents: Francois, slave of Denis Buart, and Marie Louise, *négresse* of Mr. Metoyer.

3254. MARIE THERESE
April 13, 1800, baptism of Marie Therese, a *négresse* of nine months, daughter of Marthe, *négresse* slave of Manuel Prudhomme. Godparents: Antoine, *nègre* slave of Mr. Badin, and Henriette, *négresse* slave of Manuel Prudhomme.

3255. MARIE
April 13, 1800, baptism of Marie, a *mulâtresse* of 2 months, daughter of Therese, slave of Mr. Aillot de St. Anne, and a father unknown. Godparents: Jean Baptiste, slave of Gabriel Buart, and Therese, slave of Mr. Aillot de St. Anne.

3256. MARIE
April 13, 1800, baptism of Marie, a *négresse* born January 3, daughter of Susanne, slave of Mr. Aillot de St. Anne, living in this post. Godparents: Etienne Pavie and Marie Margueritte Prudhomme.

3257. MARIE MARCELITTE
June 13, 1800, baptism of Marie Marcelitte, a *mulâtresse* of eleven months, daughter of Pelagie, *négresse* slave of Monsieur Bossié, living in this post, and of a father unknown. Godparents: Louis Levasseur and Marie Aspasie Bossié.

3258. MARIE CHRISTINE
July 6, 1800, baptism of Marie Christine, a *négresse* born May 9 in this post, daughter of Magdeleine, *négresse* slave of Demoiselle Triche, and a father unknown. Godparents: Toussaint /Metoyer/, free *mulâtre*, and Marie Anne, *négresse* slave of Mr. Badin.

3259. MARIE CILESIE
July 27, 1800, baptism of Marie Cilesie, *négrite*, born July 4, daughter of Marie Anne, slave of Marie Joseph Gagne, widow of Louis Sempré /Davion dit/, and a father unknown. Godparents: André Rambin and Anasthasie Maiou.

3260. BRIGITTE
August 3, 1800, baptism of Brigitte, a *négritte* of one year and four months, native of this post, daughter of Marie, *négresse* slave of Pierre Jarri, living at this post, and child of a father unknown. Godparents: Jean Baptiste, *nègre* of Mr. Maes, and Brigitte, slave of Mr. Morphil.

3261. MARIE POMPONE
August 17, 1800, baptism of Marie, a *mulâtresse* born March 4, 1799, daughter of Genevieve, *négresse* slave of Louis Buard, living in this post, and of a father unknown. Godparents: Placide Bossié and Marie Therese Eugenie Buart.

3262. JACQUES
September 15, 1800, baptism of Jacques, a *nègre* born the preceding day and *endoié* in his home, son of Adelaide, a *négresse* slave of Madame St. Denis, and a father unknown. Godparents: Jacques Prudhomme and Marie Margueritte Prudhomme.

3263. FRANCOISE
September 28, 1800, baptism of Francoise, a *négresse* born March 9, daughter of Celeste, *négresse* slave of Francois Perau, living in this post, and a father unknown. Godparents: Jean Louis, slave of Mr. Becon /Besson7, and Marie Jeanne, *négresse* of Mr. Henri Triche.

3264. LOUIS ALEXANDRE
October 25, 1800, baptism of Louis Alexandre, *négrillon* born March 20 in this post, son of Francoise, *négresse* of Louis Buart, and a father unknown. Godparents: Louis Alexandre, slave of Mr. Buart, and Francoise, slave of Mr. Bossié.

3265. ANTOINE
November 5, 1800, baptism of Antoine, a *négrillon* born January 11, son of Susanne, *négresse* slave of Edouard Morphil, living in this post, and a father unknown. Godparents: Edouard Cesair Morphil and Marie Louise Aspasie Morphil.

3266. MARIE JEANNE
November 9, 1800, baptism of Marie Jeanne, a *négresse* born February 6, daughter of Henriette, *négresse* slave of Me. Barthelemi Rachal, living in this post, and a father unknown. Godparents: Achile, *nègre* slave of Remis Lambre, and Victoire, *négresse* slave of Louis Rachal.

3267. CYPRIEN
November 9, 1800, baptism of Cyprien, a *mulâtre* born May 28, 1899, in this post, son of Elisabeth, *négresse* slave of Me. Barthelemi Rachal, and a father unknown. Godparents: Jean Pierre, *nègre* slave of Me. Barthelemi Rachal, and Genevieve, slave of Me. Gaspart /Fiol7.

3268. FRANCOISE
November 9, 1800, baptism of Francoise, a *négresse* born March 24, 1799 in this post, daughter of Susanne, *négresse*

slave of Louis Barthelemi Rachal. Godparents: Pierre, slave of Me. Barthelemi Rachal, and Francoise, *négresse* of Remi Lambre.

3269. FRANCOIS
November 9, 1800, baptism of Francois, a *négrillon* born April 4 in this post, son of Magdeleine, *négresse* slave of Athanase Demesiere, and a father unknown. Godparents: Nicolas, a free *mulâtre*, and Pelagie, slave of Mr. Chabuche.

3270. JEANNE FRANCOISE MAGDELEINE
November 9, 1800, baptism of Jeanne Francoise Magdeleine, born April 10, *grif*, daughter of Marie Jeanne, *négresse* of Louis Rachal. Godparents: Louis, a free *mulâtre*, and Amelie, a *négresse* slave of Mr. Tausin.

3271. JEAN BAPTISTE
December 21, 1800, baptism of Jean Baptiste, a *grife* born in this post, aged one year, son of Genevieve, a *mulâtresse* slave of Louis Totin. Godparents: Jean Baptiste, *nègre* slave of Placide Bossié, and Francoise, slave of Placide Bossié.

3272. AGNES
December 21, 1800, baptism of Agnes, a *négresse* born March 10 at this post, child of Babet, slave of Mr. Metoye, and a father unknown. Godparents: Louis Alexandre, slave of Louis Buart, and Marie, *mulâtresse* of Mr. Badin.

3273. MARIE FRANCOISE
January 12, 1801, baptism of Marie Francoise, a *négresse* born December 2, 1800, in this post, daughter of Catherinne, *négresse* slave of Francois Levasseur and a father unknown. Godparents: Jean, slave of Athanase Poissot, and Genevieve, slave of Me. Gaspart /Fio1/.

3274. MARIE FELICITE
January 25, 1801, baptism of Marie Felicite, a *négresse* born in this post on May 26, 1800, daughter of Marie, slave of Widow Triche. Godparents: Joseph, slave of Me. Triche, and Agnes, slave of Me. Triche.

3275. JOSEPH
January 25, 1801, baptism of Joseph, a *nègre* born December 9 in this post, son of Catherinne, *négresse* slave of Me. Widow Triche, and a father unknown. Godparents: Joseph, slave of Mr. Baedin, and Agnes, slave of Me. Triche.

3276. MARIE ASPASIE
February 16, 1801, baptism of Marie Aspasie, a *quarterone*, born September 29, 1801 in this post, daughter of Susanne,

[Metoyer], *mulâtresse* slave of Mr. Metoier, habitant of this post, and of a father unknown. Godparents: Jean Baptiste Etienne Pavie and Marie Therese Elisabeth Metoié.

3277. JEAN BAPTISTE MARCELIN
April 5, 1801, baptism of Jean Baptiste Marcelin, a *négrillon* born January 19, son of Louison, slave of Mr. Metoier, and a father unknown. Godparents: Jean Baptiste, slave of Mr. Badin, and Marie Louise, slave of Mr. Badin.

3278. LOUIS ISIDORE
April 1, 1801, baptism of Louis Isidore, a *négrillon* born February 23, son of Magdeleine, slave of Mr. Metoyer, and a father unknown. Godparents: Jean Baptiste Grape and Marie Louise, slave of Me. St. Denis.

3279. JEAN BAPTISTE
April 5, 1801, baptism of Jean Baptiste, a *nègre* born November 27, 1800, son of Esther, slave of Mr. Metoyer, living in this post. Godparents: Jean Baptiste, slave of Louis Buart, and Marie Victoire, slave of Mr. Maës.

3280. JEAN BAPTISTE
April 5, 1801, baptism of Jean Baptiste, a *négrillon* of one month, son of Pelagie, slave of Mr. Vilaret, habitant of this post. Godparents: Pierre, slave of Barthelemi Rachal, and Brigite, slave of Mr. Morphi.

3281. JEAN BAPTISTE
April 5, 1801, baptism of Jean Baptiste, a *nègre* of four years, born in this post, son of Heleonore, slave of Antoine Prudhomme. Godparents: Louis, slave of Mr. Fonteneau, and Marie, slave of Mr. Rouquié.

3282. CATHERINNE
April 5, 1801, baptism of Catherinne, a *négrite* of three months, daughter of Marie, slave of Mr. Fonteneau, living in this post. Godparents: Jean Baptiste, slave of Joseph Triche, and Catherinne, slave of Widow Pierre Gagné.

3283. SUSANNE
April 5, 1801, baptism of Susanne, a *mulâtresse* of three months, daughter of Francoise, slave of Mr. Rouquié, living in this post, and a father unknown. Godparents: Jean Baptiste, slave of Mr. Metoier, and Marie Jeanne, slave of Mr. Metoier.

3284. ATHANASE
April 5, 1801, baptism of Athanase, an infant of ten months, son of Genevieve, slave of Louis Gabriel Buart, and a father unknown. Godparents: Jean Baptiste, slave of Mr.

Aillot de St. Anne, and Marie, slave of Mr. Badin.

3285. JEAN BAPTISTE
April 5, 1801, baptism of Jean Baptiste, an Indian of the Aiche nation, aged 20 years, native of this post, son of Marie, an Indian, and a father unknown. Godparents: Joseph Dupre and Marie Louise Lecomte, represented by Elisabeth David.

3286. MANUEL LUCAS
April 5, 1801, baptism of Manuel Lucas, a *mulâtre* of five months, son of Pelagie, *mulâtresse* slave of Mr. Touline. Godparents: Manuel Triche and Marie Joseph Rouquié.

3287. FRANCOIS
April 5, 1801, baptism of Francois, a Conga *nègre* from the coast of Guinée, "a brute whose father and mother are unknown," about twenty years old. Godparents: Francois Rouquie and Therese Lamalathie.

3288. MARIE PERINE
April 12, 1801, baptism of Marie Perine, a *négritte* of three weeks, daughter of Marie, slave of Guillaume Chevert, habitant of this post. Godparents: Rosemon Chamart and Marie Lucie Plaisance.

3289. JEAN LOUIS
April 12, 1801, baptism of Jean Louis, a *négrillon* of one year, son of Julie, slave of Mr. Soulange Bossié, habitant of this post. Godparents: Rock, slave of Placide Bossié, and Marie Adelaide, slave of Me. St. Denis.

3290. JEAN LOUIS
April 12, 1801, baptism of Jean Louis, a *négrillon* of six months, son of Marie, *négresse* slave of Me. Widow Cadet Fort, living in this post. Godparents: Auguste, slave of Madame Cadet Fort, and Marie Louise, slave of Me. Cadet Mounion.

3291. JEAN FRANCOIS
May 24, 1801, baptism of Jean Francois, *nègre* born May 20, 1800, son of Angelique, *négresse* slave of Paul Poissot, living in this post. Godparents: Joseph Michel, slave of Remi Lambre, and Genevieve, slave of Denis Buart.

3292. JEAN BAPTISTE
May 24, 1801, baptism of Jean Baptiste, a *négrillon* born last February, son of Marie Louise, slave of Denis Buart, living in this post. Godparents: Louis, slave of Etienne Vergé, and Margueritte, slave of Mr. Metoier.

3293. MARIE AMELIE
May 24, 1801, baptism of Marie Amelie, a *mulâtresse* born March 23, a daughter of Marie, the *négresse* slave of Louis Buart. Godparents: Francois Bossié and Elisabeth Buart.

3294. MARIE FRANCOISE AMELIE
May 24, 1801, baptism of Marie Francoise, *négritte*, aged three years, native of this post, daughter of Angelique, *négresse* slave of Paul Poissot. Godparents: Antoine, the slave of Me. Widow Cadet Mounoir, and Marie Anne, slave of Francois Levasseur.

3295. CHARLES
May 24, 1801, baptism of a *nègre*, aged twenty-one years or about, native of Marguingua on the coast of Guinee, father and mother unknown. Godparents: Pierre, *nègre* slave of Mr. Trudeau, commandant, and Louison, slave of Joseph Pavie. Charles, a slave of Mr. Metoie for about eight years, had been instructed in the principles of the Catholic faith and had promised to live a Christian life.

3296. FRANCOIS DOPHINO
June 1, 1801, baptism of Francois Dophino, a *quarteron* born May 3, 1800, son of Magdeleine, *mulâtresse* slave of Widow Lecomte, and a father unknown. Godparents: Jean Francois, free *mulâtre*, and Marie Ursule, a free *mulâtresse*.*

*See note accompanying Entry 2837.

3297. JEAN BAPTISTE
June 14, 1801, baptism of Jean Baptiste, a *négrillon* born April 5 in this post, son of Louison, *négresse* slave of Joseph Pavie, and a father unknown. Godparents: Jean Louis, slave of Mr. Rouquie, and Marie Louise, slave of Mr. Armant.

3298. MARIE
July 9, 1801, baptism of Marie, *négritte* born June 22 in this post, daughter of Marie Louise, *négresse* slave of Madame Louise Margueritte, Me. St. Denis. Godparents: Francois Rambin and Marie Margueritte Prudhomme.

3299. HENRI
August 2, 1801, baptism of Henri, a *grif* born July 14 in this post, son of Marie Anne, slave of Mr. Felix Trudeau, commandant, and a father unknown. Godparents: Paul, the *mulâtre* slave of Mr. Colin, and Francoise, slave of Mr. Colin.

3300. FELICITE
August 16, 1801, baptism of Felicite, *négritte* of six weeks, native of this post, daughter of Victoire, *négresse* slave of Mr. Maës, living at this post, and a father unknown. Godparents: Gabriel, *nègre* of Mr. Trudeau, and Catherinne,

négresse of Francois Levasseur.

3301. MARIE JEANNE
August 23, 1801, baptism of Marie Jeanne, a *négritte* born in this post four months earlier, daughter of Margueritte, *négresse* slave of Mde. Jacob Lambre, and a father unknown. Godparents: Charles, slave of Remi Lambre, and Marie Jeanne, a free *mulâtresse?*.

3302. LOUIS
December 11, 1801, baptism of Louis, a *mulâtre* born November 14 in this post, son of Marie Celeste, *mulâtresse* slave of André Rambin, and a father unknown. Godparents: Louis, *nègre*, and Marie Louise, slave of Mr. Rambin.

3303. SUSANNE
May 11, 1797, burial in the cemetery of the parish of Susanne, aged twenty-one years, slave of Madame Baptiste Riche who died without receiving the sacraments.

3304. HENRI
__?__ 27, 1797, burial, in the cemetery of the parish, of Henri, aged 17?, son of Magdelaine, slave of Mr. Rambin.

3305. ZENON?
October 20, 1797, burial, in the cemetery of the parish, of Zenon?, son of Margueritte, a slave of /Marie Thérèse *ditte*/ Coincoin, a free *négresse*.

3306. ANONYMOUS
October 20, 1797, burial, in the cemetery of this parish, of a *nègre* infant of two months, *endoié*, son of Charlotte, *négresse* slave of Mr. Aliot de Ste. Anne.

3307. MARIE
November 1, 1797, burial, in the cemetery of this parish, of an infant of eight hours, *endoié*, son /*sic*/ of Marie, *négresse* slave of Mr. Rambin?.

3308. JEAN BAPTISTE
March 1, 1798, burial in the cemetery of this parish of Jean Baptiste, aged thirty years, slave of Athanase Demesiere, who died without receiving the sacraments since it was not known that he was sick.

3309. JOSEPH
August 11, 1798, burial, in the cemetery of this parish, of Joseph, aged six years, *mulâtre* son of Julie, slave of Louis Gabriel Buart.

3310. MARIE BARBE
August 13, 1798, burial, in the cemetery of this parish, of

Marie Barbe, aged give years, daughter of Julie, slave of Louis Gabriel Buart.

3311. FELICITE
September 6, 1798, burial in the cemetery of this parish, of Felicite, aged two years, daughter of Heleine, *négresse* slave of Louis Gabriel Buart.

3312. BASTIEN
September 22, 1798, burial in the cemetery of this parish, of Bastien, aged nine, son of Julie, *négresse* slave of Louis Gabriel Buart.

3313. ANONYMOUS
October 17, 1798, burial in the cemtery of this parish of an infant who died the day of his birth, "after having received the water," daughter of Pelagie, slave of Mr. De Mesieres.

3314. JULIE
November 30, 1798, burial in the cemetery of this parish of Julie, *mulâtresse* slave of Louis Buart, living in this post, who died the preceding day at the age of forty five years, after receiving the sacrament of penance.

3315. ANONYMOUS
December 29, 1798, burial, in the cemetery of this parish, of a *négrillon*, aged four days, *endoié* at home since it was not possible to carry him to the church for the ceremonies of baptism, son of Magdeleine, slave of Mr. Demesieres.

3316. ANONYMOUS
March 20, 1799, burial in the cemetery of this parish of the corpse of a Congo slave of Mr. Morphil, aged 30 years.

3317. MARIE
June 5, 1799, burial, in the cemetery of this parish, of Marie, *négresse* slave of Madame Triche, aged twenty years.

3318. ANONYMOUS
September 22, 1799, burial in the cemetery of this parish of a *négrillon* of three days, *endoié* since it was not possible to carry him to the church for baptism, son of Heleine, a slave of Louis Buart.

3319. ANONYMOUS
March, 31, 1801, burial in the cemetery of this parish of a *négrillon*, died the day of his birth, *endoié* since it was not possible to carry him to the church for baptism, son of Rose, slave of Mr. Rouquié.

3320. JEAN BAPTISTE
January 20, 1800, burial, in the cemetery of this parish, of Jean Baptiste, died the preceding day, unexpectedly, the thirty-six year old slave of Mr. Badin.

3321. JEAN LOUIS
February 7, 1800, burial, in the cemetery of this parish, of a *nègre* named Jean Louis, who died the preceding day at the age of six years, son of Pelagie, slave of Monsieur Bossié.

3322. MARIE THERESE
April 11, 1800, burial in the cemetery of this parish, of Marie Therese, died the preceding day at the age of one year, daughter of Jeanne, *négresse* slave of Dominique Davior

3323. ANONYMOUS
June 14, 1800, burial, in the cemetery of this parish, of a nine-month-old infant, *endoié* since it was not possible to carry him to the church for baptism, son of Elisabeth, slave of Monsieur Aillot de St. Anne.

3324. MELANIDE
June 15, 1800, burial, in the cemetery of this parish, of Melanide, aged six years, *négresse* slave of Mr. Rouquier, natural daughter of Rosette, also a slave of Mr. Rouquier.

3325. CHARLOT
July 30, 1800, burial in the cemetery of this parish, of Charlot, *nègre* from the coast of Guinée, who died the preceding day at the age of twenty years, after being *endoié* by Fr. Pavie when he could not be carried to the church for baptism. Deceased was a slave of Mr. Maës.

3326. ANONYMOUS
September 8, 1800, burial in the cemetery of this parish of a small *négresse* aged two weeks, who died after having been *endoié*, since it was not possible to carry her to the church for baptism, daughter of Jeanne, *négresse* slave of Dominique Simpri [dit of Davion], living at Grand Ecord.

3327. JACQUES
September 17, 1801, burial, in the cemetery of this post, of Jacques, *nègre* slave of Me. St. Denis, aged two days, son of Adelaide, *négresse* slave of Me. St. Denis.

3328. PAUL
October 10, 1800, burial in the cemetery of this parish of Paul, aged six years, who died the preceding day, *mulâtre* son of Marie Jeanne, *négresse* slave of Monsieur Bossié.

3329. JOACHIM
October 11, 1800, burial in the cemetery of this parish of Joachim, *negrê* from the coast of Guinée, who died the preceding day at the age of seventy-five years, slave of Mr. Rouquié.

3330. ROSALIE
December 10, 1800, burial in the cemetery of this parish of Rosalie, aged four years, daughter of Fanni, slave of Mr. Morphil; infant died the preceding day.

3331. PIEROT
February 24, 1801, burial in the cemetery of this parish of Pierot, aged thirty years, *nègre* from the coast of Guinée, *endoié* on the day of his death, slave of Mr. Rouquié.

3332. AUGUSTIN
March 18, 1801, burial in the cemetery of this parish of Augustin, a *mulâtre*, native of New Orleans, slave of Mr. Rouquié, who died the preceding day, by accident, at the age of 28 years.

3333. ANONYMOUS
April 10, 1801, burial in the cemetery of this parish of an infant of two days, a *négrillon* who died after having been *endoié*, since he could not be carried to the church to receive the sacrament of baptism, son of Rosette, slave of Mr. Rouquié.

3334. MICHEL
August 26, 1801, burial in the cemetery of this parish of Michel, native of the coast of Guinée, aged forty years, killed "by a clap of thunder," slave of Me. Widow Triche.

3335. ANONYMOUS
December 25, 1801, burial in the cemetery of this parish of a *négrillon* of two months, who died after being *endoié* since it was not possible to take him to the church to receive the ceremonies of baptism, son of Jeanne, slave of Dominique Davion.

3336. PEDRO CASEAUX
MARIA ANA BONTON
September 5, 1786, marriage, after one ban, of Pedro Caseaux, legitimate son of Pedro Caseaux and Theresa Christobal, a native of this parish . . . and . . . Maria Ana Bonton, native of this parish, legitimate daughter of Pedro Bonton and Francesca Botson. Witnesses: Joseph Lattier and Pedro Charpentier.

3337. JUAN BAUTISTA AILHAUD ST. ANNE
MARIA LOUISA BUARD
December 7, 1786, after one ban, marriage of Juan Bautista
Ailhaud St. Anne, native of the province of Delfinado
/Dauphine/ in France, legitimate son of Juan Antonio Ailhaud St. Anne and Maria Curnier . . . and . . . Maria
Louisa Buard, native of this parish, legitimate daughter
of Gabriel Buard and Maria Ana Rousseau. Witnesses: Luis
Carlos Deblanc, Estevan Maraffret Layssard, Estevan Pavie,
and Pedro Metoyer.

3338. CARLOS DURET
MARIE LEONORA SEBASTIEN PRUDHOMME
December 12, 1786, after two bans, marriage of Carlos Duret, native of the town of Quebec in Canada . . . and . . .
Marie Leonora Sebastien Prudhomme, native of this parish.
Witnesses: Pedro Gagnon, Francisco Rambint, Manuel Prudhomme, Guillaume Chever.

3339. JUAN BAUTISTA MORIN
JUANA RACHAL
December 12, 1786, marriage after one ban, of Juan Bautista
Morin, native of Bordeos /Bordeaux/ in France . . . and
. . . Juana Rachal, widow Rompre, native of this parish.
Witnesses: Estevan de Vaugine, Francisco Monginot, Juan
Massip and Carlos Lemoine.

3340. ANTONIO RACHAL
MARIA LUISA LEMOINE
January 6, 1787, after two bans, marriage of Antonio Rachal, native of this parish, legitimate son of Luis Rachal
and Maria Luisa LeRoy . . . and . . . Marie Luisa Lemoine,
native of this parish, legitimate daughter of Carlos Lemoine and Isabel Dupre. Witnesses: Joseph Sauvage, Mr.
Morier, and Jean Massip.

3341. IAGO DANIEL BERRIER
MARIA FRANCISCA VASCOCU
February 11, 1787, after one ban, marriage of Iago Daniel
Berrier, native of San Martin Davou, diocese of Man in
France, legitimate son of Mr. Berrier and /a blank/ . . .
and . . . Maria Francisca Vascocu, native of this parish,
legitimate daughter of Antonio Vascocu and Maria Barba
Toups. Witnesses: Francisco Prudhomme, Luis Combas,
Antonio Vascocu, and Luis Vascocu.

3342. FRANCISCO LAVESPERE
MARIA LUISA DERBANNE
April 20, 1787, after one ban, marriage of Francisco Lavespere, native of Bordeos /Bordeaux/ in France, legitimate
son of Jean Lavespere and Madelena Angeveau . . . and . . .

Maria Luisa Derbanne, legitimate daughter of Pedro Derbanne and Maria LeClerc. Witnesses: Francisco Rouquier, Francisco Bossié; Francisco Chabus and Francisco Monginot.

3343. JUAN JOSEPH MARTINEAU
MADELENA LABERY
September 6, 1787, after one ban, marriage of Juan Joseph Martineau, native of Burdeos /Bordeau͟x/ in France, legitimate son of Guillermo Martineau and Juanna Moine. . . and . . . Madelena Labery, native of this parish, legitimate daughter of Juan Bautista Labery and Juana Guedon. Witnesses: Francisco Bossié, Luis Durand, Francisco Bartolome Rachal, Mr. Chabus, Juan Bautista Grappe.

3344. MIGUEL ERNAND
MARIA OLIVER
July 11, 1787, after three bans, marriage of Miguel Ernand, native of the port of Santa Maria, legitimate son of Miguel Ernand and Josepha Jorië . . . and . . . Maria Oliver, widow Couty, native of Punta Contada /Pointe Coupée/, the legitimate daughter of Miguel Olivier and Naneta Robert. Witnesses: Pedro Lacour, Remy Poissot and Luis Totin.

3345. VALENTINO DUBOË
ROSA CHELETTE
October 8, 1787, after three bans, marriage of Valentino Duboë, native of this parish, legitimate son of Juan Bautista Duboë and Marie Josepha Clermont . . . and . . . Rosa Chelette, native of Los Alemanes /the German Coas͟t/, legitimate daughter of Miguel Cheletre and Ana Pomier. Witnesses: Joseph Latie, Felipe Frederic, Bernabe Cheletre.

3346. SILVESTRE BOSSIÉ
MARIA JUANNA LAMBRE
December 17, 1787, after one ban, marriage of Silvestre Bossie, native of the parish of San Carlos de los Alemanes, legitimate son of Francisco Bossié and Rosalia Carlos Barré . . . and . . . Maria Juanna Lambre, native of this parish, legitimate daughter of Juan Bautista Lambre and Maria Juanna Levasseur. Witnesses: Francisco Bossié, Luis Buard.

3347. PEDRO RAMIS
MARIA ANA NICOLASA LANGLOIS
February 27, 1788, after one ban, marriage of Pedro Ramis, corporal, native of Olbena in Spain, legitimate son of Antonio and Madelena Leon . . . and . . . Maria Ana Nicolasa Langlois, native of this parish, legitimate daughter of Francisco Langloy and Maria Gregoria Sta. Crux. Witnesses: Luis Borme, Francisco Lemaitre, and Benito Pescio.

3348. BENITO MONTANARY
FRANCISCA GRAPPE
April 23, 1788, after three bans, marriage of Benito Montanary, native of Nueva Orleans, legitimate son of Juan Bautista Montanary and Margarita Callon . . . and . . . Francisca Grappe, native of this parish, legitimate daughter of Alexis Grappe and Maria Luisa Guedon. Witnesses: Pedro Badin, Bernardo Dortolant, Marcos Aulay /Marcollay/ and Francisco Rambint.

3349. FRANCISCO MONGINOT
MARIA FRANCISCA BUARD
April 24, 1788, after one ban, marriage of Francisco Monginot, native of Lambesca, a town in Provensa, legitimate son of Francisco Maria Monginot and Maria Agar . . . and . . . Maria Francisca Buard, native of this parish, legitimate daughter of Gabriel Buard and Maria Ana Rousseau. Witnesses: Andres Rambint, Francisco Bossié, Bautista Buard, and Remy Lambre.

3350. IAGO LACASE
MARIA LOUISA DUPRE
May 7, 1788, after two bans, marriage of Iago Lacase, a native of Opelousas, legitimate son of Carlos Lacase and Fillis Langlois. . . and . . . Maria Louisa Dupre, native of this parish, legitimate daughter of Josephe Dupre and Maria Derbanne. Witnesses: Francisco Lavespere, Juan Bautista Buard, Luis Derbanne.

3351. JUAN BAUTISTA ANTY
MARIA FRANCISCA LEVASSEUR
June 24, 1788, after two bans, marriage of Juan Bautista Anty, native of New Orleans, legitimate son of Ignacio Anty and Catalina Guerin . . . and . . . Maria Francisca Levasseur, native of this parish, legitimate daughter of Francisco Levasseur and Maria Mader. Witnesses: Iago Levasseur, Lucas Sorel, Genoveva Sorel.

3352. JACOB HOPOK
MARIA SALVAN
July 23, 1788, after three bans, marriage of Jacob Hopok, native of Virginia, legitimate son of Jorge Hopok and of Margarita Rosee . . . and . . . Maria Salvan, native of New Orleans, legitimate daughter of Juan Salvan and Maria Luisa Lambre. Witnesses: Francisco Bossié, Louis Buard, Silvestre Bossié, Soulange Bossié.

3353. ALEXIS CLOUTIER
MARIE FRANCISCA LECOMTE
August 13, 1788, after two bans, marriage of Alexis Cloutier, native of Pointe Coupée, legitimate son of Juan

Bautista Cloutié and Maria Rachal . . . and . . . Maria Francisca LeComte, widow Dupre, native of this parish, legitimate daughter of Juan Bautista Lecomte and Margarita LeRoy.

3354. LUIS EPINET
SUSANA AULLIVAUX /OLIVO/
September 10, 1788, after one ban, marriage of Luis Epinet, native of Marena in the province of Santonge, legitimate son of Guillermo Epinet and Anna Doussaint . . . and . . . Susana Aullivaux, native of Pointe Coupée, legitimate daughter of Pedro Aullivaux and Maria Ana Riche. Witnesses: Andres Rambint, Valentino Duboë, Pierre Aullivaux, and Sebastian Aullivaux.

3355. CLAUDIO THOMAS PEDRO METOYER
TERESA BUARD
October 13, 1788, after one ban, marriage of Claudio Thomas Pedro Metoyer, native of La Rochela, parish of San Salvados, legitimate son of Nicolas Francois Metoyer and Maria Ana Drapon . . . and . . . Teresa Buard, widow Pavie, legitimate daughter of Gabriel Buard and Maria Ana Rousseau. Witnesses: Andres Rambint, Luis Buard, Bouet Laffitte, Ailhaud St. Anne.

3356. JOSEPH JEAN RIS
MARIA FRANCESCA VASCOCU
January 28, 1789, after two bans, marriage of Joseph Jean Ris, native of this parish, legitimate son of Juan Ris and Maria Juanna Chagneau . . . and . . . Maria Francisca Vascocu, widow Daniel /Berrier/, legitimate daughter of Antonio Vascocu and Maria Barba Toups. Witnesses: Francisco Rambint, Guillermo Barberoux, Juan Luis Vascocu and Andres Vascocu.

3357. ANDRES ST. ANDRÉ
MARIA RACHAL
April 20, 1789, after two bans, marriage of Andres St. André, native of Montreal, legitimate son of Iago St. André and Maria Ana Picar . . . . and . . . Maria Rachal, a native of this parish, legitimate daughter of Iago Rachal and Ursula Castel. Witnesses: Estevan Vergé, Luis Rachal, Bautista Bartolome Rachal.

3358. LUIS LAMBRE
MARIA ANA DUPRÉ
April 22, 1789, after two bans, marriage of Luis Lambre, a native of this parish, legitimate son of Juan Bautista Lambre and Maria Juana Levasseur . . . and . . . Maria Ana Dupré, native of this parish, legitimate daughter of Joseph Dupré and Maria Derbanne. Witnesses: Pedro Chaler, Pedro Baillo, Luis Bartolome Rachal.

3359. PEDRO BEAUDOUIN
       NANETE ROBIN
       September 13, 1789, after two bans, marriage of Pedro
       Beaudouin, native of this parish, legitimate son of Pedro
       Beaudouin and Maria Ana Bonton . . . and . . . Nanete
       Robin, native of this parish, legitimate daughter of Miguel
       Robin and Maria Luisa Boulé. Witnesses: Pedro Lacour,
       Joseph Latié, and Pedro Cajou?.

3360. RICHARDO SYMIS
       MARIA DE LA CONCEPTION PERES
       September 22, 1789, after three bans, marriage of Richardo
       Symis, native of the town of Brestol in England, legitimate
       son of Juan Symis and Margarita Christiy . . . and . . .
       Marie de la Conception Peres, native of San Antonio de
       Texas, legitimate daughter of Joseph Cristobal Peres and
       Maria Josepha Pelona?. Witnesses: Andres David, Pedro
       Sorel, and Bouet Lafitte.

3361. REMY LAMBRE
       SUSETA PRUDHOMME
       September 26, 1789, after one ban, marriage of Remy Lambre,
       native of this parish, legitimate son of Jacob Lambre and
       Maria Ana Poissot . . . and . . . Suseta Prudhomme, native
       of this parish, legitimate daughter of Juan Bautista Prud-
       homme and Maria Josepha Collantin. Witnesses: Francisco
       Rouquier, Gaspar Fiolle, Manuel Prudhomme, Andres Vendalay.

3362. JOSEPH HORN
       MARIA LUISA BEAUDOUIN /BODIN_7
       November 16, 1789, after three bans, marriage of Joseph
       Horn, native of York, England, legitimate son of John Horn
       and Josepha Savari . . . and . . . Maria Luisa Beaudouin,
       widow Robin, native of this parish, legitimate daughter
       of Lorenzo Beaudouin /Bodin_7 and Maria Miguel Sta. Crux.
       Witnesses: Andres David and Luis Chamarre.

3363. JOSEPH ANTONIO MARCEL DE SOTO
       MARIA BAILLO
       January 31, 1790, after two bans, marriage of Joseph An-
       tonio Marcel de Soto, native of this parish, legitimate
       son of Manuel de Soto and Maria de St. Denis . . . and
       . . . Maria Baillo, native of this parish, legitimate
       daughter of Pedro Baillo and Catalina Poissot. Witnesses:
       Manuel Prud'homme, Remy Lambre, Atanasio Poissot, Ailhaud
       St. Anne. (f)

3364. ALEXANDRO SOULANGE BOSSIÉ
       LEONORA IMEL
       February 6, 1790, after two bans, marriage of Alexandro
       Soulange Bossié, native of the parish of St. Charles on

the German Coast, legitimate son of Francisco Bossié and
Rosalia Carlos Barré . . . and . . . Leonora Ymel, legit-
imate daughter of Antonio Imel and Margarita Cheletre,
native of the parish of St. John the Baptist on the German
Coast. Witnesses: Francisco Bossié, Bartolome Campanelle,
Pablo Cheletre, and Antonio Lambre.

3365. ANDRES FREDERIC
MARIANA CHELETTRE
February 16, 1790, after one ban, marriage of Andres Fre-
deric, native of the parish of St- Charles on the German
Coast, legitimate son of Felipe Frederic and Catalina Ber-
nar . . . and . . . Widow Baillo, native of the same par-
ish, legitimate daughter of Miguel Cheletre and Barba
Pomier. Witnesses: Guillermo Lestage, Bernabe Cheletre,
Pedro Cheletre, and Francisco Leconte.

3366. PEDRO JOSEPH ALEMAN
MARIA TERESA LANGLOIS
February 16, 1790, after two bans, marriage of Pedro Joseph
Aleman, native of Bayoli in New Galicia, legitimate son of
Joseph Aleman and Maria Gertrudes Goma . . . and . . .
Maria Teresa Langlois, native of this parish, legitimate
daughter of Francesco Langloy and Maria Gregorio Santa
Crux. Witnesses: Benito Pescio, Juan Joseph St. Anne,
Francisco Lemaitre, Pedro Ramis.

3367. DOMINGO DAVION SEMPRI [dit ST. PRIX]
PELAGIE GAGNÉ
July 21, 1790, after three bans, marriage of Domingo Davion
native of this parish, legitimate son of Juan Bautista
Davion and Maria Jacinta Triche . . . and . . . Pelagia
Gagné, native of this parish, legitimate daughter of Este-
van Gagné and Maria Luisa Bertrand. Witnesses: Bernardo
Dortolant, Juan Bautista Davion, Luis Davion, Luis Bertrand

3368. AUGUSTIN FREDIEU
MARIA JUANNA SOREL
September 15, 1790, after one ban, marriage of Augustin
Fredieu, native of Toscana in Italy, legitimate son of
_____ Fredieu and Angelica Clera . . . and . . . Maria
Juanna Sorel, native of this parish, legitimate daughter
of Pedro Sorel and Maria Rosa Bossalier. Witnesses: Luis
Buard, Andres Rambint, Lucas Sorel.

3369. SALVADOR RUIS
MARIA IGNACIA ROBLEAU
September 20, 1790, after one ban, marriage of Salvador
Ruis, native of Pueblo San Luis de la Passe, in the Kingdom
of Mexico, legitimate son of Andres Ruis and Maria Nicolas
Peveyna . . . and . . . Maria Ignacia Robleau, native of

Adayes, legitimate daughter of Guillermo Robleau and Maria Isidora Sepide. Witnesses: Pedro Ramis, Francisco Sebles, Benito Pescio.

3370. ANDRES FRANCISCO VALENTIN
LUISA ANGELICA MALIGE
November 13, 1790, after 1 ban, marriage of Francisco Valentin, native of this parish, legitimate son of Francisco Valentin and Maria Luisa Totin . . . and . . . Luisa Angelica Malige, native of the Parish of Mobile, legitimate daughter of Joseph Malige and Antonio Lebrun. Witnesses: Atanasio Poissot, Luis Buard, Mr. Toisin /Tauzin/ and Francisco Rambint.

3371. LUIS VASCOCU
MARIA MADELENA PERAU
November 22, 1790, after 3 bans, marriage of Luis Vascocu, native of this parish, legitimate son of Antonio Vascocu and Maria Barba Toups . . . and Maria Madelena Perau, native of this parish, legitimate daughter of Francisco Pereau and Maria Catalina Dupre. Witnesses: Antonio Ploché, Joseph Jean Ris, Francisco Pereau, and Antonio Vascocu.

3372. JOSEPH GABRIEL TORRES
MARIA RACHAL
March 8, 1791, after one ban, marriage of Joseph Gabriel Torres, native of Los Adayes, legitimate son of Joseph Torres and Juanna Reyes . . . and . . . Maria Rachal, native of this parish, legitimate daughter of Luis Rachal and Maria Luisa Leroy. Witnesses: Andres David, Lorenzo Robequi, Benito Pescio, Francisco Felles.

3373. THOMAS BOM (BROM) /BROWN/
MARIA TEAL
March 8, 1791, after one ban, marriage of Thomas Brom, a native of the province of Pensilvania, legitimate son of Juan Brom and Margarita Onil . . . and . . . Maria Teal, native of the province of Carolina, legitimate daughter of Edwardo Teal and Rebecca Jons. Witnesses: Bautista Bartar?, Francisco Ualina?, Luis Fortin, Lucas Sorel.

NOTE: The civil divorce of this couple, dated July 2, 1792, appears in Doc. 2427, French Archives, Office of the Clerk of Court, Natchitoches.

3374. ANTONIO VASCOCU
GENEVIEVE GONIN
May 10, 1791, after three bans, marriage of Antonio Vascocu, native of this parish, legitimate son of Antonio Vascocu and Maria Toups . . . and . . . Genevieve Gonin, native of this parish, legitimate daughter of Bautista Gonin and Manuela Riche. Witnesses: Antonio Ploché, Luis Vascocu,

Bernabe Cheletre, Juan Bautista Duboë.

3375. JUAN BAUTISTA LATIÉ
MARIA PELAGIE FREDERIC
May 31, 1791, after three bans, marriage of Juan Bautista Latié, native of this parish, legitimate son of Joseph Latié and Maria Ana Verge . . . and . . . Maria Pelagie Frederic, native of the parish of St. Charles on the German Goast, legitimate daughter of Felipe Frederic and Maria Catalina Sauvage. Witnesses: Luis Tomassin, Francisca Callé, Andre David, Remy Pereau.

3376. PEDRO DUPRE
FRANCESCA LECOUR
July 2, 1791, after three bans, marriage of Pedro Dupre, native of this parish, legitimate son of Joseph Dupre and Maria Derbanne . . . and . . . Francesca LeCour, native of this parish, legitimate daughter of Don Luis LeCourt and Juanna Leroy. Witnesses: Atanasio Poissot, Estevan Vergé, Bautista Buard, Manuel Sempry /St. Prix, *dit* of Davion/.

3377. ESTEVAN DUGUET
CATALINA SALVAN
July 26, 1791, after three bans, marriage of Estevan Duguet, native of Canada, legitimate son of Bazilio Duguet and Maria Luisa Senecal . . . and . . . Catalina Salvan, native of the post of New Orleans, legitimate daughter of Juan Salvan and Maria Luisa Lambre. Witnesses: Luis Buard, Remy Lambre, Agustin Fredieu, Crisostome Pereau.

3378. FRANCISCO DAVION
MARGARITA CLOUTIÉ
August 1, 1791, after three bans, marriage of Francisco Davion, native of this parish, legitimate son of Juan Bautista Davion and Maria Jacinta Triche . . . and . . . Margarita Cloutié, native of the parish of Los Alemanes, legitimate daughter of Alexis Cloutié and Maria Rachal. Witnesses: Bautista Anty, Juan Bautista Davion, Luis Monet, Atanasio Lecour.

3379. JUAN PALVADOS
LEONORA TESSIE
August 25, 1791, after three bans, marriage of Juan Palvados, native of the post of Illineses, legitimate son of Francisco Palvados and Juanna Bernarda . . . and . . . Leonora Tessié, native of the same post, legitimate daughter of Pedro Tessié and Madelena Turpin. Witnesses: Pedro Gagne, Pedro Tessier, Francisco Rambin, Auger Tessié.

3380. ANTONIO PRUDHOMME
MARIA LAMBRE
August 31, 1791, after one ban, marriage of Antonio

Prudhomme, native of this parish, legitimate son of Juan
Bautista Prudhomme and Maria Josepha Colantin . . . and
. . . Maria Lambre, native of this parish, legitimate
daughter of Iago Lambre and Maria Ana Poissot. Witnesses:
Francisco Rouquier, Ailhaud St. Anne, Manuel Prudhomme,
and Andres Vendalay.

3381. JUAN BAUTISTA DAVION
MARIA ULALIA VASCOCU
November 3, 1791, after three bans, marriage of Juan Bautista Davion, native of this parish, legitimate son of Juan
Bautista Davion and Maria Jacinta Triche . . . and . . .
Maria Ulalia Vascocu, native of this parish, legitimate
daughter of Antonio Vascocu and Maria Barba Toups. Witnesses: Juan Bautista Davion, Antonio Vascocu, Henrique
Triche, and Andres Vascocu.

3382. JOSEPH TAUZIN
MARIA CHAMARD
November 8, 1791, after 2 bans, marriage of Joseph Tauzin,
native of the diocese of <u>Ausco</u>?* in France, legitimate son
of Gerardo Tauzin and Juanna Barthau . . . and . . . Maria
Chamard, native of New Orleans, legitimate daughter of Luis
Carlos Chamard and Maria Catalina Bardon. Witnesses: Ailhaud St. Anne, Joseph Maria Armant, Francisco Rambint,
Joseph Malige, Francisco Lacase.

*The French version of this entry, see No. 1668, identifies
Tauzin as a native of <u>Auch</u>.

3383. PEDRO BEAULIEU
MARIA TERESA BEAUDOUIN
December 12, 1791, after three bans, marriage of Pedro Beaulieu, native of the parish of Sta. Genoveva in Illinese,
legitimate son of Pedro Beaulieu and Genevova <u>Cuno</u>? (Euno?)
. . . and . . . Maria Teresa Beaudouin, native of this parish, legitimate daughter of Francisco Beaudouin and Maria
Ana Bontant. Witnesses: Benito Pescio, Juan Bautista
Duboë, Pedro Cheletre, Andres Frederick.

3384. JUAN BAUTISTA BARTOLOME RACHAL
MARIA PELAGIA BREVEL
December 19, 1791, after two bans, marriage of Juan Bautista
Bartolome Rachal, native of this parish, legitimate son of
Bartolome Rachal and Maria Lamalaty . . . and . . . Maria
Pelagia Brevel, native of this parish, legitimate daughter
of Juan Bautista Brevel and Maria Francisca Poissot. Witnesses: Alexandro Guebois, Andres Verdolay, Gaspar Fiolle,
Luis Bartolome Rachal.

3385. JUAN BAUTISTA LEMOINE
FELICITE LECASE
February 21, 1792, after one ban, marriage of Juan Bautista

Lemoine, native of this parish, legitimate son of Carlos Lemoine and Ysabel Dupre . . . and Felicité Lecase, native of the parish of Opelousas, legitimate daughter of Carlos Lecase and Felicité Langlois. Witnesses: Atanasio Poissot, Estevan Vergé, Iago Lacase, Antonio Lemoine.

3386. MIGUEL RAMBIN
MARIA TERESA MAILLIOUX
April 22, 1792, after one ban, marriage of Miguel Rambin, native of this parish, legitimate son of Andres Rambint and Francesca Clermont . . . and . . . Maria Teresa Maillioux, native of this parish, legitimate daughter of Ignacio Maillioux and Teresa Filibote. Witnesses: Lorenzo Maillioux, Francisco Rambint.

3387. JACOB PABLO /PAUL/
MARIA ANNA LAPRARIE
July 17, 1792, after three bans, marriage of Jacob Pablo, native of the province of Carolina in the United States, legitimate son of Jacob Pablo and Rachel Oberin . . . and . . . Maria Anna Laprairie, legitimate daughter of Luis Laprairie and Maria Juana Castel. Witnesses: Francois Rambin (s), Ignace Maiou (s), Louis Deville (x), Adam Hofman (x).

3388. JUAN BAUTISTA FRANCISCO* RAMBINT
MARIA JUAN-RIS
July 25, 1792, after three bans, marriage of Juan Francisco Rambint (s), aged about 36 years, legitimate son of deceased Andres Rambint and Francisca Clermont . . . and . . . Maria Juan-Ris, legitimate daughter of deceased Juan-Ris and Maria Juanna Chagneau. Witnesses: Andre Rambin (s), Pablo Mar- Caulay (s/ Paul Marcollay), Francisco Grappe (s), Miguel Chagneau.

3389. NICOLAS AUGUSTIN /METOYER/
AGNES /POISSOT/*
August 22, 1792, after one ban, marriage of Nicolas Augustin, free *mulato*, son of Maria Theresa, free *negra*, native of this parish . . . and . . . Agnes, free *mulata*, native of this parish, daughter of Francisca, *negra* slave of Monsieur Derbanne. Witnesses: Joseph Langlois, free *mulato*, Nicolas Piqueri, free *mulato*(s), Nicolas, free *negro*(x), and Pedro, *Indio* (x).

*Mme. Metoyer's surname appears in such later records as Marriage of Élisé Roques and Marie Susette Metoyer, June 26, 1820, Register 11. She was purchased and manumitted, at the age of six, by Athanase and Remi Poissot; see Docs. 1052 and 1093, French Archives, Office of the Clerk of Court, Natchitoches.

3390. CARLOS LEMOINE
JUANNA LEBRUN
September 17, 1792, after three bans, marriage of Carlos LeMoine, native of this parish, son of Carlos LeMoine and Ysabel Dupre . . . and . . . Juanna LeBrun, native of New Orleans, legitimate daughter of Guilhelmo LeBrun and of Maria Luisa Totin. Witnesses: Athanasio Poissot (x), Pedro Brosset (x), Remi Perau (x), Domingo Rachal (x).

3391. ATHANASIO LECOURT
MARIA ROSA ROBIN
September 25, 1792, after 3 bans, marriage of Athanasio Le Court, native of this parish, legitimate son of Luis LeCour de Prele and Juanna Leroi . . . and . . . Maria Rosa Robin, native of this parish, legitimate daughter of Miguel Robin and Maria Luisa Boulé. Witnesses: Gaspar Lacour (x), Pedro Beaudouin (x), Nicolas Gagné (x), Barthelemi LeCourt (x).

3392. LUIS FRANCISCO VASCOCU
MARIA GAGNE
October 22, 1792, after three bans, marriage of Luis Francisco Vascocu, native of this parish, legitimate son of Antonio Cocu and Maria Barba Toups . . . and . . . Maria Gagné, native of this parish, legitimate daughter of Pedro Gagné and Maria Davion. Witnesses: Luis Cocu (s/ Louis Vascocu), Juan Bautista Davion (x), Luis Closo (s/ Louis Closeau) and Antonio Vascocu (x).

3393. JOSEPH IAGO LATIÉ
FRANCISCA CHELETTE
October 23, 1792, after three bans, marriage of Joseph Iago Latié, native of this parish, legitimate son of Joseph Latié and Anna Vergé . . . and . . . Francisca Chelette, a native of this parish, legitimate daughter of Miguel Cheletre and Anna Barba Pomier. Witnesses: Luis Tomassin (x), Iago Fort (x), Juan Bautista Duboë (x), Francisco Lecompte (x).

3394. LUIS GUILLOI /GUILLORI/
ROSALIA
November 27, 1792, after dispensation from all three bans, marriage of Luis Guilloi, Indian, a native of Opelousas . . . and . . . Rosalia, *mestiza*, native of this parish. Witnesses: Remi Lambre (x), Luis Monet (x), Gil de la Barre (s/ Gille de la Bare).

3395. IAGO SEBASTIAN PRUDHOMME
MARIA LUISA ANTONIA /DE ST. DENIS/*
February 3, 1793, after three bans, marriage of Iago Sebastien Prud'homme, legitimate son of deceased Sebastian Prud'homme, native of this parish . . . and . . . Maria Luisa

Antonia, a daughter of a father and mother unknown, native of this parish. Witnesses: Joseph Tauzin (s), Genoveva Sorel (x), Luis Chamarre (s/ Chamard), Maria Josepha Clermont, widow of Bautista Duboë. */See note to Entry 2175/

3396.   JUAN BAUTISTA JANNOT
CECILIA LAPRAIRIE
March 19, 1793, after three bans, marriage performed with the permission of Estevan Marafret de Layssard, commandant of Rapides, between Juan Bautista Jannot, native of the town of Montreal in Canada, legitimate son of Juan Bautista Jeannot and Maria Demare . . . and . . . Cecilia Laprairie, widow of Belleouil, native of New Orleans, legitimate daughter of Luis Laprayrie and Maria Juanna Castel. Witnesses Luis Chamarre (s/ Chamard), Madame Rambin, Gille de la Barre (s), Madama Francois Rambint.

3397.   MIGUEL VINCENT
ELENA ROBLO
July 8, 1793, after three bans, marriage of Miguel Vincent, aged 25, legitimate son of Miguel Vincent and Maria Lengeven, deceased . . . and . . . Elena Roblo, aged 15 years, daughter of Guillermo Roblo, deceased, and Antonia de Ceped, his wife. Witnesses: Josef Latie (s), Luis Foovin? (Foarin?).

3398.   BERNARDO DE ORTOLAN
CATHARINA BARDON
July 22, 1793, after three bans, marriage of Bernardo De Ortolan (s/ Dortolant), captain of the cavalry at this post, legitimate son of Raimundo De Ortolant and Maria Juana Labatut, native of Bordeaux, widower of Mariana Grape . . . and . . . Catharina Bardon (s), aged about 30 years, a daughter of Raymundo Bardon and Mariana Verneuil, native of New Orleans. Witnesses: Dna. Rouquie and Dna. Arman.

3399.   DOMINGO RACHAL
MARIA ROSALIA VERCHER
January 7, 1795, after three bans, marriage of Domingo Rachal, native of this parish, legitimate son of Bartolome Rachal and Maria Lamalaty . . . and . . . Maria Rosalia Vercher, native of this parish, legitimate daughter of Luis Vercher (s/ L. Verchair) and Maria Luisa Grillet. Witnesses: Edouard Morphil (s/ Murphy), Noël Rachal (s), Maria Juana Grillet, Luis Vercher, Margarita Grillet, Michel Duffy (s); Anty (s).

3400.   ANTONIO DUBOË
MARIA JOSEPHA MALIGE
January 19, 1795, after three bans, marriage of Antonio Duboë, native of this parish, legitimate son of Juan

Bautista Duboë and Maria Josepha Clermont . . . and . . . Maria Josepha Malige, native of the parish of Mobile, legitimate daughter of Joseph Malige and Maria Antonia Le Brun. Witnesses: Bernardo Dortolant (s), Widow Rambint, Andre Rambin (s), Marie Francoise Clermont (s), Jh. Tauzin (s Mariann Bardon (s), Marie Joseph Clermont (s).

3401. DOMINGO /METOYER/
MARGUERITE /LECOMTE/*
January 19, 1795, marriage, after three bans, of Domingo, a free *mulato*, native of this parish, son of Maria Theresa, free *negra*, and a father unknown . . . and . . . Marguerite, free *mulata*, native of this parish, daughter of Maria, *negra* slave of Widow LeCompte, and a father unknown. Witnesses: Joseph, *Indio*, Madelena, *mulata*, Joseph Langloy, free *mulata*, Maria Luisa, free *negra*.

*Mme. Metoyer's maiden surname is provided in such documents as Partition of Estate of Dominique Metoyer, Natchitoches Parish Records Collection, Box 14, Folder 63, Louisiana State University Archives, Baton Rouge.

3402. HIPOLITE BORDELON
MARIA TERESA TRICHE
January 27, 1795, after three bans, marriage of Hipolite Bordelon, native of Pointe Coupée, legitimate son of Nicolas Bordelon and Adrienne Rondan . . . and . . . Maria Teresa Triche (s), native of this parish, legitimate daughter of Manuel Triche and Maria Luisa Grappe. Witnesses: Bernardo Dortolant (s), Juan Adelay, Luis Fonteneau (x) and Francisca Grappe (s).

3403. ANTONIO POISSOT
MARIA SILVILLA GUTIERES
February 3, 1795, after three bans, marriage of Antonio Poissot, native of this parish, legitimate son of Dn. Remigio Poissot and Luisa Cave . . . and . . . Maria Silvilla Gutieres, native of this parish, legitimate daughter of Miguel Gutieres and Maria Elves. Witnesses: Pablo Marcolai (s/ Paul Marcollay), Domingo Prudhomme (s), Benito Montanary (s/ Benoit Montanary), Palagia Grappe.

3404. FRANCISCO MERCIÉ
MARIA LUISA PRUDHOMME
February 16, 1795, after three bans, marriage of Francisco Mercié, native of Leon in France, legitimate son of Claudio Mercié and Margarita Barbié . . . and . . . Maria Luisa Prudhomme, native of this parish, legitimate daughter of Bastien Prudhomme and Juana Chever. Witnesses: Carlos Duret (x), Juanna Margarita Totin, Guillermo Chever (x), Maria Josepha Clermont (s).

3405. JUAN BAUTISTA LAJEUNESSE
       ISABEL BREVEL
       February 17, 1795, after three bans, marriage of Juan Bautista Lajeunesse, native of the post of Los Arcas /Arkansas_27, legitimate son of Ou_____ Billet Lajeunesse and Maria Madelena Lacroix . . . and . . . Isabel Brevel, a native of this parish, legitimate daughter of Juan Bautista Brevel and Francisca Poissot. Witnesses: Francisco La Caze (s), Atanasio Poisot, Jr. (s), Pedro Derbanne, and Eufrasia Rambint.

3406. BERTRAND PLAISANCE
       MARIA BARBA GRILLET
       April 15, 1795, after three bans, marriage of Bertrand Plaisance, native of this parish, legitimate son of Juan Bautista Plaisance and Margarita Totin . . . and . . . Maria Barba Grillet, native of this parish, legitimate daughter of Marin Grillet and Maria Luisa Brevel. Witnesses: Jn. Bautista Triche (s), Da. Dolet, Juan Francisco /Le/ Vasseur, and Maria Madelena Grillet.

3407. FRANCISCO ROUQUIER
       MARIA ANNA BUARD
       May 12, 1795, after three bans, marriage of Francisco Rouquier, a native of Puileveque, France, legitimate son of Marco Rouquier and Maria Combecave . . . and . . . Maria Anna Buard (s), native of this parish, legitimate daughter of deceased Gabriel Buard and deceased Maria Anna Rouseau. Witnesses: Francisco Bossie (s), Manuel Prudhomme (s), Atanasio Poissot; Remigio Lambre (s/ Remy Lambre), Genoveva Levasseur, L. Mongino (s). Also signed: Francois Rouquier.

3408. CARLOS LE DOUX
       LUISA EUGENIA LAMOTTE
       May 22, 1795, after three bans, marriage of Carlos LeDoux, native of this parish, legitimate son of Antoñio LeDoux and Maria Francisca Fascinde . . . and . . . Luisa Eugenia Lamotte, native of the post of Opelousas, legitimate daughter of Iago Lamotte and Juana Porret. Witnesses: Remigio Lambre (s), Sophia Oliver, Nicolas Lauve, Susana Prudhomme.

3409. PIERRE JARRY
       CECILE DUPRE
       September 15, 1795, after three bans, marriage of Pierre Jarry, native of Lice, dependancy of the Republic of Venise, major son of Michel Jarry and Marie Amien . . . and . . . Cecile Dupre, minor daughter of Robert Dupre and Manon Cavé. Witnesses: Andre Frederic, Marin Grillet (s), Marie Catherinne Frideiu, Jean Pommie, Jean Marc

Marchand (s), Franc. Lacase.

3410. JACQUES WALES /WALLACE7
MARIE HIACINTHE GANIÉ
November 16, 1795, after the publication of bans in this parish and at the Cote doche /Caddodoche7, marriage of Jacques Wales, living at the post of Cotedoche, son of Joseph Wales and Denee Bulstrong . . . and . . . Marie Hiacinthe Ganié, daughter of Etienne Ganié and Marie Louise Bertrand. Witnesses: Marie Joseph Ganié, sister, Louis Davion, brother, Pierre Ternie (s), Jullien Besson, Louis David (s), Fs. Grappé (s).

3411. JEAN BAPTISTE BUARD
MARIE GENEVIEVE LEVASSEUR
November 18, 1795, marriage of Jean Baptiste Buard, major son of deceased Gabriel Buart and Marie Anne Rousseau . . . and . . . Marie Genevieve Levasseur, daughter of Francois Levasseur and deceased Marie Mader. Witnesses: Louis Buar (x), Augustin, Jean Denis Buart, his brothers; and Francois Levasseur, her father; Baptiste Anti (s/Anty), her brother-in-law; Jean Levasseur (s), her brother; Marie Grillet, Andre Rambin (s), Marin Grillet (s/ Grillte); Metoyer (s); Murphy (s); Rouquier, the younger (s).

3412. JEAN DENIS BUART
VICTOIRE POISSOT
November 26, 1795, marriage of Jean Denis Buart (s/ Buard) native of this parish, legitimate son of deceased Gabriel Buart and Anne Rousseau . . . and . . . Victoire Poissot, native of this parish, daughter of Remi Poissot and Marie Louise Cavé. Witnesses: André Rambin (s), his brother-in-law; Jean Baptiste Buart,(s), his brother; Remi Poissot, her father; Manuel Prudhomme and Antoine Prudhomme (s) (s), her cousins; Rouquier, the younger (s); Remy Lambre (s); Murphy (s).

3413. MICHEL DENIS CASSENAVE
MARIE JEAN RIS
April 13, 1795, marriage of Michel Denis Cassenave (s), legitimate son of deceased Bernard Casenave and Renée Clavan, native of La Rochelle, parish of St. Jean . . . and . . . Marie Jean Ris, widow of Francois Rambin, legitimate daughter of Jean Ris, deceased, and Marie Jeanne Chaniau, also deceased. Witnesses: Michel Rambin (x), Jean Adelé, André Rambin (s), Michel Chanian (x), Henry Triche (s).

3414. JEAN BAPTISTE GRAPPE
GENEVIEVE SAUREL
April 21, 1795, marriage of Jean Baptiste Grappe (s), legitimate son of deceased Alexis Grape and Marie Louise

Guedon . . . and . . . Genevieve Saurel (x), legitimate daughter of deceased Pierre Saurel and Marie Rose Bosselier. Witnesses: Francois Grape (s/ Fs. Grappe), Julien Becon (s/ Jullien Besson), "Luc Sorel and Augustin, brother and brother-in-law of the bride" (s/ Augustin Fraidieu (x) and Luc Saurel (x).

3415. BASTIEN OLIVAU
HELEINE LENDRENAU
June 30, 1795, marriage of Bastien Olivau, legitimate son of Pierre Oliveau and Marie Anne Riche, native of the post of Ouachitas . . . and . . . Heleine Lendrenau (x), daughter of Jean Pierre Lendrenau and Susanne Joffrions, also living at the post of Ouachita. Witnesses: Pierre Olivau (x), his father; Joseph Marie Armand (s), Ignace Maillou (s/ Ignase Maillioux), Susanne Joffrions (s), mother of the bride, André Antoine Rambin, and Jean Adelé (s/ Jean Adlé). Also signed: Bastien Olivau (x).

3416. HENRI TRICHE
GENEVIEVE RIS
July 12, 1795, marriage of Henri Triche (s), legitimate son of deceased Manuel Triche and Marie Louise Grappe . . . and . . . Genevieve Ris, legitimate daughter of Jean Ris and Marie Jeanne Chagneau. Witnesses: Francois Grappe (s), uncle of groom, who authorizes the marriage; Louis Fontenau (x), also his uncle; Michel Chagnau (x), uncle of the bride who authorizes her marriage; Louis David (s), her friend; Jean Ris (s), her brother.

3417. JEAN LALAND
ADELAIDE VERCHER
November 3, 1795, marriage of Jean Laland, son of deceased Jean Laland and Marie Catherine Dupre . . . and . . . Adelaide Vercher, legitimate daughter of Louis Vercher and Marie Louise Grillé. Witnesses: Louis Lamalati (s/ Lamalaty); Francois Grape (s/ Grappe); Mr. Bertrand Plaisance, uncle of bride; Jean Baptiste Buart (s); and Rosalie Vercher; Anty (s).

3418. LOUIS LONGLOIS
MARIE CELESTE VERGÉ
November 23, 1795, marriage of Louis Longlois, native of Pointe Coupée, living at this post for several years, son of deceased Augustin Langlois and Marie Louise Riche, still living . . . and . . . Marie Celeste Vergé, daughter of Etienne Vergé and Marie Francoise Dupré, native of this post. Witnesses: Antoine Prudhomme (s), Jean Baptiste Anty (s), Etienne Verget and Marie Francoise Dupré, her father and mother, Pierre Dupré (s) and Lauve (s).

3419.   JEAN PIERRE CLOUTIER
        MARIE SALVANT
        January 9, 1797, marriage of Jean Pierre Cloutier, native
        of the German Coast, living for several years at this
        post, legitimate son of deceased Alexis Cloutier and Marie
        Rachal . . . and . . . Marie Salvant, native of New Or-
        leans, living in this post, legitimate daughter of de-
        ceased Jean Salvant and Marie Louise Lambre. Witnesses:
        Louis Charles Chamart, André Antoine Rambin, Placide Bos-
        sie, and Francois Lemaitre.

3420.   MARIE ATHANASE POISSOT
        MARIE LOUISE HELENE EUFROSINE PAVIE
        February 1, 1797, marriage of Marie Athanase Poissot (s),
        legitimate son of Athanase Poissot and Marie Soto . . .
        and . . . Marie Louise Helene Eufrosine Pavie (s/ Helene
        Pavie), native of this post, legitimate daughter of deceased
        Etienne Pavie and Therese Buart, living and remarried to
        Sieur Pierre Metoyer. Witnesses: Athanase Poissot, Manuel
        Prudhomme, Pierre Metoyer (s), Gabriel Buart, Denis Buard
        (s) and Murphy (s).

3421.   ANTOINE LEMOINE
        GENEVIEVE BELLEGARDE
        February 19, 1797, marriage of Antoine Lemoine, native of
        this post, legitimate son of Charles LeMoine and Elisabeth
        Dupre . . . and . . . Genevieve Bellegarde, native of the
        post of Rapides, daughter of deceased Jean Baptiste Belle-
        garde and Magdeleine Montpierre. Witnesses: Valentin
        Dessart /de Layssard/, Chevailler Poiret, Bolon Dessart
        /de Layssard/ and Jean Poiret.

3422.   PIERRE TIERRI
        MARIE ROSALIE FREDERIK
        May 27, 1797, marriage of Pierre Tierri, native of the
        post of Michel Maguire in Canada, minor and legitimate
        son of Antoine Tierri and Francoise Bequet, authorized by
        Michel Hernandes, his tutor named by the commandant of the
        post, who has declared by his letter of office under date
        of the 5th of this month that Michel Hernande will act as
        the tutor of Pierre Tierri to authorize his marriage . . .
        and . . . Marie Rosalie Frederik, legitimate daughter of
        deceased Philippe Frederik and Marie Catherine Sauvage,
        native of this parish. Witnesses: Michel Hernande,
        Barnabé Chelette, Francois Bonin /Gonin/, Andre Frederik,
        Pierre Cheletre, Francois Latié.

3423.   ETIENNE LACASSE
        DOROTHEE MASSIP
        July 4, 1797, marriage of Etienne Lacasse, native of Ope-
        lousas, living at this post, legitimate son of Charles

Lacasse and Felicité Langlois, living at Opelousas . . . and . . . Dorothée Massip, native of this parish, legitimate daughter of Jean Massip and Marie Lemoine, living at this post. Witnesses: Baltasar Brevel, Manuel Derbanne, Francois Lemaitre, and André Frederik.

3424. JEAN PAUL COUTIE
MARIE JOSEPH TORRES
July 24, 1797, marriage of Jean Paul Coutie, native of this parish, legitimate son of deceased Jean Coutie and Marie Olivié, now married to Michel Ernande and living at this post . . . and . . . Marie Joseph Torres, native of this parish, legitimate daughter of Joseph Torres and Marie Joseph de Roi. Witnesses: Michel Ernande, Pierre Chelet, Philippe Frederic, André Frederic, Athanase Poissot, who has assured us that the *vacherie* on which Sieur Joseph Torres lives is within the limits of this post.

3425. BERNARD HISSOURA
MARGUERITTE GRILLÉ
August 18, 1797, marriage of Bernard Hissoura, native of Cafalia (Tafalia) in Spain, major and legitimate son of deceased Jean Hissoura and Bernard Detchou, living in this post . . . and . . . Margueritte Grillé, widow of Remi Totin, legitimate daughter of Marin Grillé and Marie Louise Brevel. Witnesses: Jean Baptiste Theodore Grillé; Antoine Grillé, and Francois Le Maitre.

3426. LOUIS DERBANNE
FRANCOISE RACHAL
November 9, 1797, marriage of Louis Derbanne, major and legitimate son of deceased Pierre Derbanne, and Marie LeClerc, his widow . . . and . . . Francoise Rachal, legitimate daughter of deceased Barthelemi Rachal and Marie jobart Lamatie, his widow. Witnesses: Manuel Prudhomme, Pierre Chaler, Joseph Derbanne, Manuel Derbanne, Remi Lambre, Manuel Barthelemi Rachal, Louis Rachal, and Boete Lafite, Jr.

3427. JEAN BAPTISTE BUART
MARIE POISSOT
January 25, 1798, marriage of Jean Baptiste Buart, after three bans, the widower of Jeanne Levasseur and major, legitimate son of deceased Gabriel Buart and Marie Anne Rousseau . . . and . . . Marie Poissot, legitimate daughter of deceased Remi Poissot and Marie Louise Cave; both are natives of this parish. Witnesses: Elisabeth and Felicite Demeziere, Marie Charlote Mercie, Athanase Poissot, Francois Chabuche, Remi Lambre, and Jean Baptiste Anti.

3428. GASPAR LACOUR
       MARIE FELICITE BREVEL
       January 30, 1798, after three bans, marriage of Gaspar
       LaCour, legitimate son of Pierre LaCour and Marie Louise
       Verger, a native of this parish . . . and . . . Marie
       Felicite Brevel, legitimate daughter of Jean Baptiste
       Brevel and Marie Francoise Poissot, a native of this parish. Witnesses: Pierre LaCour, Remi Lambre, Athanase
       Poissot, Jean Baptiste Brevel, Nicolas Love Colin /Lauve
       dit Colin/, Jean Baptiste Derbanne.

3429. JOSEPH RABALLE
       MARIE BONTEMPS
       February 4, 1798, marriage of Joseph Raballé, widower of
       Marie Malbert, legitimate son of deceased Joseph Raballé
       and Anne Barbe? . . . and Marie Bontems, natural daughter
       of Marianne Bontems, widow of Francois Bontems*. Witnesses: Remi Lambre (s), Marie Anne Bontems, Jean Delouche,
       Pierre Baudouin, Anty (s).

       *Should be Beaudouin.

3430. JOSEPH FERRIÉ
       ELISABETH LEBRUN
       April 30, 1798, marriage, after three bans, of Joseph Ferrié, native of St. Marcel, diocese of Marseil in France,
       son of Jean Baptiste Ferrié and Margueritte Caisle? . . .
       and . . . Elisabeth LeBrun, native of this parish, legitimate daughter of Guillaume Lebrun and deceased Marie
       Louise Totin. Witnesses: Jean Baptiste Lemoine, Jean
       Joseph Martinau, Louis Rachal, Pierre Jarri.

3431. PIERRE LACOUR
       MARIE THERESE BREVELLE
       June 30, 1798, after three bans, marriage of Pierre LaCour,
       native of this parish, legitimate son of Pierre LaCour and
       Marie Louise Verge . . . and . . . Marie Therese Brevelle,
       legitimate daughter of Jean Baptiste Brevel and Marie Francoise Poissot. Witnesses: Nicolas Lauve, Jean Baptiste
       Derbanne, Jean Baptiste LaCour, Jean Baptiste Brevel, Jean
       Baptiste Anti, Pierre LaCour.

3432. PIERRE BOETE LAFITE
       URSULE GAGNE
       July 30, 1798, after three bans, marriage of Pierre Boete
       Lafite, legitimate son of Paul Boete Lafite, remarried to
       Marie Anne Sauto, and deceased Magdeleine Grape . . . and
       . . . Ursule Gagne, legitimate daughter of deceased Etienne
       Gagne and Marie Louise Bertrand, a native of this parish.
       Witnesses: Louis Lamalatie, Julien Besson, Jean Baptiste
       Anti, Louis Davion.

3433. PAUL POISSOT
MARIE LOUISE ANTI
October 6, 1798, marriage of Paul Poissot, legitimate son of deceased Remi Poissot and Louise Cave . . . and . . . Marie Louise Anti, legitimate daughter of Jean Baptiste Anti and deceased Catherine Gallien; both natives of this post. Witnesses: Remis Lambre, Manuel and Antoine Prudhomme, and Athanase Poissot.

3434. ATHANASE DUPRE
CECILE LOUISE* LECOUR
May 7, 1799, marriage of Athanase Dupre, native of this parish, legitimate son of deceased Joseph Dupre and Marie Derbanne . . . and . . . Cecile* LeCour, legitimate daughter of deceased Louis LeCour and Jeanne LeRoi. Witnesses: Louis Langlois, Pierre Dupre, Jacques Lacase, Athanase LeCour.

*The bride's name appears in the text as Cecile and in the margin as Louise.

3435. PIERRE THERNIÉ
ROSE GAGNÉ
August 20, 1799, marriage of Pierre Thernié, native of New Orleans, son of deceased Etienne Thernier and Margueritte Prudhomme, living in this post . . . and . . . Rose Gagné, native of this parish, daughter of deceased Etienne Gagné and Marie Louise Bertrand. Witnesses: Louis Lamalathi, Francois Grape, Julien Besson, Benoist Montanari.

3436. PIERRE JOSEPH MAËS
MARIE CONAN
August 22, 1799, marriage, after publication of three bans and dispensation from the impediment caused by affinity, of Pierre Joseph Maës, native of St. Amand in Flandres, a part of France, widower of Marie Anne Dartigau . . . and . . . Marie Conan, native of Bayonne in France, widow of Jean Baptiste Dartigau. Witnesses: Jean Baptiste Ailhaud St. Anne, Joseph Tausin, Louis Charles Chamart and Francois Rouquier.

3437. PIERRE VALLERI
CATHERINE
October 17, 1799, marriage, after the baptism of the groom, of Pierre Valleri of the Apalaches village, son of Carode and Marie Anne . . . and . . . Catherine, legitimate daughter of Louis and Marie Jeanne. The sacrament of penance was first administered to Catherine, and their child, Fortune, aged three, was legitimized. Godparents and witnesses were Antoine Tinsa, Louis, and Jean Baptiste Valleri. All parties were Indians of the Apalaches nation, where the ceremonies took place.

3438. JEAN BAPTISTE ARMAND
MARIE CATHERINE FREDERIK
November 26, 1799, marriage of Jean Baptiste Armand, native of this parish, legitimate son of Joseph Marie Armand and Therese Legros . . . and . . . Marie Catherine Frederik, legitimate daughter of deceased Philippe Frederik and Marie Sauvage, his widow, now living at this post. Witnesses: Joseph Marie Armand, his father; Athanase Armand, his brother; Jean Francois Frederik and Philippe Frederik, her brothers.

3439. BARTHELEMI RACHAL
MAGDELEINE GRILLET
January 7, 1800, after three bans, marriage of Barthelemi Rachal, native of this parish, legitimate son of Barthelemi Rachal and Marie Francoise Lamalathie, his widow . . . and . . . Magdeleine Grillet, legitimate daughter of Marin Grillet and Marie Louise Brevel, a native of this post. Witnesses: Bernard Hissoura; Antoine Grillet, her brother; Barthelemi Rachal, his brother, Louis Lamalathie, his uncle

3440. FRANCOIS GONIN
MARIE BARBE FREDERIQ
February 18, 1800, after three bans, marriage of Francois Gonin, native of this parish, legitimate son of Jean Baptiste Gonin and Manuel Riche . . . and . . . Marie Barbe Frederiq, native of this parish, legitimate daughter of Philippe Frederiq and deceased Barbe Cheletre. Witnesses: Barnabe Chelet; Jean Baptiste Lestage; Andre Frederiq, the uncle of the bride; and André Frederiq, her brother.

3441. BERNARD GUISARNAT
MARIE LOUISE LARENAUDIERE
September 9, 1800, after three bans, marriage of Bernard Guisarnat, native of Fean in the province of Varetous in Beard, France, legitimate son of deceased Jean Guisarnat and Catherine Borde, living for several years in this post . . . and . . . Marie Louise Larenaudiere, legitimate daughter of Pierre Larenaudiere and Jeanne Laberi, native of this parish. Witnesses: Jean Baptiste Anty and Joseph Derbanne Pierre LaRenaudiere, her father; Manuel and Dominique Rachal

3442. LAURENT MAIOU
MARGUERITE DUVAL
October 20, 1800, after one ban, rectification of marriage of Laurent Maiou, native of this parish and living here, son of Ignace Maiou and Therese Filibot, his wife, both residents of this post . . . and . . . Marguerite Duval, native of the post of Ouachita, living in this post for one year, legitimate daughter of Francois Duval and Therese Blanpan, residents of Ouachita; couple had been married by

the Ouachita commandant eighteen months earlier. Witnesses: J. Horn, Jean Marc Marchand, Pierre Maiou, Jacques Herié.

3443. JEAN BAPTISTE ANTI
MARIE CYPRIENE DERBANNE
November 26, 1800, after three bans, marriage of Jean Baptiste Anty, son of Jean Baptiste Anty and deceased Cathrine Gallien, his wife . . . and . . . Marie Cÿpriëne Derbanne, legitimate daughter of Pierre Derbanne and Marie Francoise Brevel, native of this parish. Witnesses: Joseph Tausin, Bernard Guichernat, Jean Baptiste Brevel, and Jean Baptiste Theodore Grillet.

3444. PIERRE ROBLO
MAGDELEINE PRUDHOMME
November 27, 1800, after three bans, marriage of Pierre Roblo, legitimate son of deceased Guillaume Roblo and Marie Antoine Cepedre, native of this post . . . and . . . Magdeleine Prudhomme, native of this parish, natural daughter of Bastien Prudhomme and Naillois, a *metive* Indian. Witnesses: Pierre Ternier, Jean Baptiste Theodore Grillé, Jean Baptiste Prudhomme, and Pierre Maiou.

3445. JACQUES ERRIÉ
ANASTHASIE MAILLOU
January 7, 1801, after three bans, marriage of Jacques Errié, native of New Orleans, major and legitimate son of deceased Jacques Errié and Genevieve Viger . . . and . . . Anasthasie Maillou, legitimate daughter of Ignace Maillou and Therese Flibot, native of this parish. Witnesses: Francois Rouquié, André Vascocu, Francois Perau, and Antoine Lenoir.

3446. JACQUES TERIN VERCHER
MARIE JEANNE EUPHROSINE GALLIEN
January 8, 1801, after three bans, marriage of Jacques Terin Vercher, legitimate son of Louis Vercher and Marie Louise Grillet . . . and . . . Marie Jeanne Euphrosine Gallien, legitimate daughter of Nicolas Gallien and Marie LeCour. Witnesses: Antoine Prudhomme, Nicolas Lauve, Francois Davion, Louis Derbanne.

3447. JEAN BAPTISTE VALERI /VARANGUE/
MARIE L'ASSOMPTION TORRES
January 12, 1801, after three bans, marriage of Jean Baptiste Valeri, native of this post, living at Couteil /Cotile/, post of Rapides, natural son of Marie Barbe Varangue . . . and . . . Marie L'Assomption Torres, legitimate daughter of Joseph Torres and Marie Jeanne Deroi. Witnesses: Augustin LeClerc, Jean Horne, Louis Chamart, Jacques Errié. Bans were not posted at Rapides since

no priest was stationed at that post.

3448. LOUIS /METOYER/
THERESE /LECOMTE/
February 9, 1801, after three bans, marriage of Louis, a free *mulâtre*, natural son of Marie Therese *dit* Coincoin, a free *négresse* . . . and . . . Therese, natural daughter of deceased Therese, Indian of the Canneci nation, a native of this post. Witnesses: Julien Besson; Augustin, brother of the groom; Jacques, brother of the bride, and Dominique, a free *mulâtre*.

3449. PIERRE GAGNE
MARIE JEANNE LALANDE
May 5, 1801, after three bans, marriage of Pierre Gagne, native of this parish, legitimate son of deceased Pierre Gagne, native of Canada, and Marie Louise Davion . . . and . . . Marie Jeanne Lalande, legitimate daughter of deceased Jean LaLande, native of Baione /Bayonne/ in France, and Marie Catherinne Dupre. Witnesses: Francois Perau, Dominique Davion, Jean Chrisostome Perau, and Louis Lamalathie.

3450. SIMON LEVASSEUR
MARIE JOSEPH ADELAIDE MERCIE
May 6, 1801, after three bans, marriage of Simon Levasseur, native of this parish, legitimate son of Francois Levasseur and deceased Jeanne Mader . . . and . . . Marie Joseph Adelaide Mercier, native of this parish, legitimate daughter of Louis Mercier and Louise Lefevre. Witnesses: Jean Louis Buart; Jean Baptiste Buart; Francois Perau, Francois Levasseur.

3451. ANTOINE JOSEPH /METOYER/
PELAGIE /LECOURT/*
June 1, 1801, after three bans, marriage of Antoine Joseph, a free *mulâtre*, native of this parish, natural son of Marie Therese *dite* Coincoin, a free *négresse* . . . and . . . Pelagie, a free *quaterone*, natural daughter of Marie Magdeleine, *mulâtresse* slave of Madame Widow Lecomte. Witnesses: Pierre and Augustin, free *mulâtres*, brothers of the groom; Jerome Frederic; Antoine Himel; and Dominique /Metoyer/, a free *mulâtre*.

*The maiden surname used by Mme. Metoyer is found in such documents as the marriage of Zeraphin Llorens to Marie Aspasie Metoyer, August 3, 1820, Register 11. Pelagie was purchased from her owner and manumitted, at the age of seventeen months, by Sr. Barthelemy LeCourt; see Doc. 1850, French Archives, Office of the Clerk of Court, Natchitoches.

3452. SIMEON RACHAL
MAGDELEINE LABERI
June 3, 1801, after three bans, marriage of Simeon Rachal, native of this parish, legitimate son of Louis Rachal and deceased Marie Louise De Roi . . . and . . . Magdeleine Laberi, widow of deceased Joseph Martineau, native of this parish, legitimate daughter of deceased Jean Baptiste Laberi and Jeanne Guedon. Witnesses: Louis Rachal, father of the groom; Louis Rachal, his brother; Bernard Guisarnat, Pierre La Renaudiere.

3453. JEAN BAPTISTE BREVEL
MELANIE DERBANE
August 11, 1801, after three bans announced in the churches at Natchitoches and Opelousas, and with a certificate of approval provided on July 19 by *curé* Buhat of Opelousas, marriage of Jean Baptiste Brevel, legitimate son of Jean Baptiste Brevel and deceased Francoise Poissot . . . and . . . Melanie Derbane, native of Opeloussas, living in this post, legitimate daughter of deceased Jean Baptiste Derbane and of Therese Roi, living at Opeloussa. Witnesses: Nicolas Lauve, Antoine Grillé; Jean Baptiste Grillé, and Jean Baptiste Grillé /sic/.

3454. REMI PEROT
MARIE JOSEPH GAGNÉ
September 10, 1801, after three bans, marriage of Remi Perau, native of this parish, legitimate son of deceased Francois Perot and Marie Catherinne Dupre . . . and . . . Marie Joseph Gagné, widow of Louis Davion, native of this parish, legitimate daughter of deceased Etienne Gagné and Marie Louise Bertrand. Witnesses: Louis Vascocu; Bastien Prudhomme, Basil Gagné, and Pierre Ternié.

3455. JACOB PAUL
July 17, 1792, profession of faith by Jacob Paul, a native of the province of Carolina. Witnesses: Brevel (x), Adam Hofman (x), Ignace Maillioux (s), F. Rambint (s).

3456. JACQUES UUALES /WALLACE/
November 12, 1795, profession of faith by Jacques Uuales (x), aged 24 years, native of America, living "in the post of Cote Dasse" /Caddodoche/. Witnesses: Jean Baptiste Savouie (x) and Francois Mercié (x).

APPENDIX A

GLOSSARY OF FOREIGN TERMS

bourgeois (m.)
bourgeoise (f.) — *(Fr.)* A citizen, middle-class person.

cadet — *(Fr.)* The younger of two individuals by the same name, or (mil.) a junior officer.

chirurgien or *chirurgien pour le roy* — *(Fr.)* A surgeon or doctor appointed or authorized by the government to serve at a colonial post. Since all officials served *pour le roy* or "for the king," the latter phrase is more of a figure of speech than a title of singular honor. Neither a degree in medicine nor a medical license was required of these early surgeons at Natchitoches.

creole, criollo — *(Fr., Sp.)* A person or thing native to the colony. This phrase has no racial, social, or class connotations.

cuarteron (m.)
cuarterona (f.), cartrona — *(Sp.)* A quadroon; one whose ancestry is one-fourth Negro, three-fourths Caucasian.

de la Grande Terre — *(Fr.)* Literally, "of the big country," a designation applied to Indians of a nation not identified by modern scholars. Some assume it refers to the Natchitoches Indians who lived on the large stretch of land opposite the "islands" on which the fort was built; others suggest that it refers to the Indians who occupied the high, hill country between Natchitoches and Los Adaes. Yet another possibility is suggested by the reference to Mme. Jacques Guedon as *de la Grande Terre* in Entries 340 and 342 and as a Chitimachas Indian in Entry 215.

dit (m.), dite (f.) — *(Fr.)* Literally, "called." This term signifies a "nickname" used by an individual, usually in place of his or her surname.

el gefe	(Sp.) The chief.
endoyé (m.) *endoyée (f.)*	(Fr.) Baptized by a layman when in danger of dying without a sacramental baptism. A formal baptism, in the church, was supposed to be administered as soon as possible, if the individual recovered from his illness.
fils	(Fr.) Son.
fille	(Fr.) Daughter.
garde magasin or *garde magasin du roy*	(Fr.) An official in charge of the post storehouse. Since all officials served *du roy* or "for the king", the latter phrase is more a figure of speech than a distinctive title.
griffe	(Fr.) A racial category denoting a certain percentage of Negro blood. Some authorities define a *griffe* as the offspring of a Negro and a mulatto, others as the offspring of a Negro and an Indian. Natchitoches records use the term in both meanings -- apparently as a "catch-all" phrase to indicate any individual who was not black, yet was darker than the usual mulatto.
hijo	(Sp.) Son.
metis, metive, *mestizo*	(Fr., Sp.) Offspring of an Indian and a Caucasian.
mulâtre (m.), *mulâtresse (f.)*	(Fr.) Offspring of a Negro and a Caucasian.
mulato (m.), *mulata (f.)*	(Sp.) Offspring of a Negro and a Caucasian.
mulatillo (m.), *mulatilla (f.)*	(Sp.) A young mulatto.
nègre (m.), *négresse (f.)*	(Fr.) A Negro, usually an adult.
négrillon (m.), *négrillone (f.)*	(Fr.) A Negro child.
négritte	(Fr.) A Negro girl.
negro (m.), *negra (f.)*	(Sp.) A Negro, usually an adult.
oncle	(Fr.) An uncle.
pardo, parto (m.), *parda, parta (f.)*	(Sp.) A light-colored mulatto.

quarteron (m.),   *(Fr.)* A quadroon; one whose ancestry is one-fourth Negro, three-fourths Caucasian.
quarteronne (f.)

reformé (as in   *(Fr.)* Denotes the "half-pay" troops stationed in the colony.
capitaine reformé)

subdélégué   *(Fr.)* A subdelegate, or post official who served under the commandant. At Natchitoches, the *subdélégué* usually served as the *garde magasin* as well.

APPENDIX B

CONVERSION TABLE FOR PERSONAL NAMES
FRENCH - SPANISH - LATIN - ENGLISH
AS USED IN THE REGISTERS

French	Spanish	Latin	English
Adélaïde	Adelaida		
Agathe	Agata, Agatha		
Alexis	Alexo, Alexos		
Ambroise	Ambrosio		
André	Andres		
Ange	Angel		
Angélique	Angelica, Angela		
Anne	Ana	Anna	
Antoine	Antonio	Antonio, Antonium	
Antoinette, Antoinée	Antonia		
Aspasie	Aspasia		
Athanase	Atanasio, Athanasio		
Auguste	Agusto		
Baptiste	Bautista	Baptista	
Barbe	Barba, Barbara		
Barnabé	Barnabe		Barnaby
Bernard (m.)	Bernardo		
Bernarde (f.)	Bernarda		
Basil	Basilio		
Benoit	Benito		
Brigitte	Bergita		
Casimir	Casimiro		
Catherine	Catalina, Chatarina, Catherino	Chatharina, Catharena	
Cécile	Cecilia		
Céleste	Celestia		Celeste
Césair, César, Césaire	Cesario		
Charles	Carlos	Carolum, Caroli	
Chrisostomé	Chrystosimo		
Christophe	Christobal		Christopher
Claude	Claudio		
Clémence	Clemencia	Clemencia	
de la Riviere	del Rio		
de l'Incarnation	de l'Encarnación		

French	Spanish	Latin	English
Denis (m.)	Dionisio		
Denise (f.)	Dionisia		
des Douleurs	des Dolores		
des Nieges,	des Nieves		
de la Nieges	de los Nieves	de Niebas	
des Rois, de Roy	de los Reyes		
Dominique	Domingo	Dominicus	
Dorcien	Dorcino		
Dorothée	Dorotea		
Édouard	Eduardo		Edward
Élisabeth	Isabel, Isabella, Ysabella		
Emanuelle	Emanuella		
Émelie	Emelia		
Étienne	Estevan	Stephani, Estaphanus	
Eugenie	Eugenia		
Eusebie	Eusebia		
Fanchonette	Fanconeta		
Felicité	Felicidad, Felicity		
François	Francisco		
Françoise	Francisca		
Frosine	Frosina		
Gaspard		Gaspario	
Genevieve	Genoveva, Genovefa		
Gerome, Jerome	Geronimo		
Gilbert	Gilberto, Jiliberto		
Grégoire (m.)	Gregorio		
Grégoire (f.)	Gregoria		
Guillaume	Guillelmo, Guillermo		
Hélène, Héleine	Elena, Helena		
Héloise	Eloisa, Heloisa		
Henriette	Enriqua, Henriqua		
Henry, Henri	Enrique, Henrique		
Herman	Hermano		
Hilaire	Ilario, Hilario		
Honorine	Honoria		
Hortense	Hortensia, Ortancia		
Hyacinthe	Jacinta, Hyacinta		
Ignace	Ignacio, Ygnacio		
Isidor	Isidoro		
Jacob	Jacobo	Jacobus, Jacobune	
Jacques	Santiago, Iago, Jacob, Jayme, Diego	Jacob	James
Jean	Juan	Joannis, Jeanam	
Jeanine	Juanina		

French	Spanish	Latin	English
Jeanne............	Juana	Joanna	
Joseph (m.).......	Josef, Joseph......	Josephus	
Josephe (f.)......	Josepha	Josepha	
Josephine........	Josephina		
Julien...........	Julian		
Laurens, Laurent..	Lorenzo		
Le Roy, des Roi...	de los Reyes.......	Ria	
Locadie...........	Locadia		
Louis.............	Luis..............	Ludovicus, Ludovici	
Louise............	Luisa..............	Ludovicia	
Luc...............	Lucas		
Lucille...........	Lucilla		
Lucreie...........................		Lucretia	
Madame, Mme.......	Dona, Dna..........	Madama, Domina.....	Mrs.
Madeleine........	Magdelena		
Marcel............	Marcello		
Marcellin........	Marcellino		
Marcellite.......	Marcellita		
Marguerite.......	Margarita		
Marianne..........	Mariana		
Marie.............	Maria...............................		Mary
Marin.............	Marino		
Marc, Mars........	Marte		
Marthieu..........	Matheo		
Mathilde..........	Methildy		
Maurice...........	Mauricio		
Maximilian........	Maximiliano		
Melanie...........	Melania		
Michel............	Miguel.............	Michael	
Modeste...........	Modesta		
Monique...........	Monica		
Nanette...........	Naneta		
Narcisse..........	Narcisso		
Nicolé............	Nicolosa		
Paul..............	Paulo, Pablo........................		Paul
Pelagie...........	Pelagia		
Prudhomme............................		Per Domo	
Petronille........	Petronilla		
Philippe..........	Felipe.............	Phelipa	
Pierre............	Pedro..............	Petrus, Petri	
Raymond...........	Reymundo		
Remy..............	Remigio, Remo, Remigion..........	Remigiuo	
Reynauld..........	Reynaldo		
Robert............	Roberto		
Rosalie...........	Rosalia		
Rose..............	Rosa...............	Rosa	
Saint, St. (m.)...	San, S.		

French	Spanish	Latin	English
Sainte, Ste. (f.).	Santa, Sta.		
Séraphie..........	Seraphia		
Sévère, Sévèrin...	Severio		
Silvie............	Silvilla		
Théodore..........	Theodoro, Teodoro		
Thérèse...........	Teresa, Theresa....	Theresia	
Timothée..........	Timotheo		
Toussaint.........	Todos Santos		
Ursulle...........	Ursula.............	Ursula	
Valentin..........	Valentino		
Valeri, Valery....	Valerio		
Victor............	Victoriano		
Vincent...........	Vincenze		
Victoire..........	Victoria		
Zacharias.........			Zachary

APPENDIX C

ABBREVIATIONS USED WITHIN THE REGISTERS

Dlle.	*Demoiselle* (French), equivalent to English "Miss"
Dna.	*Doña* (Spanish), equivalent to English "Mrs."
Fcois.	*François* (French, masculine)
Fcoise.	*Françoise* (French, feminine)
Franca.	*Francisca* (Spanish, feminine)
Franco.	*Francisco* (Spanish, masculine)
Jn. Bta.	*Juan Bautista* (Spanish)
Jn. Bte.	*Jean Baptiste* (French)
Ls.	*Louis* (French) or *Luis* (Spanish)
Ma.ana.	*Mariana* or *Maria Ana* (Spanish)
Mme., Mde., Mdm.	*Madame* (French), equivalent to English "Mrs."
M., Mr.	*Monsieur* (French), equivalent to English "Mr."
Rda. P.	*Reverendo padre* (Spanish), Reverend Father
S., Sn.	*San* (Spanish, masculine), saint
Sr.	*Sieur* (French), equivalent to English "Mr."
St.	*Saint* (French, masculine), saint
Sta.	*Santa* (Spanish, feminine), saint
Ste.	*Sainte* (French, fiminine), saint

INDEX

Abbé: see l'Abbé
Acadie (Canada), 1001
Achile, 3266
Acosta,
  Joseph Michel, 2864, 3050
  Maireced?, 2864, 3050
  Manuel, 2864
Adayes: see Los Adaes
Adèlaïde, 2827, 3228, 3262, 3327
Adèlaïde: see also –
  Marie Françoise Adèlaïde;
  Marie Genevieve Adèlaïde;
  Marie Héleine Adèlaïde
Adelais: see Adlé
Adelay: see Adlé
Adelé: see Adlé
Adevagar, Michele, (Dna. Joseph de Land), 744
Adlé (vars. Adelay, Adelais, Adelé, Adelee, Adelet)
  André, 2215
  Antoine, 1561, 1973
  Étienne, 1032
  François, 1807
  Jean, 3402, 3413, 3415
  Jean Baptiste (the elder), 1732
  Jean Baptiste (the younger), 1842
  Jean Baptiste Étienne, 1032-1033, 1502, 1561, 1719, 1732, 1736, 1770, 1807, 1842, 1927, 2048, 2125, 2215
  Jean Baptiste Marin, 1736
  Jean Baptiste Timothée, 1502, 1927
  Louis, 2125
  Marie Pelagie des Neiges, 2048
  Valentin, 1770, 2912
Aedek: see Saidek
Agar (Agen), Marie, (Mme. François Marie Monginot, I), 1639, 3046, 3349
Agathe, 909, 3114
Agen, Jean Baptiste, 2934
Agen, Marie: see Agar, Marie

Agnès, 2470, 3154, 3272, 3274-5
Agnès: see also Poissot, Agnès
Agustino: see Augustin
Aiche (Adaes?) Indians, 3285
Ailhaud Ste. Anne (vars. Aillot, Aliot, and Sainte Anne)
  Jean Antoine, 1599, 2006, 3337
  Jean Baptiste, 1496, 1552, 1598, 1599, 1609, 1668, 1737, 1846, 1848, 1889, 2005-2006, 2160, 2354, 2449, 2461, 2560, 2566, 2652-2654, 2667, 2703, 2721, 3086-3088, 3125, 3149, 3172, 3184, 3197, 3203, 3214, 3255-3256, 3284, 3306, 3337, 3355, 3363, 3380, 3382, 3436
  Marie Thérèse Victoire, 1599, 2006, 2875, 3184, 3323
Ailhaud Ste. Anne: see also St. Anne
Alabama, 1958
Alexandre (Alexandro), 91, 2281, 2500, 2505, 2558, 2562, 2572, 2614, 2624, 2664, 2666, 2723, 2809, 3139, 2668
Alexandre: see also François Alexandre; Louis Alexandre
Alexandre Sévèrin (Alexandro Severin), 2687
Alexis, 260, 678, 2753, 3152, 3229
Aliot: see Ailhaud Ste. Anne
Allemands: see German Coast
Alman (var. Aleman)
  Joseph, 1613, 3366
  Marie Justine, 2055
  Pierre Joseph, 1613, 2055, 2123, 3366
  Rose Mathilde, 2123
Alorge (var. Alorges)
  Charles, 209
  Jean Catherine (Mme. Pierre Victor Dupain), 204, 414, 540, 566, 665, 680, 743, 1037, 1044, 1207

Alorge (continued)
  Pierre *dit* Dizancour, 8, 40, 70,
    78, 101, 103, 154, 169, 174,
    204, 207-209, 250, 302, 313,
    325, 339-340, 346, 348, 352-
    353, 629, 717-718, 720-722,
    725, 737, 743, 808
  Pierre Guilleaume, 250, 913,
    1017, 1063
Ambroise, 560, 895
Amelie, 3270
Amelie: see also Marie Françoise
  Amelie; Emelie
Amien: see Demien
Ana: see Anne
Anastasie, 2147, 2906, 2921, 3091
André (Andres), 414, 864, 951,
  1024, 1028-1029, 2296, 2339, 2397,
  2400, 2452, 2627, 2663, 2688,
  2720, 2722, 2802, 3109, 3129,
  3205
André: see also Louis André
André, Marie (Mme. Jean Gautier)
  196, 238
Andres, Pierre, 1062
Angela: see Angélique
Angelica: see Angélique
Angélique, Indian (Mme. Charles
  Dumont), 736, 816
Angélique (Angelica, Angela), 4,
  94, 164, 258, 754, 934, 950,
  1192, 2290, 2481, 2485, 2487,
  2503, 2514, 2530, 2535, 2616,
  2724, 2776, 2778, 2793-2794,
  3099, 3101, 3182, 3291, 3294
Angevais (Angerau), Magdelaine
  (Mme. Jean Lavespere), 1518, 3342
Anglois, Catherine (Mme. Louis Vil-
  leret), 2980
Anne, Indian (Mme. Jean Baptiste
  Brevel, I), 9, 40, 41, 119, 455
Anne (Ana, Anna, Ane), 166, 198,
  513, 732, 2403, 2409, 2478, 2787,
  2918, 2920-2922, 3166, 3217,
  3250
Anne Charlotte (Ana Carlota), 2425
Anne Hyacinthe, 565
Anne Marie, 31, 323, 585, 683
Anne Rose, 223
Anti: see Anty
Antoine (Antonio), 61, 435, 438,
  441, 524, 625, 688, 889, 1023,

Antoine (continued), 1050, 1267,
  1531, 1948, 2143-2144, 2356, 2378,
  2395, 2409, 2498, 2517, 2541,
  2580, 2613, 2686, 2693, 2735,
  2781, 2784, 2798, 2812, 2823-
  2824, 2907-2908, 2929, 3119,
  3190, 3250, 3252, 3254, 3265,
  3294
Antoine, *capitaine* of the Apala-
  ches, 2825
Antoine: see also François Antoine;
  Joseph Antoine; Louis Antoine;
  Pierre Antoine; Romaine Antoine
Antoine,
  Jeanne, 688
  Joseph, 533
  Julienne, 533
  Louis, 533
  Margueritte, 688
  Marie: see Marie Louise Bastien
    de St. Denis
Antoine Celéstine (Antonio Celes-
  tino), 2337
Antoine Isidore (Antonio Isidoro),
  2504
Antoine Joseph François (Antonio
  Josef Francisco), 2513
Antoine Martin, 954
Antoine Tinsa, 2909, 3437
Antonia: see Jeanne Antoinée
Antonia Emmanuelle, 20
Antonio: see Antoine
Antony, Marie Catherine: see Marie
  Catherine (Antony) Sauvage
Anty (var. Anti, Enti),
  _____, 3399, 3417, 3429
  Ignace I, 876, 901, 988, 1041,
    1066, 1087, 1127, 1640, 1765,
    3351
  Ignace (*fils* J. B.), 1765, 2872
  Jean Baptiste, I, 1035, 1041,
    1546, 1640, 1681, 1765, 1804,
    1829, 2085, 2126, 2344, 2382,
    2974, 3378, 3411, 3418, 3427,
    3431-3433, 3441, 3351
  Jean Baptiste, II, 3443
  Louis, I, 1087, 1097, 1406, 1509,
    1573, 1765, 1933, 1984, 2038,
    2126, 2249, 2343, 2567, 2872
  Louis, II, 2872
  Louis César, 1509, 1933
  Marie Françoise Pompose, 2126

426

Anty (continued)
  Marie Genevieve Euphrasie, 1681, 2085
  Marie Hélène, 2249
  Marie Louise, 1804, 2974, 3433
  Marie Modeste, 1573, 1984
  Marie Susanne, 3179
  Silvestre, 2038
  Vallery, 1829, 2974
Apache (possibly Apalache), 2823
Apalache Indians, 1703, 1710, 1824, 2143-2156, 2518, 2740-2741, 2822-2825, 2903-2922
Aragon,
  Jean, 2207
  Joseph Augustin, 2207
Aramboule: see de Aramboule
Arcas, Los, 3405
Archeval,
  César, 2052
  Ysabel, 2052
Archives Nationales de Paris, 793
Arkansas, 3405
Arllivaux; see Olivo
Armant (var. Arman, Armand)
  _____, 1393, 1400, 2472, 2474, 2497, 3159, 3196, 3297
  _____, Dna., 3398
  Adélaïde, 2178, 2652, 2688
  Athanase, 2499, 2738, 3438
  Jean Baptiste, I, 1044, 1738, 1754, 1830, 2497, 2654, 2962, 3438
  Jean Baptiste, II, 1738
  Jean Jacob Joseph, 1819
  Jean Marie, 1526, 1754, 2549
  Joseph Marie, 1044, 1299, 1517, 1698, 1771, 1819, 1875, 1939, 2962, 3382, 3415, 3438
  Joseph Marie Felix, 1698
  Louis, 2269
  Marie Baptiste, 1737
  Marie Émilie, 1517, 1939
  Marie Fanni, 2962
  Marie Felicité Deleida, 1771
  Marie Thérèse, 1223, 1754 (see also Le Gros, Marie Thérèse)
  Pierre Ignace Joseph, 1875
  Valery, 2556, 2609, 3194
Arnand, Michel: see Ernandez, Miguel
Astasie, 3168

Athanase (Atanasio), 1245, 1486, 2268, 2325, 2330, 2367, 2389, 2478, 2485, 2532, 2540, 2557, 2562, 2660, 2758, 2785, 2789-2790, 3122, 3147, 3220, 3224, 3227, 3229-3230, 3234-3235, 3284
Athanase: see also Jean Baptiste Athanase Hilaire; Joseph Athanase
Athanase Christophe Fortune, 243, 987
Attakapas, xii, 1628, 3126
Augé, Anne (Mme. Pierre LaCour, I) 986
Auguste, 3123
Augustin (Agustino, Augustino), 486, 867, 1023, 1466, 1489, 2312, 2393, 2535, 2558, 2560, 2569, 2607, 2626, 2674, 2787, 2803, 3091, 3120, 3148, 3171, 3186, 3196, 3290, 3332
Augustine (Augustina), 571, 1487, 2330, 2533
Aullivaux: see Olivo
Aures, Jean, 386, 782
Avard (var. Avare)
  Jeanne Robert (Mme. Besson), 248, 265
  Marie Françoise, 236
  Robert, I, 30, 49, 117, 142, 168, 180, 190, 223, 236, 242, 256-257, 343, 377
  Robert, II, 265
  Widow: see Jeanne Josephe Piquery
Avenal (var. Avenel)
  George, I, 174
  George, II, 174, 181, 200, 246
  Jean Baptiste Charles, 246
  Perine, 200
Avoyelles, 1494
Azun?, Maria, 2097

Babé (Babet), 2445, 3272
Babel, 2347
Babet: see Babé and Marie Jeanne Babet
Babin La Source, Marie Genevieve (Mme. Jacques Henoul de Livaudais), 943, 995
Baca, Diego Antonio, 1759
Bachelard, Claudine (Mme. George Buard), 169

Badin (var. Baedin),
_____, Dame, 1424, 2571
_____, Dna. (the younger), 2611
Marie Serpande, 1517, 1939, 2399
Pierre, 1040, 1043, 1048, 1049, 1061, 1251, 1422, 1467, 1538, 2341, 2401, 2409, 2444, 2455, 2458, 2498, 2504, 2515, 2573, 2582, 2671, 2695, 2800, 3100, 3123, 3137, 3139, 3162, 3173, 3180-3181, 3187-3189, 3192, 3206, 3209-3210, 3241, 3245, 3252, 3254, 3258, 3272, 3275, 3277, 3284, 3320, 3348
Baillane, Marie: see Bailliot, Marie
Baillio (var. Baillane, Bailliot, Baillo, Baiou, Biou)
_____, Dlle., 1355
_____, Père, 2892
Amelie, 2889
Auguste, 1781, 3086
Élena: see Marie Héleine
Émelie: see Amelie
Héleine, 1757, 2098
Jean, 1043
Jean Louis, 1812, 2247
Marie (Mme. Joseph Antoine Marcel de Soto), 1588, 1609, 1656, 1999, 2060, 2106, 2163-2164, 2215, 2246, 2574, 2869, 3011, 3363
Marie (identity uncertain), 2950-2951
Marie Héleine, 856, 1141
Pelagie, 1700
Pierre Paul, 856, 932, 986, 991, 1030, 1043, 1054, 1060, 1075, 1141, 1173, 1287, 1590, 1609, 1700, 1757, 1762, 1781, 1790, 1808, 1812, 1996, 2370, 2385, 2598, 2869, 2889, 3011, 3358, 3363
Pierre, II, 2889
Thérèse Toinette, 932
Balasto, Josephe Christophe, 504
Ballejo, Francisco, Fr., 271, 369
Baltasar, 2327, 2352, 2381, 2548, 2650
Baltasar: see also Jean Baptiste Baltasar Monet

Baltimore, 1068
Bandichon, Marie Anne: see Marie Anne Bontemps
Baptiste (Bautista), 952, 1489, 2143, 2517-2518, 2566, 2679, 2683, 2711, 2731, 2740-2741, 2815, 3114, 3175
Baptiste: see also Jean Baptiste
Bar, Anne (Mme. Nicolas Pomier), 2833
Bar: see also Barre; de la Bare
Barbe (Barba, Barbara), 975, 2746
Barbe Rouge: see Barberousse
Barberousse (var. Barbarou, Barbaroux, Barberou, Barberoux, Barbe Rouge)
Anne Thérèse (Mme. Louis Barberousse) 1047
Guillaume, 1047, 1568, 1622, 1649, 1791, 1838, 2024, 2063, 2376, 2402, 3178
Guillaume Jean Michel, 1791
Louis, 1047
Marie Marianne Rosalie, 1838
Barbet (Barbié), Margueritte (Mme. François Mercier, I), 2858, 3404
Barbier (var. Barbié)
Étienne, I, 207, 224, 240-241, 262, 266, 317, 354, 459, 471, 830
Étienne, II (see J. B. Étienne)
Françoise dit Marechal, 55, 75, 157, 170, 207
Gaspar, 115, 230, 240, 796
Jean Baptiste Étienne, 224, 358
Marguerite (Mme. François Claude Mercier), 2858, 3404
Marie Jeanne (Mme. Jean Baptiste Hubardeau), 240, 459, 474, 615, 636, 1048, 1233
Marie Silvie, 1852
Thérèse (Mme. Guillaume Chever) 3, 37, 47, 55, 115, 224, 230-231, 245, 259, 283, 302, 536, 631, 722, 737, 801, 803, 1082
Barbo, Jeanne Marie (Mme. Joseph Louis Maldonat), 2208
Barbo, see also Gil y Barbo
Barbon, Claire Marie (Mme. Jean Aragon), 2207
Bardon, Catherine Raimond (Mme. Bernard Dortolant), 1570, 3398

Bardon (Continued),
 Marianne (Mme. Joseph Malige),
  1607, 1692, 2013, 2095, 2193,
  2258, 2886, 3400
 Marie Catherine (Mme. Louis
  Chamard), 1550, 1565, 1668,
  1963, 1977, 1982, 2100, 2545,
  2587, 2831, 2886, 3005, 3012,
  3382
 Raymond, 3398
Baré: see Bar, Barré, de la Baré
Bareta: see Barréta
Bargas, Juan Maria, 1134
Bargot: see Bergereau
Barnabé, 253, 392, 3193
Barnabé: see also Louis Barnabé
Baron,
 Marie, 474
 Pierre *dit* La Liberte, 762
Barre, Samuel, 3063
Barré (var. Boré),
 François, 1057
 Rosalie Charlotte (Mme. François
  Bossié), 1057, 1610, 1638, 2835,
  2898, 2965, 2977, 3346, 3364
Barré: see also Bar, Barre, de la
 Baré
Barréta, Luis, 1109, 1217
Barrio, Pierre, I, governor of Los
 Adaes, 355
Barrio, Pierre, II, 308
Bart?, Anne, 201
Bartar?, Bautista, 3373
Barthau (Bertheau), Jeanne, (Mme.
 Gerard Tauzin), 1668, 2831, 2886,
 3012, 3382
Barthelemy, 2276
Barthelemy: see also François
 Barthelemy
Bas, Manuel, 1059
Basil (Basilio), 2529
Bast_____, Anne (Mme. Louis Tris-
 tant), 724
Bastcocu: see Vascocu
Bastien, 3312
Bastien: see also Sebastien
Bastien, Marie Antoine: see Marie
 Louise Antoine Bastien de St.
 Denis
Bastien, Marie Louise: see Marie
 Louise Bastien Prudhomme

Batiscan, Canada, 719, 725, 734
Bayou Pierre (northwest Louisiana),
 xii, 2844, 2852, 2859, 2900, 2957,
 3011
Baton, Christophe, 785
Baudin: see Bodin, Beaudouin
Baudoin: see Bodin, Beaudouin
Baudouin, _____ Mr., 1727
Baudouin: see also Beaudouin, Bodin
Baujouin, Marie Jeanne: see Bois-
 point, Marie Jeanne
Baulieu: see Beaulieu
Bautista: see Baptiste
Bayonne, *dit* of Laberry
Beaudain: see Beaudouin, Bodin
Beaudoin: see Beaudouin, Bodin
Beaudouan, see Beaudouin, Bodin
Beaudouin (var. Baudin, Baudoin,
 Beaudain, Beaudoin, Beaudouan,
 Boduin),
 Family, 2934n
 François Pierre, 1070, 1478, 1596,
  1671, 2834, 2840, 2925-2926,
  2930, 2933-2934, 3359, 3383,
  3429
 Jean Baptiste, 2933
 Jean Nicolas, 1545, 1682, 1959,
  2086, 2223, 2834, 2933-2934
 Jean Pierre I, 1563, 1596, 1618,
  1682, 1975, 2020, 2086, 2216,
  2218, 2223, 2840, 2930, 3236,
  3359, 3391, 3429
 Jean Pierre II, 1618, 2020
 Jean Pierre (*fils* Jean Nicolas),
  2223
 Marie Angel, 2934
 Marie Anne, 2261, 2934
 Marie Carmélite, 2834
 Marie Céleste, 2216
 Marie Élizabeth (Mme. Jean Baptiste
  Denis), 1070, 1545, 1593, 1654,
  1682, 1855, 1909, 1959, 2002,
  2058, 2086, 2200, 2925, 2926
 Marie Françoise, 2218
 Marie Louise, 2840, 3362
 Marie Louise Zemire, 1682, 2086
 Marie Modeste, 2930
 Marie Thérèse (Mme. Pierre Beau-
  lieu), 1593, 1671, 2002, 2260-
  2261, 3383
 Nicolas: see Jean Nicolas

Beaudouin (continued),
  Pierre: see Jean Pierre
  Pierre, 1618, 2020, 2200
Beaulieu (var. Baulieu),
  Genevieve Cuno? (Mme. Pierre
    Beaulieu, I), 1671, 3383
  Marie Hiacinthe, 2260
  Marie Judith, 2261
  Pierre, I, 1671, 3383
  Pierre, II, 1671, 2260-2261, 3383
Beauport, Canada, 721, 982
Beaupre, *dit* of François Monecuant
Beaupres, Marie Anne (Mme. François Bourdon), 739
Bébè,
  François Oliver, 2888
  Julia, 2888
  Marie Jeanne, 2864
Beckers, Henry F., Msgr., xvii
Beçon: see Besson
Beilland, Pier__, 1585
Belhumeur, *dit* of Louis LeClerc
Bellefleur, *dit* of François Perreault and Jacques Ride
Bellegarde,
  Genevieve (Mme. Antoine Lemoine I), 2820-2821, 2924, 3421
  Jean Baptiste, 2820-2821, 2924, 3421
  Marie, 2822
Bellehunt, ____, M., 1146
Bellehunt, ____, Mme., 1146
Belleoeil, Clement *dit* du Buisson, 767
Belleouil, ____, M., 3396
Belle Rose, *dit* of Charles Dardenne
Benillot, Catherine (Mme. Pierre Grappe), 348
Benoit,
  ____ (officer), 353
  Jean, 1001
  Marie Rose (Mme. Romaine de la Fosse), 1001
  Pierre *dit* Dubois, 140
Benoist, Marie Anne (Mme. Pierre Rachal), 32, 78, 82, 180, 353, 518, 561, 721, 727, 734, 745, 752, 777
Benous, Prospère, 141
Bequet, Françoise (Mme. Antoine Thierry), 2884, 2958, 3422

Berard, ____, Mr., 989
Berard de la Gase
  Jeanne Marie, 639
  Marie, (Mme. Louis Rondin), 461, 639, 692, 740, 847, 891
Berard de la Gase: see also de la Gase
Bergean, ____, 2930
Berger: see Verger
Berger, Genevieve (Mme. Philippe du Bois), 717
Bergereau,
  Guillaume, *dit* St. Onge, 206, 227, 341
  Nicolas, 206
Bergita: see Brigitte
Bermudes, Domingo (Dominique), 731
Bermudes y de Soto: see de Soto
Bernard (Bernardo), 2358, 3141
Bernard, Catherine: see Marie Catherine Antony Bernard Sauvage
Bernard,
  Élie, I, 2819
  Élie, II, 1014, 1623, 1648, 1859, 1894, 2025, 2063, 2819
  Françoise (Mme. Pierre Hugues), 1013
  Jean, 1014
  Jeanne (Mme. François Palvados), 2947, 3379
  Joseph Célestin, 1623, 2025
  Marie Euphrasie, 1648
  Marie Joseph, 1894
  Marie Louise Euphrasie, 1648, 2063
  Pierre Landri, 2819
Bernarde (Bernarda), 1515, 2508, 2523, 2538
Bernarde: see also Ursulle Bernarde
Bernardin,
  Jean, 341
  Pierre *dit* La Bonte, 206, 341, 354
Berrier, Jacques Daniel, 1510, 1540, 3341
Bertheau: see Bartheau
Bertrand (var. Bertran),
  Benoist, 2829
  Claud *dit* Dauphine, 8, 36, 41, 80, 145, 205, 209, 235, 263, 282, 285, 305, 315, 325, 348-349, 379, 396, 540, 583, 718-719, 727, 736, 769, 989, 1062

Bertrand (continued)
  Felicité Hyacinthe, 1835
  Louis I, 1062, 1100, 1390, 1507,
    1583, 1627, 1676, 1695, 1835,
    1876, 1931, 1994, 2081, 2165,
    2322, 2829, 2950, 3054, 3367
  Louis II, 2165, 3054
  Louis François Xavier, 2950
  Louis Pierre, 1062, 2829, 2950
  Marie Hortence, 1583, 1994
  Marie Louise (Mme. Étienne Gagné),
    845, 863, 913, 1100, 1476, 1580,
    1627, 1670, 1695, 1739, 1783,
    1830, 1916, 2067, 2856, 2860,
    2952-2953, 2976, 3000
  Marie Louise (*fille* Louis), 1876,
    1991
  Marie Louise, Indian (Mme.
    Claud Bertrand): see Marie
    Louise, Indian
  Marie Pelagie Modeste, 1507,
    1931
  Marie Thérèse, 1676, 2081
  Pierre, 1739
Beson: see Besson
Besseau: see Besson
Besser, Pierre, 112, 441
Besson (vars. Beçon, Beson,
  Besseau),
  _____, 169, 172-173, 3263
  François Julien, 2846
  Jean Baptiste, I, 208, 1031
  Jean Baptiste, II, 91, 113,
    165, 168, 188, 208, 222, 248,
    263, 368, 382, 2846
  Jean Baptiste (identity un-
    certain), 2691
  Jean Baptiste Toussaint, 1825
  Jean Pierre, 248, 901, 969
  Jeanne: see Avard, Jeanne Robert
  Julien, 263, 910, 916, 1031,
    1038, 1322, 1547, 1586, 1663,
    1782, 2939, 1783, 1825, 1883,
    1960, 1997, 2073, 2425, 2647,
    2691, 2845-2846, 2852, 3091,
    3168, 3177, 3186, 3410, 3414,
    3432, 3435, 3448
  Pierre, 82, 1133
Besson:, Joseph, 1069
Bibo, _____, 744
Bidaux (Bideau), Julien François,
  263

Bigot, _____, 732
Biou: see Baillio
Bisseau: see Boisseau
Bissonet, Joseph, 3221
Bizot, Joseph, 2430
Blancpain (var. Blanpan, Blanpain),
  Joseph, 350, 527, 631, 719
  Louis Joseph, 527
  Marguerite (Mme. Pierre Raymond),
    1042,
  Thérèse (Mme. François Duval),
    2990, 3442
Bled, Marie: see Marie Françoise
  Ville Blette
Blette, 910
Blette, Manon: see Marie Françoise
  Ville Blette
Blie, Marie Françoise: see Marie
  Françoise Ville Blette
Blondin, *dit* of Louis Rachal
Bocquet, (var. Bocquets),
  Jean Baptiste, 65, 123, 130, 145,
    147, 148
  Marie Anne, 5, 43, 47
  Marie Jeanne, 65, 517
Bodin (var. Baudin, Baudoin, Beau-
  dain, Beaudoin, Beaudouan),
  Gaspard, 955, 2876
  Genoveva (Mme. Simon Goué), 1749,
    2231, 2854
  Jean Baptiste, 2876
  Jean Laurent, 2876, 2973
  Jean Pierre, 2231
  Julien, 1809
  Laurens, 893, 955, 1053, 1604,
    1749, 1809, 2854, 2876, 2973,
    3362
  Marie Louise (Mme. Michel Robin;
    Mrs. John Horn), 893, 1604,
    1882, 3362
  Marie Thérèse, 2973
Bodin: see also Beaudouin
Bodoinne, _____, 1117
Bodouin, Francine: see Marie Frozine
  Denis
Bodouin, P_____, 1545
Boispoint (Baujouin), Marie Jeanne
  (Mme. Pierre Delouche), 1086,
  2935
Boissalie, Antonia Isidora (Mme.
  Guillelmo Boissalie; Mme. Joseph
  De Lorme), 1076

Boissalie, Guillelmo, 1076
Boisseau (Bisseau), Guillaume, 191, 208-209, 250, 281, 347, 350
Boisselier (var. Boissalier, Bosselier),
  Jean, 108, 201
  Rose Marie (Mme. Pierre Joseph Sorel) 108, 427, 470, 645, 696, 857, 911, 1310, 1329, 1634, 2836, 2939, 2940, 2997, 3368, 3414
  Pierre, 201
Bom, Thomas: see Thomas Brown
Bonapont, _____ Mr., 866
Bonaventure, 523
Bonet,
  Joseph Ange, 1864
  Juero, 369
Bonnet,
  Catherinne (Dna. Pedro Gonsales), 3009
  Juan, 1816, 1864, 3009
  Juan Bautista, 1816
  Martine (Mme. Pierre Riotaur), 79, 94, 147, 751, 774
Bontemps (var. Bandichon, Bontan, Bontems, Bonton),
  François, 626
  Marie (Mme. Joseph Raballé II), 1727, 3429
  Marie Anne (Mme. François Pierre Beaudouin; Mme. Pierre Cazeau), 1070, 1478, 1596, 1671, 1727, 2834, 2840, 2925-2926, 2930, 2933-2934, 3336, 3359, 3383, 3429
  Pierre, 1478, 3336
Borde, Catherinne (Mme. Jean Guisarnat), 3006, 3441
Bordelle: see Bourdelle
Bordelon,
  Hypolite, 2941, 3190?, 3402
  Joseph Hypolite, 2941
  Nicolas, 3402
Boré: see Barré
Bormé (var. de Borme),
  _____, Sr., 2273, 2345, 2426, 2431, 2438, 2458, 2488
  Antoine, 984
  Élisabeth Clémence: see Marie Anne Élisabeth Clémence Denis

Bormé (continued),
  François Xavier, 613, 2270
  Jean Louis Caesar *dit* Provencal, 272, 282, 312, 356, 429, 453, 454, 491, 528, 531, 564, 571, 584, 613, 623, 661, 676, 717, 719, 722, 725, 734, 743, 751, 753, 808, 818, 864, 875, 1004, 1012, 1014, 1020-1023, 1027, 1380, 2283
  Joseph, 356, 1380
  Louis André, 479, 564, 851-852, 866, 914, 956, 1007, 1062, 1069, 1317?, 1534, 2280, 2285, 2298, 2300, 3347
  Manuel Clémence, 528, 552, 845, 847, 852, 869, 1734, 1763, 2307, 2415
  Pierre, 2298
Boseir: see Bossié
Bosie: see Bossié
Bosquet, Eulalie, 2233
Bosquet, Placilde, 2233
Bossan (Bossins), Étienne, 893, 988, 990
Bosselier: see Boisselier
Bosseron,
  Étienne, 297
  Pierre, 297
Bossié (var., Boseir, Bosie, Bousser, Bossier, Bozié),
  _____, 1431
  _____, Mr., 2614, 3157, 3166, 3257, 3264, 3321, 3328
  Alexandre Hildebert, 1914, 2898
  Alexandre Soulange, 1544, 1610, 1914, 2050, 2099, 2179, 2818, 2898, 2977, 3289, 3352, 3364
  Eulalie, 1605, 1620, 2011, 2022, 2038, 2098, 2167, 2179, 2233, 2783, 2843, 2977
  Eulalie Emilie, 2179
  François, 549, 1057, 1610, 1638, 2818, 2835, 2898, 2965, 2977, 3346, 3364
  François Paul, 1057, 1083, 1095, 1098, 1480, 1527, 1542, 1544, 1566, 1610, 1638, 1639, 1677, 1841, 1856, 1914, 1978, 2050, 2082, 2159, 2167, 2769, 2835, 2965, 3293, 3342-3343, 3349, 3352, 3364, 3407

Bossié (continued),
  François Placide, 2167
  Guillaume *dit* Le Brun, 1054,
    1071, 1091, 1290-1291, 1306,
    1761, 1780, 2234, 2420, 2849,
    2954, 2956, 3390, 3429
  Jean Baptiste *dit* Le Brun, 5, 25,
    36, 68, 145, 198, 375
  Jean Baptiste (*fils* François),
    1057, 1098, 1357, 1480, 1506,
    1601(bis), 1841, 1899, 1930,
    1789b
  Jean Baptiste François, 1841
  Jean Faustin Soulange, 2050
  Jean Louis César, 2818
  Jeanne *dite* Le Brun (Mme. Charles
    Lemoine II), 2056, 2187, 2214,
    2234, 2849, 2956, 3390
  Joseph de l'Epiphemie, 1677, 2082
  Louis Damas, 2965
  Manuel, 2977
  Marie (*fille* Silvestre), 1690,
    2093
  Marie (identity uncertain), 2818
  Marie Aspasie, 1566, 1978, 2898,
    2948, 3257
  Marie Élisabeth *dite* Le Brun
    (Mme. Joseph Ferrié), 1780,
    2136, 2234, 2840, 2954, 3430
  Marie Locadie, 2099
  Marie Pelagie Mélanie, 1506, 1930
  Marie Susanne, 2898
  Pamela, 3164
  Pierre *dit* Le Brun, 196, 198, 290
  Pierre Jean Baptiste, 2835
  Placide, 2099, 2167, 2197, 2233,
    3261, 3271, 3289, 3419
  Silvestre, 1431, 1479, 1544, 1620,
    1638, 1690, 2022, 2093, 2531,
    2803, 3112, 3346, 3352
  Silvestre César, 1620, 2022
  Soulange: see Alexandre Soulange
  Ulalie: see Eulalie
Bossÿ, Jean Camoin, 757
Botien: see St. André
Botson, Françoise "Fanchon" (Mme.
  Pierre Bontemps), 1478, 3336
Bouchard,
  Antoine, 719, 721, 725
  Françoise Veronique (Mme. André
    Debrande), 575, 621, 719

Bouchard (continued),
  Marie Madeleine Darvalle (Mme.
    Pierre Prudhomme), 444, 575,
    629, 676, 700, 725, 791
Bouchon, Françoise, 44
Bouillie, 1280
Boulet (var. Boulai, Boulé, Boulette,
  Bulai),
  François, 357
  Jean Baptiste Joseph *dit* Brim d'
    Amour, 357, 469, 546, 587, 589,
    656, 981, 999, 1086, 2935
  Jean Baptiste II, 656
  Joseph, 1711
  Marie Jeanne Ursulle (Mme. Jean
    Baptiste Delouche), 469, 1086,
    1563, 1897, 1975, 2113-2114, 2191,
    2935
  Marie Louise (Mme. Michel Robin II)
    589, 999, 1596, 2840, 2930, 3359,
    3391
Bourdelle,
  Nicolas, 720
  Nicolas Paul *dit* St. Nicolas, 269,
    349, 567, 631, 643, 720, 738
Bourdon,
  Francois, 739
  Marie Françoise (Mme. Jacques Levas-
    seur *dit* Jolibois; Mme. Dominique
    Monteche), 24, 37, 75, 110, 115,
    182, 192, 203, 219, 227, 236,
    240, 251, 258, 262, 272, 289,
    297, 298, 301, 307, 312, 325,
    335, 653, 663, 681, 696, 726,
    739, 742, 886, 897, 927, 928,
    957, 959, 983, 1069, 1085, 1241,
    2942
Bourguignon, *dit* of Poissot
Bousser: see Bossié
Boyer, Anne (Mme. Jacques Negle I),
  980
Bozié: see Bossié
Brasier, Pierre *dit* La Liberté, 756
Breau, Anne (Mme. Jean Benoit), 1001
Breton, Jean François, 418, 428,
  454, 542, 600, 607, 633, 672, 711,
  730, 736, 740-742, 745-746
Brevel (var. Brevelle),
  _____, 1118, 3455
  Antoine, 2406
  Baltasar, 1592, 2000, 2116, 2182,
    2988, 3423

Brevel (Continued),
  Jean Baptiste I, 9, 40, 119, 131,
    235, 339, 455, 732, 773, 2192
  Jean Baptiste II, 40, 449, 455,
    874, 902, 968, 1065, 1067,
    1077, 1118, 1295, 1474, 1672,
    1714, 1758, 1785, 1820, 1857,
    1874, 2291, 2406, 2486, 2817,
    2873, 2902, 2936, 2987, 2988,
    3001, 3010, 3074, 3094-3095,
    3384, 3405, 3428, 3431, 3443,
    3453
  Jean Baptiste III, 1758, 3453
  Magdeleine: see Marie Hélène
    Magdeleine
  Marie, 2817
  Marie Céleine, 902
  Marie Élisabeth (Mme. Jean Baptiste Tristant), 1714, 2222,
    3405
  Marie Felicité, 1820, 2873,
    2902, 3010, 3428
  Marie Françoise (Mme. Pierre
    Derbanne II), 449, 1065, 1525,
    1592, 1893, 1946, 2001, 2183,
    2259, 2406, 2988, 3443
  Marie Héleine, 874
  Marie Hélène (Henriette) Magdeleine (Mme. Jean Baptiste
    Derbanne), 902, 1077, 1508,
    1567, 1820, 1874, 1932, 2192,
    2873, 2988, 3017
  Marie Louise (Mme. Julien Rachal)
    1067, 1537, 1653, 1809, 1905,
    1955, 2057, 2182, 2221, 2404,
    2936, 2987
  Marie Louise Françoise Jeanne
    (Mme. Marin Grillet), 119, 407,
    608, 619, 641, 667, 709, 732,
    859, 929, 1002, 1040, 1067,
    1071, 1085, 1094, 1096, 1762,
    1813-1814, 2855, 2877, 2883,
    2891, 2942, 2949, 2969, 2994,
    3023, 3065, 3185, 3406, 3425,
    3439
  Marie Pelagie (Mme. J. B. Barthelemy Rachal), 968, 1508,
    1672, 1905, 1932, 2116, 2196,
    2817, 3001, 3062, 3384
  Marie Thérèse, 1785, 2933, 2987,
    2999, 3010, 3431
  Marie Victoire, 1857, 2902, 3001

Brigitte (Bergita), 2686, 2761, 2789,
  2795, 2800, 2826, 3260, 3280
Brigon, Dorothée (Mme. Joseph François Pereau), 354
Brim d'Amour, *dit* of Boulet
Briñac (Briniac), Marie (Mme. Philippe Felix Fonteneau) 1051, 2967
Brogdis?, Pedro, 1339
Broi, Jean, 484
Brom, Thomas: see Thomas Brown
Bron (Brown?), Marie (Mrs. Charles
  Tompson), 1837
Broody, Pedro, 1068
Brosset (var. Brossé, Brouté),
  Athanase, 2237
  Catherinne, 2849, 2854, 2877
  Jacques, 2877
  Jean, 1040, 2877
  Jean Baptiste, 1779, 2136, 2195,
    2854
  Jean Louis, 2935
  Marie Catherine, 1745, 2935
  Marin, 2136
  Pierre, 1040, 1614, 1745, 1779,
    2016, 2136, 2237, 2877, 3390
  Pierre César, 1614, 2016, 2837
  Silvie, 2871, 2956
Brown (var. Bom, Brom),
  John (Juan), 3373
  Marie des Nieges, 1675, 2080
  Thomas, 1675, 2080, 3373
Brown: see also Bron
Brulot, _____, 1172
Brumot (var. Brumo),
  Michel I, 988
  Michel II, 858, 988
Brunet, Marie Jeanne (Mme. François
  Cavé), 991, 2867
Bruteau, Marie (Mme. Pierre Gagnay I),
  993
Buard (var. Buar, Buart, Buhart),
  _____, 1445, 1647, 2271, 2633
  Adélaïde, 2944
  Antoine Evariste, 2137
  Augustin: see François Augustin
  Denis, 1822, 2089, 2170, 2997,
    3139, 3240, 3253, 3291-3292
  Denis Onézime, 1632, 2035
  François Augustin (*fils* J. B. Gabriel), 888, 1520, 1536, 1908,
    1941, 1954, 2374, 2530, 3059,
    3411

Buard (continued),
 François Augustin (*fils* Louis Gabriel), 1520, 1941, 2137, 3198
 Françoise (Mme. Jean Lagé), 24, 36, 54, 85, 96, 176, 522, 859, 873
 Gabriel, 3255
 Gabriel: see also Jean Baptiste Gabriel; Louis Gabriel
 Gabriel, Widow: see Marie Anne Rousseau
 George, 169
 Jacob Silvestre, 1817
 Jacques, 901
 Jean Baptiste, 948, 967, 1539, 1639, 1772, 1806, 1816, 1839, 2416, 2794, 2796, 2801, 3021, 3129, 3155, 3205, 3349, 3350, 3376, 3411, 3417, 3427, 3450
 Jean Baptiste (*fils* Louis Gabriel), 1772, 2944
 Jean Baptiste Denis, 2328, 2696, 2830, 2944, 3015, 3092, 3411, 3412, 3420
 Jean Baptiste Gabriel, 24, 66, 169, 239, 255, 274, 278, 299, 328, 335, 341, 354, 425, 433, 453, 455, 457, 497, 503, 505, 549, 591, 605, 608, 627, 641, 699, 702, 723, 732, 746, 751, 753, 888, 967, 1018, 1033, 1052, 1098, 1405, 1552, 1639, 2830, 2944, 3015, 3021, 3337, 3349, 3355, 3407, 3411-3412, 3427
 Jean Louis, 1630, 1632, 1741, 2033, 2035, 2387, 2544, 3450
 Joseph Augustin, 2137
 Louis, 3129, 3135, 3206-3207, 3261, 3264, 3272, 3279, 3293, 3346, 3355, 3370, 3377, 3411
 Louis Gabriel, 255, 433, 619, 667, 838, 888, 920, 1018, 1040, 1052, 1055, 1076, 1078, 1215, 1382, 1385, 1461, 1488, 1520, 1544, 1552, 1632, 1634, 1638, 1659, 1686, 1741, 1744, 1769, 1772-1773, 1784, 1786, 1817, 1856, 1941, 2035, 2120, 2137, 2341, 2370, 2435, 2478, 2500, 2505

Buard (continued),
 Louis Gabriel (continued), 2544, 2572, 2586, 2624, 2630, 2693, 2756, 2761, 2783, 2818, 3040, 3102, 3127, 3175, 3249, 3284, 3309-3312, 3314, 3318, 3420
 Marie, 3028, 3202
 Marie Anne (*fille* J. B.), 3015
 Marie Anne (*fille* J. B. Gabriel), 702, 2137, 2301, 2328, 2369, 2667, 2696, 2723, 2804, 3015, 3407
 Marie Catherine (Mme. André Antoine Rambin), 591, 1033, 1536, 1632, 1686, 1733, 1769, 1797, 1901, 1954, 2035, 2051, 2089, 2296, 2983
 Marie Denise, 2830
 Marie Élisabeth Josephe (Mme. Edward Murphy), 453, 1098, 1595, 1797, 2004, 2052, 2120, 2292, 2317, 2970, 2980, 2983, 3021, 3293
 Marie Françoise (Mme. François Marie Monginot II), 335, 659, 888, 921, 1639, 1741, 1899, 2138, 2416, 2496, 2830, 3021, 3046, 3208, 3349
 Marie Jeanne, 641, 1430, 1786, 1906, 2374
 Marie Louise (Mme. J. B. Ailhaud Ste. Anne), 299, 605, 920-921, 1496, 1532, 1598-1599, 1733, 1816, 1949, 2005-2006, 2120, 2341, 3337, 3398
 Marie Thérèse Eugenie (Mme. Étienne Pavie; Mme. C. T. Pierre Metoyer), 549, 1052, 1482, 1552, 1598-1599, 1630, 1677, 1751, 1785, 1822, 1856, 1899, 1917, 2005-2006, 2033, 2082, 2137, 2180, 2544, 2566, 2586, 3261, 3355, 3420
 Marie Thérèse Eugenie (*fille* Louis Gabriel), 1856, 1901, 2051, 2778, 2887, 2965
 Widow: see Marie Anne Rousseau
Bull, Catherine (Mrs. Frederick Hesser), 2983
Bureau, Jeanne (Mme. Michel Robin I), 999, 1053
Buart?, Marie, 184

Buhat, _____, Rev. Fr., 3453
Bulstrong, Onée (Denee), (Mrs. Joseph Wallace), 2856, 2952-2953, 3410
Bunel, Jacques, 462, 467, 510, 727, 863, 949, 997, 1005
Burelle (Bunelle?), _____, 857

Caddo Indian, xii, 9, 119, 205, 367, 386, 732, 781, 1000, 2255, 2998, 3410, 3456
Caddodoches Indian settlement, 3410, 3456; see also Gros Nez, St. Louis des Caddodoches
Caisle?, Margueritte (Mme. Jean Baptiste Ferrié), 3430
Caitan, _____, Rev. Fr., 3011
Cajou, Pierre, 1596, 3359
Calahorra y Sarvo, Joseph, Rev. Fr., 463, 613, 638, 984
Caldes, Franciscus, Rev. Fr., 406
Callé, Francisca, 3375
Callon (Tottin?), Marguerite, (Mme. Jean Baptiste Montanary), 1538, 3348
Campanelle: see Canpanel
Cane River (Natchitoches Parish, La.), 2928n; see also Rivière aux Cannes
Canne, Jeanne (Mme. Ponce Fiol), 1066
Canneci Indians (var. Canneis, Canneti), 187, 190, 213, 2876, 2992, 2993, 3013, 3049, 3069, 3448, 3076
Cannes Brulées (Louisiana), 729
Canon, Etienne *dit*, 97
Canpanel (Campanelle), Barthelemy, 1610, 3364
Cantalogue, Joseph, 2981
Cantalogue: see also Cantalois
Cantalois?, Joseph, 2217
Cap de la Magdeleine (Canada), 751, 1009
Capuran,
  _____, Mr., 3151
  Jooyan? (Julien?), 1913
  Joseph, 1103, 1369
  Marie Charlotte, 1641, 1913, 1951, 2866
Careb, Termette (Mme. Antoine Grillet), 732

Carle (var. Carles),
  François, 425, 457, 971, 992, 996
  François Antoine: see François Antoine Carle Le Noir
  Jean, 457, 992
  Lally: see Marie Eulalie
  Marie Eulalie "Lally", 1674, 2079
  Pierre Antoine, 971
Carlos: see Charles
Carlota: see Charlotte
Carode, Indian, 2919, 3437
Carolinas, the, xiii, 2970-2971, 3373, 3455
Case, David, 2175
Caseaux: see Cazeaux
Cashetumena, Indian, 2366
Casiano, Hermano, Brother: see Castanare, Hermano Casiano
Casimir (Casimiro), 2752
Cassel (Castel?), Françoise (Mme. Robert Mechim), 1068
Cassel (Castel?), Grégoire, 1068
Cassenave,
  Anne, 3014
  Bernard, 2861, 2946, 3014, 3413
  Denis Étienne, 2861
  Jean Baptiste, 2946
  Michel Denis, 2861, 2946, 3014, 3413
Castel: see Castelle
Castel?, Cecile (Mme. Grégoire Cassel?), 1068
Castelle (var. Castel, Castille),
  Jacques, 1704
  Jean Baptiste, 1704-1705
  Marie, 1704-1705
  Marie Françoise, 892
  Marie Françoise II, 892
  Marie Jeanne (Mme. Louis La Prairie), 3387, 3396
  Ursulle Christophe (Mme. Jacques Rachal), 855, 928, 1190, 1589, 1721, 2928, 3357
Castille: see also Ysabelle Patre and del Castillo
Castro,
  Catherine Marie, 618
  François, 618, 675
  Pierre Joseph (de Castre), 675
Catalina: see Catherine
Catharina: see Catherine

Catherine (Catalina, Catharina),
  18, 60, 151, 210, 480, 1487,
  2147-2149, 2152, 2154-2156, 2275,
  2298, 2409, 2455, 2495, 2498,
  2515, 2533, 2575, 2630, 2668,
  2681, 2755, 2760, 2765, 2805-
  2806, 2813, 2822, 2903, 2907,
  2917, 3081, 3114, 3123, 3133,
  3137, 3158, 3180-3181, 3188-
  3189, 3193, 3227, 3273, 3275,
  3282, 3300, 3437
Catherine Marie Joseph, 852
Catiche, 2628
Catiche: see also Marie Catiche,
  Marie Louise Catiche, and
  Marie Louise Catiche Metoyer
Caton, Jean Pierre *dit*, 95, 516,
  832
Caunan: see Conan
Cavaillez, _____, 1401
Cavé (var. Cavet),
  François, 991, 2867
  Louis, 2222
  Marie Jeanne "Manon" (Mme. Robert
    Dupre), 861, 1060, 2833, 2882,
    2963, 3409
  Marie Louise "Louison" (Mme. Remy
    Poissot II), 991, 1766-1767,
    1885, 2054, 2603, 2830, 2843,
    2867, 2944, 2974, 3002, 3015,
    3030, 3173, 3403, 3412, 3427
    3432
Cazeaux (var. Caseaux, Cazeau)
  Pierre I, 1478, 3336
  Pierre II *dit* Faulevant, 1478,
    3336
Cécile (Cecilia), 20, 2293, 2309,
  2323, 2341, 2401, 2444, 2455,
  2576-2577, 2599, 2706, 2715, 2790,
  2929, 3056, 3132, 3142, 3197
Cécile Genie (Cecilia Genia), 2715
Céleste (Celestia, Celestina), 2453,
  2503, 2794, 3084, 3090, 3172,
  3194, 3235, 3262
Céleste: see also Genevieve Céleste
Céleste Constance (Celestine Con-
  stancia), 2596
Célestin (Celestino), 2429, 2649,
  3183, 3210
Célestine: see also Antoine Céles-
  tine

Celicigora, Indian, 1165
Cerdas, Marie Gertrude, 100
Cerdas: see also de la Cerda
Centienne (à Centienne) *dit* of
  Pierre Jean Dolet
Cepedre: see de Zepeda
Césaire (César, Cesir, Cesario), 10,
  34, 521, 1205, 2680, 3163, 3172,
  3205
Césaire: see also Claude César; Jo-
  seph Césaire, Louis César
Ch___tron, Angélique (Mme. François
  Roujot), 526
Cha_____, Sr., 1351
Cha_____, Ursula (Mme. François Le
  Compte), 1321
Chabus (Chabais, Chabuche), François
  Barthelemy, 1504, 1518, 1527,
  1929, 2937, 2957, 3008, 3269,
  3342-3343, 3427
Chagneau (vars. Chagnau, Chagnaut,
  Chagne, Chagneaux, Chagniaux,
  Chagniot, Chagno, Chagnot, Chag-
  non, Chaigneau, Chainian, Chain-
  iau, Chainiot, Chainniot, Chaniau,
  Chanian, Chaniot, Cheniot),
  Anne (Mme. Jean Bossier), 25, 28,
    32, 82, 198, 255
  Athanas, 639
  Edmond, 306, 398
  Edmond Thomas, 322
  Éleanor (Mme. Élie Bernard), 623,
    1014, 1623, 1648, 1838, 1894,
    2025, 2063, 2819
  Étienne, 206, 400
  François, 42, 52, 80, 145, 274,
    306, 322, 398, 556, 623, 695,
    746, 807, 834, 998, 1014, 1047,
    1050, 2819
  Jeanne, 1803
  Joseph, 2850, 2881
  Joseph Michel, 2174
  Marie (Mme. Louis Rousseau), 169
  Marie (identity uncertain), 1668
  Marie Jeanne (Mme. Pierre Marion),
    14, 42, 70, 84, 185, 192, 195,
    234, 368, 515, 639, 2946
  Marie Jeanne (Mme. Guillaume Bar-
    berousse), 695, 1622, 1791,
    1030, 2024, 3356

Chagneau (continued; see preceding
  page for variations),
 Marie Jeanne (Mme. Michel Jean-
   Ris; Mme. François Frederic),
   274, 423, 443, 746, 858, 1047,
   1090, 1514, 1547, 1568, 1800,
   1937, 1960, 2861, 2938, 2978,
   3014, 3356, 3413, 3416
 Marie Jeanne (Mme. François Pievert; possibly same as preced-
   ing), 1050, 1859
 Marie Jeanne (identity uncertain),
   1724, 1842, 1894
 Marie Louise, 556, 858, 955, 998
 Michel, 1623, 1791, 1803, 2025,
   3388, 3413, 3416
Chaniau, _____, Mr., 145
Chaler (var. Chalais),
 _____, 1472
 François, 1480
 Marie Céleste, 1576, 1987
 Marie Denise, 2184
 Marie Louise (Mme. François Chaler), 1480
 Marie Séraphie, 1525, 1946
 Pierre *dit* Versailles, 1472,
   1480, 1525, 1576, 1590, 1946,
   1987, 2056, 2184, 2857, 3197,
   3358, 3426
 Pierre Ursin, 2056
Chamard (var. Chamarre, Chamart),
 André Bernard, 2235, 2688, 3005,
   3126, 3168, 3201
 Jacques Rosmond, 1565, 1977,
   2831, 3288
 Louis Charles Ives, 1565, 1604,
   1668, 1688, 1977, 2100, 2831,
   2886, 3012, 3362, 3382, 3395-
   3396, 3419, 3436, 3447
 Marie (Mme. Joseph Tauzin), 1565,
   1668, 1977, 2100, 2178, 2235,
   2831, 2886, 3012, 3070
 Michel, 2178, 2258, 2545, 2587,
   2870
Champagne, *dit* of André Debrante
Chandelarie, Maria (Dna. Joseph
   Antonio Gonsales), 2982, 3077
Channian?, _____, Mr., 3244
Channian: see also Chagneau
Charbonnet,
 _____, M., 1125

Charbonnet (continued),
 Antoine, 931, 943, 973, 995, 1020,
   1049
 Claude, 973, 995
 Jean Baptiste Barthelemy, 973, 995
 Marie Genevieve, 943
 Marie Jeanne Claudine Antoinette
   Pelagie, 973
Charles (Carlos), 483, 935, 975,
   1487, 2432, 2378, 2454, 2476-2477,
   2533, 2612, 2617, 2658, 2712,
   3098, 3145, 3251, 3295, 3301
Charles, _____, Mr., 744
Charles, Angélique: see Angelique
   Charles Dumont
Charles, Marie: see Marie Charles
   Dumont
Charles Jacques, 3098
Charlesbourg (Canada), 354
Charlot, 3325
Charlotte (Carlota), 2321, 2354,
   2378, 2399, 2476, 2511, 2524,
   3084, 3203, 3306
Charlotte: see also Anne Charlotte
Charlotte Françoise, 654
Charpentier,
 Durand, 1437
 Joseph, 1089
 Pierre, 1089, 1478, 1521, 1942,
   3336
 Thérèse, 64, 104
Charron,
 Marie Françoise Clara, 1743
 Pierre Étienne, 1743
Chateau Riche (Canada), 1091
Chatonai: see Jeanne Chatonai
Chauvin, _____, Sr., 1009
Chauzÿ: see François Chauzÿ
Chavenaut, *dit* of Matonge
Chaver: see Chever
Chelette (vars. Chelaitre, Chelatre,
   Chelet, Cheletre, Chelettre,
   Schelet, Scheletre, Schelette),
 _____, 1473
 Anne Marguerite, 2162
 Baptiste, 1625
 Barnabé: see Michel Barnabé
 François, 1625, 1635, 1664, 1884,
   1911, 2027, 2037, 2074, 2248
 Françoise (Mme. Jacques Joseph
   Lattier), 1102, 1625, 1635, 1790,

Chelette (Continued; see preceding
  page for variations),
 Françoise (Mme. Jacques Joseph
  Lattier, continued), 1792-1793,
  2037, 2248, 2373, 2379, 3393
 Jean Baptiste, 1559, 1971
 Jean Pierre, 1513, 1936
 Jeanne, 2043
 Marguerite (Mme. Antoine Himel),
  1320, 1610, 1792, 2898, 2977,
  3364
 Marie, 2961
 Marie Anne (Mme. Pierre Baillio;
  Mme. André Frederic), 1043,
  1612, 1757, 1776, 1781, 1812,
  2038, 2044, 2045, 2593, 3365
 Marie Arcene, 2257
 Marie Barbe (Mme. Philippe Felix
  Frederic II), 1054, 1532, 1601,
  1730, 1749, 1757, 1793, 1827,
  1898, 1949, 2007, 2162, 2262?,
  3003, 3061, 3440
 Marie Emmanuel, 2098
 Marie Eusebie, 2111
 Marie Françoise, 1562, 1974
 Marie Hélène, 2098
 Marie Jeanne, 3200
 Marie Josephe, 1896, 2266
 Marie Louise, 2168
 Marie Pelagie, 1884, 2958
 Marie Pierre, 2912
 Michel, 1043, 1054, 1083, 1084,
  1529, 1612, 2912-2913, 2961,
  3345, 3365, 3393
 Michel Bernabé, 1084, 1473, 1529,
  1562, 1612, 1625, 1657, 1781,
  1827, 1868, 1896, 1974, 2028,
  2098, 2257, 2526, 2812, 2961,
  2970-2971, 3345, 3365, 3374,
  3422, 3440
 P____, 1671
 Paul, 1610, 3364
 Pierre, 1083, 1513, 1559, 1612,
  1730, 1776, 1855, 1884, 1936,
  1971, 2043, 2111, 2168, 2373,
  2884, 3365, 3383, 3422, 3424
 Roi, 2903
 Rose (Mme. Valentin J. B. Dubois),
  1529, 1541, 1635, 1812, 1815,
  1827, 1957, 2037, 2247, 2526,
  2912-2913, 3345

Chelette (Continued),
 Ursulle (Mme. Pierre Clavis Saidek), 1595, 1776, 1790, 1815,
  1863, 1911, 2004, 2044, 2945,
  2970-2971
Cheniot: see Chagneau
Cheval, Catherine (Mme. Étienne
  Bosseron), 297
Chevalier, J____, 1702
Chevalier, Jacques, 32, 120-121
Chever (var. Chaver, Chevert, Sch-
  ever),
 Anne: see Jeanne
 Guillaume *dit* Dufrene, Chevalier
  de St. Agnette, 1, 3, 37, 47,
  51, 55, 88, 115, 165, 171, 189,
  203, 205, 207, 209, 302, 311,
  339-340, 342, 349, 354, 471, 566,
  615, 636, 642, 688, 722, 726,
  737, 870, 924, 980, 1010, 1082,
  1099
 Guillaume II: see Pierre Guillaume
 Jean Baptiste, 2639
 Jeanne (Mme. Pierre Sébastien
  Prudhomme), 3, 277, 281, 287,
  291, 313, 315, 420, 471, 536,
  566, 636, 722, 836, 949, 1010,
  2858, 3404
 Marie, 8, 138
 Marie Françoise (Mme. Jean Baptiste
  Prudhomme), 115, 551, 642, 737,
  800-801
 Pierre Guillaume, 302, 1082, 1088,
  1485, 1497, 1920, 3120, 3288,
  3338, 3404
 Thérèse, see Thérèse Barbier
Chinet, Hymes, 120
Chino, 1386
Chiq: see François Chiq
Chisilo, Maria Andres, 1718
Chisley (Christiÿ?), Margueritte
  (Mrs. John Symis), 1597, 3360
Chitimachas Indians, 215
Chito, 1124
Choctaw Indians, 2233
Choera, *dit* of François, *nègre*
Chopé, Indian, 2156
Christi: see Christy
Christiÿ: see Chisley
Chrisostomé, Indian, 2906
Chrisostomé: see also Christobal

Christy (var. Christi, Christie,
    Christille, Christillie),
    François, 1844
  Jacques, 997, 1060, 1591, 1808,
    1844, 1883, 2000, 2219, 2865
  Jacques Antoine, 997
  Jacques Remi, 1591, 2000
  Jean, 1908
  Jean Baptiste, 1908
  Jean Jacques, 1883
  Joseph Marcel, 2865
  Marie Denis, 2219
  Marie Euphrosine, 2892
  Marie Joseph Madeleine Isidora,
    1808, 2892
  Marguerite: see Chisley, Marguerite
Christobal, 2577, 2585, 2770
Christobal: see also Christophe
Christobal,
  Francisco Pilar (Pilio), 1548,
    1962
  Marie de l'Ascension (Dna. Pedro
    Christobal), 1548, 1962
  Pedro (Christophe), 1548, 1962
Christophe, 538, 1036
Christophe: see also Athanase
    Christophe Fortune
Christophe,
  Cécilia (Mme. Bernard Marchant),
    1079
  Thérèze (Mme. Pierre Cazeau I),
    1478, 3336
  Ursulle: see Ursulle Christophe
    Castelle
Cilesie, 3092
Cimolitte, Marie, 842
Cirose?, Jeanne (Dna. Manuel Acosta),
    2864
Civary, Jean François de, Rev. Fr.,
    105, 172
Claire: see Clermont, Le Clerc, and
    Marie Louise Claire
Clairmont: see Clermont
Claive (Clera?), Angélique (Mme.
    Fr. Fredieu), 1634, 3368
Clare: see Clermont, Le Clerc, and
    Marie Louise Claire
Clarisse (Clarissa), 2152, 2783,
    2910, 3156
Clarisse: see also Marie Louise *dite*
    Clorice

Clariso, Gilbert: see Gilbert Closeau
Claude, 36, 67, 540
Claude Cesar, 80, 160
Clauseau: see Closeau
Clavau, Felicité Renée Deforge (Mme.
    Bernard Cassenave), 2861, 2946,
    3413
Clavis, _____, 1254
Clavis: see also Saidek
Clémence (Clemencia), 869, 2415,
    2746, 3230
Clera (Claive?), Angélique, (Mme.
    Fr. Fredieu), 1634, 3368
Clermont (vars. Claire, Clairemont,
    Clairmont, Clare, Clermon, La
    Clairmont),
  Antoine, 717
  Marie Françoise (Mme. André Rambin), 417, 439, 539, 563, 633,
    654, 684, 710, 844, 937, 965,
    1033, 1056, 1069, 1688, 1770,
    2860, 2899, 3067, 3386, 3388,
    3400
  Marie Josephe Jeanne (Mme. Henri
    Richer; Mme. Jean Baptiste Dubois), 226, 242, 293, 318, 327,
    418, 456, 539, 563, 584, 606,
    621, 650, 660, 673, 717, 853,
    885, 887, 985, 1025, 1032, 1090,
    1529, 1587, 1732, 1736, 1998,
    2852, 2900, 2912-2913, 2978,
    3345, 3395, 3400, 3404
  Thérèse, 177
Clinon, Olivier *dit* L'Olive, 127
Clom, Juan Bautista, 1842
Closeau (vars. Clariso, Claudau,
    Clauso, Cloiseau, Closeau, Closo
    Closot),
  François, 839, 917
  Gilbert, 839, 1100, 1852, 2165,
    2785, 3094, 3211
  Louis, 1676, 2066, 2081, 2204,
    2784, 3107, 3392
Cloutier (vars. Cloutié, Clouquie),
  Alexis, 1546, 1922, 2254, 2743,
    2750, 2848, 3353
  Family, 2934n
  Hélène (Mme. Ambrose LeComte),
    1072, 1491, 1922, 2103, 2249,
    2344, 2748, 2930
  Henriette, 3144

Cloutier (continued),
  Jean Baptiste Alexis, 1072, 1089,
    1491, 1546, 2848, 2948, 3353,
    3378, 3419
  Jean Baptiste Sévère, 2848
  Jean Pierre, 2194, 2948, 3419
  Marguerite (Mme. François Davion),
    2103, 2194, 2931, 2948, 3378
  Marie Marguerite Zeline, 2948
  Widow: see Marie Louise Rachal
Cloutierville, 3179
Coincoin: see Marie Thérèse *dite*
  Coincoin
Cointe, Cassé, 3159
Colar, Marie Anne, 2839
Colentin: see Corantine
Colet, *dit* of Nicolas Prevot
Colet: see also du Colet
Coleta, 2295
Colin, *dit* of Nicolas Henri Lauvé
Colin, Thérèse (Mme. Albert Dolet)
  458
Collantin: see Corantine
Combas, Louis, 1510
Combe, Parine (Mme. Claude Le
  Comte), 738
Combecave, Marie (Mme. Marc Rou-
  quier), 3407
Comptois, Louise, 190
Conand (var. Caunan, Conan, Conant),
  Jean François Florentin, 2764
  Marie Anne (Mme. Jean Baptiste
    Dartigaux; Mme. Pierre Joseph
    Maes), 1673, 2078, 2257, 2959,
    3052, 3436
Condee, Marie Joseph (Mda. Pedro
  Garcia), 8, 165
Conga, 1912
Constance, 3118
Constance: see also Celeste Con-
  stance
Constance Celeste (Constancia Ce-
  lestine), 1292, 2596, 2660
Constant, Jacques, 1565, 1977
Contine, 2560, 2649, 2680
Corantine (vars. Colantin, Colen-
  tin, Collantin, Corantin, Coren-
  tine, Crontain), Marie Josephe
  Françoise Charlotte Henriette
  (Mme. Jean Baptiste Prudhomme),
  452, 565, 683, 686, 691, 714, 749,

    897, 949, 1063, 1073, 1417,
    1600, 1715, 1774, 1826, 2881,
    3018-3020, 3361, 3380
Corbier, Michel, 202
Corbier: see also de Corbier
Corde, Barbe (Mme. Joseph Rassé),
  2895
Cordoba, Nicole, 158
Corentin: see Corantine
Corretant, Marie Josephe: see Maria
  Josepha (Courretant) Torres
Cortinas, Xavier, 135
Cotedoche: see Caddodoches
Cotes, Rebecca (Mrs. Maurice Mc
  Clain), 3022
Cotile (settlement on Red River),
  2912-2913
Cottonmais, Marie Louise (Mme. Louis
  Monette), 2404
Couiaque, Marie Anne Gracien, 2905
Coulas de Sta. Theresia,
  ____, 545, 560
  Jeanne, 545
Coulas de Sta. Theresia: see also
  Sta. Theresia
Coulon de Villiers (var. Coulong),
  François, Chevalier, 943, 975,
  989, 995, 1014, 1027, 1694, 1717
Coulon de Villiers: see also de
  Villiers
Coupalon, Francisco, 2161
Courtin, Marie Louise, 2909
Couse (Couze), Marie Jeanne (Mme.
  Joseph Pavie I), 1052, 1347
Coustiel?, Iago: see Jacques Con-
  stant
Coutet, ____, 728
Couti: see Couty
Couteil, Couteille: see Cotile
Coutin?, Louis, 2260
Couty (var. Couti),
  André Paul, 3005
  Jean Baptiste, 2874
  Jean Paul I, 1528, 1716, 3423
  Jean Paul II, 1716, 2184, 2874,
    3005, 3424
Covechi,
  Denis, 1522, 1943
  Jean, 1522, 1943
Crei (Lucreie), 610
Creq: see Crete

Crete (vars. Creq, Crette),
  Marie Jeanne (Mme. Louis Anty),
    849, 1087, 1509, 1573, 1863,
    1933, 1984, 2038, 2126, 2249,
    2370, 2390, 2456, 2462, 2467,
    2872
  Pierre I, 982
  Pierre II, 849, 986, 1087, 2872,
Crevier, Agathe (Mme. Baptiste
  Gagnys), 989
Croix: see Sta. Cruz
Crux: see Sta. Cruz
Cunningham, John, Rev. Fr., xvii
Cuno? (Euno?), Genevieve, (Mme.
  Pierre Beaulieu I), 3383
Cupidon, 1464
Curnier, Marie (Mme. Jean Antoine
  Ailhaud Ste. Anne), 3337
Cusson,
  Marie (Mme. Claude Charbonnet),
    995
  Pierre, 43, 106, 180
Cyprien, 3128, 3225, 3267

D_____, Pierre, 1611
Dachanectoc, Indian, 783
Daitchou (Delche, Detchou), Bernard
  (Dna. Juan Hissoura), 2855, 2949,
  3065, 3425
Dandonau, Joseph *dit* du Sable, 42,
  132
Daniel, 327, 2897
Daniel: see also Jean Daniel
d'Arazen, Joseph, Rev. Fr., 1101-
  1103
Darban: see Derbanne
Darbone?, Marie Louise, 427
Darbonne: see Derbanne
Dardenne,
  Athanase, 547
  Charles *dit* Belle Rose, 299, 328,
    547, 634
  Marie Anne, 328
  Marie Jeanne, 634
d'Arensbourg,
  Frederick, 193-194
  Marguerite (Mme. Jacques de la
    Chaise), 191, 193-194, 220, 229
  Pelagie (Mme. Pierre Marets de
    la Tour), 221

Dartigaux (vars. Dartigeaux, Darti-
  geux, Dartigos, De Artigo),
  Jean Baptiste, 1088, 1433, 1606,
    1753, 1771, 1888, 2012, 2104,
    2294, 2305, 2349, 2353, 2398,
    2418, 2507, 2809, 2839, 2843,
    3013, 3208, 3436
  Joseph, 2835, 3052-3053
  Marie Anne (Mme. Jean Jacques Da-
    vid; Mme. Pierre Joseph Maes),
    1049, 1103, 1606, 1642, 1673,
    1707, 1727, 1731, 1737, 1801,
    1888, 1952, 2012, 2078, 2160,
    2269, 2284, 2305, 2340, 2351,
    2509, 3032, 3436
  Pierre, 1020, 1044, 1103, 1116,
    1288, 1312, 1323, 1331, 1366,
    1425, 1489, 1642, 1870, 1952,
    2305, 2349, 2357, 2396, 2398,
    2418, 2421, 2424, 2433, 2437,
    2438, 2487, 2509, 2526, 2535,
    2545, 2550, 3052, 3115, 3131
Darvalle (Dorveille) Magdeleine:
  see Magdeleine (Darvalle) Bouchard
Daublin (Reaublin, Dobin, Doblin),
  Marianne (Mme. François Closeau;
    Mme. Jean Baptiste Triche), 839,
    1006, 1285, 1316, 1340-1341, 1374,
    1468, 1731, 1774, 2377, 2386,
    2414, 2430, 2527, 2675-2677, 3081,
    3153-3154, 3188, 3274-3275, 3316,
    3334
Daublonc (var. Duriblon),
  Charles Peytavin II, 3140, 3182,
    3194
  Jean Baptiste Peytavin, 3140
Daublonc: see also De Blanc
Dauphine, *dit* of Bertrand
Dauphine, Jeanne: see Jeanne, Indian
Dauphine, Louise: see Marie Louise,
  Indian
Dauphine, Marie: see Marie Louise,
  Indian
David,
  _____, 1644
  Andres I, 1035, 2071
  Andres II, 1035, 1066, 1072, 1085,
    1091, 1094, 1597, 1604, 1661,
    1726, 2494, 2636, 3071, 3360,
    3362, 3372, 3375

David (continued),
  Élizabeth, 1693, 1726, 2096, 2885, 3087, 3118, 3285
  Frosine, 2808
  Jean Baptiste, 1049, 1675, 2080, 2824, 2964, 3014
  Jean Baptiste Mathurin, 2522
  Jean Jacques, 1005, 1049, 1819, 2340, 2396
  Louis, 957, 2808, 3083, 3410, 3416
  Maria, 3082
  Marie Eufrasie Mathurine, 2522
  Maturin, 957, 996
  Marie (Mme. Dominique LaLande), 1005
  Pierre, 996
  Ufrosina, 2195
Davion (var. d'Avion),
  Charles *dit* St. Prix, 346
  Dominique, 644, 976, 1072, 1486, 1627, 1876, 2115, 2239, 2532, 2860, 2952, 3000, 3211, 3233, 3322, 3326, 3335, 3367, 3449
  François, 837, 1593, 1882, 2002, 2103, 2157, 2194, 2484, 3000, 3378, 3446
  Jean Baptiste I *dit* St. Prix, 294, 309, 338, 346, 352, 419, 437, 532, 568, 586, 644, 653, 705, 707, 739, 745, 747?, 837, 912, 962, 993, 1022, 1051, 1058, 1062, 1100, 1195, 1249, 1258, 1627, 1667, 1835, 1886, 2273, 2326, 2367, 2381, 2411, 2506, 2829, 2860, 2950, 3000, 3367, 3378, 3381
  Jean Baptiste II (the elder), 586
  Jean Baptiste II (the younger), 912, 2103, 2115, 2220, 2224, 3381
  Jean Baptiste *fils* Dominique, 2115
  Jean Baptiste *fils* François, 2103
  Jean Baptiste (identity uncertain), 2940, 2968
  Jeanne, 532, 760
  Julien *dit* St. Prix (*alias* LeRoy *dit* Framboise), 296, 346
  Louis *dit* St. Prix, 1100, 1476, 1507, 1627, 1818, 1916, 1931,
  2239, 2807, 3064, 3097, 3122, 3147, 3259, 3367, 3410, 3432, 3454
  Manuel *dit* St. Prix, 1760, 3376
  Marie *fille* Dominique, 2860
  Marie (identity uncertain), 2322, 2367
  Marie Adelaide, 3000
  Marie Astasie, 2194
  Marie Elisabeth (Mme. Louis Bertrand), 705, 1062, 1507, 1583, 1676, 1783, 1835, 1876, 1931, 1994, 2081, 2165, 2829, 2950, 3054
  Marie Louise (Mme. Pierre Gagné), 309, 428, 432, 837, 902?, 940, 976, 993, 1523, 1608, 1651, 1701, 1760, 1818, 1886, 1944, 2014, 2066, 3043, 3180, 3243, 3282, 3392, 3449
  Marie Thérèse, 2239
de ____, Pierre, 22
de al Barado, Joseph, 158
de Anze: see de Arze
de Aramboule,
  Emmanuel, 2
  Jeanne, 2
de Arze (vars. de Anze, de Arcaze, de Arce),
  Juan I, 1074
  Juan II, 1074, 1085, 1851
  Juan Pedro, 1851
  Leonor, 1074
de Artigo: see Dartigaux
de Berban: see Derbanne
Deblanc (vars. Deblan, Daublonc, Le Blanc),
  ____, 1609, 2652, 3029
  Céleste Mathilde, 1645, 1845, 2061, 2164, 2235, 2513, 3101
  Césaire, commandant and chevalier, 271, 295, 316, 323, 332, 347, 352, 355, 399, 426, 493, 528, 553, 557, 564, 618, 638, 646, 679, 686, 722, 727, 743, 748, 749, 802
  Charle, 355
  Élisabeth Marcellite, 1645, 2061
  Jacques Maurice, 638, 802
  Jean Baptiste, 1811
  Jean Baptiste Thomas, 1866, 3101

Deblanc (continued),
  Joseph Marie Charles, 1768, 1845, 2303, 2368, 3029
  Louis Charles, commandant, 451, 557, 576, 637, 660, 686, 714, 1007, 1103, 1179, 1282, 1306, 1365, 1368, 1371, 1496, 1628, 1629, 1637, 1645, 1694, 1722, 1768, 1811, 1845, 1866, 1895, 1961, 2061, 2097, 2106, 2176-2177, 2188, 2303, 2368, 2413, 2489, 2500-2501, 2509-2510, 2513, 2518, 2561-2562, 2599, 2626, 2692, 2714-2715, 2778, 3093, 3126, 3337
  Marie Aspasie, 1637, 1961, 2176
  Marie des Douleurs: see Marie des Douleurs (Dolorite) Simone Juchereau de St. Denis
  Marie Joseph Constance, 2097
  Marie Louis César, 1768, 1811, 2176, 2246
  Marie Louise Marthe (Mme. Dufores), 1531, 1722, 1768, 1845, 1866, 1948, 2193, 2368, 2497, 3103
  Marie Mélanie (the elder), 2176
  Marie Mélanie (the younger), 2176
  Maximillian, 2177
  Pierre George César, 1895
de Borme: see Bormé
de Boustamente, Nicole (Mda. Christophe Florés), 158
Debrande (var. Debrante),
  André *dit* Champagne, 621, 719, 740
  François, 719
  Marie Josephe Veronique, 621
de Calahorra y Sarvo: see Calahorra
de Caldes (de Caldez), Francisco, Rev. Fr., 1870, 2438, 2514
de Castanare (de Castanores), Hermano Casiano, Brother, 1019-1021, 1028-1029, 1034, 1041-1042
de Castres: see Castro
de Ceped: see de Zepeda
de Corbier, _____, 169, 174
de Corbier: see also Corbier
de Coste,
  François, 844
  Marie de l'Assumption (Mme. François de Coste), 844
  Marie Françoise, 844

de Coton *dit* of du Vivier
De Coux, Jean François, 511
de Deos, Anne (Dna. Coulas de Sta. Theresia), 545
de Esmada (de Strada), Francisco, 104
de Falsinthe: see Fazende
Deforge, Felicité: see Clavau, Felicité Renée (Deforge)
Degagne, Catherinne (Mme. Joseph Marie Mercier), 2955
de Garcie: see Garcia
de Grenade, Nicola, 22
de Grenade: see also le Grenade
Deguisancourt, Marie (Mme. Charles Alorge), 209
Deil (Teal?),
  Isaac, 2142
  John, 2142
  Leticia, 2142
Deil: see also Teal
Dejarnul?, _____, Sr., 990
Dejones, Rebecca: see Rebecca D. Jones
de Juchereau: see de St. Denis
de Kerelecq: see Kerlerecq
de la Aintelle, Pierre Isabelle, 675
de la Baré (Barre), Gille, 3394, 3396
de la Campa, Jean Gregorio, 144, 522
de la Cerda (var. Cerda, Cerdas, de la Serda, de la Sert, La Sert), Maria Gertrudes (Dna. Joseph Gonzales), 13, 100, 168
de la Cerda: see also de la Sert
de la Chaise,
  _____, 1011
  Anne Marie, 38
  Charles Auguste, 193
  Jacques, 7, 10, 11, 13, 19, 36, 38, 59-63, 73, 84-85, 134, 140, 144, 150-152, 162, 166-167, 178, 182, 193, 210, 214, 216, 220-221, 225, 229, 233, 367
  Louis Antoine, 73
  Marie Loüise, 7, 63
  Marie Marguerite, 229, 2329, 2347
  Rose: see Rose Juchereau de St. Denis
Delacise, Marie Monet, 3011
de la Creoz, Maria (Dna. Andres Villareal), 1019

444

de la Creoz: see also Sta. Cruz
de la Croix: see Sta. Cruz and La Croix
de la Ferrebeyre, Michel (Dna. Joseph Goutierrez), 994
de la Fosse,
  Pierre, 1001
  Romaine, 1001
de la Fosse: see also Fosse
de la Gase (var. de la Gace),
  Ignace, 740, 829?
de la Gase: see also Berard de la Gase
de la Grande Air: see de la Grande Terre
de la Grande Terre, Jeanne, Indian (Mme. François Dion Despres Derbanne), 4, 13, 128, 148, 168, 207, 350, 513, 516
de la Grande Terre, Marie Anne Thérèse, Indian (Mme. Jacques Guedon), 215, 340, 342, 348, 454
de la Haye, Jeanne (Mme. Joseph Le Court), 984
de Laissard: see Layssard
de La Lane: see Goutierrez
de la Malathi: see La Malathy
de la Motte, Nicolas, 1713
de la Motte: see also La Motte
de Land, Joseph, 744
de Land: see also Goutierrez
de la Peña: see Loppes de la Peña
de la Perriere: see La Perriere
de la Porte, Marie Françoise (Mme. Charles Pellerin I), 718
de la Renaudiere: see La Renaudiere
de la Rivière (del Rio), Marie Jeanne Louise, (Mme. Charles La Renaudiere; Mme. Jacques Hubert), xiii, 286, 316, 525, 567, 615, 872, 980, 992, 1002, 1012, 1015, 1037, 1074, 1080, 1161, 2890, 3007
de la Roche: see La Roche
de la Ronde, Pierre, chevalier, 356, 524-525, 535, 539-540, 550, 558, 561, 568, 577-578, 586, 590, 655, 665, 722, 734
de la Sta. Crux: see Sta. Cruz
de la Sert,
  ____, 660
  Joseph Michel, 660
  Jean Baptiste, 660

de la Sert: see also de la Cerda
de la Tour, Pierre Marets (vars. Mariet, Marel), 8, 13, 27, 38, 46, 56, 59, 65, 75, 124, 132, 134, 136, 141, 146-147, 157, 167, 183, 192, 205, 210, 221
de la SS. Trinidad, Joseph Marie, Rev. Fr., 995
de la Vez, Marie Jeanne (Mme. Christophe Naler?), 334
del Castillo, Josef Antonio, 1074
del Castillo: see also Castelle
Delche: see Daitchou
Delec, Louise (Mme. Pierre Sorel), 735
Delessart: see Layssard
Delincour (vars. Delincourte, Detincourt),
  César, 720
  Marie (Mme. Adrien Leger; Mde. Nicolas Paul Bourdelle), 412, 426, 560, 567, 611, 643, 648, 1002
de Lisle, Marie Élizabeth (Mme. Claude Bertrand), 989
de Livaudais: see Henoul de Livaudais
De Lorme,
  Joseph I, 1076
  Joseph II, 1076
de los Reyes, Juanna (Dna. Joseph Courretant Torres), xiii, 1558, 1713, 1750, 1970, 2864, 2870, 2874, 3005, 3372, 3424, 3447
Delouche,
  Anne, 2935
  Family, 2934n
  Jacques, 2191
  Jean Baptiste, 1086, 1563, 1832, 1897, 1975, 2113-2114, 2191, 2698, 2935, 3429
  Jean Louis, 1897
  Julien, 2114
  Marie Felicité, 1563, 1975
  Michel, 2191
  Pierre (the elder), 1086, 2935
  Pierre (the younger), 2113
del Rio: see de la Rivière
Delvaux, Jean, Rev. Fr., xv, 1500, 1555, 2700-2701, 2736, 3223-3224, 3229, 3233
de Macarti: see Macarti

Demare, Marie (Mme. Jean Baptiste Jannot I), 3396
de Marmolejo, Ildephonous Joseph, Rev. Fr., 347
de Mersier, _____, 738
de Mézières (vars. Demeiziere, De Mesiere, de Mezier, de Meziere, De Mezierres, De Mezzer, Messieres, Meziere, Mezieres, Mezzer),
  Antoine Marie, 468, 2302, 2388
  Athanase I: see Athanase Christophe Fortunat
  Athanase II: see Marie Pelagie Athanase
  Athanase Christophe Fortunat, 185, 233, 243, 267, 271, 347, 355, 405, 413, 468, 489, 493, 499, 523-524, 547, 582, 630, 640, 648, 654, 679, 691, 701, 708, 880, 885, 909-910, 922, 937-939, 975, 995, 1030, 1108, 1115, 1131, 1166, 1171, 1180, 1184, 1187, 1218, 1225, 1292, 1500, 1698, 1709, 2278, 2286, 2295, 2304, 2310, 2312, 2315, 2320, 2347, 2359
  Césaire Marie, 679, 939, 1019, 1183, 2319
  Coleta, 2631
  Elisabeth Marie Felicité, 271, 523, 2313, 2844, 3427
  Jacques, 2256, 2311, 2329, 2371, 2380, 2468, 2828
  Louis Christophe Claude, 347
  Louis Françoise Marie, 405
  Marie, 1187
  Marie Jean Jacques, 880
  Marie Joseph, 939, 2314, 2359, 2394, 2439, 2499
  Marie Nicolas Zozime, 937, 2295, 2306, 2347, 2359, 3082
  Marie Pelagie Athanaise (female), 630
  Marie Pelagie Athanase (male), 405, 447, 489, 640, 680, 691, 2371, 2394, 2410, 2439, 2499, 2601, 2609, 2697, 2811, 2847, 3128, 3269, 3308, 3313, 3315
  Marie Petronille Feliciane: see Marie Petronille Feliciane Juchereau de St. Denis

de Mézières (continued),
  Marie Stephanie Pelagie, 489
  Zozime: see Marie Nicolas Zozime
Demien (Amien), Marie (Mme. Michel Jarri), 2882, 3409
Demond, Sara (Mme. Abraham Gonin), 985
De Mont: see Dumont
De Mouy (var. du Muy),
  Marguerite (Mme. Jean Baptiste Roujot), 1027, 1110
  Marie Élizabeth, 1706, 1714, 1719, 1725
  Maurice, 1065, 1071
Denes (vars. Denette, Denis),
  Jean Baptiste, 356
  Marie Anne Élisabeth Clémence (Mme. Jean Louis Cesar Bormé), 329, 434, 453, 490, 528, 542, 552, 553, 564, 584, 613, 682, 705, 848, 865, 2243, 2283
Denes: see also Denis
Denis, 2155
Denis, chief of Apalaches, 2143, 2155, 2495, 2517, 2740-2741
Denis,
  Athanase, 2925
  Jean Baptiste I, 1070, 1083, 2925-2926
  Jean Baptiste II, 1070, 1593, 1654, 1742, 1855, 1909, 1959, 2002, 2058, 2200, 2325, 2925-2926
  Jean Pierre, 2200
  Louis Evrie, 2200
  Marguerite, 1855, 2925
  Marie, 1593, 2002
  Marie Deneige, 2926
  Marie Eufrosine, 1959
  Marie Nanette, 1654, 2058
Denoié, _____, 3037
de Noÿot, Ignace, 692
De Ortolan: see Dortolant
De Pre: see Dupre
de Prelle: see LeCourt de Prelle
Depres, Marianne, 1545
De Pres: see also Dupre
Deragon,
  Maria Apolonia (Dna. Francisco Gonsales), 2982, 3077
  Simon, 2982, 3077
Derancourt de St. Amand, Gilbert, 839, 848, 995

446

Derban, Marguerite (Mme. Joseph
  Laurent), 1078
Derbanne (vars. Darban, Darbone,
  Darbonne, De Berban, Derban,
  Dervan, Dervanne, Dervin,
  d'Herbanne)
  ____, infant, 495
  ____, Mlle. 35
  ____, Mr., 69-70, 80, 82, 99,
    160-161, 167, 189, 197, 234,
    237, 344, 1492-1493, 3099-3100,
    3171
  André (Antoine) François, 604
  Cidonie, 2827
  François, *fils* Gaspard, 672
  François, *fils* J. B. Gaspard,
    2873
  François /Guyon *dit*/ Dion Despres
    13, 128, 148, 168, 207, 350,
    513, 514
  Gaspard I, 89, 260, 270, 284, 303,
    307, 321, 350, 357, 534, 548,
    554, 589, 604, 612, 662, 665,
    672, 689, 728, 740, 982, 999,
    1000, 1002, 1017, 1037, 1058,
    1065, 1075, 1077, 1081, 1325,
    1377, 1746, 1766, 2318, 2462,
    2845, 2873, 2968, 2988, 3092?
    3166?
  Gaspard II, 321, 594, 1554, 1617,
    1881, 1966, 2019, 2197, 2845,
    2968, 3092?
  Jean *dit* Despres, 113, 171, 534
  Jean Baptiste *fils* Gaspard, 548,
    1037, 1064-1065, 1075, 1087,
    1462, 1508, 1567, 1704, 1712,
    1932, 1979, 2192, 2377, 2456,
    2473, 2873, 2988, 3428
  Jean Baptiste *fils* Gaspard II,
    1554, 1966
  Jean Baptiste *fils* Jean Baptiste,
    1874
  Jean Baptiste *fils* Pierre, 3453
  Jean Baptiste Dion, 4, 13, 18-19,
    26, 45, 69, 83, 87-90, 92, 97-
    98, 100, 116-117, 163, 168,
    207, 224, 230, 548, 741
  Jean Pierre, 944
  Jeanne; see Jeanne de la Grande
    Terre
  Joseph, 2065, 2583, 3426, 3441

Derbanne (continued),
  Louis, 1539, 1576, 1588, 1987,
    1999, 3350, 3426, 3446
  Louis Étienne (Olier?), 1592,
    2001
  Louis Solastie, 2192
  Magdeleine (Dna. Joseph Antoine
    Goutierrez de la Lane), 972
  Manuel, 2173, 2827, 2863, 3423,
    3426
  Marie (Mme. Jean Christy), 1908
  Marie (identity uncertain), 874,
    972
  Marie, *fille* Gaspard, 1881
  Marie Anastasie, 1567, 1979
  Marie Aspasie, 2183
  Marie Cÿprienne, 1893, 2936,
    3239, 3443
  Marie de l'Incarnation (Mme. Jo-
    seph Dupre; Mme. Jean Marchant)
    407, 411, 416, 674, 741, 853,
    903, 930, 970, 1017, 1057,
    1064, 1079, 1308, 1480, 1539,
    1590, 1709, 1752, 1794, 2862,
    3350, 3358, 3376, 3434
  Marie des Nieges *fille* Gaspard,
    1617, 2019
  Marie Deneige *fille* Jean Baptiste,
    2988
  Marie Jeanne (Mme. François
    Manne), 57, 69, 76, 83, 89,
    148-149, 321
  Marie Louise Margueritte (Mme.
    Étienne Barbier; Mme. Louis An-
    toine de St. Denis), 90, 98,
    207, 224, 240, 260, 268, 270,
    280, 317, 350, 459, 525, 535,
    632, 689, 879, 1419, 1486, 1592,
    1722, 1874, 2001, 2175, 2444,
    2512, 2532, 2542, 3104, 3251,
    3262, 3278, 3289, 3298, 3327
  Marie Louise Margueritte (Mme.
    Françoise Lavespere), 689, 1419,
    1518, 1533, 1588, 1650, 1700,
    1752, 1766, 1950, 1999, 2065,
    2173, 2393, 2857, 3017, 3342
  Marie Placide, 2197
  Marie Rose, 2845
  Marie Susanne, 2968
  Marie Victoire (Mme. Pierre Cha-
    ler), 421, 1480, 1525, 1576,

Derbanne (continued),
  Marie Victoire (Mme. Pierre Chaler, continued), 1767, 1781, 1857, 1946, 1987, 2056, 2184, 2275, 2316, 3035
  Mélanie (Mme. Jean Baptiste Brevel III), 3453
  Michel, 2259
  Paul Alexandre, 1508, 1932
  Pierre I, 98, 261, 266, 298, 338, 350, 421, 423, 432, 452, 653, 689, 855, 879, 901, 944, 972, 980, 982, 1065, 1122, 1203, 1220, 1324, 1346, 1394, 1442, 1455, 1459, 1477, 1480, 1518, 1752, 2054, 2056, 2275, 2290, 2316, 2356, 2375, 2392-2393, 2402, 2432, 2445, 2452, 2480, 2485, 2529, 2536-2537, 2583, 2591, 2672, 2684, 2699, 2857, 3017, 3026, 3047, 3119, 3342, 3389, 3426
  Pierre II (Pierrite), 879, 1065, 1383, 1480, 1539, 1592, 1752, 1893, 2001, 2183, 2259, 3253, 3405, 3443
Derbanne: see also Durbannes
de Reggio, Brigida, 1866
Derneville, Élisabeth Pompone (Mme. Louis Charles Deblanc), 1370, 1629, 1637, 1645, 1694, 1722, 1768, 1811, 1845, 1866, 1895, 1961, 2061, 2097, 2176-2177, 2241, 2495, 2517
de Roblat, Jean *dit* La R____, 357
De Roi: see Le Roy, de los Reyes
Deroie, Maria Ana, 1705
de Rosier, *dit* of Renaud
Derroven, Étienne, 1047
Derry, La., 2928n
de St. Amand: see Derancourt de St. Amand
de St. Denis (vars. de St. Denys, St. Denis, Jucherot de St. Denis, Juchereau de St. Denis),
  ____, 827, 1181, 2273, 2286
  Emmanuella: see Emmanuella Maria Stephania Sanchez Navarro
  Louis Antoine Juchereau I, commandant and chevalier, 7, 10-12, 16-17, 20, 23, 27, 31, 33, 34, 45, 48, 53, 56, 62, 64, 74, 101-103, 106, 112, 144, 151, 155-156, 166, 178, 183, 187-188, 195, 202, 211, 213, 218, 225, 229, 243, 347, 355, 367, 369, 464, 731, 832, 2546
  Louis Antoine Juchereau II, 72, 222, 273, 286, 310, 317-318, 323, 333, 355-356, 422, 450, 456, 463, 474, 527, 538, 557, 572, 613, 879, 1021, 1029, 1200, 1722
  Marguerite: see Marie Louise Marguerite
  Marie, 225, 253, 267, 286, 347, 538
  Marie des Douleurs (Dolorite) Simone Juchereau (Mme. César de Blanc), 243, 273, 323, 326, 330-332, 337, 355-356, 524, 533, 545, 557, 574, 579, 592, 602, 613, 618, 638, 649, 671, 673, 679, 680, 802
  Marie des Nieges (Mme. Emanuel Antonio Bermudez y de Soto), 16, 112, 279, 295, 304, 310, 316, 332, 406, 450, 464, 468, 485, 490, 527, 531, 556, 564, 569, 572-573, 576, 581, 624, 638, 646, 671, 731, 784, 860, 877, 1011, 1609, 1694, 1697, 2383, 2844, 2869, 2957, 3011, 3363
  Marie Eleonore, 332
  Marie Gertrude Juchereau, 48
  Marie Louise Antoine Bastien (Mme. Jacques Sebastien Prudhomme), 1486, 1492, 1558, 1567, 1970, 1979, 2175, 2532, 2536, 3094, 3395
  Marie Louise Marguerite Juchereau (Mme. Pierre Coutoleau Duplessis) 58, 229, 233, 305, 514, 519-520, 522, 668, 744
  Marie Petronille Feliciane Juchereau (Mme. Athanase de Mézières) 16, 33, 38-39, 53, 74, 271, 347, 390, 547
  Marie Rose Juchereau (Mme. Jacques de la Chaise), 2, 7, 37, 56, 73, 134, 144

de St. Denis (continued),
  Pierre Antoine Juchereau, 183
    253, 279, 329-331, 406, 533,
    556-557, 564, 574, 576, 645,
    650, 671, 673, 735, 826, 1296
  Widow: see Emmanuella Maria
    Stephania Sanchez Navarro,
    and Marie Louise Marguerite
    Derbanne
de St. Denys (de St. Denis) *dit*
  of Pierre Rachal
de St. Denys, Louis (soldier), 120
de Sta. Crux: see Sta. Cruz
de Salomee, Ursulle (Mme. Cesar
  Delincour), 720
De Sauto: see de Soto
de Sorel: see Sorel
de Soto (vars. De Sauto, De Zoto,
    Sautau, Sauto, Sotho, Soto)
  Emanuel Antonio Marcel Bermudez
    y, 406, 450, 464, 485, 490,
    579, 581, 592, 602, 624, 646,
    671, 731, 733, 735, 784, 823,
    860, 862, 919, 921, 1011, 1248,
    1609, 2283, 2324, 2844, 2869,
    2956, 3011, 3363
  Eulalie Marie Anne (Mme. Paul
    Bouet Laffitte), 490, 1524,
    1569, 1575, 1611, 1847, 1890,
    1986, 2015, 2046, 2106, 2128-
    2129, 2163, 2324, 2358, 2380
    2844, 2957, 2976, 3024, 3432
  Joseph Antoine Marcel, 671, 1493,
    1524, 1609, 1645, 1656, 1866,
    1945, 2060-2061, 2106, 2164,
    2246, 2324, 2537, 2727-2728,
    2776, 2779-2781, 2795, 2798,
    2865?, 2869, 3011, 3159, 3363
  Joseph François, 485
  Joseph Marcel II, 2164
  Louis Joseph Firmin, 464
  Marcel: see Joseph Antoine Mar-
    cel and Joseph Marcel
  Marie, 406, 422, 464, 1628,
    1785, 2192, 2202
  Marie Anne: see Eulalie Marie Anne
  Marie des Douleurs, 1656, 2060,
    2869
  Marie Emmanuel (Mme. Athanase
    Poissot), 624, 960, 1011, 1603,
    1637, 1778, 1823, 1847, 1961,
    2010, 2060, 2867, 2887, 3420

de Soto (continued)
  Maria Josepha (Dna. Domingo
    Bermudes), 731
  Marie Josephe Damasene, 406, 1713,
    1750, 2359
  Marie Louise Cilesie, 2106
  Marie Monet, 3011
  Remy Euph____ Marcel, 2869
  Severine Antoine Gertrude, 860
des Rois: see de los Reyes and Le
  Roy
de Sotos, Jeanne, 692
Destase?, _____, Mr., 3250
de Strada: see Francisco de Esmada
Detchou: see Daitchou
de Terrepui, _____ Verschiers,
  250, 340, 342, 361, 366, 369
Detincourt: see Delincourt
de Torres,
  François, 158
  Marc, 158
de Torres: see also Torres
Detuile (vars. Detui, Detuil),
  Catherinne Claire, 2828
  Françoise, 2879
  Guillaume Jacob, 2879
  Jacques (Jacob), 2828, 2879, 3058,
    3060
  Julie, 3058
  Margueritte (Mme. Pierre Hufe-
    rogue), 2828
Detuile: see also Dutihl
de Vaugine,
  Étienne I, commandant, 1063, 1097,
    2436, 2442, 2445, 2471, 2478,
    2503, 2528, 2538, 3339
  Étienne II, 1515, 2496
  François Nuisman, 2464, 2470
  Françoise, 2396
  Silesia, 2436, 2449, 2470-2471
Dever, Marie (Mrs. William Mechim),
  1068
Deville, Louis, 3387
de Villers Blet: see Ville Blette
de Villiers, Louis, Chevalier,
  2313-2314
de Villiers: see also Coulon de
  Villiers
des Jeans, Jean: see Jean Mader *dit*
  Jean dos Jeans
des Pagnet, Marguerite (Mme. Charle
  de Blanc), 355

Despres, Antoine, 728, 738, 746
Despres: see also Dupre
de Visote, Jeanne (Mme. Guillaume Poirier), 456
de Vivier: see du Vivier
de Zepeda (vars. Cepedre, de Ceped, de Zeperda, Seperda, Sepide), Maria Antonia Isidora (Dna. Guillermo Robleau), 1636, 1744, 1788, 1828, 3369, 3397, 3444
d'Herbanne: see Derbanne
d'Huberdeaux: see Huberdeau
Diciz, 2340
Didier, Jacques, Rev. Fr., 637
Dionesio: see Denis
Dizancour, *dit* of Pierre Alorge
Doblin: see Daublin
Docla, *dit* of Nicolas, *nègre*
Dolet (vars. Dolar, Dolé, Dolis, Dulé),
  Albert, 458, 510
  Jean Pierre I, 491, 1064, 1364, 1519, 1569, 1577, 1872, 1940, 1988, 2015, 2429, 2639, 2752, 2859, 2893, 3138
  Jean Pierre II, 1872
  Louis Neuville, 1519, 1940
  Marie Louise: see Marie Louise Toutin
  Marie Louise Denis, 1577, 1988
  Pierre Jean *dit* à Centienne, 439, 458, 491, 510, 990, 1064
Dollet?, Luis, 2410
Dolores: see Marie Françoise de Dolores
Dominique (Domingo), 2431, 2433, 2491, 2546, 2588, 2606, 2718, 2742, 3087
Donado, Herman, 1021
Donado, _____, Rev. Fr., 1041
Donato Bello, _____, Sr., 1000
Dophino: see François Dophino
Dormoy, Françoise (Mme. Jean Baptiste Malbert I), 728
Dorothée (Dorotea), 2278, 2326, 2675, 2699, 2762, 2787, 2863
D'Ortolant (vars. De Ortolan, De Ortolant, Dortolant, Ortholan, Ortolan, Ortolant, Ortolon),
  Bernard, 1026, 1031, 1038, 1304, 1516, 1538, 1580, 1627, 1728, 1782, 1848, 1902, 1938, 1991, 2193, 2319, 2365, 2422, 2581, 2648, 3348, 3367, 3398, 3400, 3402
  François, 1902
  Jean Baptiste, 1687, 1728, 2090, 2417
  Jean Pierre Julien Raymond, 1782
  Marie Athanase, 1848
  Raymond, 1026, 3398
Dorveille (Darvalle): see Bouchard
Doucet, François *dit* Eustache, 291, 357, 937, 1024, 1026, 1030, 1034, 1045, 1053, 1055, 1176, 1301, 2277, 2310, 2364
Doussaint, Anne (Mme. Guillaume Epinette), 1549, 3354
Drapon (Dupron), Marianne (Mme. Nicolas François Metoyer), 1552, 3355
Dreux, _____, 864, 2097
du _____, Hyves, *cadet*, 35
Dubardeau: see Hubardeau
Dubie?, Genevieve (Mme. François Lebeuf), 2212
Dubois, *dit* of Pierre Benoit
Dubois (vars. Duboë, Duboi, du Bois, Dubos),
  _____, 1432, 1457, 3048
  Adalaïde Locadie, 2198
  Anne Barbe, 1541, 1957, 2910
  Antoine, 2228
  Antoine Philippe, 884, 1090, 1561, 1973, 2069, 2228, 2852, 2900, 3400
  Aspasie, 2127
  César, 1587, 1998
  Élisabeth (Mme. Julien Rondain), 1, 122, 518
  François Emerand, 2900
  François Isidor, 1514, 1937
  Françoise, 539, 772
  Hyves (Mme. Nicolas Prevot), 24, 49, 86
  Jacques, 121
  Jean Baptiste *fils* Philippe, 418, 439, 456, 539, 584, 606, 656, 673, 684, 717, 723, 730, 741, 753, 772, 779, 853, 884, 887, 893, 981, 985, 1011, 1015, 1025, 1032-1033, 1056, 1084, 1090-1091, 1239, 1446, 1514, 1529, 1541,

Dubois (continued),
Jean Baptiste *fils* Philippe (continued), 1732, 1736, 1937, 1957, 2852, 2900, 2912-2913, 2978, 3345, 3400
Jean Baptiste *fils* Valentin J. B., 2247
Jean Baptiste François, 418, 1090, 1409, 1457, 1514, 1587, 1657, 1671, 1799, 1937, 1998, 2044-2045, 2069, 2098, 2127, 2196, 2900, 2978, 3048, 3167, 3374, 3383, 3393
Jean Baptiste Josue, 2069
Julien Leandre, 2852
Marie Baltilde, 1635, 2037, 2913
Marie Euphrosine, 2978
Marie Genevieve (the elder), 584, 779
Marie Genevieve (the younger; Mme. Jean Baptiste Étienne Adlé), 606, 942, 1032, 1502, 1561, 1732, 1736, 1807, 1842, 1927, 1973, 2048, 2125, 2215, 2852
Marie Pompone, 3170
Marie Rose, 2913
Philippe, 717
Pierre, 1549
René, 114, 129, 148, 153, 174, 339, 381, 515
Théodore, 965, 1001
Valentin, 2912
Valentin Jean Baptiste, 673, 1529, 1541, 1635, 1770, 1957, 2037, 2247, 2905, 2908, 2912-2913, 3345, 3354
du Buisson, *dit* of Clement Belleoeil
du Burdeau: see Huberdeau
Duc: see Le Duc
Duchet (vars. Dugue, Duguet),
Basile, 1659, 3377
Étienne, 1791, 2159, 3377
François Étienne, 2159
Duchil: see Dutihl, Detuile
du Colet, _____, 237
du Colet: see also Colet
Du Cote (var. Ducodere),
Louis Pellerin, 256, 326, 347, 356
Margueritte Caiote (Mme. Jean Baptiste Ferrier), 2954

Duffy, Michel, 3399
Duforet (var. Du Fores),
_____, Mr., 3104
_____, Da., 3084
Dufosset, Jean Valentin, 2177
Du Frene (Dufresne), *dit* of Chever
Dufrene, Guillerma: see Jeanne Marguerite Toutin (Mme. Pierre Guillaume Chever)
Dugue, _____, 673
Dugue: see also Duchet
Dumont (vars. De Mont, Dumons),
Catherine (Mme. Jacques Vercher), 1009
Charles, 736
Marie Angélique Charles (Mme. Joseph Verger; Mme. Jacques Turpot), 28-29, 41, 54, 76, 93, 107, 116, 219, 259, 281, 303, 350, 357, 662, 666, 718, 728, 729, 736, 816, 981-982, 1017
Marie Charles (Mme. Henry Trichel), 22, 72, 88, 101, 105, 116, 186, 346, 352, 365, 816, 1000, 1006
Marie Elizabeth (Mme. Jean Baptiste Denes), 356
du Muy: see de Mouy
Dupain (var. Dupin),
Antoine, 54, 79, 173
Jeanne (Mme. Baptiste du Vivier), 410, 751, 1038
Marie Felicité (Mme. Jean Baptiste Armant), 680, 946, 1037, 1044, 1704, 1754, 1771, 2318
Marie Jeanne *dit* Riotaur (vars. Rioteau, Rioter, Riotor, Riotord; Mme. Julien Rondin), 21, 79, 92, 109, 139, 147, 199, 232, 276, 288, 537, 601, 633, 988, 1046
Pierre *dit* Riotaur, 147, 743, 751
Pierre, 3019
Pierre Manuel Victor, 680, 742, 752, 808, 1011, 1037, 1044, 1056, 1063, 1207, 1633, 1643, 2036, 2040, 2355
Dupard, _____, 831
Dupare,
Guilhaumme, 1643, 2040
Louis Guilhaumme, 1643, 2040
Duplessis (vars. Duplaisis, Duplecis, Duplecy),
Emmanuelle (Mme. René Henri Le Boeuf), 300, 530, 643, 994

Duplessis (continued),
  Jean, 643
  Louise: see Marie Louise Marguerite Juchereau de St. Denis
  Marie Elves? (Dna. Michel Goutierrez), 2843, 3002, 3403
  Pierre Coutoleau, 58, 170, 172, 208, 513, 516, 519-520, 744
  Pierre Louis, 530, 620, 1045, 1066, 1082
Dupont, Anne (Mme. Pierre David), 996
Dupre (vars. De Pre, De Pres, De Pret, Despres, Dupree, Dupres, Duprez),
  ____, 668, 1306
  ____, Mda., 2441, 2450, 2454, 2468, 2480, 2503
  A____, Rev., 2623, 2749
  Anne Marie, 861, 1060
  Antoine Baptiste, 954
  Athanase, 2227, 2890, 3434
  Barbe Élisabeth, 846
  Cécile (Mme. Pierre Jarri), 2074, 2111, 2114, 2263, 2698, 2882, 3075, 3409
  Élisabeth (Mme. Jean Baptiste Garein; Mme. Charles Le Moine I), 50, 543, 723, 730, 854, 892, 930, 1030, 1237, 1505, 1679, 2820-2821, 2841, 2849, 2885, 2923-2924, 2956, 2959, 2995-2996, 3051, 3340, 3385, 3390, 3421
  François, 1709
  Françoise, 2893
  Jacques *dit* La Suisse, 21, 49-50, 131, 153, 341, 354, 723, 729, 730, 741, 999
  Jean Baptiste I, 408, 455, 593, 612, 666, 729, 790, 850, 876, 901, 930, 954, 986, 999, 1060, 1093, 1150, 1152, 1208, 1234, 1240, 1255, 1264, 1269, 1758, 2308, 2325, 2326, 2336, 2342, 2362, 2382, 2403-2404
  Jean Baptiste II, 408
  Jean Baptiste *fils* Joseph, 1752
  Jean Baptiste (identity uncertain), 2221, 2251
  Jean David, 1794

Dupre (continued),
  Joseph I, 21, 407, 411, 509, 674, 741, 853, 901, 903, 970, 1017, 1058, 1060, 1064, 1079, 1168, 1210, 1263, 1279, 1283, 1539, 1590, 1647, 1705, 1709, 1714, 1740, 1745, 1752, 1757, 1794, 2326, 2336, 2862, 3350, 3358, 3376, 3434
  Joseph II, 674, 1058, 1275, 1740, 1840, 2519
  Joseph III, 1840, 3229-3230, 3237, 3285
  Joseph, Mda., 2519
  Marguerite, 3106
  Marianne (Mme. Jean Louis Lambre), 1577, 1590, 1662, 1887, 1959, 1988, 2057, 2072, 3358
  Marie (the elder), 411
  Marie (the younger), 1283
  Marie (identity uncertain), 1653, 1711, 2200, 2237, 2339, 2529, 2833, 2882
  Marie Anne Rose (Mme. Jean Pierre Dolet), 903, 1064, 1519, 1577, 1834, 1872, 1940, 1988, 2429, 2859, 2862, 3406
  Marie Catherine (Mme. Joseph François Barthelemy Pierre Pereau; Mme. Jean Lalande), 247, 341, 354, 416, 470, 541, 591, 593, 690, 846, 934, 997, 1005, 1031, 1061, 1081, 1092, 1556, 1699, 1843, 1968, 2832, 2845-2846, 2850-2851, 2865, 2951, 2968, 2979, 2989, 3016, 3417, 3449, 3453
  Marie Delaide, 2862
  Marie de l'Assumption, 433
  Marie Françoise (Mme. Étienne Verger), 1017, 1533, 1684, 1740, 1778, 1950, 2088, 2893, 3080, 3418
  Marie Josephe *fille* J. B. (the elder), 612, 790
  Marie Josephe *fille* J. B. (the younger), 666
  Marie Josephe *fille* Joseph, 853
  Marie Louise (Mme. Jacques La Caze), 1479, 1539, 1594, 1699, 1794, 1804, 1824, 1840, 1868, 1872,

Dupre (continued),
  Marie Louise (Mme. Jacques La
    Caze, continued), 1908, 2003,
    2102:, 2171, 2191, 2336, 2375,
    2531, 2857, 2894, 3350
  Marie Marcellite, 2102
  Marie Osite, 2227
  Marie Robert (Mme. Jean Pomier),
    1060, 1582, 1742, 1993, 2074,
    2171, 2833, 2963, 3036
  Pierre, 970, 1577, 1647, 1988,
    2102, 2227, 2362, 2862, 3376,
    3418, 3434
  Robert, 49, 593, 861, 991, 1060,
    2366, 2833, 2882, 2963, 3409
  Thérèse, 876
Dupron, Marianne: see Drapon
Durand,
  ____, *charpentier* (possibly
    Charpentier, Durand), 1437
  Louis, 990, 1373, 1527, 3343
Durbanes, Marie (Mme. Pierre du
  Roques), 2895
Durbanes: see also Derbanne
Duret, Charles, 1497, 3338, 3404
Durci, François, 2888
Duriblon: see Daublonc
Duroche, Marion (Mme. Jean Baptiste
  Pievert), 1050
Du Roque,
  Nicolas, 2895
  Pierre, 2895
  Victoire Constance, 2895
du Sablé, *dit* of Joseph Dandonau
Dutihl (vars. Duchil, Duetiel, Du-
  til), Marie Monique (Mme. Pierre
  Dartigaux), 1049, 1103, 1642,
  1819, 1867, 1952, 2424, 2587,
  2629, 2634, 2670, 2702, 2707,
  2719-2720, 2722
Dutihl: see also Detuile
Duval,
  ____, *dit* la Couronne, 768
  François, 2990, 3442
  Margueritte (Mme. Laurent Mail-
    lioux), 2990, 3004, 3442
du Verge: see Verger
Du Vivier (var. de Vivier),
  Jean Baptiste *dit* de Coton, 410,
    751, 990, 1038
  Marie Louise (Mme. Jean Baptiste
    La Renaudiere), 410, 1038

du Vivier (continued),
  Michel Rochelos, 751
Edmond, Catherine (Mme. Jean Hazes
  I), 205
El Cour: see Le Court
Elbé, Rebecca (Mrs. Hezekiah Russ),
  2980
Elena: see Hélène
Eleonore (Eleonora, Leonora), 709,
  2671, 3173, 3281
Eleonore: see also Marie Héleine
  Eleonore
Elie, Pierre, 2819
Élisabeth (Isabelle, Ysabel), 155,
  265, 483, 896, 935, 2346, 2350,
  2355, 2361, 2363, 2366, 2385,
  2407, 2415, 2469, 2652, 2739,
  2792, 2802, 3088, 3117, 3141,
  3184, 3233-3234, 3253, 3267,
  3323
Émelie: see Amelie, Marie Thérèse
  Émelie
Emmanuel, 370, 685
Emmanuel: see also Manuel
Emmanuelle: see Antonia Emmanuelle
Emperear, Marie (Mme. Jacques An-
  toine Christy), 997
Enriqueta: see Henriette
Epinette (var. Epinet),
  Guillaumme, 1549, 3354
  Louis, 1549, 3354
Erld,
  David, 2140
  Martin, 2139
  Mary Noemy, 2141
  Richard, 2139-2141
Ernandez (vars. Arnand, Ernand, Er-
  nandes, Hernandes),
  ____, 2121, 2189
  Jeanne: see Juana Hernandez
  Miguel I, 1528, 3344
  Miguel II, 1528, 2189, 2191, 2259,
    2864, 2960, 3344, 3422, 3424
Ernandez: see also Hernandez
Errié,
  Jacques I, 3445
  Jacques II, 3445, 3447
Errié: see also Herié
Ertase, Guillaume, 3135, 3136
Es: see Hazes
Esclavon, André, 1199

453

Esteban (Estevan): see Étienne
Esther (Ester), 2421, 2487, 2675,
  2692, 2797, 3200, 3279
Etie, Felicité, 2139-2142, 2153,
  2739
Étienne (Esteban, Estevan), 95,
  262, 437, 478, 754, 906, 909,
  950, 1225, 2144-2146, 2151-2152,
  2204, 2390, 2460, 2596, 2689-
  2690, 2904, 3100, 3216, 3230,
  3253
Étienne: see also Joseph Étienne
Étienne, chief of the Apalaches,
  2903, 2917, 2921
Étienne *dit* Canon, 97
Étienne *dit* Pierrot du St. Totin,
  102
Étienne, Louise: see Marie Louise
  Marguerite Derbanne (Mme. Étienne
  Barbier)
Étienne Noel (Estevan Noel), 2647
Eugene (Eugenio), 2553, 3161, 3210
Eulalie (Eulalia, Ulalia), 2703,
  3214, 3242
Eulalie: see also Lalie, Marie
  Lalie
Euno?(Cuno?), Genevieve (Mme.
  Pierre Beaulieu I), 3383
Eusebe: see Henri Eusebe
Eveque, Jeanne (Mme. Jean Bernard),
  1014
Eustache, *dit* of Doucet
Eustache, ____, Rev. Fr., 347, 350,
  355, 381-382, 386, 731, 741, 769
Evrie, Luis, 2200
Ezernack: see Guisarnat

Falsinthe: see Fazende
Fanchon, 519
Fanie Venus, 3213
Fanilian, 513
Fanni, 3155, 3165, 3242, 3330
Fanni: see also Fanie Venus,
  Marie Anne Fanni
Fasecoche, Catherine (Mme. George
  Avenal I), 174
Fasindthe: see Fazende
Fatin, 691
Faulevant, *dit* of Pierre Cazeau II
Favarre, Anne (Mme. Claude Le Duc),
  340

Favrot, ____, Mr., 3027
Fayart (vars. Fallyar, Feauyried?,
  Fayard),
  Jean *dit* La Lamette, 252, 272
  Marie Anne, 252
  Marie Louise, 272
Fazanga, ____, 1189
Fazende (vars. de Falsinthe, Fal-
  sinthe, Fasindthe, Fasinth,
  Fassenthe),
  Antoine, 435, 448, 468, 496, 498,
    625, 630, 845, 863-864, 867, 994
  Gabriel, 701, 704
  Jacques *dit* Morien, 880, 908,
    1224
  Marie Françoise (Mme. Antoine
    François Le Doux), 405, 435,
    447-448, 451, 481, 489, 492, 630,
    953, 1020, 1702, 3408
  Marie Pelagie (Mme. Athanase de
    Mézières), 405, 413, 446, 468,
    489, 590, 630, 679, 684, 701,
    704, 708, 880, 937, 1180, 1500
Feauyried: see Fayart also
Feauyried,
  Jean, 292
  Jean Louis, 292
Febi, 2751
Febles (Feble, Felles, Fibles, Se-
  bles), François, 1636, 1674, 2079
  3369, 3372
Federik: see Frederic
Felibot: see Filibot
Feliciane, 31, 46, 378
Felicité (Felicidad, Felicity), 946,
  2153, 2418, 2483, 2548, 2739, 2966,
  3083, 3105, 3114, 3129, 3132-3133,
  3191, 3234, 3248-3249, 3251, 3300,
  3311
Felipe: see Philippe
Felix, 447
Felles, Francisco: see Febles
Ferrier (var. Ferrié),
  Jean Baptiste, 3430
  Jean Baptiste *fils* Joseph, 2954
  Joseph, 2954, 3430
Fhelipot: see Filibot
Fibote: see Filibot
Fifi, *dit* of A____ Langlois
Filhiol: see Fiol
Filibert: see Philibert

Filibot (Felibot, Fhelipot, Fibote, Filibote, Flibot, Philipot, Thilibou, Tibau, Tibaud), Marie Thérèse (Mme. Ignace Maillioux I), 1511, 1602, 1687, 1701, 1724, 1803, 1853, 1934, 2009, 2090, 2899, 2992, 3386, 3442, 3445
Filk., Daniel, 2232
Fiol (vars. Filhiol, Fiolle),
  Gaspard, 847, 947, 955, 1058, 1066, 1094, 1571, 1600, 1672, 1981, 2463-2464, 2469, 2567, 3091?, 3361, 3384
  Ponce, 1066
Fisot, ____, Widow, 258
Fisot: see also Phizot
Fleming, Marie Eugenia (Mrs. Barnaby Murphy), 1098, 3021
Fleur, Marie Thérèse, 187
Fleur: see also Flore
Flibot: see Filibot
Flondor, Jean Baptiste *dit*, 26, 262
Flore, Jean, 187
Flore: see also Fleur, Florés
Florentin (Florentino), 2650
Florés,
  Christophe, 158
  Francisco, 2723, see also Florio
  Xaviere Dominique (Dna. François de Torres), 158
Floriant, Antoine, 744
Florien,
  Juana Helena, 1811
  Juan Bautista, 1811
Florio, Francisco, 2697, 2707, 2709, see also Florés
Foarin? (Foovin?), Luis, 3397
Fonceca, Visente, 3033
Fondelique, Marie Genevieve (Mme. Étienne Adlet), 1032, 1561, 1973?
Fonteneau (vars. Fonteno, Fontenot),
  Felix, 1051
  Fontenel, 3124
  Jean, 1833, 2979
  Jean Baptiste, 1543, 1958
  Jean Sévèr, 3170
  Lesure (Lenure), 2949, 3065
  Louis, 1051, 1250, 1543, 1777, 1833, 1889, 1958, 2049, 2125, 2146-2148, 2150, 2156, 2417, 2490, 2524, 2558, 2640, 2851, 2950, 2967, 3170, 3186, 3241, 3243, 3281-3282, 3402

Fonteneau (continued),
  Marie Eufrosine, 2049
  Marie François Louis, 1777
  Marie Modeste, 1889, 2888, 2979
  Marie Thérèse, 2967
  Philippe Felix, 1051, 2967
  Simon, 1833
Fontenette (vars. Fontenele, Fontenelle),
  Jacques, 931, 958
  Marie Genevieve, 931, 956, 1709, 1715, 2295, 2302, 2306, 2312, 2315, 2319, 2327
Foovin? (Foarin?), Luis, 3397
Foret, Frank S., Rev. Fr., xvii
Foriente (Fouente?), Joseph, 2943
Fort,
  André, 2262
  Jacques, 1039, 1102, 1336, 1574, 1649, 1746, 1865, 1985, 2064, 2170, 2262, 2882, 2963, 3073, 3079, 3169, 3393
  Jean Denis Jacque, 2170
  Louis, 1649, 2064
  Marie, 2263
  Marie Françoise, 1102, 3023, 3169
  Marie Jacques, 2836
  Marie Louise Modeste, 1865
  Marie Marthe, 1746, 2113, 2170, 2812, 3114
  Pierre (the elder), 1039
  Pierre (the younger), 1574
Fort Pontchartrain, 719
Fortain (var. Fortin),
  Jean Antoine, 1720
  Louis I, 1011
  Louis II, 1012, 1068, 1274, 1720
Fortune, 2822, 3437
Fortune: see also Athanase Christophe Fortune, Jean Baptiste Fortune
Fosse, Pierre *dit* Tourangeau, 8, 76, 87, 90, 226, 228, 248-249, 289, 304, 333, 519-520, 759
Fouente, Louis, 3039
Fouente: see also Foriente
Fraidieu: see Fredieu
Framboise, *dit* of Le Roy
Francesco, Bernarda (Mme. Gaspar Vagar), 1342
Francisca: see Françoise
Francisco: see François

455

François (Francisco), 11, 14, 33,
    48, 52, 57, 95, 111, 117-118,
    149-150, 253, 291, 626, 653, 677,
    755, 820, 960, 1021-1022, 2271,
    2282, 2286, 2367, 2377, 2418,
    2441, 2464, 2481, 2484, 2511,
    2514, 2546, 2595, 2612, 2618,
    2625, 2644, 2670, 2673, 2678-
    2679, 2695, 2697, 2708, 2713,
    2715, 2725, 2730-2731, 2742, 2754,
    2760, 2762, 2780, 2790, 3134,
    3138, 3153, 3180, 3188-3189, 3211,
    3244, 3249, 3253, 3269, 3271,
    3287
François: see also Antoine Joseph
    François, Jacques François, Jean
    François, Joseph François, Louis
    François
François dit Choera, 111, 2546,
    2590
François Alexander, 3240
François Antoine (Francisco Antonio),
    2508, 2511, 3136
François Barthelemi, 3188
François Chauzÿ, 763
François Chiq (Francisco Chiq),
    2613
François Dophino, 3296
François, Gilles, dit Jolis Garcon,
    34, 64, 68, 300
François Honoré (Francisco Honore),
    2705
François Jean Baptiste, 2826
François Joseph Marie (Francisco
    Joseph Maria), 2755
François Michel (Francisco Miguel),
    2310
François Thomas (Francisco Thomas),
    2374
François Zenon (Francisco Zenon),
    2694
Françoise (Francisca), 6, 99, 484,
    824, 925, 939, 951, 2143, 2146,
    2148, 2151-2152, 2155-2156, 2276,
    2286, 2299, 2316, 2332, 2336,
    2345-2346, 2351, 2362, 2375, 2379,
    2386, 2404, 2412, 2419, 2454,
    2480, 2490, 2519-2520, 2526-2527,
    2539, 2547, 2565, 2569-2570, 2578,
    2595, 2620, 2643, 2721, 2724,
    2730, 2732, 2741, 2749, 2772-2773,
    2790, 2826, 2897, 2914-2918, 2920,
    2984, 3095, 3099-3100, 3106, 3139,
    3145, 3153, 3160, 3175, 3190,
    3212, 3216, 3220, 3222, 3225,
    3228, 3237, 3245, 3249, 3263-3264
    3268, 3283, 3299, 3389
Françoise: see also Charlotte Fran-
    çoise, Jeanne Françoise Magdeleine,
    Marie Jeanne Françoise
Françoise dite Sangonette, 1059
Françoise Genevieve, 924
Françoise Marie (Francisca Maria),
    2763
Françoise Rosalie, 3100
Frape d'Abord, Jacques dit, 84
Frederic (vars. Federik, Federique,
    Frederico, Frederiq, Frederique),
    _____, Dame, 1691
    André fils Philippe I, 1612, 1671,
        1779, 1790, 1793, 1798, 2111,
        2162, 2262, 2370, 2646, 3365,
        3383, 3409, 3422-3424, 3440
    André, fils Philippe II, 1793, 3169,
        3440
    Antoine fils Philippe I, 1276
    Antoine fils Philippe II, 3061
    Antoine Soulange, 1601, 2007
    François, 1265, 1547, 1800
    François fils Philippe I, 2853
    François Henry, 1265, 1800
    Jean Baptiste (the elder), 1753
    Jean Baptiste (the younger), 1832,
        2958
    Jean François, 1550, 1963, 2168,
        3438
    Jerome, 3451
    Marguerite Reine (Mme. Pierre Che-
        lette), 1083, 1512, 1559, 1742,
        1832, 1855, 1884, 1936, 1971,
        2043, 2111, 2168
    Marie, 1898
    Marie Barbe (Mme. François Gonin),
        1827, 2942, 3003, 3440
    Marie Catherine, 1798, 2853, 2962,
        3438
    Marie Genevieve, 1032, 1561, 1973
    Marie Magdeleine Euphemie, 1550,
        1963
    Marie Marguerite, 2162
    Marie Pelagie (Mme. Jean Baptiste
        Lattier), 1574, 1658, 1691,
        1985, 2169, 2853

Frederic (continued; see preceding
    page for variations),
  Marie Pelagie *fille* Philippe II,
    1898, 2041, 2053, 2094, 2999,
    3375
  Marie Rosalie (Mme. Pierre Thierrie), 1559, 1971, 2101, 2169,
    2884, 2958, 3422
  Philippe I, 1054, 1083, 1211-1212,
    1414, 1550, 1612, 1658, 1753,
    1798, 1832, 1963, 2853, 2884, 2958,
    2962, 3365, 3375, 3422, 3438
  Philippe II, 1054, 1083, 1293,
    1513, 1529, 1532, 1582, 1601,
    1749, 1793, 1827, 1898, 1936,
    1949, 1993, 2007, 2162, 2373,
    2942, 3003, 3061, 3345, 3439,
    3440
  Philippe III, 1532, 1949
Fredieu (vars. Fraidieu, Fredier,
    Frideiu),
  _____, 3045
  Anastasie, 1660, 2068
  Antoine, 2997
  Augustin, 1634, 1659-1660, 2043,
    2068, 2117, 2236, 2240, 2649,
    2666, 2756, 2836, 2997, 3045,
    3368, 3377, 3414
  Augustin César, 2117
  Fr., 1634, 3368
  Jean Baptiste Isaac, 2836
  Marie Olivier, 2240
  Marie Catherinne, 3409
Fromantin, Jean, 665
Fuenta, A. Bx. Pedro, Rev. Fr., 1500

Gabriel, 66, 701, 938, 2505, 2575,
    3176, 3300
Gabriel: see also Jean Gabriel
Gaidon: see Guedon
Gagné (vars. Gagnay, Gagnys, Gane,
    Ganié, Ganier, Gannie),
  _____, Sr., 1010, 1138
  Anne, 1830, 3014
  Baptiste, 989
  Basil, 3454
  Bernard Simeon, 1580, 1991
  Étienne, 913, 989, 1100, 1392,
    1476, 1580, 1627, 1670, 1695,
    1739, 1783, 1830, 1916, 1991,
    2067, 2856, 2860, 2952-2953,
    2976, 3000, 3034, 3367, 3410,
    3432, 3435, 3454
  Jean Baptiste *fils* Étienne (the
    elder), 1476, 1916
  Jean Baptiste *fils* Étienne (the
    younger), 1670, 2067
  Jean Baptiste *fils* Pierre, 1886
  Jeanne, 2239
  Joseph, 1608, 2014
  Julien, 1523, 1944
  Louis, 1651, 2066
  Louis Basil, 1695, 2856, 2860
  Manuel, 1760
  Marie, (Mme. Louis François Vascocu), 1676, 2081, 3392
  Marie Élisabeth, 1783
  Marie Françoise Roselie "Rose"
    (Mme. Pierre Ternier), 1739,
    2185, 2245, 2807, 3000, 3435
  Marie Hyacinthe (Mrs. Jacob Wallace), 976, 1608, 2014, 2856,
    2952-2953, 3410
  Marie Josephe (Mme. Louis Davion;
    Mme. Remy Pereau), 1100, 1523,
    1835, 1891, 1944, 2860, 2976,
    3064, 3259, 3410, 3454
  Marie Joseph *fille* Pierre, 1701
  Marie Joseph Henriette, 1818,
    2952
  Marie Louise, 976, 1670, 2067,
    3081
  Marie Suzette Angélique, 1608,
    2014
  Nicolas, 3391
  Pelagie (Mme. Dominique Davion),
    1627, 2066, 2115, 2165, 2239,
    2860, 3000, 3367
  Pierre I, 993
  Pierre II, 902, 940, 976, 1523,
    1608, 1651, 1701, 1760, 1818,
    1886, 1944, 2014, 2066-2067,
    2515, 2625, 3043, 3137, 3379,
    3391, 3449
  Pierre III, 940, 3449
  Pierre (identity uncertain), 1523,
    1944
  Pierre Étienne, 913
  Susanne, 2194
  Ursulle (Mme. Louis Pierre Paul
    Bouet Lafitte), 1507, 1931, 2115,
    2856, 2976, 3432

Gagnon (var. Gañon),
  ____, Dame, 1421
  Jean, 1137
  Marie Louise, 1485, 1920, 2765
  Pierre I, 1091
  Pierre II, 1091, 1485, 1497, 1547, 1920, 1960, 3338
  Pierre Nagsan, 1547, 1960
Gagnon: see also Gagné, Gignon
Gallien (var. Galien),
  Jean Baptiste, 3238
  Joseph, 675
  Louis, 2427
  Louis *fils* Nicolas, 1616, 2018
  Louis Manuelle, 2253
  Louis Neuville, 2254
  Marie Adèlia, 2986
  Marie Catherine (Mme. Jean Baptiste Anty), 1041, 1765, 1804, 1829, 2343, 2974, 3433, 3443
  Marie Jeanne (Anne) Eufrosine, 1521, 1942, 2932, 3013, 3446
  Marie Ursulle, 2931
  Nicolas, 1097, 1521, 1616, 1829, 1942, 2018, 2253-2254, 2848, 2931, 2948, 2986, 3235, 3446
  Pierre, 721
  Pierre Noel, 721, 1041, 1097, 2931, 2986
Ganier, ____, 1260, 1298, 2400
Ganier: see also Gagné
Gañon: see Gagnon
Garcia (vars. de Garcie, Garcie, Gassile),
  Juan Bautista Antonio: see Juan Bautista Antonio Garcia Raymundo
  Juana Victoria (Mme. François Le Moine; Mme. Louis Lamalathy), 8, 110, 165, 177, 197, 203, 228, 245, 276, 752, 996, 1038, 1066
  Luice, 158
  Maria Antonia (Raymund), (Dna. Juan Bonnet), 1816, 3009
  Pierre (Pedro), 8, 165
  Parence, 183
Garcon, ____, 2365
Garcon: see also Gascon
Garein (var. Garien),
  Jean Louis *dit* La Verdure, 723, 730, 771
  Luc, 723

Garonne, ____, 838
Gas, ____ (de la Gase?), 829
Gascon, ____, Mda., 2510
Gascon: see also Garcon
Gaspard, 230, 284, 343, 3127
Gassile, Antoinette Remande: see Maria Antonia (Raymund) Garcia
Gaunet, François, 3112
Gauthier (var. Gautier),
  Agnès, 196
  Guillaume René, 311
  Jean I, 114, 196, 238
  Jean II, 238
  Julienne, 622
  Louise Pelagie, 28
  Marie, 114
  Marie Louise (Mme. Jean Gauthier), 114
  Michel, 339
  René *dit* La Fleure, 280, 311, 339, 622
Gauthier: see also Gotie
Gay, Magdeleine (Mme. René Dubos), 129
Genevieve (Genovefa), 95, 99, 149-150, 197, 582, 635, 906, 938, 1493, 1904, 2150, 2158, 2270, 2289, 2311, 2323, 2385, 2394, 2428, 2448, 2451, 2474, 2525, 2537, 2690, 2736, 2743, 2754, 2757, 2760, 2770-2772, 2792-2793, 3091, 3102, 3154, 3165, 3173, 3176, 3195, 3212, 3233, 3250, 3261, 3267, 3271, 3273, 3284, 3291
Genevieve: see also Françoise Genevieve
Genovieve (Genoveva) Celeste, 2190
Genevieve Thérèse (Genoveva Teresa), 2700
Genovefa: see Genevieve
Gens des Gens: see Jean des Jeans
Gentin, Marguerite, (Mme. Françoise LeMoine I), 8
George: see Jorge
Geraygne?, Françoise? (Mme. Jean Valentin), 990
German Coast (Les Allemands), La., 249, 726, 729, 742, 753, 980, 1043, 1054, 1060, 1083, 1612, 1638, 1658, 1930, 1974, 2167, 2963, 3348, 3364, 3375, 3378
Gignon (var. Ginan),
  Anne Marie (Mme. Louis Gignon), 612

Gignon (continued),
  Louis, 612, 1142
Gignon: see also Gagnon
Gillard: see Guilhard
Gillot: see Guillot
Gil y Barbo (Varvo), Antoine, 439
Ginan: see Gignon
Go____, Marguerite (Mme. Pierre
  Gotie), 735
Gôme (Goma), Marie Gertrude,
  (Mme. Joseph Alman), 1613, 3366
Gonin (vars. Gonier, Gonain,
    Gonit, Gonite),
  Abraham, 985
  François, 1562, 1974, 2101, 2122,
    3003, 3174, 3422, 3440
  Jean Baptiste, 854, 887, 926,
    942, 981, 985, 1084, 1657,
    2878, 2961, 3003, 3374, 3440
  Jean Pierre, 926
  Marie Deneige Manuel, 3003
  Marie Genevieve (Mme. Antoine
    Vascocu II), 942, 1490, 1562,
    1657, 1921, 1974, 2027, 2122,
    2266, 2785, 2878, 3003, 3146,
    3374
  Marie Joseph (Mme. Michel Bernabé
    Chelette), 887, 1084, 1562,
    1625, 1896, 1974, 2028-2029,
    2098, 2257, 2961, 3009
  Marie Louise (Mme. Pierre Gonin),
    926
  Pierre, 926
Gonzales (vars. Gonsale, Gonsales),
  ____, 1469
  Bernard, 3009
  Francisco, 2982, 3077
  Jean François Antoine, 2982, 3077
  Joseph, commandant of Los Adaes),
    13, 168
  Joseph Antoine, 2982, 3077
  Manuel, 1581, 1992
  Marie Josephe Thérèse, 3009
  Pierre, 3009
  Victoria Margarita (Mme. Jean Baptiste Dion Derbanne), 13, 51,
    83, 168, 244, 674, 741
Gotie,
  Marie Rose (Mme. Jean Baptiste Sorel), 735
  Pierre, 735

Gotie: see also Gauthier
Goudeau,
  François, 2, 14, 16, 29, 33, 43,
    63, 119, 143?, 145, 175, 178-
    179, 194, 205
  Marguerite, 194
Goué,
  Jean Baptiste, 2854
  Joachim, 2854
  Marie Rosalie, 2231
  Narcise (Mme. Joachim Goué), 2854
  Simon, 2231, 2854
Goutier: see Gauthier, Goutierrez
Goutierrez (vars. Goutier, Goutiere,
    Goutierez, Goutierre, Guetiernez,
    Gutieres, Gutierrez),
  ____, M., 1157, 1159, 1163
  Jean, 1159
  Joseph, 994
  Joseph Antoine, de la Lane, 972
  Joseph Michel, 994
  Joseph Pierre, de la Lane, 972
  Marie, 1157
  Marie Francisca, 2410, 2475
  Maria Juana, 2075, 2524
  Marie Silvie (Mme. Antoine Poissot),
    2224, 2843, 3002
  Martin, de Land, 668, 744, 1162,
    1703, 1718
  Michel, 2843, 3002, 3403
Goutierrez: see also de Land
Gracien,
  Genevieve, 2914
  Marie Anne: see Marie Anne Gracien
    Couiaque
Grande Ecore (Red River, La.), 2228,
  3326
Grande Terre: see de la Grande Terre
Grandissa, Marie: see Marie Eve Le
  Roy
Grandmaison, ____, 557
Grappe (vars. Gappe, Grap, Grape),
  Alexis, 260, 268, 319-320, 348,
    440, 473, 486, 578, 657-658,
    678, 687, 708, 736, 843, 895,
    901, 904, 996, 998, 1001, 1003,
    1004, 1007, 1021, 1023, 1026,
    1051, 1538, 2939-2940, 2967,
    3348, 3414
  Alexis, Mme. or Widow: see Guedon,
    Marie Louise Marguerite

Grappe (continued),
  François, 319, 487, 659, 837,
    885, 900, 1038, 1047, 1061,
    1080, 1583, 1735, 1743, 1777,
    1902, 1994, 2047, 2110, 2210,
    2506, 2808, 2941, 2964, 3082-
    3083, 3121, 3133, 3167, 3387,
    3410, 3414, 3416-3417, 3435
  Jean Baptiste I, 925, 1527, 1543,
    1665, 1696, 1728, 1805, 1861-
    1862, 1958, 2075, 2264, 2365,
    2656, 2836, 2939-2940, 3084,
    3118, 3123, 3278, 3343, 3414
  Jean Baptiste II, 2264, 2381
  Marie Anne (Mme. Bernard D'Ort-
    olant), 657, 916, 1026, 1426,
    1516, 1695 - 1696, 1728, 1782,
    1848, 1938, 2285, 3398
  Marie Françoise (Mme. Benoist
    Montenary), 1502, 1524, 1538,
    1586, 1739, 1743, 1782, 1787,
    1825, 1889, 1927, 1945, 1997,
    2047, 2207, 2224, 2332, 2337,
    2348, 2383, 2411, 2506, 2648,
    2819, 2940, 3348, 3402
  Marie Louise (Mme. Emmanuel Tri-
    chel), 320, 893, 900-901, 924,
    944, 961-962, 1000, 1583, 1586,
    1735, 1787, 1805, 1858, 1994,
    1997, 2046, 2125, 2938, 2941,
    3402, 3416
  Marie Madeleine (Mme. Paul Bouet
    Laffitte), 477, 487, 578, 885,
    910, 922, 936, 947, 968 - 969,
    1007, 1257, 1696, 1716, 1747,
    3432
  Marie Onésime, 2940
  Marie Pelagie (Mme. Louis Fonte-
    neau), 708, 1051, 1543, 1611,
    1735, 1755, 1777, 1889, 1902,
    1958, 2015, 2048-2049, 2939,
    2967, 3403
  Pierre, 348
  Pierre Leandre, 2939
  Widow: see Marie Louise Marguerite
    Guedon
Gray,
  Martin, 2739
  Maria (Mary), (Mrs. Richard Erld),
    2139-2141
Grégoire (Gregorio), 45, 2510

Grégoire Silvestre (Gregorio Silves-
  tre), 2760
Greneau, Emmanuel, 2977
Grenoble, *dit* of Pierre Ternier
Grillet (vars. Grillé, Grillier),
  Antoine, 732, 3439, 3453
  Antoine *fils* Marin, 1614, 1775,
    1869, 2016, 2229, 2994, 3425
  Élisabeth Termette, 667
  Hélèn, 2119
  Jean Baptiste Théodore, 1579,
    1814, 1990, 2765, 2855, 2877,
    3146, 3425, 3443-3444, 3453
  Marguerite (Mme. Remis Toutin;
    Mme. Bernard Hissoura), 1071,
    1499, 1584, 1655, 1798, 1869,
    1925, 1995, 2059, 2119, 2373,
    2465-2466, 2855, 2949, 2994,
    3399, 3425
  Marie, 3411
  Marie Barbe (Mme. Bertrand Pierre
    Plaisance), 1585, 1614, 1869,
    1996, 2016, 2203, 2753, 2883,
    2969, 3044, 3406
  Marie Françoise (Mme. Louis Bar-
    thelemy Rachal), 859, 1094,
    1495, 1579, 1631, 1850, 1924,
    1990, 2134, 2891, 2195
  Marie Jeanne (Mme. François Le
    Vasseur), 1096, 1503, 1775,
    1779, 1928, 2855, 2982, 3395
  Marie Josephe (Mme. Pierre Bros-
    set), 407, 1039, 1614, 1745,
    1779, 2016, 2136, 2237
  Marie Louise (Mme. Louis Vercher),
    608, 1009, 1693, 1730, 1775,
    1813, 1877, 2096, 2871, 2975,
    3399, 3417, 3446
  Marie Magdeleine (Mme. Barthelemy
    Rachal II), 1762, 2942, 2994,
    3105, 3406, 3439
  Marie Thérèse (Mme. Jacques Le
    Vasseur II), 729, 1085, 1585,
    1662, 1996, 2072, 2229, 2942
  Marin *dit* Sauterelle, 407, 455,
    608, 641, 667, 732, 859, 929,
    985, 1002, 1018, 1033, 1039,
    1044, 1052, 1054, 1065, 1067,
    1071, 1085, 1094, 1096, 1313,
    1412, 1762, 1814, 2373, 2423,
    2442, 2465, 2491, 2616, 2620,

Grillet (continued),
  Marin (continued), 2724, 2753,
    2855, 2877, 2883, 2891, 2942,
    2949, 2969, 2994, 3023, 3065,
    3105, 3185, 3406, 3409, 3411,
    3425, 3439
  Thérèse Barbe?, 929
Gros: see Le Gros
Gros Nez, village of the Caddo
  Indians, 367, 386
Guadalajara, Mexico, 3033
Guaidon: see Guedon
Guerboi (Guerbois), Louis Alexandre,
  1672, 2700, 3384
Guedon (vars. Gaidon, Guaidon,
  Güeydon),
  ____, 473
  Jacques dit Nantois, 126, 208,
    215, 340, 342, 348, 454
  Louise, 1723, 2047
  Louise Marguerite: see Marie
    Louise Marguerite
  Marguerite, 1728
  Marie Anne (Mme. Joseph Jean
    Baptiste Le Duc; Mme. Nicolas
    Laignon), 254, 275, 282, 294,
    300, 329, 340, 409, 440, 488,
    551, 792, 1003, 1008, 1013,
    1764, 2943, 3031, 3078
  Marie Jeanne Susanne (Mme. Charles
    Toutin; Mme. Jean LaBerry), 251,
    268, 301, 342, 429, 454, 458,
    491, 529, 555, 596, 659, 699,
    890, 969, 1048, 1070, 1080,
    1088, 1092, 1099, 1483, 1527,
    1555, 1756, 1761, 1780, 1871,
    1900, 1918, 1967, 2751, 2754,
    2832, 2838-2839, 2890, 2927,
    2972, 2989, 3007-3008, 3077,
    3343, 3452
  Marie Louise, 409, 1777, 3348
  Marie Louise Marguerite (Madeleine),
    (Mme. Jean Baptiste Besson; Mme.
    Alexis Grappe), 188, 208, 222,
    248, 254, 263, 319-320, 348,
    473, 476, 486, 578, 596, 657,
    658, 678, 708, 843, 880?, 904,
    918, 1007, 1021, 1023, 1026,
    1031, 1051, 1155, 1175, 1185,
    1352, 1379, 1410, 1413, 1452,
    1538, 1663, 1890, 2073, 2298,
    2300, 2322, 2337, 2366, 2431,
    2443, 2510, 2548, 2552, 2656,
    2678, 2846, 2939-2940, 2967,
    3189, 3414
Guenard, Marie (Mme. Michel Le Moine),
  730
Gueri: see Thierry
Guerin (var. Guerine),
  Catherine (Mme. Ignace Anty), 1041,
    1087, 1640, 2872, 3351
  Pierre, 123
Guerin: see also Pierre dit Guerin
Guetiernez: see Goutierrez
Guichernat (Guicherand): see Guisarnat
Guilhard, Antoine, 1429
Guilhaume César, 55
Guilhaume dit Malbouroug, 88
Guillaume (Guillermo, Guillelmo),
  910, 2376, 2455, 2504, 2515, 2571,
  2617, 2640, 2665, 3104, 3173, 3181,
  3192
Guillori (vars. Guillari, Guilloi),
  Louis, Indian, 2863, 3013, 3394
  Marie, Indian, 2863
  Marie Felicité, Indian, 3013
Guillot (vars. Gilot, Gilote, Gillot),
  Agathe (Mme. Simon Gilot), 352
  Marie Louise Françoise (Mme.
    Charles Davion; Mme. Étienne Le
    Roy; Mme. Henry Trichel), 6, 30,
    68, 97, 102, 105, 117, 191, 309,
    561, 590, 727, 738, 795, 984
  Simon, 352
Guilmain, Jeanne (Mme. Pierre de la
  Fosse), 1001
Guisarnat (vars. Guichernat, Guiche-
  rand),
  Bernard, 3006-3007, 3141, 3441,
    3443, 3452
  Jean, 3006, 3441
  Pierre Bernard, 3006
Gutierrez: see Goutierrez
Guyol, Élizabeth (Mme. César De
  Blanc), 399

Ha___, Etienne, 346
Hace, 2740-2741
Hagu?, Carlos, 2739; see also Huoot,
  Charles
Halock, Barbe, 1601; see also Vil-
  dek, Barba Reyna

Hamaicta, Indian, 2145
Hautié, Sophie: see Holié, Sophie
Hazes (vars. Es, Haiezes, Haiszes,
  Haszes, Heszes, Hazeszes),
  Jean I, 205
  Jean II, 170, 205, 342, 349
Hebert (var. Heberd),
  François, 2448
  Jacques, 905, 983
Hebert, see also Hubert
Héleine (Hélène, Helena, Elena),
  442, 882, 2150, 2277, 2291, 2333,
  2344, 2368, 2413, 2490, 2513, 2646,
  2799, 2804, 3082, 3087, 3129, 3188,
  3207, 3214, 3311, 3318
Héleine Magdeleine, 2363
Heleonore: see Eleonore
Henoul de Livaudais,
  Antoinette (Mme. Antoine Charbonnet), 943, 995
  Jacques, 943, 995
  Marie Genevieve (Mme. François
    Coulon de Villiers), 943, 995
Henoul de Livaudais: see also Babin
  de Livaudais
Henri (Henry, Henrique), 2553, 3299,
  3304
Henri Eusebe, 3164
Henriette (Enrieta, Enriqueta, Henriqua), 2397, 2479, 2802, 2907,
  3106, 3199, 3254, 3266
Henry, Marie Josephe, 857
Hernandes (var. Hernandez),
  Etroied? (Dna. Pedro Sta. Cruz),
    2870
  Juana (Dna. Mathieu y Varvo),
    733
  Juana (Dna. Joseph Maria Ortiz),
    1095
Hernandes: see also Ernandes
Herié, Jacques, 3442
Herié: see also Errié
Hervé, François, 319, 417, 560?
Hesser,
  Antoine Christian, 2983
  Christian, 2983
  Frederick, 2983
Hewitt: see Huoot
Hiacinth: see Hyacinth
Hilaire: see Jean Baptiste Athanase
  Hilaire

Himel (vars. Himle, Himmle, Humel,
  Hymel, Imel, Imil, Ymel),
  Antoine, 1086, 1320, 1532, 1601,
    1610, 1792, 1949, 2007, 2179,
    2818, 2898, 2963, 2977, 3113,
    3364, 3451
  François, 1898
  Jean Louis, 1320
  Marie Eleonore (Mme. Alexandre Soulange Bossié), 1610, 1912, 2050,
    2099, 2179, 2818, 2898, 2977,
    3364
  Marie Françoise, 1792, 2099, 2868,
    2961
Hipolito: see Hypolite
Hissoura (var. Hitchoura),
  Bernard I, 2839, 2855, 2875, 2949,
    3065, 3425
  Bernard II, 2855, 3439
  Juan, 2855, 2949, 3065, 3425
  Marie Delisse, 2949, 3065
Hitta, Marie Gertrude, 439
Hochel, Nancy (Mrs. John Covechi),
  1522, 1943
Hofman, Adam, 3387, 3455
Holié, Sophie, 2957, 2969, 3020
Honoré (Honorio), 2506, 2788, 2795,
  2805, 3092, 3135, 3244
Honoré: see also François Honoré,
  Jean Baptiste Honoré
Hoopoock (vars. Hoopok, Hopak, Hopok, Houpok),
  George (Jorge), 1544, 3352
  Jean Louis, 1630, 2033
  Jean Jacob: see John Jacob
  Jean Silvestre, 1605, 2011
  John Jacob, 1542, 1544, 1605,
    1630, 2011, 2033, 3352
Horn (var. Horne),
  John I, 1604, 3362
  John II (John Joseph), 1604, 3362,
    3442, 3447
Houadre, Guillaume: see Warden, William
Huberdeau (vars. d'Huberdeau, d'Huberdeaux, Dubardeau, Du Burdeau,
  Hubardeaux),
  Jean Baptiste, 459
  Jean Baptiste, Widow, 1411
  Marie Louise Silvie (Mme. Louis
    Toutin), 474, 1048, 1814, 2225-
    2226, 2689, 3095-3096

Huberdeau (continued; see preceding page for variations),
  Pierre, 432, 459, 472, 474, 1048, 1233
Hubert,
  Jacques, 989, 997, 1015
  Jean Baptiste, 1015
  Marie Françoise (Mme. Antoine Bouchard), 719, 725
  Marie Marthe (Mme. Jean Baptiste Denis I), 1070, 2925-2926
Hubert: see also Hebert
Huferogue,
  Catherinne Claire, 2828
  Pierre, 2828
Huferogue: see also Ofenogue
Huguefoy, Marie (Mme. Françoise Lamontagne), 2226
Hugues,
  François *dit* Tonau, 1013, 1548, 1962
  Pierre, 1013
Humel: see Himel
Huoot, Charles (Carlos), 2139-2142, 2153; see also Hago?, Charles
Hyacinth (Jacinto), 543, 2295, 2368, 3196
Hyacinth: see also Joseph Marie Hyacinth
Hyacinthe: see Anne Hyacinthe, Rosalie Hyacinthe
Hymel: see Himel
Hÿnes, Marie (Dna. Antonne Pagnot), 572
Hypolite (Hipolito), 2436
Hyves, 35

Iago: see Jacques
Ignace, 475
Illinois, 1020, 2178, 3051, 3379
Imel (Imil): see Himel
Ines, 2386
Infante, Joseph Diaz, Rev. Fr., 443, 464-465, 473
Isabella: see Élisabeth
Isidore, 2595
Isidore: see also Antoine Isidore, Louis Isidore
Isle Brevelle (Isle à Brevel), La., 2623, 2928n, 3239

Isle d'Oriant, Canada, 721
Isle d'Orleans, Canada, 354

Jacinto: see Hyacinth
Jacob (Jacobo), 823, 2145, 2290, 2297, 2408, 2747, 2751
Jacques (Santiago, Iago), 75, 84, 157, 162, 178, 220, 467, 487, 559, 686, 775, 953, 1059, 2311, 2332, 2365, 2371, 2380, 2435, 2440, 2462, 2504, 2540, 2581, 2669, 2675-2676, 2685, 2727, 2758, 2761, 2771, 2777, 2804-2805, 2903, 2993, 3085, 3093, 3098, 3125, 3149, 3161, 3174, 3185, 3230, 3234, 3262, 3327, 3448
Jacques: see also Charles Jacques, Joseph Jacques, Louis Jacques René
Jacques *dit* La Ramée, 20, 156
Jacques François, 42
James: see Jaymé
James Henry (Jayme Enrique), 2490
Janisse (Janis), Antoine, 536, 582
Janneton, 2825
Jannot (var. Jeannot),
  Jean Baptiste I, 3396
  Jean Baptiste II, 3396
Janot, 64, 155, 519
Jaquatzin, Indian, 2516
Jarri,
  _____, 3075
  Marie Rose, 2263
  Michel, 2882, 3409
  Pierre, 2263 2833, 2882, 3075, 3260, 3409, 3430
  Pierre II, 2882
Jasmin, *dit* of Pierre, 70, 514
Jaymé, 2459
Jayme Enrique: see James Henry
Jean (Juan), 436, 923, 1481, 2153, 2293, 2346, 2361, 2363, 2398, 2442, 2563, 2570, 2591, 2619, 2629, 2663, 2672, 2681, 2716-2718, 2729, 2733, 2780-2782, 3120, 3125, 3156, 3191, 3198, 3273
Jean: see also Pierre Jean
Jean *dit* Janot, 64, 155
Jean *dit* Le Jeunesse, 96
Jean Antoine, 602
Jean Baptiste: see also François Jean Baptiste

Jean Baptiste (Juan Bautista), 19, 188, 338, 440, 444-445, 627-628, 661, 663, 710, 850, 862, 1021-1023, 1028-1029, 1055, 1479, 1487-1488, 2152, 2158, 2294, 2407, 2437, 2445, 2456, 2461, 2481, 2485, 2489, 2494, 2501, 2522, 2503, 2523, 2528, 2531, 2533, 2574, 2591, 2633, 2635, 2639, 2671, 2683, 2691, 2694, 2706, 2719, 2746, 2748, 2796, 2803, 2808, 2811, 2905-2906, 2929, 3092, 3097, 3106-3108, 3130, 3143, 3170, 3172, 3201, 3212, 3214, 3217, 3236-3237, 3245, 3255, 3260, 3271, 3277, 3279, 3285, 3292, 3297, 3308, 3320
Jean Baptiste *dit* Flondor, 26, 35, 100, 262
Jean Baptiste Athanase Hilaire (Juan Bautista Atanasio Hilario), 2411
Jean Baptiste Augustin (Juan Bautista Augustin), 2434
Jean Baptiste Fortune, 3140
Jean Baptiste Honoré (Juan Bautista Honore), 2791
Jean Baptiste Louis (Juan Bautista Luis), 2335
Jean Baptiste Marcelin, 3277
Jean Baptiste Valleri, Indian, 2910-2911, 3437
Jean Daniel, 553
Jean des Jeans, *dit* of Jean Mader
Jean François (Juan Francisco), 222, 600, 885, 2396, 2500, 2525, 2662, 2724, 2998, 3208-3209, 3291, 3296
Jean Gabriel, 605
Jean Joseph, 862
Jean Louis (Juan Luis), 583, 900, 925, 979, 1021, 1023, 1028, 1791, 2274, 2301, 2320, 2376, 2440, 2444, 2492, 2512, 2555, 2561, 2568, 2573, 2582, 2599, 2692, 2721, 2734, 2744, 2767-2769, 2809, 3133, 3137, 3177, 3263, 3289-3290, 3297, 3321
Jean Noel, 3111
Jean Pierre (Juan Pedro), 550, 558, 765, 1021, 1913, 2298, 2302, 2366, 2479, 2496, 2527, 2646, 2756, 2807, 3243, 3267
Jean Pierre *dit* Caton, 39, 95, 516, 832
Jean Pierre Nolbert (Juan Pedro Nolbert), 2661
Jean-Ris (vars. Jean-Rit, Riche, Riese, Ris, Ryse),
———, Dna., 2076
Françoise, 1198
Joseph, 443, 1090, 1564, 1568, 1587, 1666, 1791, 1800, 1976, 1998, 2076, 2174, 2386, 2842, 2901, 2938, 3356, 3416
Marie, 1247
Marie (Mme. Jean Baptiste François Rambin; Mme. Michel Denis Cassenave), 1623, 2025, 2069, 2448, 2525, 2861, 2946, 3014, 3388, 3396, 3413
Marie Aspasie, 2842
Marie Celeste, 1666, 2076
Marie Eleonore (Leousa), (Mme. Jean Baptiste François Dubois), 1090, 1514, 1587, 1800, 1937, 1998, 2069, 2127, 2198, 2228, 2386, 2402, 2978, 3048
Marie Genevieve (Mme. Henry Triche II), 1678, 1859, 2083, 2127, 2190, 2213, 2656, 2938, 2941, 3416
Marie Pelagie Belazin, 2174
Michel I, 443, 746, 1090, 1107, 1568, 2842, 2861, 2938, 2946, 2978, 3014, 3356, 3413, 3416
Michel II, 858
Jeanne (Juana), 44, 63, 69, 125, 152, 185, 231, 235, 287, 292, 314-315, 451, 479, 750, 908, 952, 1023, 1034, 1477, 2298, 2304, 2310, 2320, 2328, 2338, 2360, 2371, 2434-2435, 2534, 2572-2573, 2578, 2582, 2613, 2626-2627, 2657, 2693, 2705, 2713-2714, 2732, 2786, 2801, 3049, 3130, 3189, 3195, 3211-3221, 3322, 3326, 3335
Jeanne, Indian (Mme. Pierre Louis Bertrand), 1062, 2829, 2950
Jeanne Antoinée (Juana Antonia), 2454

Jeanne Chatonai, 3220
Jeanne Françoise Magdeleine, 3270
Jeannot: see Janot
Jerome, Louise (Mme. Louis Raymond), 1016
Joachim, 3329
Jobar (vars. Jobarre, Jobard, Joubar, Joubard, Joubart, Jubar), *dit* of La Malathy
Jobart, Charles, 259
Jocolone, 260
Joffrions, Susanne, 3415
Jolibois, *dit* of Le Vasseur
Joli Coeur, Remy *dit*, 93, 164
Jolis Garcon, *dit* of Gilles François
Jones (Dejones, Jons), Rebecca D., (Mrs. Edward Teal), 2945, 2970-2971
Jorge, 2684
Jorie, Josephe: see Jouë, Josepha
Jorin?, _____, Sr., 2439
Jory, Miguel, 2113
Joseph (Josef), 935, 1303, 2282, 2298, 2331, 2346-2347, 2409, 2412, 2430-2431, 2465, 2567, 2579, 2589, 2594, 2619, 2622, 2630, 2642, 2657, 2667, 2684, 2705, 2730, 2743, 2749, 2776, 2779, 2789, 2795, 2823, 2903-2905, 2909, 2914, 3083, 3102, 3115, 3131, 3148, 3150, 3162, 3166, 3171, 3187, 3195, 3206, 3215, 3232, 3243, 3274-3275, 3307, 3401
Joseph: see also Antoine Joseph François, François Joseph Marie, Jean Joseph, Louis Joseph, Pierre Joseph
Joseph Antoine (Josef Antonio), 53, 2364, 2410
Joseph Athanase (Josef Atanasio), 2644
Joseph Césaire, 3091
Joseph Étienne, 2206, 3088
Joseph François, 195
Joseph Jacques (Josef Santiago), 2329
Joseph Louis (Josef Luis), 2372
Joseph Manuel, Indian, 1703
Joseph Michel, 3173, 3176, 3203, 3291
Joseph Marie Hyacinth (Josef Maria Jacinto), 2303

Joseph Placide, 3094
Joseph Valery, 3088
Josephe: see Magdeleine Josephe, Marie Barbe Joseph
Josephine: see Marie Françoise Josephine
Jouannis, de Lissard, 2404
Jouë, Josepha (Dna. Miguel Ernandes I), 1528, 3344
Joupin, Marie (Mme. Julien Rondin I), 147
Jourdan (Jourdain), *dit* of Edmond Thomas
Juan: see Jean
Juana: see Jeanne
Juchereau de St. Denis: see de St. Denis
Judith (Judit), 82, 2423, 2453
Julie (Julia, Juliana), 2289, 2335, 2390, 2428, 2492, 2527, 2544, 2761, 3102, 3289, 3309-3310, 3312, 3314
Julien (Julian), 31, 35, 298, 323, 372, 378, 1167, 2432, 2670, 3147
Julien: see also Pierre Julien
Justine, 906
Juzaud,
_____, 347
Cyprien, 386
Juzaud: see also Juchereau:

Kaskaskia, Illinois, 206, 725, 730
Keniguinne, Eve: see Marie Eve Le Roy
Kerlerec (vars. de Kerelecq, Kerelecq),
Charlotte de Boete, 463
Louis, chevalier, 405
Kiava, Elisabeth (Mme. David Ottemare?), 2879
Kindrie, _____, Mr., 2297
Kintrie, Francisca (Mme. Andres Poirier), 1020
Knotts, Irby L., xvii

La _____, Perrete (Mme. Jean Laignon), 1003
Laba, Ignacio, Maria, Rev. Fr., 472, 475-488

Labattut, Marianne (Marie Jeanne),
   (Mme. Raymond D'Ortolant), 1026,
   3398
l'Abbé, Jeanne, 204, 237, 256
Laberry (vars. Labayrie, Laberhi,
   Laberi, Labery),
   ____, Dame, 1680, 2084
   Etienne, 454
   Jean Baptiste *dit* Bayonne, 429,
      454, 458 494, 857, 890, 918,
      969, 983, 990, 992, 1000, 1003,
      1004, 1006, 1008, 1015, 1026,
      1029, 1043, 1048, 1051, 1054,
      1064, 1071, 1080, 1088, 1092,
      1099, 1154, 1227, 1483, 1487,
      1527, 1755, 1780, 1918, 2272,
      2282, 2287, 2330, 2345, 2389,
      2414, 2421, 2428, 2459-2460,
      2502, 2507, 2533, 2600, 2619,
      2661, 2681, 2712-2713, 2832,
      2838-2839, 2890, 2927, 2972,
      2989, 3007-3008, 3343, 3452
   Jeanne (Mme. Pierre La Renaudiere),
      1080, 1504, 1572, 1646, 1871,
      1929, 1983, 2062, 2189, 2252,
      2330, 2360, 2423, 2460, 2469,
      2890, 3006-3007, 3441
   Marie, 1530, 1873, 1947, 2995
   Marie Françoise (Mme. Barthelemy
      Rachal *fils* Louis), 890, 1088,
      1530, 1900, 1947, 2030, 2131,
      2459, 2473, 2841, 2927, 3008
   Marie Josephe (Mme. Louis Rachal
      II), 1099, 1501, 1555, 1624,
      1833, 1926, 1967, 2138, 2252,
      2430, 2839, 2972
   Marie Louise, 494
   Marie Louise Agathe (Mme. François
      Pereau), 429, 1092, 1483, 1556,
      1802, 1918, 1968, 2045, 2110,
      2161, 2294, 2309, 2507, 2832,
      2858, 2989
   Marie Louise Magdeleine (Mme. Jean
      Joseph Martianeau; Mme. Simeon
      Rachal), 969, 1504, 1527, 1624,
      1788, 1929, 2026, 2464, 2468,
      2838, 2937, 3343, 3452
   Pierre, 1076, 2529
La Bonte, *dit* of Pierre Bernardin
La Borde, Mathieu, 1050
Labride?, Pierre, 1047

La Brüe (var. Le Brüe),
   Catherine (Mme. Jean Boisselier;
      Mme. Godeau?), 108, 143
   Ferdinand, 143
   Marie, 143
La Brüe: see also Le Brun
La Bryere, Chief of Na_____
   Indians, 385
La Camite, Indian, 2204
La Caze (vars. La Case, La Casse),
   ____, Mr., 2613, 2631
   Charles, 1539, 1679, 2885, 2894,
      2996, 3350, 3385, 3423
   Etienne, 2894, 3423
   Felicité (Mme. Jean Baptiste Le
      Moine), 1679, 2129, 2238, 2885,
      2996, 3385
   François, 980, 982, 1049, 1668,
      1892, 2762, 2866, 3382, 3405,
      3409
   Jacques, 1539, 1679, 2171, 2238,
      2763, 3350, 3385, 3434
   Marie Céleste, 2894
la Cha____, Mr., 1139
La Chaise: see de la Chaise
La Choix: see La Croix
La Claire, Marie Françoise *dite*
   Robard, 614
La Claire: see also Le Clerc
La Clairmont: see Clermont
Lacoste (LaCone), Pierre, 998,
   1013, 1035, 1726
La Cour,
   Émelie (Mme. Pierre Baillio II),
      2889
   Gaspard, 2038, 2873, 2902, 3010
      3092?, 3391, 3428
   Jean Baptiste, 2889
   Magdelaine (Mme. Joseph Marie
      Charles Deblanc), 3029
   Marie, 1711
   Marie Amelie, 2902
   Marie Parr?, 2177
   Pierre I, 986, 3428
   Pierre II, 493, 840, 986, 1075,
      1077, 1086, 1121, 1294, 1510,
      1528, 1573, 1596, 1708, 1711,
      1863, 1984, 2249, 2467, 2840,
      2902, 2987, 2999, 3010, 3344,
      3359, 3431
   Pierre III, 3431

La Cour (continued),
  Pierre *fils* Gaspard, 3010
La Cour: see also Le Court
la Couronne, *dit* of Duval
La Croix, *dit* of _____ Thomas, soldier
La Croix (vars. de la Croix, La Choix),
  Marie Anne (Mme. François Chagneau), 77, 238, 249, 252, 274, 290, 306, 322, 556, 623, 695, 998, 1014, 1047, 1050, 1376, 2819
  Marie Madelena (Mme. Ou___ Billet Tristant), 3405
La Cruz: see de la Creoz, Sta. Cruz
Ladé, Louis, 1005
La Douceur, *dit* of Piere Sebastien Prudhomme
Laffitte (vars. Lafite, Laffite, Lafitte, Le Fite),
  François Bouet, 1007
  François Manuel Boete, 2957
  Jean Baptiste, 1696
  Joseph Marie César, 1524, 1945
  Louis Bouet, 2163
  Louis Pierre Paul Bouet, 1570, 1597, 1787, 1890, 1981, 2422, 2953, 2976, 3426, 3432
  Manuel, 3024
  Marianne (Mme. François Bouet Laffitte), 1007
  Marie des Neiges Hyacinthe, 1890, 2953
  Marie Felicité Bouet, 2844
  Marie Josephe, 1847
  Marie Magdeleine Bouet, 2976
  Marie Pompose, 1611, 2015
  Marie Thérèse Rosalie Hyacinthe, 1747
  Paul Bouet, 1007, 1015, 1027, 1039, 1256, 1257, 1286, 1524, 1542, 1552, 1575, 1611, 1646, 1696, 1716, 1747, 1847, 1890, 1945, 1986, 2015, 2046, 2062, 2163, 2383, 2521, 2844, 2956, 2976, 3024, 3130, 3355, 3360, 3432
  Pierre: see Louis Pierre Paul Bouet
La Fille, 2682

La Fleur, _____, 822
La Fleure, *dit* of René Gauthier
La Font,
  Catherine (Mme. Jean Baillio), 1043
  Jean Baptiste, 764
  Jeanne (Mme. Pierre Massipe), 1030, 2959
Laforet, Maria Josepha, 1831
La Forme, *dit* of Ignace Anty
La Forré,
  Élisabeth St. Germaine, 2205
  Joseph, 2205
La France, *dit* of Jacques Turpot
La Garenne, Françoise (Phizot), (Mme. Jean Fayard), 252, 272
La Gase, _____, 443
La Gase: see also Berard de la Gase
Lagé (var. Lager),
  Antoine, 54
  Jean *dit* La Rose, 24, 54, 96, 169, 176, 206, 522
  Jean Gabriel *dit* La Rose, 24, 549, 605, 859
  Louis, 176
  Marie Louise (Mme. Charles Dardenne), 299, 328, 522, 547, 627, 634
Lagé: see also Leger
Lagnon (Lagneau): see Laignon
La Grenade, Antonio, 1335
Laignon (var. Lagneau, Lagnon, Naions),
  Jean, 1003
  Nicolas, 1003-1004, 1007-1008, 1013, 1026, 1051, 1080?, 1723, 1837, 3031, 3078
Laisar?, Enrique, 2303
Laisard: see Layssard
La Jeunesse, *dit* of Tristant
Lake a la Vase (near Natchitoches), 769
La Lamette, *dit* of Jean Fayart
La Lande,
  _____, Sieur, 690
  Dominique, 1005
  Jacques, 1699
  Jean I, 1005, 1081, 1554, 1556, 1699, 1825, 1966, 1968, 3417, 3449
  Jean II, 3417

La Lande (continued),
　Jean Pierre, 1887, 3160
　Marie, 2197, 2851
　Marie Jeanne, 2110, 3449
La Lande: see also Goutierrez de Land
La Lanne, Jean Josephe (Mme. Jean Marinne), 668, 819?
La Liberté, *dit* of Pierre Baron, Pierre Brasier
La Lime, *dit* of Charles Pellerin, François Le Maitre
La Malathy (vars. de la Malathi, Lamalati, Lamalathi, Lamalathie, Lamalaty, Lamatti, Lamaty, Malathi),
　Jacques, 165
　Jeanne: see Juana Victoria Garcia
　Louis I *dit* Jobard (with variations), 109, 165, 176-177, 182, 197, 203, 245, 254, 276, 301, 408-409, 551, 699-700, 716, 726, 730, 737, 739, 742, 747, 751, 752, 825, 946, 960, 996, 1025, 1035, 1038, 1066, 1092, 1729, 2284
　Louis II *dit* Jobard (with variations), 177, 957, 1495, 1858, 1924, 2163, 2608, 2760, 3124, 3417, 3432, 3435, 3439, 3449
　Marie *dit* Jobard, 600
　Marie Françoise Louise (Mme. Barthelemy Rachal I), 203, 460, 482?, 716, 752, 883, 933, 1094, 1389, 1672, 1708, 1751, 2610, 2802, 2817, 2871, 2891, 2975, 2994, 3001, 3068, 3117-3118, 3166, 3266-3268, 3384, 3399, 3426, 3439
　Marie Jeanne (Mme. Maturin David; Mme. Andres David), 276, 838, 957, 996, 1035, 1726, 2567, 3071
　Thérèse (Mme. Ignace Anty; Mme. Gaspar Fiol), 245, 436, 462, 855, 876, 1066, 1510, 1571, 1675, 1726, 1765, 1858, 1933, 1981, 2080, 2109, 2116, 2395, 2608, 2700, 2964, 2967, 2972, 3243, 3267, 3287
Lamb,
　Antoine, 745
　Nicolas, 745
Lambert, Nicolé, 964

Lambre (vars. Lamber, Lambra),
　_____, Dna., 2182, 2551, 2594, 2621, 2680
　_____, Sr., 1843
　Antoine, 1610, 1620, 1828, 2022, 2498, 3364
　Catherine Pelagie (Mme. François Paul Bossié), 963, 1057, 1506, 1566, 1677, 1744, 1772-1773, 1806, 1823, 1841, 1860, 1880, 1914, 1930, 1978, 2050, 2082, 2167, 2293, 2372, 2397, 2835, 2881, 2889, 2965, 3019
　Jacob, 3163
　Jacob Jacques, 416, 431, 445?, 455, 457, 559, 570, 575, 632, 702, 726, 752-753, 933, 956, 959, 1018, 1028, 1030-1031, 1043, 1057, 1059, 1073, 1169, 1212, 1236, 1302, 1600, 1607, 1700, 1817, 2274, 2307, 2321, 2334, 2346, 2350, 2360-2361, 2366, 2374, 2378, 2384, 2399, 2407-2408, 2412, 2435, 3018-3020, 3361, 3380
　Jacques *fils* Jacob Jacques, 959
　Jacques *fils* Jean Baptiste, 978
　Jean Baptiste I, 424, 436, 457, 614, 681, 742, 883, 945, 977, 978, 992, 997, 1018, 1039, 1057, 1073, 1214, 1278, 1318, 1590, 1638, 1741, 1784, 2293, 2338, 2352, 2390, 2405, 2428, 2442, 2462, 2473, 2492, 2500-2502, 2512, 2835, 3346, 3358
　Jean Baptiste II, 424, 941, 952, 963, 1048, 1078, 1186, 1314
　Jean Baptiste (identity uncertain), 2965
　Jean François, 632, 1522
　Jean Jacque, 2242
　Jean Louis, 1519, 1566, 1590, 1662, 1690, 1940, 1943, 1978, 2057, 2072, 2093, 2301, 2390, 2405, 2925, 3203, 3358
　Joseph Louis, 1677, 1784, 2082, 2137, 2965, 2977, 3158
　Marianne, 445
　Marie (identity unvertain), 1515, 1522, 1551, 1061, 1903, 1943, 1964, 1978, 2049, 2181, 2387, 2492, 2498, 2538, 2574, 2591

Lambre (continued),
  Marie (Mme. Antoine Prudhomme), 3018-3019, 3380
  Marie *fille* Remy (the elder), 2881
  Marie *fille* Remy (the younger), 3020
  Marie Anne Cephalide, 2128, 2181
  Marie Catherine (Mme. Manuel Prudhomme), 1551, 1745, 1753, 1784, 1892, 1964, 3055
  Marie Jeanne (Mme. Silvestre Bossié), 1503, 1520, 1620, 1638, 1690, 1914, 1928, 1941, 1620, 2093, 3346
  Marie Louise Margueritte (Mme. Jean Salvan), 1061, 1542, 1544, 1659, 2850-2851, 2948, 2979, 3352, 3377, 3419
  Marie Madeleine, 570
  Marie Rose (Mme. Louis Gabriel Buard), 681, 901, 903, 951, 1018, 1520, 1536, 1632, 1741, 1772, 1817, 1828, 1841, 1856, 1941, 1954, 2035, 2137, 2180, 3040
  Marie Thérèse Eugenie, 1690, 2093
  Martin, 726, 742, 753
  Remy, 431, 1061, 1066, 1073, 1443, 1450, 1458, 1496, 1600, 1609, 1639, 1659, 1660, 1692, 1810, 1817, 1823-1824, 1880, 1903, 2068, 2095, 2128, 2242, 2393, 2568, 2575, 2579, 2605, 2617-2618, 2621, 2632, 2637, 2657-2660, 2682, 2774, 2788-2789, 2806, 2881, 2989, 3018, 3020, 3150, 3152, 3171, 3176, 3197, 3210, 3212, 3266, 3268, 3291, 3301, 3349, 3361, 3363, 3377, 3394, 3407-3408, 3412, 3426-3428, 3433
La Mé: see Lemée
Lamontagne, François, 2226
  François, 2226
  Jacques, 2226
Lamotte,
  Jacques, 3408
  Louise Eugenie (Mme. Ange Charles François Marie Le Doux), 3408
  Marguerite (Mme. Jean Toutin), 342

La Motte: see also de la Motte
Lamoure, Catherine (Dna. Pedro Gonsales), 3009
la Movilien, Magdalena, Indian, 2143
Langelier, Magdeleine (Mme. Louis Fortain I), 1012
Langes,
  Françoise (Mme. Joseph Langes), 1581, 1992
  Joseph, 1581, 1992
Langlois (vars. Langloi, Langloy, Longlois),
  A____ *dit* Fifi, 1439
  Charles, 1174
  Felicité (Mme. Charles La Caze), 1539, 1679, 2885, 2894, 2996, 3350, 3385, 3423
  Fillis: see Felicité
  François *dit* Sans Regret, 611, 647, 712, 740, 747, 877, 964, 1082, 1097, 1100, 1105, 1106, 1534, 1613, 2433, 2447, 2451, 2452, 2519, 3004, 3347, 3366
  François Antoine Grégoire, 877
  Jean Baptiste, 747
  Joseph, 2800, 3389, 3401
  Louis, 2893, 3418, 3434
  Louis Auguste (Augustin), 1158, 1717, 2424, 2893, 3418
  Margarita, 2651
  Marianne Nicolé (Nicolosa), (Dna. Pedro Ramis), 964, 1534, 1689, 2055, 2092, 2123, 2172, 2186, 2188, 2447, 2520, 3347
  Marie, 2042, 2866, 3004
  Marie Charlotte, 2866
  Marie Euphrosine, 3004
  Marie Louise *fille* Louis, 2893
  Marie Louise *fille* Louis Auguste, 1674, 1717, 2079
  Marie Thérèse (Mme. Pierre Joseph Alman), 1581, 1613, 1992, 2055, 2123, 2943, 2973, 3366
  Perrine Isabelle, 712
la Perrier (var. de la Perriere),
  Louis Antoine, 845
  Louis George Monjonan, commandant, 845, 848, 989
La Pointe, Marie (Mme. Louis St. Germaine), 1628-1629, 2031-2032

La Prairie (vars. Laprarie, Laprayrie),
   Cécile (Mme. ____ Belleouil; Mme. Jean Baptiste Jannot), 3396
   Louis, 3387, 3396
   Marie Anne (Mrs. Jacob Paul II), 3387
Laquesane, Marie (Mme. Reynauld Lestage), 1025
La R____, *dit* of Jean de Roblat
La Ramée, Jacques *dit*, 20, 156
La Renaudiere (vars. de la Renaudiere, La Renadiere, La Regnaudiere, La Renodiere, Larnodiere, Larnoidier, L'arnordiere, Lernodier, Regnaudiere, Renaudiere), ____, 1161, 1648, 2001, 2063, 3161, 3210
   Agnes (Mme. Guillaume Bergereau), 196, 206
   César, 316
   Charles, 15, 200, 246, 286, 316, 525, 567, 615, 706, 872, 980, 992, 1002, 1012, 1015, 1038, 1074, 1080, 2890, 3007
   Charles Philippe, 1572, 1983
   Françoise (Dna. Juan de Arze), 1074, 1759, 1821, 1851, 2371, 2376, 2398, 2400
   Jean Baptiste *fils* Charles, 706, 1038, 1047, 1062, 1080, 1101, 1502, 1871, 1927, 2899
   Jean Baptiste *fils* Pierre, 2189
   Jean Ignace Maximilian, 1821
   Jean Pierre François Sévèrin, 1504, 1929
   Marie, 1229
   Marie *fille* Charles, 567, 1720, 2365
   Marie Adélaïde, 2890
   Marie Aspasie, 3007
   Marie Clémence, 478, 1002, 1572, 1983
   Marie Françoise (Mme. Pierre Benoist; Mme. George Avenal), 52, 114, 174, 181, 200, 246
   Marie Louise (Mme. Jacques Negle; Mme. François Carle), 286, 410, 480, 872, 971, 980, 992, 2200, 2260, 2890
   Marie Louise (Mme. Bernard Guisarnat), 1871, 3006, 3441

La Renaudiere (continued),
   Marie Magdeleine (Mme. Louis Fortain II), 615, 1012, 1720, 1851, 2270
   Marie Magdeleine *fille* Pierre, 2252
   Marie Roselie, 1646, 2062, 3007
   Perrine Pivert (Widow Philippe La Renaudiere): see Perrine Pivert
   Philippe, 174, 206
   Pierre, 525, 971, 1091-1092, 1504, 1572, 1646, 1851, 1871, 1929, 1983, 2062, 2189, 2252, 2459, 2469, 2474-2475, 2890, 3006-3007, 3441, 3452
La Ritte (La Rotte), Marie de Niege *dite*, Indian, 104, 345
La Rivière, Jean Baptiste, 508, 706, 710
La Rivière: see also de la Rivière
Larnodiere: see La Renaudiere
La Robert: see Jeanne Josephe Picquery (Mme. Robert Avard)
La Roche (var. de la Roche),
   François, 1008, 1012, 1024
   Pierre, 1024
La Rose, *dit* of Lagé
La Rotte: see La Ritte
La Rouble?, ____·, 355
La Sert: see de la Sert, de la Cerda
Lassis, Marie, 3167
La Suisse, *dit* of Jacques Dupre
Lattier (vars. Latier, Latiore, Lattié, Lattir),
   Catherine (Mme. Luis Thomassino), 840, 1075, 1484, 1578, 1867, 1897, 1919, 1989, 2053, 2121, 2230, 2248, 2875, 2981
   François, 1578, 1989, 2169, 2218, 3422
   Jacques Joseph, 905, 3393
   Jean, 981
   Jean Baptiste I, 977, 1559, 1658, 1691, 1971, 2053, 2094, 2169, 2999, 3375
   Jean Baptiste II, 2169, 2853
   Joseph, 840, 905, 977, 981, 985, 986, 1009, 1075, 1083, 1478, 1484, 1529, 1596, 1658, 1691, 1867, 1919, 2094, 2853, 2875, 2981, 3336, 3345, 3359, 3375, 3393, 3397

Lattier (continued),
  Joseph *fils* Jean Baptiste, 2999
  Joseph François, 2248
  Marie Deloise, 2853
  Marie Rose Brigitte, 1691, 2094
  Sophie, 2221, 2256
Laurens (Lauriat), Pierre, 204
Laurent (Lorenzo), 1034, 2371
Laurent (vars. Lauran, Lorand),
  Jeanne (Mme. René Gauthier), 280,
    311, 339
  Joseph, 1078, 1087, 1879
  Marie Françoise, 1879
  Pierre, 339
  Simon, 1078
Laurine, 3171
Lauve, Nicolas Henri *dit* Colin,
  2886, 2902, 2969, 3160, 3245,
  3249, 3299, 3408, 3418, 3428,
  3446, 3453
Lawrence, Augustin, 1129
La Verdalay, 1672
L'Avergne,
  Jean, 517
  Marie, 517
La Verdure, *dit* of Jean Louis Garein
Lavespere (var. Lavispere),
  François, 1518, 1525, 1533, 1539,
    1789, 1650, 1946, 1950, 1999,
    2065, 2173, 2857, 3017, 3171,
    3342, 3350
  Hilaire, 2173
  Jean François, 1518, 2857, 3017,
    3342
  Marie Aimé, 1588, 1999
  Marie Felicité, 1533, 1950, 2963
  Marie Héleine, 3017
  Marie Mélanie, 1650, 2065
  Pierre, 2857
La Vidette, *dit* of Renauld
La Vidette Boudin, *dit* of François
  Le Moine
La Violette, *dit* of Vigneron
Laybe, François Dominique, 146
Laybe: see also Leibe
Layssard (vars. de Laissard, de Layssard, Delessart, Dessart, and
    Laisard),
  Bolon, 3421
  Étienne Maraffret, 1496, 1337
  Nicolas Maraffret, 921, 994
  Valentin, 1531, 1948, 2820, 3421

Layssard: see also de Lissard Jouannis
Le Bel,
  Anne Marie (Mme. Henrÿ Le Bel),
    515
  Henrÿ, 515, 521
  Jeanne, 515
Le Blanc,
  _____, Sieur, 2282, 2299, 2435,
    2490
  Louis I, 1861-1862
  Louis II, 1861
  Marie Lucilla, 1862
Le Boeuf (vars. La Beuf, Le Beuf),
  Eugene, 2212
  François, 2212
  Jean Louis, 530, 1045, 1332
  Marie Françoise, 300, 1846
  Marie Jeanne, 2752
  Marie Louise (Dna. Joseph Michel
    Goutierrez), 994
  René Henry, 300, 530, 994
  Simon, 2212
Le Bos, Isabelle (Mme. Pierre Laurent), 339
Le Bru, Françoise, 485
Le Brüe: see La Brüe
Le Brun, *dit* of Bossié
Le Brun,
  _____, Mme. 239, 278
  _____, Mr., 5, 66-67
  Marie Antoine (Mme. Joseph Malige),
    2852, 2900, 3370, 3400
Le Case: see La Caze
Le Clerc (vars. Claire, Le Claire, Le
    Clert),
  Augustin, 3447
  Louis *dit* Belheumeur, 988, 992,
    1315
  Marie Anne Louise (Mme. Pierre
    Derbanne), 421, 689, 879, 944,
    970, 1065, 1518, 1554, 1893,
    1966, 2054, 2857, 3017, 3026,
    3047, 3185, 3342, 3426
Le Comte (vars. Le Compte, Le Conte),
  Ambroise, 560, 1491
  Ambroise *fils* Jean Baptiste, 428,
    1072, 1558, 1804, 1840, 1922,
    1970, 2742, 2746, 3176, 3223,
    3225, 3227, 3230-3234
  Claude, 738

Le Comte, (Continued),
  François, 1085, 1321, 1612,
    3365, 339
  Jacques, 3096, 3218
  Jean Baptiste *fils* Claude, 428,
    651, 738, 947, 984, 999, 1058,
    1072, 1307, 1546, 1738, 2289,
    2411, 2848, 3353
  Jean Baptiste *fils* Ambroise,
    1491, 1922, 2868, 2936, 2986
  Margueritte (Mme. Dominique
    Metoyer), 2868, 2992-2993,
    3025, 3224, 3401
  Marie Celeste, 2205
  Marie Françoise (Mme. Joseph Dupres II; Mme. Alexis Cloutier),
    1058, 1546, 1840, 2342, 2362,
    2848, 3228, 3353
  Marie Louise, 2404, 2928
  Marie Louise Marguerite (Mme.
    Jean Baptiste Dupre; Mme. Louis
    Monet), 651, 999, 1093, 1491,
    1493, 1537, 1557, 1616, 1758,
    1810, 1844, 1865, 1885, 1922,
    1969, 2018, 2118, 2168, 2325,
    2403-2404, 2537, 2602, 2641,
    3142-3143, 3285, 1955
  Marie Thérèse (Mme. Louis Metoyer),
    2447, 2992, 3448
  Ursula de _____, 1321
  Widow: see Marguerite Le Roy
LeCourt de Prelle (vars. El Cour, Le
  Cour, La Cour, de Presle),
  _____, 2482
  Athanase, 1654, 2058, 2216, 2482-2483, 2516, 2641, 2862, 3228,
    3231, 3378, 3391, 3434
  Barthelemy Le Roy, 488, 984,
    2102, 2253, 2255, 2931, 3013,
    3232, 3391, 3451
  Cecile (Louise), 2227, 2254-2255,
    2483, 3232, 3434
  Family of, 2934n
  Françoise (Mme. Pierre Dupre),
    1521, 1548, 1647, 1942, 1962,
    2102, 2227, 2484, 2862, 3376
  Jacques, 2973
  Jacques Eloy, 2255
  Jean Baptiste Athanase, 2255, 2932
  Jean Baptiste Le Roy, 707, 984,
    2931-2932
  Jean Louis Matthias, 264, 270, 287,
    292, 314, 337, 347, 356, 386,
    414, 434-435, 451, 463, 475-476,
    535, 557, 588, 649, 654, 665,
    682, 693, 734, 743, 749, 984,
    1097, 1153, 1647, 2276-2279, 2342,
    2343, 2391-2392, 2446, 2862, 2931,
    2986, 3376, 3391, 3434
  Joseph (Seigneur de Presle), 984
  Joseph Valleri, 2255, 2837
  Louis: see Jean Louis Matthias
  Louis Césaire, 2255, 2641
  Marie, 1738, 1829, 2279, 2391, 3223
  Marie Antoinette Le Roy (Mme. Nicolas Gallien), 466, 984, 1097,
    1521, 1616, 1942, 2018, 2253-2254, 2931, 2986, 3446
  Marie Barbe, 2255, 3096
  Marie Louise, 2255, 2837
  Neuville, 2255
  Pelagie (Mme. Antoine Joseph Metoyer), 2482, 2880, 3451
Le Cour: see also La Cour
Le Doux (var. Le Du),
  Ange Charles François Marie, 463,
    1734, 3408
  Antoine François I, 492, 1020,
    1228, 2333, 3408
  Antoine François II, 405, 434,
    438, 446, 466, 481, 492
  Étienne Valery, 1763
  François, 1027, 1725, 1763
  Gabriel Antoine, 1702
  Jean Baptiste François, 1725
  Marie Françoise (Mme. Joseph Poirier), 1020, 1702, 1734, 2820
  Pierre, 1027
Le Duc *dit* Ville Franche (var. Duc),
  Claude, 340
  Claude *fils* Joseph J.B., 282
  Daniel, 275
  Jean Baptiste, 294, 442, 1864
  Jeanne Élisabeth, 329, 786
  Jeanne Felicité (Mme. François
    Hugues), 442, 640, 1013
  Joseph, 254
  Joseph Jean Baptiste, 254, 274,
    282, 294, 329, 340, 348, 409,
    551, 640, 786, 792, 1003, 1008,
    2943
  Marie Françoise, 551

Le Duc *dit* Ville Franche (continued),
  Marie Joseph, 792
  Marie Louise (Mme. François Le Maitre), 1008, 1665, 1723, 1761, 1802, 1837, 1846, 1915, 1972, 2075, 2186, 2943, 3066, 3072
Lefebvre, Marie (Mme. Jean Baptiste Besson I), 208
Le Fevre (vars. Le Feuvre, Levevre),
  Angélique (Mme. Michel Rochelos du Vivier), 751
  Antoine, 1068, 1080, 1095
  Marie Louise (Mme. Louis Mercier), 1852, 1891, 2039, 2132, 2955, 3450
  Pierre, 2955
Le Fite: see Laffitte
Leger,
  Adrien *dit* Piedferme, 251, 720, 1002
  Jean Baptiste Adrien *dit* Piedferme, 585, 643, 713, 1002, 1572, 1720, 1983
  Jean Ignace *dit* Piedferme, 1821
  Marie (Richard), (Mme. Jacques Detuil), 2828
  Thomas, 219, 249, 339
Leger: see also Lagé
Le Gros (Gros, Le Gro), Marie Thérèse (Mme. Joseph Marie Armant), 1517, 1606, 1692, 1717, 1737, 1754, 1771, 1819, 1875, 1939, 2095, 2962, 3438
Leibe, Joseph Dominique, 359
Leibe: see also Laybe
Le Jeunesse, Jean *dit*, 96
Le Jeunesse: see also La Jeunesse
Le Maitre (vars. Le Maistre, Lemetre),
  Baptiste, 1761
  Feliciane Théophile, 2186
  François I, 1008, 2943
  François II (Louis), *dit* La Lime, 1008, 1068, 1534, 1560, 1613, 1665, 1723, 1761, 1802, 1846, 1915, 1972, 2075, 2172, 2186, 2256, 2943, 3066, 3347, 3366, 3419, 3423, 3425
  Ignace, 1665, 2075

Le Maitre (continued),
  Jean Baptiste, 1846
  Jean Jacques, 2256
  Marianne Artemise, 1560, 1972
  Marie Euphrosine, 1915
  Marie Françoise, 2218
  Marie Thérèse, 2943, 3072
  Nicolas, 1560, 1723, 1972, 2752
  Victoire Constance, 1560, 1802, 1972, 2895, 3002, 3122
Le Major, *dit* of Charles _____, 124
Lemée (vars. La Mé, La Mée, Le May),
  Antoine, 844, 873, 923, 995, 1002, 1012
Le Moine,
  Antoine I, 854, 1679, 1873, 2820-2821, 2924, 3385, 3421
  Antoine II, 2820
  Charles I, 730, 854, 930, 1030, 1070, 1230, 1237, 1498, 1505, 1594, 1679, 1748, 1801, 2003, 2129, 2214, 2820-2821, 2841, 2849, 2885, 2923-2924, 2956, 2959, 2995-2996, 3051, 3339-3340, 3385, 3390, 3421
  Charles II, 2234, 2849, 2954, 2956, 3390
  Charles *fils* Antoine, 2924
  François I, 8
  François II *dit* La Vidette Boudin, 8, 133
  Héleine, 2956
  Jean Baptiste I, 930, 1679, 1834, 2129, 2238, 2841, 2885, 2956, 2996, 3385, 3430
  Jean Baptiste II (the elder), 2129
  Jean Baptiste II (the younger), 2885
  Jeanne (Mme. Guillaume Martineau), 1527, 2937, 3343
  Marie, 2238, 2323
  Marie Caroline, 2996
  Marie Denise, 2238
  Marie Louise (Mme. Jean Baptiste Massipe), 1030, 1327, 1482, 1557, 1617, 1748, 1801, 1834, 1873, 1917, 1969, 2019, 2040, 2104, 2187, 2236, 2894, 2959, 3423
  Marie Louise (Mme. Antoine Rachal), 1505, 1594, 2003, 2070, 2214,

Le Moine (continued),
  Marie Louise (Mme. Antoine Rachal; continued), 2841, 2923, 2926, 2995-2996, 3340
  Marie Louise (identity uncertain), 1883, 2820
  Marie Louise *fille* Charles II), 2234
  Marie Susanne, 2849
  Michel, 730, 3051
  Remy, 2821
Lemoine, Russell, Rev. Fr., xvii
Lendrenau,
  Hélène (Mme. Sebastien Olivo), 3415
  Jean Pierre, 3415
Lengevin, Maria (Dna. Miguel Vincent), 3397
Le Noir,
  Anne (Mme. Françoise Le Noir), 1046
  Antoine, 1046, 1511, 1674, 1759, 1934, 3445
  François, 1046
  François Antoine Carle, 1674, 2079
Leon, Madelena (Dna. Antonio Ramis), 1534, 3347
Leonard,
  Catherine (Mme. Jean Monteche), 349, 739
  Marie Anne (Mme. Jean Baptiste La Cour), 2889
Leonet (Lionnois), *dit* of Jean Baptiste Samuel
Lequinte, Louis, Indian, 3069
Lernodier: see La Renaudiere
Le Roy (vars. de Roi, Le Roi),
  Barthelemy: see Barthelemy Le Court
  Étienne *dit* Framboise, 6, 30, 97, 102, 105, 191, 727, 738, 984
  Jean Baptiste: see Jean Baptiste Le Court
  Jeanne (Mme. Jean Louis Matthias Le Court de Prelle), xiii, 30, 269, 288, 296, 319, 338, 466, 488, 530, 532, 550, 558, 568, 578, 635, 640, 647, 652, 665, 670, 707, 984, 1097, 1153, 1647, 2862, 2931, 2986, 3376, 3391, 3434

Le Roy (continued),
  Julien *dit* Framboise: see Julien Davion *dit* St. Prix
  Louise Françoise Guillot: see Marie Louise Françoise Guillot
  Marguerite (Mme. Jean Baptiste Le Comte), 191, 428, 594, 597, 607, 609, 651, 703, 707, 738, 984, 999, 1058, 1072, 1307, 1546, 1904, 2482, 2539, 2541, 2557, 2559, 2565, 2569, 2623, 2744-2745, 2747-2749, 2754, 2848, 2930-2935, 3144, 3223-3237, 3296, 3353, 3401, 3451
  Marie, 537, 948
  Marie Antoinette: see Marie Antoinette LeCourt
  Marie Eve (Grandissa, Keniguinne), (Mme. Martin Lambre), 726, 742, 753
  Marie Jeanne (Mme. Pierre La Roche), 1024
  Marie Louise (Mme. Louis Rachal I), 105, 419, 465, 481, 534, 562, 586, 588, 603, 652, 655, 665, 682, 716, 727, 843, 948, 984, 1067, 1088, 1099, 1423, 1501, 1505, 1810, 1849, 1926, 2838-2839, 2841, 2923, 2927, 2936, 2972, 2987, 2991, 3008, 3340, 3372, 3452
  Pierre Laurent: see Pierre Laurent LeCourt
Le Roy: see also de los Reyes
Le Sage, Pierre, 205
Le Saussaye?,
  Jacques, 907
  Marie Frosine Pelagie, 907
Les Allemands: see German Coast
Lestache, Isabelle (Mme. Étienne Laberry), 454
Lestache: see also Lestage
Lestage (vars. Lestache, Lestase),
  Agathe, 1356, 1490, 1921
  Barthelemy, 1831, 2961
  Bernabé, 1868
  François, 1799
  Guillaume, 904, 1025, 1032, 1354, 1356, 1490, 1603, 1612, 1719, 1755, 1799, 1831, 1868, 1896, 1921, 2010, 2101, 2686, 3042, 3174-3175, 3365

Lestage (continued),
  Jean Baptiste, 1603, 1755, 2010, 2029, 2098, 3440
  Jean Étienne, 1719
  Marguerite (Mme. Jean Vercher), 1870, 2461, 2463
  Marie Emmanuel, 1603, 2010
  Marie Rosalie Brigitte, 2101
Reynauld, 1025
Le Vasseur (vars. Le Vassau, Levassaux, Levassere, Vasseur),
  _____, M., 2318, 2407, 2687, 3181
  _____, Mde., 1631, 2034
  Baptiste, 2782
  Catherine (Mme. Jean Baptiste Morin), 289, 471, 886, 941, 983, 1078, 1188
  Cécile (Mme. Jean Piserot), 241, 424, 437, 443, 460, 472, 582, 610, 626, 672, 685, 694, 945
  Charles François, 110, 258, 423, 470, 526, 609, 908, 927, 966, 1055, 1061, 1083, 1096, 1197, 1319, 1333, 1338, 1503, 1640, 1681, 1729, 1767, 1773, 1792, 1806, 1879, 1928, 2085, 2334, 2363, 2370, 2456, 2494, 2543, 2584, 2765, 2982, 3077, 3158, 3273, 3294, 3300, 3351, 3411, 3450
  François, 1427
  Françoise, 630, 694
  Jacques *dit* Jolibois, 37, 75, 110, 176, 192, 208-209, 236, 241, 245, 251, 284, 289, 312, 465, 726, 742, 983, 1069, 1085, 2942
  Jacques *fils* François, 966
  Jacques Joseph François, 312, 901, 966, 978, 1069, 1078, 1085, 1094, 1096, 1334, 1503, 1585, 1640, 1662, 1903, 1928, 1996, 2072, 2229, 2297, 2334, 2363, 2456, 2942, 3351
  Jean François, 2601, 3406, 3411
  Louis *fils* François, 1729, 2119, 2687, 3122, 3257
  Louis *fils* Jacques Joseph François, 1662, 2072
  Magdeleine, 814
  Manuel Simeon, 1773, 2942

Le Vasseur (continued),
  Marguerite Modeste, 1806
  Marie, 197
  Marie Anne, 966, 977
  Marie Françoise (Mme. Jean Baptiste Anty), 1640, 2085, 2126, 2334, 2405, 2494, 3351
  Marie Genevieve Jeanne (Mme. Jean Baptiste Buard), 1655, 1681, 2059, 2085, 2456, 2687, 3407, 3411, 3427
  Marie Jeanne (Mme. Jean Lambre), 192, 424, 526, 555, 559, 585, 595, 606, 681, 742, 836, 911, 933, 978, 1018, 1057, 1314, 1590, 1638, 1721, 1784, 2835, 2966, 3346, 3358
  Marie Judith, 2229
  Marie Louise, 927
  Marie Ursulle, 1503, 1928
  Pierre Manuel, 2942
  Pierre Siriac, 1585, 1996
  Remy Victor, 1903
  Simon, 3450
  Thérèse (Mme. Jacob Jacques Lambre), 37, 312, 549, 570, 616, 632, 726
L'Eveille, Indian, 379
Leveille, Pierre, 412, 675
L'Eveilles, Pierre *dit* 87
Leven?, Magdeleine: see Leon, Madelena
Leveque,
  _____, Monsignor, 3219-3222
  Charles François, 734
  Jeanne (Mme. Élie Bernard I), 2819
  Maturin, 734
Levevre: see Lefevre
Lionnois (Leonet), *dit* of Jean Baptiste Samuel
Lisette, 417, 581, 670
Livaudais: see Henoul de Livaudais, Babin de Livaudais
Livo: see Olivo
Liÿonard: see Leonard
Llorens, Zéraphin, 3451
Locovis, Joseph, 2190
Locavia, Thérèse, 111
L'Olive, *dit* of Olivier Clinon
Lomard, Marie Françoise (Mme. Antoine Lamb), 745

Longlois: see Langlois
Longuera: see Noguerra
Loppes de la Peña, Joseph, 2097
Lorand: see Laurent
Lorence, Augustin, 1022
Lorenza, Francisca, 2160
Lorenzo: see Laurent
Lorrina, 2379
Los Adaes (var. Adaes, Adailles, Adais, Aidaie, Los Adais, Los Adayes), xi, 2, 8, 13, 105, 135, 144, 187, 308, 347, 355, 406, 443, 463, 473, 493, 522, 580, 580, 613, 733, 747, 860, 877, 1045, 1267, 2172, 2199, 2202, 2863, 2982, 3077, 3369, 3372
Louet?, _____, 738
Louis (Luis), 182, 234, 257, 283, 351, 448, 486, 588, 597, 600, 619, 750, 882, 1259, 1493, 1703, 2145, 2154, 2156, 2158, 2285, 2291, 2299, 2316-2317, 2321, 2349, 2443, 2450, 2486, 2547, 2552, 2554, 2564-2565, 2588, 2591, 2620, 2637, 2657, 2677, 2693, 2713, 2743, 2770-2773, 2915, 3086, 3134, 3144, 3150, 3158, 3177, 3199, 3225, 3246-3247, 3270, 3281, 3292, 3302, 3437; 2354, 2439
Louis: see also Jean Baptiste Louis, Jean Louis, Joseph Louis
Louis Alexandre (Luis Alexandro), 310, 1488, 1910, 2478, 2534, 2572, 2662, 2668, 3135, 3207, 3240, 3264, 3272
Louis André (Luis Andres), 2654
Louis Antoine (Luis Antonio), 221, 317, 574
Louis Barnabé (Luis Barnabe), 2645
Louis César (Luis Cesar), 295, 1515, 2538, 2565, 3226, 3237
Louis François, 244
Louis Isidore, 3278
Louis Jacques René, 863
Louis Joseph (Luis Josef), 19, 2443
Louis Nicolas, 851
Louis Pierre, 516, 917
Louis Robert (Luis Roberto), 2425, 2524
Louis Sebastien, 531

Louis Thomas (Luis Tomas), 2387, 2655
Louis Zenon (Luis Zenon), 2541
Louisburg, Canada, 1044
Louise (Luisa), 80, 160, 270, 378, 535, 561, 920, 934, 987, 1824, 1904, 2150, 2158, 2361, 2406, 2482-2483, 2486, 2512, 2571, 2580, 3095, 3175
Louise: see also Marie Thérèse Louise
Louise *dite* Jocolone, 260
Louise Cirena, 646
Louise Marguerite, 98, 305, 323
Louise Reine, 576
Louise Susanne, 90, 163
Louisiane, Anne, 677
Louison, 212, 834, 3141, 3209, 3215, 3227, 3277, 3295, 3297
Lucas: see Manuel Lucas
Lucas, Jeanne, 3041
Luce (Lucia), 2585
Lucovisi (Lucoviq), Joseph, 2205, 2241
Lucreie, 202, 602; see also Crei
Lugue,
 Jean, 2896, 2960
 Marie Eugenie, 2960
Luis: see Louis
Luisa: see Louise
Lunot, Susanne (Mme. François Debrande), 719
Lutheran Faith, 769

M. Congo, 1910
Macarti (de Macarti), Baptiste, 1866
Macarti: see also Miro y Macarti
Macarty, Jean Jacques, 105, 107, 119, 141, 169, 981
Macipe: see Massipe
Macti, Indian, 2920-2922
Mader (vars. Madere, Madern, Maderne),
 Cécile, 506, 694
 François Daniel, 552
 Jean I *dit* Jean des Jeans, 96, 184, 228, 238, 241, 249, 252, 277, 308, 342, 393, 457, 506-507, 552, 571, 598, 627, 663-664, 694, 739, 742, 798, 821

Mader (continued),
  Jean II, 249, 341, 522, 798
  Jeanne (Mme. François Carle), 277, 425, 457, 908
  Marie Françoise, 598
  Marie Jeanne (Mme. Charles François Le Vasseur), 308, 927, 945, 966, 1096, 1338, 1640, 1729, 1773, 3351, 3411, 3450
  Reine Jeanne, 228, 362
Maderne: see Mader, Materne, Modern
Maderne, Marie: see Marie Thili
Maes (vars. Mas, Mes),
  Jean Baptiste, 1606, 2012
  Louise Josephine, 2160
  Marie Genevieve Agathe, 1673, 2078, 2835, 2971
  Marie Victoire, 1606, 2012
  Pierre Joseph I, 1103, 1407, 1517, 1606, 1642, 1673, 1939, 1952, 2012, 2078, 2160, 3022, 3032, 3101, 3208, 3216, 3260, 3279, 3300, 3325, 3436
  Pierre Joseph II, 1642, 1673, 1952, 2078
Magdeleine (Madalena, Magdalana), 477, 922, 2143, 2151, 2391, 2401, 2408, 2412, 2446, 2480, 2482, 2546, 2676-2677, 2685, 2709, 2744-2745, 2758, 2779, 2768, 2786, 2847, 2965, 3107, 3109, 3127, 3146-3147, 3164, 3178, 3181, 3199, 3225-3226, 3244, 3269, 3278, 3296, 3304, 3401
Magdeleine: see also Héleine Magdeleine, Jeanne Françoise Magdeleine, Marie Josephe Magdeleine, Marie Thérèse Magdeleine
Magdeleine Josephe, Indian, 476
Magnon, _____, 1418
Magnon, _____, Mme. 3240
Mailier: see Meillier
Maillioux (vars. Mailliou, Maillou, Mailliouxe, Maiou, Malloux, Mayeux, Maÿou, Mayoux)
  _____, 1687
  Cécile, 1853
  Ignace I, 1076, 1511, 1602, 1701, 1724, 1803, 1853, 1934, 2009, 2090, 2899, 2990-2991, 3386, 3387, 3415, 3442, 3445, 3455

Maillioux (continued),
  Ignace II, 1602, 1687-1688, 2009
  Jean Baptiste Dorcin, 1687, 2090
  Laurent I, 1688, 1853, 2124, 2219, 2261, 2990, 3386, 3442
  Laurent II, 2990
  Marie Hyacinthe Anastasie, 1803, 2090, 2899, 3259
  Marie Louise (Mme. Jacques Errié), 1511, 1934, 2990, 3445
  Marie Thérèse (Mme. Michel Antoine Rambin), 1688, 1724, 1853, 2039, 2124, 2209, 2213, 2265, 2727, 2899, 2991, 3128, 3386
  Pierre, 2245, 2265, 2704, 3342, 3444
Mairgay (Mingui), Françoise Anne (Mme. François Le Maitre), 1008, 2943
Malathi: see La Malathy
Malbert (vars. Malber, Malbort),
  Alexis, 658
  Angélique, 1685, 1712, 2091
  Élisabeth, 452
  Jean Baptiste I, 728
  Jean Baptiste II *dit* Sans Facon, 452, 500, 658, 711, 728, 736, 875, 961, 1024, 1039, 1712, 2834, 2933-2934
  Jean Baptiste III (the elder), 587
  Jean Baptiste III (the younger), 961
  Marie Anne Louise (Mme. Joseph Rabalé), 1494, 1601 (bis), 1685, 1923, 2008, 2091
  Marie De Neige (Mme. Jean Nicolas Beaudouin), 2223, 2834, 2933-2934
  Marie Françoise (Mme. François La Roche; Mme. Jacques Fort), 711, 1024, 1039, 1102, 1574, 1649, 1712, 1746, 1985, 2064, 2170, 2262, 2997, 3073, 3079, 3290
  Marie Jeanne, 875
Malbouroug, Guillaume *dit*, 88
Maldonat,
  Joseph Louis, 2208
  Marc Maximilian, 2208
Malige,
  _____, Dna. 2606, 2639

Malige (continued),
  Heloise Seraphine, 1692, 2095
  Joseph, 1401, 1607, 1668, 1680,
    1692, 2013, 2084, 2095, 2193,
    2228, 2258, 2615, 2852, 2900,
    3370, 3382, 3400
  Joseph Noel, 1607, 2013
  Louis Bernard, 2193
  Marie Jeanne Anne, 2258, 2900
  Marie Josephe (Mme. Antoine Philippe Dubois), 2228, 2232,
    2755, 2852, 2900, 3400
  Marie Louise Angélique (Mme. André François Valentine), 1680,
    2084, 3370
  Michel Cyprien, 2258
Malloux: see Maillioux
Mandeville, ____, 1289
Manne,
  François I, 148
  François II, 57, 83, 91, 99, 110,
    148-149, 153
  Marie Louise, 83, 421
Manon, 516
Manuel (Manual), 2408, 2497, 2512,
  2568, 2576, 2578, 2591, 2603-
  2604, 2618, 2632, 2638, 2682,
  2750, 2761, 3111
Manuel: see also Emmanuel, Joseph
  Manuel, Noel
Manuel Lucas, 3286
Manuela, 2518
Maraffret: see Layssard
Marcel, 278
Marcellin (Marcellino), 2757, 3181,
  3206; see also Jean Baptiste
  Marcelin
Marchand (var. Marchant),
  Bernardo, 1079
  Jean, 145
  Jean, 1079, 1308
  Jean Marc, 3409, 3442
  Marianne (Marie Anne), 80-81,
    145, 521
Marcollay, Paul, 1538, 2355, 2946,
  3348, 3388, 3403
Marcou, Marie (Mme. Jean Plaisance), 1004
Marechal, *dit* of Barbier
Maret, Pierre de la Tou: see de la
  Tour

Marguerite (Margarita), 27, 201,
  331, 403, 486, 505, 519, 527, 594,
  607, 631, 703, 715, 919, 2144,
  2148, 2284, 2291-2292, 2294, 2308,
  2326, 2339, 2369, 2389, 2407, 2432,
  2473, 2477, 2493, 2508, 2518, 2521,
  2527, 2558, 2581-2583, 2589, 2670,
  2711, 2717, 2725, 2742, 2745, 2758,
  2799, 2808, 2815, 2823-2825, 2837,
  2880, 2904-2906, 3090, 3092, 3109,
  3117, 3129, 3148, 3150, 3163, 3166,
  3171, 3182, 3185, 3187, 3194, 3249,
  3252, 3292, 3301, 3305, 3315
Marguerite Victoire, 665, 947
Maria: see also Marie
Maria Antonia, 1309
Maria Cécile, 197
Maria de la Assomption, 2648
Maria de los Nieves y Maria Ana, 2448
Maria Elena: see Marie Héleine
Maria Gro, 1191
Maria Lorenzo, 1703
Mariana: see Marie Anne
Marie (Maria), 12, 26, 35, 45, 56,
  100, 103-104, 118, 189, 211, 262,
  389, 514, 521, 616, 628, 698, 748,
  755, 830, 899, 915, 2274, 2286,
  2290, 2299, 2301, 2329, 2337, 2357,
  2359, 2364, 2366, 2410-2411, 2416-
  2417, 2420, 2424, 2432-2433, 2435,
  2455, 2468, 2484, 2488, 2490, 2493,
  2499, 2502, 2509, 2550, 2554, 2557,
  2564, 2600, 2612, 2622, 2624, 2644,
  2659, 2702, 2711, 2718-2720, 2733-
  2734, 2743-2744, 2746-2747, 2750,
  2762-2763, 2767, 2774, 2776, 2788-
  2789, 2809, 2811, 2823, 2827, 2993,
  3092, 3106, 3119-3120, 3123, 3126,
  3133, 3135-3136, 3138, 3153, 3155,
  3163, 3169, 3175, 3180, 3183, 3190-
  3191, 3193, 3195, 3199, 3206, 3210,
  3224, 3226-3227, 3239-3240, 3243,
  3245-3246, 3250, 3255-3256, 3260,
  3272, 3274, 3281-3282, 3284-3285,
  3288, 3290, 3293, 3307, 3316, 3401
Marie Adèlaïde (Maria Adelaida),
  2510, 2598, 2683, 3202, 3251, 3289,
  3298
Marie Agnès, 3149: see also Marie
  Agnès Poissot
Marie Amelie, 3293

Marie Anaselite, 3213
Marie Angélique (Maria Angelica), 432, 2714, 3113
Marie Anita (Maria Anita), 2611
Marie Anne (Marianne, Mariana), 10, 15, 71, 95, 113, 154, 171, 450, 521, 592, 609, 611, 664, 678, 787, 851, 864, 866, 871, 1021, 1036, 1166, 2144, 2273, 2313, 2328, 2345, 2352, 2373, 2382, 2393, 2420, 2426, 2480, 2510-2512, 2515, 2528, 2543, 2561-2562, 2579, 2584, 2591, 2604, 2611, 2619, 2633, 2664, 2674, 2708, 2712, 2719, 2731, 2736, 2747, 2751, 2777, 2800, 2804, 2807, 2813, 2824-2825, 2908, 2919, 2929, 2985, 3097, 3120, 3124, 3130, 3139, 3148, 3163, 3174, 3186, 3189, 3196, 3202, 3258-3259, 3294, 3299, 3437
Marie Anne Fanni, 3124
Marie Anne Thérèse, Indian: see Marie Anne Thérèse de la Grande Terre
Marie Anore, 417
Marie Antoine, 112
Marie Aspasie, 3276
Marie Augustine (Maria Augustina), 2569
Marie Aureile, 2985
Marie Barbe (Maria Barba or Barbara), 74, 156, 376, 2488, 3102, 3159, 3310
Marie Barbe Joseph, Indian, 1824
Marie Catherine, 3178
Marie Catiche (Maria Caticha), 2643
Marie Cécile (Maria Cecilia), 2768
Marie Celesie: see Marie Silesie
Marie Céleste (Maria Celestia or Celestina), 1526, 2392, 2549, 2591, 2609-2610, 3211, 3238, 3246, 3302
Marie Christine, 3258
Marie Claire, Indian, 2204
Marie Constance (Maria Constancia), 2707; see also Marie Octance
Marie de Douleurs, 337
Marie de la Dolores, 1904
Marie de l'Ascension, 3125

Marie de l'Assumption, 433
Marie (Maria) Deleisa, 2388
Marie des Nieges (Maria de los Nieves), 2744, 2281, 3203
Marie Denise (Maria Deneise), 2281
Marie des Nieges *dit* La Rotte (La Ritte), 345
Marie, Diego, 3165
Marie Echine, Indian, 216
Marie Edé (Maria Edé), 2609
Marie Eleonor (Maria Elonor, Eleonard, Heleonore, Leonora), 330, 2505, 2666, 2806, 3104, 3156-3157, 3187
Marie Élisabeth, 2985
Marie Esther (Maria Ester), 2314
Marie Eugenie (Maria Eugenia), 2394
Marie Fanchonette (Maria Fanconeta), 2635
Marie Fani, 3116
Marie Felicité (Maria Felicidad), 2545, 2587, 3274
Marie Felix (Maria Felix), 2659
Marie Françoise, Indian (Mme. Pierre Raymond), 1016, 1101, 2901
Marie Françoise (Maria Francisca), 11, 43, 48, 85, 162, 190, 239, 253, 258, 307, 565, 648, 677, 820, 916, 967, 1488, 1492, 2286, 2334, 2338, 2348, 2422, 2471, 2475, 2504, 2530, 2534, 2536, 2546, 2597, 2615, 2631, 2658, 2704, 2721, 2723, 3127, 3151, 3157, 3160, 3162, 3193, 3199, 3206, 3215, 3218, 3252, 3273
Marie Françoise Adèlaïde (Maria Francisca Adelaida), 2701
Marie Françoise Amelie, 3294
Marie Françoise de Dolores, 2539, 2542
Marie Françoise Josephine, 3215
Marie Frozine (Maria Frozina), 1493, 2537, 2555, 2696
Marie Genevieve (Maria Genoveva), 2319, 2327
Marie Genevieve Adèlaïde, 3126
Marie Genevieve Rosalie, 956
Marie Gertrude, 48, 100
Marie Héleine (Maria Helena, Elena), 426, 2303, 2369, 2419, 2601, 2653
Marie Héleine Adèlaïde, 2444, 3154
Marie Héleine Eleonore (Maria Elena Leonora), 2665

479

Marie Henriette, Indian, 58
Marie Honore, 569
Marie Hortense (Maria Hortensia), 2548
Marie Hyacinthe (Maria Jacinta), 2322, 2353
Marie J____, 906
Marie Jeanne (Maria Juana), 261, 269, 296, 333, 423, 425, 585, 599, 614, 885, 900, 924, 953-954, 960, 975, 1028, 1710, 1912, 2153, 2289, 2291, 2302, 2319-2320, 2331, 2340, 2348, 2359, 2365, 2376, 2377, 2387, 2402, 2414, 2421-2422, 2440, 2442, 2467, 2478, 2485-2486, 2494, 2496, 2507, 2510, 2528, 2540, 2597, 2603, 2635-2636, 2642, 2672, 2679, 2697, 2706, 2710, 2729, 2735, 2748, 2795-2796, 2798, 2800, 2803, 2814-2815, 2847, 2998, 3093, 3100, 3103, 3111-3112, 3169, 3176, 3177, 3180, 3184, 3191, 3197, 3200, 3204, 3217, 3220, 3223, 3229-3230, 3235, 3263, 3266, 3270, 3283, 3301, 3328, 3437
Marie Jeanne Babet (Maria Juana Babé), 2710
Marie Jeanne Françoise (Maria Juana Francisca), 2422
Marie Josephe (Maria Josefa), 554, 582, 669, 899, 916, 2380, 2384, 2423, 2450, 2491, 2495, 2664, 2684, 2753, 2758, 2911, 2915, 2919, 3105, 3108, 3138, 3185-3186, 3219
Marie Josephe Magdeleine (Maria Josefa Madelena), 2425
Marie Judith, 3101, 3131
Marie Julie, 878
Marie Julien, 592, 787
Marie Lalie, 3157
Marie l'Ascenscion: see Marie de l'Ascension
Marie Leonore, 956
Marie Louise (Maria Luisa), 5, 68, 75, 77, 81, 157, 218, 233, 257, 279, 325, 343, 520, 534, 543, 577, 581, 655, 693, 841, 862, 882, 896, 904, 920, 939, 946, 1489, 1910, 2268, 2271, 2296, 2300, 2306, 2327, 2341, 2381-2382, 2388, 2404-2405, 2418, 2427, 2429, 2441, 2444-2445, 2449-2450, 2458, 2472, 2481, 2487, 2489, 2497, 2506, 2514-2515, 2522, 2526, 2532, 2535, 2541-2542, 2545-2547, 2555-2556, 2568, 2580, 2588-2589, 2602, 2614, 2617-2618, 2624, 2632-2633, 2645, 2666, 2690, 2694-2695, 2712, 2738, 2748, 2763, 2766-2767, 2786-2788, 2792, 2809, 2903, 2908, 2922, 3082, 3097, 3100, 3104, 3113, 3127, 3131, 3134, 3138, 3144-3145, 3153, 3159, 3162, 3167, 3186, 3192, 3196, 3198, 3208, 3218-3219, 3240-3241, 3253, 3277-3278, 3290, 3292, 3297-3298, 3302, 3401
Marie Louise, Indian (Mme. Claud Bertrand *dit* Dauphine), 36, 40, 46, 71, 75, 78, 80, 91, 103, 235, 263, 282, 285
Marie Louise *dite* Clorise, 3198
Marie Louise *dite* Mariotte, 3202
Marie Louise Catiche (Maria Luisa Catiche): see Marie Louise Catiche Metoyer
Marie Louise Claire, 2966
Marie Louise Marthe (Maria Luisa Marta), 2749
Marie Magdeleine (Maria Madelena), 326, 446, 542, 841, 947, 2412, 2542, 2876, 2973, 3451
Marie Marcelle, Indian, 167
Marie Marcelitte, 3257
Marie Marguerite (Maria Margarita), 2399, 3104
Marie Marianne, 578
Marie Marthe (Maria Martha), 2502, 2665, 3103, 3156
Marie Mélanie, 3192
Marie Modeste, Indian (Mme. Jean Laurent Bodin), 2391, 2876, 2897, 2973
Marie Monique, Indian, 3076
Marie Nanette, Indian: see Anne, Indian (Mme. Jean Baptiste Brevel I)
Marie Octance (Maria Octancia), 2413
Marie Osite, 2964
Marie Perine, 3288
Marie Pompose (Pompone), Indian, 1678, 2083, 3261
Marie Reine des Anges, 3203

Marie Rosalie, Indian, 2998, 3013
Marie Rose (Maria Rosa), 573,
  2309, 2336, 3499, 2662, 3119
Marie Sally (Maria Saly), 2659
Marie Sally Felix (Maria Saly
  Felix), 2659
Marie Silesie (Marie Celesie, Maria
  Silesia), 2449, 2768, 3110, 3233,
  3259
Marie Sirine (Maria Sirina), 2351
Marie Susanne (Marie Susette,
  Maria Susana, Maria Suseta),
  2279, 2402, 2559, 2629, 2640,
  2747, 3167
Marie Thérèse, Indian (Mme. Jacques
  Guedon): see Marie Anne Thérèse
  de la Grande Terre
Marie Thérèse (Maria Teresa, Maria
  Theresa), 187, 413, 568, 922, 979,
  1023, 2298, 2300, 2307, 2354,
  2358, 2443, 2632, 2766, 3111,
  3130, 3204, 3207-3208, 3212, 3222,
  3254, 3322
Marie Thérèse *dit* Coincoin, 225,
  484, 820, 862, 921, 2130, 2283,
  2324, 2383, 2426, 2489, 2623,
  2764, 2791, 2897, 2984, 2992-
  2993, 3148, 3252, 3305, 3389,
  3401, 3448, 3451
Marie Thérèse Emelie (Maria Teresa
  Emelia), 2765
Marie Thérèse Louise, 2632
Marie Thérèse Magdeleine, 2847
Marie Ursulle, Indian, 670, 2255,
  2837, 2932, 2984, 2985, 3096,
  3296
Marie Victoire (Maria Victoria),
  2722, 3116, 3279
Mariet: see de la Tour
Marin, 1348, 1912
Marin: see also Marinne
Marin, _____, Mme., 819
Marinero (Marmero?), Marie, (Dna.
  André Rodrigues), 3027
Marinette, Indian, 391
Marinne,
  Jean, 668
  Marie de l'Incarnation, 668
Marion (vars. Marionau, Marionnau),
  _____, Mr., 3134
  Jeanne: see Marie Jeanne Chagneau

Marion (continued),
  Louis, 77, 81, 190, 197, 244, 255
  Pierre, 14, 77, 81, 85, 185, 234,
    240, 368
Marly (Marli), *dit* of Sorelle
Marmoulet, _____, Rev. Fr., 105
Martancour, Marie Thérèse (Mme. Jean
  Baptiste Ville Blette), 205, 349
Marthe, Anne Marie Philippe: see
  Anne Marie Philippe
Marthe (Marta), 2500-2501, 2692,
  2708, 2735, 3135-3136, 3254
Marthe: see also Marie Louise Marthe
Marthos y Navarreti, Angel, Gov., 490
Martianeau: see Martineau
Martiaueau: see Martineau
Martier, Pierre, 410
Martin: see also Antoine Martin
Martin,
  Adrien (Mme. Jean Bernardin), 341
  Céleste, 2107
  John, 2108
  Joseph, 1894, 2198
  Marie, 2243
  Maria Frozina, 2107
  Marie Anne (Mrs. Elie Robinson),
    1625, 1661, 2027-2029, 2071
  Zachary I, 2107-2109, 2243
  Zachary II, 2109
Martineau (vars. Martianeau, Marti-
  nau),
  Guillaume, 1527, 2937, 3343
  Jean Joseph, 1527, 1624, 2026,
    2838, 2937, 3220-3221, 3343,
    3430, 3452
  Joseph François, 2937
Masc: see Metz
Masipe: see Massipe
Masse, _____, Mr., 581
Maurin (Morin), Jean Baptiste, 1498,
  3339
Maurin: see also Morin
Massipe (vars. Macipe, Masipe, Mas-
  sip, Mazipe),
  Antoine Paksan, 2041
  Élisabeth, 1834
  Dorotea, 1748, 2104, 3423
  Étienne, 1482, 1917
  François Charles, 2236
  Jean Baptiste, 1030, 1086, 1327,
    1399, 1482, 1498, 1505, 1557,
    1748, 1801, 1834, 1873, 1917,

481

Massipe (continued),
　Jean Baptiste (continued), 1969,
　　2041, 2104, 2187, 2236, 2323,
　　2894, 2959, 3340, 3423
　Marguerite, 2924
　Marie, 2959
　Marie Jeanne, 1873
　Marie Louise, 1557, 1969
　Marie Teotis, 2104
　Pierre, 1030, 2924, 2959
　Pierre *fils* Jean Baptiste, 1801,
　　2959
　Remy (Remigio) Silvestre, 2187
　Theotista, 1327
Materne, Marie Jeanne (Thili),
　(Mme. Jean Mader), 228, 241, 249,
　274, 277, 308, 333, 457, 507,
　552, 598, 694
Mathiane, 637
Mathias, ____, Rev. Fr., Vicar General, 168
Mathieu André, 637
Matin, Marie: see Marie Martin
Matonge, ____, Sr., *dit* Chavenaut,
　1213
Matuliche, Geronimo, 1123
Maurice (Moricio, Mauricio), 2680,
　2801, 3198
Maurine, Marie Gertrude (Mme. Louis
　Césaire Le Court), 2641
Maxiama, Indian, 2154
Mayeux: see Maillioux
Mayou: see Maillioux
Maytaye: see Metoyer
Mechim,
　Robert, 1068
　William, 1068
Meillier (vars. Mailier, Meiller,
　Meslier, Mesliers, Miliere),
　Catherine (Mme. Jean Philippe
　　Pierre Prudhomme; Mme. Pierre
　　Alorge), 51, 62, 179, 204, 250,
　　289, 302, 566, 642, 722, 724,
　　725, 737, 749, 1056, 1273
　Catherine (mother of Mme. Prud-
　　homme), 209
Melanide, 3324
Melanide: see also Melanie
Melanie (Melania), 2810
Melonne?, Madeleine (Mme. Joseph De
　Lorme I), 1076

Melrose, La., 2623
Menard,
　____, Mr., 935
　Marie Joseph (Mme. Louis Christophe
　　Claude de Mézières), 347
Mendoza, ____, 1104
Mercier (var. Mercié),
　Agathe Dorthine, 2858
　Agnès (Mme. Jean Baptiste Morin I),
　　983
　Felicité, 1891
　François Claude, 2858, 3404
　François II, 2132, 2217, 2858,
　　3404, 3456
　François *fils* Louis, 2955
　Joseph Marie, 2955
　Louis, 1852, 1891, 2039, 2132,
　　2955, 3450
　Louis Nicolas, 2039
　Marie Charlotte, 3427
　Marie Françoise, 2217
　Marie Josephe (Mme. Joseph Renoy),
　　1516, 1564, 1938, 1976
　Marie Josephe Adèlaïde, 1852, 2955,
　　3450
　Marie Louise, 2132
　Nicolas, 2039
Merier, Francisco, 1785
Merles, Marie (Mme. Jean Carles),
　457, 992
Meschi?, Thomas, 121
Metoyer (vars. Maytaye, Metayé, Me-
　toié, Metoier, Metoyé),
　Antoine Joseph, 2324, 2539, 2791,
　　2837, 2984, 3132, 3182, 3451
　Augustin: see Nicolas Augustin
　Augustin II, 2984
　Catiche: see Marie Louise Catiche
　Claude Thomas Pierre, 1010, 1044,
　　1297, 1420, 1449, 1488-1490,
　　1496, 1552, 1598-1599, 1921,
　　2005-2006, 2051, 2180, 2283,
　　2383, 2426, 2556, 2596-2597,
　　2643-2644, 2662-2664, 2704,
　　2706, 2709-2711, 2766-2768,
　　2770-2772, 2775, 2783, 2791,
　　2796-2797, 2993, 3057, 3109,
　　3111, 3113, 3155-3156, 3177?,
　　3183, 3198-3200, 3209, 3248,
　　3250, 3253, 3272, 3276-3279,
　　3283, 3292, 3295, 3337, 3355,
　　3411, 3420

Metoyer (continued),
  Dominique I, 2130, 2643, 2645, 2703, 2714, 2745, 2868, 2992, 2993, 3025, 3401, 3448, 3451
  Dominique II (the elder), 3025
  Dominique II (the younger), 2868
  Family Genealogy, 2623, 2749
  François, 2489
  François Benjamin, 2180
  Jean Baptiste Augustin (the elder), 3089
  Jean Baptiste Augustin (the younger), 2897
  Jean Baptiste Louis, 2992, 3144
  Joseph, 2993
  Louis, 1904, 2447, 2623, 2749, 2764, 2766, 2826, 2992, 3089, 3179, 3248, 3448
  Louis, Widow, 2447; see also Marie Thérèse Le Comte
  Marie, 2596
  Marie Aspasie (Mme. Zéraphin Llorens), 3451
  Marie Barbe, 3179
  Marie Eulalie, 2283
  Marie Françoise Roselie, 2383
  Marie Louise Catiche, 2623
  Marie Modest Nicolas Augustin, 2130
  Marie Rose, 2749
  Marie Susanne, 921, 2304, 2392, 2434, 2559, 2623, 2642, 2650, 2703, 2737, 2764, 2993, 3089, 3132, 3179, 3248, 3272
  Marie Susette (Mme. Élisé Roques), 3389
  Marie Thérèse Elisabeth, 2051, 2861, 2891, 3276
  Nicolas Augustin, 921, 1489, 2130, 2304, 2392, 2434, 2480, 2560, 2623, 2642, 2702, 2736, 2749, 2762, 2811, 2897, 2984, 3089, 3110, 3149, 3389, 3448, 3451
  Nicolas François, 1552, 3355
  Pierre I, see Claude Thomas Pierre
  Pierre II, 2559, 2737, 2847, 2985, 3144, 3451
  Pierre Toussaint, 2426, 3258
  Pierre Victorin, 1598, 2005
  Théophile, 2447
Metz, (Masc, Mase), Marie Barbe, (Mme. Pierre Pomier), 1060, 2963

Meunier (Munier), *dit* of Toutin
Mezieres: see de Mézières
Michel (Miguel), 595, 2575, 2637, 2698, 2806, 2910, 3110, 3158, 3197, 3334
Michel: see also François Michel, Joseph Michel, Pierre Michel
Michel,
  Joseph Vincent, 2241
  Pierre, 1574, 1985
  Rosalia (Vincent), 2185
  Vincent, 2241
Michiels, Philip F., Rev. Fr., xvii
Mies, Milande (Mme. François Boulet), 357
Miglaane: see McClain
Miguel, Pierre (Pedro), see Michel
Milhet, Marie Marguerite Catherine (Mme. Pierre Rousseau), 1512, 1888, 1895, 1935
Milkain,
  Marie Rebecca, 2232
  Noble, 2232
Millet: see Milhet
Millican: see Milkain
Mills,
  Clay, xvii
  Danny, xvii
  Donna, xvii
  Gary B., Dr., xvii
Milston, Elena (Helen), 1906
Mingui, Françoise: see Mairgay
Miro, Estevan, governor, 1845
Miro y Macarti, Céleste, 1845
Mobile, Alabama, 1027, 1032, 3370
Modern?,
  François, 1569
  Marie Josephe Frozine, 1569, 1980
  Michel, 1571, 1981
  Pierre, 1570, 1982
Modeste (Modesta), 2801
Moguet, Marie Catherine (Mme. Jean Baptiste Langlois), 747
Moine: see Le Moine
Monecuant, François *dit* Beaupre, 769
Monet (vars. Monette, Monnet),
  Claude, 353
  Dorothée, 2326, 2699, 3143-3144, 3218, 3221-3222
  Jean Baptiste Baltasar, 2650, 3219

Monet (continued)
  Louis I, 466, 488, 562, 1067,
    1093, 1464, 1537, 1557, 1615-
    1616, 1649, 1955, 1969, 2017-
    2018, 2064, 2118, 2326, 2404,
    2551-2553, 2580, 2602, 2650,
    2679, 2923-2929, 3142-3145,
    3217-3222, 3236, 3378, 3394
  Louis II, 2404
  Pierre, 1099
  Pierre Mathieu *dit* St. Morice,
    353, 720, 730, 811, 1093
Monette's Ferry (Cane River, La.),
    2928n
Mongeot: see Mongot
Mongino, L., 3407
Monginot,
  François Marie I, 1639, 3046,
    3349
  François Marie II, Dr., 1496,
    1498, 1501, 1518, 1617, 1638,
    1641, 1678, 1926, 1951, 2019,
    2083, 2138, 2180, 2612, 2705,
    2733-2735, 2755, 2830, 3046,
    3125, 3131, 3339, 3342, 3349
Mongot (Mongeot), 557, 634, 695
Monique (Monica), 2305, 2638, 2707,
    2709, 2769, 3161
Monjonan de la Perriere: see la
    Perriere
Monnet: see Monet
Monpierre: see Montpierre
Montaige: see Monteche
Montanary (vars. Montenari, Monte-
    nary),
  Benoist, 1538, 2047, 2207, 2829,
    2846, 3130, 3348, 3403, 3435
  Jean Baptiste, 1538, 3348
  Marie Hélène Pompose, 2047
Montbrun, _____, 727
Monteche (vars. Montaige, Montege,
    Monteje, Montexely, Montez),
  Dominique, 314, 320, 342, 349,
    353, 421, 454, 457-458, 460-
    461, 469, 472, 576, 596, 610,
    616-617, 644, 681, 721, 738-
    739, 745, 747, 752, 886, 897,
    959, 1018, 1021, 1023, 1070,
    1238, 1241, 1281, 1722, 2291,
    2298-2299, 2320, 2376
  Jean, 349, 739

Monterrey, Mexico, 1019
Montes,
  Dominique, 465, 809, 1004; see
    also Dominique Monteche
  Mariann (Widow Dominique Montes),
    465
  Theresia Jacoba, 465
Montpierre (Monpierre), Magdeleine,
    (Mme. Jean Baptiste Bellegarde),
    2820-2821, 2924, 3421
Montreal, Canada, 1089, 1589, 3037,
    3396
Morales,
  Joseph Manuel, 1684, 2088, 2202
  Manuel Athanase, 2202
  Marie Françoise, 1684, 2088
Moreau, Pierre, 2520
Morein, Marie Madeleine (Mme. Ma-
    turin L'Eveque), 734
Morelle, Élisabeth Anne (Mme. An-
    dres David I), 1035
Morien (Morier?), *dit* of Jacques
    Fazende
Morier,
  _____, Mr., 1143, 3340
  Marie (Mme. Pierre Gallien), 721
Morille, Marie Anne (Dna. Simon
    Deragon), 2982
Morin,
  _____, Mr., 1505
  Agnes, 886
  Ines (Ynes), 2338
  Jean Baptiste I, 983
  Jean Baptiste II, 886, 941, 963,
    983, 1078, 1470, 1879, 1891,
    2492; see also Jean Baptiste
    Maurin
  Joseph, 2913
  Juan, 1019
  Maria Francisca (Dna. Joseph
    Villareal), 1019, 1718, 1764
  Marie Jeanne (Mme. Joseph Lau-
    rent), 941, 1078, 1879
  Ynes: see Ines
Morin: see also Maurin
Morine,
  Henry Gilles, 186
  Jean Antoine, 186
Morire, _____, 405
Morire: see also Morier
Moro, Paulle, 563

Moro: see also Moreau
Morphi (Morphil): see Murphy
Morvant,
   Jounne, 2892
   Marie Euphrosine, 2892
Mounoir (Mounion),
   ____, Mme., 3290, 3294
   Henri, 3041
   Michel, 3041
Moville, François, 111
Mulon, François, 3241
Munier: see Meunier
Murphy (vars. Morphi, Morphil),
   Barnaby, 1098, 3021
   Edward, 1098, 1363, 1480, 1595,
     1906, 2004, 2052, 2598, 2696,
     2725-2730, 2758, 2980, 3021,
     3063, 3108, 3116, 3125, 3150,
     3165, 3183, 3185, 3187, 3242,
     3260, 3265, 3280, 3316, 3330,
     3399, 3412, 3420
   Edward César, 2052, 2120, 2970,
     3116, 3265
   Marie Louise Élisabeth Aspasie,
     2120, 3116, 3265
   Marie Françoise Eugenie, 3021

Macdonogh (Magdonogh), Jacques, 71,
   84, 124, 126, 128, 134, 135, 140,
   146-148, 154, 160
McClain (var. Miglaane),
   Françoise Élisabeth, 3022
   Jacques, 3022
   Maurice, 3022

Nacogdoches, Texas, 1231, 1962,
   2892, 3011
Nailloi, Indian, 2245, 3444
Naions, Nicolas: see Nicolas Laignon
Naler (Valer?),
   Christophe, 334
   Marie Jeanne, 334
Nanette (Naneta), 244, 579, 1569-
   1571, 1678, 1980-1982, 2083,
   2364, 2638
Nanette, Indian: see Anne, Indian
Nanthe: see Guedon *dit* Nantois
Nantois, *dit* of Guedon
Narcis, 3223

Nassario, Joseph, 3038
Natchez, Mississippi, 793, 1050,
   2225
Navarre, Robert, 130
Navarre: see also Sanchez Navarro
Nebel?, Genevieve, 1387
Negle,
   Jacques I, 980
   Jacques II, 872, 980
   Jacques Charles, 872
New Orleans, Louisiana, xii, 341,
   745, 749, 991, 1006, 1033, 1041,
   1061, 1078-1079, 1542, 1544, 1659,
   1668, 1930, 1961, 1987, 2047, 2097,
   2176, 3215, 3332, 3348, 3352, 3382,
   3396, 3398
Nicolas, 62, 152, 217, 865, 2148,
   2150-2151, 2308, 2438, 2441, 2454,
   2813-2814, 2915-2916, 3146, 3245,
   3269, 3389
Nicolas: see also Louis Nicolas
Nicolas *dit* Docla, 82, 161
Nicolas Augustin, 2304; see also
   Nicolas Augustin Metoyer
Nicolas Piqueri: see Piqueri
Noel: see Emmanuel, Jean Noel, Man-
   uel
Noguerra (vars. Longuera, Nogueira),
   Domingo, 1053, 1074, 1095
   Juan, 1095
Noir: see Le Noir
Noiyan, ____, 2269
Nolbert: see Jean Pierre Nolbert
Normant, Cécile (Mme. Joseph Marie
   Armant), 1044
Nuerin, Marie (Mme. Jean Baptiste
   David), 1049

Oberin, Rachel (Mrs. Jacob Paul I),
   3387
Ofenogue, Julie, 2879
Ofenogue: see also Huferogue
Old River (Natchitoches Parish, La.),
   2928n
Olivau, Élisabeth, 2212
Olivau: see also Olivo
Olivaut, Marie Anne (Mme. Pierre
   Étienne Charron, 1743
Oliver, Sophie, 3400
Olivier (var. Ollivier),
   Anne (Mme. Jean Lugue), 2896, 2960,

Olivier (continued),
  Marie, 2121, 2189, 2191, 2222, 2259, 2896
  Marie Françoise (Mme. Jean Paul Couty I; Dna. Miguel Ernandez), 1528, 1716, 3005, 3344, 3424
  Michel, 1528, 2309, 2896, 2960, 3344
Olivo (vars. Arllivaux, Arlliveaux, Aullivaux, Aulliveaux, Livo),
  Catherine (Mme. Louis Le Blanc), 1861-1862
  Pierre, 1549, 3354, 3415
  Roselie, 1861
  Sebastien, 1549, 3354, 3415
  Susanne (Mme. Louis Epinette), 1549, 1915, 3354
Olsup, Anne (Mrs. Edmond Querk), 2233
Onil (O'Neal?), Marguerite (Mrs. John Brown), 3373
Onésime, 3182
Onstance: see Constance
Opelousas, Louisiana, 1051, 1101-1103, 1679, 1909, 2015, 3394, 3423, 3453
Opelousas Indians, 3013, 3394
Ortiz,
  Joseph Maria, 1095
  Maria Francisca (Dna. Domingo Noguerra), 1095
Ortholan: see D'Ortolant
Ottemare (Ottemane?),
  David, 2879
  Marie (Mme. Guillaume Jacob Detui), 2879
Ouachita (post in northeast Louisiana), xii, 1861-1862, 2205, 2225-2226, 2241, 2896, 2960, 2990, 3415, 3442
Ouales: see Wallace
Ouin (Ouen), Indian, 2904, 2920

Pabla: see Pauline
Pablo: see Paul
Page, Louise (Mme. Michel Brumot I), 988
Pagnot,
  Antonne, 572
  Marie Antoinite, 572

Pain,
  Daniel, 275, 277, 283, 288, 293, 327, 347, 353, 355, 415, 430, 438, 444?, 457, 493, 526-527, 553, 580, 590, 649, 661, 693, 704, 717, 722, 743, 749, 841, 848, 851, 865, 869, 882, 913, 923, 974, 984, 995, 1003
  François Daniel, 430, 477, 526, 552
  Jean Baptiste Augustin, 974
  Louis, 478, 649, 841
  Marie Adèlaïde Victoire, 704
  Marie Élisabeth Rosalie, 848
  Marie Françoise, 430
  Marie Pelagie, 479, 590, 714, 839, 841, 851, 866, 867, 878, 914, 923, 973-974, 995
Palvados (Palvado),
  Felicité, 2105
  François, 2947, 3379
  Jean, 2105, 2211, 2947, 3379
  Marie Honorine, 2947
  Marie Joseph, 2210
Pantaleon, ____, 3172
Papillault (Papilleau), Charles, 426
Paschal, Marie (Mme. François Goudeau), 175, 178-179, 194
Pascio: see Pescio
Patre, Petronila Ysabelle *dite* Castille (Dna. Juan Joseph de Sta. Cruz), 747, 1045
Paul (Pablo), 1023, 2451, 2682, 2727, 3112, 3299, 3328
Paul (Pablo),
  Jacob I, 3387
  Jacob II, 3387, 3455
Pauline (Pabla, Pablina), 264, 1913, 2600, 2685, 3151
Pavie (var. Pavia),
  ____, Rev. Fr., 3059, 3061, 3325
  Antoine, 1435
  Étienne, 878, 1040, 1044, 1049, 1052, 1071, 1093, 1098, 1103, 1120, 1242, 1284, 1344, 1347-50, 1378, 1482, 1496, 1751, 1763, 1774, 1786, 1822, 1899, 1917, 2445, 2449, 2475, 2477, 2522, 2887, 3141, 3337, 3420
  Jean Baptiste Étienne, 1899, 2669, 2798, 3184, 3256, 3276
  Joseph I, 1052, 1347

Pavie (continued),
  Joseph II, 1052, 2415, 3209, 3215, 3295, 3297
  Marie Josephe, 1786
  Marie Louise Héliene Eufrosine, 1822, 2669, 2796-2797, 2887, 3420
  Pierre, 2887
Pedro: see also Pierre
Pedro, _____, Rev. Fr., 355
Pejobsans (Pejobson): see Robinson
Pelagie (Pelagia), 963, 2308, 2408, 2431, 2443, 2488, 2504, 2523, 2548, 2553, 2605, 2614, 2663, 2740, 2752, 2759, 2769, 2797, 2803, 2805, 3081, 3084-3085, 3118, 3121, 3128, 3162, 3205, 3226, 3247, 3257, 3269, 3280, 3286, 3313, 3321
Peletier, Margueritte (Mme. Michel Gauthier), 339
Pellerin,
  Charles I, 718
  Charles II *dit* La Lime, 718, 1330
Pellerin du Cote, Louis Gerard, 326, 356, 544
Pelona (Pelone), Marie Josephe (Dna. Joseph Christophe Perez), 1597, 3360; see also Pologne
Pennsylvania: 1010, 1068, 2983, 3373
Per _____, Marie Nicole (Dna. André Remis), 1636
Per Domo: see Prudhomme
Pereau (vars. Perau, Perault, Pereaut, Pero, Perot, Perox, Perrau, Perrault, Perro, Perrot) *dit* Vildec (vars. Vildaigre, Vildecque, Vildeque),
  Family, xiv
  François I: see Joseph François
  François II: see Joseph François Barthelemy Pierre
  François III; see François Barthelemy
  François IV, 2161
  François Barthelemy, 541, 1081, 1092, 1483, 1556, 1844, 1918, 1968, 2045, 2110, 2161, 2832, 2989, 3011, 3016, 3263, 3371, 3445, 3449-3450

Perau (continued),
  Jean Baptiste, 1483, 1918
  Jean Chrisostomé I, 690, 1061, 1553, 1659, 1663, 1843, 1887, 1965, 2073, 2210, 2367, 2850-2851, 2979, 3377, 3449
  Jean Chrisostomé II, 2850
  Jean Chrisostomé Faustine, 1887
  Jean Louis Pierre, 2851
  Jeanine Anesie, 2110
  Joseph Aimable, 1663, 2073
  Joseph François, 354
  Joseph François Barthelemie Pierre, 354, 411, 541, 593, 690, 846, 936, 997, 1005, 1031, 1061, 1081, 1092, 2832, 2845-2846, 2850-2851, 2865, 2951, 2968, 2979, 2989, 3016, 3454
  Louis, 2045
  Marie, 2210-2211
  Marie Aimée *fille* Jean Chrisostomé, 2210
  Marie Aimée *fille* François, 2989
  Marie Anne, 416, 2845
  Marie Anne Dorothée (Mme. Jacques Christi), 593, 997, 1591, 1748, 1808, 1844, 1883, 2000, 2219, 2326, 2846, 2865
  Marie Catherine, 1556, 1968
  Marie Catherine Felicité, 1843
  Marie Céleste, 2832
  Marie de l'Incarnation (Mme. Julien Besson), 1031, 1476, 1825, 1916, 2321, 2381, 2846, 2865
  Marie Josephe (Mme. Gaspard Derbanne II), 1081, 1554, 1617, 1808, 1854, 1966, 2019, 2197, 2425, 2845, 2968
  Marie Magdeleine Barthe (Mme. Jean Louis Vascocu), 936, 1881, 2133, 2166, 2219, 2240, 2756, 2951, 3016, 3371
  Marie Modeste, 2979
  Remy, 846, 1553, 1591, 1854, 1965, 2000, 2166, 2187, 2869, 3375, 3390, 3454
  Remy Cazimir, 1553, 1965
  Titis, 3172
Perez,
  Joseph Christophe, 1597, 3360
  Marie de la Concession (Mrs. Richard Symis), 1597, 3360

Perot: see Pereau
Perreault, François *dit* Bellefleur, 361
Perrier, _____, 346
Perrier: see also de la Perriere
Perrine (Perrina),1526, 2549, 2599, 3199
Peruce, 2628
Pescio (Pascio, Pessyo), Benoit, 1613, 1636, 1689, 2092, 2110, 2123, 2651, 3347, 3366, 3369, 3372, 3383
Petit, Anne (Mme. Luc Garein), 723
Peveyna, Maria Nicolas (Dna. Andres Ruis), 3369
Philadelphia, Pennsylvania, 1010, 2983
Philibert (Filibert), Luc Gaspard, 1499, 1655, 1925, 2059
Philippe (Felipe), 2287, 2867
Philippe (Philipelau, Philiplau), Anne Marie (Marthe), (Mme. Jacques Dupre; Mme. Remy Poissot), 21, 49-50, 107, 153, 184, 227, 247, 267, 290, 306, 313, 341, 354, 449, 455, 483, 529, 541, 723, 729-730, 741, 753, 861, 978, 991, 999, 1011, 1271, 2287
Phizot, Françoise (La Garenne), (Mme. Jean Fayart), 252, 272
Phizot: see also Fisot
Phoebe: see Febi
Picard,
    Joseph, 209
    Marianne (Mme. Jacques Botien *dit* St. André), 1589, 2928, 3357
Picquery: see Piquery
Piedferme, *dit* of Leger
Philipot, Teresa: see Filibot, Marie Thérèse
Pierot, 3331
Pierran, 1487
Pierre (Pedro), 12, 46, 65, 89, 101, 106, 137, 163, 166, 237, 261, 266, 344, 371, 384, 434, 513, 620, 908, 1029, 1184, 1910, 2289, 2298, 2300, 2322, 2345, 2373, 2407, 2414, 2421, 2426, 2428, 2442, 2446, 2456, 2458, 2463, 2488, 2509, 2543, 2550, 2554, 2584, 2597, 2620, 2646, 2649, 2661, 2726, 2729, 2732, 2750, 2774-2775, 2779, 2786, 2788, 2792-2793, 2799, 2814, 2922, 3057, 3090, 3108, 3154, 3160, 3183, 3237, 3268, 3280, 3295, 3389
Pierre: see also Jean Pierre, Louis Pierre
Pierre Antoine, 273
Pierre Jean (Pedro Juan), 2351
Pierre Joseph (Pedro Josef), 2320, 2438, 2628, 2634
Pierre Julien, 372
Pierre Michel, Indian, 304
Pierre Noi___, 373
Pierre Prince, 1021, 1022-1023
Pierre Valleri, Indian, 2919, 2922, 3437
Pierre *dit* Guerin, 59, 151, 826
Pierre *dit* Jasmin, 70, 154, 514
Pierre *dit* L'Eveilles, 87, 412?
Pierre *dit* Pierot, 345
Pierrot, 579, 1432; see also Pierot
Pierrot du St. Totin, Étienne *dit*, 102
Pievert,
    François, 1050, 1838, 1859
    Jean Baptiste 1050
    Marie Jeanne, 1859
Pipe, Bernardo, 1070
Piquery,
    _____, Mr., 297
    Jeanne Josephe (Mme. Robert Avard), 19, 109, 119, 180, 223, 236, 242, 262, 264
Piqueri, Nicolas, free man of color, 3389
Piserot (vars. Piseros, Pisserault),
    Jean, 472, 865, 901, 945, 983, 1113
    Jean Pierre, 945
    Jeanne Marie, 472, 952, 1003
Pivert, Perrine (Mme. Philippe La Renaudiere), 15, 52, 93-94, 164, 174, 206
Placide: see Joseph Placide
Plaisance (var. Plaisante),
    Bertrand Isaac, 2969
    Bertrand Pierre, 1788, 2203, 2689, 2883, 2969, 3044, 3406, 3417
    Jean Baptiste I, 1004, 1082, 1756, 2753, 2757, 2883, 2954, 2969, 3404

Plaisance (continued),
  Jean Baptiste II, 1756, 2203
  Louis, 3044
  Marie Lucile (Lucie), 2203, 3288
  Marie Susanne, 2883
  Mathieu, 1004
Plauché (vars. Ploché, Plocher),
  Antoine, 1540, 1622, 1657, 1956, 2024, 2201, 3374
  Étienne Henry, 2201
  Jean Baptiste Balthasar, 1622, 2024
  Jean Placide, 2201
  Louis Célestin, 1540, 1956
  Marie Ecué, 2201
Poeÿ farré, _____, 995
Pointe Blanche, Canada, 3037
Pointe Coupée, Louisiana, 1027, 1030, 1065, 1072, 1097, 1528, 1939, 2126, 3344, 3353-3354, 3402, 3418
Poiret, Marie Françoise Chevailler: see Marie Françoise LeDoux
Poirier (vars. Poiret, Poirié, Poriè, Porret, Poyrie),
  Andres, 1020
  Anne, 2918
  Antoine, 931
  François, 1850
  Guillaume, 456
  Jean Baptiste, 1850, 2225-2226, 2906-2907, 2912-2913, 2918, 3421
  Joseph, Chevalier, 1020, 1702, 1734, 3421
  Marie Françoise, 1734
  Marie Françoise Hélène, 1734
  Marie Joseph, 1702
  Vincent, 456, 931, 1850
Poissot (vars. Poisoi, Poisot, Poisotte, Poissau, Poisseau, Poisson),
  _____, Sieur, 2339, 2358, 2998, 3163, 3191
  Antoine, 2224, 2843, 3002, 3403
  Athanase I, 267, 850, 874, 932, 936, 1011, 1064, 1073, 1077, 1605, 1609, 1637, 1647, 1656, 1697, 1778, 1794, 1823, 1847, 1893, 1961, 1979, 2011, 2060, 2181, 2237, 2380, 2450, 2481, 2487, 2708, 2716-2718, 2731, 2867, 2881, 2887, 3039, 3156, 3165, 3195, 3273, 3363, 3370, 3376, 3385, 3389-3390, 3407, 3420, 3424, 3427-3428, 3433
  Athanase II: see Marie Athanase
  Marie *fille* Remy I, 247, 753, 1073, 2184, 2385
  Marie *fille* Remy II, 2944, 3427
  Marie, identity uncertain, 2834
  Marie (male), 3151
  Marie Agnès (Mme. Nicolas Augustin Metoyer), 1434, 1479, 2130, 2451-2452, 2531, 2897, 2984, 3089, 3179, 3389
  Marie Anne (Mme. Jacob Lambre), 184, 416, 431, 656, 690, 702, 753, 854, 856, 871, 883, 1466, 1471, 1600, 1607, 2013, 2440, 2456, 2466, 2476-2478, 2488, 2502, 2504-2505, 2508, 2511, 2514, 2527-2528, 2577, 2881, 3018-3020, 3249, 3301, 3361, 3380
  Marie Athanase, 1567, 1697, 2844, 2887, 3405, 3420
  Marie Catherine (Mme. Pierre Baillio), 431, 449, 840, 856, 932, 1173, 1609, 1700, 2869, 2889, 3011, 3363
  Marie Céleste, 2224
  Marie Françoise (Mme. Jean Baptiste Brevel II), 227, 408, 411, 449, 455, 874, 902, 968, 1065, 1067, 1077, 1672, 1714, 1756, 1785, 1820, 1857, 2817, 2873, 2902, 2936, 2987-2988, 3001, 3010, 3074, 3384, 3405, 3428, 3453
  Marie Louise Modeste, 1885
  Marie Marcellite, 2867
  Marie Victoire (Mme. Jean Denis Buard), 1767, 2251, 2794, 2830, 2942, 3015, 3242, 3412
  Paul, 1766-1767, 2885, 2974, 3291, 3294, 3432
  Pelagie, 3002
  Pierre (the elder), 290, 394
  Pierre (the younger), 313, 892, 901, 929, 970
  Pierre Etionne, 2887

Poissot (continued; see preceding
page for variations),
  Remy I *dit* Bourguignon, 93, 107,
    153, 184, 206, 227, 247, 267,
    278, 290-291, 306, 313, 341,
    354, 394, 431, 445, 449, 454-
    455, 483, 529, 541, 543, 555,
    607, 666, 669, 697-698, 709,
    717, 723, 740, 746, 753-754,
    755, 846, 861, 896, 901, 928,
    934, 954, 981, 991, 995, 999,
    1004, 1011, 1017-1018, 1031,
    1073, 1077, 1085-1119, 1192,
    1261, 1266, 1271, 1343, 1375,
    1697, 1699, 2287, 2294, 2300,
    2361, 2385, 2429, 2481, 2486,
    2867, 3389
  Remy II, 107, 856, 991, 1017,
    1262, 1492, 1528, 1644, 1766-
    1767, 1885, 2054, 2530, 2536,
    2604, 2615, 2792-2794, 2830,
    2843, 2867, 2944, 2974, 3002,
    3015, 3030, 3119, 3344, 3403,
    3412, 3427, 3432
  Remy (Remi) *fils* Antoine, 2843
  Remy (Remi) *fils* Paul, 2974
  Roque Remy Silvestre, 1823, 2164,
    3117, 3213
  Theotis, 2054
Pologna (Pologne, Polonia), Maria,
  (Dna. Joseph Manuel Morales),
  1684, 2088, 2112, 2202
Pologna (see also Pelona
Pomier (vars. Pomié, Pommier),
  _____, Sr., 1300, 2467, 2523
  Anne Barbe (Mme. Michel Chelette)
    1043, 1054, 1083-1084, 1513,
    1529, 1541, 1582, 1612, 1762,
    1799, 1896, 1936, 1957, 1993,
    2912-2913, 2961, 3345, 3365,
    3393
  Denise, 2833, 3036
  Felicité, 2963
  Jacques, 2963
  Jean I, 1060, 1070, 1481, 1582,
    1664, 1742, 1815, 1993, 2074,
    2171, 2263, 2833, 2963, 3036,
    3409
  Jean II, 1582, 1993
  Louis, 2171
  Marie, 1742, 2493

Pomier (continued),
  Marie Euphrasie (Eufrosine), 1664,
    2074
  Nicolas, 2833
  Pierre, 1060, 2963
Pomiles?, _____, Mr. 1361
Porié: see Poirier
Porret, Jeanne (Mme. Jacques La
  Motte), 3408
Pouillet, Jeanne (Mme. Jean Marchand),
  145
Poupard, Michel (Mme. François Trou-
  part), 736
Poyrie: see Poirier
Pradier, _____, Mr., 569
Prevost (var. Prevot),
  _____, 25
  Anne, 25
  Nicolas I *dit* Colet, 5, 62, 86
  Nicolas II, 86
  Nicole, 86
  Pierre, 86
Prevot de Guarre, Marie Anne, 261
Prevotiere: see Provatiere
Prieto, Juan, 463, 485
Prince, 2611, 3090, 3106; see also
  Pierre Prince
Provatiere (var. Prevotiere),
  Jeanne (Mme. René Gautier), 199,
    622
  Julianne, 622
Provencal, *dit* of Jean Louis Caesar
  Bormé
Prox, Claire (Mme. Jean Antoine Mo-
  rine), 186
Prudhomme (vars. Prud'homme, Per
  Domo),
  _____, 475, 1114, 1160, 1206,
    1209, 1243, 1337, 1912, 2268,
    2270, 2351, 2458, 2489, 2515,
    3055, 3199
  Anne "Nanette" (Mme. Louis Guil-
    haume Dupare), 949, 1643, 1830,
    1878, 1880, 2040, 2418, 2420
  Antoine *fils* Pierre Sebastien,
    536
  Antoine *fils* Jean Baptiste I,
    2181, 2413, 2419, 2423, 2574,
    2593, 2694, 2726, 2773, 2790,
    2799, 2805, 3018, 3020, 3114,
    3138-3139, 3148, 3161-3162,

Prudhomme (continued),
  Antoine *fils* J. B. I (continued),
    3191, 3247, 3251, 3281, 3380,
    3412, 3418, 3433, 3446
  Bastien: see Pierre Sebastien
  Catherina, 471
  Dominique, 897, 2183, 2351,
    2594, 3403
  Emmanuel: see Pierre Emmanuel
  Family, xiii
  François I, 179, 1056, 1101, 1447,
    1510, 1621, 1641, 1683, 1715,
    1791-1792, 1836, 1878, 1951,
    2023, 2087, 2209, 2859
  François II, 1796
  François *fils* Jean Baptiste I,
    1715
  Françoise (Mme. François Barbier),
    207
  Françoise Veronique, 575
  Jacques Sebastien, 1907, 2175,
    3262, 3395
  Jean Baptiste I, Dr., 231, 422,
    583, 599, 642, 683, 714, 737,
    749, 800-801, 868-869, 897,
    949, 1001-1002, 1006, 1023,
    1044, 1056, 1063, 1073, 1103,
    1132, 1244, 1358, 1600, 1715,
    1754, 1826, 2299, 2419, 2881,
    3018-3020, 3361, 3380
  Jean Baptiste II (the elder),
    642, 800
  Jean Baptiste II (the younger),
    714
  Jean Baptiste *fils* Pierre Sebastien, 836, 3444?
  Jean Baptiste *fils* François, 1621,
    2023
  Jean Baptiste (identity uncertain), 2986
  Jean Baptiste, Widow, 1417; see
    also Marie Josephe Françoise
    Charlotte Henriette Corantine
  Jean Jacques, 3018
  Jean Philippe Pierre, 47, 51, 172,
    179, 209, 722, 724-725, 737,
    749, 1056
  Jean Pierre, 676
  Jean Pierre Manuel, 1880
  Jeanne Thérèse (Mrs. William Warden), 566, 868, 870, 958, 971,
    1010

Prudhomme (continued),
  Louis Narcisse, 1551, 1964
  Magdeleine, 700
  Magdeleine Bastien, 2245, 3444
  Marguerite, 629, 791
  Marguerite (Mme. Etienne Ternier),
    3435
  Marguerite Victoire (Mme. Pierre
    Tristant), 51, 420, 629, 647,
    688, 724, 804, 894
  Maria Ana Desirée, 2181
  Marie Célestine Bastien, 1669,
    2077
  Marie Charlotte Modeste, 1641,
    1951
  Marie de la Nieges, 1878
  Marie Eleonore Bastien (Mme.
    Charles Duret), 636, 1497
  Marie Emmanuel Césaire, 1836
  Marie Josephe, 1907
  Marie Louise (Mme. François Rouquier), 422, 1063, 1512, 1580,
    1633, 1643, 1708, 1811, 1826,
    1860, 1935, 1991, 2036, 2040,
    2108, 2135, 2242, 2280, 2349,
    2354, 2355, 2357, 2413, 3019
  Marie Louise Bastien (Mme. François Mercier), 1669, 2077,
    2217, 2858, 3404
  Marie Louise Euphrasie, 1683,
    2087
  Marie Marguerite *fille* Jacques,
    2175
  Marie Marguerite (identity uncertain), 3256, 3262, 3298
  Marie Pompone, 2859
  Marie Thérèse Rosalie, 2209
  Nanette: see Anne
  Narcisse, 2891, 3239
  Pierre: see Jean Philippe Pierre
  Pierre II, 235, 575, 621, 629,
    676, 725, 737, 791
  Pierre Emmanuel, 1063, 1072,
    1353, 1454, 1475, 1497, 1508,
    1551, 1600, 1609, 1727, 1836,
    1860, 1932, 1964, 2049, 2570,
    2576, 2638, 2665, 2777, 2786-
    2787, 2889, 3055, 3120, 3134-
    3136, 3138, 3148, 3246, 3251,
    3254, 3338, 3361, 3412, 3363,
    3380, 3407, 3420, 3433

Prudhomme (continued),
  Pierre Sebastien I, 420, 471,
    566, 636, 700, 722, 836, 1010,
    1345, 2858, 3395, 3404
  Pierre Sebastien II, 420, 2245,
    2858, 3444, 3454
  Susanne "Suzette" (Mme. Remy
    Lambre), 1526, 1600, 1633,
    2036, 2128, 2242, 2549, 2881,
    3020, 3361, 3408
  Susanne *fille* Antoine, 3019
  Thérèse, 1760, 1907, 2377
  Widow, 1367, 1372
Punta Contada: see Pointe Coupée

Quebec, 350, 354, 721, 982 - 983,
  989, 993, 1091, 1497, 3338
Quieri, Pierre, 3242
Qoinquin: see Marie Thérèse *dite*
  Coincoin
Querk,
  Anne Eulalia, 2233
  Edmond, 2233
Quingelte, Jean, 2243

Rabalé (vars. Rabalai, Rabalais, Ra-
    ballé),
  Angélique Domicile, 1685, 2091
  Anne Barbe? (Mme. Joseph Rabalé I),
    3429
  Joseph I, 3429
  Joseph II, 1415, 1494, 1601 (bis),
    1685, 1923, 2008, 2091, 2834,
    3429
  Margueritte, 1601 (bis), 2008
  Marie Jeanne (Anne), 1494, 1923
Rachal (var. Rachalle),
  _____, 1631, 3062
  Adélaïde, 2267
  Antoine, 2214
  Antoine François Marie, 481, 1505,
    1594, 1905, 2003, 2041, 2070,
    2214, 2841, 2923, 2926, 2995-
    2996, 3340
  Antoine Narcisse, 2070
  Athanase, 2817
  Barthelemy I, 460, 482?, 752, 883,
    984, 1094, 1125, 1219, 1226,
    1672, 1708, 1751, 1820, 2291,
    2308, 2350, 2397, 2408, 2817,
    2871, 2891, 2975, 2994, 3001,
    3068, 3384, 3399, 3426, 3439
  Barthelemy II, 933, 1092, 2034,
    2994, 3439
  Barthelemy *fils* Louis I, 603,
    1088, 1099, 1530, 1626, 1900,
    1947, 2030, 2034, 2131, 2838,
    2927, 3008
  Barthelemy (identity uncertain),
    2070, 2255, 2493, 2610, 2817,
    2826, 3205, 3280, 3439
  Barthelemy, Dlle., 1649, 2064,
    1388
  Barthelemy, Mde., 1389
  Barthelemy Ruben, 1530, 1947
  Cyprien, 2936
  Dominique, 1721, 3390
  Dominique Barthelemy, 460, 2134,
    2267, 2395, 2404, 2871, 2975,
    3399, 3411
  Edouard Octave, 2839
  Élisabeth, 1900, 2927, 2937
  Étienne François, 1759, 2250,
    3068
  Felicité, 1810
  François Barthelemy, 3343
  François Célestin, 3008
  François Dorcien, 1626, 2030
  François Isaac, 3001
  Françoise, 2927
  Jacques, 32, 670, 855, 928, 1072,
    1190, 1270, 1589, 1721, 2928,
    3357
  Jacques Remy, 928, 1270
  Jean Baptiste *fils* Antoine, 2841
  Jean Baptiste *fils* Julien, 1849
  Jean Baptiste Barthelemy I, 883,
    1097, 1589, 1672, 1814, 1849,
    1865, 2116, 2131, 2384, 2196,
    2817, 3001, 3062, 3357, 3384
  Jean Baptiste Barthelemy II, 2116
  Jean Joseph, 1624
  Jeanne (Mme. Charles François Le-
    veque; Mme. Rompré; Mme. Jean
    Baptiste Maurin), 180, 583,
    734, 1498, 3339
  Jeanne, *fille* Barthelemy *fils*
    Louis, 2838
  Julien, 419, 1067, 1537, 1653,
    1809, 1905, 1955, 2057, 2182,
    2221, 2936, 2987

Rachal (continued),
  Julien II, 1905
  Louis I, 419, 481, 562, 597, 610,
    682, 703, 727, 843, 870-871,
    948, 1041, 1067, 1088, 1099,
    1423, 1505, 1530, 1589, 1810,
    1900, 1947, 2838-2839, 2841,
    2923, 2927, 2936, 2972, 2987,
    2995, 3008, 3340, 3357, 3372,
    3452
  Louis II *dit* Rat, 682, 1067,
    1089, 1099, 1444, 1501, 1555,
    1624, 1813, 1926, 1967, 2138,
    2252, 2839, 2972, 3152, 3452
  Louis *fils* Antoine, 2923
  Louis *fils* Julien, 1537, 1955
  Louis *fils* Louis Barthelemy, 1631,
    2034
  Louis (identity uncertain), 2477,
    2622, 2995, 3098, 3143, 3204,
    3266, 3270, 3426, 3430
  Louis Barthelemy, 716, 1066, 1087,
    1094, 1096, 1495, 1579, 1590,
    1631, 1672, 1924, 1990, 2134,
    2195, 2399, 2891, 3268, 3358,
    3384
  Louis Gerome, 2975
  Louis Joseph Bernard, 2839
  Manuel, 2995
  Manuel Barthelemy, 2196, 2267,
    2607, 2699, 3426, 3441
  Manuel Hilaire, 2196
  Maria del Pilar, 2157
  Marie *fille* Jacques (Mme. André
    St. André), 1589, 1615, 2017,
    2250-2251, 2928, 3357
  Marie *fille* Louis (Dna. Joseph
    Gabriel Torres), 948, 2157,
    2199, 3372
  Marie (identity uncertain), 2516,
    2530, 2923, 3097
  Marie Adèlaïde, 2972
  Marie Agathe, 2195
  Marie Aimée, 2267
  Marie Anne, 2221
  Marie Élisabeth, 246, 257, 275,
    314, 353, 518, 623, 625, 745,
    1093
  Marie Euphrosine, 1579, 1990
  Marie Françoise Artemise, 2134
  Marie Françoise Barthelemy (Mme.
    Louis Derbanne), 1576, 1987,
    2131, 2134, 2173, 2183, 2196,
    2204, 2250, 2607, 2610, 2975,
    3151, 3426
  Marie Jeanne, 482
  Marie Josephe Eufrosine, 2138
  Marie Joseph François, 1501, 1926
  Marie Lolitte, 1653, 2057
  Marie Louise (Mme. Pierre Noel
    Gallien; Mme. Jean Baptiste
    Alexis Cloutier; Mme. Pierre
    Charpentier), 78, 721, 1041,
    1072, 1089, 1097, 1546, 2372,
    2427, 2848, 2931, 2947, 2986,
    3353, 3378, 3419
  Marie Louise *fille* Louis, 843,
    1495, 1882, 1924, 3204
  Marie Luce (Louise), 1786, 1924,
    3117
  Marie Mélanie, 1555, 1967
  Marie Olive, 2994
  Marie Ozite (Ausite), 2182
  Marie Suzanne, 2871
  Narcisse, 2891
  Noël, 3399
  Pierre *dit* St. Denis, 6, 32, 78,
    82, 103, 180, 353, 389, 518,
    721, 727, 734, 745, 752, 793
  Pierre *fils* Barthelemy, 1708
  Pierre *fils* Julien, 2987
  Remy, 2131
  Silvestre, 1594, 2003
  Simeon, 2199, 2923, 3222, 3452
  Thérèse, 855
Rachalli, _____, 1384
Raimond: see Raymond
Raimond, Catherine: see Catherine
  Raimond Bardon
Rambin (var. Rambint),
  _____ Dame or Widow, 1621, 2023,
    2071, 3396, 3400
  _____, Sr., 2353, 2453, 2566,
    3192, 3211, 3304
  Adèlaïde: see Marie Françoise
    Adèlaïde
  André *fils* Michel (the elder),
    2213
  André *fils* Michel (the younger),
    2991
  André Antoine I, 414, 417, 456,
    563, 604, 606, 633, 684, 710,

Rambin (continued),
  André Antoine I (continued), 723,
    725, 741, 745, 873, 965, 980,
    982, 1003, 1007, 1024-1025,
    1032-1033, 1039, 1052, 1056,
    1069, 1688, 2859, 2899, 2991,
    3067, 3386, 3388
  André Antoine II, 1033, 1090,
    1098, 1101, 1381, 1398, 1536,
    1549, 1552, 1634, 1639, 1686,
    1733, 1769, 1797, 1839, 1901,
    1954, 2051, 2089, 2213, 2215,
    2296, 2335, 2397, 2653, 2655,
    2759, 2778, 2782, 2797, 2983,
    3164, 3259, 3302, 3349, 3354-
    3355, 3400, 3411-3413, 3415,
    3419
  Euphrasie: see Marie Louise Euphrasie
  François: see Jean François
  François Augustin, 1536, 1954,
    2759
  Jean Baptiste *fils* André Antoine
    I, 684
  Jean Baptiste *fils* André Antoine
    II, 1839
  Jean Baptiste Azenor, 2899
  Jean Baptiste Denis, 1686, 2089
  Jean Baptiste François, 633, 1032,
    1069, 1497, 1538, 1568, 1668,
    1688, 1707, 1733, 1878, 2048,
    2453, 2525, 2616, 2678, 3298,
    3338, 3348, 3356, 3370, 3379,
    3382, 3386-3388, 3455
  Louis André, 1769, 3204
  Louise, 1807, 2388, 2419
  Louise Rose, 2353
  Marie, 833, 2124
  Marie Antoinette Barbe, 439
  Marie Barbe (Mme. François Prudhomme), 1683, 1769, 1796, 1836,
    1878, 1951, 2023, 2087, 2209,
    2335, 2351, 2356, 2859
  Marie Françoise Adélaïde, 1797,
    2198, 2598, 2654, 2704, 2726,
    2759, 2782, 2870, 2946, 2983,
    3121, 3126, 3155, 3174, 3213
  Marie Joseph, 563
  Marie Louise Euphrasie (Euphrosine),
    1602, 1683, 1773, 1822, 2009,
    2087, 2246, 2556, 2653, 2655,
    2428, 2798, 2831, 2966, 2978,
    3022, 3089, 3194, 3405
  Marie Thérèse Ozite, 1901
  Michel Antoine, 873, 1602, 1621,
    1688, 1901, 2009, 2023, 2124,
    2213, 2265, 2899, 2991, 3386,
    3413
  Michel Laurent, 2124
  Pierre Hipolite, 2265
  Rosalie (Mme. Jacques Le Vasseur),
    1069, 1085, 1334, 1836, 1839
  Théodore, 965
Raminez, Pedro, Rev. Fr., 731
Ramis,
  _____, Mr., 2651, 3099
  Antonio, 1534, 3347
  Pedro, 1534, 1613, 1636, 2042,
    2055, 3347, 3366
Raphael, 2581, 3208
Rapides, post of (Louisiana), xii,
  984, 1824, 2247, 2495, 2516-2518,
  2737, 2861, 2889, 3421
Rassé,
  Joseph, 2895
  Marie Manuel (Mme. Nicolas du
    Roque), 2895
Rat, *dit* of Louis Rachal II
Raymond,
  Louis, 1016, 1042
  Madeleine (Mme. André Vascocu),
    1101, 1535, 1619, 1953, 2021,
    2161, 2220, 2297, 2842, 2901
  Pierre, 1016, 1042, 1101, 2901
Raymond: see also Raimond
Raymundo, Juan Bautista Antonio Garcia, 2437
Reaubliu, Marianne: see Marianne
  Daublin
Red River, 2928n
Reggio: see de Reggio
Regis, 2686
Regnaudiere: see La Renaudiere
Reinevint?, Pedro, 167
Remigio: see Remy
Remis,
  Andre, 1636
  Salvador, 1636
Remond, Aviette (Dna. Ignace de la
  Gase), 740
Remond: see also Raymond
Remy (Remis, Remigio), 2362, 2375,
  2466, 3168, 3217
Remy *dit* Joli Coeur, 93, 164

Renau,
    ———, 3095
    Jean, 3087
Renaud,
    Jean Baptiste *dit* de Rosier, 334
    Nicolas, 1913
Renaudiere: see La Renaudiere
Renauld, Louis: see Renaux, Louis
Renauld, Nicolas *dit* La Vidette, 367
Renaux, Louis, 234
René: see Louis Jacques René
Renoy (var. Renoi),
    Bernard, 1516, 1938
    Joseph, 1516, 1564, 1938, 1976
    Joseph André, 1564, 1976
Reobleau: see Robleau
Rescua, 2517-2518
Retint (Rutin), Jeanne, (Mme. Jean Brosset), 1040, 2877
Reyes: see de los Reyes
Riber, Marie (Mrs. Ridechelle Warden), 1010
Richard,(var. Richart),
    Isabeau (Mme. François Manne I), 148
    Marie (Widow Jacob Detuil), 3058, 3060
    Maria de la Conception (Dna. Mestre? Richard), 2042
    Marie Hortense, 2042
    Mestre?, 2042
Riché (vars. Richer, Richet),
    Antoine, 942, 1221
    Baptiste, 3180
    Baptiste, Mme. 3146, 3303
    Emmanuelle (Mme. Jean Baptiste Gonin; Mme. Guillaume Lestage), 318, 887, 942, 985, 1025, 1084, 1490, 1603, 1651, 1719, 1755, 1799, 1868, 1921, 2010, 2101, 2878, 2956, 3003, 3042, 3183, 3198, 3374, 3440
    Henri, 226, 242, 293, 318, 395, 404, 456, 717, 985, 1025
    Jean, 717, 828
    Jeanne Joseph, 242
    Marie, 715, 887, 926
    Marianne (Mme. Pierre Olivo), 1550, 3354, 3415
    Marie Jeanne (Mme. Vincent Poirier), 293, 395, 418, 456, 706, 931, 1850

Riché (continued),
    Marie Louise (Mme. Louis Augustin Langlois), 1717, 2893, 3418
    Pierre Henry, 226, 364
Riche: see also Jean-Ris
Ridé, Jacques *dit* La Belle Fleur, 1016, 1204, 1724
Riese: see Jean-Ris
Riotaur (vars. Rioteau, Rioter, Riotor, Riotord), *dit* of Dupain
Riovoiranne, Françoise (Mme. Jean Lattier), 981
Ris: see Jean-Ris
Rivière: see de la Rivière
Rivière aux Cannes, settlement on Red River, 984, 2928n, 2934n
Rivoire, Laurent, 652
Robard, *dite* of Marie Françoise La Claire
Robequi, Lorenzo, 3372
Robert: see Robert Avard and Louis Robert
Robert,
    Anne "Nanette" (Mme. Michel Olivier), 1528, 2896, 2950
    Jeanne (Mme. Louis Robert), 1854
    Jeanne: see Jeanne Avard
    Louis, 1854
    Minanette?: see Anne "Nanette"
    Remy, 1854
Robin,
    Anne, 2200
    François, 1882, 3004
    Marie, 1578, 1618, 1989, 2020, 2216, 2253
    Marie Anne "Nanette" (Mme. Pierre Beaudouin), 1484, 1563, 1596, 1618, 1654, 1682, 1919, 1975, 2020, 2058, 2086, 2216, 2218, 2840, 2930, 3359
    Marie Rose, 3231, 3236, 3238, 3391
    Michel I, 999, 1053
    Michel II, 999, 1053, 1596, 1882, 2520-2521, 2840, 2930, 3359, 3391
    Nanette: see Marie Anne
Robinson (vars. Pejobsans, Pejobson),
    André David, 1661, 207
    Elie Martie, 1625, 1661, 2027-2029
    Jean Baptiste, 1625, 2029
    James Isaac, 1625, 2027
    William, 1625, 2028

Roblat: see de Roblat
Robleau (vars. Reobleau, Roblau, Roubleau, Roublet, Roublot),
 Antonio, 1828
 Guillermo, 1636, 1744, 1788, 1828, 3369, 3397, 3444
 Helena (Mme. Michel Vincent), 1744, 2132, 2185, 2241, 3168, 3397
 Maria Isidora, 1788
 Maria Ignacia (Dna. Salvador Ruis), 3369
 Miguel, 1147, 1268
 Miguel, Dna., 1147
 Pedro, 2185, 3444
Roc (Rock), 2763, 3157, 3289
Roc: see also Rocque, Roque
Roche, Parthe (Mrs. Charles Tompson), 3022
Roche: see also La Roche
Rocque, _____, Sr., 1182
Rodriguez (vars. Rodrigue, Rodrigues),
 André, 3027
 Angélique (Mme. Pierre Crete I), 982
 Antoine *dit* Pagnau, 167
 François, 3027
 Jeanne (Anne) de Dieu (de Dios), (Dna. Coulas de Sta. Theresia; Dna. François Dominique Laybe; Dna. Joseph Seyena); 34?, 146, 545, 650, 733
Roi: see Le Roy, de los Reyes
Roi,
 François, 2955
 Thérèse (Mme. Jean Baptiste Derbanne), 3453
Romaine (Romano), 2276
Romaine Antoine *dit* Souris?, 210
Romero, _____, Rev. Fr., 984
Rompré, _____, Mr., 1498
Romual, 3146
Rondain (vars. Rondan, Rondin, Rondien),
 Clemence, 847
 Dominique François, 461
 Emmanuel, 1
 François, 232
 Jeanne (the elder), 79, 139
 Jeanne (the younger), 288, 402
 Julien I, 147

Rondain (continued),
 Julien II, 1, 79, 92, 109, 139, 147, 175, 199, 212, 217, 232, 236, 276, 280, 288, 298, 339, 350, 352-353, 391, 529, 537, 601, 719, 722, 727, 729, 799, 988, 1046
 Julien III, 601
 Louis I, 461, 501, 537, 591, 622, 692, 740, 847, 891,
 Louis II (the elder), 692
 Louis II (the younger), 891
 Marie (Mme. Michel Brumot II; Mme. Antoine Le Noir), 537, 988, 1046, 1511, 1674, 1934
 Marie Jeanne, 199, 360
Rondau, Marie (Mme. Chaniau), 145
Rondeau,
 Adrienne (Mme. Nicolas Bordelon), 2941, 3402
 Cécile (Mme. Pierre Le Doux), 1027
Ronne (Rouvieres?), Anne (Mme. Joseph Bormé), 356, 1380
Roque, Élisé, 3389
Roque, see also du Roque, Rock
Rosalie (Rosalia), 2343, 2505, 2637, 2640, 2651, 2656, 2863, 3100, 3110, 3170, 3241, 3330, 3394
Rosalie: see also Françoise Rosalie, Marie Genevieve Rosalie
Rosalie Hyacinthe (Rosalia Jacinta), 2417
Rose (Rosa), 900, 2315, 2477, 2756, 2806, 2810, 3319
Rose: see also Anne Rose
Rose, Anne (Mme. Jean Baptiste Hubert), 1015
Rosee, Marguerite (Mrs. George Hoopock), 1544, 3352
Rosette, 3160, 3324, 3333
Roubleau: see Robleau
Rougere, Marie Genevieve (Mme. Pierre Gagnon I), 1091
Roujot (vars. Rougeau, Rougeot),
 François, 526
 Jean Baptiste, 661, 663, 974, 1001, 1012, 1020, 1027, 1063, 1071, 1085, 1089, 1091, 1110, 1707, 1724, 2471
 Margarita (Mme. François Le Doux), 1027, 1725, 1763

Roujot (continued),
  Marie Jeanne (Mme. Daniel Pain), 292-293, 308, 430, 438, 526, 580, 599, 634, 649, 661, 676, 693, 695, 704, 848, 875, 973, 974, 995
  Modeste, 2278, 2333
Roujot: see also Rousseau
Rouleau, Charlotte (Mme. Jean Baptiste Hubardeau I), 459
Roupre: see Rougere
Rouquier (vars. Rouquer, Rouquié, Rouquire),
  _____, 3028
  François, 1063, 1073, 1093, 1463, 1512, 1518, 1551, 1600, 1633, 1807, 1826, 1939, 1964, 2036, 2128, 2135, 2209, 2607, 2668-2669, 2673-2674, 2683, 2685, 2810, 2832, 2896, 2972, 3015, 3019, 3028, 3120, 3160, 3193, 3202, 3215-3216, 3252, 3281, 3283, 3287, 3297, 3319, 3324, 3329, 3331-3333, 3342, 3361, 3380, 3407, 3436, 3445; 1860
  Jean François Marie (Marin), 1826, 2135, 2701, 2949, 3065, 3411-3412
  Marc,(Mars), 1063, 3407
  Marcellite, 2949, 3065
  Marguerite, 1909
  Marie (Mme. Marc Rouquier), 1063, 1362
  Marie fille François, 1860, 2874, 2986, 3008
  Marie Aimée, 2989
  Marie Anne, 1512, 1935, 2701, 3124
  Marie Josephe, 1633, 2036, 3286
  Marie Josephe Henriette, 2135
Rousseau (vars. Rousau, Rousaux, Rouseau, Rousot, Roussau, Roussot),
  Gabriel, 2235
  Louis, 169
  Marie Anne (Mme. Gabriel Buard), 15, 66, 113, 169, 176, 239, 299, 328, 335, 453, 467, 549, 591, 593, 608, 641, 657, 664, 702, 888, 1018, 1033, 1052, 1098, 1111, 1222, 1235, 1246, 1277, 1311, 1451, 1453, 1488, 1552, 1639, 1686, 2089, 2292, 2296, 2317, 2328, 2364, 2369, 2388, 2432, 2434, 2476, 2493, 2534, 2546-2547, 2563, 2578, 2588-2589, 2636, 2645, 2655, 2830, 2944, 3015, 3021, 3337, 3349, 3355, 3407, 3411-3412, 3427
  Marie Hortense Anasthasie, 1888
  Nicolas, 1888
  Pierre Jorge, 1103, 1486-1487, 1500, 1512, 1888, 1895, 1935, 2554
Rousseau: see also Roujot
Rouvieres?, Anne: see Anne Ronne
Roy, Antoine, 780
Roy: see also Roi, Le Roy
Rubei, _____, Sgt., 510
Ruis,
  Andres, 3369
  Barbara Victoria, 712
  François, 712
  Salvador, 3369
Russ,
  Isecaie (Hezekiah), 2980
  Tebité (Tabitha), (Mme. Abraham Vileret), 2980
Rutin: see Retint
Ryse: see Jean-Ris
Ryse, Bernardo, 2358

Saboye, Juan Bautista, 1095
Saccalé, Indian, 2911
Saidek (vars. Aedek, Saidec, Saidet, Saydek, Seideik),
  Eleonore Clavis, 1911
  Jean Baptiste, 2044
  Louis, 2118
  Marie Élisabeth, 1595, 2004
  Marie Françoise Clavis, 1790
  Marie Louise Clavis (Mrs. Christopher Teal), 1776, 2970-2971
  Marie Rose Clavis (Mrs. James Teal), 1815, 2945
  Pierre Clavis I, 1595, 1776, 1790, 1815, 1863, 1911, 2004, 2044, 2118, 2945, 2970-2971
  Pierre Clavis II, 1863
  Reine Pierre Clavis, 3086, 3112
St. Agnette, Chevalier de: see Guillaume Chever
St. Amand: see Derancourt de St. Amand
Saint Amour, Marie (Mme. Joseph Charpentier), 1089

St. André,
    André, 1589, 1615, 2017, 2250-2251, 2928, 3357
    Jacques Botien *dit*, 1589, 2928, 3357
    Jacques II, 2928
    Marie Adrienne, 1615, 2017
    Marie Louise Osite, 2928
    Marie Victoire, 2251
    Onésime, 2250
St. Anne, Jean Joseph, 1613, 3366
St. Anne: see also Ailhaud Ste. Anne
St. Augustine (parish on Isle Brevelle, Natchitoches), 2623
St. Charles (parish on German Coast of Louisiana), 1054, 1083, 1612, 1638, 1658, 2167, 3364, 3375
St. Cire, 3056, 3142
St. Croix: see Sta. Cruz
St. Denis, *dit* of Pierre and Jacques Rachal
St. Denis (St. Denys): see also de St. Denis
St. Geme: see Ste. Geme
St. Germaine,
    Charles Étienne, 1629, 2032
    Élisabeth: see Élisabeth La Forré
    Louis, 1628-1629, 2031-2032
    Louis Joseph, 1628, 2031
    Marie Louise, 2205
St. John the Baptist (parish on German Coast), 1930, 1974, 3364
St. Louis des Caddodoches, xii; see also Caddo
St. Marcel, ____, Mr., 3213
St. Morice, *dit* of Mathieu Monet
St. Nicolas, *dit* of Nicolas Paul Bourdelle
St. Onge, *dit* of Guillaume Bergereau
St. Pierre (parish on German Coast of Louisiana), 249
St. Prix, *dit* of Davion
Ste. Anne: see Ailhaud Ste. Anne
Ste. Anne (parish in Canada), 734
Ste. Geme,
    Joseph, 1506, 1930
    Marie (Mme. Jean Baptiste Bossié), 1506, 1930
Ste. Genevieve, Illinois region, 1070, 1671, 3383
Saintpris: see Davion *dit* St. Prix

Sali, 3248
Saltillis (Saltillo), Mexico, 744
Salvage,
    Luis, Indian, 1710
    Catalina, Indian, 1710
Salvant (var. Salvan),
    Catherine (Mme. Étienne Duchet), 1659, 2159, 3377
    Jean, 1061, 1542, 1544, 1659, 2850-2851, 2948, 2979, 3352, 3377, 3419
    Marie (Mme. Jean Pierre Cloutier), 2948, 3419
    Marie (Mrs. Jacob Hooppock), 1542, 1544, 1605, 1630, 2011, 2159, 2850, 3352
    Marie Louise Margueritte (Mme. Jean Chrisostomé Pereau), 1061, 1553, 1663, 1843, 1887, 1965, 2033, 2073, 2210, 2384, 2401, 2647, 2850-2851, 2979
    Marie Louise, 2382
Samuel, Jean Baptiste *dit* Leonet or Lionnois, 444, 2332, 3049
Samuel, Marie Blac, 3049
San Antonio de Bexar, Texas, 1500, 1597
San Fernand, Texas, 1500
San Luis de la Passe, Mexico, 1636, 3369
Sanchez (vars. Sanche, Sanches, Senches),
    Emmanuela Maria Stephania Sanchez Navarro (Mme. Louis Antoine Juchereau de St. Denis), 1, 7, 16, 20, 23, 31, 60, 72-73, 108, 193, 202, 244, 253, 266, 269, 271, 273, 279, 287, 295, 304, 347, 355, 371-372, 376, 383-384, 392, 523, 528, 531, 538, 544, 565, 569, 574, 576, 579, 592, 611, 616, 624, 731, 758, 761, 763, 787, 789, 817, 820
    Joseph, 677
    Margarita, 2135
    Maria Antonia (Dna. Diego Antonio Baca), 1759
    Philipe, 1128
Saneta Crux: see Sta. Cruz
Sans Cartier, Thomas *dit*, 92
Sans Fason, *dit* of Jean Baptiste Malbert

Sans Quartier, Indian, 214
Sans Regret, *dit* of François Langlois
Santa Maria, port of, 3344
Sta. Cruz (vars. Croix, Croux, Crux, de la Creoz, de la Croix, de la Sta. Crux, de Sta. Crux, Saint Croix, St. Croix, Saneta Crux, Santa Crouse, Santa Crux, Sta. Croix),
  Juan Joseph, 747
  Juan Maria, 2172, 2870
  Juan Pedro, 2172
  Justine Adèlaide, 2870
  Maria Matilda, 1689, 2092
  Maria Michaela Roselia (Dna. Laurens Bodin), 893, 955, 1053, 1064, 1749, 1809, 2231, 2519, 2521, 2854, 2876, 3362
  Maria de l'Incarnation (Dna. Francisco Castro), 618, 675
  Maria Gregoria (Mme. François Langlois; Mme. Pierre Duplessis), 712, 747, 877, 964, 1045, 1534, 1613, 1703, 3004, 3347, 3366
  Pierre, 2870
Sta. Theresia, Marie Antoinette Rodrigue, 650
Sta. Theresia: see also Coulas
Santiago, 1181, 2260
Santiago: see Jacques also
Sarpy, Jean Silvestre, 2135
Saurelle: see Sorelle
Sautau: see de Soto
Sauterelle, *dit* of Marin Grillet
Sauvage,
  Joseph, 1505, 3340
  Marie Catherine (Antony) Bernard, (Mme. Philippe Frederic I), 1054, 1083, 1550, 1612, 1658, 1753, 1798, 1832, 1963, 2094, 2129, 2853, 2884, 2958, 2962, 3365, 3375, 3422, 3438
Savari (Sencais?), Josephe (Mrs. John Horn I), 1604, 3362
Savarin, Marie Louise (Mme. Pierre Lefevre), 2955
Savouie, Jean Baptiste; 3456; see also Saboye
Saydek: see Saidek
Schelet (Schelettre): see Chelette
Schever: see Chever

Sebastien (Bastien), 2272, 2501-2502, 2544, 2585, 2600, 2659, 2671, 2710
Sebastien: see also Louis Sebastien
Sebles, Francisco: see Febles
Seideik: see Saidek
Selinas?, Juana Isabel (Dna. Juan Morin), 1019
Sencais (Savari?), Josephe (Mrs. John Horn I), 1604
Senecal, Marie Louise (Mme. Basile Duchet), 1659, 3377
Seperda: see de Zepeda
Sévèrin: see Alexandre Sévèrin
Seyena,
  Joseph, 733
  Manuella (Dna. Manuel y Varvo), 733
Shreveport, Louisiana, xii
Sierra, Pedro, 159
Silvin (Silvano), 2290, 3224
Silvestre, 2677, 3099, 3123
Silvestre: see also Gregoire Silvestre
Sioucheppe, Honnorée (Mme. François Visiant), 998
Smith, Nicolas, 3053
Soles (Soulé), Theresa (Dna. Luis Thomassino I), 1075, 2875, 2981
Solis, François Antoine, 860, 877
Solomon, Indian, 2149
Sompoy? (St. Prix?), Manuel, 1647
Sophie (Sophia), 2563, 2609, 2702, 2799, 3161
Sorel (vars. de Sorel, Saurelle, Sorelle) *dit* Marli (Marly, Marlie),
  Dominique, 2240, 2264
  François Antoine, 470
  Jean Baptiste, 735
  Louis, 1688
  Luc, 1634, 2117, 3350, 3368, 3414
  Marguerite, 696, 1178
  Marie Genevieve (Mme. Jean Baptiste Grappe), 857, 1543, 1564, 1660, 1958, 1976, 2000, 2068, 2264, 2474, 2616, 2691, 2738, 2939-2940, 3351, 3395, 3414
  Marie Jeanne (Mme. Augustin Fredieu), 911, 1553, 1634, 1660, 1965, 2043, 2068, 2117, 2236, 2240, 2264, 2433, 2472, 2601, 2836, 2963, 2997, 3045, 3368

Sorel (continued),
  Marie Stéphanie, 645
  Pierre Joseph, 412?, 427, 645, 696,
    735, 857, 911, 988, 1074, 1178,
    1310, 1329, 1395, 1448, 1546,
    1597, 1634, 1640, 2470, 2836,
    2937-2940, 2997, 3360, 3368, 3414
  Pierre II, 1329
Sotho: see de Soto
Soulé: see Soles
Souris, *dit* of Romaine Antoine
Stanislas, _____, Rev. Fr., 995
Stanislas, 1492, 2536
Stasie: see Anastasie
Strase,
  _____, 412
  Jeanne, 412
  Marie, 412
Susana: see Susanne
Susanne (Susana, Susanna), 98, 285,
  351, 600, 950, 954, 958, 1465,
  2190, 2280, 2292, 2507, 2603,
  2621, 2626, 2629, 2734, 2737,
  740, 2804, 2822, 2910, 3092,
  3098, 3149-3150, 3152, 3205,
  3207, 3221, 3256, 3265, 3268,
  3283, 3303
Symis,
  John, 1597, 3360
  Richard, 1597, 3360

Taborda, Madelena (Dna. Juan No-
  guerra), 1095
Tampson: see Tompson
Tapaltaque (dependency of Nacog-
  doches), 2892
Tauré: see Torres
Tauzin (vars. Tausin, Toisin, Tozin),
  _____, 3070
  Adélaide, 2178, 3012, 3140
  Euphrasie Catherinne, 2831
  Gerard, 1668, 2831, 2886, 3012,
    3382
  Henri Evariste?, 2886
  Joseph, 1607, 1668, 2013, 2100,
    2178, 2235, 2257, 2688, 2831,
    2886, 3012, 3140, 3270, 3370,
    3382, 3395, 3400, 3436, 3443
  Louis Eugene, 3012
  Louis Joseph, 2100, 3012, 3164

Tauzin (continued),
  Victoire Matilde, 2235
Teal (vars. Teel, Tiel),
  Celeste Rebeca (Mrs. Zachary Mar-
    tin), 2107-2109, 2243
  Christopher I, 2107, 2970-2971
  Christopher II, 2970
  Edward, 2945, 2970-2971, 3373
  James (Jacques), 2109, 2945
  James (Jacques) II, 2945
  Jean Baptiste, 2971
  Marie (Mrs. Thomas Brown), 1675,
    2080, 3373
Teal: see also Deil, Tille
Tenant?, _____, 1170
Teresa: see Thérèse
Ternier (vars. Ternié, Thernié,
    Thernier),
  Étienne 3435
  Pierre *dit* Grenoble, 1683, 2667,
    3107, 3147, 3178, 3244, 3410,
    3435, 3444, 3454
Terpuÿ: see de Terrepuy
Terri____, Marie Magdeleine (Mme.
  Jacques Le Saussaye?), 908
Tessier (vars. Teissier, Tessié,
    Texier),
  Auger, 3379
  Eleonora (Mme. Jean Palvados),
    2105, 2211, 2947, 3379
  Jean Baptiste, 2008, 2211, 2933
  Joseph, 2105, 2186
  Pierre, 2211, 2947, 3379
Tete Platte, la, Indian, 781
Texier: see Tessier
Thawrete?, Anne Louise (Dna. Joseph
  Michel de la Sert), 660
Theincour: see Delincour
Théodore Antoine, 919
Theotise, 3219
Theré?, Marie Thérèse (Mme. Pierre
  du Pain), 743
Thérèse (Teresa Theresa), 36, 344,
  415, 462, 631, 868, 870, 935,
  938, 958, 962, 1022, 1055, 1125,
  2277, 2288, 2297, 2318, 2322,
  2325, 2357, 2363, 2367, 2370,
  2372, 2392, 2403, 2427, 2446-
  2447, 2450, 2452, 2494, 2529,
  2552, 2596, 2673, 2767, 2773,
  2775, 2992, 3094, 3130, 3152,
  3172, 3197, 3255, 3448

Thérèse: see also Genevieve Thérèse
Thierry (vars. Gueri, Tierri),
  Antoine, 2884, 2958, 3422
  Jean Pierre Basil, 2958
  Marie des Anges, 2884
  Pierre, 2884, 2958, 3422
Thili, Marie Jeanne: see Marie Jeanne Thili Materne
Thily, Marguerite (Mme. Thomas Leger), 249
Thilibou: see Filibot
Thomas, 2147, 2149, 2154-2155, 2902
Thomas: see also François Thomas, Louis Thomas
Thomas, _____ dit La Croix, 788
Thomas dit Sans Cartier, 92
Thomas, Edmond dit Jourdan, 306, 322
Thomas, Marie, 311, 322
Thomassine (vars. Thomasino, Thomassino, Tomacine, Tomassin, Tomassino, Tomazin, Toumasin),
  Catherine Ann, 1484, 1919
  Césaire, 2875
  Joseph Jerome, 2981
  Luis I, 1075, 2875, 2981
  Luis II, 1075, 1416, 1484, 1578, 1644, 1897, 1919, 1989, 2053, 2121, 2230, 2875, 2981, 3375, 3393
  Louis Gabriel, 2230
  Louis Joseph, 1416, 1867
  Marie Pelagie, 2053
  Marie Reine, 2121
  Thérèse Ozite, 1578, 1989, 2981
Thompson: see Tomcin, Tompson
Tibau: see Filibot
Tibot, Nicolas, 1701
Tibot: see also Filibot
Tierri: see Thierry
Tille, Marie, 2232
Tille: see also Teal
Tinsa: see Antoine Tinsa
Todos Santos: see Toussaint
Toisse, 99
Tomacine: see Thomassine, Tomcin, Thompson
Tomassino: see Thomassine
Tomcin,
  _____, 2225
  Jean, 2225

Tomcin: see also Tompson, Thomassine
Tompson (var. Tampson),
  Charles, 1837, 3022
  Joseph Nicolas, 1837
  Marthe (Mrs. Jacques McClain), 3022
Tonant, _____, 1170
Tonau, dit of François Hugues
Torres (vars. de Torres, Tauré, Torre),
  Joseph Corretant), 1558, 1713, 1750, 1970, 2864, 2870, 2874, 3005, 3200, 3372, 3424, 3447
  Joseph Gabriel, 2199, 3372
  Maria Anna (Dna. Maria Juan Sta. Cruz), 2172, 2870
  Maria Antonia, 1558, 1970
  Marianne, 2895
  Maria de l'Assomption (Mme. Jean Baptiste Valeri Varangue), 3447
  Maria Felicidad, 2199, 3201
  Maria Josepha (Mme. Jean Paul Couty), 2157, 2874, 3424
  Maria Juliana Sention (de l'Ascension), 1750
  Maria Paula de los Dolores (Dna. Maireced? Acosta), 1713, 2865, 3050
Torres: see also de Torres
Totain (Totin): see Toutin
Tottan, Marguerite (Mme. Jean Baptiste Montanary), 1538, 3348
Touaa, Indian, 2914-2918
Touline, _____, Mr., 286
Toups (var. Tups),
  Jean Louis, 842
  Marie Barbe (Mme. Antoine Jean Vascocu), 842, 914, 1101, 1232, 1568, 1657, 1667, 1706-1707, 2842, 2878, 2901, 2951, 3016, 3341, 3356, 3371, 3374, 3381, 3392
Tourangeau, dit of Pierre Fosse
Tournedoe, Fanchette (Mme. Jean Lavergne), 517
Toussaint (Todos Santos), 383, 2751, 3099
Toutin (vars. Totain, Totin, Tottan, Toutain),
  Charles I dit Meunier, 251, 301, 335, 342, 348, 458, 555, 596,

Toutin (continued),
    Charles (continued), 657, 659, 770, 778, 806, 815, 1004, 1048, 1070
    Charles II, 251, 778
    Charles Célestin, 2119
    François, 659, 951, 1626, 1756, 2027, 2330
    Gabriel, 770
    Jean, 342
    Jeanne Marguerite (Mme. Jean Baptiste Plaisance; Mme. Guillaume Chever), 596, 880, 1004, 1082, 1485, 1626, 1669, 1756, 1818, 2030, 2077, 2272, 2331, 2615, 2832, 2839, 2883, 2954, 2969, 3404, 3406
    Leon Bruno, 1655, 2059
    Louis, 301, 880, 1048, 1088, 1145, 1391, 1528, 2316, 2321, 2331, 2460, 2822-2823, 2927, 3201, 3271, 3344
    Marie Agathe, 1499, 1925
    Marie Josephe Honorine, 1584, 1995, 2203, 2757
    Marie Louise (Mme. Pierre Dolet; Mme. François Valentin, Mme. Guillaume Bossier *dit* Le Brun), 268, 409, 429, 441, 458, 491, 918, 1064, 1091, 1291, 1306, 1780, 2849, 2954, 2956, 3370, 3390, 3430
    Remy, 1869
    Remy Ebutrin, 555, 1071, 1094, 1428, 1499, 1584, 1655, 1802, 1869, 1925, 1995, 2059, 2119, 2347, 2465-2466
Traofar, Magdalena, 484
Trichel (vars. Triché, Trichele, Trichely, Trichle),
    ____, 2280, 2302, 3258
    Adam, 352
    Alexis Hilaire de Leri, 1858
    Baptiste, 2785, 3189
    Emmanuel *fils* Henri, 72, 532, 588, 595, 635, 664, 685, 962, 993, 998, 1000, 1006, 1025, 1031, 1039, 1048, 1202, 1253, 1586, 1731, 1735, 1747, 1787, 1805, 1858, 1912, 1997, 2046, 2347, 2395, 2431, 2443, 2784, 2883, 2938, 2941, 3084-3085, 3128, 3286, 3402, 3416

Trichel (continued),
    Emmanuel *fils* Jean Baptiste, 1731
    Étienne, 1774
    Felicité Modest, 1586, 1997
    François, 2878
    Françoise, 1735, 2784
    Henri *fils* Adam, 22, 28-29, 58, 72, 107, 116, 177, 186, 296, 307, 309, 346, 350, 352, 357, 365, 436, 454, 597, 609, 625, 635, 696, 715, 718, 720, 728-729, 734, 744-745, 747, 816, 889, 960, 964, 981, 986, 993, 1000, 1006, 1135, 1193, 2284
    Henri *fils* Emmanuel, 1584, 1667, 1995, 2813-2815, 2938, 2978, 3263, 3381, 3413, 3416
    Hyacinthe: see Marie Hyacinthe
    Jean Baptiste *fils* Henri, 116, 420, 427, 458, 594, 944, 993, 996, 999-1000, 1006, 1017, 1051, 1130, 1194, 1285, 1316, 1340-1341, 1731, 1774, 2298, 2331, 2345
    Jean Baptiste (identity uncertain), 3406
    Jeanne Elisabeth (Mme. Adam Trichel), 352
    Joseph, 2208, 2389, 2966, 3081, 3121, 3282
    Manuelle, 2248
    Marie Cilesie Lolitte, 2046
    Marie Françoise, 2105
    Marie Henry: see Marie Hyacinthe
    Marie Josephe, 1584, 1876, 1886, 1995, 2117, 2265, 2883
    Marie Hyacinthe (Mme. Jean Baptiste Davion), 294, 309, 346, 419, 532, 577, 586, 644, 705, 816, 837, 912, 993, 1062, 1100, 1627, 1667, 2829, 2860, 2950, 3000, 3367, 3378
    Marie Melanide, 2938
    Marie Seleusia Hyacinthe, 1787
    Marie Thérèse (Mme. Hypolite Bordelon), 1729, 1748, 1805, 1862, 2208, 2938, 2941, 3083, 3402
    Pierre, 22
    Pierre Andres, 1805, 3002
    Thérèse?, 1374
    Widow: see Marianne Daublin
Tristant,
    Jean Baptiste *dit* La Jeunesse, 2222

Tristant (continued),
  Jean François, 647, 804
  Louis, 724
  Marie Felicité, 2222
  Marie Thérèse, 894
  Ou___ Billet *dit* Lajeunesse, 3405
  Pierre *dit* La Jeunesse, 647, 724,
    804, 894
Troupart, François, 736
Troupart: see also Turpot
Trudeau (var. Trudo),
  Felix, commandant, 3141,
    3196, 3295, 3299-3300
  Pierre, 1005
Tups: see Toups
Turpin,
  Jean Baptiste, 836
  Magdeleine (Mme. Pierre Tessier),
    2947, 3379
Turpot, Jacques *dit* La France, 662,
  687, 736; see also Troupart
Turpot, Marie Louise, 662

Ualina?, Francisco, 3373
Ulalia: see Eulalie
Ungle, _____, governor of Los Adaes,
  463
Unidentified,
  __anant, 1196
  Anonymous (Indian), 136, 142, 213,
    235, 499-500, 508-509, 758, 761,
    776, 1143-1144, 1151-1152, 1171,
    1196, 1299, 1360, 1402, 1428,
    2516, 2551
  Anonymous (*métis*), 496, 503, 617,
    687, 809
  Anonymous (*mulâtre*), 1139, 1227,
    1282, 1311, 1324, 1353, 1375,
    1383, 1385, 1400, 1420, 1422,
    1434, 1455
  Anonymous (*nègre*), 256, 368, 497-
    498, 699, 806-807, 818, 824-825,
    1108, 1111-1116, 1119-1120, 1122,
    1126, 1130-1132, 1135, 1138,
    1154-1156, 1168, 1175, 1179,
    1185, 1194-1195, 1197, 1199,
    1201-1203, 1206, 1209-1210, 1212,
    1214-1215, 1218, 1220, 1222,
    1226, 1234-1236, 1238-1240, 1242-
    1243, 1246, 1248-1251, 1255,

Unidentified (continued),
  Anonymous (*nègre*, continued),
    1261-1264, 1266, 1277-1278,
    1284-1286, 1312-1313, 1318-1319,
    1322-1323, 1328, 1331, 1337,
    1340-1341, 1346, 1349-1350,
    1352, 1361, 1366-1373, 1378-
    1379, 1382, 1401, 1405, 1407,
    1410-1411, 1413, 1433, 1442-
    1445, 1447, 1449-1450, 1452-
    1454, 1458-1459, 1461, 1463,
    1468, 1474-1475, 3306, 3316,
    3318-3319, 3326, 3333, 3335
  Anonymous (race unknown), 747, 784,
    789, 827, 835, 1148, 1150, 1169,
    1272, 1297, 1336, 1343, 1348,
    1354, 1377, 1390, 1403, 1436,
    1438, 1440-1441, 1456, 1467,
    1652, 2446, 2523, 3313, 3323
  Anonymous (white), 440?-442?, 473,
    502, 812, 1231, 1252, 1359, 1396
  _____, Antoine, 441, 868
  _____, Antonio ___ana___, 1149
  _____, Baptiste, 1460
  _____, Barthelemy, Mda., 2479
  _____, Charles *dit* Le Major, 124
  _____, Claude, 67
  D___, Pierre, 1306
  _____, Emanuel, 1581, 1992
  _____, Francisco, 2754
  _____, François, 894
  _____, François X, 909
  _____, Françoise, Dlle, 1575, 1986
  _____, Gabriel, 813
  _____, Gaspart, Mr., 3091
  _____, Genevieve, 1591
  _____, Gertrude, 860
  _____, Gil, 2114
  _____, Helena, 442
  _____, Iago (Jacques), 2191
  _____, Jean, 911
  _____, Jean Baptiste Étienne, 2861
  _____, Jean Louis?, 1216
  _____, Jeanne, 26, 30
  _____, Jeanne de Dieu, 34
  _____, Jh., Dame, 1397
  _____, Joseph, 1650
  _____, Joseph Maria, 1789
  _____, Louis, 1653
  _____, Lucretia, Signora Doña, 167
  _____, Marguerite, 189

503

Unidentified (continued),
_____, Maria Ana, 2430
_____, Maria Barbara, 2144-2145, 2150, 1892
_____, Maria Céleste, 2112
_____, Maria Gertrudes, 2199
_____, Maria de los Nieves, 2188
_____, Maria Genovefa, 1698
_____, Marie, 232, 909, 1625, 1665
_____, Marie, 396
_____, Marie Adèlaïde Bautiste, 2217
_____, Marie Barbe, 2262
_____, Marie des Nieges (de Niebes), 1601 (bis), 2008
_____, Marie Françoise, 67, 967
_____, Marie Jeanne, 482, 580, 941
_____, Marie Louise, 902, 925, 1306
_____, Marie Rose, 2, 544, 620,
_____, Marie Thérèse, 894
_____, Nicole des Douleurs, 23
_____, Paul, 1575, 1986
_____, Solomon, 1892
_____, Susanne, 1892
_____, Thérèse, 23
_____, (La) Thomas La Concepion, 461
Ursulle (Ursula), 1326, 1489, 2318, 2438, 2476, 2514, 2524, 2534, 2716, 3125, 3134, 3214, 3246
Ursulle Bernarde (Ursula Bernarda), 2508
Uualis: see Wallace

Vagar, Gaspar, 1305, 1342
Valdek (var. Veldek),
Guillaume, 1669
Guillerma (Mme. Guillaume), 2587
Valdek: see also Pereau *dit* Vildec
Valentin (var. Valentine, Vallentin),
_____, Rev. Fr., 406, 464, 638, 984,
André François, 1680, 2084, 2400, 3370
François, 918, 990, 1091, 3370
Jean, 990
Joseph, 1680, 2084
Marie Thérèse (Mme. Pierre Gagnon), 918, 1091, 1485, 1547, 1848, 1864, 1920, 1960
Valer: see Naler

Valeri, 3121
Valeri: see also Jean Baptiste Valleri; Joseph Valery; Pierre Valleri
Vandal,
Antoine, 573, 727, 729
Marguerite, 571
Varangue (var. Varange),
_____, Dna., 2690
_____, Mr., 3245
Jean Baptiste Valeri, 3447
Marie Barbe, 3447
Varraque, _____, Dna., 2635
Varvo: see Gil y Barbo
Vascocu (vars. Bastcocu, Cocu, Vasicoueul, Vastcocu, Vascueul),
_____, Sieur, 2210
André, 1042, 1045-1046, 1050, 1053, 1101, 1535, 1568, 1619, 1667, 1764, 1953, 2021, 2220, 2275, 2292, 2323, 2332, 2339, 2351, 2842, 2901, 3356, 3381, 3445
André Jean Baptiste, 2220
Antoine, 1657, 1666, 2076, 2122, 2266, 2608, 2878, 3371, 3374, 3381, 3392
Antoine François, 2122
Antoine Jean, 415, 842, 914, 1019, 1022, 1029-1030, 1034, 1041-1042, 1045-1046, 1050, 1053-1054, 1059, 1076, 1101, 1136, 1140, 1232, 1540, 1568, 1657, 1666-1667, 1706-1707, 1956, 2272, 2337, 2842, 2878, 2901, 2951, 3016, 3341, 3356, 3370, 3374, 3381, 3392
François, 3016
François Donatien, 2266
Héleine, 2878
Jean Baptiste, 2951
Jean Louis, 842, 1568, 1729, 2133, 2166, 2317, 2335, 2338, 2357, 2360, 2369, 2372, 2878, 2951, 3016, 3356, 3371, 3374
Jean Vital, 2133
Joseph André, 2901
Louis, 2166
Louis François, 914, 1535, 1619, 1657, 1953, 2021, 2133, 2266, 2307, 2352, 3392, 3454
Marie Eulalie, 1535, 1667, 1953, 2174, 2829, 3016, 3107, 3381

Vascocu (continued),
　Marie Françoise (Mme. Jacques Daniel Berrier; Mme. Joseph Jean-Ris), 1510, 1540, 1568, 1666, 1956, 2076, 2122, 2166, 2174, 2220, 2842, 3341, 3356
　Marie Jeanne, 1140, 1706-1707
　Marie Modeste, 1535, 1953, 2901
　Marie Rose, 1136, 1706-1707
　Marie Thérèse (Mme. Antoine Ploché), 1540, 1622, 1956, 2021, 2201
　Marie Thérèse *fille* André, 1619, 2021, 2024
Vasseur: see Le Vasseur
Vauchere: see Vercher
Vaugine: see de Vaugine
Veldek, Francisco Guillermo, 2077; see also Valdek, Vildec
Vency (Veney?), 2520-2521
Venus, 3159
Venus: see also Fanie Venus
Vercher (vars. Vauchere, Verchair, Verchaire),
　____, Dna. 2636
　____, Mr., 2461
　Catherine, 2453
　Deleita, 1730
　Étienne: see Étienne Verger
　Jacques, 1009
　Jacques Therin (Zuirino), 1813, 2871, 3098, 3105, 3446
　Jean Baptiste Beloni, 1693
　Jean Louis, 1079, 1870, 2096, 2463, 2491
　Jean Pierre, 1693, 1775, 2096, 2975
　Joseph *fils* Louis, 1877
　Joseph (identity uncertain), 1881, 2436, 2472
　Louis, 1009, 1040, 1065, 1067, 1096, 1693, 1730, 1775, 1813, 1877, 2096, 2871, 2975, 3399, 3417, 3446
　Marie Adélaïde, 1579, 1730, 1990, 2230, 2968, 3417
　Marie Gertrude, 1870
　Marie Rosalie (Mme. Dominique Barthelemy Rachal), 1499, 1646, 1877, 1925, 2062, 2267, 2491, 2871, 2975, 3399, 3417

Verchur (Verschiers) de Terrepuy: see de Terrepuy
Verdalay (Verdolay, Vendalay), Andres, 2129, 3361, 3380, 3384
Verger (vars. Vergaire, Vergé),
　____, 1647
　____, Mme. 1740
　Angélique Dumont: see Angélique Charles Dumont
　Deletta: see Deleita Vercher
　Étienne I, 259, 437, 480, 546, 548, 903, 968, 991, 1017, 1058, 1070, 1081, 1086-1087, 1440, 1533, 1589, 1679, 1684-1685, 1740, 1778, 1872, 1950, 2088, 2091, 2375, 2893, 3080, 3239, 3292, 3357, 3376, 3385, 3418
　Étienne II, 1778
　Guillaume, 281
　Jacques: see Jacques Vercher
　Joseph I, 28-29, 76, 147, 172-173, 175, 199, 219, 259, 281, 303, 350, 353, 357, 511, 517-518, 546, 718, 728-729, 766, 816, 981-982, 1017
　Joseph II, 219, 554, 961, 991, 1092, 1494, 1885, 1923; see also Joseph Vercher (identity uncertain)
　Louis: see Louis Vercher
　Marie (Mme. Charles Pellerin), 29, 250, 546, 548, 554, 662, 718, 905
　Marie (identity uncertain), 1650, 2065
　Marie Anne (Mme. Jean Baptiste Joseph Boulet; Mme. Joseph Lattier), 28, 357, 469, 546, 589, 604, 656, 840, 905, 977, 981, 999, 1075, 1086, 1658, 2853, 2875, 2935, 2981, 3375, 3393, 2223
　Marie Céleste (Mme. Louis Langlois), 1573, 1615, 1740, 1984, 2017, 2229, 2893, 3418
　Marie Élisabeth Josephe (Mme. Jean Baptiste Dupre), 175, 408, 452, 612, 666-667, 729, 850, 876
　Marie Françoise "Manon" (Mme. Gaspard Derbanne I), 284, 303, 321, 350, 587, 604, 644, 713, 1037,

Verger (continued),
  Marie Françoise (continued), 1077, 1080, 1519, 1940, 2845, 2873, 2968, 2988
  Marie Jeanne (Anne) Catherine (Mme. Jean Baptiste Malbert), 76, 452, 469, 554, 587, 658, 687, 711, 728, 849, 875, 961, 1024, 1039, 1494, 1712, 1746, 1923, 2834, 2933-2934
  Marie Louise (Mme. Pierre Crete; Mme. Pierre La Cour), 303, 849, 982, 986, 1087, 1711, 2872, 2902, 3010, 3428, 3431
Verneuil, Mariana (Mme. Raymond Bardon), 3398
Veronique (Veronica), 2813
Verrier, _____, 346
Versailles (Versally), *dit* of Pierre Chaler
Verschiers de Terrepuy: see de Terrepuy
Viard, François, 517, 520
Vichÿ, Nicole (Mme. Nicolas Bourdelle), 720
Victoire (Victoria), 838, 882, 1029, 2154, 2389, 2400, 2406, 2414, 2421, 2428, 2661, 2722, 2780-2781, 2824, 2911, 3115, 3152, 3216, 3243-3244, 3266, 3300
Victoire: see also Marguerite Victoire
Viger,
  Genevieve, 3445
  Jeanne (Mme. Nicolas Bergereau), 206
Vigneron, Jean François *dit* La Vidette, 366
Vilaret: see Vileret
Vildaigre (Vildec), *dit* of Pereau
Vildec, *dit* of Pereau
Vildek, Barba Reyna, 2007; see also Halock, Barbe
Vileret (Vilaret, Vilerel),
  _____, Mr., 3280
  Abraham, 2980
  Abraham Edouard, 2980
  Louis, 2980
Vilfranche: see Ville Franche
Villa Franca: see Ville Franche
Villard, Pierre, 998, 1014, 1024, 1156, 1201, 2309, 2333

Villareal,
  Andres, 1019
  Andres *hijo* Josef, 1764
  Josef, 1019, 1164, 1718, 1764
  Joseph Domingo, 1718
Ville Blette (vars. Bled, Blet, Blie, Blette, de Viel Blet, deVillers Blet, de Vilblette, Vilblette, Bille Blet),
  Jean Baptiste, 205, 349
  Marie Françoise "Manon" (Mme. Jean Haszes, Mme. Dominique Monteche), 59, 87, 205, 314, 320, 349, 430, 794
Ville Franche, *dit* of Le Duc
Ville Vieille, Nicole (Mme. Robert Navarre), 130
Villiere, _____, Sieur, 1014
Vincense, 2495
Vincent,
  Miguel I, 3397
  Miguel II, 2185, 3397
  Rosalia, 2185
Visiant,
  François, 998
  Honoré, 998
Vitry, _____, Rev. Fr., 6, 168
Voson, Chatharina, 465

Wallace (vars. Ouales, Uuales, Wales, Wallece),
  Benjamin, 1906
  Étienne Césair, 2856
  Jacob (Jacques), 2856, 2952-2953, 3410, 3456
  Jacques II, 2952
  Joseph, 2856, 2952-2953, 3410
  Josue, 1906
  Pierre Neuville, 2953
Warden (var. Houadre),
  Ridechelle, 1010
  William (Guillaume), 1010
Williams, John G., Mrs., xvii

Ymel: see Himel
Ysabel: see Élisabeth
y Varvo,
  Manuel, 733
  Mathieu, 733

y Varvo: see also Gil y Barbo

Zenon, 2802, 3305
Zenon: see also François Zenon,
    Louis Zenon
Zosime (Zosimo), 2306

www.ingramcontent.com/pod-product-compliance
Lightning Source LLC
Chambersburg PA
CBHW050423240426
43661CB00055B/2256